LAKES

**Chemistry
Geology
Physics**

LAKES
Chemistry
Geology
Physics

Edited by
Abraham Lerman

With Contributions by
P. Baccini, M. A. Barnes, W. C. Barnes,
C. J. Bowser, T. B. Coplen, G. T. Csanady,
H. P. Eugster, L. A. Hardie, K. J. Hsü,
D. M. Imboden, B. F. Jones, K. Kelts,
S. Krishnaswami, D. Lal, A. Lerman,
F. J. Pearson, Jr., R. A. Ragotzkie, P. G. Sly,
W. Stumm

Springer–Verlag
New York   Heidelberg   Berlin

Abraham Lerman
Department of Geological Sciences
Northwestern University
Evanston, Illinois 60201
USA

Library of Congress Cataloging in Publication Data
  Main entry under title:
  Lakes—chemistry, geology, physics.
    Includes bibliographies and index.
    1. Lakes.   2. Limnology.   I. Lerman, Abraham.
    GB1603.2.L34 551.4'82 78–17842
    ISBN 0–387–90322–4

© 1978 by Springer-Verlag New York Inc.

Printed in the United States of America.

9 8 7 6 5 4 3 2 1

ISBN 0–387–90322–4 Springer-Verlag   New York

ISBN 3–540–90322–4 Springer-Verlag   Berlin   Heidelberg

Introduction—
Man's Limnetic Drive

The modern man gravitates to lakes much more strongly than his immediate economic needs require. The word recreation is often used to describe man's attraction to lakes and his tendency to be near water. But the tendency is deeper than recreational: the appeal is primarily aesthetic, and one of the measures of the value assigned by man to lakes is the gradients of land prices, generally decreasing from the lake shores landward. Numerous and ancient are the attempts of man to bring a water environment into his midst. Garden pools, ponds, artificial lakes, and fountains are expressions of a desire to have a body of water nearby or expressions of what may be called the *limnetic drive* of human nature. A purely utilitarian water structure, such as a drinking fountain or a storage cavern, requires neither expanse nor elaborate ornamentation. The fountains and ponds adorned with tile mosaics, sculpture, or architectural monuments served to impart the symbolism of religious or historical events, not necessarily connected with water, although the combined appeal to eye of such water plus stone structures has retained its value in the course of centuries.

The title *Lakes: Chemistry, Geology, Physics,* listing in alphabetical order three fields of science in relation to lakes, may convey an idea of an encyclopedic treatise dealing systematically with the variety of chemical, geological, and physical processes in lakes. The volume, however, is neither a treatise nor a handbook in a usual sense: it brings together under one cover some of the more important aspects and newer developments in the fields of chemical, geological, and physical limnology. "Some," as it would be difficult to assemble in one volume everything that has been new to limnology in the last 10 to 20 years. The qualification "the more important aspects" is, to a degree, a subjective judgment: selection of the topics for the book was determined not only by what is important or new in limnology, but also by the readiness of the contributing authors to commit themselves to writing and publication schedules.

The 11 chapters of the volume address themselves to the following subjects: heat budgets of lakes (R. A. Ragotzkie); dispersal and water circulation (G. T. Csanady); sedimentation and sediment transport (P. G. Sly); man-produced chemical perturbations of lakes (W. Stumm and P. Baccini); organic matter in lake sediments (M. A. Barnes and W. C. Barnes); radiochronology of lakes (S. Krishnaswami and D. Lal); mineralogy of lake sediments (B. F. Jones and C. J. Bowser); saline brine lakes (H. P. Eugster and L. A. Hardie); calcium carbonate precipitation in lakes (K. Kelts and K. J. Hsü); stable isotope studies of lakes (F. J. Pearson and T. B. Coplen); and chemical models of lakes (D. Imboden and A. Lerman). It is the editor's privilege to point out that, in addition to the strong interests in lake research, virtually all of the contributing authors have to their record achievements and expertise in fields other than limnology.

The readership at whom the book is aimed is composed of scientists, engineers, and the public of graduate students in limnology and related fields of environmental sciences. Each chapter of the book presents some of the fundamentals of the field it deals with and discusses the more recent developments within it. Through this approach it was thought possible to combine the features that are useful in instruction, such as in graduate seminars, with the more advanced presentation of the state of the art. The diversity of the subject matter of the individual chapters requires from the reader a variable degree of familiarity with limnology in general and with the fundamentals of such disciplines as hydrodynamics, organic and physical chemistry, mineralogy, geochemistry, and sedimentology. Depending on the field and presentation style of the contributors, some of the chapters are cast in a fairly general expository style whereas some go into greater depths of detailed treatment.

As the title of the volume implies, the book deals with the nonbiological sides of limnology. Its emphasis is on inorganic processes and those biogeochemical processes that can be looked at in terms of the macroscopic mechanisms to which geologists, physicists, and chemists are accustomed in their dealings with the global environments. The biology of lakes has always been, and is, a traditionally strong and popular field of limnology. The dependence of life in lakes on the phenomena of the inorganic world, such as light penetration in water, oxygen dissolution, flow of nutrients, and climate, was recognized early and has ever since been part and parcel of the numerous systematic studies of lakes. The multidisciplinary studies of lake systems, as they have been emerging in recent years, differ from the nineteenth- and earlier twentieth-century limnology more in their measure and scope than in their conceptual principles. Determining how the inorganic environment and lake ecosystems interact, and how they relate one to another through cause and effect and through feedback mechanisms, are common goals of diverse lake studies. The scale of environmental changes taking place in industrial societies is a new phenomenon to which many lake systems are exposed. The triangle Man–Physical environment–Aquatic biota has understandably become a major area of public concern, legal deliberations, and scientific research.

We owe to the biological limnology our present knowledge of the living world of lakes, knowledge that is broad and deep but, perhaps disappointingly, excludes from the biota mermaids, mermen, and other creatures of phylogenetically uncertain origins, besung by poets as having lakes for their abode. Fascination before the beauty of a water surface in a natural setting and the mystery of the unseen subsurface world nourish the intellectual curiosity of man. Expressions of the intellectual curiosity in various forms, ranging from mythical to rationally scientific, combine, as in Goethe's poetry, in poems of mermaids luring fishermen into deeps and in the more sober philosophical verses on water as an ultimate source of all things.

The technology and grand construction scales of this century have brought about further expressions of man's limnetic drive. The damming of rivers and control of their flow have created thousands of reservoirs, many of which compete in size and setting with large lakes. Clearly, considerations of energy use, agriculture, fisheries, shipping, and human recreation have played important but varying roles in the decision to create a lake at one site or another. The statistics of the 1970s estimate the total volume of man-made water reservoirs in the world at less than 5000 km^3, and the total surface area in the vicinity of 100,000 km^2. These dimensions are comparable within a factor of two to the volume and area sizes of such great lakes as Lake Michigan or Lake Huron. The potential increase in number and size of man-made lakes is large, as at the limit most of the river water flowing into the oceans can be made to reside longer on the continents. So far, however, the increase in the water-storage capacity of the land surface due to man's activity is far from affecting the water residence time on land on a global scale, and the more important concerns still center around the quality of the immediate environment of the man-made lakes, just as is the case of the natural lakes.

The expanding technological culture of man and his limnetic drive place higher demands on his integrated knowledge of nature, to preserve the existing and forestall the unwanted. To this end, even a slightly better understanding of the chemistry, geology, and physics of lakes is a step in the desired direction.

Evanston, Illinois   Abraham Lerman

Contents

List of Contributors

Dr. Peter Baccini
Department of Chemistry
University of Neuchatel, and
Institute for Water Resources and Water
    Pollution Control
Swiss Federal Institute of Technology
8600 Duebendorf, Switzerland

Dr. Mary A. Barnes
Department of Geological Sciences
University of British Columbia
Vancouver, B.C., Canada

Dr. William C. Barnes
Department of Geological Sciences
University of British Columbia
Vancouver, B.C., Canada

Dr. Carl J. Bowser
Department of Geological Sciences
University of Wisconsin
Madison, Wisconsin 53706 USA

Dr. Tyler B. Coplen
U.S. Geological Survey
Reston, Virginia 22092 USA

Dr. Gabriel T. Csanady
Woods Hole Oceanographic Institution
Woods Hole, Massachusetts 02543 USA

Dr. Hans P. Eugster
Department of Earth and Planetary Sciences
The Johns Hopkins University
Baltimore, Maryland 21218 USA

Dr. Lawrence A. Hardie
Department of Earth and Planetary Sciences
The Johns Hopkins University
Baltimore, Maryland 21218 USA

Dr. Kenneth J. Hsü
Geological Institute
Swiss Federal Institute of Technology
8092 Zurich, Switzerland

Dr. Dieter M. Imboden
Institute for Water Resources and Water
    Pollution Control
Swiss Federal Institute of Technology
8600 Duebendorf, Switzerland

Dr. Blair F. Jones
U.S. Geological Survey
Reston, Virginia 22092 USA

Dr. Kerry Kelts
Geological Institute
Swiss Federal Institute of Technology
8092 Zurich, Switzerland

Dr. S. Krishnaswami
Physical Research Laboratory
Navrangpura, Ahmedabad, India

Dr. Devendra Lal
Physical Research Laboratory
Navrangpura, Ahmedabad, India

Dr. Abraham Lerman
Department of Geological Sciences
Northwestern University
Evanston, Illinois 60201 USA

Dr. F. J. Pearson, Jr.
U. S. Geological Survey
Reston, Virginia 22092 USA

Dr. Robert A. Ragotzkie
Marine Studies Center
University of Wisconsin
Madison, Wisconsin 53706 USA

Dr. Peter G. Sly
Canada Centre for Inland Waters
Burlington, Ontario, Canada

Dr. Werner Stumm
Institute of Aquatic Sciences, and Institute for
    Water Resources and Water Pollution
    Control
Swiss Federal Institute of Technology
8600 Duebendorf, Switzerland

Chapter 1

Heat Budgets of Lakes

Robert A. Ragotzkie

Introduction

The heat budget of a lake can best be described as its integrated, thermal response to its external physical climate. Unlike oceans where large-scale advective processes play a major role in the heat exchange processes, lakes are individual entities, each responding slightly differently to its external climate. Viewed in this manner a lake can be considered as a recording climatic instrument. Properly calibrated, this natural climatic indicator can yield information about the climate of a region over periods ranging from a few days or a season to an entire year.

The primary *internal* characteristics of lakes which determine their climatic response are mean and maximum depth, fetch, basin shape, and relative exposure to wind. The primary *external* factors to which a lake responds are radiation (both short- and longwave), air temperature, humidity, stability of the air above the lake surface, and wind. For frozen lakes ice thickness, snow depth, and albedo (reflectivity) are critical factors.

In this chapter we will examine how the *internal* characteristics of lakes determine their thermal interaction with *external* meteorological factors. The analysis of the heat balance of lakes will provide the model framework for demonstrating and explaining this interaction.

Basic concepts

In dealing with the heat balance of a lake it is important to keep in mind that all the major processes which account for heat flow into or out of a lake occur at or near the surface. In shallow lakes significant amounts of heat are exchanged seasonally with the bottom sediments, but since the net annual heat flow into and

out of the sediments is zero or nearly so, this term can be omitted for the present. Therefore the analysis of the heat balance will consist of those processes by which heat enters or leaves the lake at its surface plus the change in heat content of the lake itself.

The heat balance of an unfrozen lake can be simply expressed as

$$Q_T = Q_R + Q_L + Q_S \tag{1}$$

where Q_T = rate of change of heat stored in lake,

Q_R = net radiation,

Q_L = latent heat of evaporation, and

Q_S = sensible heat exchange.

All rates will be expressed as cal/cm²/day.

The equation states simply that change in the lake's heat content is equal to the algebraic sum of radiation processes, evaporation, and conduction to the atmosphere. Other terms will be considered later to deal with special situations.

The most easily observed and understood heat balance term is the heat stored in the lake. Though this term seems straightforward enough, the definition of heat storage was the source of much confusion in early heat budget studies. It would appear at first glance that the heat content of a lake could be obtained simply by use of a vertical temperature sounding and by integrating the temperature over the entire depth. Because the bottom of a lake slopes downward toward the deepest point, the area of the various layers of a lake decreases with increasing depth. Thus the top meter of the lake constitutes a great deal more volume than the bottom meter at the deepest point. To get around this difficulty it is customary to calculate a "unit lake" using the lake's hypsometric curve. In this way each layer is weighted for its relative area, taking the surface area as unity. From these weighting factors the amount of heat contained in each successive layer can be obtained by multiplying the mean temperature of the layer times the relative area of that layer. A "unit lake'' then is a column of water with a surface area of 1 cm² and tapering downward to some small fraction of a square centimeter at the deepest portion of the lake. By this procedure the heat content per unit area of the entire lake is accurately computed.

An alternative method of taking the average depth of the lake times the average temperature of the water column is sometimes used. However this procedure does not take into account the decrease in temperature with depth in a stratified lake. Although it is theoretically correct to use this method for unstratified and hence isothermal lakes, caution should be observed because so-called unstratified lakes often exhibit temporary stratification in summer and are usually somewhat stratified during the period of ice cover.

Thermal properties of water

The thermal behavior and heat balance of lakes depend in many ways on the unique thermal properties of water itself. For liquid water the primary properties of interest are its density–temperature relationship, freezing point, heat capacity, and latent heat of fusion and vaporization. The anomalous density–temperature relationship is a critical factor in the thermal behavior of lakes. At normal atmospheric pressure water attains its maximum density of 1.000 at 3.94°C. Above and below this temperature the density decreases in a complex exponential way (Figure 1). The occurrence of the maximum density of water at about

4°C above its freezing point of 0°C has a major influence on the way lakes cool and ultimately freeze over. Figure 1 also shows that the rate of decrease of density increases with increasing temperature. This means that a much less steep vertical temperature gradient is required to produce a given hydrostatic stability at high temperatures than near 4°C. For example, about the same stability is produced by a 1°C difference between 26 and 27°C as by a 6°C difference between 4 and 10°C.

Water has an exceptionally high heat capacity. At 0°C the value at normal atmospheric pressure is 1.01 cal/g/°C. Though this value varies slightly with temperature the differences are small enough to be neglected in heat balance studies. Since the density of water is nearly 1.00 throughout the temperature range normally encountered in lakes, we can approximate the volumetric heat capacity for water at 1.0 cal/cm³/°C without incurring a significant error.

The latent heat of evaporation for water varies with temperature, but for most lake heat budget studies a value of 590 cal/g is adequate. The latent heat of fusion (freezing) is 80 cal/g.

Heat exchange processes

Radiation

Radiation is the transfer of energy by electromagnetic waves. All matter not at a temperature of absolute zero sends out or emits radiation. The total quantity of radiation increases with the temperature of the emitting substance. In addition hotter substances emit radiation at shorter wavelengths (higher energy) than cooler substances. Thus the sun emits high-intensity radiation in the shorter (visible and ultraviolet) wavelength portion of the spectrum while radiation from the earth is in the form of longer (infrared) wavelengths at a much lower intensity.

For our purposes it is convenient to divide radiation into two types: solar radiation which is primarily shortwave at the earth's surface and which varies in intensity with time of day, season, and latitude, and terrestrial or longwave radiation. Solar radiation passes through the atmosphere with relatively little absorption although considerable scattering occurs. At the surface of water, ice, or snow some of this incoming solar radiation is reflected. The proportion which is reflected is termed the albedo of the substance. An albedo value of 1.0 means that 100% is reflected and a value of zero means that none is reflected. The albedo of water varies with the angle of incidence. Except at low angles of incidence water has a very low albedo of about 0.03 to 0.05. Therefore, most of the energy of solar radiation penetrates the

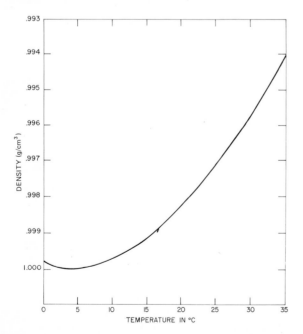

FIGURE 1.   Relationship between temperature and density of fresh water.

surface of the water. For this reason deep water appears nearly black when viewed from above. Ice surfaces have a higher albedo which varies a great deal depending on the nature of the surface. Fresh snow is very reflective and may have an albedo of 0.7 to 0.9, that is up to 90% of the energy from the sun is reflected by snow.

Solar radiation which penetrates the surface of the water (or overlying ice and snow cover) is absorbed by the water. However, as water is relatively transparent to light in the visible spectrum, this absorption, and hence heating of water itself, takes place over a considerable depth. The depth distribution of the radiation heating is exponential in form:

$$I_z = I_0 e^{-kz} \tag{2}$$

where I = intensity of radiation,
   z = depth, and
   k = extinction coefficient, usually expressed as m^{-1}.

In most lakes most of the solar radiation penetrating the surface is absorbed in the first few meters. However, in very clear lakes significant solar heating of the water may occur at depths of 10 m or more.

Because of its relatively low absolute temperature, radiation emitted by liquid water is mostly in very longwave or far infrared region. Emission of longwave radiation from the surface of the lake is given by the Stefan–Boltzmann Law, simply expressed as:

$$R_L = \sigma \epsilon T^4 \tag{3}$$

where R_L = total longwave energy emitted,
   σ = constant = 0.817×10^{-10} cal/cm^2/min/°C^4,
   ϵ = emissivity (black body = 1), and
   T = temperature on the Kelvin scale.

Thus the longwave radiation is proportional to the fourth power of the absolute temperature and to the emissivity of the substance. Water has an emissivity of about 0.97 or nearly that of a "black body." Only the very near surface of the water of a lake, the top 10 to 100 μm, emits radiation to the overlying atmosphere.

Clouds being usually made up of liquid water droplets are nearly opaque and hence strongly absorbent of longwave radiation emitted by the surface of a lake. Clouds and to a lesser extent the atmosphere itself also emit radiation which is in turn absorbed by the surface of the earth including lakes. This is termed back radiation.

Combining all these radiation streams leads to the concept of net radiation which is the algebraic sum of all radiation terms.

$$R_{net} = R_s + R_{refl} + R_L \uparrow + R_L \downarrow \tag{4}$$

where R_s R_{refl} are the visible shortwave incoming and reflected radiation energies.

It is possible to measure these terms directly by means of upward and downward facing solarimeters and a longwave net radiometer or in combination by a net radiometer which senses and integrates both upward and downward long- and shortwave radiation. However, because of the difficulties of instrument maintenance and calibration and also the tediousness of data handling, such direct observations are usually done only for short periods, i.e., a few days or less. Instead solar radiation records from nearby meteorological stations are used for the incoming solar radiation term and corrected for average reflectivity. Longwave radiation is more complicated in that the temperature of the overlying air and water vapor as well as the presence or absence of clouds play a major role in determining the net longwave radiation flux at the surface of a lake. Although longwave emission by the lake increases with water temperature, back radiation from the overlying atmosphere also increases with air temperature and humidity. Since water vapor capacity of the air increases exponentially, the net result is that the back radiation tends to increase with temperature more than the outgoing radiation emitted by the lake itself. Therefore, it is generally observed that total outgoing longwave radiation tends to *decrease* with increased temperature of air and water. Sverdrup *et al.* (1946) show this relationship in graphical form (Figure 2). Cloud cover further reduces the outgoing longwave term. An empirical relationship for this term given by Sverdrup *et al.* (1946) states that

$$R_{L\ effective} = R_{L\ clear}(1 - 0.083K), \tag{5}$$

where K is cloud cover in tenths expressed on a scale of 0 to 10.

Clearly the estimation of the radiation terms is a complex and less than precise business, but, as will be apparent later in this chapter, radiation plays a major role in the heat budget of a lake. Therefore, every effort should be made to evaluate these terms.

Sensible heat

Transfer of sensible heat between a lake and the atmosphere takes place by a combination of conduction and convection. Heat is transferred across the water's surface by conduction to or from the air at the air/water boundary. This conduction occurs only in a very thin layer of water or air at the boundary itself and depends directly on the temperature gradient across that boundary. From laboratory experiments Twitchell (1976) found that in the water the conducting layer is about 0.13 cm. and in the air about 0.4 cm. Beyond these regions, sensible heat is transferred by turbulence or convective processes in both the air and the water.

These processes are in turn controlled by wind and the stability of the overlying air. Because the water

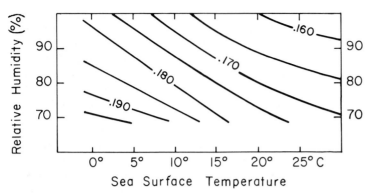

FIGURE 2.   Effective back radiation in g/cm²/min from the sea surface to a clear sky. Represented as a function of sea-surface temperature and relative humidity of the air at a height of a few meters. From Sverdrup, 1946.

temperature of a lake tends to lag behind that of the air, air stability varies with the seasons. In the spring, when the water is colder than the air, the overlying air is cooled from below and tends to be stably stratified. In this situation wind action on the lake itself is reduced and at times almost eliminated, thus sharply reducing heat transfer. In contrast, in the fall when the lake is generally warmer than the air, convection is favored and sensible heat transfer to the air is enhanced.

Evaporation

Evaporation is a major means of heat loss by lakes. The high latent heat of vaporization for water, about 590 cal/g, must be supplied directly from heat stored in the water itself. Hence the cooling power of evaporation is very large.

The process of evaporation occurs somewhat analogously to sensible heat transfer. At the air/water boundary water molecules escape directly to the air. Again this part of the process occurs only in the top layer of water molecules, the "skin" of the water, and affects only the immediate boundary layer of the air. The rate of vaporization depends directly on the vapor pressure gradient across the air/water boundary usually expressed as $\Delta e/\Delta z$ where Δe is the vapor pressure difference in millibars and Δz is the vertical height between the two measurements. Above this layer wind and vertical mixing remove the water vapor from the boundary layer, thus maintaining the vapor pressure gradient. Because of the requirement of wind mixing of the overlying air, evaporation is greatest when the overlying air is neutrally stable or unstable.

Bowen ratio

The direct measurement of sensible heat transfer and evaporation is quite difficult and requires continuous and detailed monitoring of wind, air and water temperature, and humidity. It is both difficult and expensive to maintain such a monitoring program for long periods. Therefore, the alternative and most commonly used approach is by use of the Bowen ratio (Bowen,

1926). Defined as the ratio between sensible heat transfer and evaporation, the method assumes that the eddy diffusivity for both heat and water vapor are the same. It is then possible to evaluate the Bowen ratio directly from water temperature and atmospheric temperature and humidity.

$$B = \frac{Q_S}{Q_L} = 0.66^{p/1000} \frac{T_w - T_a}{e_w - e_a} \qquad (6)$$

where B = Bowen ratio,
p = atmospheric pressure in mb,
T_w = water temperature,
T_a = air temperature,
e_w = equilibrium vapor pressure of water (derived from T_w), and
e_a = water vapor pressure of air.
By substituting the Bowen ratio in the basic heat budget Eq. (1) we obtain

$$Q_T = Q_R + Q_L(1 + B) \qquad (7)$$

and solving for Q_L, one can then obtain the sensible heat term, Q_S, directly from Eq. (6).

Bottom conduction

Heat flow from geothermal sources deep within the earth averages about 1 μcal/cm²/sec. On an annual basis this heat source adds about 30 cal/cm²/year to most lakes. In Lake Mendota this heat source is about 0.1% of the annual heat budget. In shallower lakes with smaller heat budgets the percentage will be slightly higher, but is generally less than 0.5%. Except in meromictic lakes this heat source is insignificant and can be ignored in lake heat budget studies.

Heat flows through the bottoms of lakes in response to seasonal changes of water temperature. Heat flows from the water to the sediments during the summer and early fall and then back into the water during the winter. The amount of heat involved in this seasonal exchange depends mostly on the seasonal temperature range of the water in contact with the bottom and secondarily on the thermal properties of the bottom sediments or underlying rock. From extensive temperature measurements of bottom sediments Scott (1964) calculated the winter heat flow from this source for nine lakes in Wisconsin. His values ranged from 940 cal/cm^2 for South Trout Lake, a deep lake with a quite cold hypolimnion, to 1590 cal/cm^2 for Lake Mendota whose hypolimnion temperature reaches 10°C or more.

This seasonal heat exchange between lakes and their sediments is exactly out of phase with the annual water temperature cycle, withdrawing heat during the summer and adding heat during the winter. In the summer this source is only a small percentage of the total heat content of the water and is generally ignored in the evaluation of a lake's summer heat budget. During the winter when the lake is covered with ice and the water temperature is below 4°C, the warm bottom sediments are a significant source of heat.

Thermal behavior of lakes

Though the view of a lake as a natural climatic instrument is attractive in its simplicity, a lake's overall thermal response and resulting heat balance is the result of an exceedingly complex interaction of many thermal and dynamic processes. In order to explain these processes, their interaction, and their effects on a lake's response we will examine the annual thermal cycle of a moderately deep temperate lake.

Starting in the spring shortly after the disappearance of ice cover, the water of the lake attains a temperature of 4°C. At that time the lake is neutrally stable and the water is isothermal from surface to bottom. Warming at or near the surface then occurs, primarily by solar radiation. The warmed surface water is mixed downward by wind action. Initially mixing usually extends throughout the entire depth of the lake because the weak stability resulting from temperature gradients near 4°C is easily overcome by the kinetic energy supplied by the wind. Thus the incoming heat is distributed uniformly throughout the lake and for all but the deepest lakes the water remains isothermal as the temperature rises several degrees above 4°C.

As surface heating by solar radiation continues, the warmer, near surface water becomes sufficiently buoyant to resist complete vertical mixing. The action

of the wind continues, however, and under the combined influence of surface heating and wind mixing a relatively shallow layer of isothermal water develops. Below this layer the vertical temperature gradient and hence the hydrostatic stability is much increased. This stable layer is called the thermocline. The process of thermocline formation is illustrated in Figure 3.

The thermocline effectively separates the warmer, surface mixed layer (epilimnion) from the deeper, cooler layer (hypolimnion). At first the thermocline is shallow, often forming only 2 or 3 m below the surface. Periods of strong winds result in deeper mixing and the thermocline descends. Lighter winds and continued heating may then form a new warm layer and shallow thermocline. This process often repeats, and it is not uncommon for several thermoclines to exist simultaneously during this time of the year. Eventually the warm surface layers are consolidated and a single thermocline develops which persists throughout the entire summer and early fall.

The lake is now stably stratified with most of the incoming heat being trapped in the epilimnion by the thermocline. During the remaining summer heating season the lake continues to gain heat by radiation. Some of this heat is lost by evaporation and sensible heat transfer to the atmosphere, but most of it is stored in the epilimnion.

In late summer the rate of heat loss by evaporation and sensible heat exceeds the radiation input and the lake begins to cool. Since the cooling occurs at the surface, the cooler and denser surface water descends convectively and cooling occurs throughout the entire epilimnion. As the temperature of the epilimnion decreases, stability is reduced and the thermocline begins to descend again. In autumn the temperature of the epilimnion decreases to nearly that of the hypolimnion, and eventually strong winds mix the two layers and the lake again becomes isothermal, but this time at a higher temperature than in spring. Continued surface cooling proceeds by evaporation and increasing sensible heat loss to the atmosphere. These transfer processes are greatly enhanced by the unstable condition of cool air overlying the relatively warm water of the lake causing vigorous convection of the atmospheric boundary layer.

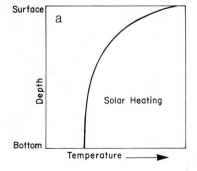 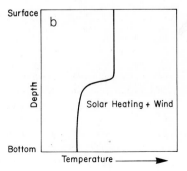

FIGURE 3. Formation of the thermocline. Note that the heat content is the same in (a) and (b), but the temperature gradient, hence the stability of the water at mid-depth, has been sharply increased by wind mixing of the surface layer.

When the entire lake has cooled to 4°C it might be expected that further cooling would stabilize the surface layer and a reverse thermocline would form. However, the very small change in density per °C near 4°C is easily overcome by the wind action, and the lake remains isothermal as it continues to cool below 4°C.

Ice formation cannot begin until water reaches its freezing point of 0°C. In a lake exposed to varying winds and continuous cooling, there eventually occurs a period of calm and strong outward heat flow. At this time a thin, stable layer of water develops at the surface and a temperature of 0°C is quickly reached. Further heat loss at this point removes the heat of fusion and ice begins to form. Usually this process occurs first in shallow and protected bays. However, since the entire lake reaches this critical stage in an isothermal condition, ice formation often occurs suddenly, and the entire lake may become ice covered in

a few hours. Generally the first ice cover forms at night when calm conditions are most likely to prevail and when strong outgoing radiation augments the evaporative and sensible heat loss to the atmosphere. However, lakes are sometimes seen to freeze in late afternoon during a clear calm period and when the net radiation balance changes from positive (inward) to negative (outward). By this process lakes can theoretically freeze over at any time after the water reaches 4°C, but observations show that owing to wind action freezeup usually does not occur until the average water temperature is significantly below 4°C.

The temperature at which lakes freeze over is closely related to their fetch (Figure 4). Very small lakes and ponds freeze when their bulk water temperature is between 2 and 3°C, while larger lakes cool to 1°C or less before freezing. In lakes with a fetch greater than 2 km or so (Figure 4a) the effect of fetch is less pronounced than in smaller lakes (Figure 4b).

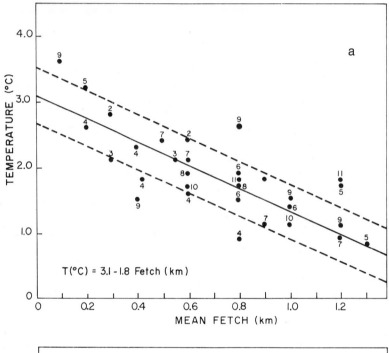

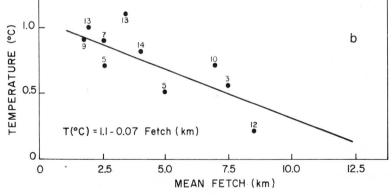

FIGURE 4.   Relationship between water temperature at the time of freezeup and fetch for Wisconsin lakes. Numbers above points are mean depths in meters. From Scott, 1964.

According to the regression equation determined for the larger lakes, lakes with a fetch of 15 km or greater normally reach 0°C before freezing. This is certainly true for the Great Lakes and has also been observed to be true for Lake Winnebago, Wisconsin, which has a mean fetch of 27 km (Scott, 1964).

Once the lake becomes ice covered the entire heat exchange process and the lake's thermal response changes. Heat loss now occurs only at the surface of the ice by outgoing longwave radiation and conduction of sensible heat to the atmosphere. Evaporation or sublimation from the surface of the ice or snow occurs, but generally at a much slower rate than from the open water. The ice sheet also isolates the lake from mixing by wind action. Heat flow within the lake and exchange with the atmosphere is almost entirely by conduction and radiation. Heat is added to the bottom water by conduction of heat stored in the sediments and is lost from the surface by conduction to the bottom of the ice whence it is conducted upward through the ice cover to be lost from the ice surface mainly by longwave radiation and to a lesser extent by sublimation and sensible heat transfer to the atmosphere. Sunlight penetrating the ice cover adds heat by absorption in the upper portion of the water. As soon as the lake freezes over the water of the lake ceases to undergo a net loss of heat and actually begins to warm by the combined processes of bottom conduction and solar radiation. Some of this heat is lost from the ice surface and is expressed as growth of the thickening ice sheet.

The next major change in the lake's thermal response occurs when the first snow covers the ice. At this time the upward conduction of heat is sharply reduced because of the low thermal conductivity of snow. Secondly, the snow surface is highly reflective and the albedo of the lake surface increases to 0.7 or higher. Snow is also much less transparent to short-wave solar radiation. This means that much of the solar radiation is reflected or absorbed by the snow and less penetrates the snow and ice cover to warm the underlying water. It is readily seen that these processes—reduced conduction loss and reduced radiation input—tend to compensate each other. As a result, solar heating continues and this together with heat gain from bottom conduction results in continued slow warming of the water. As the snow cover becomes deeper, the water of the lake is increasingly isolated thermally from the atmosphere. In regions of heavy snowfall the rate of ice formation slows down because of the insulating effect of the snow even though the atmospheric climate is severe. In some cases the weight of the snow depresses the ice below the level of the water and flooding of the ice occurs. This water combines with the snow and freezes thus developing a layer of gray ice beneath the snow and over the clear lake ice.

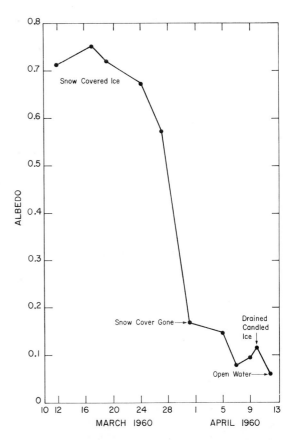

FIGURE 5. Albedo of Lake Mendota preceding ice breakup. Measurements are hemispheric albedo measured from an aircraft. From Bauer and Dutton, 1960.

With the onset of spring, the snow cover softens and begins to melt. Most of the melted snow evaporates to the atmosphere, but final melting may result in a layer of slush and water on the ice. This condition seldom lasts very long, and shortly the ice is exposed and the water of the lake is then subject to increasing heating by solar radiation which by early spring is increasing rapidly.

Melting of the ice is accomplished mostly by the conduction from the warming underlying water plus direct solar radiation. Final destruction of the ice cover is signalled by the separation of the vertically oriented ice crystals. This process, known as "candling," occurs when the ice thickness has decreased to 20 cm or less. The surface of the ice takes on a dull gray appearance and the ice is said to be "rotten." The albedo decreases sharply to a value of 0.1 or less, thus enhancing the absorption of solar radiation and further melting. When "candling" is complete and the interstices of the crystals are completely thawed, the water drains downward, and the ice appears grayish-white in color and the albedo increases slightly (Figure 5). At this point the physical integrity of the ice sheet is essentially destroyed, and the next strong wind causes the ice to break up. As soon as the ice is broken up, wind action on the lake causes vertical mixing of the water and the transport of warmer bottom water to the surface where it loses heat to the melting ice. This entire process—breakup and melting—usually takes place in a single day although large northern lakes may retain a partial ice cover for some days before the entire process is completed.

The lake now proceeds to warm rapidly under the influence of strong solar radiation, and, since the density of water increases as its temperature rises to 4°C, complete vertical mixing occurs convectively aided by wind action until the entire body of the lake has reached 4°C. The cycle then begins anew.

Heat balance of lakes

Comparison of the heat budgets of two temperate lakes in the same location, one deep and stratified and one shallow and unstratified, illustrates the effects of lake morphometry on their thermal response to climate. Lakes Mendota and Wingra are both located at Madison, Wisconsin. Lying at 43° N. latitude, these lakes are subject to a moderately continental temperate climate characterized by warm summers and quite cold winters. Depending on their depth, lakes in the region usually freeze in late November to late December and break up in late March to early April.

Lake Mendota is a typical dimictic temperate lake. It has a maximum depth of slightly more than 25 m, a mean depth of 12.1 m, and a fetch of about 8 km. The lake stratifies in May and the thermocline gradually descends to about 11 m. Surface cooling begins in

early August and by November the thermocline has completely disappeared and the lake is again isothermal.

Lake Wingra is a shallow nonstratified lake with an average depth of 1.6 m and except for several spring holes is generally less than 3 m deep. It has a fetch of 2 km and does not develop a permanent thermocline. Because of its shallowness and lower heat storage capacity Lake Wingra freezes several weeks before Mendota.

The annual cycle of heat storage in Lakes Mendota and Wingra (Figures 6 and 7) show the effects of lake depth on heat budget. Both lakes are subject to the same climate yet the heat storage during the ice-free period in Mendota reaches about 25,000 cal/cm² while Lake Wingra barely reaches 4200 cal/cm². Even during the ice-covered period the water of Lake Mendota gains about 3500 cal/cm² while Wingra gains only about 1000 cal/cm². At the time of ice breakup the water temperature of Lake Wingra averages over 6°C while that of Mendota averages about 3°C. The difference in total storage arises from the much larger heat capacity of Lake Mendota thus enabling that lake to store the heat from incoming solar radiation at a lower temperature.

Ice cover is treated as "negative heat" storage and is calculated from the amount of heat required to melt it. A more detailed discussion of the ice-covered period is given later in this chapter.

The individual heat exchange processes which combine to produce the observed heat storage cycle for Lake Mendota are shown in Figure 8. The net radiation term follows a nearly sinusoidal curve in phase with the solar radiation and is the primary source of heat for the lake during the entire year. Evaporation

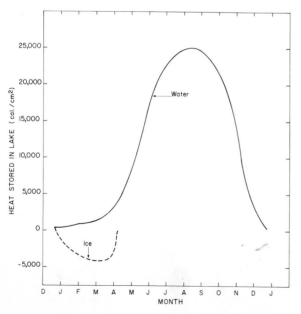

FIGURE 6.   Annual cycle of heat storage in Lake Mendota based on 27-year mean water temperatures and ice thicknesses from Birge as compiled by Dutton and Bryson, 1962. Storage in water during ice-covered period from Scott, 1964. Lake Mendota is a stratified lake with a mean depth of 12.1 m.

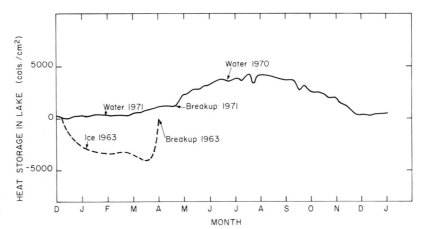

FIGURE 7. Annual cycle of heat storage in Lake Wingra based on data for 1970–71 from Koonce, 1972. Negative heat stored in ice for 1962–63 from Scott, 1964. Lake Wingra is an unstratified lake with a mean depth of 1.6 m.

accounts for most of the heat loss, particularly from June through November, and sensible heat exchange is important only in the fall when maximum temperature gradients exist between the warm water and overlying cold air. The rate of change of heat storage is, of course, the algebraic sum of these three terms. Though the curves in Figure 8 appear somewhat confusing, the climatic response of the lake can be viewed quite simply by dividing the year into separate periods.

During the winter and spring Lake Mendota is clearly acting as a net radiometer, integrating the net incoming radiation and retaining nearly all the heat as storage. Starting in May when the surface water temperature is increasing rapidly, evaporation plays a much more important part in the heat balance. From

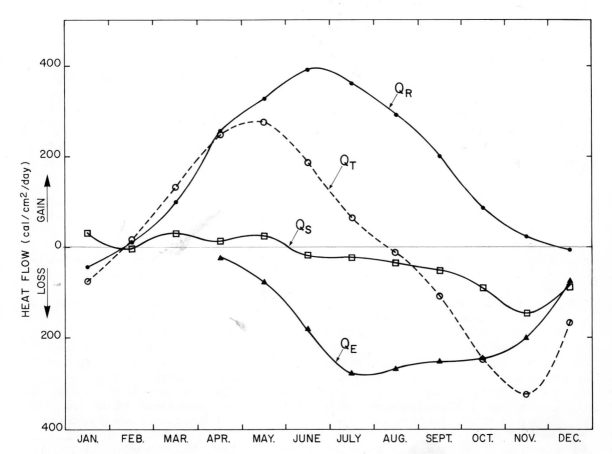

FIGURE 8. The annual course of the major heat budget terms for Lake Mendota. Data are from Dutton and Bryson (1962) and are based on 27 years of water temperature records from Birge. Symbols are from Eq. (1).

May until October the rate of change of heat storage almost exactly parallels the rate net radiation input but the curves are offset by the rate of evaporation loss. Finally in October and November increased sensible heat loss to the air occurs, owing to the strong temperature gradient between the warm lake surface and the overlying air. During this period evaporation loss decreases slightly so that the rate of storage remains parallel to the net radiation curve from June through November.

In summary, the heat budget of Lake Mendota during its ice-free period is dominated by the net radiation term. The departure of the lake's heat storage term from the net radiation term during the summer and early fall is almost entirely accounted for by evaporation. Sensible heat loss plays a minor role except briefly during the fall.

Frozen lakes

Once a lake freezes over its thermal response to climate and its heat budget change radically. Immediately upon completion of the ice cover, the evaporation and sensible heat losses which characterize the fall cooling season of the ice-free lake nearly cease, and radiation becomes the primary heat exchange process between the lake and the atmosphere. Net radiation is strongly outgoing and results in more or less steady ice growth during the period December through February. Sunlight which penetrates the ice cover and even thin to moderate snow cover heats the water beneath the ice.

With the addition of snow cover the heat exchange processes between the lake and its surroundings as well as within the lake itself become much more complex. Many more storage terms are involved and the means by which heat enters and leaves the lake are much less obvious. To visualize this complicated heat flow situation the diagram in Figure 9 will be helpful. Sensible heat is stored in the water, ice, and snow. Latent heat is stored in the ice and snow. Recalling the convention to base heat content on a base of 0°C, it is obvious that both sensible and latent heat in the ice and snow must be calculated as "negative heat." The "negative" sensible heat in snow and ice is obtained from the product of its temperature below 0°C, its total mass per square centimeter, and the specific heat for ice (0.5 cal/°C/g). The mass of ice per unit area is equal to its thickness times its density (0.917 g/cm³). For snow the total water content must be determined by field measurements of density or by melting a core of known cross-section. Latent heat is equal to the mass of ice or snow per unit area times 80 cal/g, the latent heat of fusion for water.

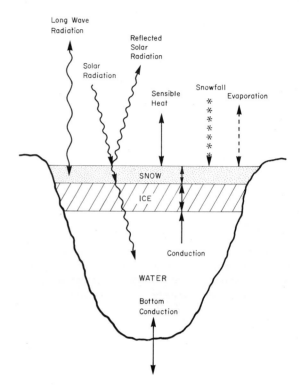

FIGURE 9.   Heat flows in a frozen lake.

Ice growth occurs by heat loss from outgoing longwave radiation from the surface of the snow. Heat enters the water by solar radiation which penetrates the ice as well as light to moderate snow cover. Some of this heat is stored as indicated by increasing water temperature throughout the winter and some is lost by conduction to the overlying ice. The net effect is a decrease in the total heat content of the lake even though heat storage in the water increases steadily throughout the winter. Some heat is also gained by conduction from the bottom sediments in which heat has been stored during the summer.

Sensible and latent heat exchange between the snow surface and the air continue but are relatively minor terms in the heat budget. Finally, snow falling on the ice represents negative latent heat which will eventually have to be balanced by heat income before the lake loses its ice cover in the spring.

Scott (1964) in a comprehensive study of the winter heat budgets of 53 lakes in Wisconsin found that frozen lakes respond to differences in climate, but that this response is significantly modified by the size and depth of the lakes. Maximum ice thickness increases with the severity of the climate, but the effects of lake depth and fetch as well as the snow depth often mask the climatic effects, particularly for small, shallow lakes. For lakes with a fetch of less than 1.5 km the maximum ice thickness decreases with fetch. Similarly lakes with a mean depth of less than 4 m have slightly less ice than deeper lakes. Increasing snow depth by virtue of its insulating effect results in less ice formation. The snow depth effect is undoubtedly interrelated with the effects of fetch owing to the tendency for very small lakes to retain deeper snow cover whereas on larger lakes wind action blows some of the snow off the lakes and packs the remaining snow thus reducing its insulating effect.

The formation of gray ice is another complicating factor in the winter lake heat budget. When the total snow load exceeds the buoyancy of the ice, the ice sheet is forced downward and water rising through cracks and fissures floods the surface of the ice beneath the snow. Freezing of the resulting slush produces a layer of gray ice. This phenomenon changes the thermal properties of the combined ice and snow cover. The total thickness of the ice is increased, and the thermal conductivity of the combined ice and snow cover is increased, thus allowing an increase in the rate of heat loss from the underlying water. Although gray ice is only about one-quarter as transparent to sunlight as clear ice, it is nevertheless nearly five times more transparent than an equal thickness of snow (Table 1). Therefore, flooding of the ice and formation of gray ice increases the amount of solar

TABLE 1.   Average Absorption Coefficients for Light of Ice and Snow. Values From Scott, 1964

Substance	Absorption coefficient (cm^{-1})
Clear ice	0.015
Gray ice	0.067
Snow (1–6 cm deep)	0.30–0.34
Snow (7–15 cm deep)	0.24

radiation reaching the underlying water thus tending to increase its heating rate. The two effects—increased conductivity of the ice and snow cover and increased transparency to solar radiation—tend to cancel each other so the net effect on the heat content of the lake is probably small.

In contrast to the period of ice growth which occupies most of the winter season, the period of ice wastage or melt is relatively short, lasting only a few weeks in temperate lakes and somewhat longer in subarctic lakes. Little or no ice wastage occurs until the snow cover disappears. Once the snow has gone, a period of much increased heating of the water by solar radiation begins. Some of this heat is immediately used to melt the ice by conduction from the water to the ice. This effect is much more pronounced in shallow lakes where under-ice water temperatures often

FIGURE 10.   Broken candled ice blown on shore by wind during ice breakup.

exceed 4°C. Scott observed that during wastage the ice sheet continues to lose heat by net radiation and nearly all the heat for melting is derived from the solar-heated underlying water. During the final stage of melting there is some sensible heat transfer from the air resulting in surface melting. Final weakening of the ice sheet by melting in the interstices between the vertical ice crystals and "candling" of the ice sets the stage for rapid destruction of the ice sheet by the wind. Much of this ice is blown ashore where it may do considerable damage to shore structures (Figure 10). The remaining broken ice often melts in less than a day as the water of the lake begins to mix vertically, bringing the heat stored in the deeper water to the surface. However, as there is also strong incoming solar radiation at this time and usually relatively warm overlying air, both of which provide heat for melting of the ice, the amount of heat derived from the heat stored in the water is difficult to evaluate. The brief decrease in water temperature of 1°C or less which might be expected to occur during final breakup has not been reliably observed because of the difficulty in monitoring water temperatures immediately before and during the breakup.

Antarctic lakes

In the dry valleys of Victoria Land in eastern Antarctica there exist a number of permanently frozen lakes. Most of these are shallow and contain very little liquid water, but two, Lakes Bonney and Vanda, are quite deep and have a number of interesting thermal features (Ragotzkie and Likens, 1964). Lake Bonney, located in Taylor Valley, is made up of two basins, one 4.8 km long and the other 2.6 km in length. Its maximum depth is 32.2 m. Lake Vanda, located in Wright Valley, is 5.0 km in length and has a maximum depth of 66.1 m.

Both lakes are covered with about 4 m of snow-free ice, but their internal thermal structures are radically different (Figure 11). Estimates of several of the heat budget terms during the Antarctic summer revealed that both lakes gain heat by net radiation and lose heat by direct evaporation (sublimation) from the surface of the ice.

The bulge in Lake Bonney's vertical temperature structure reaches 7.8°C at 13 m and is most likely caused by solar heating. The ice is exceedingly clear and 6% or more of the incident solar radiation penetrates the ice. Despite this mid-depth temperature maximum the water column is hydrostatically stable because of increasing salinity with depth.

The temperature structure of Lake Vanda is not as easily explained. The warmest water (>25°C) is at the

bottom, and there are four isothermal, isohaline layers separated from each other and from the ice and bottom of five layers of stratified water. This amazingly strong inverse thermal stratification is more than compensated by increasing dissolved salt with depth, and the lake is hydrostatically stable. Apparently Lake Vanda is receiving heat by conduction from the bottom which moves slowly upward by conduction through the stratified layers and by convection through the isothermal layers. This heat is then conducted through the ice and is lost from the ice surface (Figure 12).

The heat balance of Lake Vanda during about 1 month during the summer (Table 2) is dominated by net radiation (gain) and evaporation (loss) with lower values for bottom conduction and ice melt. During a 3-month period from late November to late February, the temperature of the top 10 m of water increased by

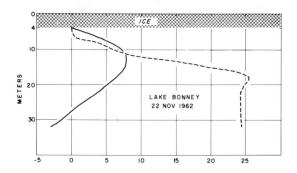

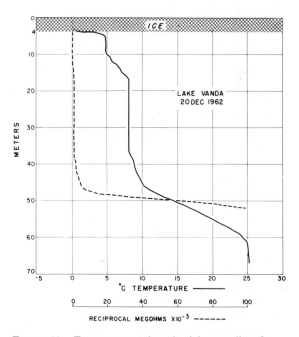

FIGURE 11.   Temperature and conductivity soundings for Antarctic Lakes Bonney and Vanda. Conductivity values are corrected for temperature and standardized for 18°C. From Ragotzkie and Likens, 1964.

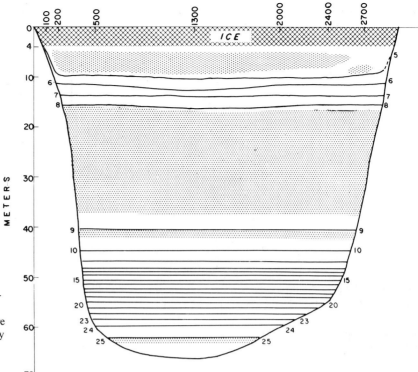

FIGURE 12. Temperature cross-section for Lake Vanda for 20 December 1962. Shaded areas are layers of convection separated by strong gradients of temperature and dissolved solids. From Ragotzkie and Likens, 1964.

about 1°C representing a heat gain of about 17 cal/cm²/day about the same rate as the ice melt term (~20 cal/cm²/day). Although the available data are not sufficient to even estimate the total annual heat budgets of these lakes, this limited analysis of their summer heat budgets suggests that the heat budgets of permanently frozen lakes is almost entirely restricted to changes in ice thickness and that the water plays a minor role. The anomalous temperature structures, permanent ice cover, and exposure to the extremes of polar climate, particularly radiation, of these lakes make them especially interesting subjects for heat budget studies.

Synthesis of the heat budget

In the preceding sections we have discussed the analysis of the heat budgets of lakes, the heat exchange processes which are involved, and the physical and thermal behavior of lakes. It is now possible to analyze the problem from the synthetic or model approach. We will show how a first estimate of the heat budget of a lake can be obtained with a minimum of observational data and without regular year-round *in situ* monitoring of the lake itself.

First of all the thermal cycle of the lake is divided into two periods: the ice-covered period and the ice-free period.

Ice-covered period

In a comprehensive study of lake ice, snow cover, albedo, and climate by members of the Department of Meteorology at the University of Wisconsin–Madison, the progress of the freezeup and breakup of lake ice was observed in the region from Madison, Wisconsin (43° N. latitude) to the Arctic Circle (67° N. latitude) and from the Hudson Bay (90° W. longitude) to Great Bear Lake (120° W. longitude) (Ragotzkie and McFadden, 1962; McFadden, 1965). These observations were made entirely from reconnaissance aircraft provided by the U.S. Navy, using visual observation, continuous time-lapse movie and still photography, and airborne radiometers.

One of the most striking results of this study was that the freezing of lakes is closely correlated to the running mean air temperature of the preceding period.

TABLE 2. Heat Balance for Lake Vanda during the Period 28 November 1962 to 20 December 1962. Heat Flow Values in cal/cm²/day. From Ragotzkie and Likens, 1964

Process	Gain	Loss
Net radiation	110	
Evaporation (sublimation)		125
Conduction from bottom	44	
Storage as ice melt		20+[a]
Total	154	145

[a]Does not include internal melt of ice sheet.

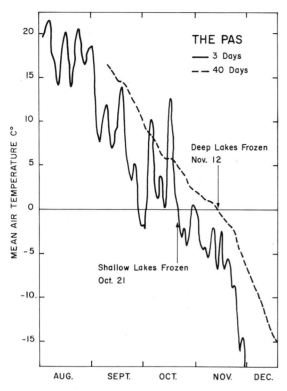

FIGURE 13.   Comparison of lake freezing dates and the 3- and 40-day running mean air temperatures at the Pas. Manitoba, 54° N. latitude for 1961. From McFadden, 1965.

For shallow lakes in the 1- to 3-m-depth range, freezing occurred very close to the date when the 3-day running mean of the mean daily air temperature passed through 0°C and remained mostly below 0°C for the winter. Deep lakes in the range of 6 to 15 m in depth froze when the 40-day running mean of the mean daily air temperature reached 0°C. An example of the results of the 1961 observations near the Pas, Manitoba, at 54° N. latitude is shown in Figure 13. The results of the entire study, summarized in Table 3, show that with few exceptions the freezing date of a lake can be estimated within a day or two if the approximate depth of the lake is known.

By reversing the correlation it is apparent that if the freezing date of a lake is known and a record of mean daily air temperatures is available the lake can be classified as deep or shallow, an important piece of information when synthesizing the heat budget during the ice-free season.

Very deep or very large lakes such as Great Slave, Great Bear, Baker, Dubawnt, Winnipeg, and Reindeer, because of their very large heat storage capacity and extensive exposure to wind, freeze later in the season. The Laurentian Great Lakes, with the exception of Lake Erie, which is quite shallow, rarely freeze over completely due to their great depth and very large heat storage capacity.

Thawing and breakup of lake ice is a much more complicated event. The processes which result in the final breakup of a lake's ice cover are entirely different from those which result in freezing. As discussed earlier, snow cover with its high albedo protects lake ice from solar insolation. Once the snow cover is

TABLE 3.   Comparison of Freeze Dates and Mean Air Temperature

		Deep lakes			Shallow lakes		
Station and N. latitude	Year	Freeze date	40-day mean air T (°C)	Days lead (+) or lag (−) of freezeup vs 40-day (0°C)	Freeze date	3-day mean air T (°C)	Days lead (+) or lag (−) of freezeup vs 3-day (0°C)
Lynn Lake (57°)	1961	25 Oct	−0.5	<−1	—	—	—
The Pas (54°)	1961	12 Nov[a]	0.0	0	21 Oct	−0.4	<−1
Winnipeg (50°)	1961	25 Nov	−0.1	<−1	3 Nov	−1.3	<−1
Kenora (50°)	1961	21 Nov	+0.7	+2	6 Nov	−3.1	<−4
Madison (43°)	1961	16 Dec[b]	−1.7	−3	—	—	—
Baker Lake (64°)	1963	7 Oct	0.0	0	—	—	—
Ennadai (61°)	1963	3 Nov	−0.2	<−1	21 Oct	0.0	0
Lynn Lake (57°)	1963	20 Nov[b]	+1.2	+1	29 Oct	+1.9	+3
The Pas (54°)	1963	—	—	—	4 Nov	+2.0	+7
Kenora (50°)	1963	1 Dec	+0.9	+1	15 Nov	−0.3	−3
Madison (43°)	1963	18 Dec[b]	−2.2	−3	30 Nov[b]	−1.1	<−1

[a]Freezing date obtained by extrapolation.
[b]Freezing line observed at station location.
From McFadden, 1965.

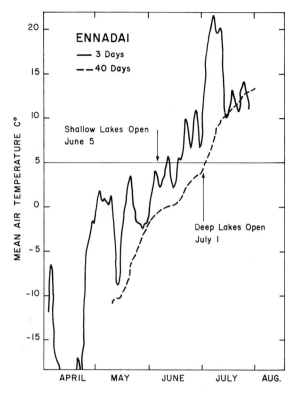

FIGURE 14.   Comparison of lake ice breakup dates and the 3- amd 40-day running mean air temperatures at Ennadai, N.W.T., 61° N. latitude for 1964. From McFadden, 1965.

gone, solar heating of the water melts the ice sheet, but final breakup is generally triggered by a sustained windy period. Despite these complications a running mean air temperature of +5°C is a reasonably good predictor of lake ice breakup. Deep lakes in the region studied tended to breakup when the 40-day running mean reached +5°C and shallow lakes lost their ice when the 3-day running reached +5°C. Figure 14 shows an example of the ice breakup observations. The breakup of shallow lakes was less predictable on the basis of air temperature alone. The 3-day running mean of air temperature ranged from 2 to 13.3°C at breakup, but, as air temperatures are rising rapidly during this time of year, use of the +5°C threshold does not result in errors of more than a few days in estimating the date of breakup (Table 4). Caution should be exercised in using this method for estimating ice breakup date. Wind storms or lack of wind can result in an earlier or later breakup. Direct observations, either by ground observers or aerial reconnaissance, are preferable.

Since lakes freeze over when their entire water mass is $1 \pm 1°C$, the heat content of the water at the time of freezing is nearly zero (based on 0°C as the zero heat base). Heating of the water proceeds very slowly during the ice-covered period (Figures 6 and 7). Although this term cannot be estimated from airborne reconnaissance, it can be roughly estimated by using measured heating rates for shallow and deep lakes in similar climates and latitudes.

Negative heat stored in the ice cover itself tends to be the same for all the larger lakes exposed to the same climate. Therefore, ice thickness records for one or two of the larger lakes of a region provide reasona-

TABLE 4.   Comparison of Opening Dates and Mean Air Temperature

		Deep lakes			Shallow lakes		
Station and N. latitude	Year	Thaw date	40-day mean air T (°C)	Days lead (+) or lag (−) of breakup vs 40-day (5°C)	Thaw date	3-day mean air T (°C)	Days lead (+) or lag (−) of breakup vs 3-day (5°C)
Madison (43°)	1963	3 Apr[a]	<3.0	+14	3 Apr[a]	13.3	−10
The Pas (54°)	1963	22 May	4.9	<+1	—	—	—
Lynn Lake (57°)	1963	2 Jun	4.4	+3	23 May	6.9	<−1
Ennadai (61°)	1963	24 Jun	4.6	+2	6 Jun	10.8	−4
Baker Lake (64°)	1963	—	—	—	25 Jun	5.5	<−1
Brochet (58°)	1964	1 June[b]	3.9	+7	—	—	—
Ennadai (62°)	1964	1 July	4.3	<+2	5 Jun	3.4	+5
Yellowknife (63°)	1964	7 Jun	5.2	<−1	—	—	—
Snare Rapids (63°)	1964	8 Jun	5.1	<−1	—	—	—
Contwoyto (66°)	1964	—	—	—	10 Jun	2.0	+10

[a]Thawing line observed at station.
[b]Opening date obtained by extrapolation.
From McFadden, 1965.

bly good estimates for the other lakes. Reservoirs with fluctuating water levels or flowages with rapid flow through of water are exceptions and are not included in this attempt to synthesize the heat budget of a lake.

Ice-free period

Breakup of the candled ice cover usually occurs quickly under the influence of wind and the ice may disappear completely within a day or two. This rapid melting of the ice cover, which may be 10 to 20 cm thick, might be expected to result in a slight cooling of the water of the lake. However, this cooling, if it occurs, has not been reliably observed because of the difficulty of measuring the water temperature in the days immediately before breakup. Nevertheless it must be assumed that some of the heat required to melt the ice is derived from the underlying water, but the exact amount depends on the thickness of the ice at breakup and the intensity of solar insolation on the day or two when melting occurs.

In any case, at the beginning of the ice-free season the heat content of the lake is quite low. As the lake is isothermal immediately after ice out, a quite good estimate of heat content can be obtained from a single measurement of the near surface water away from remnant shore ice or shallow bays. Multiplying this value by the mean depth of the lake yields the heat content per unit area.

The course of the spring and summer heating cycle is a function first of the climate and second of the morphometry of the lake itself. Under given climatic conditions the maximum surface temperature attained by a lake is affected very little by its depth. Therefore the primary factor affecting the maximum heat content of a lake is its average depth. For a stratified lake the effective depth controlling heat content is the depth of the thermocline. The reasons for this are twofold. First the thermocline isolates the deeper hypolimnion from the heat sources at the surface, thus greatly reducing the heat transfer into that portion of the lake, and second the area of the lake at levels below the thermocline and hence the volume of the "unit lake" is much less than the portion above the thermocline. This effect is shown in Figure 15 where the annual heat budget for Lake Mendota is plotted against depth. That portion of the lake below the average summer thermocline, 11 m, has an annual heat budget of about 20% of the lake as a whole. In the epilimnion or mixed layer, the water temperature is nearly isothermal except during prolonged calm periods. Therefore, the heat content of the epilimnion can be estimated directly from the surface water temperature if the depth of the thermocline, and the hypsometric curve are known. The heat content of the entire lake will be somewhat greater than this value but probably not more than 20% greater except in very deep lakes.

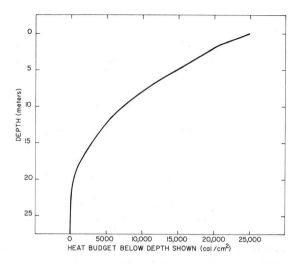

FIGURE 15.   Annual heat budget of Lake Mendota as a function of depth based on 27 years of temperature records from Birge; heat budget data are calculated by Dutton and Bryson, 1962. See text for further explanation.

For an unstratified lake, i.e., either a very shallow lake or a very large lake of intermediate depth, a reasonably good estimate of heat content can be obtained from the product of the surface temperature and the mean depth.

To synthesize the heat budget of lake during the ice-free period, then, all that is needed is a record of the surface water temperature and either the mean depth for unstratified lakes or the summer thermocline depth for stratified lakes. In addition the hypsometric curve is needed for stratified lakes in order to correct for the decrease in area with depth.

Surface water temperatures can, of course, be measured directly by conventional thermometer. However, it is not always possible for an observer to visit many different lakes at regular intervals throughout the ice-free season especially if the lakes are relatively inaccessible. A much more efficient and powerful method is the use of an airborne infrared radiometer. The state of the art of remote sensing of surface water temperatures by infrared radiometer has advanced rapidly in recent years, and surface water temperatures can now be measured with an error of less than 1°C under most conditions. Errors from atmospheric and particularly water vapor absorption must be taken into account, but in nontropical regions airborne measurements made from an altitude of 1000 ft or less are generally accurate within 1°C even without atmospheric correction. For further discussion of this technique see Ragotzkie and Bratnick (1965), Clark (1964), or Scarpace et al. (1975). By use of this technique it is relatively simple to obtain the surface temperatures of a large number of lakes even in relatively inaccessible regions by regular flights throughout the ice-free period. Peterson (1965) analyzed airborne radiometric surface temperatures of 300 lakes in central Canada. As expected he found that shallow lakes tended to be warmer in the spring and deep lakes were warmer in the fall. Unfortunately as no flights were conducted during mid-summer no maximum heat content estimates could not be made.

Lake depths present a slightly more complex problem although once known, repeated observations are not necessary. If ice freezing dates are known lakes in a region can be characterized as shallow or deep by correlation with running mean air temperatures as described previously. For shallow lakes we need the mean depth.

The mean depth of a lake is generally obtained from a detailed bathymetric map of the basin. As such maps are rarely available for remote lakes, an alternate method is needed. An indirect estimate of the mean depth of a lake can be obtained from the primary period of the surface seiche. By Merian's formula the period of a seiche is given by:

$$T = 2L/(n\sqrt{gh}) \qquad (8)$$

where T = period of the seiche,
 L = length of the lake
 g = acceleration of gravity,
 h = mean depth of the lake, and
 n = number of nodes.

If the lake is reasonably simple in form, the primary or uninodal seiche is usually dominant and $n = 1$. The mean depth can then be calculated directly from the seiche period. It is relatively simple to determine the primary seiche period by means of a water level recorder located at one end of a lake. Under very primitive conditions the seiche period can also be obtained by manually recording visual observations of lake level over a period of time and then analyzing the record for the primary period of lake level fluctuation. A major virtue of this approach is that a boat is not needed so any lake which can be reached on foot or by seaplane can be "sounded" from the shore. The method was tested on ten different lakes (Stewart, 1964) with known average depths ranging from 2.1 to 20.2 m and lengths ranging from 0.3 to 13.7 km. The standard error of estimate of mean depth using the seiche period was 0.6 m.

For shallow lakes the mean depth is the only parameter we need to combine with the surface water temperatures to obtain the heat content. For deep, and hence stratified lakes, we need to know the summer thermocline depth when the heat content is at or near its maximum. It would appear that this information could only be obtained by repeated vertical temperature soundings thus defeating the entire purpose of a heat budget synthesis from minimal data. Although a great deal of work has been done on the depth of the thermocline or mixing layer in lakes and oceans, most approaches are highly mathematical or require exten-

sive observational data. In attempt to simplify this problem, the temperature structures of a number of lakes in Wisconsin and central Canada were monitored throughout the spring and summer seasons. From this extensive body of data a very simple relation emerged which related the depth of the summer thermocline to the maximum unobstructed fetch of the lake.

$$D_{th} = 4\sqrt{F} \qquad (9)$$

where D_{th} = depth of thermocline in meters and
 F = fetch in kilometers.

The observations leading to this simple relationship are illustrated in Figure 16. It is interesting that the relation seems to hold over a range of lake sizes from 0.1 to over 20 km. No effect of lake orientation could be found, but there was a tendency for thermoclines in sheltered lakes to be shallower and in exposed lakes to be slightly deeper than predicted. Thus, for deep lakes the depth of the summer thermocline can be estimated within a meter or so solely by reference to an outline map or aerial photograph from which the fetch can be determined.

To complete the synthetic calculation of the summer heat budget of a stratified lake we need the hypsometric curve of the lake's basin. Though no indirect method exists for determining the detailed bathymetry of a particular lake, inspection of the hypsometric curves for a number of lakes reveals that the basins of many lakes are V-shaped or nearly so. Though exceptions to this generalization certainly exist, the assumption of a V-shaped basin is a reasonable first estimate of lake basin shape. Such a first estimate of a hypso-

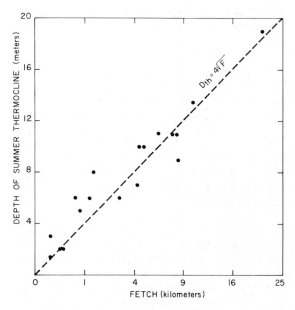

FIGURE 16.   Relationship between summer thermocline depth and fetch. Dashed line shows relationship $D_{th} = 4\sqrt{F}$.

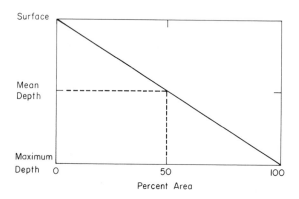

FIGURE 17.   Hypsometric curve for a V-shaped lake. Mean depth is obtained from the primary period of the surface seiche.

metric curve can be constructed by taking the mean depth, obtained from the seiche period, as equal to the depth at which the area is 50% of the surface area and connecting that point with the zero depth–100% area point with a straight line. This line is extended to the zero percent area point which arbitrarily defines the maximum depth as twice the mean depth. The procedure is illustrated in Figure 17.

We now have all the elements to synthesize a heat budget for a lake during the ice-free period. For shallow unstratified lakes the heat content per unit area is taken as the product of the surface temperature and the mean depth (volumetric heat capacity 1.0 cal/cm³):

$$\Sigma H_s = T_{sfc} \cdot \overline{D} \quad (\text{cal/cm}^2) \quad (10)$$

For stratified lakes the heat content calculation includes the surface temperature, the depth of the thermocline, and a hypsometric term. If the linear hypsometric curve for a V-shaped lake basin is used, the heat content can be expressed as:

$$\Sigma H_s = T_{sfc} \cdot D_{th}/2. \quad (11)$$

By taking half of the thermocline depth the linear hypsometric term is included.

The heat storage of a lake (H_s) on the dates of ice breakup and freezeup can be obtained from the mean water temperature times the mean depth. If aerial radiometric temperature measurements are not available, the mean water temperature at breakup can be taken as 2 to 3°C for deep lakes and 4 to 6°C for shallow lakes. Water temperature at freezeup can be estimated from the fetch (Figure 4).

In summary the annual heat storage cycle of a lake can be synthesized from the dates of ice breakup and freezeup, surface temperatures obtained by airborne radiometer, mean depth from the period of the surface seiche, thermocline depth from the fetch, and the assumption of V-shaped basin and a linear hypsome-

tric curve. Winter heat storage requires direct measurement of ice thickness, but by aerial observations of snow cover and albedo the periods of ice growth and wastage can be determined.

Admittedly such a synthesis is crude and represents only a first estimate of the annual course of the heat storage term and thermal structure of a lake. However, it provides a model for the calibration of lakes as climatic indicators. The ice phenology of lakes provides an estimate of mean air temperature and surface water temperature, and heat content in the early season is a good measure of net radiation. Zones of sharp climatic gradients or regions of climate homogeneity can be readily identified from ice phenology and water surface temperatures. The synthetic model also provides estimates of lake parameters such as mean depth, thermocline depth, water temperature, and length of ice cover which are of interest to biological and chemical limnologists. Finally the synthetic model provides a more systematic approach to the study of the heat budgets of lakes.

References

Bauer, K. G., and J. A. Dutton. (1960). *Flight Investigations of Surface Albedo*. Tech. Rep. No. 2, Contract DA-36-039-SC-8082, Department of Meteorology, University of Wisconsin. 68 pp.

Bowen, I. S. (1926). The ratio of heat losses by conduction and by evaporation from any water surface. *Phys. Rev.,* **27**:779–787.

Clark, J. (Ed.). (1964). *Techniques for Infrared Survey of Sea Temperature*. Bur. Sport Fish. and Wildlife Circ. No. 202.

Dutton, J. A., and R. A. Bryson. (1962). Heat flux in Lake Mendota. *Limnol. Oceanogr.* **7** (1):80–97.

Koonce, J. F. (1972). Seasonal succession of phytoplankton and a model of the dynamics of phytoplankton growth and nutrient uptake. Ph.D. Thesis, University of Wisconsin–Madison.

McFadden, J. A. (1965). *The Interrelationship of Lake Ice and Climate in Central Canada*. Tech. Rep. No. 20, Nonr 1202 (07), Department of Meteorology, University of Wisconsin–Madison. 120 pp.

Peterson, J. T. (1965). *On the Distribution of Lake Temperatures in Central Canada Observed From the Air*. Tech. Rep. No. 22, Nonr 1202 (07), Department of Meteorology, University of Wisconsin–Madison. 35 pp.

Ragotzkie, R. A., and M. Bratnick. (1965). Pp. 349–357. Infrared temperature patterns on Lake Superior and inferred vertical motions. *Proc. 9th Conf. Great Lakes Res.,* University of Michigan Great Lakes Res. Div., Publ. 13.

Ragotzkie, R. A., and G. E. Likens. (1964). The heat balance of two antarctic lakes. *Limnol. Oceanogr.* **9**:412–425.

Ragotzkie, R. A. and J. D. McFadden (1962). Operation

Freeze-up: *An aerial reconnaissance of climate and lake ice in central Canada*. Tech. Rep. No. 10, Nonr 1202 (07). Department of Meteorology, University of Wisconsin–Madison. 26 pp.

Scarpace, F. L., R. P. Madding, and T. Green III. (1975). Scanning thermal plumes. *Photogrammetr. Eng. Remote Sensing*. **4** (10):1223–1231.

Scott, J. T. (1964). *A Comparison of the Heat Balance of Lakes in Winter*. Tech. Rep. No. 13, Nonr 1202 (07), Department of Meteorology, University of Wisconsin–Madison. 133 pp.

Stewart, R. (1964). On the estimation of lake depth from the period of the seiche, *Limnol. Oceanogr.* **9** (4):606–607.

Sverdrup, H. V., M. V. Johnson, and R. H. Fleming. (1946). *The Oceans*. Prentice–Hall, New York, NY. 1087 pp.

Twitchell, P. F. (1976). Water–air boundary investigations. Ph.D. Thesis, Oceanography and Limnology, University of Wisconsin–Madison. 154 pp.

Chapter 2

Water Circulation and Dispersal Mechanisms

G. T. Csanady

Introduction

Water motions in lakes are mostly caused by the wind. Random variability of the wind and the geometrical complexity of natural lake basins combine to produce temporally changing and spatially nonuniform water motions. The human mind cannot fully comprehend the complexity of these motions even in principle, because an infinite number of parameters are necessary for their full description, and simplifying strategies must be adopted. One time-honored approach is some form of averaging, the reduction of complexity to a few statistics. For example, monthly mean current patterns may be studied in a basin, or current records obtained at a single location subjected to spectral analysis. However, some of the details removed by statistical processing can be of interest in their own right, or their effects may be important in some practical problem such as pollution.

An alternative, fruitful approach is to focus on some conspicuous feature of lake behavior and distill from complex reality a relatively simple, identifiable *distinct phenomenon.* An example from classical limnology is the *seiche* or periodic lake level oscillation. For the purpose of understanding an identified phenomenon, one first constructs a simple *conceptual model,* that is, an imaginary lake idealized to the point where a few parameters suffice to describe its behavior. A successful conceptual model contains just enough complexity to simulate the phenomenon of interest realistically, that is, in such a way that some *quantitative* correspondence between model and prototype behavior may be exhibited. A hierarchy of conceptual models of increasing complexity may then be developed to refine understanding and to improve the accuracy of quantitative simulation. There are of course clear limits to this approach, because any given phenomenon interacts with many others. A point of diminishing return is soon reached as a conceptual model is made more complex.

Yet another approach is to analyze observations and determine *budgets* of momentum and kinetic energy for a whole lake, or for selected portions of it. This sometimes exposes the physical causes of observed motions with particular clarity.

In recent years considerable progress has been registered in lake hydrodynamics through the conceptual model approach. Much of the work related to Lake Ontario, where the International Field Year on the Great Lakes (IFYGL), an 18-month observational study was carried out in 1972–73. Some advances have also been made in understanding mean circulation, and even momentum and kinetic energy budgets. Most recent work concerned large lakes and large scale motions, the behavior of which had previously been almost completely unknown.

The present chapter concentrates on these recent advances in lake hydrodynamics and attempt a synthesis of them into a coherent intellectual framework. The fundamentals of the subject are well covered in classical texts, such as those of Proudman (1953) and Hutchinson (1957). After a very brief summary of fundamental principles and equations, this chapter will deal with new insights and new empirical knowledge. Most of this is derived from IFYGL and is especially relevant to lakes so large that the earth's rotation is important in their hydrodynamics. Even so, it is not possible to cover all that is new and interesting, only what is well established in fact and understanding.

Fundamental equations

Experience has shown that medium and large scale water motions in lakes are well described by the equations of motion simplified according to the hydrostatic and Boussinesq approximations. Moreover, the linearized forms of these equations, in which advective momentum fluxes are neglected, are usually quite successful in accounting for observed currents, surface elevations, or thermocline movements. Momentum fluxes due to motions of a much shorter time scale than the inertial period appear as Reynolds stresses in these equations. Reynolds stress, analogous to the viscous stress, is the transport of momentum by turbulent velocity fluctuations. However, only those Reynolds stress components representing shear stress in horizontal planes are practically significant. The vertical gradients of these stresses are important momentum sources or sinks in the horizontal equations of motion. They derive their high magnitude from wind stress and bottom stress and from the relatively rapid variation of these stresses in the vertical. The hydrostatic approximation reduces the number of momentum equations to be considered to two, and the Boussinesq approximation allows the effects of internal density differences to be described by a dynamic height term:

$$D = \int_z^0 \frac{\rho - \rho_0}{\rho_0}\, dz \qquad (1)$$

where ρ_0 is reference density and $z = 0$ is the undisturbed free surface.

The Reynolds stresses in horizontal planes along the two horizontal coordinates, τ_x and τ_y, are conveniently converted to the kinematic quantities.

$$F_x = \tau_x/\rho_0, \ \ F_y = \tau_y/\rho_0.$$

With these concepts and simplifications the linearized equations of motion and continuity are:

$$\frac{\partial u}{\partial t} - fv = -g\frac{\partial(\zeta + D)}{\partial x} + \frac{\partial F_x}{\partial z}$$
$$\frac{\partial v}{\partial t} + fu = -g\frac{\partial(\zeta + D)}{\partial y} + \frac{\partial F_y}{\partial z} \qquad (2)$$
$$\frac{\partial u}{\partial x} + \frac{\partial v}{\partial y} + \frac{\partial w}{\partial z} = 0.$$

Here $f = 2\Omega \sin \phi$ is the Coriolis parameter, with Ω = angular speed of the earth and ϕ = latitude. The effects of the earth's rotation are quite conspicuous in some phenomena observed in large lakes. The symbol ζ denotes free surface elevation above hydrostatic equilibrium. Strictly speaking, this should include a term accounting for atmospheric pressure variations, $\zeta = \zeta_s + \zeta_a$, where ζ_s is actual surface displacement from equilibrium and

$$\zeta_a = \frac{p_a}{\rho_0 g}. \qquad (3)$$

However, the horizontal variations in atmospheric pressure, p_a, over a lake can usually be neglected. This will be understood below.

Eqs. (2) may be regarded as three equations for the three velocity components u, v, and w, noting that to the linearization approximation

$$\frac{\partial \zeta}{\partial t} = w(0). \qquad (4)$$

To solve Eqs. (2) for given boundary conditions it is necessary to specify the distributions $D(x,y)$, $F_x(x,y,z)$, and $F_y(x,y,z)$ either as externally impressed fluxes or parameterize them in terms of the velocities. The density of lake water is for all practical purposes a function of temperature alone, so that D depends on the temperature distribution, which is subject to the heat conduction equation. If advective terms and other horizontal fluxes are neglected analogously to Eq. (2), the heat conduction equation reduces to

$$\frac{\partial T}{\partial t} = -\frac{\partial q}{\partial z} \qquad (5)$$

where T is temperature and $q = Q_H/\rho_0 c_p$ is "kinematic" vertical heat flux, with Q_H vertical heat flux in ordinary units such as kcal m^{-2} sec $^{-1}$, and c_p specific heat at constant pressure. The neglect of advective terms in this equation is not as readily justifiable as in Eq. (2): over the short term the divergence of the horizontal advective heat transport (uT, vT) is often much greater than the divergence of the vertical flux q. A corresponding alternative simplification of the heat conduction equation, valid mainly for short term phenomena, is then:

$$\frac{dT}{dt} = 0 \qquad (6)$$

where d/dt indicates the total derivative. The temperature of fluid particles thus remains conserved in the course of their motion. An equilibrium density distribution may then be prescribed and various dynamical problems solved on the assumption that fluid particles retain their density. A class of conceptual models based on this approximation makes use of a two-layer approach, the lake being idealized as consisting of a light epilimnion and a heavy hypolimnion, an abrupt change of density taking place at the thermocline. The latter is taken to be of vanishing thickness. In using such models one must keep in mind that Eq. (6) constitutes a rather drastic simplification, valid to an adequate approximation at most for a few days, and often only for a few hours.

Parameterization of Reynolds stresses

One of the principal difficulties in modelling water movements in lakes remains that the turbulent processes giving rise to Reynolds stresses are very incompletely understood, especially in the presence of stratification. The best present evidence is that well away from boundaries and stable interfaces the classical Austausch hypothesis is a realistic approximation, so that stresses may be parameterized as

$$F_x = A \frac{\partial u}{\partial z} \qquad F_y = A \frac{\partial v}{\partial z} \qquad (7)$$

where A is a momentum exchange coefficient, expressible as the product of an eddy length scale and an eddy velocity scale. In the interior region of turbulent flow, in a well-mixed water column these two scales may be taken to be constant.

The wind exerts a stress τ_0 on the water surface, usually calculated from a quadratic drag formula:

$$\tau_0 = c_d \rho_a V^2 \qquad (8)$$

where c_d is drag coefficient, ρ_a is air density, and V is wind speed at some reference level (often 10 m: c_d is then the "10-m drag coefficient"). A kinematic form of this stress is convenient:

$$u_*^2 = \frac{\tau_0}{\rho_0}. \qquad (9)$$

Here u_* is known as the friction velocity, and ρ_0 is the previously used reference density (of water). A typical value of the drag coefficient in Eq. (8) is 1.6×10^{-3}, so that a 7 m sec^{-1} wind evokes a stress of 1 dyn cm^{-2}, and a friction velocity of $u_* = 1$ cm sec^{-1}, a value which may be taken as typical.

Immediately below the free surface an analogue of the turbulent wall layer is present, within which the velocity changes rapidly, but the stress remains much the same as at the surface. Present understanding of turbulent flow within this zone is minimal so that one usually avoids predicting what the actual surface velocity is under given external circumstances. In the interior region of the flow, typically a meter or more below the surface, the eddy velocity scale is u_*, the length scale proportional to the mixed depth h (total depth for a fully mixed column, depth above the thermocline otherwise). For mixed depths of the order of 20 m an approximate formula for the Austausch coefficient is (Csanady, 1972a)

$$A = \frac{u_* h}{20}. \qquad (10)$$

There is no reliable information on stresses exerted at a thermocline. In many problems, however, neglecting any interface stresses gives realistic results for short periods.

At a solid bottom (at $z = -h$) a quadratic drag formula similar to Eq. (8) applies with good approximation. Stating this in component form,

$$F_x = c_d u W \qquad F_y = c_d v W \qquad (11)$$

where $W = (u^2 + v^2)^{1/2}$ is velocity magnitude and u, v are velocity components *above* a wall layer within

which rapid velocity changes take place. In practice the bottom wall layer is typically 1 m deep, much as its analogue at the free surface. The bottom drag coefficient [c_d in Eq. (11)] is a function of bottom roughness and its typical magnitude is 2×10^{-3}. Empirical evidence on bottom drag coefficients is very scarce.

Calculations of the velocity distribution within the *interior* region of turbulent flow may thus be made imposing surface and bottom conditions, equating the stresses according to Eq. (7) with those from Eqs. (8) and (11). It is important to remember that this does not resolve the wall layers: the "surface" velocity calculated in this manner is actually velocity some distance below the surface, and the "bottom" velocity refers to the flow just outside the bottom wall layer. It is emphasized here that the classical zero-velocity (no-slip) bottom boundary condition, coupled with a constant eddy viscosity, gives quite unrealistic results.

Transport equations

The uncertainties affecting Reynolds stresses provide powerful incentive for avoiding the necessity of quantifying them. Because only vertical gradients of the stresses enter Eq. (2) as significant accelerations, a plausible step is to integrate these equations with respect to depth. The depth-integrated or *transport* equations contain components of the horizontal transport or depth-integrated volume flux:

$$U = \int_{-h}^{\zeta} u \, dz \qquad V = \int_{-h}^{\zeta} v \, dz \qquad (12)$$

where $z = -h(x, y)$ is the lake bottom. These quantities are subject to the following equations, obtained from Eq. (2) by integration:

$$\frac{\partial U}{\partial t} - fV = -g \left(h \frac{\partial \zeta}{\partial x} + \frac{\partial Z}{\partial x} \right) + F_{xo} - F_{xh}$$

$$\frac{\partial V}{\partial t} + fU = -g \left(h \frac{\partial \zeta}{\partial y} + \frac{\partial Z}{\partial y} \right) + F_{yo} - F_{yh}$$

$$\frac{\partial U}{\partial x} + \frac{\partial V}{\partial y} = -\frac{\partial \zeta}{\partial t} \qquad (13)$$

where $Z = \int_{-h}^{0} D \, dz$ is the integrated dynamic height term. Most frequently the transport equations are used in connection with simple models, in which the water column is assumed homogeneous: in that case $Z = 0$. Subscripts o and h refer to surface and bottom stresses.

Equations similar to Eq. (13) may be written down for 2, 3, etc., layer models, the density being assumed constant layer by layer. Two-layer models, for example, have been extensively discussed by Proudman (1953).

Vorticity equation

Some phenomena cannot be modelled realistically using the linearized Eqs. (2). An alternative approach is to regard the fluid column well mixed (at least layer by layer) so that the velocity components u, v are assumed constant with depth. From the full (nonlinear) equations of motion and continuity an equation may then be derived for the vertical component of vorticity:

$$\omega = \frac{\partial v}{\partial x} - \frac{\partial u}{\partial y}. \quad (14)$$

The equation applies to fluid columns of depth h, which may vary not only in space but also following the motion of fluid columns:

$$\frac{d}{dt}\left(\frac{\omega + f}{h}\right) = \frac{1}{h}\frac{\partial}{\partial x}\left(\frac{F_{yo} - F_{yh}}{h}\right) \\ - \frac{1}{h}\frac{\partial}{\partial y}\left(\frac{F_{xo} - F_{xh}}{h}\right). \quad (15)$$

The quantity $(\omega + f)/h$ is known as the "potential vorticity." Eq. (15) states that this quantity varies following the motion of a fluid column as the curl of the net external force (stress at the top less stress at the bottom, divided by depth). In the absence of such stresses, potential vorticity is conserved. Thus when a fluid column is stretched, i.e., h increases, $\omega + f$ must also increase. Since f is constant for all practical purposes over horizontal distances encountered in almost all lakes, positive vorticity is generated. Conversely, squashing of a water column generates negative vorticity.

The potential vorticity equation is advantageously used in place of one of the nonlinear momentum equations, when momentum advection may not be ignored.

Setup and seiche

A brief discussion of some results of classical limnology will illustrate the notions of *identified phenomenon* and *conceptual model* introduced earlier. Observations of lake levels have shown that a steady wind causes a "setup" of the lake surface, the downwind end standing higher than the upwind one. A simple conceptual model is a rectangular basin of constant depth containing water of constant density and being subject to wind stress directed parallel to the x axis.

Eqs. (13) show that a static equilibrium is possible in which the transports and bottom stresses are zero and the wind stress is balanced by a surface elevation gradient of magnitude

$$\frac{d\zeta}{dx} = \frac{u_*^2}{gh}. \quad (16)$$

For a "typical" wind stress of $\rho u_*^2 = 1$ dyn cm^{-2} and a depth of 100 m, Eq. (16) gives an elevation gradient of 10^{-7} or 1 cm in 100 km. Strong winds on shallow water produce a steeper gradient. Eq. (16) agrees in order of magnitude with observation, although there are a number of complications associated with wave run-up on the downwind shore and with the variable depth distribution.

Lake level observations also show that the sudden application or disappearance of wind stress causes lake level oscillations, known as "seiches." The same simple conceptual model, rectangular basin of constant depth filled with homogeneous fluid, also provides a good first order description of the seiche. Eqs. (13) have free oscillatory modes of motion as solutions. The calculated frequencies agree quite well with observed ones. The method of excitation may be elucidated by solving the "initial value problem," i.e., by determining the model's response to a suddenly imposed wind. These results have been discussed many times in the literature and there is no need to dwell upon them here.

Refinements of the simplest seiche model account for effects of variable depth, irregular basin outlines, Coriolis force, and bottom friction. Some interesting recent advances are contained in papers by Platzman (1972), Rao and Schwab (1976), and Mortimer and Fee (1976).

These remarks complete the introductory portion of this chapter. We now turn to a more substantive discussion of recent advances.

Wind-driven coastal currents

As public interest arose in water pollution problems in North America in the 1960s, more and more observations of water movements were made in the Great Lakes, in nearshore as well as in deeper waters. A consensus quickly grew up that the main motive force of these motions was the wind, and it was also realized that the wind stress was exerted mainly during episodes of strong winds in relatively short bursts. The observed motions exhibited formidable complexity, but a picture emerged that current meters placed within a few kilometers from shore were exposed to a different "population" of currents than those in deep water (Birchfield and Davidson, 1967; Malone, 1968; Jones, 1968). Specifically, current speeds in the shore zone were found to be relatively high, of order 30 cm sec^{-1} or more, especially following storms, and the direction of the motion was parallel to the shore for a dominant fraction of time. By contrast, in deeper water currents tended to be weaker (although not always and not everywhere), and the direction of motion was more uniformly distributed over all directions of the compass. More systematic studies of the nearshore zone in Lake Ontario (Csanady, 1972c; Blanton, 1974) resulted in the explicit recognition that a "coastal boundary layer" (CBL) existed, within which the flow was rectified by the shore and tended to be fairly energetic. The width of the CBL could be put at 7 km at one location, in somewhat the same inexact way as other boundary layer thicknesses are usually judged.

One factor which complicates matters considerably is the seasonal march of stratification in lakes, the warming of nearshore waters early in spring, and the formation of a seasonal thermocline later. The density differences so created have some important dynamic effects, as will be discussed in detail below. However, the above described wind-driven coastal currents were present with or without such density differences, so that a mechanism must exist for their generation in homogeneous water.

The next few sections shall attempt to elucidate this mechanism. Putting the argument into the logical framework defined in the Introduction, it runs as follows. We distill from observation the distinct phenomenon of the wind-driven longshore current, occupying a coastal boundary layer of a few kilometers width, where the water column is no more than a few tens of meters deep. A simple conceptual model is developed to explain the dynamics of such a current in a closed basin in *homogeneous* water, to be known as a *topographic gyre*. It is shown that the model describes quantitatively the main features of observed coastal currents. Certain refinements and extensions of the model are then discussed to extend its range of application or to show its limitations.

Topographic gyre model

Consider at first a closed basin of arbitrary shape and depth distribution, over which a wind stress constant in time (but arbitrarily distributed in the horizontal plane) is imposed suddenly at $t = 0$. Neglect the Coriolis forces for the time being and write the depth-integrated equations of motion and continuity for the volume transport components U, V, linearized, and with the hydrostatic approximation assumed, as follows:

$$\left.\begin{aligned} \frac{\partial U}{\partial t} &= -gh\frac{\partial \zeta}{\partial x} + F_x \\ \frac{\partial V}{\partial t} &= -gh\frac{\partial \zeta}{\partial y} + F_y \\ \frac{\partial U}{\partial x} + \frac{\partial V}{\partial y} &= -\frac{\partial \zeta}{\partial t} \end{aligned}\right\}, \quad (17)$$

where F_x, F_y are the components of the wind stress divided by density as used in the preceding sections,

$h(x, y)$ is the water depth, and ζ the surface elevation from equilibrium. The linearization does not apply in the immediate vicinity of the shores where $h \to 0$, but in dealing with relatively large-scale motions this complication may be safely ignored. However, the absence of bottom friction terms in Eqs. (17) is justifiable only in the initial period of response, before significant velocities develop. At later times F_{bx}, F_{by} have to be added to the right-hand side of the first and second of Eqs. (17), leading to a slightly more complex model.

The brief earlier discussion of seiches has shown that these equations describe the behavior of an oscillating system. The response of the basin to a suddenly imposed wind stress may be regarded as consisting of a directly "forced" component (a particular solution of the above equations) and of free modes of oscillations or seiches. The latter are short-period motions of relatively low velocity, swamped in the coastal zone by the much stronger and much more persistent directly wind-driven coastal currents. It is only the forced component of the solution which can model the observed wind-driven coastal currents. Curiously, very little attention has been paid in the oceanographic literature so far to the forced solution of Eqs. (17), in contrast to seiches on which there is an overwhelming wealth of information. The only forced solution of Eqs. (17) which has often been quoted is the static setup of a constant depth basin, briefly mentioned above, in which the lake surface is an inclined plane:

$$\zeta = \frac{F_x}{gh}x + \frac{F_y}{gh}y, \quad U = 0, \quad V = 0. \quad (18)$$

This solution does not satisfy Eq. (17) for nonuniform depth.

For a realistic depth distribution a more complex time-independent elevation distribution $\zeta(x, y)$ may be found. The structure of Eqs. (17) suggests that in this case U and V should be linear functions of time, i.e.,

$$U = At, \quad V = Bt \quad (19)$$

where A, B = function (x, y).

Substituting into Eqs. (17), we find

$$\left.\begin{aligned} A &= -gh\frac{\partial \zeta}{\partial x} + F_x \\ B &= -gh\frac{\partial \zeta}{\partial y} + F_y \\ \frac{\partial A}{\partial x} + \frac{\partial B}{\partial y} &= 0 \end{aligned}\right\} . \quad (20)$$

The boundary conditions are that the normal components of the transport vanish at the shores at all times t, so that the same condition applies to the accelerations A, B. If, subject to these conditions, Eqs. (20) may be solved, the solution yields a time-independent surface level distribution accompanied by a nontrivial transport distribution, increasing linearly with time.

It is not difficult to demonstrate that such solutions

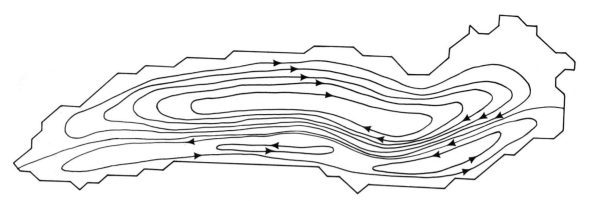

FIGURE 1.   Transport-streamline pattern of wind-driven flow in Lake Ontario. From Rao and Murty (1970).

may, in fact, be found. The third of Eqs. (20) may be satisfied by introducing a streamfunction for the accelerations:

$$A = \frac{\partial \Psi}{\partial y}, \; B = -\frac{\partial \Psi}{\partial x}. \tag{21}$$

The boundary condition at the shores is now $\Psi =$ constant, a streamline coincides with the coastline. Eliminating ζ from the first two of Eqs. (20), we find

$$\frac{\partial}{\partial x}\left[\frac{1}{gh}\left(\frac{\partial \Psi}{\partial x} - F_y\right)\right]$$
$$+ \frac{\partial}{\partial y}\left[\frac{1}{gh}\left(\frac{\partial \Psi}{\partial y} - F_x\right)\right] = 0. \tag{22}$$

This equation may be integrated without difficulty in principle. Numerical models of frictionally controlled steady-state circulation are based on a very similar equation and the calculated flow patterns are qualitatively very similar to what one finds from Eq. (22). A sample solution of this kind due to Rao and Murty (1970) is shown in Figure 1. It refers to Lake Ontario, the depth contours of which are shown in Figure 2, acted upon by a west wind. The real topography was used in the calculations with only slight smoothing. The wind stress was taken to be spatially uniform in the example of Figure 1, but more complex stress distributions are easily handled on a computer.

The characteristic feature of streamline patterns calculated from Eq. (22) is the appearance of closed gyres lying to either side of the deepest axis of the basin. The *upwind* legs of these gyres coincide with and occupy the deep water, while the downwind legs are found in the two shore zones. This pattern appears even though the wind stress is uniform in space, a case for which the forced solution in a constant depth basin involves no motion at all. Clearly, therefore, the appearance of the gyres is tied to the depth distribution or *topography* of the basin floor, hence the terminology "topographic gyres."

The special case of long and narrow basins

To analyze the physical factors underlying the generation of closed gyres by a steady and uniform wind, it is convenient to simplify the above conceptual model still further and consider only basins much longer than they are wide, which contain a considerable central or *trunk* region with *parallel shores and depth contours.* An idealized model of such a basin is sketched in Figure 3, which is seen to represent the main features of the previous example, Lake Ontario, reasonably faithfully. We place the x axis along the length of the basin and consider the forced motion produced by a constant wind stress acting along this same axis $F_x = F$, $F_y = 0$, suddenly imposed at time zero. To be determined is the transport distribution in a cross-section ($x =$ constant plane) within the trunk region.

At any cross-section (whether in the trunk region or not) integration of the third of Eqs. (20) over a region to one side of the cross-section yields by the divergence theorem and in virtue of the boundary conditions:

$$\int_{y_1}^{y_2} A \, dy = 0, \tag{23}$$

where y_1 and y_2 are the coordinates of the shores. In the trunk region, $x_1 < x < x_2$, one may seek a solution wherein transport is parallel to the boundaries and depth contours, i.e., $B = 0$. Because also $F_y = 0$, the second of Eqs. (2) shows $\partial \zeta / \partial y = 0$, i.e., the surface elevation is constant in a cross-section. The first of Eqs. (20) shows:

$$A = -gh\frac{d\zeta}{dx} + F, \; x_1 < x < x_2. \tag{24}$$

Integrating this equation over the cross-section, and observing Eq. (23), it is possible to calculate the elevation gradient:

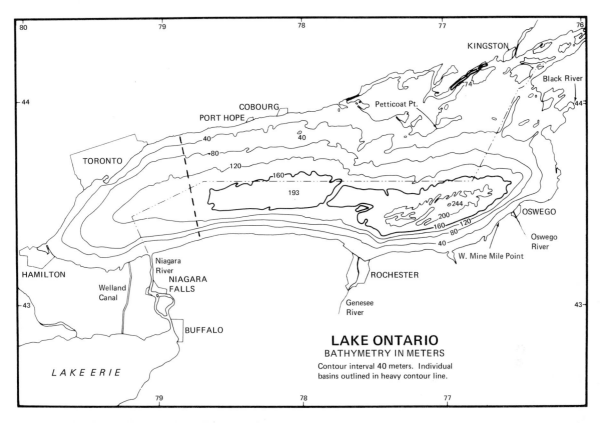

FIGURE 2a.   Depth contours in Lake Ontario, after Sweers (1969). Oshawa–Olcott cross section is shown by dashed line east of Toronto.

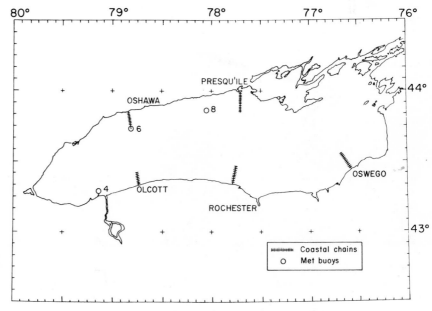

FIGURE 2b.   Locations of coastal chains and key meteorological buoys in Lake Ontario during IFYGL.

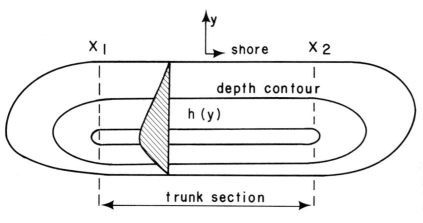

FIGURE 3. Schematic diagram of long and narrow basin with regular "trunk" section in which depth contours are parallel.

$$\frac{d\zeta}{dx} = \frac{Fb}{gS}, \ x_1 < x < x_2, \qquad (25)$$

where $b = y_2 - y_1$ is the width of the lake and S is its cross-sectional area:

$$S = \int_{y_1}^{y_2} h \ dy. \qquad (26)$$

Returning to Eqs. (24) and (19), we may now write the transport in the trunk region as

$$U = Ft\left(1 - \frac{hb}{S}\right), \ x_1 < x < x_2. \qquad (27)$$

It may be verified directly that Eqs. (25) and (27) constitute a solution of Eqs. (17) for the trunk region of a long and narrow basin.

The simple relationship of Eq. (27) is illustrated in Figure 4 using the depth distribution of Lake Ontario at the center of its apparent trunk region, south of Coburg, as an example. The transport distribution may be simply described as a rescaled and displaced depth distribution. The calculated transport is zero where $h = S/b$, which is the *average* depth of the section. The elevation gradient $d\zeta/dx$ is the same as would be produced by the wind in a basin of constant depth, equal to the average depth. Along the locus of the average depth the wind stress and pressure gradient are in exact balance and no downwind or upwind flow is produced. In shallower water the wind-stress is greater than the total gravity force $gh \ d\zeta/dx$ due to the surface slope, and the water accelerates downwind. In deeper water the pressure gradient dominates and a return flow develops.

The transport distribution in the remainder of the basin may now also be elucidated qualitatively. Recalling that by Eqs. (21) and (22) the A, B distribution may be represented by a streamline pattern, streamlines in the trunk region may be determined to correspond to the calculated transport pattern. This yields relatively densely spaced lines both at the center and at the shores, pointing in opposite directions, however. In the end regions the streamlines must close:

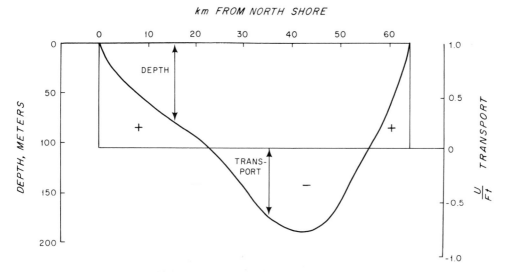

FIGURE 4. Distribution of depth and theoretical longshore transport in a trunk section of Lake Ontario.

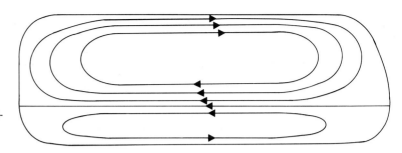

FIGURE 5.   General appearance of wind-forced transport streamlines in long and narrow lakes.

the details depend on the depth distribution, but the appearance of a "double-gyre" pattern follows regardless of these details. Figure 5 illustrates this qualitative inference, which is, of course, also in accord with the numerical calculations for a more realistic example, the character of which was illustrated in Figure 1. The location of the closed gyres is indeed seen to be controlled by the depth distribution, i.e., the *topography* of the basin.

Eq. (27) also shows that the downwind transport is proportional to *Ft,* which is the *impulse* (time-integral) of the wind-stress. The units of the stress-impulse and of depth-integrated transport are equal, both having the physical dimension of L^2T^{-1}. Near shore, where the depth is much less than the average depth, the transport is nearly equal to the windstress impulse, in the frictionless model. The physical reason for this is that the adverse pressure gradient is determined by the average depth. The total pressure-gradient force is proportional to the local depth and in the shallow shore zone is thus negligible in comparison with the wind stress. Therefore virtually all of the latter's impulse is absorbed by the water column, increasing its total momentum almost exactly by the amount of the wind stress impulse.

Intuitively, one is more inclined to think of water particle velocities than of depth-integrated transport. An *average* velocity may be obtained on dividing transport by depth. For the idealized trunk region of Figure 3, such an average velocity distribution is illus-

trated in Figure 6. The solid line shows the distribution calculated from Eq. (27) which contains singularities at the shores, where the depth tends to zero. The broken line is a conjecture showing likely effects of friction, to be discussed further below.

Whatever the exact effects of friction, the calculated velocity distribution is characterized by relatively strong coastal currents and relatively weak return flow. Realistic values of wind stress impulse are a few times 10^4 cm² sec⁻¹. A wind stress of 1 dyn cm⁻² (a "typical" value, caused by about a 7 m sec⁻¹ wind) acting for 10 hr produces an impulse of 36,000 cm² sec⁻¹. In a basin of an average depth of about 100 m, waters shallower than 10 m hardly "feel" the pressure gradient force, as already pointed out. Distributing an impulse of 36,000 cm² sec⁻¹ over a depth of 10 m results in an average velocity of 36 cm sec⁻¹. This indeed is of the same order of magnitude as the speed of "typical" observable coastal currents. By contrast, average return flow velocities (along the upwind legs of the topographic gyres) are an order of magnitude less, because a similar transport is there distributed over a depth an order of magnitude greater. Now it so happens that many different physical factors produce velocities of the order of 3 cm sec⁻¹ in lakes—among them several modes of seiches. Thus the return flow is likely to be submerged into a very noisy background. On the other hand, the directly wind-driven coastal currents stand out as easily identifiable, distinct phenomena.

FIGURE 6.   Depth-average longshore velocity in Lake Ontario trunk section due to a wind impulse of $Ft = 20{,}000$ cm² sec⁻¹.

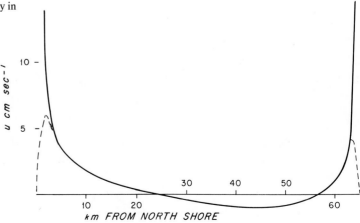

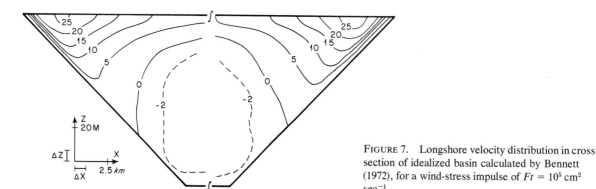

FIGURE 7.   Longshore velocity distribution in cross section of idealized basin calculated by Bennett (1972), for a wind-stress impulse of $Ft = 10^5\ \mathrm{cm^2\ sec^{-1}}$.

The above discussion is based mainly on two of my own papers, Csanady (1973a, 1975a). However, credit for the first clear explanation of directly wind-driven coastal currents in homogeneous water belongs to Bennett (1972, see also 1974). His conclusions are best exhibited by some diagrams incorporating the results of numerical calculations for an idealized long and narrow basin, also including a reasonably realistic representation of internal friction. Although this is in some ways a more complex conceptual model than discussed above, it makes the same points physically. A velocity distribution calculated by Bennett is shown in Figure 7, using various "typical" magnitudes for wind-stress impulse, etc. and an idealized cross-sectional shape. This illustration confirms the earlier result that wind-driven coastal current velocities may be expected to be of the order of 30 cm sec^{-1}, while the speed of compensating return flow in deep water is only of the order of 3 cm sec^{-1}.

Comparison with observation

Because of the idealizations of the topographic gyre conceptual model and of the unavoidable imperfections of field measurements, one can expect to find only rough agreement of wind-stress impulse and depth-integrated momentum where water depth is much less than average, and that with allowances for losses which may reasonably be attributed to friction. As the water depth tends to the cross-sectional average, the depth-integrated longshore momentum should tend to zero. Clearly it takes a fairly detailed survey of the coastal boundary layer to make such a demonstration.

The observations carried out during the International Field Year (IFYGL) on Lake Ontario provided for the first time a sufficiently detailed set of data for testing models of the above kind. The main sources of information for this purpose were the coastal chain studies (Csanady, 1972c), carried out at several locations both on the south and north shores. The coastal chain observations yielded the current velocity distributions in chosen cross-sections, extending from the shores to 10–14 km into the lake. There was sufficient resolution to give reasonable estimates of depth-integrated transports and their distribution in the key nearshore bands. During well-defined storms the winds were more or less uniform over the whole lake and the wind stress impulse could be estimated with acceptable accuracy from meteorological data.

Two clear-cut wind stress impulses occurred early in August 1972, during the second alert period of IFYGL. We shall focus here on the response of the lake during these episodes, as determined by the ob-

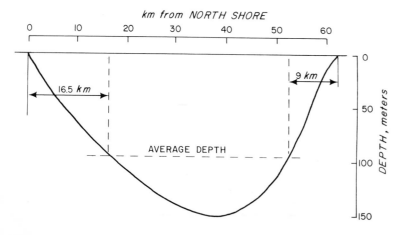

FIGURE 8.   Depth distribution of Lake Ontario along Oshawa–Olcott cross section.

servations in the Olcott–Oshawa cross-section, approximately 90 km east of the western tip of the lake, in a more or less regular trunk region (in the sense of the simple theory discussed before).

The depth distribution of the lake in this section is shown in Figure 8. Late on 6 August a 7-hr weak easterly storm occurred with hourly winds of up to 6 m sec^{-1}. The total estimated westward wind stress impulse for this storm was approximately

$$Ft = 25,000 \text{ cm}^2 \text{ sec}^{-1}.$$

Another stronger and oppositely directed wind stress impulse was exerted on the water on 9 August, with hourly winds of up to 15 m sec^{-1}, lasting some 10 hr and yielding a total estimated wind stress impulse of (counting westward impulse as positive)

$$Ft = -90,000 \text{ cm}^2 \text{ sec}^{-1}.$$

Detailed current distributions during stormy weather could not always be determined but have been obtained at Oshawa on 8 and 10 August and at Olcott on 10 August. Depth-integrated transports in the shore-parallel direction, calculated from the observations, are shown in Figures 9 and 10. The dotted line in Figure 9 shows the change in transport from 8–10 August, presumably directly caused by the wind stress impulse on the 9th.

Except for fairly obvious effects of friction and some minor irregularities, the observations show a transport distribution very much as expected from theory. The maximum transports agree well in order of magnitude with the wind stress impulse estimate. The strongest support for the theory comes from the observation that the integrated transports tended to

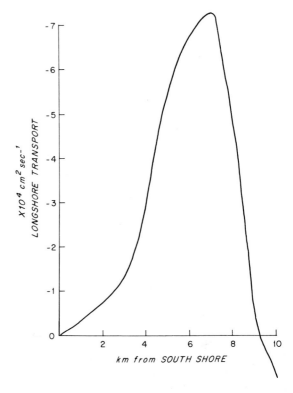

FIGURE 10.   Transport distribution off Olcott, August 10, 1972.

zero near the locus of the average depth both along the north and the south shores. The detailed theoretical transport distribution (for comparison with the data) may be taken to be the depth curve in Figure 8, with the horizontal line labeled "average depth" as the abscissa, and the ordinate appropriately rescaled. The discrepancy between theory and observation is of course strong in very shallow water, where frictional effects are likely to be dominant, but this is to be expected.

We may therefore take the "topographic gyre" conceptual model to be verified, in the sense that it supplies a first order description of a variable depth basin's transient response to a wind stress impulse. A desirable refinement of the model would be to consider effects of friction, at least bottom friction. Furthermore, in order to explore the likely limitations of the model, one would like to assess the effects of the Coriolis force.

Effect of bottom friction

If the water column is vertically well mixed, a quadratic friction law based on average velocity constitutes a realistic representation of bottom stress. In the *trunk* region of a long and narrow basin illustrated in Figure

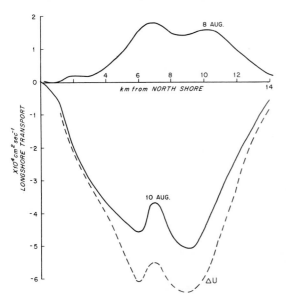

FIGURE 9.   Observed transport distribution along Oshawa coastal chain following two storm episodes in August 1972.

3, where $V = 0$, the longshore transport is then subject to

$$\frac{\partial U}{\partial t} = -gh\frac{d\zeta}{dx} + F - c_d \frac{U}{h}\left|\frac{U}{h}\right| \qquad (28)$$

$$\int_{-y_1}^{y_2} U\,dy = 0 \qquad (29)$$

where c_d is a drag coefficient, of order 2×10^{-3}.

Here $d\zeta/dx$ is again independent of y or t, so that the first equation is easily integrated with respect to time, and yields:

$$\frac{U}{U_a} = \frac{1 - e^{-t/t_f}}{1 + e^{-t/t_f}} \qquad (30)$$

where

$$U_a = hc_d^{-1/2}\left(F - gh\frac{d\zeta}{dx}\right)^{1/2}$$

$$t_f = \frac{h^2}{2c_d U_a} = \frac{h}{2}c_d^{-1/2}\left(F - gh\frac{d\zeta}{dx}\right)^{-1/2}.$$

The physical interpretation of U_a and t_f is, respectively, asymptotic longshore transport velocity and frictional adjustment time. At times large compared to t_f the longshore transport tends to U_a. Note that both U_a and t_f are depth dependent. The above relations, as written down, are valid for $U > 0$, possible only where $F - gh\,d\zeta/dx > 0$. Where the pressure gradient overwhelms the wind stress, $gh\,d\zeta/dx - F > 0$, the signs of the terms under the square roots reverse and

both U and U_a are negative, i.e., point in a direction opposite to F.

On substituting the result of Eq. (30) into the second of Eqs. (29), we find an expression from which the longshore elevation gradient $d\zeta/dx$ may be calculated for any given time t, and for a prescribed depth distribution $h(y)$. At short times $t \to 0$ the results of the previous section are recovered. For t large compared to t_f, an asymptotic steady-state transport distribution is approached, which is qualitatively rather similar to the initial one, schematically illustrated in Figure 5, except that the locus of zero transport shifts to a depth *greater* than average, $h_b > h_a$. In this depth the longshore pressure gradient again balances the wind stress:

$$\frac{d\zeta}{dx} = \frac{F}{gh_b}.$$

This asymptotic gradient is less than the initial one, corresponding to a reduced intensity of the whole topographic gyre. The stress of the wind, integrated over the whole width of the basin, is now balanced partly by the adverse pressure gradient or setup and partly by bottom friction. Most of the frictional force arises in shallow water, where velocities are high.

Figure 11 shows the asymptotic transport distribution calculated from Eqs. (29) and (30) for the cross section of Lake Ontario already illustrated in Figure 4. A bottom drag coefficient of $c_d = 2 \times 10^{-3}$ was used and a steady wind stress of 1 dyn cm^{-2} assumed. The

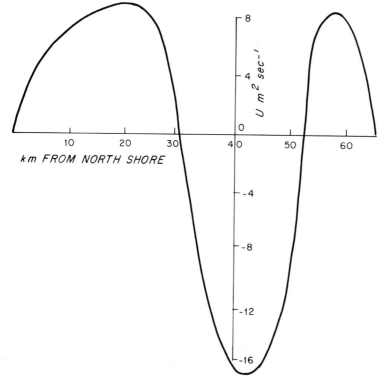

FIGURE 11. Calculated transport distribution in trunk section of Lake Ontario under frictional equilibrium conditions with west wind.

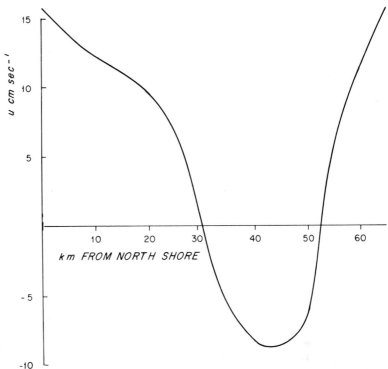

u cm sec^{-1}

km FROM NORTH SHORE

FIGURE 12.   Calculated depth averaged velocity in frictional equilibrium flow.

depth at which the transport vanishes is about 150 m now, i.e., some 40% greater than in the frictionless initial state. The asymptotic elevation gradient is therefore about 70% of the initial setup. Figure 10 shows the asymptotic distribution of average velocity U/h, which is now finite at the shore and features relatively higher return flow velocities, but over a smaller central section.

The calculations of Rao and Murty (1970) were based on the equivalent of Eqs. (28), and the assumption of steady state, so that theirs is an asymptotic transport distribution. In Figure 1 it may indeed be verified that the locus of zero transport in the trunk section is more or less as illustrated in Figure 11.

The practical significance of the asymptotic frictionally controlled flow pattern is somewhat undermined by calculating the frictional adjustment time t_f for water of the order of 100 m depth. This turns out to be several days, or rather longer than a steady wind usually blows. For the maximum depth of 192 m shown in Figure 4, $c_d = 2 \times 10^{-3}$, $F = 1$ cm^2 sec^{-2}, the value of t_f is in excess of 4 days. The usual duration of a storm is of the order of 8 hr, or about $0.1 t_f$. The frictionless, initial response is under such circumstances likely to be a better approximation to what is observed than the asymptotic state. The opposite is true only in water less than 10 m deep.

In such very shallow water the currents set up by the wind then also decay in a similarly short time. From Eqs. (29) it is also possible to calculate the decay of the motion on the cessation of the storm. The

exercise is elementary and shows that the time-scale of decay is again $h/\sqrt{c_d F}$, or of the order of a few hours in water a few meters deep.

The frictional influences noted earlier in the observational evidence may now be interpreted in terms of the above results. Near shore one may neglect the pressure gradient and assume that an asymptotic transport distribution is present, so that, from Eq. (30):

$$U \cong h \sqrt{\frac{F}{c_d}}. \qquad (31)$$

The quantity under the square root sign is an asymptotic average velocity, a "typical" value of which is 20 cm sec^{-1}. The depth may be taken to increase linearly with distance from shore:

$$h = sy \qquad (32)$$

where the bottom slope s usually lies between 10^{-3} and 10^{-2}. In the cross section shown in Figure 8 it is 6 $\times 10^{-3}$ on the north shore and 1.1×10^{-2} on the south shore. According to Eq. (31) the transport should then grow linearly with distance from shore, about as $0.1y$ on the north shore and $0.2y$ on the south shore (in c.g.s. units). On the north shore, in the August 10 data, this is indeed the case. However, on August 8 on the north shore and on August 10 on the south shore, a more severe reduction of transport takes place at the shore. This may be partly explained by the fact that the August 8 survey was carried out some 6 hr after the cessation of the storm, while the August 10 south shore survey was taken also at a time when the wind speed was already markedly lower than at the peak of the storm. In addition it is also relevant that the slope *very* near the south shore is much less than the value quoted above, and that the transport distribution in fact roughly mirrors the depth distribution close to shore, as it should according to Eq. (31). On the whole, the quantitative agreement is quite good between the observations and the crude extension of the topographic gyre conceptual model to frictional influences. We emphasize again that this could only be expected in a well-mixed water column, which however, is often present very close to shore in a storm.

A final point to be made is that the frictional effects are only appreciable in shallow water and that the frictional equilibrium model illustrated in Figure 1 or 11 definitely does not agree with the observational evidence in deep water. The locus of zero transport is, as already seen, as predicted by the frictionless theory. Return flow velocities in deep water are closer to the frictionless prediction of order 3 cm sec^{-1}, than to that of the frictional equilibrium model, cf. Figure 12, which shows velocities close to 10 cm sec^{-1}. All this is consistent with the inferences made from the frictional adjustment time, which was found to be much longer than the duration of a typical storm.

Effect of the Coriolis force

Having established the basic correctness of the topographic gyre conceptual model, it is worth exploring briefly the likely complications due to the rotation of the earth, which introduces Coriolis forces into the equations of motion. We continue to confine our attention here to enclosed shallow seas which are much longer than they are wide. In such cases, the onshore–offshore transport V is likely to remain much less than the longshore transport U, because the shore constraints remain powerful. In the previous sections we have found solutions with exactly zero onshore–offshore transport. When the Coriolis force associated with longshore flow acts on the fluid, one must expect *some* onshore–offshore displacements, but, subject to later verification, it is reasonable to postulate these to be small, $V_0 \ll U_0$, where U_0, V_0 are "typical" values of longshore and offshore transport.

The Coriolis force introduces the terms $-fV$, $+fU$ into the left-hand side of the first and second Eqs. (17), respectively. For small V and wind stress alongshore, the second equation then becomes approximately:

$$fU = -gh \frac{\partial \zeta}{\partial y} \qquad (33)$$

which expresses geostrophic balance between longshore transport and offshore pressure gradient. This balance requires the surface level to rise to the right of the flow, causing higher levels to develop along the right-hand shore than along the left, looking down current. The greatest cross-flow gradients develop where the average velocity U/h is highest, i.e., in the coastal boundary layers. Corresponding to a 10 cm sec^{-1} average velocity, with $f = 10^{-4}$ sec^{-1}, the elevation gradient is $\partial \zeta/\partial y = 10^{-6}$ or 1 cm in 10 km. Given that the coastal boundary layer width is of order 10 km, along the right-hand shore of a basin (looking along wind) the surface has to rise by an amount of the order of 1 cm, while it has to drop by a similar amount on the left-hand shore.

The volume of water which has to be transferred from one shore to the other in order to establish these cross-flow gradients is thus of order 10^6 cm^3 per unit length of the shoreline. The transfer has to take place on the time scale of inertial adjustment, i.e., f^{-1} or 10^4 sec, requiring a cross-basin volume transport of $V = 10^2$ cm^2 sec^{-1}. This is indeed small compared to the typical value of U which, as we have seen, was a few times 10^4 cm^2 sec^{-1}. In the longshore momentum balance the term fV is of order 10^{-2} cm^2 sec^{-2}, which is small compared to the other terms (all of order 1 cm^2 sec^{-2}). This verifies that the direct Coriolis force influence on the longshore balance of forces is negligible—on the time scale of a few hours. There are some surprising effects on a longer time scale to which we shall turn in the next few sections.

Spontaneous current reversals

Most coastal zone observations in Lake Ontario during IFYGL showed coastal currents originally established by the wind in various stages of decay. There were, however, exceptions: especially during prolonged quiescent periods following a wind stress impulse, it was noticed that the flow, instead of decaying slowly due to frictional dissipation, spontaneously reversed direction in certain locations along the shore line. Thus it happened that in one section of the basin the longshore flow was still following the previous wind stress impulse, while elsewhere it had *reversed* without significant influence from the wind. The current was every bit as strong after reversal as before. Moreover, an analysis of observations taken at several coastal locations revealed that the coastal current reversal progressed from one location to the other in a *counterclockwise* (cyclonic) sense around the basin. The apparent speed of propagation was of the order of 40 km day^{-1}, or 50 cm sec^{-1}, so that a full cycle around Lake Ontario would have taken something like 15 days. Spectral analysis of current observations at a fixed location (Blanton, 1974) showed a marked periodicity at 14–16 days.

The spontaneous reversal of a coastal current carrying massive momentum is a spectacular event and it is even more remarkable that it should progress at a more or less well-defined speed in one sense only around a closed basin. It seems immediately likely that this preference for one sense of propagation has something to do with the rotation of the earth. Remembering the cross-flow elevation gradients associated with these currents (which may be assumed to be present to balance the Coriolis force), it is clear that a small-amplitude elevation–depression pattern must also propagate along the shore together with the direct-reversed current pattern. Slowly and cyclonically propagating small-amplitude level disturbances have been detected in Lac Léman and Lake Michigan, for example, well before the discovery of spontaneous coastal current reversals (Mortimer, 1953, 1963). Hamon (1962) discovered similar slowly propagating sea level anomalies on the Australian coast. These were attributed by Robinson (1964) to what we now call topographic waves. Along the west coast of North America similar phenomena were also observed (Cutchin and Smith, 1973) and attributed to topographic waves. A complication in interpretation arises from the fact that in a stratified fluid another slowly propagating wave (the internal Kelvin wave) is possible and it is usually not possible to tell from sea level data alone which type of slow wave causes the disturbance. From water intake temperature data Mortimer (1953, 1963) has been able to show that in the episodes discussed by him an internal Kelvin wave at least accompanied the level disturbances. In the light of later discussion it will become clear that even this does not exclude the possibility that a topographic wave was also present, along with the internal Kelvin wave. In the case of the sea level anomalies off Australia and Oregon, there is even less reason to believe that the level variations were alone due to topographic rather than internal Kelvin waves or vice versa.

Internal Kelvin waves are discussed further below. A full understanding of the current reversal episodes observed during summer in Lake Ontario requires both conceptual models, topographic and internal Kelvin waves. In at least some episodes, however, the observed phenomena had the character of the topographic wave uncomplicated by an internal Kelvin wave. In other words the stratification played no significant dynamical role and the wave form was more or less as one would have expected it to be in a homogeneous fluid. To account for slowly propagating current reversals in *homogeneous* water, a wave-like model is therefore needed in which the Coriolis force plays a prominent role, but stratification does not. The development of such a model is pursued in the next four sections.

The topographic wave conceptual model

Consider a long and straight coastline coincident with the x axis. Let depth contours run parallel to the shore, so that depth is a function of offshore distance only, $h = h(y)$. The wave-like phenomenon to be modelled has a frequency σ, *low* compared to the inertial frequency f, and it is accompanied by *small* surface elevation amplitudes at the shores. This also implies onshore transports V much smaller than longshore ones, U. Yet, in the transport equations with Coriolis force included the term fV cannot be ignored in comparison with $\partial U/\partial t$, which is of order σU, because, although $V << U$, also $\sigma << f$. However, $\partial V/\partial t = $ order σV may be safely ignored compared to fU. In the continuity equation the term $\partial \zeta/\partial t$ is also neglected on account of the low frequencies and small elevation amplitudes expected. These simplifications leave the following form of the transport equations:

$$\frac{\partial U}{\partial t} - fV = -gh \frac{\partial \zeta}{\partial x}$$

$$fU = -gh \frac{\partial \zeta}{\partial y} \qquad (34)$$

$$\frac{\partial U}{\partial x} + \frac{\partial V}{\partial y} = 0.$$

No forcing term has been included. Any wave-like motions are assumed to be started by some initial flow pattern, of the topographic gyre type, which had been set up by a prior wind stress impulse.

A full discussion of Eqs. (34) has been given by Gill and Schumann (1974). A stream-function, $\psi(x,y,t)$ may be introduced such that

$$U = \frac{\partial \psi}{\partial y} \qquad V = -\frac{\partial \psi}{\partial x}. \qquad (35)$$

Eqs. (34) may then be reduced to

$$\frac{\partial^2}{\partial t \partial y} \left(\frac{1}{h} \frac{\partial \psi}{\partial y} \right) - \frac{f}{h^2} \frac{dh}{dy} \frac{\partial \psi}{\partial x} = 0. \qquad (36)$$

The boundary condition at the shore is that the x axis is a streamline, while at large distances from the shore the longshore transport becomes negligible. Therefore:

$$\psi = 0 \qquad \text{at} \qquad y = 0$$

$$\frac{\partial \psi}{\partial y} = 0 \qquad \text{as} \qquad y \to \infty. \qquad (37)$$

A solution to Eq. (36) may be found by the method of the separation of the variables, i.e., assuming

$$\psi(x,y,t) = \phi(x,t)\,\lambda(y). \qquad (38)$$

Substitution into Eq. (36) yields

$$\frac{d}{dy}\left(\frac{1}{h}\frac{d\lambda}{dy}\right)\frac{\partial\phi}{\partial t} - \frac{f}{h^2}\frac{dh}{dy}\lambda\frac{\partial\phi}{\partial x} = 0. \qquad (39)$$

Regarding this as an equation for ϕ, its coefficients are independent of y if

$$c\,\frac{d}{dy}\left(\frac{1}{h}\frac{d\lambda}{dy}\right) = -\frac{f}{h^2}\frac{dh}{dy}\lambda \qquad (40)$$

where c is a constant. The equation for $\phi(x,t)$ takes the simple form:

$$\frac{\partial\phi}{\partial t} + c\,\frac{\partial\phi}{\partial x} = 0. \qquad (41)$$

Starting off with an arbitrary distribution $\phi_0(x)$ at $t = 0$, Eq. (41) may be satisfied by

$$\phi = \phi_0(x - ct) \qquad (42)$$

so that the distribution ϕ_0 propagates with a speed c in the *positive* x direction without change of shape.

The value of c is not arbitrary, but must be such that the homogeneous equation [Eq. (40)] has a solution satisfying the boundary conditions derivable from Eq. (37):

$$\begin{aligned} \lambda &= 0 & y &= 0 \\ \frac{d\lambda}{dy} &= 0 & y &\to \infty. \end{aligned} \qquad (37a)$$

This poses an eigenvalue problem of a standard kind. For a given, physically reasonable depth distribution, an infinite set of wave speeds c_n, $n = 1, 2, 3 \ldots$ arise, each of which is associated with its own eigenfunction $\lambda_n(y)$, which one may regard the waveform of the nth order wave.

The eigenfunctions $\lambda_n(y)$ form an orthogonal set so that an arbitrary initial distribution $\lambda_0(y)$, which satisfies the boundary conditions [Eq. (37a)], may be expanded in terms of them. This enables one to solve the initial value problem: a given impulsively established transport distribution [which of course satisfies Eq. (37)] is expanded in terms of the eigenfunctions. Each of these then represents a wave, travelling with speed c_n in the positive x direction. A combination of all the waves describes the subsequent history of the disturbance. That c_n is positive for all n follows from the structure of Eq. (40), for monotonically increasing depth (and positive f: in the southern hemisphere waves travel in the *negative* x direction). Physically, the "positive" x direction is such that the wave leaves the shore to the right. In a closed basin the wave thus travels in a cyclonic (anticlockwise, in the northern hemisphere) sense.

Further mathematical details, including the method of calculating wave modes forced by specific wind stress impulses are given by Gill and Schumann (1974). As already remarked, the problem is a classical one in applied mathematics with a considerable literature. For a reasonably simple initial transport distribution it is easily deduced that only the lowest few modes ($n = 1, 2$, etc.) are excited at significant amplitude. For simplicity, in later discussion we shall focus mainly on the behavior of the fundamental wave, $n = 1$.

That the pattern of flow described by the above solution of Eqs. (34), for a given c, say $c = c_1$, is indeed a "wave" in the customary sense is clear from the above, especially from Eq. (41). It is also evident from Eq. (40) that the existence of this kind of motion is tied to depth variations, i.e., to the *topography* of the shore zone: for $h =$ constant one finds $\zeta = 0$, $U = 0$ everywhere. The precise values of $c_1, c_2 \ldots$, etc. are determined by the depth distribution, the only other physical factor which enters Eq. (40) being the Coriolis parameter f. For zero f the result is the same as for constant depth: no wave of the above kind is possible. On account of the importance of topography for this wave it is called a "topographic wave." The importance of the Coriolis force is most sharply brought into focus by vorticity arguments (cf. later) which show that the topographic wave is a member of the class of "vorticity waves" possible in a rotating fluid.

A simple shore-zone model

In order to elucidate the physical characteristics of topographic waves further, it is instructive to make some calculations for a particularly simple shore-zone, consisting of a beach of constant shape, joined at $y = \ell$ to a constant depth basin. Figure 13 illustrates how the cross-section of Lake Ontario south of Oshawa may be idealized in this manner.

Over the constant depth portion the right-hand side of Eq. (40) vanishes, so that the boundary condition $d\lambda/\partial y = 0$ must be applied at $y = \ell$. All motion in the topographic wave is thus confined to the sloping portion of the shore. For a shore-zone of constant slope, $h = sx$, with $s =$ const. Eq. (40) becomes:

$$y\,\frac{d^2\lambda}{dy^2} - \frac{d\lambda}{dy} + \frac{f}{c}\lambda = 0. \qquad (43)$$

It is noteworthy that this equation does not depend on the magnitude of the bottom slope s. Indeed, all explicit physical parameters may be removed from it by introducing the new variable $\eta = fy/c$, in terms of which the equation reads

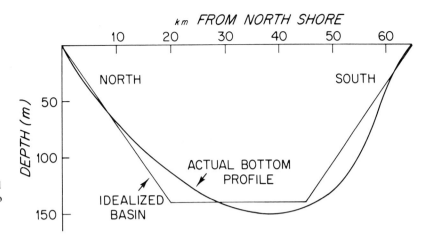

FIGURE 13.   Actual and idealized depth distribution in Lake Ontario along Oshawa–Olcott cross-section.

$$\eta\lambda'' - \lambda' + \lambda = 0 \qquad (43a)$$

where primes denote differentiation with respect to η. The solution of this equation, satisfying the boundary condition at the shore, is:

$$\lambda = A\eta J_2(2\sqrt{\eta}) \qquad (44)$$

with A an arbitrary constant and $J_2(\ )$ a Bessel function. The boundary condition of vanishing $d\lambda/dy$ at $y = \ell$ may then be satisfied by

$$J_1\left(2\sqrt{\frac{f\ell}{c}}\right) = 0. \qquad (45)$$

The Bessel function $J_1(\ )$ has an infinite number of zeros, the first few at arguments:

$$3.832, 7.016, 10.173, \text{etc.}$$

Corresponding to these zeros the wave propagation velocities c_i ($i = 1, 2, 3 \ldots$) are found:

$$\frac{f\ell}{3.67}, \frac{f\ell}{12.30}, \frac{f\ell}{25.87}, \text{etc.}$$

In a shore zone of 20 km width, given $f = 10^{-4} \text{ sec}^{-1}$ for example, the lowest order wave has speed $c_1 = 54.5 \text{ cm sec}^{-1}$. Higher order waves are much slower, $c_2 = 16 \text{ cm sec}^{-1}$, $c_3 = 7.7 \text{ cm sec}^{-1}$ etc.

Without loss of generality the amplitude of the long-shore wave profile $\phi(x - ct)$ may be arbitrarily taken as unity. The distribution of longshore transport in a transect where $\phi = 1$ is

$$U = \frac{d\lambda}{dy} = A\frac{f}{c}\sqrt{\eta}J_1(2\sqrt{\eta}) \qquad (46)$$

while the surface elevation may be calculated to be

$$\zeta = A\frac{f^2}{gsc}\left[J_0(2\sqrt{\eta}) - J_0\left(2\sqrt{\frac{f\ell}{c}}\right)\right] \qquad (47)$$

where the integration constant has been determined from the condition that $\zeta = 0$ at $y = \ell$. This result

enables one to relate the stream-function amplitude A to elevation amplitude at shore, ζ_0:

$$A = \frac{gsc\zeta_0}{f^2\left[1 - J_0\left(2\sqrt{\frac{f\ell}{c}}\right)\right]}. \qquad (48)$$

The depth-average velocity is U/sy or

$$u = A\frac{f^2}{sc^2}\frac{1}{\sqrt{\eta}}J_1(2\sqrt{\eta}). \qquad (49)$$

The shore-amplitude of this is:

$$u_0 = A\frac{f}{sc^2} = \frac{g\zeta_0}{c\left[1 - J_0\left(2\sqrt{\frac{f\ell}{c}}\right)\right]}. \qquad (50)$$

To calculate some typical magnitudes consider the lowest order wave of speed $c_1 = 54.5 \text{ cm sec}^{-1}$ in the sample shore-zone illustrated in Figure 13, of width $\ell = 20$ km, slope $s = 7 \times 10^{-3}$. Both the surface elevation ζ and the depth-average velocity u decrease in this fundamental wave monotonically from a maximum at the shore to zero at $y = \ell$. For a shore amplitude ζ_0 of 1 cm Eq. (50) yields a velocity amplitude u_0 of 12.8 cm sec^{-1}. Note that such a velocity should be easier to observe than an elevation of 1 cm. There are many other types of motion which produce elevation changes of this or greater order (seiches, for example), so that a 1-cm elevation signal is buried in a great deal of noise. A velocity signal of 13 cm sec^{-1}, on the other hand, is comparable to directly wind-driven current velocities and is likely to stand out.

The depth-integrated transport in the fundamental wave is zero both at the shore and at $y = \ell$, and has a single maximum in between at $fy/c = 1.446$. The value of the maximum is

$$U_m = 0.312\frac{gs\zeta_0}{f}. \qquad (51)$$

Given the typical quantities assumed in the example above this becomes $2.2 \times 10^4 \text{ cm}^2 \text{ sec}^{-1}$, comparable to the longshore transport caused by a wind stress of 1 dyn cm^{-2} acting for about 6 hr.

One may now envisage the generation of topographic waves in a closed basin as follows. A wind stress impulse sets up a topographic gyre, the high velocity portions of which occur along the two shores parallel to the wind, in bands comparable to the beach width ℓ. As geostrophic balance is established, the level rises slightly on the right-hand shore and drops on the left-hand shore. If the velocity amplitude of the

wind driven coastal currents is u_0, the magnitude of the shore elevation/depression ζ_0, necessary for geostrophic balance, may be calculated by setting Coriolis force equal to offshore pressure gradient:

$$fu_0 = \text{order } g \frac{\zeta_0}{\ell}. \tag{52}$$

Proceeding around the perimeter of the basin, one encounters positive elevations on one section of the shoreline, negative ζ in other places, and a full wave

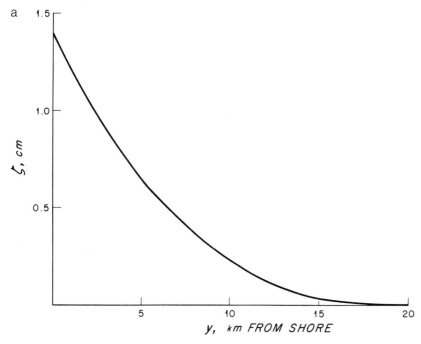

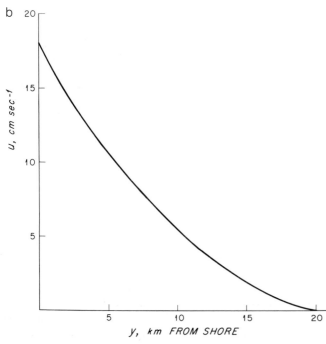

FIGURE 14.   Properties of topographic wave along north shore of idealized basin: (a) surface elevation, (b) longshore velocity, for an arbitrary shore elevation amplitude of 1.4 cm.

pattern stretching around the perimeter. In other words in a topographic gyre, pressure gradients are generated in the longshore direction by geostrophic adjustment, which are *not* balanced by any other force and must accelerate the fluid. If the length of basin perimeter is L, the longshore wavenumber is $k = 2\pi/L$ and longshore elevation gradients are of order

$$k\zeta_0 = \text{order } k \frac{f u_0 \ell}{g} \qquad (53)$$

using the estimate of Eq. (52) for ζ_0. This corresponds to a horizontal acceleration of $gk\zeta_0 = \text{order } kfu_0\ell$ which, if directed against the original direction of flow of the wind-driven current, annihilates its momentum in a period of order $u_0/gk\zeta_0 = \text{order } (kf\ell)^{-1}$. The reciprocal of this period is an estimate of the frequency with which the pressure disturbance may be thought to change:

$$\sigma = \text{order } kf\ell. \qquad (54)$$

If these changes occur in a wave-like manner, the speed of propagation is $\sigma/k = \text{order } f\ell$. The results of the qualitative arguments embodied in Eqs. (52)–(54) are then clearly equivalent to the more exact results calculated for an idealized shore zone in Eqs. (46)–(50). The wave propagation velocity was $c_1 = f\ell/3.67$ (for the fundamental wave). Substituting this into Eq. (50) one finds the equivalent of Eq. (52), with the magnitude of the constant filled in.

In the Lake Ontario example a reasonable estimate of effective perimeter length is 600 km. With the above numerical data this yields a calculated period of 12.7 days.

The distribution of surface elevation, longshore velocity, and transport, calculated for the idealized shore zone of Figure 13 with an aribtrary shore elevation amplitude of 1 cm, is illustrated in Figure 14. The peak transport occurs at 7.9 km from shore. The magnitude of this is such that its generation could be due to a moderate prior wind stress impulse.

Vorticity balance

Further insight into the wave-like propagation of a wind-induced topographic gyre may be obtained by some general arguments based on the vorticity equation [Eq. (15)]. That equation shows that when a wind stress is applied over a lake of nonuniform depth, vorticity of the depth-averaged flow is generated at the rate

$$\text{curl } (\tau/\rho h),$$

where τ is wind stress vector, and h is variable depth. Thus, when a constant wind suddenly begins to act in the direction of the longer axis of a lake, vorticity of

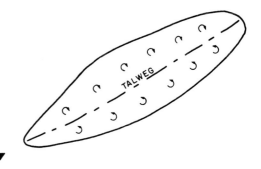

FIGURE 15.   Generation of vorticity by wind in a lake of variable depth. The "Talweg" (valley way in German) is the line connecting points of greatest depth in each cross-section.

opposite sign develops on either side of the greatest depth (the "Talweg"), as illustrated in Figure 15, τ/h being large near either shore and small in the center. Specification of a vorticity distribution determines the flow pattern in the basin by a well-known hydrodynamic theorem. The vorticity distribution illustrated in Figure 15 induces the double-gyre flow pattern in a long and narrow lake of simple depth distribution discussed above (see Figure 5).

The discussion of the topographic gyres did not take into account Coriolis force. However, before significant velocities develop, the Coriolis force may certainly be neglected; therefore, the same initial pattern tends to be set up with or without rotation.

Once flow velocities are appreciable, rotational effects may be expected to appear and to be most important where the flow crosses depth contours. This is the case mainly near the ends of longish basins, where each half of the double gyres must close. Here, at the downwind end, the fluid is forced from shallow to deep parts of the basin, from deep to shallow at the upwind end, both left and right of the Talweg. As the fluid begins to cross depth contours, changes in h must be balanced by changes in vorticity ω. It is simplest to think of an initial vorticity distribution $\omega_0(x,y)$ established impulsively by wind stress, with no wind acting afterwards. The potential vorticity $(f + \omega_0)/h$ is then conserved for each water column. The initial vorticity ω_0 is positive on the right hand grye and negative on the left hand one. At the downwind end of both gyres the fluid is moving from shallow to deep parts of the basin, that is, the depth h of each column is increasing. This requires an increase in $f + \omega$, that is, with constant f, a change from ω_0 to $\omega_0 + \Delta\omega$, with $\Delta\omega$ positive. By the same token, a negative vorticity increment is generated at the upwind end of the lake. For the right-hand (cyclonic) gyre this means that its downwind end is reinforced, the vorticity increasing from $\omega_0 + \Delta\omega$, while its upwind end is weakened and *partially cancelled* by the negative vorticity increment. The anticyclonic gyre is weakened at the downwind end and strengthened at the upwind end.

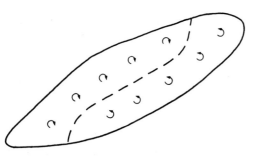

FIGURE 16.   Modification of initial vorticity distribution due to the rotation of the earth.

Thus, the line which separates cyclonic from anticyclonic vorticity (which coincides initially with the Talweg) sweeps upwind along the left-hand shore from the downwind end, downwind on the right-hand shore from the upwind end, so that a short time later the regions of cyclonic and anticyclonic vorticity are arranged as shown in Figure 16. In other words, the double-gyre flow pattern begins to rotate counterclockwise under the influence of the Coriolis force, after having been set up by the wind. If friction did not destroy this pattern, one would expect it to continue rotating around the basin.

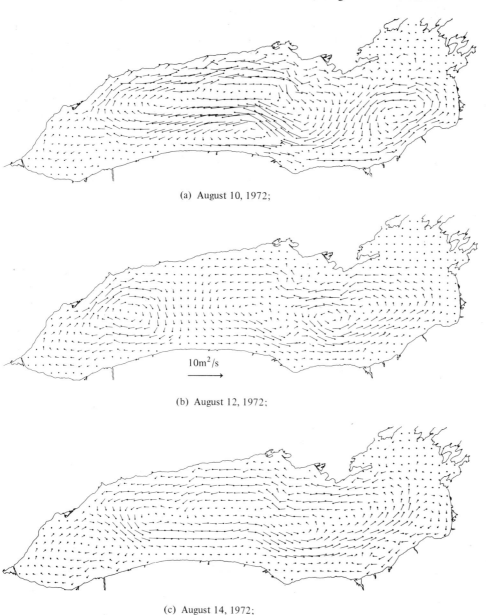

(a) August 10, 1972;

$10 m^2/s$

(b) August 12, 1972;

(c) August 14, 1972;

FIGURE 17.   Numerically calculated rotation of depth-integrated transport in Lake Ontario, following a westerly storm. From Simons, 1974.

The same phenomenon may also be understood in terms of the ''second-class'' motions of a fluid, some very illuminiating examples of which were discussed by Ball (1965). The elliptical paraboloid considered by Ball is, in fact, a reasonable model of a long lake. His illustrations show a rotation of the flow pattern much as demonstrated here in Figures 15 and 16. Numerical models also reproduce such effects (Simons, 1974, 1975). Figure 17, due to Simons, shows numerically calculated rotation of the transport streamline pattern in Lake Ontario.

The above arguments are akin to those of Longuet-Higgins (1968) on a double Kelvin wave. As Longuet-Higgins points out, topographic waves are vorticity waves similar in dynamical character to Kelvin and Ross by waves.

Comparison with observation

Detailed coastal zone observations were carried out along the north shore of Lake Ontario during IFYGL, at Oshawa and Presquile (see Figure 2, above). Following eastward wind impulses, a topographic wave may be expected to propagate from the eastern end of the lake to Presquile in about 2 days, according to the propagation speed given by theory, and then to Oshawa in another 2 or 3 days. The main ''signature'' of the topographic wave should be a reversal of the flow extending to the entire water mass occupying the coastal zone (and not only to the warm layer on top, as happens in an internal Kelvin wave), the amplitude of

the reversed current being comparable to the down-wind coastal current originally generated by the storm.

Such events were clearly observable on several occasions during IFYGL. Figure 18, from Csanady (1976), shows the velocity distribution on October 13, 1972 off Oshawa, 5 days after a massive eastward wind impulse. The velocities are all westward and peak at a value about half as large (30 cm sec^{-1}) as was the maximum wind-driven current immediately upon cessation of the wind. The slower flow in the top layer is the remainder of a baroclinic coastal jet (cf. later) which still flows toward the east relative to the water below, having been also produced by the storm 5 days previously. The flow reversal at Oshawa began to develop 4 days after the storm, 2 days after it was noticeable at Presquile. Note that the amplitude of the reverse flow decayed appreciably at 12–14 km from shore, in accordance with the topographic wave conceptual model. The quantitative correspondence between the simple model and observation is clearly good.

The previously noted 14-day periodicity of currents at Oshawa (Blanton, 1974) may also be ascribed partly to topographic waves.

Coastal jets

By focusing attention on depth-integrated transport we have so far avoided the problem of how momentum is distributed in the vertical. Some interesting and

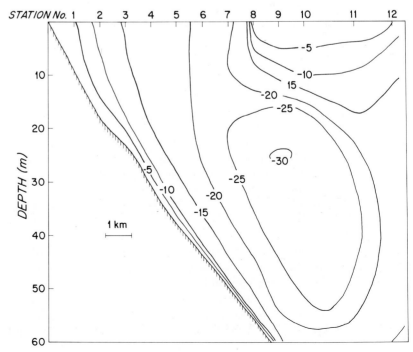

FIGURE 18.   Longshore velocity (cm sec^{-1}) in a cross-section off Oshawa, Ontario, October 13, 1972. Negative values designate westward velocity, while previous wind impulse was eastward.

important contrasts between the upper and lower portions of the water column arise in the presence of density stratification. In fresh water, at mid-latitudes stratification is only present seasonally, insolation during the warmer months of the year producing a warm and light surface layer bounded below (at a typical equilibrium depth of 10–30 m) by a seasonal thermocline.

Thermoclines are regions where the temperature varies rapidly in the vertical, implying a similarly rapid variation of density. In such strongly stratified regions the force of gravity suppresses turbulence. The vertical transfer of wind-imparted momentum is thus inhibited, so much so that the shear stress in horizontal planes within the thermocline is usually small. Although this is not true all of the time or everywhere, many useful dynamical deductions on water motions in lakes may be made by postulating vanishing shear stress within the thermocline.

Most of the coastal zone observations already discussed were collected when a summer thermocline was present. Details of the evidence not so far discussed showed that at least at some distances from shore the momentum of the wind-induced coastal current was concentrated in the top, warm portion of the water column above the thermocline. This concentration of momentum in a relatively shallow layer resulted in increased velocities, compared to their depth-averaged values. The region where such concentration was pronounced occupied a band of order 5 km width. Their high velocity, shallow depth, and narrow width make it appear appropriate to describe these flow structures as "jets," and, in view of their location, to refer to them as "coastal jets."

Coastal jets have been found to be generated by longshore wind stress impulses. They were also associated with characteristic thermocline displacements: coastal jets leaving the shore to the *right* were associated with a sharp downward tilt of the thermocline and opposing jets with an *upward* tilt.

A simple conceptual model of the coastal jet phenomenon may be constructed by invoking the two-layer approximation and neglecting stress at the thermocline. The equations of motion and continuity are used in a depth-integrated form, transports for top and bottom layers being considered separately. This kind of model was introduced into the literature by Charney (1955a) in connection with investigations of Gulf Stream dynamics.

Simple coastal jet conceptual model

Consider a seminifinite water body bounded by a straight coastline coincident with the x axis, while the y axis points out to sea. Assume that the water depth

is a constant $H = h + h'$, a slightly lighter top layer of equilibrium depth h lying over denser water of depth h'. The fractional density defect $\epsilon = (\rho' - \rho)/\rho'$ is small, of order 10^{-3}. Let a wind begin to blow at time $t = 0$, exerting a stress $\tau_0 = \rho F$ at the water surface, directed parallel to the coast, constant in space and in time for $t > 0$. All primed quantities shall refer to the bottom layer.

The linearized equations of momentum and mass balance integrated over depth separately for top and bottom layers are:

Top layer
$$\begin{cases} \dfrac{\partial U}{\partial t} - fV = -gh\dfrac{\partial \zeta}{\partial x} + F \\[2ex] \dfrac{\partial V}{\partial t} + fU = -gh\dfrac{\partial \zeta}{\partial y} \\[2ex] \dfrac{\partial U}{\partial x} + \dfrac{\partial V}{\partial y} = -\dfrac{\partial}{\partial t}(\zeta - \zeta') \end{cases}$$

$$(55)$$

Bottom layer
$$\begin{cases} \dfrac{\partial U'}{\partial t} - fV' = -gh'\dfrac{\partial \zeta}{\partial x} \\[1ex] \qquad\qquad + gh'\epsilon\dfrac{\partial}{\partial x}(\zeta - \zeta') \\[2ex] \dfrac{\partial V'}{\partial t} + fU' = -gh'\dfrac{\partial \zeta}{\partial y} \\[1ex] \qquad\qquad + gh'\epsilon\dfrac{\partial}{\partial y}(\zeta - \zeta') \\[2ex] \dfrac{\partial U'}{\partial x} + \dfrac{\partial V'}{\partial y} = -\dfrac{\partial \zeta'}{\partial t} \end{cases}$$

where U, V, U', V' are depth-integrated velocities or volume transports (separately for top and bottom layers) along x and y, and ζ' is the vertical displacement of the thermocline from its equilibrium position.

Boundary conditions at the coast $y = 0$ are such that the normal transports U, U' vanish. At infinity $y \to \infty$ we postulate vanishing surface and interface elevations.

The above sets of three equations each for top and bottom layers are clearly coupled through the presence of both ζ and ζ' in either set. It is, however, possible to produce two linear combinations of the two sets in such a way that the resulting sets of equations are uncoupled *normal mode* equations of the form:

$$\begin{aligned} \frac{\partial U_n}{\partial t} - fV_n &= -gh_n\frac{\partial \zeta_n}{\partial x} + F_n \\[1ex] \frac{\partial V_n}{\partial t} + fU_n &= -gh_n\frac{\partial \zeta_n}{\partial y} \\[1ex] \frac{\partial U_n}{\partial x} + \frac{\partial V_n}{\partial y} &= -\frac{\partial \zeta_n}{\partial t} \end{aligned}$$

$$(56)$$

where h_n is an appropriate "equivalent depth," although it may also be regarded as a factor modifying gravity. These are transport equations for a *homogenous* fluid of depth h_n. Eqs. (56) arise from adding a constant α_n times the first set of three Eqs. (55) to the second set of three, so that the composite variables are

$$U_n = \alpha_n U + U'$$
$$V_n = \alpha_n V + V'$$
$$\zeta_n = \alpha_n(\zeta - \zeta') + \zeta' \qquad (57)$$
$$F_n = \alpha_n F.$$

These linear transformations, when introduced into Eqs. (55), result in a set of equations of the form of Eq. (56), provided that $\alpha_n(n = 1,2)$ is a root of Stokes' equation:

$$\alpha^2 + \left(\frac{h'}{h} - 1\right)\alpha - \frac{h'}{h}(1 - \epsilon) = 0. \qquad (58)$$

The corresponding equivalent depths are then

$$h_n = h'\epsilon(1 - \alpha_n)^{-1}. \qquad (59)$$

The above separation of the problem into normal modes is exact under the postulated conditions. The physical properties of the normal mode equations are best exhibited, however, using approximate values of the roots $\alpha_{1,2}$, valid for small values of the density defect ϵ. The two roots are, expanded in powers of ϵ:

$$\alpha_1 = 1 - \frac{\epsilon h'}{h + h'} + 0(\epsilon^2)$$
$$\alpha_2 = -\frac{h'}{h} + \frac{\epsilon h'}{h + h'} + 0(\epsilon^2) \qquad (60)$$

with corresponding equivalent depths, to the lowest order only:

$$h_1 = h' + h + 0(\epsilon)$$
$$h_2 = \frac{\epsilon h h'}{h + h'} + 0(\epsilon^2). \qquad (61)$$

To lowest order in ϵ, the normal mode equations [to be called respectively "surface" or "barotropic" ($n = 1$) and "internal" or "baroclinic" ($n = 2$) modes] are now written in terms of the original variables, according to Eq. (57), but multiplied for convenience by a constant factor in the case of the internal mode:

"Surface" mode
$$\frac{\partial(U + U')}{\partial t} - f(V + V') = -g(h + h')\frac{\partial\zeta}{\partial x} + F$$
$$\frac{\partial(V + V')}{\partial t} + f(U + U') = -g(h + h')\frac{\partial\zeta}{\partial y}$$
$$\frac{\partial(U + U')}{\partial x} + \frac{\partial(V + V')}{\partial y} = -\frac{\partial\zeta}{\partial t} \qquad (62)$$

"Internal" mode
$$\frac{\partial U'}{\partial t} - fV' = -g\epsilon\frac{h h'}{h + h'}\frac{\partial\zeta'}{\partial x} - \frac{h'}{h + h'}F$$
$$\frac{\partial V'}{\partial t} + fU' = -g\epsilon\frac{h h'}{h + h'}\frac{\partial\zeta'}{\partial y}$$
$$\frac{\partial U'}{\partial x} + \frac{\partial V'}{\partial y} = -\frac{\partial\zeta'}{\partial t}.$$

The approximate surface mode equations are exactly what applies to a homogeneous fluid of depth h

$+ h'$, acted upon by a wind stress ρF, along the x axis. In this mode (and to order ϵ^0) the fluid does not "feel" the density defect of the top layer. The internal mode equations are identical in form to the surface mode ones, when applied to motions of the *bottom* layer of fluid alone, i.e., as if the thermocline were a free surface, but with gravity reduced by a factor of $\epsilon h/(h + h')$. Also the effective force acting on the bottom layer is *opposite* in direction to the applied wind stress, and its magnitude is reduced by the factor $h'/(h + h')$. The reduction in gravity is by a large factor, while the effective stress is not much different from that acting at the surface. One may therefore at once suspect that very large thermocline displacements may be produced. The opposite direction of the effective force in the internal mode has generally the consequence of producing opposite surface and thermocline displacements.

The full solution of the problem posed (suddenly imposed wind) contains some inertial oscillations and an aperiodic part describing a "coastal jet" structure near shore and Ekman drift far offshore. Full details are given by Crépon (1967, 1969); here only the *aperiodic* part of the response will be discussed. Solving the approximate normal mode equations (62) separately, and adding the results, one arrives at the particular solution (correct to order $\epsilon^{1/2}$)

$$u = \frac{U}{h} = \frac{Ft}{h + h'}\left[e^{-y/R_1} + \frac{h'}{h}e^{-y/R_2}\right] \qquad (63)$$
$$v = \frac{V}{h} = -\frac{F}{f(h + h')}\left[1 - e^{-y/R_1} + \frac{h'}{h}(1 - e^{-y/R_2})\right]$$
$$\zeta = -\frac{Ft}{fR_1}\left[e^{-y/R_1} + \frac{h'}{h}\frac{R_2}{R_1}e^{-y/R_2}\right]$$
$$u' = \frac{U'}{h'} = \frac{Ft}{h + h'}\left[e^{-y/R_2} - e^{-y/R_1}\right]$$
$$v' = \frac{V'}{h'} = -\frac{F}{f(h + h')}\left[1 - e^{-y/R_1} - (1 - e^{-y/R_2})\right]$$
$$\zeta' = -\frac{Ft}{fR_2}\frac{h'}{h + h'}\left[e^{-y/R_2} - \frac{R_2}{R_1}e^{-y/R_1}\right].$$

Here u, v, etc. are velocities averaged over the two layers separately (which are easier to visualize than transports), and R_1 and R_2 are surface and internal radii of deformation:

$$R_1 = f^{-1}\sqrt{g(h + h')} \qquad (64)$$
$$R_2 = f^{-1}\sqrt{g\epsilon h h'/(h + h')}.$$

These radii scale the widths of regions within which the contributions of the two modes of motion contribute to velocities and to surface and thermocline elevations. The latter, and *longshore* velocities increase in direct proportion to time, or more descriptively, to the impulse Ft of the wind stress. The *onshore–offshore* velocity is constant in time and reduces to zero on approaching the coast within a band of scale width R_1

and R_2, referring to the contribution of the surface and internal mode, respectively.

Very close to shore, $y << R_2$ [note that $R_2 << R_1$, by Eq. (64)], the onshore velocities v, v' in either layer are negligible. The longshore velocities are, on the other hand, to a high degree of approximation:

$$u = \frac{Ft}{h}$$
$$u' = 0 \qquad (y << R_2). \tag{65}$$

In other words, the impulse of the wind stress is distributed over the top layer only. The physical reason is contained in the fourth of Eqs. (55): in the absence of pressure gradients along x (and of friction at the interface), bottom layer longshore velocity can only be generated by Coriolis force due to onshore–offshore flow. Because of the shore constraint this is zero and hence the water of the bottom layer must remain constant.

At intermediate values of y, $R_2 << y << R_1$, onshore–offshore velocities are approximately

$$v = -\frac{F}{f(h + h')}\frac{h'}{h}$$
$$v' = +\frac{F}{f(h + h')} \qquad (R_2 << y << R_1). \tag{66}$$

The total offshore transport is thus zero, $vh + v'h' = 0$, inflow in the top layer (if F is positive) being balanced by outflow in the bottom layer. Longshore velocities are in this same intermediate region:

$$u = \frac{Ft}{h + h'} = u' \qquad (R_2 << x << R_1). \tag{67}$$

The impulse of the wind stress has here been distributed evenly over the entire water column. Within the bottom layer this has happened through the medium of the Coriolis force, because by the fourth of Eqs. (55) (of which the right-hand side is zero):

$$U' = \int_0^t f\,V'\,dt = \frac{Ft}{h + h'}\,h' \tag{68}$$

having substituted bottom layer onshore transport from Eq. (66). The total offshore displacement in the bottom layer is thus just sufficient to produce the required longshore transport through the action of the Coriolis force.

Far from shore, $y >> R_1$, longshore velocities are zero, the bottom layer is completely at rest, and Ekman drift in the top layer balances wind stress.

Turning now to surface and thermocline elevations, these are seen to increase in proportion to time, or rather to wind stress impulse, and are present at any distance not large compared to R_1. Because $R_2 << R_1$, thermocline elevations are large, but only close to shore, $y << R_2$. It is easily shown that the total depletion of bottom layer water near shore, beneath the rapidly sinking part of the thermocline, is exactly

TABLE 1.   "Typical" Data Assumed in Coastal Jet Model

Total depth $h + h'$	10^4 cm	Wind force $\tau_0\,\rho = F$	1 cm² sec²
Top layer h	2.10^3 cm	Surface mode radius of deformation R_1	316 km
Bottom layer h'	8.10^3 cm		
Effective gravity ϵg	2 cm sec²	Internal mode radius of deformation R_2	5.66 km
Coriolis parameter f	10^{-4}/sec		

what is flowing offshore in the "intermediate" region [Eq. (66)]. It is also easily checked that this water is transferred to a region of scale-width R_1 (where the thermocline is being slowly raised) from an interior region of scale width R_2 (where it is rapidly sinking). Corresponding to the much larger extension of the R_1 region, the elevation of the thermocline there at any instant is small compared to its depression over the R_2 region.

The surface elevation is raised (by a positive F) over both R_1 and R_2 regions, to the total extent required by the Ekman drift far offshore. At the shore, however, the rise is greater than if the fluid were homogenous. Even if R_2/R_1 is small (of order $\epsilon^{1/2}$), this extra elevation may be detectable, because the combined factor $h'R_2/hR_1$ may not be much smaller than unity.

Note also that, given time independent onshore–offshore flow, the Coriolis force of longshore flow at any instant is balanced by onshore–offshore pressure gradients. The momentum balance along y is thus geostrophic, with both longshore flow and offshore pressure gradient increasing linearly in time.

The above results are best appreciated if one considers "typical" magnitudes of the quantities involved. Table 1 lists plausibly assumed values of the independent parameters characterizing lakes. The ratio of the radii of deformation is seen to be typically about 50, while the magnitude of R_1 is so great that $y >> R_1$ is not a realistic part of the model: no lake is more than 1000 km wide. However, the nearshore and intermediate regions may be realistically described by this model. The validity of the results must be re-

TABLE 2.   Some Characteristics of Two-Layer Coastal Jet, after 6 hr Wind

	Close to shore $y << R_2$	Intermediate $R_2 << y << R_1$	Far $y << R_1$
u cm sec^{-1}	10	2	0
v cm sec^{-1}	0	−4	−5
ζ cm	6.46	6.32	0
u' cm sec^{-1}	0	2	0
v' cm sec^{-1}	0	1	0
ζ' cm	−275	5.06	0

FIGURE 19.   Schematic picture of coastal
jet development in two-layer fluid.

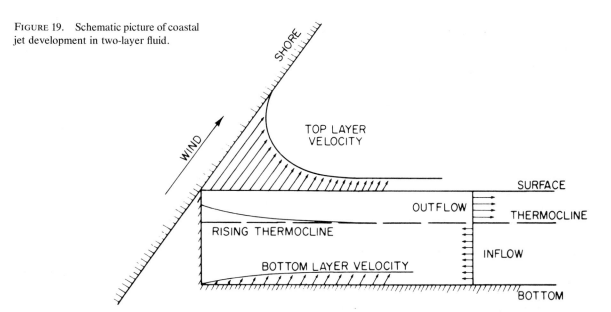

stricted to an initial period, because of the linearliza-
tion and other simplifications adopted. The calculations apply for $t = 2 \times 10^4$ sec, or just under 6 hr.

Eqs. (63) show that the offshore velocities are
scaled by $F/f(h + h')$ and the longshore ones by $Ft/(h + h')$: these become 1 and 2 cm sec^{-1}, respectively,
with the above assumptions. Surface elevations are
proportional to $Ft/fR_1 = 6.32$ cm and thermocline
elevations to $[Ft/fR_2][h'/(h + h')] = 283$ cm. The
most conspicuous effect of the wind is clearly the
movement of the thermocline, which rapidly outgrows
the linearizing assumption of $|\zeta'| << h$. Calculated
characteristics are listed in Table 2. A "baroclinic"

coastal jet is found near shore (confined to the top
layer, and associated with an inclined thermocline)
and "barotropic" coastal currents in the intermediate
region (evenly distributed over the depth, and associated with a surface slope). Figure 19 is an attempt to
illustrate the properties of the two-layer coastal jet
structure with a wind tending to produce upwelling.
The opposite wind produces an opposite jet and a
downwelled thermocline, of otherwise the same characteristics. Figure 20 shows the same situation in a
long channel. The channel width b is assumed to be
large compared to R_2, but small compared to R_1. This
is a slightly improved conceptual model because it

FIGURE 20.   Coastal jets in canal model.

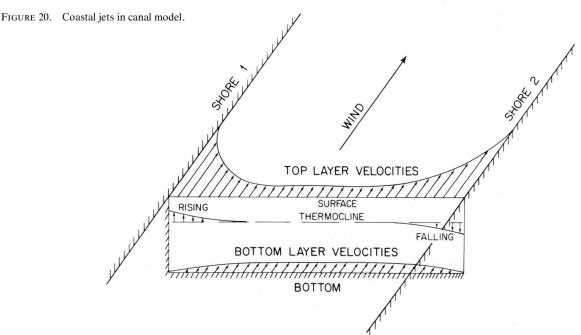

does away with the unrealistic $y \gg R_1$ region. The calculations are much the same as in the above simplest model. This figure shows both an upwelling and a downwelling, the intermediate R_1 region occupying most of the basin width.

The flow characteristics in the simple coastal jet conceptual model may be summed up as follows:

(1) The longshore momentum acquired from the wind stress impulse is concentrated in the top layer, within a region of width of order R_2 from shore. This is a fairly direct consequence of the frictionless thermocline assumption, in a coastal zone where crossflow is prevented by the shore. The scale width over which this occurs, R_2, however, could not be intuitively foreseen, as it arises from an intricate interplay of stratification and Coriolis force.

(2) The fast current in the top layer within the R_2 region is in geostrophic balance with the thermocline tilt, on top of a stationary bottom layer. Such balance therefore requires that the upwelled or downwelled thermocline separating the two layers have a considerable inclination.

(3) Outside the R_2 region, onshore–offshore displacements in the bottom layer generate longshore velocity by the medium of the Coriolis force. In effect the longshore momentum gained from the wind is thus evenly distributed over the entire water column, exactly as if vigorous vertical mixing had taken place.

Observations on coastal jets

Clear examples of coastal jets have been observed in Lake Ontario during IFYGL, following eastward wind stress impulses which frequently occur during the summer. A set of five coastal zone observations around the lake (at locations illustrated earlier, Figure 2) is shown in Figure 21. These observations were made immediately following a wind stress impulse Ft of approximate magnitude 25,000 cm² sec⁻¹, which acted on a lake close to hydrostatic equilibrium.

Along the south shore, i.e., to the right of the wind, a thermocline downtilt developed with an amplitude of order 5 m, with an apparent e-folding distance of order 5 km. The internal radius of deformation R_2 was close to 5 km. Eq. (63) gives a maximum thermocline displacement a little under 5 m and a longshore velocity in the top layer of 25 cm sec⁻¹. At the core of the jet, the observed average velocity in the top layer is about equal to this at Olcott and slightly higher at Rochester and Oswego, the total momentum of the flows is higher (33,000 and 43,000, respectively) than the wind impulse estimate. This was presumably due to momentum advection (Csanady, 1975b). With a few minor discrepancies, the main features of these observed

coastal jets clearly conform to the simple conceptual model discussed above.

On the north shore during the same episode there is upwelling and there are associated coastal jets leaving the shore to the left. However, apparently due to the shallowness of the thermocline, only a fraction of the wind-imparted momentum is found in the jets. Some of this may have been lost by momentum advection (the same mechanism that increased the momentum of the south shore jet), but it is also likely that some other loss mechanisms intervened. Later in the season, when the thermocline is deeper, better agreement with the coastal jet model was found also on the north shore.

Spontaneous thermocline movements near shore

The characteristic large nearshore uptilts and downtilts of the thermocline have generally been found to persist long after the wind dies down which originally set up the coastal jets and the thermocline structure associated with them. However, it was also observed that if a quiescent period follows the winds, the zones occupied in a closed basin by uptilt and downtilt, respectively, propagate counterclockwise around the basin. At given locations the thermocline is observed to move spontaneously up or down by a distance of the order of 10 m. At fixed depths large temperature changes occur as the thermocline moves up or down. Thus at waterworks intakes, temperatures suddenly rise or fall as a warm or cold "front" passes by. Clear descriptions of the propagation of warm fronts around Lake Michigan have first been given by Mortimer (1963).

One would expect that a change from a thermocline uptilt to a downtilt or vice versa is accompanied by a reversal of the coastal jet. Geostrophic balance requires coastal jet reversal and the persistence of the new thermocline shape indicates such balance. The expectation was explicitly confirmed during IFYGL (Csanady and Scott, 1974). Spontaneous up or down movements of a character as just discussed were observed in Lake Ontario in a nearshore band of order 5 km width, associated with coastal jet reversals.

The large amplitude nearshore thermocline movements and associated coastal jet reversals are analogous to the phenomena interpreted above in terms of the topographic wave conceptual model. Not surprisingly they may also be interpreted in terms of an analogous model, the internal Kelvin wave. This is again a shore-trapped mode of motion, occurring in a stratified rotating fluid. A simple two-layer idealization adequately accounts for many of the observed phenomena.

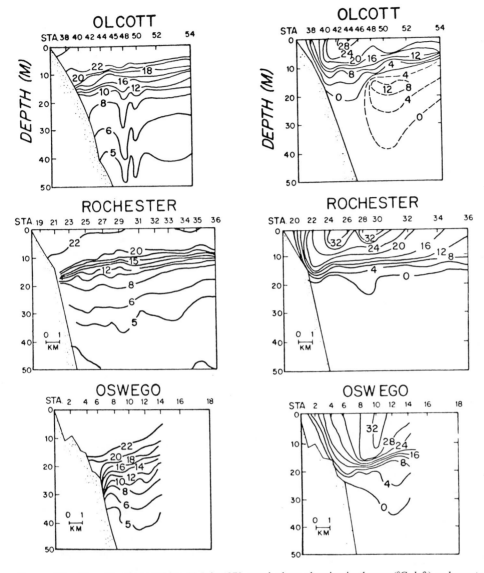

FIGURE 21.   Example of coastal jet, 23 July 1972, south shore showing isotherms (°C, left) and constant longshore velocity contours (cm sec⁻¹). Direction of flow is such as to leave shore to the *right*.

The internal Kelvin wave conceptual model

Consider a semiinfinite body of fluid, $y > 0$, bounded by a coastline coincident with the x axis. Suppose that a light layer of equilibrium depth h overlies a heavy layer of constant equilibrium depth h'. The internal mode equations [4 to 6 of Eq. (62)] then describe the dynamics of any thermocline oscillations. Eliminating U' and V' from these equations by taking curl and divergence, an equation for thermocline displacement ζ' is obtained:

$$\frac{\partial^2 \zeta'}{\partial t^2} - c^2 \left(\frac{\partial^2 \zeta'}{\partial x^2} + \frac{\partial^2 \zeta'}{\partial y^2} \right) + f^2 \zeta' = 0 \qquad (69)$$

where $c^2 = \epsilon g h \dfrac{h'}{h + h'} = f^2 R_2^2$. Shore-trapped waves on the thermocline, of artibrary form, are described by the equation

$$\zeta' = \phi(x - ct)e^{-y/R_2} \qquad (70)$$

with $\phi(\ )$ an arbitrary longshore amplitude distribution which propagates along the x axis. It is readily verified that Eq. (70) is a solution of Eq. (69). It is also clear that Eq. (70) satisfies a boundary condition at infinity appropriate to a shore-trapped flow structure, in that ζ' decays to zero at distances large compared to the internal radius of deformation R_2. The remaining question is whether or how the boundary condition of zero flow across the coast can be satisfied.

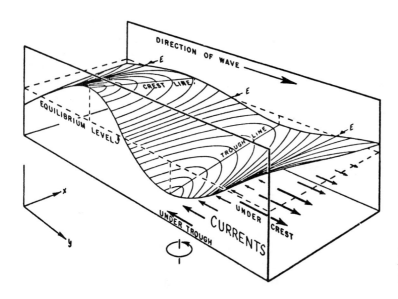

FIGURE 22.   Portion of a Kelvin wave traveling along a narrow channel, from Mortimer (1971).

From Eqs. (62) one may express V' as follows:

$$\frac{\partial^2 V'}{\partial t^2} + f^2 V' = - c^2 \left(\frac{\partial^2 \zeta'}{\partial t \partial y} - f \frac{\partial \zeta'}{\partial x} \right)$$
$$+ \frac{h'}{h + h'} fF. \quad (71)$$

To represent a free wave, let $F = 0$. Substitution of Eq. (70) into Eq. (71) shows the right-hand side of Eq. (71) to vanish; note, however, that an oppositely propagating wave, $\zeta' \sim \phi^*(x + ct)$, does not lead to this result. Onshore–offshore transport is zero at *all* y in waves described by Eq. (70) and the boundary condition at the shore is clearly satisfied. The wave within which this is true propagates along the *positive* x axis, i.e., it leaves the coast to the right. If the straight coast of this model is regarded as an idealization of the shores of a large closed basin, the wave is seen to travel in a counterclockwise or cyclonic sense.

The Kelvin wave is a classical conceptual model, discussed in most oceanographic texts. Its internal mode manifestation discussed here is characterized by

$$-U = U' = c\zeta' \quad (72)$$

so that oscillatory motion parallel to the coast accompanies thermocline displacements, the motions being of opposite sense in top and bottom layers. An examination of Eqs. (55), taking into account the above developed characteristics of the internal Kelvin wave, shows that the balance of forces in the offshore direction is geostrophic. An offshore surface slope balances the Coriolis force of longshore motion in the top layer. The thermocline slope (of a sense opposite to the surface slope) more than balances the effects of the surface slope in the bottom layer, and establishes an offshore pressure gradient necessary there for the geostrophic balance of the oppositely directed bottom layer flow. In the longshore direction the balance of

forces is exactly as in long waves (seiches) without rotation: the longshore surface slope is responsible for the acceleration $\partial u/\partial t$. The wave propagation velocity c not being a function of wavelength, a Kelvin wave of arbitrary form travels without distortion.

Properties of internal Kelvin waves are illustrated in Figures 22 and 23, from Mortimer (1971) and Csanady (1972c), respectively.

Generation of internal Kelvin waves

It is clear from Eq. (70) that the structure of flow in an internal Kelvin wave is very similar to the structure of the coastal jet discussed in some detail above. In both these models the flow is predominantly longshore, geostrophic, and confined to a nearshore band of scale width R_2. Without further investigation one might

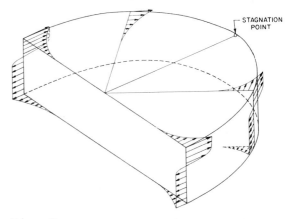

FIGURE 23.   Perspective sketch of velocity distribution in the first baroclinic Kelvin wave, with half basin cut away, from Csanady (1972c).

then suppose that a coastal jet flow structure, impulsively established in a closed basin by a wind stress episode and then left alone, would result in the excitation of internal Kelvin waves, much as topographic gyres lead to topographic waves. The simplicity of the constant depth model allows one to exhibit the connection in detail with relatively little algebra.

In order to discuss the initial value problem, excitation of internal Kelvin waves by a suddenly imposed wind stress, it is necessary to find a solution of the internal mode equations [last three of Eqs. (62)] with the forcing term retained. The following simple solution is readily discovered:

$$\zeta' = -\frac{Fx}{\epsilon gh} e^{-y/R_2}$$

$$U' = fR_2 \frac{Fx}{\epsilon gh} e^{-y/R_2} \qquad (73)$$

$$V' = \frac{h'}{h + h'} \frac{F}{f} (1 - e^{-y/R_2}).$$

This solution is the equivalent of a static *setup* in a nonrotating closed basin by a steady wind, except that at the thermocline it becomes a *set down*. As pointed out earlier, the effective direction of the forcing term is reversed in the internal mode. Given rotation, however, the setdown is not constant in an offshore direction, but decays to a negligible value at distances much larger than the internal radius of deformation. Furthermore, the setdown is not static, but is accompanied by longshore and offshore motion. The longshore flow is in geostrophic balance with the offshore pressure gradient, and decays to zero at large distances from the shore. The offshore flow is zero at the coast and becomes the Ekman drift necessary to balance the wind stress far offshore.

Consider now the initial behavior of the bottom layer in a two-layer fluid, after a longshore wind stress is suddenly imposed. At time zero the thermocline is in its equilibrium position, and the water is at rest. These initial conditions may be satisfied by adding a free wave solution to the time-independent solution of Eq. (73). An appropriate simple free wave of the general form given by Eq. (70) is

$$\zeta'_k = \frac{F}{\epsilon gh} (x - ct) e^{-y/R_2}. \qquad (74)$$

This internal Kelvin wave is accompanied by a longshore flow distribution $U'_k = c\zeta'$ [see Eq. (72)], and no offshore flow. Adding the internal Kelvin wave to the solution of Eq. (73) one arrives at

$$\zeta' = \frac{Ft}{fR_2} \frac{h'}{h + h'} e^{-y/R_2} \qquad (75)$$

which is exactly as found in the discussion of the coastal jet [Eq. (63)], neglecting the small contribution of the surface mode. The internal mode contribution

to the coastal jet flow structure may thus be regarded as the sum of a static solution and a Kelvin wave.

The significance of this result emerges on considering what happens on the cessation of the wind. The static solution then reverts to zero, while the internal Kelvin wave remains, and continues to propagate along the coast in a cyclonic sense.

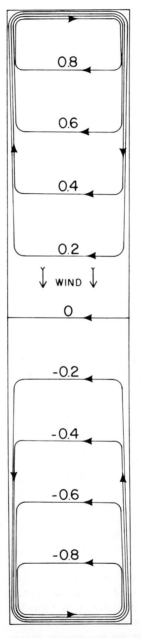

FIGURE 24.   Nondimensional streamfunction for baroclinic flow produced by steady wind in 5:1 rectangle, the width of which equals 15 radii of deformation. Suddenly imposed wind produces this forced pattern plus a sequence of waves, including internal Kelvin waves, from Csanady and Scott (1974).

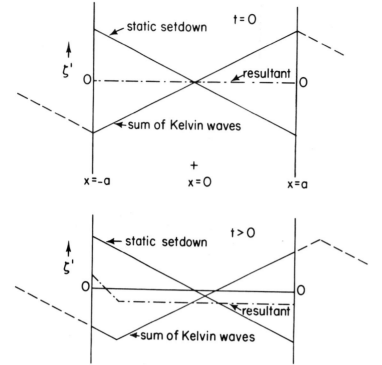

FIGURE 25a.   Combined effect of static thermocline displacements and triangular Kelvin wave. At $t = 0$ the resultant is exactly zero, the thermocline being at rest. At later times ζ' is constant along most of the shore and its value increases in direct proportion to time, except that behind the Kelvin wave peak a reversal gradually develops. This diagram shows thermocline elevations on the *right-hand* shore (looking downwind).

For specific simple closed basin shapes it is possible to work out the details, although the algebra becomes much lengthier than in the above simple discussion. Calculations of this kind for various simple "Model Great Lakes" have been published by Csanady (1968, 1972b), Birchfield (1969), Csanady and Scott (1974), and others. Illustrations of idealized internal Kelvin wave behavior taken from these papers are shown in Figures 24 and 25.

Comparison with observation

The presence of long internal Kelvin waves in large lakes has first been clearly demonstrated by Mortimer (1963) in what must surely be classed as one of the great contributions to physical limnology. Mortimer examined the records of water works intake temperatures around Lake Michigan and was able to demonstrate the progression of a warm front around the southern and southeastern portions of the lakeshore. Figure 26 shows one of Mortimer's illustrations. This event was produced by a northerly wind impulse, which created a downtilt in the thermocline on the western shore and an uptilt on the eastern. Subsequently, the end of the warm zone moved around the lake from Waukegan to Muskegon in a counterclockwise sense at a speed of 1.6 to 1.9 km hr^{-1}. A realistic idealization of the basin consists of a 15-m-deep top layer and a 60-m-deep bottom layer, with a density contrast of 1.74×10^{-3}. This yields $c = 1.6$ km hr^{-1}, in agreement with observation.

It was pointed out above that the coastal jets accompanying internal Kelvin waves are (nearly) in geostrophic equilibrium. Therefore a jet leaving the shore to the right is accompanied by a slight rise of surface level at the shore, while a jet of opposite direction produces a slight level drop. The magnitude of the drop or rise is 1.5 cm for a typical coastal jet speed of 30 cm sec^{-1} and a typical current width of 5 km. While the rise or drop is small, it is nevertheless observable, because, owing to the slow progression of the Kelvin wave, the level change is relatively persistent and emerges on filtering out faster oscillations. Mortimer (1963) was able to show this phenomenon for Lac Leman, Switzerland. As Figure 27 illustrates, a surface elevation wave propagates around the lake in a counterclockwise sense, at a speed of approximately 1.7 km hr^{-1}. The bottom dotted line shows the Geneva water works intake temperature, accurately in phase with local water level. The amplitude of the temperature wave is about 8°C and that of the surface level about 1.5 cm. A realistic idealization of this basin is: top layer depth 15 m, bottom 85 m, density contrast 1.54×10^{-3}, and hence internal wave celerity $c = 1.6$ km hr^{-1}, in good agreement with observation.

The above facts strongly suggest that reversing coastal jets accompany Kelvin wave-like progression of thermocline uptilt or downtilt. Direct confirmation

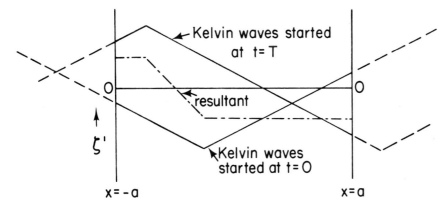

FIGURE 25b. Combination of triangular Kelvin waves after removal of wind stress. The resultant pattern propagates without change of shape along the shore. Kelvin wave started at $t = T$ by the removal of stress is the mirror image of the wave started at $t = 0$ by the imposition of stress, but is displaced by the distance covered in time T, from Csanady and Scott (1974).

for this was obtained in Lake Ontario during IFYGL. Figures 28 and 29 from Csanady and Scott (1974) shows the progression of thermocline and coastal jet development in a counterclockwise sense in an episode in late July 1972. The structure of coastal jets after the first day of this eastward wind impulse (July 23) was already shown above (Figure 21). Eastward winds continued until July 27 and were followed by a quiescent period. Particularly clear is the progression of flow reversal along the south shore. On the 27th the flow is already westward at Olcott, in spite of 5 days of strong eastward wind stress. The eastward coastal jet is still strong at Rochester, showing a remarkable parting of the waters in between. By July 31 the eastward jet at Rochester also gives way to strong westward flow. Both at Olcott and Rochester the thermocline tilts strongly upward. At Oswego the flow is on the point of reversal and the thermocline is in the process of upward movement.

The speed of propagation in this episode is again about 1.7 km hr^{-1}, which is close to internal wave celerity in a realistic idealized model of the lake. The width of the coastal jets is close to the corresponding radius of deformation of about 5 km. As already pointed out, the momentum of the initially generated coastal jet is comparable to the impulse of the wind stress. The agreement between observation and simple conceptual model is gratifying, although there is one complication: at least on the north shore, a topographic wave accompanies the internal Kelvin wave. Fortuitously, the two waves travel approximately at the same speed. That this is not always true may be seen by referring to an earlier illustration (Figure 18) shown in connection with topographic waves. Following an October storm episode, the topographic wave-induced flow reversal reached the coastal survey area off Oshawa, while th coastal jet was still moving in the original eastward direction relative to the waters

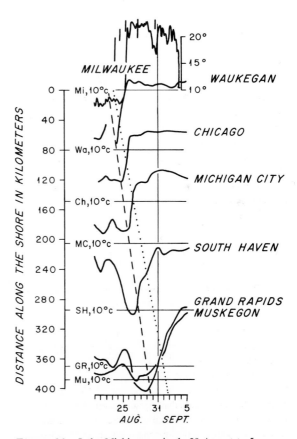

FIGURE 26. Lake Michigan, episode 20 August to 5 September 1947: extracts from waterworks intake-temperature records plotted in counterclockwise order around the basin and with vertical spacing corresponding to distance between intakes along the shoreline. The broken and dotted lines provide estimates of the speed of a presumed internal Kelvin wave, from Mortimer (1963).

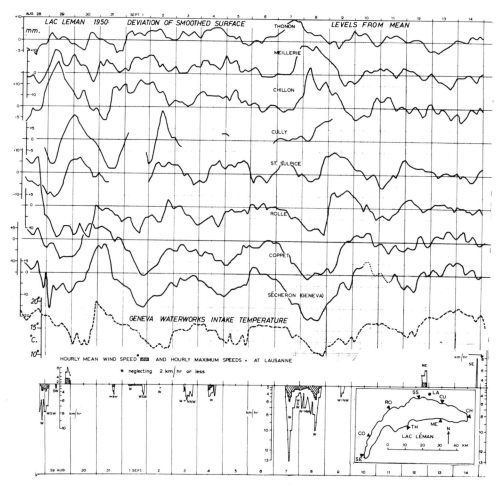

FIGURE 27.   Fluctuations in surface level after short periodicities have been removed by a smoothing process derived from water-level records at a number of stations around Lac Léman (Switzerland and France) during the period 28 August to 14 September 1950. The position of the stations is indicated by the coded inset map, and the records are plotted in counterclockwise order around the basin. Also plotted are Geneva waterworks intake temperature and hourly mean and maximum wind speeds at Lausanne, Switzerland, from Mortimer (1963).

below. In other words, the internal Kelvin wave lagged behind, presumably on account of reduced density contrast so late in the season, which affects wave celerity.

Near-inertial oscillations of currents and thermocline

Mortimer (1963) has also drawn attention to another type of wave motion prominent in large lakes, one that has a period slightly below the inertial. Inertial oscillations constitute a well-known mode of motion, possible in the ocean far from shores. In these oscillations, taking place at exactly a period $T_p = 2\pi/f$, no pressure gradients appear, and the Coriolis force constantly accelerates the fluid in a direction 90° to its instanta-

neous motion. Certain wave-like motions observed by Mortimer in Lake Michigan had a period close to the inertial. They were first evident in temperature records at water works intakes. Temperature oscillations at a period somewhat below $T_p \cong 17$ hr suggested that the thermocline moved up and down in the vicinity of water intakes by several meters. Thermocline oscillations of this kind imply horizontal pressure gradients in the fluid and require a conceptual model different from the simple inertial oscillation for its explanation. The relevant model is the internal Poincaré wave.

Later research revealed that internal oscillations of this type are prominent mainly in the center portion of large lakes under summer conditions. Thermocline motions of several meters amplitude occur, accompanied by moderately fast currents, changing in phase from one side of the thermocline to the other. Distinct modes of the thermocline motion may be identified,

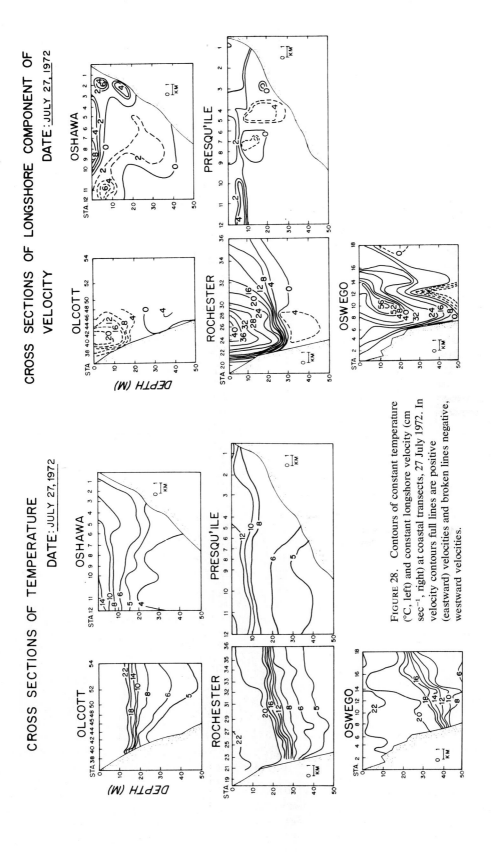

FIGURE 28. Contours of constant temperature (°C, left) and constant longshore velocity (cm sec⁻¹, right) at coastal transects, 27 July 1972. In velocity contours full lines are positive (eastward) velocities and broken lines negative, (westward) velocities.

54   G. T. Csanady

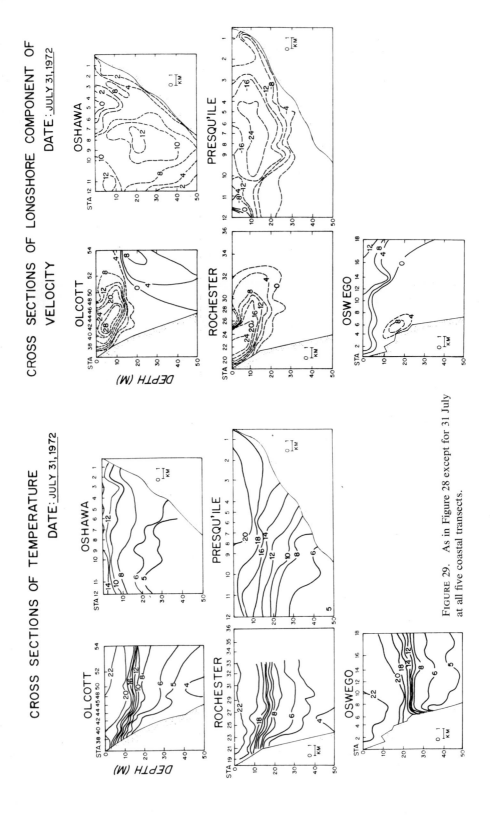

FIGURE 29. As in Figure 28 except for 31 July at all five coastal transects.

the most energetic waves having three to five nodes across Lake Michigan. The waves are excited by storms, much as other lake oscillations.

This type of long thermocline wave may be understood in terms of a conceptual model based again on a two-layer basin of constant depth set into motion by the wind. The internal Poincaré wave is the rotational analogue of the internal seiche familiar from small lakes, but it is found in basins large enough for the earth's rotation to play a dominant role in determining the frequency and structure of the seiche.

The internal Poincaré wave conceptual model

Consider a long channel with straight side walls, the centerline of which conincides with the x axis. Side-

walls are at $y = \pm b/2$. The channel contains a two-layer fluid of equilibrium depth h (top) and h' (bottom).

Internal mode oscillations in the channel obey the fourth to sixth of Eqs. (62). To model the observed near-inertial motions described above a solution with the characteristics of standing waves may be sought. One finds that Eqs. (62) and the side-wall boundary conditions of zero normal transport are satisfied by the internal Poincaré wave:

$$\zeta' = a_n \sin \frac{n\pi y}{b} \cos \sigma_n t$$

$$U' = \frac{a_n fb}{n\pi} \cos \frac{n\pi y}{b} \cos \sigma_n t \qquad (76)$$

$$V' = \frac{a_n \sigma_n b}{n\pi} \cos \frac{n\pi y}{b} \sin \sigma_n t$$

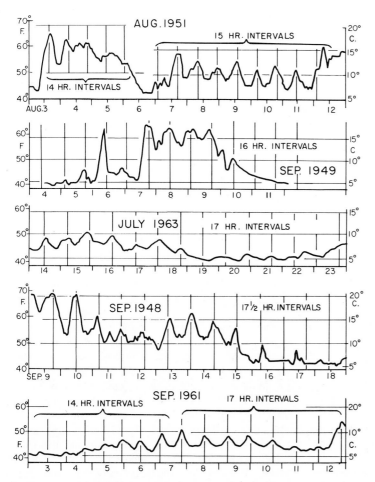

FIGURE 30.   Lake Michigan: "periodic" fluctuations in temperature (hourly means or hourly readings) at the municipal filtration plant intake at Milwaukee, Wisconsin, during selected episodes. The mean periodicity assigned to each episode is estimated as a "best fit" by eye, from Mortimer (1971).

with a_n an arbitrary thermocline displacement amplitude and

$$\sigma_n^2 = f^2 + \frac{n^2\pi^2c^2}{b^2}. \qquad (77)$$

Note also that top layer transports are $U = -U'$, $V = -V'$. These expressions satisfy the boundary condition of zero V' (and V) at $y = \pm b/2$, if $n = 1, 3, 5. \ldots$

The exact character of the motions described by Eq. (76) depends strongly on the value of the quantity fb/c, which one may regard as either nondimensional channel width or nondimensional rotational speed of the earth. When this quantity is small, the effects of rotation are negligible and the frequency of oscillations becomes, from Eq. (77), $\sigma_n \cong n\pi c/b$, which is transverse seiche frequency in a nonrotating channel. At the same time the amplitude of transverse motions V' becomes large compared with that of longitudinal motion U'. In the contrary case of large fb/c, the frequency σ_n approaches the inertial frequency f for the fundamental mode $n = 1$ and some other lower modes, and the U' amplitude approaches the V' amplitude, with the particle orbits becoming circular. This limit is close to the inertial oscillation with period $2\pi/f$, which is a well-known simple model of motion in a rotating fluid far from any boundaries. However, in contrast to that simple model, in an internal Poincaré wave there are also significant thermocline motions.

To take some typical numbers, assume a top layer depth of 10 m and a velocity amplitude of 30 cm sec^{-1}, in a channel 30 km wide, at mid-latitudes, $f = 10^{-4}$ sec^{-1}. In the fundamental mode $n = 1$, the corresponding thermocline displacement amplitude is about 3 m, certainly far from negligible.

Larger amplitude Poincaré waves occur mainly following storms, after which they decay with a half-life of order of several inertial periods. Their generation may be simply modelled using Eq. (62) and assuming that a wind stress is suddenly imposed at time $t = 0$ and removed at $t = T$. The solution of the initial-value problem for a straight infinite channel of constant depth is immediate and yields the thermocline oscillation amplitudes (Csanady, 1973b):

$$a_n = \frac{h'}{h + h'}\frac{8F_y}{\sigma_n^2 b}\sin\left(\frac{\sigma_n T}{2}\right). \qquad (78)$$

This is valid for a cross-wind. Longshore winds are somewhat less effective, the excited amplitudes being f/σ_n times the above result for a_n.

Most effective in exciting a given Poincaré-wave mode is a wind stress episode lasting for half a wave period, π/σ_n. As already seen, in a large lake at mid-latitudes the lowest modes have periods close to 17 hr, which should be excited best by wind stress impulses

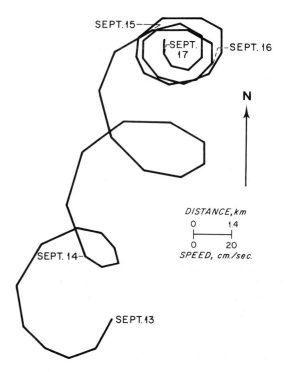

FIGURE 31.   Currents at 20 km from eastern shore of Lake Michigan, in water 60 m deep. Shoreline orientation is NNW to SSE, from Verber (1966).

of about 8-hr duration. Fortuitously, this is in fact the typical lifetime of a strong wind stress episode at mid-latitudes. Given the typical wind stress value of 3 dyn cm^{-2} in such stronger blows, Eq. (78) yields an amplitude of about 2 m for each excited mode assuming quantities typical of Lake Michigan.

It is also interesting to consider the distribution of amplitudes a_n for increasing mode number n. Given a large enough nondimensional width fb/c, the frequency σ_n remains close to f for the lowest few values of n, according to Eq. (78). However, the relationship being quadratic in n, the frequency soon begins to increase and the second term on the right of Eq. (78) rapidly comes to dominate the relationship. As σ_n increases, a_n decreases on account of the multiplier σ_n^{-2} in Eq. (78) and initially also because $\sin(\sigma_n T/2)$ decreases. Thus a_n is relatively large and nearly constant for the first few modes n, but for these only, in a large lake. In a small lake, by contrast, the amplitudes decrease with n as 1:9:25: . . . , so that the fundamental mode is of much more overwhelming importance.

The details of the mathematical solution also show that, as the wind stress is imposed, it begins to accelerate the water along the direction of the stress, without affecting the local free surface level or the thermocline elevation. The shores, however, prevent perpendicular water movement and cause surface/thermocline level changes, at first in their immediate vicinity, then farther out: this action is the cause of surface and internal seiche generation. For the case of constant depth, the effects of shores may be studied in the simplest way using a semiinfinite ocean model, as shown by Crépon (1967, 1969). The shores signal their presence with a wave propagation velocity c in the internal mode. Before the arrival of a pulse from the nearest shore, i.e., for $t < y/c$, if y is the distance from the nearest shore, the water does not "know" that there are shores, i.e., the surface/thermocline elevation remains unaffected. Crépon shows some illuminating diagrams illustrating this effect.

In the case of a long lake the pressure pulses emitted by the end walls reach the center of the lake in a much longer period than those from the side walls. For internal seiches the total time interval of practical interest is from zero to a few inertial periods: beyond that the oscillations decay. A wave on the thermocline reaches a distance of about $20R_2 = 20c/f$ in $20/2\pi \approx 3$ inertial periods. In Lakes Michigan and Ontario R_2 in mid-summer is of the order of 5 km. Hence, excepting end regions of a length of about 100 km, the excitation of internal seiches cannot be seriously affected by the presence of end walls. This argument justifies the use of the infinite channel model and defines its limitations.

Comparison with observation

One prominent signature of internal Poincaré waves is that at a given location and at a fixed depth close to the equilibrium depth of the thermocline large temperature oscillations occur at a period slightly below the inertial. Mortimer (1963) showed that this took place at a number of municipal water intakes on Lake Michigan. A later large-scale survey of the same lake conducted by the Federal Water Quality Administration (FWQA) during the mid 1960s provided more striking evidence at a large number of locations. An illustration of fixed-point temperature oscillations is shown here in Figure 30 from Mortimer (1971).

The FWQA survey also showed how currents behaved at mid-lake. Verber (1966 and earlier references) documented in a series of papers the observed near-inertial oscillations of currents during summer stratification. Figure 31 shows a progressive vector diagram based on fixed point current meter observations, which indicates that water particles were moving at times in nearly circular orbits. The phase of these oscillations was observed to change across the thermocline; Figure 32, from Mortimer (1963), illustrates this effect.

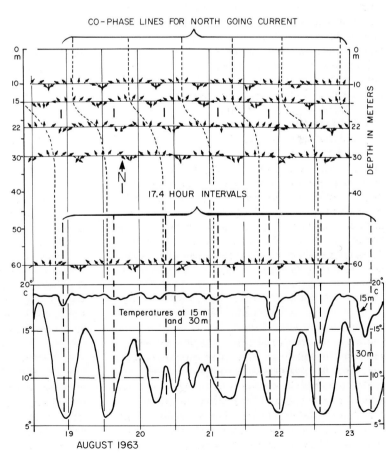

FIGURE 32. Lake Michigan, station 8, 19–23 August 1963. Current directions at five depths (10, 15, 22, 30, and 60 m; adapted from U.S. Dept. Int., 1967, Figure 6-3), compared with temperatures at two depths (15 and 22 m), from Mortimer (1971).

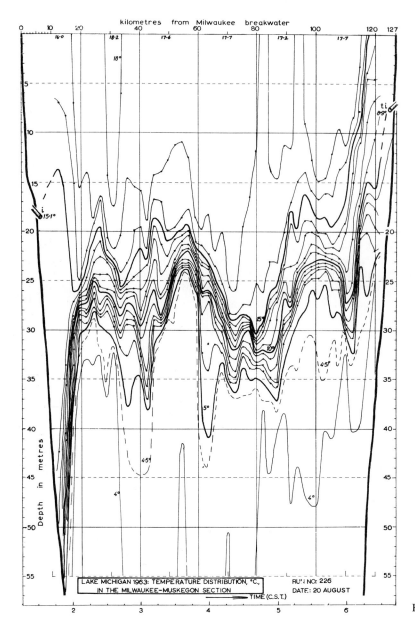

FIGURE 33.   From Mortimer (1968).

The larger scale structure of the termocline surface associated with such oscillations shows considerable complexity. Figure 33 illustrates isotherm depths observed from a car ferry crossing Lake Michigan (Mortimer, 1968). It is remarkable that such a complex picture, certainly aliased due to the fact that the ferry took 5.5 hr to cross the lake, still provides information on the model structure of the waves involved. Mortimer (1968) has shown that by overlaying chosen isotherms observed on successive runs the wave-like nature of the pattern is strikingly demonstrated. This is shown here in Figure 34, taken from Mortimer's report.

In Lake Michigan Poincaré waves with one, three, and five nodes were found in this manner to be present prominently enough to indicate nodes in such cross-sections. In Lake Ontario, which is considerably narrower (65 versus 120 km), IFYGL observations reported by Boyce and Mortimer (1976) showed a somewhat simpler cross-lake structure in which only the one- and three-node waves were present. Figure 35 from an earlier manuscript by Boyce (1972) illustrates this finding. These results are in accord with the theoretical result to the effect that the nondimensional basin width determines how many of the lowest modes are excited with significant amplitude.

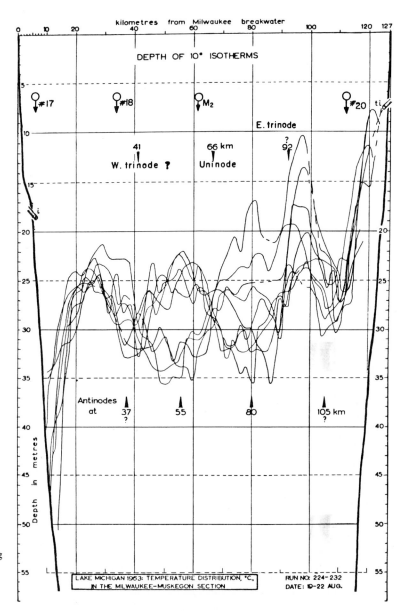

FIGURE 34. Distribution of the 10° isotherm in the Milwaukee-Muskegon cross-section of Lake Michigan during nine consecutive runs of the railroad ferry, S.S. "Grand Rapids" 19–22 August, 1963, from Mortimer (1968).

Mortimer (1963) has shown furthermore that internal Poincaré waves arise in response to storms. The amplitude of the observed Poincaré waves is, however, greater by about a factor of two than follows from the simple theory discussed above. The complexity of natural lake basins is no doubt partly responsible for this. Apart from the questions remaining regarding their excitation, the internal Poincaré wave conceptual model certainly may be taken to account for some prominent observable phenomena. Many other observations since Mortimer's pioneering studies have confirmed his findings and demonstrated that, outside the coastal band, large lakes in summer have a

current regime actually dominated by internal Poincaré waves.

The coastal boundary layer

In several phenomena discussed above a distinction arose between a nearshore zone and "mid-lake," i.e., a zone outside some nearshore band. From several points of view it is appropriate to speak of a "coastal boundary layer" in large lakes, of a typical width of 10 km.

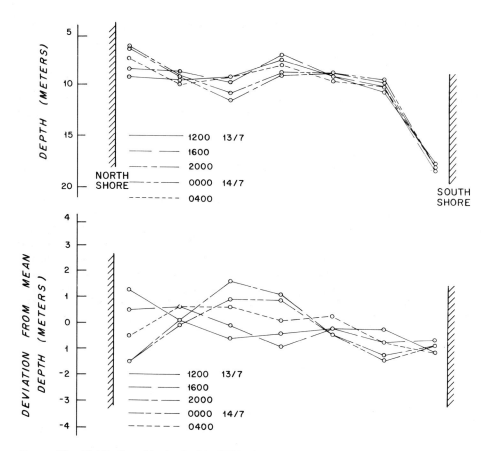

FIGURE 35.   Distribution of the depth of the 10C isotherm across Lake Ontario from Oshawa to Olcott during the International Field Year on the Great Lakes, July 1972. Top graph shows actual depths and bottom graph departures from the mean depth at 4-hr intervals. Three nodes are clearly recognizable, from Boyce (1972).

Theoretically, an explanation for the occurrence of boundary layers of any kind lies in the fact that the highest space derivatives in the governing nondimensional differential equations are multiplied by a small factor (Carrier, 1953). In the case of frictional boundary layers the small factor is the reciprocal Reynolds number in the equations of motion. When the rotation of the earth is important, the equations of motion are best made nondimensional in such a way that the Coriolis force comes to be of order unity. The shear stress terms are then multiplied by the turbulent analogue of the Ekman number which is again small and suggests the existence of boundary layers both at the bottom and near horizontal boundaries. If we neglect these terms, the next highest space derivatives are in the nonlinear terms, which are multiplied by the Rossby number. This is again a small quantity if the length scale is chosen so as to represent lake-wide motions. Thus, "inertial" boundary layers may be expected to occur near the shores, similar to those discussed by Charney (1955b).

If one neglects both frictional and inertial terms, the equations of motion and continuity may be reduced to a linear second-order differential equation for the small displacements ζ of the free surface, or of the thermocline. This equation, in a nondimensional form, is

$$\frac{\partial^2 \zeta}{\partial t^2} - \frac{R^2}{L^2} \nabla_1^2 \zeta + \zeta = 0. \tag{79}$$

where R is surface or internal radius of deformation and L is typical basin dimension.

The highest space derivatives in this equation are multiplied by the factor R^2/L^2. For barotropic motions this factor is invariably of order unity whether in oceans or in the Great Lakes and therefore the flow does not have a boundary layer character. The ratio R^2/L^2 is, however, small for baroclinic motions, in which case geostrophic adjustment to the presence of the shores occurs in a band of scale width R_2. This, therefore, becomes a kind of baroclinic boundary layer, in which the coastal jets of the theoretical models were found to occur.

Even for barotropic frictionless motions at low Rossby number, the peculiar geometry of the shore zone leads to a singularity at the point where the free surface intersects the sloping bottom. The highest order space derivative in Eq. (79) in this case is multiplied by a factor containing the water depth h. Sufficiently close to the shore this becomes small enough to produce singular behavior, one manifestation of which is that topographic waves may occur.

Thus, it is clear the motion in the shore-zone should have a boundary layer character for several reasons. An interplay of the different physical effects referred to above is indeed likely to produce a boundary layer of unusually complex structure.

The above deductions are based on some successful conceptual models, related previously to corresponding observed phenomena. Their aggregate effect becomes noticeable in studying the *climatology*, i.e., various statistical properties, of currents near shore, and in comparing this with the climatology of offshore currents. Some illuminating studies of this kind appeared in the literature in recent years, to be surveyed briefly in the next section.

Current climatology nearshore and offshore

The first clear distinction between current regimes observed near and far from shore has apparently been drawn by Verber (1966). In the course of the large scale experiment conducted by the FWQA in Lake Michigan (referred to above), a number of current meters were deployed, covering the whole lake in a more or less even grid pattern. Some of the meters were near shore in shallow water. In classifying the types of current regimes observed, Verber notes that "straightline flow" is always found near shore, while far from shore the currents generally oscillate in all directions. Figure 36 taken from Verber's paper illustrates the typical current behavior by means of a progressive vector diagram near shore: typical offshore currents were shown before in Figure 31.

The same data were later analyzed in greater detail by Birchfield and Davidson (1967) and Malone (1968). Spectra at stations far from shore were dominated by a large peak at frequencies slightly above inertial, while close to shore most of the energy was in low-frequency motions (Figure 37, after Birchfield and Davidson, 1967). According to Malone (1968), there is a "large current component nearly parallel to the coast" at nearshore meters. The percentage of energy in the near-inertial peak is three times less near shore than offshore.

All this early evidence on the distinct character of the coastal zone became consolidated and placed into perspective by work during and in preparation for the International Field Year on the Great Lakes. Moored

current meter observations (Weiler, 1968) have shown that the kinetic energy of surface currents peaks some 8 km from shore. Blanton (1974) has corroborated this finding and showed that the percentage of energy in long period motions falls dramatically between 8 and 10 km from shore (Figure 38). Blanton (1975) has also demonstrated that the onshore–offshore component of the surface currents nearshore is much smaller than the longshore current, typically by a factor of 5. Sato and Mortimer (1975) note that in Lake Michigan, as in Lake Ontario, the coastal zone is the "repository of most of the lake's kinetic energy."

The prevalence of longshore flow and the weakness of onshore–offshore velocities has important consequences for the nearshore dispersal of effluents (Csanady, 1974). Effluent plumes tend to hug the shores and to remain trapped in the shore zone for long distances. Figure 39 illustrates Rhodamine B plumes generated by dyeing the cooling water outflow of a power station on Lake Huron. Most of the mass exchange between the coastal boundary layer and offshore waters was

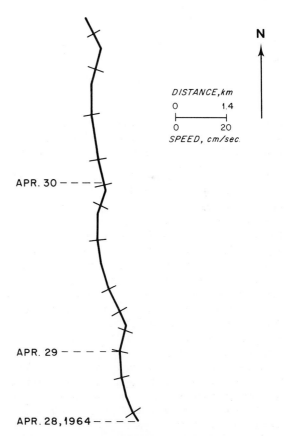

FIGURE 36.   Currents observed at a station about 5 km from western shore of Lake Michigan, April 1964, showing 2-hr progressive vectors. Shoreline orientation is parallel to the mean current direction, the depth of water 22 m, from Verber (1966).

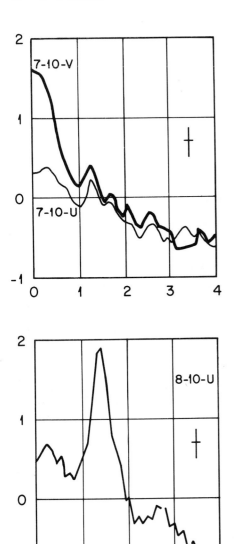

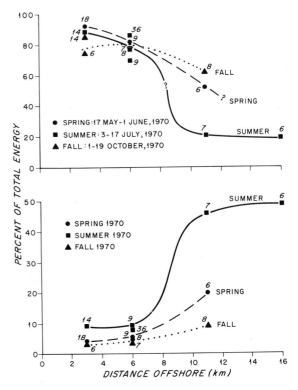

FIGURE 38.   Energy in long period motions (top, period >3 days) versus inertial oscillations (bottom, period 16 to 18 hr), as percentage of total energy. Current meters were moored at depths as noted adjacent to data points (meters), from Blanton (1974).

FIGURE 37.   Current spectra at a nearshore (top) and an offshore station (bottom), 5 and 30 km from the western shore of Lake Michigan, in depths of 22 and 97 m. The top graph shows the longshore (v) and offshore (u) components of near-surface velocity. At the offshore station both had very similar spectra and only the u spectrum is shown. Abscissa is cycles per day and ordinate 10-base log of energy density in cm² sec⁻². Large peak at offshore station occurs at local inertial frequency of 17.8 hr. Note large amount of low frequency energy in longshore velocity near shore, from Birchfield and Davidson (1967).

observed to take place on those occasions when the coastal current reverses direction. Reversals take place roughly with the frequency of weather cycles (typically every 4 days), although, as was pointed out earlier, there are also spontaneous coastal current reversals unrelated to the wind. In any event, the large changes of thermocline elevation accompanying flow reversal near shore amount to a practically complete water mass renewal near shore. Dye plumes were observed to disappear without trace during such mass exchange episodes, almost as if a chance event annihilated them. Thus, while currents persist in one direction, pollutants travel alongshore within the coastal zone, but the coastal waters are bodily removed during thermocline readjustment.

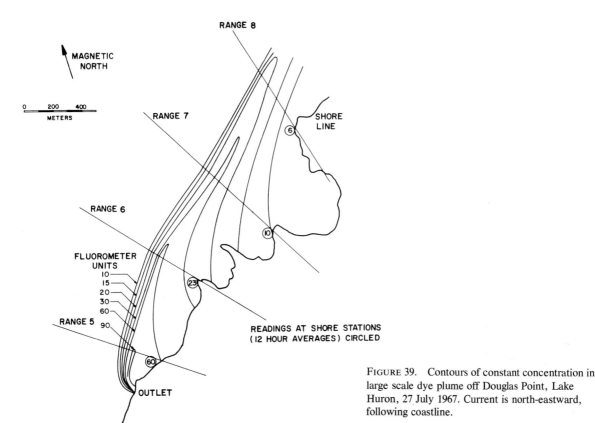

MAGNETIC
NORTH

0   200   400
METERS

RANGE 8

RANGE 7

SHORE
LINE

⑥

RANGE 6

⑩

FLUOROMETER
UNITS
10
15
20
30
60
90

RANGE 5

㉓

READINGS AT SHORE STATIONS
(12 HOUR AVERAGES) CIRCLED

⑥⓪

OUTLET

FIGURE 39.   Contours of constant concentration in large scale dye plume off Douglas Point, Lake Huron, 27 July 1967. Current is north-eastward, following coastline.

References

Ball, F. K. (1965). Second-class motions of a shallow liquid. *J. Fluid Mech.,)* **23**:545–562.

Bennett, J. (1972). On the dynamics of wind-driven lake currents. Ph.D. thesis, University of Wisconsin, Madison.

Bennett, J. (1974). On the dynamics of wind driven lake currents. *J. Phys. Oceanogr.,* **4**:400–414.

Birchfield, G. E. (1969). The response of a circular model Great Lake to a suddenly imposed wind stress. *J. Geophys. Res.,* **74**:5547–5554.

Birchfield, G. E., and D. R. Davidson. (1967). A case study of coastal currents in Lake Michigan. Pp. 264–273. *Proc. 10th Conf. Great Lakes Res.,* Univ. Michigan, Ann Arbor, MI.

Blanton, J. O. (1974). Some characteristics of nearshore currents along the north shore of Lake Ontario. *J. Phys. Oceanogr.,* **4**:415–424.

Blanton, J. O. (1975). Nearshore lake currents measured during upwelling and downwelling of the thermocline in Lake Ontario. *J. Phys. Oceanogr.,* **5**:111–124.

Boyce, F. M. (1972). Temperature transects of Lake Ontario. Manuscript, Canada Centre for Inland Waters, Burlington, Ontario.

Boyce, F. M., and C. H. Mortimer. (1976). Temperature distributions across Lake Ontario. Center for Great Lakes Studies, Univ. Wisconsin, Milwaukee, draft report. 362 pp.

Carrier, G. F. (1953). *Boundary Layer Problems in Applied Mechanics.* Vol. 3. Academic Press, New York, NY. Pp. 1–19.

Charney, J. G. (1955a). The generation of oceanic currents by the wind. *J. Marine Res.,* **14**:477–498.

Charney, J. G. (1955b). The Gulf Stream as an inertial boundary layer. *Proc. Nat. Acad. Sci. USA,* **41**:731–740.

Crépon, M. (1967). Hydrodynamique marine en regime impulsionnel. *Cah. Oceanogr.,* **19**:847–880.

Crépon, M. (1969). Hydrodynamique marine en regime impulsionnel. *Cah. Oceanogr.,* **21**:333–353; 863–877.

Csanady, G. T. (1968). Motions in a model Great Lake due to a suddenly imposed wind. *J. Geophys. Res.,* **73**:6435–6447.

Csanady, G. T. (1972a). Frictional currents in the mixed layer at the free surface. *J. Phys. Oceanogr.,* **2**:498–508.

Csanady, G. T. (1972b). Response of large stratified lakes to wind. *J. Phys. Oceanogr.,* **2**:3–13.

Csanady, G. T. (1972c). The coastal boundary layer in Lake Ontario. *J. Phys. Oceanogr.,* **2**:41–53; 168–176.

Csanady, G. T. (1973a). Wind-induced barotropic motions in long lakes. *J. Phys. Oceanogr.,* **3**:429–438.

Csanady, G. T. (1973b). Transverse internal seiches in large, oblong lakes and marginal seas. *J. Phys. Oceanogr.,* **3**:439–447.

Csanady, G. T. (1974). Mass exchange episodes in the coastal boundary layer, associated with current reversals. *Rapp. P.-v. Réun. Cons. Int. Explor. Mer,* **167**;41–45.

Csanady, G. T. (1975a). Hydrodynamics of large lakes. *Ann. Rev. Fluid Mech.* **7**:357–386.

Csanady, G. T. (1975b). Lateral momentum flux in boundary currents. *J. Phys. Oceanogr.*, **5**:705–717.

Csanady, G. T. (1976). Topographic waves in Lake Ontario. *J. Phys. Oceanogr.*, **6**:93–103.

Csanady, G. T., and J. T. Scott. (1974). Baroclinic coastal jets in Lake Ontario during IFYGL. *J. Phys. Oceanogr.*, **4**:524–541.

Cutchin, D. L., and R. L. Smith. (1973). Continental shelf waves: Low frequency variations in sea level and currents over the Oregon continental shelf. *J. Phys. Oceanogr.*, **3**:73–82.

Gill, A. E., and E. H. Schumann. (1974). The generation of long shelf waves by the wind. *J. Phys. Oceanogr.*, **4**:83–90.

Hamon, B. V. (1962). The spectrums of mean sea level at Sydney, Coff's Harbour and Lord Howe Island. *J. Geophys. Res.*, **67**:5147–5155.

Hutchinson, G. E. (1957). *A Treatise on Limnology.* Vol. I. John Wiley, New York, NY. 1015 pp.

Jones, I. S. F. (1968). Surface layer currents in Lake Huron. Pp. 406–411. *Proc. 11th Conf. Great Lakes Res.*, Int. Assoc. Great Lakes Res.

Longuet-Higgins, M. S. (1968). Double Kelvin waves with continuous depth profiles. *J. Fluid Mech.*, **34**:49–80.

Malone, F. D. (1968). An analysis of current measurements in Lake Michigan. *J. Geophys. Res.*, **73**:7065–7081.

Mortimer, C. H. (1953). The resonant response of stratified lakes to wind. *Schweiz. Z. Hydrol.*, **15**:94–151.

Mortimer, C. H. (1963). Frontiers in physical limnology with particular reference to long waves in rotating basins. *Great Lakes Div. Publ.* (University of Michigan), **10**:9–42.

Mortimer, C. H. (1968). *Internal Waves and Associated Currents Observed in Lake Michigan during the Summer of 1963.* Spec. Rep. No. 1, Center for Great Lakes Studies, University of Wisconsin, Milwaukee.

Mortimer, C. H. (1971). *Large-Scale Oscillatory Motions and Seasonal Temperature Changes in Lake Michigan and Lake Ontario.* Spec. Rep. No. 12, Center for Great Lakes Studies, University of Wisconsin, Milwaukee.

Mortimer, C. H., and E. J. Fee. (1976). Free surface oscillations and tides of Lakes Michigan and Superior. *Phil. Trans. Roy. Soc. London A,* **281**:1–61.

Platzman, G. W. (1972) Two dimensional free oscillations in natural basins. J. Phys. Oceanogr. *2,* 117–138

Proudman, J. 1953. *Dynamical Oceanography.* Wiley, New York, NY. 409 pp.

Rao, D. B., and T. S. Murty. (1970). Calculation of the steady-state wind-driven circulation in Lake Ontario. *Arch. Meteor. Geophys. Bioklim.,* **A19**:195–210.

Rao, D. B., and D. J. Schwab. (1976). Two dimensional normal modes in arbitrary enclosed basins or a rotating earth: Application to Lakes Ontario and Superior. *Phil Trans. Roy. Soc. London A,* **281**:63–96.

Robinson, A. R. (1964) Continental Shelf Waves and the response of sea level to weather systems. J. Geophys. Res. *69,* 367–368.

Sato, G. K., and C. H. Mortimer. (1975). *Lake Currents and Temperatures Near the Western Shore of Lake Michigan.* Univ. Wisconsin–Milwaukee, Center for Great Lakes Studies, Spec. Rep. No. 22.

Simons, T. J. (1974). Verification of numerical models of Lake Ontario: Part I. Circulation in spring and early summer. *J. Phys. Oceanogr.,* **4**:507–523.

Simons, T. J. (1975). Verification of numerical models of Lake Ontario. II. Stratified circulations and temperature changes. *J. Phys. Oceanogr.,* **5**:98–110.

Sweers, H. E. (1969). *Structure, Dynamics and Chemistry of Lake Ontario.* Marine Sciences Branch, Dept. Energy, Mines and Resources, Ottawa. 227 pp.

Verber, J. L. (1966). Inertial currents in the Great Lakes. Pp. 375–379. *Proc. 9th Conf. Great Lakes Res.*

Weiler, H. S. (1968). Current measurements in Lake Ontario in 1967. Pp. 500–511. *Proc. 11th Conf. Great Lakes Res.* Int. Assoc. Great Lakes Res.

Chapter 3
Sedimentary Processes in Lakes

P. G. Sly

Introduction

The formation and behavior of lacustrine sediments is
dominated by the interaction of a number of physical
processes whose relative importance is influenced,
particularly, by the form of the basin, its orientation
and size, and by climatic conditions. The range of lake
types and their sedimentary characteristics are widely
diverse. Despite apparent differences, however, it is
important to realize that essentially the same relationships may be used to express sediment response to
dynamics forces in almost all lake systems.

Sedimentary processes in lake systems differ from
those of marine systems in three major aspects: (1)
Despite the great size of a few lakes, the small size of
most lakes significantly limits the generation of long-
period wind waves and therefore maintains such energy levels much below that of marine systems; the
occurrence of sorted coarse sands and gravels is
largely confined to shallow water areas. (2) Lakes are
essentially closed, or nearly closed systems, with respect to sediment transport and, because the ratio
between land drainage and lake area is often high,
sediment loadings and sedimentation rates appear substantially higher than in marine environments, even
when accumulation is restricted almost entirely to fine
sediments (typically mid-lake sedimentation rates are
at least 10 times that of oceanic environments). Geo-
logically speaking, therefore, most lakes are transitory
features. (3) Lakes are almost tideless, tidal currents
are generally negligible, and littoral zones are much
reduced or absent.

Almost certainly, the occurrence of lake sediments
has been a common feature of past depositional environments and perhaps more frequently than suggested
by the existing geological records (Hough, 1963);
based only upon sedimentological evidence, however,
it is difficult to be sure whether or not ancient sediments are of lacustrine or marine origin unless there is
clear evidence of basin closure, generally rapid deposition, and restricted littoral development. As discussed by Feth (1964) and by Picard and High (1972),
it is essential to consider all additional evidence, especially geochemical and paleontological, in order to
establish ancient lake sediments; salt water lakes are
not uncommon, but true freshwater seas are not
known to exist.

In the following review and discussions the underlying theme seeks to link and associate the various
factors which influence sedimentary processes and to
show how, and under what circumstances, they may
be characterized. Further, to gain a proper appreciation of the role of sediments within lake systems it is
essential to understand the more important relationships between particle size, composition, and geochemical behavior.

In this contribution, work carried out by the author
in the Laurentian Great Lakes (North America) has
been extensively used to illustrate many of the discussion points and to provide examples.

Lake types

Lake types, based upon their mode of origin, are an
important guide to the sedimentary processes within
them and suggest such characteristics as basin form,
source materials and materials availability, and the
likely magnitude of physical forces affecting lake dynamics; the various approaches used to classify the

forms of lake basins have been examined and considered in detail by Hutchinson (1957).

Tectonic mechanisms have been responsible for very large-scale movements which (in late Miocene times) caused the formation of vast inland seas in southeast Europe and southern Asia, remnants of which include the Aral, Caspian, and Black Seas. In East Africa, a smaller crustal sag accommodates Lake Victoria and examples of rift valley lakes include: Tahoe (California), Baikal (USSR), Tanganyika and Nyasa (East Africa), and the Dead Sea.

Lakes of volcanic origin are often deep and usually smaller than those of tectonic origin. They may be formed by lava damming (e.g., Lake Kivu and the Sea of Galilee) and by crater explosion and collapse (e.g., Crater Lake, Oregon).

Lakes formed as a result of landslides are mostly of a temporary nature because of the susceptibility of the dam material to erosion.

Lakes formed as a result of glaciation may have been produced in a number of ways: by ice damming (Farrand, 1969, late-glacial Lake Duluth; Gustavson, 1975, proglacial Lake Malaspina, Alaska); by drainage barriers formed of moraine materials (Finger Lakes, New York); by ice scour (Canadian and Scandinavian Shield areas); by freeze–thaw effects at the head of glaciated valleys (Cirque Lakes); and by valley glaciation which produced long, narrow, and deep lakes such as the fiord lakes of many high latitude regions of both northern and southern hemispheres. In areas of glacial drift, kettle lakes frequently fill small depressions which originally accommodated ice residuals. In North America, additionally, all of the large lakes bordering the Canadian Shield (Great Bear, Great Slave, Athabasca, Winnipeg, and the Laurentian Great Lakes) owe much of their origins to the effects of repeated glaciation.

Fluvial action may produce oxbow and levee lakes as a result of channel shifting, or by deposition of sediment barriers in delta areas or at sites of tributary inflow. In marine areas the accumulation of beach sands may similarly close valleys and embayments, and form coastal lagoons (Steers, 1953). Lakes may also develop as a result of aeolian effects, where blown sands may impound small lakes and lagoons (Les Landes, southern France) or, as an erosional agent, wind-excavated deflation basins may be formed (Reeves, 1966).

The largest man-made lakes have been constructed, usually, by building dams across existing drainage systems (e.g., Lake Mead, Arizona; Lake Kariba, Zambia); however, many smaller lakes have formed in disused quarries and other mining operations.

Other lake types include those formed as a result of solution effects, by ponding of organic materials, by permafrost melting, or in meteorite craters.

Basin changes

Changes with time

The form of existing lakes depends not only upon the form of the original basin but upon subsequent tectonic and isostatic movements, and upon the accumulation of infilling material (or subsequent removal during glaciation). Changes which affect the physical regime of lakes may be separated into four distinct types: (1) basin-wide effects which are caused by climatic change; (2) basin-wide effects which are produced by changes in water level; (3) basin-wide effects which are related to expansion or shallowing, due to natural erosion–accumulation trends; and (4) local changes which affect only part of a basin, such as the migration of deltas, formation of spits and bars, or modification of inflow due to drainage change.

In the Laurentian Great Lakes major changes in sedimentary processes may be related both directly and indirectly to climatic influence. Despite the fact that the region has been subject to repeated glaciation during the Pleistocene only fragmentary evidence remains of deposits formed prior to the last Wisconsin Stage (Karrow, 1963, 1967 and 1969, and Karrow et al., 1961). Presumably ice movement during succeeding glacial advances removed or reworked any previously existing materials. Sediment accumulation in early postglacial times also differs markedly from that of the present; the glaciolacustrine clays (and varved deposits formed near the ice front) in Lake Superior (Reid, 1961; Dell, 1974), for example, are in marked contrast to the largely unstructured recent muds, now accumulating (Mothersill, 1971; Sly and Thomas, 1974).

Changes in sedimentation which are related to both major and minor variations in water level, within the Laurentian Great Lakes, are well illustrated by a number of features (Sly, 1973a). In the Lake Ontario basin the presence of a beach bar at about +30 m above lake level at Hamilton has been related to the high-level glaciolacustrine Lake Iroquois (Karrow, 1963), dated at about 12,000 years B.P. and a submerged beach bar at an elevation of approximately −70 to −79 m below lake level in western Lake Ontario and dated about 11,000 years B.P. (Lewis, 1969) has been related to a low lake stage, following withdrawal of ice from the easterly drainage outlet of the lake.

Also, in the Lake Ontario basin, the presence of extensive but thin (1–5 cm) sand and silty-sand layers, immediately above glaciolacustrine clays and (often) below recent deep water mud accumulations (Lewis and McNeely, 1967; Sly and Lewis, 1972), provides strong supporting evidence of a rapid shallowing which was followed by deepening, consistent with known lake stages.

Shoreline migration in the Great Lakes basin continues at the present time as isostatic rebound causes tilting and uplift, such that the north shore of Lake Superior is rising relative to the south by as much as 0.46 m/100 years (Kite, 1972a,b); further east, the outlet of Lake Ontario is rising at a rate of about 0.37 m/100 years (Sly and Lewis, 1972). By comparison, relative movements in the Lake Erie basin are estimated at about 0.05 m/100 years (International Great Lakes Levels Board, 1973).

In situations of basin-wide filling it is often not possible to differentiate the effects of fluctuating inputs, water level changes, and local response. However, for example, in the western basin of Lake Erie where accumulation rates exceed 0.5 cm/year (Kemp and Thomas, 1976) and where shoreline erosion is resulting in regression at rates of up to 1.5 m/year (Great Lakes Levels Board, shoreline and physical characteristics, Canadian Federal Department Public Works; surveys and unpublished data, Haras, 1972), significant changes will have taken place during the past 2000 years while water levels have remained stable. Based upon such values, it may be estimated that the western basin of the lake has shallowed by about 35–40%, and that its surface area has increased by some 15–20%. Recent, unpublished core data (Kemp, personal communication) from Lake Erie suggest that sediment accumulation may not have been continuous throughout the past 2000 years; however ^{37}Cs and ^{210}Pb isotope data suggest that breaks in the most recent accumulation represent only a minor portion of the cored sequence.

Within the Laurentian Great Lakes there are also many examples of local changes in sedimentary conditions. The development of the Toronto Islands in Lake Ontario (Lewis and Sly, 1971) has recently formed an extensive lagoonal area of low-wave energy. In eastern Lake Erie, Long Point continues to extend southeastwards at a rate of about 7 m/year, and thereby adds an additional 6–8% to the area of the existing protected bay on its north side, each 100 years. On the south shore of Lake Erie, at Presque'Isle peninsula, a corresponding eastward migration of about 5.5 m/year was recorded by Berg and Duane (1968), prior to the implementation of methods of shore stabilization.

In many lakes, also, the deposition of delta sediments at the mouth of inflowing streams is of major significance. For example in Lillooet Lake, British Columbia, the delta of the Lillooet River is presently advancing into the lake which is about 140 m (460 ft) deep and 2 km wide, at a rate of about 10 m/year (Gilbert, 1975), the Terek delta in the Caspian Sea is presently advancing as much as 300 m/year (Holmes, 1955), and in Lake Mead the delta of the Colorado River advanced at a rate of nearly 3000 m/year between 1939 and 1948 (Sundborg, 1964).

Infilling

The form of an existing lake basin provides no more than a guide to total sediment accumulation, although great thicknesses may accumulate in rift valley lakes; for example, the Dead Sea where more than 4000 m (13,000 ft) of sediments (mostly precipitates) have been deposited since Miocene times (Neev and Emergy, 1967) and Lake Tahoe (also less than 20 km wide) which has accumulated more than 200 m of material during the past two million years (Hyne *et al.*, 1972). In Lake Geneva (Switzerland) nearly 200 m of sediment (glacial and recent) overlie bedrock (Serruya, 1969), in British Columbia the narrow basin of Lillooet Lake (Gilbert, 1975) contains nearly 200 m of fill and, in Japan, Lake Yogo has nearly 200 m of fill in a valley only 1 km wide (Nakao and Horie, 1975).

Of course, in glaciated regions much of the lake fill may be represented by glacial till or material of nonlacustrine origin (Clague, 1975). Even so, in the Laurentian Great Lakes, as much as 60 m of glaciolacustrine and recent muds have been deposited in parts of the lake basins during the past 10–12,000 years (Sly and Lewis, 1972; Sly, 1976).

Although Hutchinson (1957) developed a variety of formulations to express lake morphometry in numeric form, such terms are of limited use as a means of expressing sediment accumulation. While small lakes may behave as single systems, almost all large lakes respond as a complex of subbasins (Thomas *et al.*, 1972, 1973), each of which may be of significantly different size, form, and depth, yet which, in some lakes, may be separated by only minor differences in lake bed relief.

The shape and depth of lake basins undoubtedly affects the circulation of water within them, and therefore has a particular influence upon the distribution and deposition of fine clay and silt particulates. Although the concept of sediment focusing (Lehman, 1975) expresses this relationship and further explores the geometry of sediment accumulation in idealized basins, Figure 1 shows clearly that this is but one of a number of controlling factors which influence sediment response. The distribution of sediments in large man-made lakes is further modified by the operating characteristics of such reservoirs (Sundborg, 1964; Borland and Miller, 1960).

Sediment accumulation in small lakes, where the effects of wave action are minimal, differs somewhat from that of large lakes where wave energies may represent a significant portion of the total dynamic energy of the system. In small lakes, energy levels may be sufficient only to provide partial and selective transport of incoming sedimentary materials.

The accumulation of sedimentary deposits in small lakes basins, of similar size and origin (such as ice

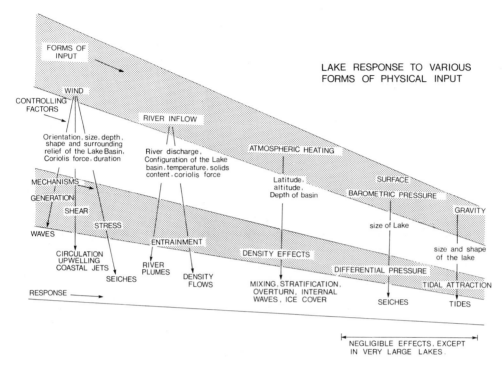

FIGURE 1.   Lake response to various forms of physical input.

scour lakes), may show much similarity over wide areas, where controlling factors remain the same. However, although the distribution of sediment facies will reflect the aging and shallowing of an idealized lake basin, the sedimentary history of large lake basins and changes in the relief of their surrounding watersheds appear to be distinct and individual.

Lake response to various forms of physical input

General relationships

The preceding introduction and general outline of lake types and basin changes has implied that a variety of physical forces interact, in different ways, in a diversity of basin forms, of different size. In Figure 1 an attempt is made to show how these, and other, factors influence the effects of wind, river inflow, atmospheric heating, surface barometric pressure, and gravity; barometric pressure and gravitational influence being, generally, of least importance.

The fetch and duration of wind influence the generation of waves, which are particularly responsible for the erosion and transport of coarse particulates in lake basins. As a result of wind shear, water movements such as circulation (deflected to the right in the north-

ern hemisphere by Coriolis force) and upwelling and coastal jets (Csanady, 1966; see also Chapter 2) also develop in lake basins and have the capacity to selectively transport finer particulates of silt and clay size, most of which are already in suspension or have been resuspended by wave motion. Lake waters may also respond to wind stress by piling up at one end of a basin in the form of a temporarily inclined water surface, and which subsequently oscillates as a function of the length and depth of the basin. By raising water levels such seiches may amplify wave effects and streams of sediment transport.

In addition to the influence of controlling factors such as basin configuration, solids content, and temperature (density) of river inflow, the effects of river input may differ substantially depending upon both the rate of discharge and the relative quantities of bed and suspended load. A further influence is the degree to which river inflow is maintained in entrained phase and to which horizontal and vertical shearing may result in turbulent mixing, and subsequent diffusion. Under some conditions river inflow may remain discrete as a result of density separation, and particulates may be carried substantial distances through the lake basin with little settling or diffusion. Rivers may act as a driving force, maintaining and amplifying lake circulation, and locally there may be sufficient current velocity to cause subaqueous erosion but, usually, their plumes represent the distal portion of sediment transport streams which enter the lake basin from the surrounding land drainage area.

The effects of atmospheric heating may be seen in the thermal and density structure of lakes. When stratified, there may be sufficient density difference between water masses that very fine particulates are kept in suspension; fines already in suspension may become transported by the host waters during periods of vertical mixing, overturn, and upwelling (Mathews, 1956). Periods of ice cover are usually associated with still-water conditions and may enhance opportunities for the settling of very fine particulates which would otherwise remain in suspension as a result of normal water motion.

Seiches associated with differences in surface barometric pressure rarely occur on their own and are usually considered to be part of the wind-seiche response. Such differential pressure effects can be felt only by extensive water bodies which are large enough to respond to atmospheric pressure gradients across a continuous water surface.

Measurable tides occur only in the larger lakes, but tidal currents may add to the overall circulation on a local basis.

Controlling factors

Size and shape

There is a more-or-less complete gradation of size of lake bodies from the Caspian Sea, with an area of 436,000 km² (Van der Leeden, 1975), to lakes of the smallest size (measured in m²), although, as shown in Figure 2, the Caspian is exceptional. The largest lakes are those of tectonic or structural origin, and those associated with major glacial effects (Laurentian Great Lakes). Another group of lakes are also long and deep, but very narrow (glaciated valley lakes, fiord lakes, and the largest man-made reservoirs), and therefore represent rather specialized sedimentary conditions. By far the greatest number of lakes occur as relatively shallow depressions in the form of ice scour lakes, cirques, oxbow and levee lakes, kettle lakes, wetland lakes, lagoons, and the smaller man-made lakes.

In Figure 2 the ratios between length and width are given for lakes greater than 2500 km² (about 1000 miles²) plotted in order of decreasing size (data from Gresswell and Huxley, 1965). Although the elongated form of some rift valley lakes (e.g., Baikal, Nyasa, Tanganyika) and some man-made lakes (e.g., Kariba) is clearly evident, generalities do not hold for all or, even, most large lakes. It is also clear that great size

does not necessarily imply great depth (see Gresswell and Huxley, 1965, for description of large lakes, and Van der Leeden, 1975, for selected statistics). The reporting of lake dimensions and areas varies greatly in the literature because of errors, differences in methods used to compute such values, and rounding-off and conversions between English and metric units. Some of the data in Figure 2, which has been based upon information from Gresswell and Huxley (1965), appear at variance with reports by other authors; for the purpose of general comparison such variance is not of major concern. However, specific text references to the size and form of lakes have been given elsewhere, where deviation from Figure 2 values appears significant.

Lake Baikal is the deepest lake with a water depth of about 1610 m (5300 ft), Lake Tanganyika has a depth of 1470 m (4825 ft) (Capart, 1949), and the Caspian Sea has a depth of 945 m (3103 ft) (Van der Leeden, 1975). On the other hand, Lake Victoria has a maximum depth of only 79 m (260 ft) (Kendall, 1969), and Lakes Chad and Eyre partly or completely dry out. On a comparative basis, the Great Salt Lake (Utah) has an area of between 2600 and 5200 km² (1–2000 miles²) and a depth of less than 11 m, and Lake Kivu with an area of about 2700 km² has a maximum depth of 489 m (1600 ft) (Van der Leeden, 1975). Crater Lake (Oregon), with an area of only about 52 km², is more than 580 m (1900 ft) deep.

The size of a lake basin largely controls the amount of wave energy by limiting fetch, and in long and narrow lake basins wave action is usually directed heavily at the ends of the basin. The depth of lake basins is also important with respect to the development of nearshore zones where wave shoaling and refraction contribute substantially to the development of long shore sediment transport streams (Rukavina, 1976). In broad shallow lakes typical offshore conditions never develop and wave generation is restricted by bed effects.

Lake surface and land drainage relationships

The nature and size of watersheds surrounding lake basins has a major influence on the input of sedimentary materials and, to some extent, their transport and deposition within a lake. Regions of high relief are often typified by very variable river inflows and strongly peaked sediment loads, which are frequently composed of an abundance of coarse particulates (Church and Gilbert, 1975) as, for example, the intermittent deposition of coarse particulates in Lake Biwa sediments (Yamamoto, 1975). Low-gradient watersheds are generally characterized by less extreme fluctuations of inflow, with contributed materials often

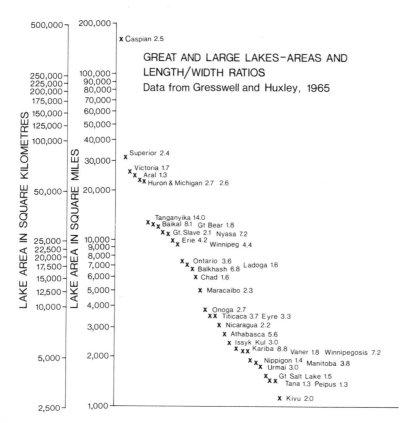

FIGURE 2.   Great and large lakes: areas and length/width ratios.

lacking in coarse particulates (subject to modification under flood events).

The following examples illustrate the great range of such area ratios expressed as lake surface area/land drainage area:

Lake Eyre (Australia) lake area (Johns and Ludbrook, 1963)	9,300 km²	ratio 1:140
Lake Champlain (U.S.) (Hunt and Henson, 1969)	1,130 km²	1:17.0
Lake Geneva (Switzerland) (Serruya, 1969)	600 km²	1:14.0
Lake Titicaca (South America) (Gilson, 1964)	7,600 km²	1:8.0
Lake Ontario (North America) (IJC Report, 1969b)	19,000 km²	1:3.4
Lake Erie (North America) (IJC Report, 1969a)	25,800 km²	1:2.9
Lake Victoria (South Africa) (Kendall, 1969)	68,800 km²	1:2.8
Lake Tahoe (U.S.) (Hyne et al., 1972)	500 km²	1:1.6

The effects of various land surface area/land drainage area relationships depend also upon the sediment yield of the land area. Sediment yield in drainage basins is largely carried into receiving lake systems by river and stream inflow, in the form of bed and sus-

pended load components. Measurements of bed loads, however, are difficult to obtain (actual or by difference) and, at present, there appears no adequate formulation to properly express bed load transport (Church and Gilbert, 1975). Under extreme conditions, coarse fraction bed load may represent > 90% of the total sediment discharge; in most cases, however, bed load represents only a small part of the total sediment load.

In Canada, most of the Fraser River basin which lies between the Coastal and Rocky Mountains carries a suspended sediment concentration, expressed as annual suspended load/annual stream flow, of 200–400 mg/liter (Stichling, 1973). The St. Lawrence drainage basin, of much less relief, carries only 50–200 mg/liter of suspended sediment concentration, while smaller lowland drainage areas have less than 50 mg/liter of suspended sediment concentration (Walling, 1977).

By comparison, data from the Rhone River entering Lake Geneva (data modified after Serruya, 1969) suggest that concentration levels are about 470 mg/liter and discharge concentrations for the Rhine River, entering Lake Constance, are of the same magnitude (Müller, 1966).

Sediment yield, as erosion, is considered further with respect to climatic controls.

Lake orientation

Wind and associated wind duration provide the driving force for the generation of waves and for much of the circulation in lakes. In these respects orientation of lakes relative to dominant wind fields has a major influence upon both fetch and period. In the Laurentian Great Lakes, Fricbergs (1970) and Rukavina (1976) have demonstrated the influence of wind on sediment transport, and, most recently, Håkanson (1977) has discussed the significance of fetch and orientation on sediment response in Lake Vanern (Sweden). In an apparent paradox, Livingston (1954) reported on a group of shallow lakes (generally less than 10 m deep) in northern Alaska, whose long axis appeared to have developed perpendicular to the direction of dominant wind. It was demonstrated, however, that since the sediment load which is current transported is dependent upon the power of the current velocity, the ends of an initially circular basin would be scoured out at a greater rate than the downwind shore, and the upwind shore would receive cuspate depositional forms as a result of eddy transport. Lakes formed by this mechanism, in suitably erodable materials, remained essentially similar in both size and shape. By comparison it was also suggested that the Carolina Bays (Odum, 1952) could have developed only as deflation basins which were later water filled, if orientation was clearly parallel to the dominant wind at the time of formation.

Thermal structure and density effects

In lakes the density structure of water masses is controlled by temperature, solids, and dissolved solids content (Sherman, 1953), and the effects of density stratification are particularly important with respect to the movement of fine particulates. In fresh waters the temperature of maximum density is about 4°C at the surface (Hutchinson, 1957) and decreases under pressure, for example, to about 3.4°C at a depth of 500 m.

Under seasonal conditions, as surface waters cool (or warm) to about 4°C vertical mixing of the water mass occurs. With further cooling, ice forms at the surface but densities remain relatively high at the bottom where temperatures are still close to 4°C. During the summer months, when surface water temperatures exceed 4°C, surface waters are similarly less dense than bottom waters and maintain stable density stratification; warm surface (epiliminion) waters are usually separated from deep cool (hypolimnion) waters by a sharp thermal gradient (thermocline).

Most lakes in temperate regions mix vertically twice a year as spring and fall overturns (dimictic lakes). High-latitude and mountain lakes, however, may not warm above 4°C, mixing, vertically, only once a year (monomictic lake Stanwell-Fletcher, Rust and Coak-

ley, 1970). Similarly, low-latitude lakes may not cool below 4°C, and also mix, vertically, only once a year. Meromictic lakes remain stable and density stratified and do not overturn (Lake Tanganyika, Capart, 1952), and they are frequently controlled by gradients in dissolved solids content or by salinity gradients produced as a result of freshwaters overlying saline waters.

In some lake areas the high solids content of inflowing waters (often associated with thermal density effects, as well) may produce underflow conditions as discussed by Gilbert (1975) in Lillooet Lake and by Lara and Sanders (1970) in Lake Mead.

Climatic factors

Climatic factors are seen to influence lake basins in many ways. The precipitation and evaporation balance maintains water levels, and fluctuations in lake basins often appear greatest where land surface to lake area ratios are greatest. Arid conditions in the land drainage areas amplify sediment yield to inflowing streams.

In well-forested areas such as the southern Canadian Shield annual surface erosion rates are quoted at about 0.01 mm/year (Slaymaker and McPherson, 1973), rising to 0.05 mm/year in agricultural areas in the Canadian watersheds of Lakes Erie and Ontario (Ongley, 1976). These values are in marked contrast to those from the Red Deer River badlands in Alberta where rates of up to 17 mm/year have been noted by Campbell (1973) and from North Dakota where erosion rates of 10–19 mm/year have been recorded (Schumm, 1956). Hadley and Schumm (1961) have reported extremes as high as 46 mm/year for some basins in the western United States.

As a further comparison it is interesting to note that erosion rates in the basins of the St. Lawrence River (Canada) and the Colorado River (U.S.) show approximately the same order of difference as do the measurements of suspended sediment concentrations in each of these two basins:

	Suspended sediment concentration	Denudation rate
St. Lawrence River Basin	50–200 mg/liter	0.01–0.055 mm/year
Badlands (Western U.S.)		> 20 mm/year
Colorado River	10,000 mg/liter	
(Entering Lake Mead based upon 145 × 10⁶ tons of suspended sediment, 13.2 × 10⁶ acre ft run-off. Howard, 1960)		
Order of magnitude difference	1,000	1,000

In cold climate areas the presence of winter ice cover will substantially reduce or nullify wave action and may modify circulation patterns such that quiet water conditions persist, allowing the deposition of very fine particulate materials. In addition, the transport of coarse materials by ice rafting (Pelletier, 1969) and ice push (Tsang, 1974, 1975) may be significant long-term contributors to sediment accumulation in basins of widely differing size. Ice cover may also provide shoreline protection during winter periods (Dickie and Cape, 1974), but under freeze–thaw conditions weathering effects may reduce even the most resistant rock materials to fragments easily available to lacustrine erosion processes.

Over-lake weather conditions, particularly local storms and high winds, are strongly influenced by the relief of the land surrounding the lake surface, and lakes in deeply incised valleys, fjord lakes, rift valley lakes, and crater lakes may be subject to severe and localized storms often with extremely high winds passing along the entire length of the water surface (e.g., Lake Baikal, Kozhov, 1963). Despite the relatively short duration of such winds they may have considerable impact on local shore erosion, sediment transport, and deposition.

In addition to the immediate effects of weather on lakes, lakes of large size, such as Lake Victoria (Kendall, 1969), may have a strong feed-back effect thereby causing significant local weather and climatic modification.

Physical inputs and sediment response

In Figure 3 the interaction between waves, currents, and sediments is expressed in diagramatic form. The influence of waves is modified by the effects of fetch, duration, incidence, and bathymetry, and likewise the influence of currents is also modified by basin configuration, velocity, direction, and density.

The sediment response to the imposed shear stress, resulting from wave and current action is, itself, controlled by additional factors such as particle size, cohesive strength, and bed form.

The form of sediment response in terms of erosion, transport, and deposition therefore represents a final integration of the interaction between external forces and the particulate fraction.

For convenience, sedimentary processes responding to the various forms of physical input are considered separately in nearshore transitional and offshore regions.

Beach and nearshore

In the nearshore region surface waves interact with bottom sediments in two ways: (1) as breaking waves in the beach zone, and (2) in that zone only affected by the orbital velocities of water motion, beyond the breaker zone. The beach zone comprises a narrow vertical range, either side of the water plane, and is, in

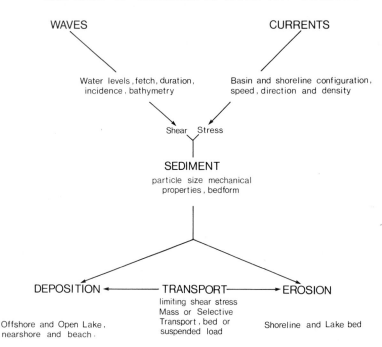

FIGURE 3. Response of sediments to waves and currents.

TABLE 1. Potential Wind Wave Influence on Bottom Sediments

Fetch (km)	Continuous wind speed				Continuous wind speed			
	74	56	37	28	74	56	37	28 (Kph)
	40	30	20	15	40	30	20	15 (knots)
	Significant wave heights ($\frac{1}{3} H$) (m)				Wave base (WB)—approx 25% of wave length (m)			
600	7.3	4.9	2.6	1.6	77	53	35	24
500	7.0	4.7	2.5	1.6	68	50	31	22
400	6.4	4.4	2.4	1.5	59	45	27	20
300	5.8	4.0	2.3	1.4	50	39	22	17
200	5.0	3.4	2.0	1.3	41	31	18	15
100	3.8	2.7	1.6	1.2	29	22	14	12
50	2.9	2.1	1.3	0.9	20	15	10	8
20	2.1	1.5	1.1	0.6	12	10	6	4.5
10	1.5	1.2	1.0	< 0.5	9	6.5	4.5	3
5	1.2	0.9	0.8	—	6	4.5	3	2
2	1.0	0.6	< 0.5	—	3	3	1.5	—

part, related to wave height. Just offshore of the beach zone there remains an area which becomes progressively less affected by wave energy where, at a depth of one-quarter wave length, motion is about 21%; at a depth of one-half wave length, motion is about 4% of that of the surface (for every one-ninth of the wave length the orbital motion is approximately halved).

When considering the influence of wave action, therefore, the two zones may be viewed together.

A detailed analysis of wave-induced shear stress acting upon bottom sediments has been given by Riedel et al. (1972) and Komar and Miller (1973). Krishnappen and Skafel (1976) used this approach to develop an analysis of the interaction of waves with Point Pelee shoal sediments in Lake Erie.

For simplicity, however, the depth at which wave-induced shear stress exceeds the critical shear stress of bed materials (wave base) and becomes an important factor in terms of sediment response is here defined as that depth of water corresponding to not less that 25% of available wave motion (based upon significant wave period). In Table 1 a series of values for this approximated wave base (WB 25%) is given for fetch distances of from 2 to 600 km, for selected wind speeds, based on the development of significant waves (deep water) after Bretschneider (1952). Bergs (1965) concluded that wind waves generated in Lake Huron appeared to conform to the wave-case predictions of Bretschneider (1958) for wave heights of 1 m or greater. It was noted, however, that subsurface water particle movement appeared to depart from accepted theory.

In a similar approach Sly (1973b) showed that approximately 5% of the area of the Great Lakes (excluding Lake Erie) would be affected, and that perhaps as much as 25% of Lake Erie would be so affected. In broad shallow lakes, such as Lake Balaton in Hungary (Györke, 1973) which has a mean depth of 3.3 m, wave action may affect the bottom sediments over almost the entire lake area (600 km²). The significance of wind wave energies is considered, further, in a comparison of energy levels within lakes (Figures 5 and 6).

The distribution of surficial sediments in both Lake Ontario and Lake Huron has been described by Thomas et al. (1972, 1973) who have clearly demonstrated that the sand-sized materials occur almost exclusively in the shallower shoreline and nearshore areas, where they form 32 and 38%, respectively, of the total sediment composition of each of these two lakes. In Lake Ontario it has been suggested (Jonys, unpublished data) that about 55% of the sand-sized material is contributed from river inflows; the remaining 45% therefore, must be accounted for by processes active in the nearshore zone.

In the nearshore area wave action provides some of the transport energy and most of the erosional energy; such activity has two major components: (1) longshore drift, and (2) onshore–offshore migration. The lack of sand particulates in most Great Lakes deep-water sediments (Thomas et al., 1972) indicates that the onshore–offshore process is limited in extent and only rarely provides a "sediment escape" from what is otherwise an essentially "closed system" in the nearshore.

While the development of beach forms under marine conditions has been widely documented by numerous authors, the development of lacustrine beach systems has been less well studied. Krumbein and Slack (1956) commented upon the great variability, narrowness, and complexity of lake beach deposits along the Lake Michigan shore, and Cook (1970) commented further that "Certain differences seem to exist in the hydrodynamic regimes of high and low energy shorelines. While directional inequalities in wave-induced oscillations are not pronounced in the nearshore zone of an ocean beach, shoreward surges are notably dominant in lakes or wave tanks. Also, rip currents are not well developed along low energy beaches, and water may return offshore by other means. These disparities cast doubt on the applicability of sand transport models for oceanic coasts to protected lacustrine shores."

Lewis and Sly (1971), in a study of the Toronto Islands in Lake Ontario, used sediment mean size and sorting to develop approximations of equal wave energy in the nearshore zone and Coakley (1972) used similar data in the form of trend surface displays to establish nearshore sediment response at Point Pelee, Lake Erie. Based on limited data there appears to be reason to suggest that beach sediments in nontidal regimes may be characterized by the "null point theory" (Miller and Zeigler, 1964); at present, however, this remains conjectural and the precise controls of water level, water table, wave height, incidence, and material availability have not been clearly established and differentiated from the better known oceanic beach systems (Harrison et al., 1968; Harrison, 1968) where tidal range is such an important influence.

In the Laurentian Great Lakes, movement of sediments by longshore drift has been documented by many authors, among them Berg and Duane (1968), Rukavina (1969, 1970), and Hands (1970), and shore erosion has been reported by Coakley and Cho (1972) and Gelinas and Quigley (1973); nearshore studies from Lake Diefenbaker were also reported by Coakley and Hamblin (1970).

Bajorunas (1970) studied littoral transport phenomena in southern Lake Huron where wave duration was found to be the significant variable if less than about 12 hr, while effective shoreline length (20 km) became a critical control for more extended time periods. The dimensional analysis indicated that transport rates increased with the square root of the sediment size (fine to medium sands). It was found that the theoretical equations [e.g., material transported = $(KH^2L \cos \alpha)/8$ where K = coefficient depending upon material size and steepness of beach, H = wave height, L = wave length, α = angle incidence of wave approach, (Bascom, 1964)] which utilized wave energy, angle of approach, and shoreline length could give a reasonable estimate of sediment movement if wind, waves, and currents held the same general direction. However, in the complex wave and current environment of the nearshore, such estimates could fail, and, in such cases, current speed and direction became the determining factor. Murray (1970) demonstrated, in addition, that sediment fall velocities in turbulent fields were reduced by as much as 30% when compared to still water conditions (particle size tested, 2.0 mm), a factor further contributing to the mobility of coarse particulates. Local variations in the shoreline frequently caused currents and waves to oppose, and under such conditions the data showed a strong correlation between sediment transport and current speed. There appeared to be no upper limit to this relationship.

As an example of this latter point Freeman et al. (1972) discussed the effects of a severe storm surge at Sarnia, also in southern Lake Huron, during August 1971. During this storm approximately 60,000 m³ of sandy material were eroded, but only about 25,000 m³ were later redeposited on shore; the remainder was almost certainly transported southwards, likely by a persistent longshore current having a continuing velocity in excess of 30 cm/sec.

Onshore–offshore movements

Recently Davis et al. (1972) and Fox and Davis (1976) compared the ridge and runnel topography of ocean beaches with those of Lake Michigan beaches and clearly established a similarity of form.

The study of lake beach responses under storm conditions, by Fox and Davis (1970) has further illustrated the onshore–offshore pattern of sediment migration and has confirmed this as a typical response to high-incident wave approach where there is adequate availability of material. Mothersill (1970) supported this interpretation and has shown that the offshore transport has resulted in significantly negative skewed sediments (coarse materials) in the troughs or runnels, while the bars or ridges remain positively skewed and exhibit low standard deviation, unimodel and fine-grained sand populations.

Fricbergs (1970) provided an interesting demonstration that eroded material may not continue in transport within a longshore current. In a review of the contribution of materials to the build-up of Toronto Islands from Scarborough Bluffs, it was noted that the bluffs yield approximately 300,000 m³ of material a year, by erosion. Despite this considerable quantity of material only about 19,000 m³ or 6% actually became incorporated "downstream" in the Toronto Islands; the remainder, being of insufficient size, appears to have been maintained in turbulent suspension and transported outwards and offshore from the immediate source area.

Based upon available data it therefore appears that nearshore and beach response in the lacustrine environment is substantially similar to that of marine systems where equations for wave-generated longshore currents and sediment transport rates have been recently reviewed by Komar (1976); because of limited fetch and lack of tidal regimes, energy levels in marine systems are usually much higher than in lakes.

The onshore–offshore movement of sediment in lakes is likely further amplified by seiche effects, although no measurements are available to indicate the increased rate of sediment transport attributable to such a cause. Seiches are particularly important in large lakes and, for example, in the Laurentian Great Lakes maximum ranges of from 0.76 m in Lake Huron to 2.56 m in Lake Erie have been recorded (McDonald, 1954). Oscillation periods in Lake Erie are from 14 to 16 hr, and less for Lake Ontario.

The development of depositional structures (Reineck and Singh, 1973) and of wave-formed sedimentary structures (Clifton, 1976) in lake sediment bear many similarities with marine counterparts, but it should be noted, in most lake systems, that high-current velocities are of localized occurrence and that water level fluctuations are of long duration as they are associated with seasonal cycles.

Delta areas

River deltas provide another sedimentary environment, distinct from beach and beach bar systems, but within the nearshore zone. In the Laurentian Great Lakes the bird's foot delta of the St. Clair River and the delta bar of the Niagara River offer two very different examples of delta types.

The sediments transported through the St. Clair system are derived directly from the shores and bed of southern Lake Huron and sediment transport is high, particularly in response to storm conditions (as described by Freeman et al., 1972). Duane (1967) indicated that the upper reaches of the St. Clair channel are remarkably stable, thus helping to maintain a high suspended load concentration throughout. Mandelbaum (1966) considered that particle size availability had a strong influence on the development of the St. Clair delta, and has suggested that positively skewed sediments might be related to the proximity of inlet, and negative skew to the complex of wave and current influences in the outer parts. It was estimated that only about 60% of the input material was retained in the delta. Thomas (1971) and Thomas et al. (1977) have further confirmed that significant quantities of St. Clair River (southern Lake Huron) material enter the Detroit River and finally accumulate in western Lake Erie. The St. Clair delta is building out into Lake St. Clair, which is mostly less than 4 m deep and about 40 km in width, and which lies between Lakes Huron and Erie. It has many features in common with the delta plain of the Mississippi delta (Gould, 1970).

The sedimentary processes of the Niagara River delta are quite different from those of the St. Clair. Much of the bed of the lower Niagara River is bedrock, with an extremely uneven bed form. The river carries only a moderate total load of material, and Sutton et al. (1970) have estimated that a recurved,

subaqueous delta, covering approximately 50 km² and averaging about 1.5 m in thickness, has been deposited at the mouth of the river (there is some evidence to suggest that the present rate of accumulation of coarse materials has decreased). This delta area is subject to the predominantly west–east longshore sediment transport and has been further modified by complex wave and current activities. Active sands have been recorded to a depth of about 15–20 m which is comparable to observations made off Toronto by Lewis and Sly (1971). The delta front appears to have built out over some form of preexisting feature (possibly part of an earlier delta front formed during an interglacial period) and has developed a steep frontal slope with water depths increasing rapidly to more than 110 m. The delta is characterized by the development of a frontal offshore bar, and shoreward of this the subaqueous form is crossed by a complex of ridges and open and closed channels.

The formation of slump structures, particularly where deltas are building out into deeper water, is a common feature of lakes of all sizes. Slumping occurs principally when foreset beds become oversteepened but may not occur when underflow conditions extend the transport of coarser fractions. Slump features have been reported by Matthews (1956) in Garibaldi Lake, by Fulton and Pullen (1969) in upper Arrowhead Lake, and by Gilbert (1975) in Lillooet Lake; large-scale features have been reported by Walker and Massingill (1970) from the Mississippi delta and by Mathews and Shepard (1962) from the Fraser delta.

The development of deltas in smaller lakes and reservoirs appears to follow essentially the same pattern as in larger lakes, but on a smaller scale (and with less modification due to wave effects); mathematical expressions for sediment deposition have been provided by Sundborg (1964) and Church and Gilbert (1975).

Transitional region

This region is of variable width and depth range; its shoreward beginning may be generally marked by the cessation of sorting and transport phenomena related to sand-size particulates; its lakeward boundary, however, merges almost imperceptibly into the adjacent deep mid-lake zone.

Generally speaking, fine sand represents less than 10% of the total sediment population of this zone, while silt and clay are variably mixed with no marked separation, as might be enhanced by flocculation in the marine environment (Favejee, 1951).

The most significant sedimentary processes in this zone are related to circulation, upwellings (largely related to tilting of the thermocline), and the impact of large-scale inflows by rivers. Csanady (1966) showed, based upon mean field concentration, that horizontal diffusion of particulates was largely related to the effects of complex currents, whereas vertical diffusion was related to the influence of eddies. In addition, turbidity currents, slump movements, and shear effects reflect special cases of sedimentary processes which effect only limited areas.

Whereas the nearshore and shoreline region may be considered as the marginal or "shelf" facies of large lakes, the transitional region is more analogous to the "slope" facies of continental margins. Indeed, in many of the Laurentian Great Lakes (Superior, Michigan, Georgian Bay, and Ontario), the "slope" feature is well defined and is commonly marked by an increasing lake floor gradient which often extends to depths much in excess of 100 m.

However, the relief and expression of the bathymetric slope frequently associated with this zone differs markedly from lake to lake and even within lakes and reflects not only major differences in the bedrock geology (Hough, 1958) but also the postformation histories of each distinct basin.

Baroclinic and barotropic influences

In large lakes the baroclinic circulations, superimposed upon the regional geostrophic pattern, show relatively high velocities (Csanady and Pade, 1968, 1969; Scott *et al.*, 1971; Blanton, 1974) of up to 50 cm/sec and more, at or near the surface.

Such currents have been observed to a depth of about 35 m and to a distance between 4 and 8 km offshore, along the south shore of Lake Ontario, near Oswego. Scott *et al.* (1971) have also commented upon the mass transport of such currents and have estimated that the average daily transport may be 2.4 km³/day. Such a flow would be between four to six times greater than that of the Niagara River inflow.

Studies on barotrophic circulations suggest that similar rates of motion may also apply.

In Lake Erie, Burns and Ross (1972) reported that epilimnion currents exceeded 45 cm/sec and, although hypolimnion currents as great as 95 cm/sec were recorded, it appears general that epilimnion flow exceeds hypolimnion flow by about an order of magnitude.

It is not presently possible to correlate sediment distributions with specific baroclinic or barotropic regimes, largely because of the variability and impersistence of such flows. Examples may be used, however, which show preferred relationships with certain conditions.

McAndrews (1972) in a discussion on the presence of pollen grains in Lake Ontario sediments has been able to trace the dispersal pattern of fines from the Black River (Eastern Lake Ontario) and has shown how such materials could be incorporated into one of the main circulatory gyres (geostrophic) of the main

lake. This tracing provides a means for following the complex intermixing of river and lake waters and ultimate transport into the deep mid-lake zone.

A further example of such tracing may be seen in the composition distribution of bottom sediments in western Lake Ontario, and their relation to the source, the Niagara River. The use of trace element geochemistry (Thomas, 1972; Holdrinet *et al.*, in press) has shown that fine muds (mixtures of silt and clay) can be followed as they slowly deposit out of suspension following along and adjacent to the lake's south shore and extending eastward toward Rochester. That all such fines are not restricted to this transport path is also evidenced by the incorporation of some similar materials in the mid-lake sediments.

In western Lake Erie, (Thomas *et al.*, 1977, and unpublished data) has shown, based upon geochemical (heavy metals and organic contaminants) and particle size relationships, that suspended materials entering the lake from the Detroit River retain distinct and separate transport paths within the lake depending upon which side of the river they occur during inflow. Such distinction in transport pathways is remarkable, particularly when recognizing the severe mixing which is experienced in this part of the lake as a result of frequent wave action. In central Lake Erie where the transitional zone extends fully across the lake, Hartley (1968) and Burns and Ross (1972) have demonstrated the persistence of variable cross-lake bottom flows which maintain a strong northerly component to their movement, particularly in the area just east of Point Pelee. Lewis (personal communication and unpublished data) and Sly and Lewis (1972) have evidence for the continuing dispersal of fine materials northward in this same general area, and in the form of extending muddy bottom deposits.

Studies by a number of authors, in southern Lake Michigan, notably, Ayres and Hough (1964), Gross *et al.* (1970), Linebach *et al.* (1970), Kennedy *et al.* (1971), Shimp *et al.* (1971), and Gross *et al.* (1972), have exemplified similar features in particular the distribution of fines in relation to the kinetics of inflow and the lakeward prograding of materials.

Upwelling and tilt

Upwelling phenomena are commonly observed in many lakes and Lee (1972) defined parts of the north shore of Lake Ontario as being influenced frequently by such conditions. Cronan and Thomas (1972) and St. John *et al.* (1972) in a study of sediments taken at depths of from 30 to 60 m in the same area found that lag sands were Fe–Mn coated, and implied that bed materials were receiving chemical precipitate from upwelling waters in an area otherwise characterized by nondeposition. Such observations strongly suggest, although physical processes still dominate sediment accumulation in regions of deeper lake waters, that geochemical processes may also play an important role.

Influence of river inflow

Although each of the Laurentian Great Lakes receives inflow from a number of sources, the extent of such influences is relatively minor when compared with the dynamics of the St. Marys River, the St. Clair-Detroit River, and the Niagara River. Lake Michigan exchanges with Lake Huron through the Straits of Mackinac but without the unidirectional flow of a "stream" system. As an example, it is estimated that the total discharge of the Niagara River averages about 5500 m³/sec and ranges between 3400 and 6950 m³/sec. The river velocity at its point of inflow to Lake Ontario varies between 80 and 300 cm/sec with a generalized flow of about 100 cm/sec. The Niagara River maintains a fairly consistent eastward flow along the south shore of Lake Ontario and acts as an important driving force (comparable to that described by Loucks, 1972) for the circulatory system of the lakes. The computed circulation patterns of Simons and Jordan (1971) add further evidence to support this.

In many lakes the development of sediment plumes is particularly associated with the dispersal of suspended loads in surface waters, which enter the lake from river inflow during periods when inflowing waters are less dense than receiving waters because of temperature difference. However, under certain conditions sediment plumes may also develop as a result of complex current flow around shoreline features and an interesting example of this has been given by Haras *et al.* (1976) off Point Pelee in Lake Erie (Figure 4).

In lakes of differing size it is therefore apparent that the smaller the lake the less significant are the effects of wave action in sediment transport; whereas, for a given river inflow, the greater the inflow the stronger its effect will be upon sediment transport within the lake.

The occurrence of density flows has been recorded in many lakes. In mid-latitudes the discreet transport of sediment-laden water, as a density flow, is a common feature during the spring run-off and early summer when the inflow of river waters has a different temperature to that of the main lake body. Forel (1895) in one of his classic studies on Lac Leman (Lake Geneva) described the extensive density flow associated with the Rhone River input and the coherence of this discrete water mass. Dussart (1948) extended this work, and Vollenweider (1956) described a similar extensive density plume associated with the input of the Toce River into Lake Maggiore. However, the best known studies on density flows have been reported by Anderson and Pritchard (1951), Howard, (1960), and Gould (1960) in Lake Mead. More re-

cently, studies by Brodie and Irwin (1970) have described deposition from active density currents in Lake Wakatipu (New Zealand), and Church and Gilbert (1975) have discussed the mechanics of bottom and underflow conditions with particular reference to deep lakes. As a general characteristic the density flows are remarkable in their coherence and longitudinal extent.

The development of trough-like features or canyons related to underflow conditions or density and turbidity flows has been recorded from locations receiving high input loadings of relatively coarse (sand) materials, for example, the Black Sea (Trimonis and Shimkus, 1970); in Lake Geneva the Rhone inflow channel, across the delta surface, is clearly defined by an extensive, longitudinal deposit of sand (Houbolt and Janker, 1968).

The presence of such erosional features, however, tends to be limited to rather specialized environmental conditions. Although density–turbidity currents are frequently produced in lakes as a result of underflow conditions at a point of river input, it should be appreciated that turbidity flows may be triggered by bank collapse or the effects of subaqueous slumping, as noted by Ludlam (1969).

Offshore region

The primary characteristics of this zone are great water depth, a generally uniform cover of recent clayey muds (clay size materials comprising as much as 40% or more of the total sediment), and a slow-moving circulation of the overlying water mass.

In lakes of extreme depth or of unique bathymetry, bottom water stagnation (Ström, 1955) also may be of concern.

In the Laurentian Great Lakes, as has been demonstrated by Thomas *et al.* (1972 and 1973), deep lake deposits may be separated into a number of distinct depositional subbasins. Such basins appear to be limited by both strong relief features and yet, also, by almost imperceptible rises that are themselves often characterized by slightly coarser materials (which reflect both "nondepositional" and/or winnowing conditions).

In some cases there is good evidence to suggest that these deep, mid-lake depositional zones reflect a "cell"-like structure which may be present in the more general geostrophic circulation of the main lake as a whole. In other cases the separation of subbasins may reflect other as yet unidentified influences, such as the convection circulation proposed by Gould and Budinger (1958).

Thomas (1969a) and Thomas *et al.* (1972 and 1973) have provided strong support for the separation of deep basin facies from other lacustrine zones and they have shown that an increasing inorganic carbon con-

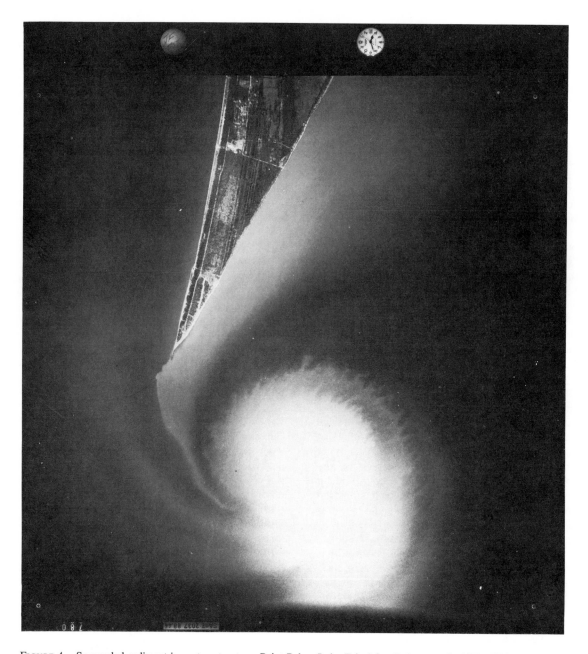

FIGURE 4.   Suspended sediment in vortex structure, Point Pelee, Lake Erie (after Bukata *et al.*, 1974, 1975).

tent is related to the high percentage of silt size fractions, and that organic carbon increases with clay content; similar observations have been made in other deep lakes, in particular the study by Bordovskiy (1969) on the sediments of the central Caspian. Although most of the inorganic carbon related to silt size fractions appears to be in the form of calcium carbonate, the mechanisms of its formation and deposition remain uncertain. Brunskill (1969) described processes of high carbonate precipitation in Fayetteville Lake, New York, but its meromictic structure repre-

sents a special situation. It is known, however, that calcium carbonate precipitation also occurs in many other large and deep lakes (Lac Leman, cited by Thomas *et al.* 1972).

In general most of the deep mid-lake zone deposits observed are composed of soft, apparently structureless clayey muds, with occasional and impersistent black sulfide banding. The presence of sulfide banding is probably associated with bacterial activity.

Sedimentation rates are generally low and Thomas *et al.* (1972) have estimated average rates of 114, 139, and 309 g/m²/year within three of the larger mid-lake subbasins of Lake Ontario. These figures are comparable to those quoted by Bordovskiy (1969) of about 360 g/m²/year in the Caspian, and by Kendall (1969) of about 200 g/m²/year in Lake Victoria. In Lake Kinneret, Stiller and Assaf (1973) recorded the accumulation of detrial carbonates which dominate the composition of bed materials. The principle source was defined as the Jordan River and rates of accumulation decreased from source. Settling trap experiments (cited from then unpublished work by Serruya) gave values of from 220 to 60 g/m²/year.

In some lakes settling of extremely fine particulate materials may not, in fact, take place. Mathews (1956), in a study of Garibaldi Lake, reported on the presence of finely divided rock flour in the form of a cloudy suspension occurring at considerable depth. Based upon settling rates of about 1 hr/ft and 37 days/ft for particulates ranging in size from 3.5 to 0.35 μm (25 and 75 percentiles, respectively), it was shown that settling times of from 15 weeks to 30 years would be required to deliver such fines to depths of 300 ft under calm conditions.

It would seem therefore, in most lakes subject to some form of continuing circulation and upwelling, that settling of extremely fine particles is not possible. Only under conditions of extended ice cover and limited inflow could sufficiently calm conditions persist long enough to allow the accumulation of such fines.

In some lakes the presence of electrolytes in the water mass may allow fine particulate materials to adhere together in groups, thereby allowing fine materials to settle more rapidly as a result of flocculation.

In Lake Mead, Sherman (1953) demonstrated flocculation in response to "salinity" effects and showed that, while particles larger than 24 μm in size settled mostly as individual grains, particles less than 24 μm in size were often aggregated in the form of floccules. The smallest floccules had least bulk density (about 1.3 at a mean size of 0.5 μm) and the largest floccules had greatest bulk density (about 2.3–2.4 at mean size approaching 100 μm); the largest floccules also had the largest mean size of individual particles and had the least floccule porosity. Flocculated materials having a high water content (low bulk density) are therefore likely to be composed of fine materials.

Holmes (1967), in a study of Lake Windemere, demonstrated the flocculation of postglacial organic-rich sediments comprising about 20% organic matter. In this work it was noted that the most significant aspect of fine material decomposition was related to hydration with the upper size limit of this effect being about 20 μm; it was suggested that there might be some relation between this size limit and the upper limit of flocculation, noted at about 25 μm.

In both Lake Mead and Lake Windemere the upper limit of particle size subject to flocculation appears similar.

The effective upper limit of flocculation in seawater was also noted at about 25 μm by Favejee (1939).

Energy levels

Lacustrine and marine comparisons

In Figure 5, mean particle size in phi units [$\phi = -\log_2$ (particle diameter in millimeters)] is plotted against depth (meters) for bottom sediment size data representing both marine and lacustrine environments. The Great Lakes data are largely drawn from publications by Thomas *et al.* (1972, 1973, 1976), Baltic Sea data have been derived from Seibold (1967), and the remainder from Pelletier (1973). Assuming that the decrease in the particle size with depth is a reasonable analogy of decreasing physical energy in the system, the data show, on a depth comparative basis, that energy levels in marine systems are substantially higher than in lakes.

In the smaller lakes (Lake St. Clair) or shallower lake areas (west and central basins of Lake Erie),

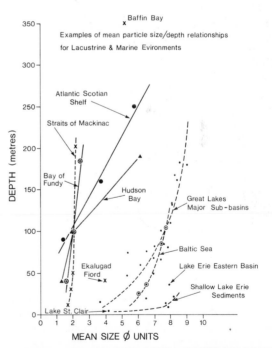

GREAT LAKES DATA FROM CANADA CENTRE FOR INLAND WATERS, BURLINGTON ONTARIO ; BALTIC SEA DATA FROM SEIBOLD (1967), MARINE DATA FROM PELLETIER (1973), AND STRAITS OF MACKINAC DATA FROM LAUFF et al., (1961)

FIGURE 5.   Examples of mean particle size against depth relationships for lacustrine and marine environments.

energy levels decrease rapidly with depth. Data from the subbasins of Lakes Huron, Ontario, and Superior show similarity with deep water data from the Baltic. The divergence between Baltic Sea and Laurentian Great Lakes data at shallower depths, however, may be more apparent than real because of bias resulting from a limited Baltic Sea data base. Generally speaking, Baltic Sea and Laurentian Great Lakes data show similar sediment characteristics.

Although bed materials are substantially coarser in the area of the Atlantic Scotian Shelf, the similarity of the slope, compared to Laurentian Great Lakes data, suggests that differences are mostly related to relative energy scales rather than to major differences in the slope at any particular depth. In each of these areas, therefore, it may be suggested that energies derived from wind waves and energies derived from currents are somewhat proportional.

The steep line slope of data from the Bay of Fundy strongly suggests that current activity provides an effective driving force at all depths, even when surface wave action may be fetch limited. By comparison, slope data from the Straits of Mackinac (between Lakes Michigan and Huron) derived from Lauff et al. (1961) show a very similar relationship. Wind waves, in the Straits of Mackinac, are probably of less (relative) significance than in the Bay of Fundy, a situation suggested by slight divergence in the two data sets, in shallow water. At depth, however, the currents in the Straits of Mackinac appear to lose less energy than do the water masses in the Bay of Fundy.

In Hudson Bay, energy levels in deep waters suggest rather limited current activity.

Comparison within lake systems

In Figure 6 mean particle size and percentage clay content are plotted against depth for three locations in the Laurentian Great Lakes (Sly, 1975): Kingston, at the eastern end of Lake Ontario, Niagara, at the western end of the Lake Ontario, and Tobermory, which lies in the area of interchange between Lake Huron and Georgian Bay. Figure 6 shows that a mean size of 1ϕ occurs at a depth of 5 m at Niagara, 17 m at Kingston, and 20 m at Tobermory; conversely, a mean size of 8ϕ occurs at a depth of 120 m at Niagara, 45 m at Kingston, and 120 m at Tobermory.

A comparable trend may be seen in the percentage clay data (where 30% clay content is found at depths of 30, 48, and 70 m at Kingston, Tobermory, and Niagara, respectively). These data imply that surface wave action is strongest at Tobermory and least at Niagara (despite the length of fetch at Niagara this site is dominated by offshore winds). The greatest rate of loss of dynamic energy with depth occurs at Kingston; the least rate of loss occurs at Niagara, which suggests strongly that sustained transport of silt and clay parti-

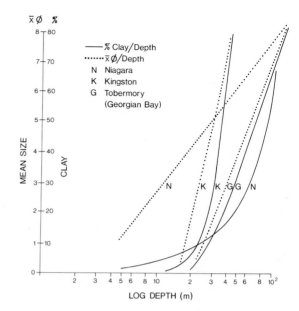

FIGURE 6.   Mean particle size, percentage clay, and depth relationships; Laurentian Great Lakes data (modified after Sly, 1975).

culates is associated with the presence of significant current activity.

In considering the potential effects of wave generation and its influence in shallow waters, approximations such as developed in Table 1 are of value only if direction of effective fetch (Håkanson and Ahl, 1976; Håkanson, 1977) can be determined.

Implications from particle size analyses

Figure 7 shows a plot of standard deviation against particle size (phi units) for the Niagara site, Lake Ontario (Sly, 1977). Standard deviation reflects sorting in the central part of size distribution curves and shows clearly that best sorting is achieved for sediments having a mean of about 2.5ϕ (0.17 mm). Similar curves have been developed for many other lake sediments: Lake Maggiore (Damiani, 1972), Lake Geneva (Vernet et al., 1972), Bay of Quinte (Damiani and Thomas, 1974); they also confirm that best sorting is achieved in the sand size fraction (at about 2.5ϕ) and that lesser improved sortings occur in both coarser and finer particulates.

This distribution conforms to that anticipated from the erosion-transportation regimes as defined by Hjulström (1939), Sundborg (1956), and Sundborg (1967). The best sorted materials (about 2.5ϕ) correspond to those sand-size particles requiring least erosional velocity to start in motion. Very fine particulates (clays) improve in sorting as a result of selective transport and deposition; coarse fractions (gravels) also improve in sorting, as a result of the selective winnowing of fine materials.

Surface sediments having equivalent size and sorting characteristics may be used, therefore, to show that the integrated dynamic energy levels to which they respond are sensibly the same; Lewis and Sly (1971) used this approach based on point data in a study of the Toronto waterfront, and Coakley (1972) used a similar approach in a trend surface analysis of sediment response at Point Pelee (Lake Erie). Data based on nearly instantaneous bottom samples suggest that size and sorting characteristics conform most closely with wave field effects (Miller and Ziegler, 1964), but that return flows (rip currents) modify the nearshore distributions. While standard deviation/size relationships provide a useful model analogy for energy conditions to which sediments respond in aqueous systems, two important deficiencies must be accepted: (1) the standard deviation is rather insensitive to variations in the tails of size distribution curves, and (2) mean size may retain the same value despite changes in the mixture. The use of higher order statistical moment measures such as skewness and kurtosis, however, may partially overcome such problems.

The distribution of skewness in Laurentian Great Lake sediments has been interpreted by Thomas *et al.* (1973) as the mixing of silt with the end member populations of sand and clay, where silt in sand produces a positive skew and silt in clay produces a negative skew. Further, the addition of gravel to sand member populations reduces skewness but, with eventual dominance of gravels, trends lead to increasing positive skewness (Damiani and Thomas, 1974).

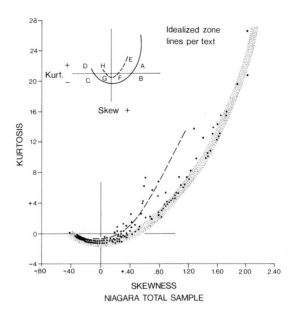

FIGURE 8.   Skewness and kurtosis relationships, Niagara site, Laurentian Great Lakes (after Sly, 1977).

An approach to zero skewness is suggestive of mixed populations.

Measurements of standard deviation define the dispersion in the central two-thirds of the distribution curve; kurtosis, on the other hand, provides a comparison of the sorting of the tails of the distribution curve, relative to the central portion, and is very sensitive to even minor departures from normal distribution. As stated by Folk and Ward (1957), the introduction of silt into the end member populations of sand or clay (Spencer, 1963) results in deterioration in the sorting of the tails of distribution curves, while sorting in the central part remains good; this is typified by conditions of positive kurtosis, often approaching high values in extreme end member populations (sands and clays). Mixed population samples with a higher standard deviation are typified by kurtosis values of zero or less (see also Mothersill, 1975) [following previous practice kurtosis measures are normalized (Coakley and Beal, 1972; Jaquet and Vernet, 1976)].

In publications by Thomas *et al.* (1972, 1973) and by Damiani and Thomas (1974), it was shown to be possible to describe skewness and kurtosis relationships in the form of a single curve which effectively described sediment energy relationships in decreasing order, by means of four components denoted ABCD. However, as a result of the author's more detailed sampling it has been possible to develop a further refinement, where additional components (EFGH) have been established by separating those samples, from the previous sectors, which contain gravel (Figure 8). These additional components (E–H) therefore likely include both lag deposits (produced by erosion rather than deposition) and the higher energy gravel fractions.

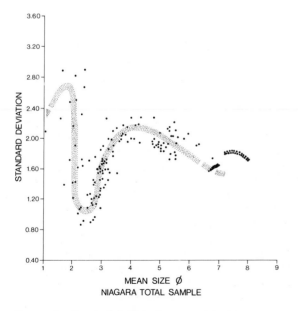

FIGURE 7.   Standard deviation/mean particle size relationships Niagara site, Laurentian Great Lakes (after Sly, 1977).

It is felt that the curve relationships as shown in Figure 8 offer a powerful means of relating sediment energy relationships in different lakes which, by means of a nondimensional expression, are common to all aqueous systems. The curve sectors ABCD are essentially equivalent to those of Thomas *et al.* (1972, 1973), but with gravel materials excluded. The components of this curve therefore reflect a continuous energy decline as would be experienced in a lacustrine system essentially free from erosional conditions. Such an interpretation is further supported by the work of Davaud (1976), on the Lac de Morat (size, approximately 3 × 8 km × 45 m deep), who demonstrated an almost exact fit against the original Laurentian Great Lakes data given by Thomas *et al.* (1972, 1973).

The curve components EFGH incorporate all remaining sample materials in which gravels occur and, therefore, with the exception of materials of "external" origin (e.g., tills and ice rafted sediments), they represent mostly the occurrence of winnowed and lag deposits, and turbidity and slump deposits, the individual characteristics of which are established by reference to other particle size or structural characteristics.

The development of progressively higher energy lag deposits may be shown by gravel–sand and gravel–clay relationships. As velocities increase (Sundborg, 1956; Terwindt *et al.,* 1968), winnowing of particulates progressively leaves behind a lag composed, initially, of gravel and very fine sand and silt, then coarse gravel and silt, and finally very large gravel (cobbles) and clay.

The presence of silts and silty clays in sand–gravel deposits suggests the development of deposits under more than one hydraulic regime, such that fine materials accumulate and partially mix with coarser bed materials as a result of a decrease in water velocities

(such conditions can develop as a result of season fluctuations in lake levels, or as a result of seasonal changes in the hydrographs of inflowing rivers or streams).

Spatial variance

Despite the recovery of many thousands of bottom sediment samples from lacustrine and marine environments few distributions and sediment characteristics have been subjected to statistical verification. Håkanson (1974) showed how a mathematical model could be used to develop numerical expressions for topographic roughness of lake beds and Sly (1975) used real depth data as part of an analysis of variation, at chosen sites in the Laurentian Great Lakes, which also incorporated mean particle size and some geochemical composition.

Table 2 (modified after Sly, 1975) shows Student's t test values for coefficients of variation (v) for groups of samples having regular grid spacings (30–3000 m) at Site 1, Niagara, and Site 2, Tobermory. In Table 2 t values of 2.2 or less suggest that the data populations, which are under comparison, are essentially the same. If, however, values lie between 2.2 and 3.0 the populations are likely different (at the 5% probability level); values between 3.0 and 4.0 exceed the 1% probability level and values greater than 4.0 imply that data population differences are highly significant (at the 0.1% probability level). Table 2 compares the ability of different sample spacings to express similar natural populations; although the similarities between the more closely spaced data sets are generally greater than for more widely spaced sets, this is not always so.

In Table 3, v values for depth (meters), mean particle size ($\phi\bar{x}$), and composition concentrations of total

TABLE 2.   Spatial Variations: Sites 1 and 2

Site number	Parameter	*t values of v for selected parameters at sites 1 and 2*			
		3000 m/1000 m spacing	*1000 m/300 m spacing*	*300 m/100 m spacing*	*100 m/30 m spacing*
1	Depth	5.2	4.6	2.8	0.9
2	Depth	4.4	4.3	3.8	2.4
1	$\bar{x}$	2.1	2.1	2.1	0.6
2	$\bar{x}$	0.2	1.0	1.0	0.7
1	Na	0.9	2.1	1.1	1.1
2	Na	0.6	1.3	0.8	0.3
1	K	4.2	3.0	1.4	0.2
2	K	0.2	0.4	0.1	1.4
1	Hg	2.8	1.2	0.2	1.0
2	Hg	1.2	0.4	0.7	0.4

Data from Sly, 1975.

TABLE 3. Spatial Variations of Selected Parameters vs Depth

Site number	Range of $\bar{x}$ depth (m)	Averaged v values for depth and for mean particle size ($\phi\bar{x}$) as related to selected depth ranges, for sites 1 and 2					Averaged v values for K and for Hg as related to selected depth ranges, for sites 1 and 2				
		v values for depth at grid spacing					v values for K at grid spacings				
		3000 m	1000 m	300 m	100 m	30 m	3000 m	1000 m	300 m	100 m	30 m
1	10–20	57.0	18.6	6.2	4.3	1.2	16.5	11.6	6.2	4.5	3.3
1	30–40	75.0	38.8	11.0	2.6	1.6	19.5	13.1	4.3	1.2	3.3
1	60–80	39.8	9.4	2.8	1.2	0.5	13.4	6.1	1.5	0.6	0.5
2	30–40	42.3	14.3	2.8	1.8	2.6	17.8	16.1	19.0	17.2	20.1
2	50–60	42.1	7.4	3.4	1.2	0.7	5.0	15.7	5.6	13.0	10.3
2	100–120	21.4	1.2	2.2	1.4	0.4	7.7	9.1	3.5	5.8	2.3
		v values for mean particle size ($\phi\bar{x}$)					v values for Hg				
1	10–20	29.3	22.3	11.1	7.7	8.7	101.1	44.4	35.2	30.1	52.1
1	30–40	43.0	8.5	2.5	5.0	3.0	75.2	32.7	6.4	7.5	27.9
1	60–80	7.8	1.5	2.4	1.0	2.1	22.8	12.8	12.5	18.4	6.4
2	30–40	50.8	28.5	21.3	25.6	119.1	98.6	89.4	73.6	102.7	108.2
2	50–60	19.2	43.3	52.9	56.8	39.2	25.0	64.7	42.2	28.7	25.0
2	100–120	6.5	3.5	4.8	7.7	1.7	71.2	74.4	68.8	56.7	45.9

Data from Sly, 1975.

K and Hg are given for different depth ranges at sites 1 and 2. Bathymetry may be adequately defined by data returns spaced about 100 m apart and, as would be expected in depositional environments, it seems clear that variation for a given spacing decreases with depth.

Variations in composition concentrations show closer relationships to particle size than to depth.

Such data suggest that while the bathymetry of lake basins may be adequately described (at different scales) by data based upon a simplistic view of decreasing complexity with depth, samples which are used to describe sedimentological and geochemical characteristics represent more complex data populations and associations.

Sediment facies

The distribution of materials of different particle sizes in aqueous systems not only reflects the influence of the physical inputs controlling the system but, itself, influences the chemical composition of accumulating sediments (Thomas, 1973).

In the coarser particle sizes rock fragments and mineral forms remain largely inert during processes of erosion, transport, and deposition, and their dispersal may closely represent that of a conservative substance (Thomas, 1969b; Mankiewicz et al., 1975); typically heavy metals may be transported and deposited as major or minor mineral constituents under such conditions.

Finer particulates, however, show progressively more "geochemical activity," and, as noted by För-

stner (1977), slight alkalinities in normal surface waters may be sufficient for the formation and precipitation of hydroxides, carbonates, sulfides, and phosphates of heavy metals.

In the finest materials, sorption and cation exchange are particularly important on particles with large surface areas and virtually all amorphous colloidal materials of both organic and inorganic composition have high cation exchange capacities. The selective transport and accumulation of heavy metal and persistent organic contaminants is therefore particularly related to the presence of clay minerals and organics in the finer size fractions.

Bearing such relationships in mind Thomas et al. (1977), using both and R mode factor analysis and a Q mode analysis, developed a series of material facies for Lake Erie sediments which linked both particle size and chemical composition. These facies proved to be very sensitive indicators of environmental conditions and correlated well with known water quality. Of particular interest were the definition of a carbonate facies characterized by detrital materials and three distinct clay facies represented by normal, reduced, and highly contaminanted materials.

The observable physical characteristics of the sediments lead to a similar identification of the main facies types (Sly, 1977).

Clearly the relationships between particle size and sediment geochemistry reflect the close integration of physical and geochemical processes in lakes, although sediment mixing (Jernelov, 1970; Schindler et al., 1977) may further modify fine sediment particle size and geochemical profiles near the surface of sediment cores.

Summary

Sedimentary processes in lakes are strongly influenced by physical factors; in large lakes wind wave generation and circulation dominate sediment response, and in small lakes river inflow and circulation dominate response.

Lakes are essentially closed systems in which materials availability and the input of materials from land drainage exert a strong influence upon accumulation. In some lakes particle size fractions may be limited in their occurrence; in such cases this may be related either to a scarcity in supply (see also Wolfe, 1964) or to the natural hydraulics of the lake system.

Rates of sedimentation in lakes are generally much higher than in marine environments and sedimentary sequences may show differences which reflect the various origins of each type of lake basin. The accumulation of sediments in lake basins frequently exhibits temporal variations related to changes in climatic regime, water levels, infilling, or local modifications by bathymetric features (e.g., deltas, spits, bars, etc.).

The erosion, transport, and deposition of coarse materials is mostly confined to the shallow nearshore zone except where underflow, turbidity, or slump conditions provide mechanisms to carry such materials into deeper waters.

The distribution and accumulation of fine materials is particularly influenced by the morphology of lake basins and the temperature (density) structure of the water mass.

The distribution of lake sediments occurs in response to the effects of a complex of integrated water movements including circulation, upwelling, and flow, and rarely shows correlation with specific motion unless of persistent or unique character (e.g., turbidity flows).

The accumulation of very fine clay particulates requires that lake water masses remain essentially motionless (as under prolonged ice cover) or that conditions exist in which materials may flocculate.

Relationships between depth and particle size, and between standard deviation (sorting) and particle size, may be used as a means of comparing relative "energy" levels in lacustrine or marine environments. Relationships between skewness and kurtosis provide a nondimensional expression of sediment/"energy" response which may be applied to all lacustrine and marine environments in which materials are of detrital origin.

The use of sedimentary models (Miller, 1954) for the analysis of sedimentary environments may be based upon the physical characteristics of particulate materials, or may variously incorporate geochemical characteristics. The use of an integrated sedimentological and geochemical facies concept provides a strong tool for illustrating the close associations between sedimentological and geochemical processes in lakes.

ACKNOWLEDGMENTS.   The author gratefully acknowledges the many valuable discussions with colleagues at the Canada Centre for Inland Waters (Burlington, Ontario) and in particular P. E. Hamblin for assistance in preparation of material concerning the physical factors influencing sediment response. The valuable criticisms and review by R. L. Thomas were particularly useful during the preparation of materials covering sediment energy level relationships and sediment facies.

References

Anderson, E. R., and D. W. Pritchard. (1951). Physical limnology of Lake Mead. Navy Electronics Lab. Rept. No. 258. 152 pp.

Ayers, J. C., and J. L. Hough. (1964). Studies of water movements and sediments in southern Lake Michigan: Part II. The surficial bottom sediments in 1962–1963. Univ. Mich., Great Lakes Res. Div. Spec. Publ. No. 19. 47 pp.

Bajournas, L. (1970). Littoral transport and energy relationships. Pp. 787–798. *Proc. Twelfth Conf. Coastal Engineering,* Washington.

Bascom, W. (1964). *Waves and Beaches—the Dynamics of the Ocean Surface.* Doubleday, New York, NY. 267 pp.

Berg, D. W., and D. B. Duane. (1968). Effect of particle size and distribution on stability of artificially filled beach, Presque'isle Peninsula, Penn. Pp. 161–178. *Proc. Eleventh Conf. Great Lakes Res.,* Int. Assoc. Great Lakes Res.

Bergs, A. (1965). Surface waves and subsurface particle movement due to waves. Pp. 291–298. Pub. No. 13. Great Lakes Res. Div., Univ. Michigan, Ann Arbor, MI.

Blanton, J. O. (1974). Some characteristics of nearshore currents along the north shore of Lake Ontario. *J. Phys. Oceanogr.,* **4**:415–424.

Bordovskiy, O. K. (1969). Organic matter of recent sediments of the Caspian Sea. *Oceanol. Acad. Sci. USSR, Trans. Am. Geophys. Union,* **9**(6):799–807.

Borland, W. M., and C. R. Miller. (1960). Distribution of sediment in larger reservoirs. *Trans. Am. Soc. Civ. Eng.* (Paper 3019), **125**:166–180.

Bretschneider, C. L. (1952). The generation and decay of wind waves in deep water. *Trans. Am. Geophys. Union* **33**:381–389.

Bretschneider, C. L. (1958). Revisions in wave forecasting. Pp. 30–67. *Proc. Sixth Conf. Coastal Engineering Council on Wave Research.* The Engineering Foundation.

Brodie, J. W., and J. Irwin (1970). Morphology and sedimentation in Lake Wakatipu, New Zealand. *N. Z. J. Marine Freshwater Res.* **4**:479–496.

Brunskill, G. J. (1969). Fayetteville Green Lake, New York. II. Precipitation and sedimentation of calcite in a meromictic lake with laminated sediments. *Limnol. Oceanogr.,* **14**:830–847.

Bukata, R. P., W. S. Haras, J. E. Brunton, and J. P. Coakley. (1974). Satellite, airborne and ground-based observations of suspended sediment transport off Point Pelee in Lake Erie. Presented at *Conf. on Human Environment,* Poland. Pub. l974. Unpub. manuscript series, Canada Centre Inland Waters, Burlington, Ont. 9 pp.

Bukata, R. P., W. S. Haras, and J. E. Brunton. (1975). The application of ERTS-1 digital data to water transport phenomena in the Point Pelee–Rondeau area. *Verh. Int. Verein. Limnol.,* **19**:168–178.

Burns, N. M., and C. Ross. (1972). Project Hypo, an intensive study of the Lake Erie central basin hypolimnion and related surface water phenomena. Canada Centre Inland Waters Paper No. 6. U.S. Environ. Prot. Agency. Tech. Rep. No. TS-05-71-208-24. 182 pp.

Campbell, I. A. (1973). Accelerated erosion in badland environments. Pp. 18–27. *Proc. Hydrol. Symp. Univ. Alberta, Fluvial Processes and Sedimentation.* Nat. Res. Counc. Canada, Ottawa.

Capart, A. (1949). Sondages et carte bathymétrique. Exploration hydrobiologique du lac Tanganyika (1946–7). *Inst. Roy. Sci. Nat. Belg.,* **2**:(2). 16 pp.

Capart, A. (1952). Le milieu géographique et géophysique. Exploration hydrobiologique du lac Tanganyika. *Inst. Roy. Sci. Nat. Belg.,* **1**:3–27.

Church, M., and R. Gilbert. (1975). Proglacial fluvial and lacustrine environments. Pp. 22–100. In: A. V. Jopling and B. C. McDonald (eds.), *Glaciofluvial and Glaciolacustrine Sedimentation.* Soc. Econ. Palaeon. and Min. Special Pub. 23, Tulsa, OK.

Clague, J. J. (1975). Late Quaternary sediments and geomorphic history of the southern Rocky Mountain trench, British Columbia. *Can. J. Earth Sci.,* **12**:595–605.

Clifton, H. E. (1976). Wave formed sedimentary structures—a conceptual model. Pp. 126–148. In: R. A. Davis and R. L. Ethington (eds.), *Beach and Nearshore Sedimentation.* Soc. Econ. Palaeon. and Min. Special Pub. 24, Tulsa, OK.

Coakley, J. P. (1972). Nearshore sediment studies in western Lake Erie. Pp. 330–343. *Proc. Fifteenth Conf. Great Lakes Res.,* Int. Assoc. Great Lakes Res.

Coakley, J. P., and G. S. Beal. (1972). SEDAN—A computer program for sediment particle size analysis. Canada Dept. of the Environ., Inland Waters Directorate. Rep. Series 20, Ottawa. 33 pp.

Coakley, J. P., and H. K. Cho. (1972). Shore erosion in western Lake Erie. Pp. 344–360. *Proc. Fifteenth Conf. Great Lakes Res.,* Int. Assoc. Great Lakes Res.

Coakley, J. P., and P. F. Hamblin. (1970). Investigation of bank erosion and nearshore sedimentation in Lake Diefenbaker. Canada Centre for Inland Waters Rep. Series, Burlington, Ontario. 18 pp.

Cook, D. O. (1970). Models for nearshore sand transport. Pp. 210–216. *Proc. Thirteenth Conf. Great Lakes Res.,* Int. Assoc. Great Lakes Res.

Cronan, D. S., and R. L. Thomas. (1972). Geochemistry of ferromanganese oxide concretions and associated deposits in Lake Ontario. *Geol. Soc. Am. Bull.,* **83**:1493–1502.

Csanady, G. T. (1966). Dispersal of foreign matter by the currents and eddies of the Great Lakes. Pp. 283–294. Pub. No. 15 Great Lakes Res. Div., Univ. Michigan, Ann Arbor, MI.

Csanady, G. T., and B. Pade. (1968). Coastal jet project. Environmental Fluid Mechanics Lab. Rep. No. 1. Great Lakes Inst. Rep. No. PR36: Univ. Waterloo. 27 pp.

Csanady, G. T., and B. Pade. (1969). Coastal jet project. Environmental Fluid Mechanics Lab. Rep. No. 2: Univ. Waterloo. 8 pp.

Damiani, V. (1972). Studio di un ambiente fluvio-lacustro sulla base di una analisi granulometrica dei sedimenti: Fiume Toce e bacino delle isole Barromee (Lago Maggiore). *Mem. Ist. Ital. Idrobiol.,* **29**:37–95.

Damiani, V., and R. L. Thomas. (1974). The surficial sediments of the Big Bay Section of the Bay of Quinte, Lake Ontario. *Can. J. Earth Sci.,* **11**:1562–1576.

Davaud, E. (1976). Contribution a l'etude geochemique et sedimentologique de depots lacustres recents (Lac de Morat, Swisse). Ph.D. Thesis, Univ. Geneve, No. 1745. 129 pp.

Davis, R. A., W. T. Fox, M. O. Hayes, and J. C. Boothroyd. (1972). Comparison of ridge and runnel systems in tidal and non-tidal environments. *J. Sed. Petrol.,* **42**:413–421.

Dell, C. I. (1974). The stratigraphy of northern Lake Superior late-glacial and postglacial sediments. Pp. 179–192. *Proc. Seventeenth Conf. Great Lakes Res.,* Int. Assoc. Great Lakes Res.

Dickie, G. J., and D. F. Cape. (1974). The effect of winter processes on the shoreline of Point Pelee National Park, Industrial Res. Inst. Univ. Windsor, Ontario. Project 7-44. Prepared for Dept. of Environment, Inland Waters Directorate. 56 pp.

Duane, D. B. (1967). Characteristics of the sediment load in the St. Clair River. Pp. 115–132. *Proc. Tenth Conf. Great Lakes Res.,* Int. Assoc. Great Lakes Res.

Dussart, B. (1948). Recherches hydrographiques sur le lac Léman. Pp. 187–206. Ann. Station Centr. Hydrobiol. Appl., F2, 2.

Farrand, W. R. (1969). Quaternary history of Lake Superior. Pp. 181–197. *Proc. Twelfth Conf. Great Lakes Res.,* Int. Assoc. Great Lakes Res.

Favejee, J. Ch. L. (1939). Quantitative X-ray analysis of some Dutch soils. *Meded. Lanbouw.,* **43**:43–51.

Favejee, J. Ch. L. (1951). The origin of the "Wadden" mud. *Meded. Lanbouw.,* **51**:113–141.

Feth, J. H. (1964). Review and annotated bibliography of ancient lake deposits (Pre-Cambrian to Pleistocene) in the western States. U.S. Geol. Survey Bull. 1080. 119 pp.

Folk, R. L., and W. C. Ward. (1957). Brazos River Bar: A study in the significance of grain size parameters. *J. Sed. Petrol.,* **27**:3–26.

Forel, F. A. (1895). *Le Léman: Monographic limnologique.* Vol. 2. *Mécanique, Chimie, Thermique, Optique, Acoustique.* F. Rouge, Lausanne. 651 pp.

Förstner, U. (1977). Forms and sediment associations of trace metals. In: H. Shear and A. E. P. Watson (eds.), pp. 219–213 *Proc. Workshop of Fluvial Transport of Sediment Associated Nutrients and Contaminants.* Sponsored by the Int. Joint Commission, Kitchener, Ontario (October 1976).

Fox, W. T., and R. A. Davis. (1970). Profile of a storm-wind, waves and erosion on the southeastern shore of Lake Michigan. Pp 233–241. *Proc. Thirteenth Conf. Great Lakes Res.,* Int. Assoc. Great Lakes Res.

Fox, W. T., and R. A. Davis. (1976). Weather patterns and

(86)

coastal processes. Pp 1–23. In: S. A. Davis and R. L. Ethington (eds.), *Beach and Nearshore Sedimentation.* Soc. Econ. Palaeon. Min., Special Pub. 24, Tulsa, OK.

Freeman, N. G., T. S. Murthy, and W. S. Haras. (1972). A study of a storm surge on Lake Huron. *Coll. Abstr. Third Canadian Oceanographic Symposium,* Burlington. 21 pp.

Fricbergs, K. S. (1970). Erosion control in the Toronto area. Pp. 751–755. *Proc. Thirteenth Conf. Great Lakes Res.,* Int. Assoc. Great Lakes Res.

Fulton, R. J., and M. J. L. T. Pullen. (1969). Sedimentation in Upper Arrow Lake, British Columbia. *Can. J. Earth Sci.,* **6**:785–790.

Gelinas, P. J., and R. M. Quigley. (1973). The influence of geology on erosion rates along the north shore of Lake Erie. Pp. 421–430. *Proc. Sixteenth Conf. Great Lakes Res.,* Int. Assoc. Great Lakes Res.

Gilbert, R. (1975). Sedimentation in Lillooet Lake, British Columbia. *Can. J. Earth Sci.,* **12**:1697–1711.

Gilson, H. C. (1964). Lake Titicaca. *Verh. Int. Verein. Limnol.,* **15**:112–127.

Gould, H. R. (1960). Turbidity currents. Pp. 201–207. In: *Comprehensive Survey of Sedimentation in Lake Mead, 1948–49.* U.S. Dept. Interior, Geol. Surv. Prog. Paper 295.

Gould, H. R. (1970). The Mississippi delta complex. Pp. 3–30. In: J. P. Morgan, (ed.), *Deltaic Sedimentation Modern and Ancient.* Soc. Econ. Palaeon. Min. Special Pub. 15., Tulsa, OK.

Gould, H. R., and T. F. Budinger. (1958). Control of sedimentation and bottom configuration by convection currents, Lake Washington, Washington. *J. Marine Res.,* **17**:183–198.

Gresswell, R. K., and A. Huxley. (1965). *Standard Encyclopedia of the World's Rivers and Lakes.* Putnam, New York, NY. 384 pp.

Gross, D. L., J. A. Linebach, W. A. White, N. J. Ayer, C. Collinson, and H. V. Leland. (1970). Preliminary stratigraphy of unconsolidated sediments from the southwestern part of Lake Michigan. Illinois Geol. Survey Environ. Geol. Note No. 30. 20 pp.

Gross, D. L., J. A. Lineback, N. F. Shimp, and W. A. White. (1972). Composition of Pleistocene sediments in southern Lake Michigan, USA. Pp. 215–222. Section 8 Rep. Twenty-fourth International Geology Congress, Montreal.

Gustavson, T. C. (1975). Bathymetry and sediment distribution in proglacial Malaspina Lake, Alaska. *J. Sed. Petrol.,* **45**:450–461.

Györke, O. (1973). Hydraulic model study of sediment movement and changes in the bed configuration of a shallow lake. Pp. 410–416. *Proc. Helsinki Symp. Hydrology of Lakes,* IAHS-AISH Pub. No. 109.

Hadley, R. F., and S. A. Schumm. (1961). Sediment sources and drainage basin characteristics in the upper Cheyenne River basin. Pp. 187–198. U.S. Dept. Interior, U.S. Geol. Survey Water Supply Paper 1531-B.

Håkanson, L. (1974). A mathematical model for establishing numerical values of topographical roughness for lake bottoms. *Geogr. Annaler,* **56(A)**:183–200.

Håkanson, L. (1977). The influence of wind, fetch and water depth on the distribution of sediments in Lake Vanern, Sweden. *Can. J. Earth Sci.,* **14**:397–412.

Håkanson, L., and T. Ahl. (1976). Vättern-recenta sediment och sedimentkemi. Statens Naturvårdsverk. pm 740, NLU Rept. 88, Uppsala. 164 pp.

Hands, E. B. (1970). A geomorphic map of Lake Michigan shoreline. Pp. 250–265. *Proc. Thirteenth Conf. Great Lakes Res.,* Int. Assoc. Great Lakes Res.

Haras, W. S., R. P. Bukata, and K. K. Tsui. (1976). Methods for recording Great Lakes shoreline change. *Geosci. Can.,* **3**:174–184.

Harrison, W. (1968). Prediction of beach change. Pp. 209–235. In: C. Board, R. J. Chorley, P. Haggett, D. R. Stoddart, and E. Arnold (eds.), *Progress in Oceanography* (2).

Harrison, W., E. W. Rayfield, J. D. Boon, G. Reynolds, J. B. Grant, and D. Tyler. (1968). A time series from the beach environment. ESSA Res. Lab. Tech. Mem. AOL, 1, Miami, FL. 28 pp.

Hartley, R. P. (1968). Bottom currents in Lake Erie. Pp. 398–405. *Proc. Eleventh Conf. Great Lakes Res.,* Int. Assoc. Great Lakes Res.

Hjulström, F. (1939). Transportation of detritus by moving water. In: P. D. Trask, (ed.), *Recent Marine Sediments Symposium.* Amer. Assoc. Petrol. Geol., Tulsa, OK.

Holdrinet, M. Van H., R. Frank, R. L. Thomas, and L. J. Hetling. (1978). Mirex in the sediments of Lake Ontario. J. Great Lakes Res., (in press).

Holmes, A. (1955). *Principles of physical geology.* Thomas Nelson, London. 532 pp.

Holmes, P. W. (1967). Sedimentary studies of late Quaternary material in Windermere Lake (Great Britain). *Sed. Geol.,* **2**:210–224.

Houbolt, J. J. H. C., and J. B. M. Jonker. (1968). Recent sediments in the eastern part of the Lake of Geneva (Lac Léman). *Geol. Mijnbouw.,* **47**:131–148.

Hough, J. L. (1958). *Geology of the Great Lakes.* Univ. Illinois Press, Urbana, IL. 313 pp.

Hough, J. L. (1963). Geological and sedimentary characteristics of the freshwater environment. Pp. 134–139. Proc. Pub. No. 10, Great Lakes Res. Div., Univ. Michigan, Ann Arbor, MI.

Howard, C. S. (1960). Character of inflowing water. Pp. 103–113. In: *Comprehensive Survey of Sedimentation in Lake Mead, 1948–49.* U.S. Dept. Interior. Geol. Surv. Prof. Paper 295.

Hunt, A. S., and E. B. Henson. (1969). Recent sedimentation and water properties, Lake Champlain. Pp. 21–35. In: *New York State Geol. Assoc. Guidebook to Field Excursions.* Forty-first Annual Meeting.

Hutchinson, G. E. (1957). *A treatise on Limnology; Geography, Physics and Chemistry.* Wiley, New York, NY. Vol. 1. 1015 pp.

Hyne, N. J., P. Chelminski, J. E. Court, D. S. Gorsline, and C. R. Goldman. (1972). Quaternary history of Lake Tahoe, California–Nevada. *Geol. Soc. Am. Bull.,* **83**:1435–1448.

International Great Lakes Levels Board (1973). Regulation of Great Lakes water levels. Report to the Int. Joint Commission (Ottawa and Chicago). 294 pp.

International Joint Commission (IJC) (Report to) (1969a). *Pollution of Lake Erie, Lake Ontario, and the International Section of the St. Lawrence River.* Vol. 2. *Lake Erie.* 316 pp.

International Joint Commission (IJC) (Report to) (1969b).

Pollution of Lake Erie, Lake Ontario, and the International Section of the St. Lawrence River. Vol. 3. *Lake Ontario and the International Section of the St. Lawrence River.* 329 pp.

Jaquet, J.-M., and J.-P. Vernet. (1976). Moment and graphic size parameters in the sediments of Lake Geneva (Switzerland). *J. Sed. Petrol.,* **46**:305–312.

Jernelöv, A. (1970). Release of methyl mercury from sediments with layers containing inorganic mercury at different depths. *Limnol. Oceanogr.,* **15**:958–960.

Johns, R. K., and N. H. Ludbrook. (1963). Investigation of Lake Eyre. Pp. 1–34. Dept. Mines South Australia Geol. Surv. Rep. 24 (Part 1).

Karrow, P. F. (1963). Pleistocene Geology of the Hamilton–Galt area. Ontario Dept. Mines, Geol. Rep. No. 16, Toronto. 68 pp.

Karrow, P. F. (1967). Pleistocene geology of the Scarborough area. Ontario Dept. of Mines, Geol. Rept. 46. 108 pp.

Karrow, P. F. (1969). Stratigraphic studies in the Toronto Pleistocene. *Geol. Assoc. Can. Proc.,* **20**:4–16.

Karrow, P. F., J. R. Clark, and J. Terasmae. (1961). The age of Lake Iroquois and Lake Ontario. *J. Geol.,* **69**:659–667.

Kemp, A. L. W., and R. L. Thomas (1976). Cultural impact on the geochemistry of the sediments of Lakes Ontario, Erie and Huron. *Geosci. Can.,* **3**:191–207.

Kendall, R. L. (1969). An ecological history of the Lake Victoria basin. *Ecol. Monogr.* **39**(2):121–176.

Kennedy, E. J., R. R. Ruch, and N. F. Shimp. (1971). Distribution of mercury in unconsolidated sediments from southern Lake Michigan. Illinois Geol. Survey Environ., Geol. Note No. 44. 19 pp.

Kite, G. W. (1972a). An engineering study of crustal movement around Lake Superior. Inland Waters Directorate, Dept. Environ. Tech. Bull. 62, Ottawa. 101 pp.

Kite, G. W. (1972b). An engineering study of crustal movement around the Great Lakes. Inland Waters Directorate, Dept. Environ., Tech. Bull. 63, Ottawa. 57 pp.

Komar, P. D. (1976). Evaluation of wave generated longshore current velocities and some transport rates on beaches. Pp. 48–53. In: R. A. Davis and R. L. Ethington (eds.), *Beach and Nearshore Sedimentation.* Soc. Econ. Palaeon. Min., Special Pub. 24, Tulsa, OK.

Komar, P. D., and M. C. Miller. (1973). The threshold of sediment movement under oscillatory water waves. *J. Sed. Petrol.,* **43**:1101–1110.

Kozhov, M. M. (1963). *Lake Baikal and its life.* W. Junk, the Hague. 344 pp.

Krishnappan, B. G., and M. G. Skafel. (1976). Interactions of waves with the Pelee Shoal sediments. Unpub. Rep. Canada Centre Inland Waters, Burlington, Ontario. 20 pp.

Krumbein, W. C., and H. A. Slack. (1956). Relative efficiency of beach sampling methods. U.S. Army Corps Eng., Beach Erosion Board Tech. Mem. 90. 43 pp.

Lara, J. M., and J. I. Sanders. (1970). The 1963–4 Lake Mead Survey. U.S. Dept. Interior, Bur. Reclam. Rep. REC-OLE-70-21. 172 pp.

Lauff, G. H., E. B. Henson, J. C. Ayers, D. C. Chandler, and C. F. Powers. (1961). The bottom sediments of the Straits of Mackinac Region. Pub. No. 6. Great Lakes Res. Div., Univ. of Michigan, Ann Arbor, MI. 69 pp.

Lee, A. H. (1972). Some thermal and chemical characteristics of Lake Ontario in relation to space and time. Inst. Environ. Sci. Eng. Great Lakes Inst. Div. Rept. EG-6. Univ. Toronto, Toronto, Ontario. 162 pp.

Lehman, J. T. (1975). Reconstructing the rate of accumulation of lake sediment, the effect of sediment focusing. *Quat. Res.,* **5**:541–550.

Lewis, C. F. M. (1969). Quaternary geology of the Great Lakes. Report on Activities, Part A: April to October 1968. Pp. 63–64. R. G. Blackadar, (ed.). Geol. Survey of Canada, Paper No. 69-1A.

Lewis, C. F. M., and R. M. McNeely. (1967). Pp. 133–142. Survey of Lake Ontario bottom deposits. *Proc. Tenth Conf. Great Lakes Res.,* Int. Assoc. Great Lakes Res.

Lewis, C. F. M., and P. G. Sly. (1971). Seismic profiling and geology of the Toronto waterfront area of Lake Ontario. Pp. 303–354. *Proc. Fourteenth Conf. Great Lakes Res.,* Int. Assoc. Great Lakes Res.

Lineback, J. A., N. J. Ayer, and D. L. Gross. (1970). Stratigraphy of unconsolidated sediments in the southern part of Lake Michigan. Illinois Geol. Survey Environ., Geol. Note No. 35. 35 pp.

Livingston, D. A. (1954). On the orientation of lake basins. *Am. J. Sci.,* **252**:547–554.

Loucks, R. H. (1972). Estuary–ocean exchange. *Proc. Coastal Zone Seminar,* Bedford Inst. Oceanogr. Dartmouth, Nova Scotia. (1):63–71.

Ludlam, S. D. (1969). Fayetteville Green Lake, New York. III. the laminated sediments. *Limnol. Oceanogr.,* **14**:848–857.

McAndrews, J. H. (1972). Pollen analyses of the sediments of Lake Ontario. Pp. 223–227. Sect. 8. Twenty-fourth Int. Geol. Congress, Montreal.

McDonald, W. E. (1954). Variation in Great Lakes levels in relation to engineering problems. Pp. 249–257. *Proc. Fourth Conf. Coastal Engineering.* Council on Wave Research, Univ. California, Berkley, CA.

Mandlebaum, H. (1966). Sedimentation in the St. Clair River delta. Pp. 192–202. Pub. 15. Great Lakes Res. Div., Univ. Michigan, Ann Arbor, MI.

Mankiewicz, D., J. R. Steidtmann, and L. E. Borgman. (1975). Clastic sedimentation in a modern alpine lake. *J. Sed. Petrol.,* **45**:462–468.

Mathews, W. H. (1956). Physical limnology and sedimentation in a glacial lake. *Geol. Soc. Am. Bull.,* **67**:537–552.

Matthews, W. H., and F. P. Shepard. (1962). Sedimentation of the Fraser River delta, British Columbia. *Am. Assoc. Petrol. Geol. Bull.,* **46**:1416–1443.

Miller, R. L. (1954). A model for the analysis of environments of sedimentation. *J. Geol.,* **62**:108–113.

Miller, R. L., and J. M. Ziegler. (1964). A study of sediment distribution in the zone of shoaling waves over complicated bottom topography. Pp. 133–153. In: R. L. Miller (ed.), *Papers in Marine Geology.* Shepard Commemorative Vol.

Mothersill, J. S. (1970). Relationship of grain size modes to nearshore sedimentary environments, Lake Superior, Ontario. *Can. J. Earth Sci.,* **8**:522–526.

Mothersill, J. S. (1971). Limnogeological studies of the eastern part of the Lake Superior basin. *Can. J. Earth Sci.,* **8**:1043–1055.

Mothersill, J. S. (1975). Lake Chad: Geochemistry and sedimentary aspects of a shallow polymictic lake. *J. Sed. Petrol.,* **45**:295–309.

Müller, G. (1966). The new Rhine Delta in Lake Constance. In: M. L. Shirley and J. A. Ragsdale (eds.), *Deltas in Their Geological Framework*. Houston Geological Society, Houston, TX. 251 pp.

Murray, S. P. (1970). Settling velocities and vertical diffusion of particles in turbulent water. *J. Geophys. Res.*, **75**:1647–1654.

Nakao, K., and S. Horie. (1975). Pp. 71–75. Sedimentary structure near Lake Yogo inferred from electrical depth sounding. In: S. Horie (ed.), *Palaeolimnology of Lake Biwa and the Japanese Pleistocene*. Univ. Press., Tokyo. Vol. 3.

Neev, D., and K. O. Emery. (1967). The Dead Sea—depositional processes and environments of evaporites. Bull. 41., Min. Devel. Geol. Survey, State of Israel, Jerusalem. 147 pp.

Odum, H. T. (1952). The Carolina Bays and a Pleistocene weather map. *Amer. J. Sci.*, **250**:263–270.

Ongley, E. D. (1976). Sediment and nutrient yield from Great Lakes tributary drainage, Canada. *Geosci. Can.*, **3**:164–168.

Pelletier, B. R. (1969). Submarine physiography, bottom sediments, and models of sediment transport. Pp. 100–135. In: *Earth Science Symp. Hudson Bay*. Nat. Advis. Comm. Res., Geol. Survey Canada, Ottawa. GSC Paper 68-53.

Pelletier, B. R. (1973). A re-examination of the use of the silt/clay ratios as indicators of sedimentary environments: a study for students. *Maritime Sed.*, **9**(1):1–12.

Picard, M. D., and L. R. High. (1972). Criteria for recognizing lacustrine rocks. Pp. 108–145. In: J. K. Rigby and W. K. Hamblin (eds.), *Recognition of Ancient Sedimentary Environments*. Special Pub. No. 16. Soc. Econ. Palaeon. Min.

Reeves, C. C. (1966). Pluvial lake basins of West Texas. *J. Geol.*, **74**:269–291.

Reid, J. R. (1961). Investigation of bottom cores from north and south-central Lake Superior. Pp. 126–144. *Proc. Fourth Conf. Great Lakes Res.*, Int. Assoc. Great Lakes Res., Pub. No. 7. Univ. Michigan, Ann Arbor, MI.

Reineck, H. E., and I. B. Singh. (1973). *Depositional sedimentary Environments*. Springer-Verlag, New York, NY. 439 pp.

Riedel, H. P., J. W. Kamphius, and A. Brebner. (1972). Measurement of bed shear stress under waves. *Proc. Thirteenth Conf. Coastal Engineering*, Vancouver. 1:587.

Rukavina, N. A. (1969). Nearshore sediment survey of western Lake Ontario, methods and preliminary results. Pp. 317–324. *Proc. Twelfth Conf. Great Lakes Res.*, Int. Assoc. Great Lakes Res.

Rukavina, N. A. (1970). Lake Ontario nearshore sediments. Whitby to Wellington, Ontario. Pp. 266–273. *Proc. Thirteenth Conf. Great Lakes Res.*, Int. Assoc. Great Lakes Res.

Rukavina, N. A. (1976). Nearshore sediments of Lakes Ontario and Erie. *Geosci. Can.*, **3**:185–190.

Rust, B. R., and J. P. Coakley. (1970). Physical–chemical characteristics and postglacial desalination of Stanwell–Fletcher Lake, Arctic Canada. *Can. J. Earth Sci.*, **7**:900–911.

Schindler, D. W., R. Hesslein, and G. Pipphut. (1977). Interactions between sediments and overlying waters in natural oligotrophic and experimentally eutrophied Pre-Cambrian Shield Lakes. In: H. L. Golterman (ed.), *Proc. SIL-UNESCO Symp*. Interaction between sediments and freshwater, Amsterdam (1976). Junk. Pp. 235–243.

Schumm, S. A. (1956). The role of creep and rainwash on the retreat of badland slopes. *Am. J. Sci.*, **254**:693–706.

Scott, J. T., P. Jekel, and M. W. Fenlon. (1971). Transport in the baroclinic coastal current near the south shore of Lake Ontario in early summer. Pp. 640–653. *Proc. Fourteenth Conf. Great Lakes Res.*, Int. Assoc. Great Lakes Res.

Seibold, E. (1967). La Mer Baltique prise comme modèle de géologie marine. *Rev. Géogr. Phys. Géol. Dyn.*, (2), **IX**(5):371–384.

Serruya, C. (1969). Problems of sedimentation in the Lake of Geneva. *Verh. Int. Verein. Limnol.*, **17**:209–218.

Sherman, I. (1953). Flocculent structure of sediment suspended in Lake Mead. *Trans. Am. Geophys. Union*, **34**:394–406.

Shimp, N. F., J. A. Schleicher, R. R. Ruch, D. B. Heck, and H. V. Leland. (1971). Trace element and organic carbon accumulation in the most recent sediments of southern Lake Michigan. Illinois Geol. Survey Environ. Geol. Note. No. 41. 25 pp.

Simons, T. J., and D. E. Jordan. (1972). Computed water circulation of Lake Ontario for observed winds 20 April–14 May 1971. Canada Centre Inland Waters Publ., Burlington. 17 pp.

Slaymaker, H. O., and H. J. McPherson. (1973). Effects of land use on sediment production. Pp. 159–183. *Proc. Hydrol. Symp. Fluvial Processes and Sedimentation*, Univ. Alberta. Nat. Res. Counc. Canada, Ottawa.

Sly, P. G. (1973a). Sediment processes in Great Lakes. Pp. 465–492. In: *Proc. Hydrology Symp. Fluvial Processes and Sedimentation*, Univ. Alberta. Nat. Res. Counc. Canada, Ottawa.

Sly, P. G. (1973b). The significance of sediment deposits in large lakes and their energy relationships. Pp 383–396. In: *Proc. Symp. Hydrology of Lakes*, IAHS-AISH Pub. 109, Helsinki.

Sly, P. G. (1975). Statistical evaluation of recent sediment geochemical sampling. *Proc. IX Internat. Cong. Sedimentology*, Nice.

Sly, P. G. (1976). Lake Erie and its basin. *J. Fish. Res. Board Can.*, **33**:355–370.

Sly, P. G. (1977). Sedimentary environments in the Great Lakes. In: H. L. Golterman (ed.), *Proc. SIL-UNESCO Symp*. Interactions between sediments and freshwater, Amsterdam (1976). Junk. Pp. 76–82.

Sly, P. G., and C. F. M. Lewis. (1972). The Great Lakes of Canada—Quaternary geology and limnology. Guide Book Trip A43: Twenty-fourth Internat. Geol. Congress, Montreal. 92 pp.

Sly, P. G., and R. L. Thomas. (1974). Review of geological research as it relates to an understanding of Great Lakes limnology. *J. Fish. Res. Board Can.*, **31**:795–825.

Spencer, D. W. (1963). The interpretation of grain-size distribution curves of clastic sediments. *J. Sed. Petrol.*, **24**:151–158.

St. John, B. E., P. G. Sly, and R. L. Thomas. (1972). The importance of sediment studies in western lakes as a key to basin management. Pp. 145–174. *Proc. Symp. on Lakes of Western Canada*. Univ. Alberta, Edmonton.

Steers, J. A. (1953). *The Sea Coast*. New Naturalist Series, Collins, London. 276 pp.

Stichling, W. (1973). Sediment loads in Canadian rivers. Pp. 38–72. *Proc. Hydrol. Symp. Fluvial processes and sedimentation*, Univ. Alberta. Nat. Res. Counc. Canada, Ottawa.

Stiller, M., and G. Assaf. (1973). Sedimentation and transport of particles in Lake Kinneret traced by ^{137}Cs. Pp. 397–403. *Proc. Helsinki Symp. Hydrology of Lakes*, IAHS-AISH Pub. No. 109.

Ström, K. (1955). Waters and sediments in the deep of lakes. *Mem. Inst. Ital. Idrobiol.*, Suppl. **8**:345–356.

Sundborg, A. (1956). The River Klarälven, a study of fluvial processes. *Geogr. Annaler*, **38**-2:127–316.

Sundborg, A. (1964). The importance of the sediment problem in the technical and economic development of river basins. *Ann. Acad. Reg. Sci. Uppsala*, **8**:33–52.

Sundborg, A. (1967). Some aspects on fluvial sediments and fluvial morphology. I. General views and graphic methods. *Geogr. Annaler*, **49A**:333–343.

Sutton, R. G., T. L. Lewis, and D. L. Woodrow. (1970). Pp. 308–318. Nearshore sediments in southern Lake Ontario, their dispersal patterns and economic potential. *Proc. Thirteenth Conf. Great Lakes Res.*, Int. Assoc. Great Lakes Res.

Terwindt, J. H. J., H. N. C. Breusers, and J. N. Svasek. (1968). Experimental investigation on the erosion-sensitivity of a sand–clay lamination. *Sedimentology*, **11**:105–114.

Thomas, H. E. (1960). Drainage basin tributary to Lake Mead. Pp. 21–30. In: *Comprehensive Survey of Sedimentation in Lake Mead, 1948–49*. U.S. Dept. Interior, U.S. Geol. Survey. Prof. Paper 295.

Thomas, R. L. (1969a). A note on the relationship of grain size, clay content, quartz and organic carbon in some Lake Erie and Lake Ontario sediments. *J. Sed. Petrol.*, **39**:803–809.

Thomas, R. L. (1969b). The qualitative distribution of feldspars in surficial bottom sediments from Lake Ontario. Pp. 364–379. *Proc. Twelfth Conf. Great Lakes Res.*, Int. Assoc. Great Lakes Res.

Thomas, R. L. (1971). Report on the occurrence and distribution of mercury in the sediments of Lake St. Clair. Unpublished Report. Canada Centre Inland Waters, Burlington, Ontario. 11 pp.

Thomas, R. L. (1972). The distribution of mercury in the sediments of Lake Ontario. *Can. J. Earth Sci.*, **9**:636–651.

Thomas, R. L. (1973). The distribution of mercury in the sediments of Lake Huron. *Can. J. Earth Sci.*, **10**:194–204.

Thomas, R. L., A. L. W. Kemp, and C. F. M. Lewis (1972). Distribution composition and characteristics of the surficial sediments of Lake Ontario. *J. Sed. Petrol.*, **42**:66–84.

Thomas, R. L., A. L. W. Kemp, and C. F. M. Lewis. (1973). The surficial sediments of Lake Huron. *Can. J. Earth Sci.*, **10**:226–271.

Thomas, R. L., J.-M. Jaquet, and A. Mudroch. (1975). Sedimentation processes and associated changes in surface sediment trace metal concentrations in Lake St. Clair, 1970–1974. *Proc. Internat. Conf. Heavy Metals in the Environment*, Nat. Res. Counc. Can. and Univ. Toronto, Toronto (October 1975). Pp. 691–708.

Thomas, R. L., J.-M. Jaquet, A. L. W. Kemp, and C. F. M. Lewis. (1976). Surficial sediments of Lake Erie. *J. Fish. Res. Board Can.*, **33**:385–403.

Thomas, R. L., J.-M. Jaquet, and R. Froidevaux. (1977). Sedimentation processes and geochemical facies in Lake Erie. Presented at *SIL-UNESCO Symp*. Interactions between sediments and freshwater. Amsterdam, 1976. Unpub. Manuscript Series, Canada Centre Inland Waters, Burlington, Ontario. 10 pp.

Trimonis, E. S., and K. M. Shimkus. (1970). Sedimentation at the head of a submarine canyon. *Oceanol. Acad. Sci. USSR. Trans. Am. Geophys. Union*, **10**(1):74–85.

Tsang, G. (1974). Ice piling on lake shores, with special reference to the occurrences on Lake Simcoe in the spring of 1973. Inland Waters Directorate, Scientific Series No. 35, Ottawa. 12 pp.

Tsang, G. (1975). A field study on ice piling on shores and the associated hydrometeorological parameters. Pp. 93–110. *Proc. Third Int. Symp. Ice Problems*, Hanover, NH.

Van der Leeden, F. (1975). Water resources of the world—selected statistics. Water Inf. Centre, Pt. Washington, NY. 568 pp.

Vernet, J.-P., R. L. Thomas, J.-M. Jaquet, and R. Friedli. (1972). Texture of the sediments of the Petit Lac (Western Lake Geneva). *Ecolgae Geol. Helv.*, **65**:591–610.

Vollenweider, R. A. (1956). L'influenza della torbidita provocata dalle acque di piena nel bacino di Pallanza (Lago Maggiore). *Mem. Inst. Ital. Idrobid.*, **9**:85–111.

Walker, J. R., and J. V. Massingill. (1970). Slump features on the Mississippi Fan, northeastern Gulf of Mexico. *Geol. Soc. Am. Bull.*, **81**:3101–3108.

Walling, D. E. (1977). Natural sheet and channel erosion of Unconsolidated Source Material (Geomorphic Control, Magnitude and frequency of transfer Mechanisms). In: H. Shear and A. E. P. Watson (eds.), *Proc. Workshop of fluvial transport of sediment-associated nutrients and contaminants*, sponsored by the Int. Joint Commission, Kitchener, Ontario (October 1976). Pp. 11–36.

Wolfe, R. G. (1964). The dearth of certain sizes of materials in sediments. *J. Sed. Petrol.*, **34**:320–327.

Yamamoto, A. (1975). Grain sizes of the core sediments and variations of palaeoprecipitation in Lake Biwa during the last three hundred thousand years. Pp. 209–225. In: S. Horie (ed.), *Palaeolimnology of Lake Biwa and the Japanese Pleistocene*. Vol 3. Otsu Hydrobiol. Station, Kyoto Univ., Otsu, Japan.

Chapter 4
Man-Made Chemical Perturbation of Lakes

W. Stumm and P. Baccini

Introduction

Pollution may be defined as an alteration of man's surroundings in such a way as they become unfavorable to him. This implies that pollution is not solely a matter of the addition of contaminants or pollutants to the environment, but it can also result from other direct or indirect consequences of man's actions. Most of the energy utilized by our industrial society for its own advantage (heat production, manipulation of the landscape, urban construction, agriculture, forestry, geological exploitations, construction of dams) ultimately affects the ecosystems and creates chemical perturbations. Man—as a terrestrial being—interferes primarily with the terrestrial environment; because of the interdependence of the land and water ecosystems and because of the extreme sensitivity of the latter, the stress imposed upon the environment by civilization becomes primarily reflected in the aquatic ecosystems.

Interdependence of land and water ecosystems

Man interferes more and more with cycles that couple land, water, and atmosphere. In Figure 1 we illustrate schematically with the help of a few selected physical, chemical, and biological attributes some interdependences of land and water. For example, a technological energy input into a terrestrial ecosystem (e.g., deforestation, conversion of grassland into cropland, intensification of agricultural production, land amelioration) reduces the quantity of biomass (decrease in vegetation cover); this in turn affects the microclimate and reduces evapotranspiration thus increasing rain runoff and rates of erosion and siltation. Accelerated nutrient cycles and faster transport of soil constituents increase sedimentation rates and lead to enrichment with nutrients of surface waters followed by changes in chemical and biological composition of the aquatic habitats. Obviously, a lake ecosystem has physical, chemical, biological, and geological inputs and outputs.

A substantial amount of the disposals and discards of society reaches lakes. The ratio of pollutant fluxes to natural fluxes increases with increasing civilizational activity. The quality of water bodies generally reflects the range of human activities within their catchment area. In a broad sense, potential perturbation of lakes may be related to population density and energy dissipation in the drainage area of the lake. Figure 2 shows the relationships among per caput energy consumption, population density, and energy consumption per unit area for various countries. These data may be compared with the mean biotic energy flux (energy fixed by photosynthesis) and the input of solar energy to the surface of the earth. Perturbation of an ecosystem is indicated when energy flux by civilization exceeds markedly biotic energy flux. As Figure 1 shows, this is the case in most countries of the northern hemisphere.

Chemical perturbation of a lake may be related to the population density in the drainage area of the lake, to the surrounding factor (drainage area/lake area), to the per caput waste production—or more generally to the per caput energy production, and to the reciprocal of the mean depth of the lake. Thus the potential loading, J, of a lake in units of wastes produced or energy consumed per volume of lake water per unit of time may be given by:

$$J = \frac{\text{capita}}{\text{drainage area}} \frac{\text{drainage area}}{\text{lake area}} \frac{1}{\text{lake depth}}$$
$$\cdot \frac{\text{waste production or energy consumption}}{\text{capita}} \cdot (1 - \eta) \quad (1)$$

where η is the effectiveness of environmental protection measures (recycling, waste retention, waste treatment). In Table 1, loading parameters are compared for some lakes.

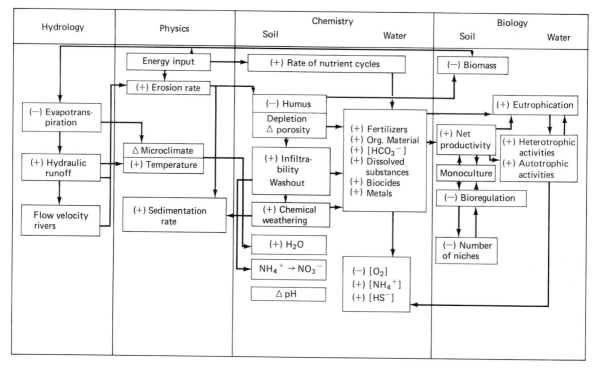

FIGURE 1.　Interdependence of land–water systems.

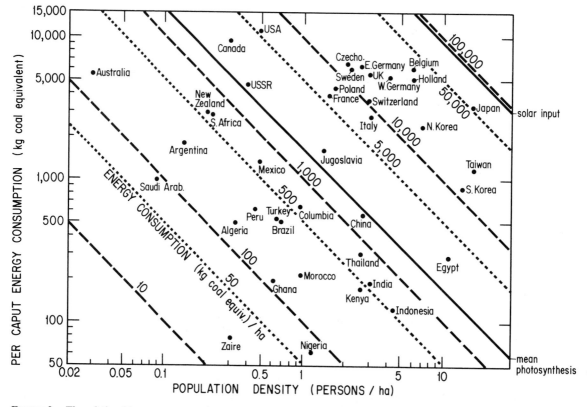

FIGURE 2.　The relationships among per capita energy consumption, population density, and energy consumption per unit area (or pollution potential), for different countries in 1972. Note: The area of each country includes only FAO-defined agricultural areas (cf. Li, 1976).

TABLE 1. Comparison of Loading Parameters of Some Lakes

Lake	Country	Surrounding factor[a]	Mean depth (m)	Inhabitants (km^{-2})	Inhabitants per m^3 lake volume	Energy consumption per lake volume (kcal/m^3/day)
Greifensee	Switzerland	15	19	441	348	37.4
Plattensee	Hungary	10	3	~60	200	20
Lake Washington	USA	~15	18	~50	42	9.8
Lake Constance	Switzerland/Germany/Austria	19	90	114	24	2.5
Lago di Lugano	Switzerland/Italy	11	130	264	22.3	2.2
Lake Biwa	Japan	4.5	41	~150	16	1.5
Lago Maggiore	Switzerland/Italy	26	175	92	13.7	1.1
Lake Winnipeg	Canada	35	13	~3	8.1	1.53
Lake Geneva	Switzerland/France	13	154	94	7.9	0.8
Lago di Como	Italy	22	185	~60	7.1	0.5
Lake Titicaca	South America	14	~100	~40	5.6	0.02
Lake Victoria	Africa	3	40	~70	5.1	0.04
Brienzersee	Switzerland	37	179	23	4.7	0.49
Lago di Garda	Italy	4	150	~50	1.3	0.1
Lake Baikal	USSR	17	730	~5	0.6	0.01
Lake Tanganjika	Africa	4	572	~50	0.3	0.003
Lake Inari	Lapland	12	~50	0.5	0.1	0.01
Lake Superior	USA/Canada	1.5	145	~5	0.05	0.01

[a]Drainage area/lake area.

Transport paths

For every substance to be transported into a lake, we like to know the source functions, the transport routes, the reservoirs, and the chemical and biological processes. The main transport paths are the rivers and the atmosphere. The particulate load of rivers is about three to five times the dissolved loads.

A significant part of the flux of dissolved and suspended materials transported by the rivers results from erosion and chemical denudation. These fluxes may have increased substantially because of changes in land use and acidification of rain. The transformation of forest to croplands and grazing areas as well as road building increase erosion rates by as much as one order of magnitude. Degens et al. (1976) have estimated from Black Sea sediment cores rates of soil erosion in the drainage area of the Black Sea, a region characterized by its diversity comprising all transitions between arid and humid climates or lowlands or mountainous areas. The present denudation rate is ca. 100 tons km^{-2}. High levels in sedimentation rates from A.D. 200 to the present time were accounted for by agricultural activities and deforestation. It appears from these data that agricultural activities have accelerated soil erosion by a factor of about 3. Although most pollutants that enter a lake are moved into the lake by rivers, industrial outfalls, and drainage, for some pollutants transport through the atmosphere must not be underestimated. The atmosphere is a significant and fast conveyor belt acting over large distances for various products of fossil fuel combus-

tion (oxides of sulfur and nitrogen, hydrocarbons, heavy metals, acidity), for exhausts of steel production (fine particles), for emissions of volatile oxides from the production of cement (As, B, Pb, Se, Zn), for some radioactive substances released from nuclear reactors and weapon tests, and for halogenated hydrocarbons (DDT, PCBs, hexachlorobenzene, compounds transported mainly in the vapor phase). Some pollutants (soil components, fertilizers) are moved into lakes through the action of wind. Periodic rainfalls sweep out all materials from a height of 5 km (Goldberg, 1972). Assuming an average rainfall of m cm yr^{-1}, the flux of materials per unit to the lake and its drainage area is $F = mC$ g cm^{-2} $year^{-1}$ where C is the pollutant concentration in g/cm^3 of rain.

Winchester and Nifong (1971) have attempted to compare river input with atmospheric input for Lake Michigan (Table 2). Air seems to be in this case a significant source for pollution by Co, Cu, Mn, Ni, Pb, Ti, V, and Zn.

Factors regulating the chemical composition of lake water systems

Man-produced perturbations in the existing chemical conditions in lakes have created a need for models of water composition capable of describing present and future states of water systems. Fresh waters vary in chemical compositions; but these variations are, at

TABLE 2.   Comparison of Inputs by Rivers and by Air into Lake Michigan

Element	Input[a] (ton yr⁻¹)	Air pollution inventory (ton yr⁻¹)	Ratio[b] ≳ 10
Ag	10	3	
Al	13,000	45,000	
As	65	(44)	?
B	330	4	
Ba	330	210	
Be	—	5	?
Br	650	725	
Ca	490,000	37,000	
Cd	—	12	?
Cl	250,000	635	
Co	6.5	50	X
Cr	33	100	
Cu	230	3,200	X
Fe	(22,000)	86,000	?
Ga	3	(4.4)	
K	75,000	15	
Mg	134,000	5,500	
Mn	230	4,600	X
Mo	33	46	
Na	200,000	1,400	
Ni	10	1,000	X
P	650	150	
Pb	100	2,200	X
S	180,000	680,000	
Se	6.5	(20)	(X)
Si	44,000	59,000	
Sn	—	13	?
Sr	2,000	5	
Ti	100	2,400	X
V	29	610	X
Zn	650	3,900	X

[a] Estimated average stream flow into Lake Michigan = 32.6 km³ yr⁻¹.

[b] If the ratio air pollution inventory/stream input ≥ 10, there is reason to expect a major input to the lake by the atmospheric route. Such cases are indicated by "X"; "?" denotes elements where data are lacking or uncertain.
From Winchester and Nifong (1971).

least partially, understandable if the environmental history of the water, its pollution, and the rock–water–atmosphere systems are considered.

Many constituents of the earth's crust are thermodynamically unstable in the presence of water and the atmosphere; rocks react primarily with $CO_2(g)$ and H_2O, for example:

$$CaCO_3 + CO_2 + H_2O \rightleftarrows Ca^{2+} + 2HCO_3^- \quad (2)$$
$$\text{calcite}$$

$$NaAlSiO_8(s) + CO_2 + 5\tfrac{1}{2}H_2O \rightleftarrows Na^+ + HCO_3^-$$
$$\text{Na-feldspar}$$
$$+ 2H_4SiO_4 + \tfrac{1}{2}Al_2Si_2O_5(OH)_4(s) \quad (3)$$
$$\text{kaolinite}$$

$$3Ca_{0.33}Al_{4.67}Si_{7.33}(OH)_4(s) + 2CO_2 + 2H_2O$$
$$\text{montmorillonite}$$
$$= Ca^{2+} + 2HCO_3^- + 8H_4SiO_4 + 7Al_2Si_2O_5(OH)_4(s).$$
$$\text{kaolinite}$$
$$(4)$$

The rock type in the drainage area of the lake determines to a large extent the inorganic composition of the lake water. In Table 3A chemical analyses are presented (from Garrels and Mackenzie, 1971) of river waters whose drainages are dominated by certain rock types. Thus, lake water draining from a limestone area is very much like that of the Danube, because reactions such as (2) predominate; and lake water in a crystalline area is very much like the Nile River, because the chemical composition is regulated more by reactions such as (3) and (4). Table 3B gives plausible weathering reactions and their extent per liter of water which lead to a chemical composition representative of the average surface water in North America.

Figure 3 illustrates the various processes that affect the chemical composition of the lake water. Appreciation of some of the variables that regulate the chemical composition can be obtained by considering some simple equilibrium and steady-state mass balance models (Figure 4).

Equilibrium models

In an imaginary experiment, rocks (e.g., calcite, dolomite, kaolinite, Na- and K-feldspars) are mixed with H_2O and exposed to an atmosphere containing CO_2. With the help of the equilibrium constants for the pertinent reactions, the chemical equilibrium composition of the water can be calculated (Table 4).

In the real system, equilibrium may not be attained; then the equilibrium composition gives the boundary conditions toward which closed systems must proceed however slowly. Kramer (1967) has shown that the Great Lakes fit to a good first approximation a model involving calcite, dolomite, apatite, kaolinite, gibbsite, and Na- and K-feldspars with air of $p_{CO_2} = 3.5 \times 10^{-4}$ atm and water at 5°C. Kramer's equilibrium predictions are less successful for anions than for cations, however, and his best results are normalized to match observed concentrations of chloride and sulfate (Table 4). Schindler (1967), Garrels and Mackenzie (1971), White et al. (1963), Feth et al. (1964), and others have shown that simple solubility acid base and redox equilibria may control major and minor constituents in fresh waters. Obviously the rates of many reactions are too slow to attain equilibrium in the real systems. In considering equilibria and kinetics in lake systems it is useful to recall that different time scales need to be identified for different reactions. As shown by Morgan (1967), and Stumm and Morgan (1970) there exist for

TABLE 3.   Control of Inorganic Water Composition by Chemical Weathering Processes

A. Composition (mg/liter) of fresh water types (taken from Garrels and Mackenzie, 1971)

	Limestone terrain Danube River	Argillaceous terrain Amazon River at Obidas	Crystalline terrain Nile River	Salty Rio Grande River at Laredo, Texas
SiO_2 [a]	5.6	10.6	20.1	30
Ca^{2+}	43.9	5.4	15.8	109
Mg^{2+}	9.9	0.5	8.8	24
Na^+	2.8	1.6	15.6	117
K^+	1.6	1.8	3.9	6.7
HCO_3^-	167.0	17.9	85.8	183.0
SO_4^{2-}	14.7	0.8	4.7	238.0
Cl^-	2.4	2.6	3.4	171.0

B. Plausible chemical weathering processes leading to a chemical composition representative of the average surface water in North America

Process	HCO_3^-	SO_4^{2-}	Cl^-	Ca^{2+}	Mg^{2+}	Na^+	SiO_2	Change by weathering for 1 liter of water (mmol)
			(mmol/liter)					
$2NaAlSi_3O_8(s) + 2CO_2 + 2H_2O = Al_2Si_4O_{10}(OH)_2(s)$ $+ 2Na^+ + 2HCO_3^- + 2SiO_2$	0.14	—	—	—	—	0.14	0.14	0.14 Feldspar
$MgCa(CO_3)_2(s) + 4CO_2 = Mg^{2+} + Ca^{2+} + 4HCO_3^-$	0.56			0.14	0.14			0.14 Dolomite
$CaCO_3(s) + CO_2 + H_2O = Ca^{2+} + 2HCO_3^-$	0.44			0.22				0.22 $CaCO_3$
$\{CaSO_4 \cdot 2H_2O\}(s) = Ca^{2+} + SO_4^{2-} + 2H_2O$		0.19		0.19				0.19 Gypsum
$\{NaCl\} = Na^+ + Cl^-$			0.13			0.13		0.13 NaCl
Addition of rain water	0.04	0.01	0.10	0.02	0.01	0.09	0.01	Rain
Final composition (mmol/liter)	1.18	0.20	0.23	0.57	0.15	0.36	0.15	

[a]Dissolved SiO_2 is present as H_4SiO_4.

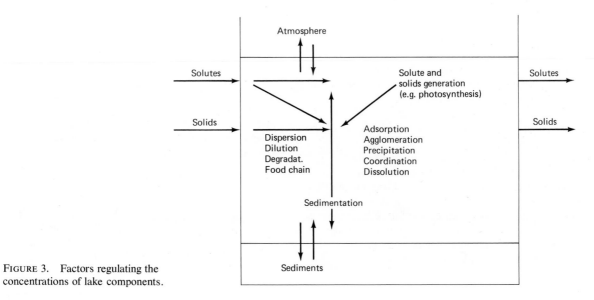

FIGURE 3.   Factors regulating the concentrations of lake components.

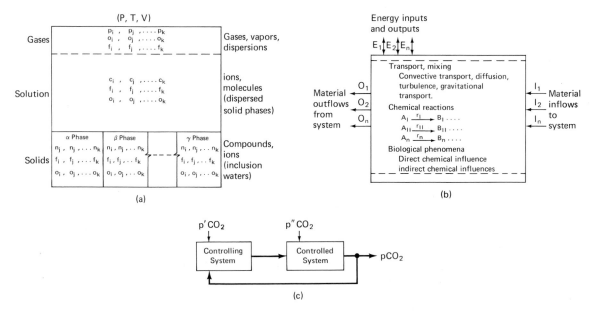

FIGURE 4.   Generalized models for the description of natural water systems. (a) Equilibrium models establish boundary conditions toward which aquatic environments must proceed, however slowly. (b) Steady-state model permits the description of the time-invariant conditions of dynamic and open systems. (c) Living systems and ecosystems may be controlled by negative feedback (homeostasis).

all kinds of systems regions or environments where equilibrium is approached, even though gradients exist throughout the systems as a whole. When the residence time is sufficiently large relative to the appropriate time scale of the reaction, the time invariant condition of the well-mixed volume considered approaches chemical equilibrium.

If on the other hand the reaction rate is slow in comparison to the residence time of the water, the concentrations of chemical species in lake waters are also controlled by the rates of inputs and removals of dissolved and particulate matter (Figure 3; see also Chapter 11).

Mass balance models

Mass balance models provide a flow diagram and thus a dynamic description of a lake system. The various inputs of natural materials or of pollutants from the catchment area by rivers and drainage and from the atmosphere are compared with the fluxes out of the lake (into sediments, into outflowing river, or into the atmosphere). Figure 5 gives a simple example.

In a *steady state,* input of a chemical species to a lake is balanced by its removal, and its concentration in lake water remains time invariant. Under simplifying assumptions (one-box model of a well-mixed lake, evaporation balanced by rain, no removal by spray), the steady-state chemical balance can be formulated (Vollenweider, 1969; Lerman, 1974) as

$$J = fJ - \frac{Q}{V} C \qquad (5)$$

where J is the rate of input of a chemical species into the lake (e.g., g/m³ of lake water/year); f is a fractional value and fJ is the fraction of input that is being removed from water into sediments (or into a standing crop of biota); C is the concentration in lake water (g/m³); $\frac{Q}{V} C$ represents the rate of removal by outflow from a hypothetically well-mixed lake; Q is the outflow rate from the lake per unit of time (m³ yr⁻¹); and V is the lake volume (m³). Because V/Q is the residence time of the water in the lake, τ (years), the steady-state concentration is

$$C = J(1 - f)\tau. \qquad (5)$$

Thus, as shown by Lerman and others, the rate of input (J) and water residence time (τ) determine the steady-state concentration of a chemical species in the lake. If the species is involved in other removal processes (sedimentation or biological uptake), f must also be known. Within the scope of a steady-state model, each element or compound, E, is characterized by its residence time τ_E:

$$\tau_E = \frac{C V}{J} = \frac{\text{total mass } E \text{ in lake}}{\text{rate of input of } E}. \qquad (6)$$

In lakes it is often convenient to define a relative residence time τ_{Rel} (Stumm and Morgan, 1970):

$$\tau_{Rel} = \tau_E/\tau = 1 - f. \qquad (7)$$

The relative residence time of an element or compound decreases with increasing reactivity (incorpora-

TABLE 4.   Equilibrium Models for the Chemical Composition of Natural Waters[a]

Phases	Composition (concentration given as $-\log M$)							
	H^+	HCO^-	Ca^{2+}	Mg^{2+}	H_4SiO_4	Na^+	K^+	P_{total}
Aqueous solution, calcite[b]	9.9	4.1	3.9	—	—	—	—	
Aqueous solution, calcite, $CO_2(g)$	8.3	3.0	3.3	—	—	—	—	
Aqueous solution, calcite, $CO_2(g)$, kaolinite, Ca-montmorillonite	8.3	3.0	3.3		3.6			
Aqueous solution, calcite, $CO_2(g)$, dolomite, apatite, calcite, kaolinite, gibbsite, Na-feldspar, K-feldspar[c]	8.32	2.85	3.00	3.45	4.8	4.2	5.3	7.14

[a]Variables: $t = 25°C$; $p_{CO_2} = 3 \times 10^{-4}$ atm.
[b]$CO_2(aq)$ and H_2CO_3 are treated as nonvolatile acids; in order to define the system, it is assumed that $[Ca^{2+}] = \Sigma[CO_2]$ ($\Sigma[CO_2] = [CO_2(aq)] + [H_2CO_3] + [HCO_3^-] + [CO_3^{2-}]$); total pressure = 1 atm.
[c]Kramer's equilibrium model for the composition of the Great Lakes (Kramer, 1967). The following condition is imposed on the model: $[Cl^-] + 2[SO_4^{2-}] = 1.3 \times 10^{-3}\ M$; $t = 5°C$.

tion into biomass, suspended solids, or precipitates). Most substances entering lakes are nonconservative (i.e., have a residence time different from that of water). All these substances that are strongly adsorbed on suspended matter or become incorporated into settling biomass have small relative residence times. The residence time of a substance or element is regulated by the loss through the outlet and by the loss

through nonhydrological processes of elimination (e.g., sedimentation):

$$\frac{1}{\tau_E} = \frac{1}{\tau_W} + \frac{1}{\tau_S} \qquad (8)$$

where τ_S is the residence time for the nonconservative pathway (e.g., the residence time of the settling constituent) and τ_w is the residence time of water. Rela-

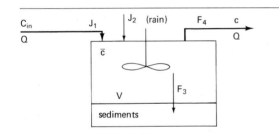

J_i = inputs [kg year^{-1}]
F_i = fluxes out [kg year^{-1}]
V = volume of lake [m^3]
Q = inflow or outflow rate [m^3 year^{-1}]
c = concentration of soluble species
C = conc. of species in suspended matter [mg kg^{-1}]
D = distribution coefficient = $\dfrac{C}{c}$ [m^3 kg^{-1}]
P = sedimentation rate [kg year^{-1}]

Mass balance:
$J_1 = Q\,C_{in}$; $F_3 = CP = DcP$
$F_4 = Q\,C$
$v\dfrac{dc}{dt} = J_1 + J_2 - F_3 - F_4$

$\dfrac{dc}{dt} = \dfrac{Qc_i + J_2}{V} - C\left(\dfrac{Q + DP}{V}\right)$

$c(t) = C_o \exp\left(-\dfrac{Q+DP}{V}\,t\right) + \dfrac{QC_{in} + J_2}{Q + DP}\left[1 - \exp\left(-\dfrac{Q+DP}{V}\,t\right)\right]$

At steady state:
$t \rightarrow \infty\ c(t) = \bar{c}$

$\bar{c} = \dfrac{QC_{in} + J_2}{Q + DP}$

Comparison with field data in Greifensee
($V = 1.25 \times 10^8$ m^3, $Q = 8.9 \times 10^7$ m^{3}year^{-1}, $P = 3.7 \times 10^7$ kg year^{-1})

Metal	C_{in} mg m^{-3}	D kg^{-1}	J_2 (rain) kg year^{-1}	$\bar{c}$ calculated mg m^{-3}	$\bar{c}$ measured mg m^{-3}
Zn	19.8	25	1316	3.1	4.1
Pb	3.2	120	1376	0.4	0.60
Cu	3.8	35	224	0.4	1.0
Cd	0.1	65	6	0.01	0.06

FIGURE 5.   Mass balance model exemplified for heavy metals in Greifensee. Data from Tschopp (1977).

tive residence times for Na^+ and Cl^- are very close to 1.0. Lerman and Weiler (1971) have determined that less than 0.5% of the input rates of Na^+ and Cl^- in the Great Lakes were removed into the sediments. The rates of removal of phosphorus to lake floor sediments are of the order of 25–50% of input load ($\tau_{Rel} = 0.5$–0.75) under aerobic conditions. ^{137}Cs and heavy metal ions also behave in a nonconservative way: they are strongly adsorbed on suspended materials and have residence times approaching those of suspended matter ($\tau_{Rel} \approx 0.10$–0.6). The flux of materials into and out of the sediments usually accounts for a significant fraction of the lake budget (Lerman and Brunskill, 1971; Lerman, 1974; Mortimer, 1971).

In most lakes, the rates of inputs have increased and consequently concentrations of many constituents are not time invariant. Nevertheless, steady-state models give useful limits for comparison purposes, i.e., concentrations that were obtained if the rate of input was kept constant for a time period of approximately $3\tau_E$. The shorter the residence time, the faster the system adjusts to steady state after the onset of a new constant input rate.

Interactions between organisms and abiotic environment

Organisms and their abiotic environment are interrelated and interact with each other. An understanding of this interrelationship is a prerequisite for an understanding of the factors that regulate the chemical composition of a lake and of the ways lake ecosystems are chemically perturbed. The biosphere often reacts very sensitively to a chemical perturbation; sometimes it mitigates and sometimes it amplifies the chemical impact.

Maintenance of life results from solar energy; in a lake, a small portion of the light energy is used in algal photosynthesis and becomes stored in the form of organic material. Some of this organic matter becomes oxidized, liberating energy in order to support the life processes of heterotrophic decomposer (bacteria, fungi) and consumer (animals) organisms. These latter organisms decompose the unstable products of photosynthesis through energy-yielding redox reactions. In a balanced ecological lake system, a mutual interaction between the activities of photosynthetic and heterotrophic organisms, a near stationary state between production and destruction of organic matter as well as between production and consumption of oxygen seems to be maintained (Figure 6).

$$CO_2 + 2H_2O$$
$$+ \text{ energy} \underset{\text{respiration}}{\overset{\text{photosynthesis}}{\rightleftharpoons}} CH_2O + O_2 \quad (9)$$

Because other nutrients participate in the reaction, a more involved equation may be used—on the basis of

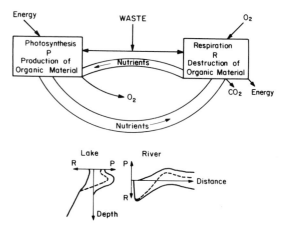

FIGURE 6.   Balance between photosynthesis and respiration. A disturbance of the P–R (photosynthesis–respiration) balance results from vertical (lakes) or longitudinal (rivers) separation of P and R organisms. An unbalance between P and R functions leads to pollutional effects of one kind or another: depletion of O_2 if $P<R$ or mass development of algae if production rates become larger than the rates of algal destruction by consumer and decomposer organisms ($R<P$).

the C, N, and P ratios in marine plankton—to characterize photosynthesis, P, and respiration, R, reactions in the aquatic environment:

$$106CO_2 + 16NO_3^- + HPO_4^{-2} + 122H_2O$$
$$+ 18H^+ \,(+ \text{ trace elements, energy})$$

$$P \updownarrow R$$

$$C_{106}H_{263}O_{110}N_{16}P_1 + 138O_2. \quad (10)$$
$$\text{algal protoplasma}$$

The balance between production and destruction of organic material in a lake can be characterized by

$$I + P \approx R + E$$

where I and E are import and export, respectively, of organic matter and P and R are the rate of photosynthetic production and heterotrophic respiration (rate of destruction of organic material). The flux of energy through the system is accompanied by cycles of nutrients and other elements. As does every ecosystem, a lake and its surroundings contain a biological community (primary producers, various trophic levels of decomposers and consumers) in which the flow of energy is reflected in the trophic structure and in material cycles. In a complex ecological community, all its members play their part in cycling nutrients; they are interlocked by various feedback loops.

The balance between photosynthesis and respiration is largely responsible for regulating the redox intensity of the lake waters. Photosynthesis may be conceived as a process producing localized centers of

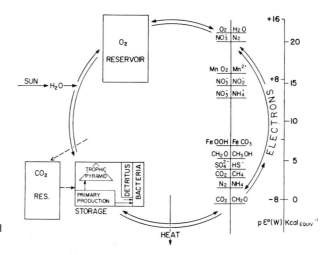

FIGURE 7. Photosynthesis and biochemical cycle.

highly negative $p\epsilon$ and a reservoir of oxygen (Figure 7) (Stumm and Stumm-Zollinger, 1971).

Redox processes and redox equilibria

Only a few elements—C, N, O, S, H, Fe, Mn—are predominant participants in aquatic redox processes. When comparisons are made between calculations for an equilibrium redox state and concentrations in the aquatic dynamic environment, the implicit assumptions are that the biological mediations are operating essentially in a *reversible* manner at each stage of the ongoing processes or that there is a metastable steady state that approximates the partial equilibrium state for the system under consideration. As shown in Figure 8, the nonphotosynthetic organisms tend to restore equilibrium by catalytically decomposing the unstable products of photosynthesis through energy-yielding redox reactions, thereby obtaining a source of energy for their metabolic needs.

Although conclusions regarding chemical dynamics may not be drawn from thermodynamic considerations, it appears that most relevant redox reactions, except possibly those involving N_2, are biologically mediated in the presence of suitable and generally ubiquitous microorganisms. A redox intensity scale in Figure 8 gives the sequence of reactions observed in an aqueous system at various $p\epsilon$ values (pH = 7). The various redox combinations are listed in Figure 8.

Although aqueous solutions do not contain free electrons, it is possible to define a (hypothetical) electron activity, $p\epsilon = -\log\{e^-\}$; the latter is related via the Nernst equation to the redox potential (oxidation intensity), E_H, of the system.

$$p\epsilon = \frac{E_H}{2.3RT/F} = \frac{E^0}{2.3RT/F} + \frac{1}{n}\log\frac{\Pi\{ox_i\}^{n_i}}{\Pi\{red_i\}^{n_i}}. \quad (11)$$

In an equilibrium system containing a number of redox couples of known total concentration, the activity of each redox species is a function of $p\epsilon$. Since

many redox processes are very slow in reaching equilibrium and do not couple with one another readily, it is possible to have several different apparent redox levels in the same local environment.

In natural waters redox reactions tend to occur in order of their thermodynamic possibility. In a lake, the organic products of photosynthesis settling into the deeper waters act as reductants (supplying electrons) leading to a sequential "titration" of the various

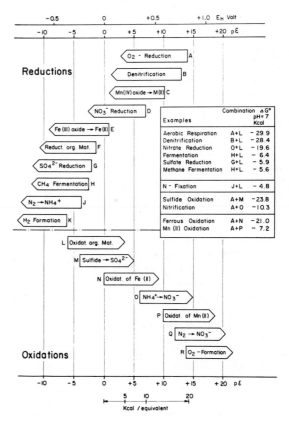

FIGURE 8. Biologically mediated redox processes calculated for pH = 7.

TABLE 5.   "Redox Titration" by Photosynthetically Produced Organic Matter (Settling Biological Debris)[a]

Oxygen utilization (respiration)
$$\frac{1}{4}\,CH_2O + \frac{1}{4}\,O_2 = \frac{1}{4}\,CO_2 + \frac{1}{4}\,H_2O \tag{1}$$
Denitrification
$$\frac{1}{4}\,CH_2O + \frac{1}{5}\,NO_3^- + \frac{1}{5}\,H^+ = \frac{1}{4}\,CO_2 + \frac{1}{10}\,N_2 + \frac{1}{2}\,H_2O \tag{2}$$
Nitrate reduction
$$\frac{1}{4}\,CH_2O + \frac{1}{8}\,NO_3^- + \frac{1}{4}\,H^+ = \frac{1}{4}\,CO_2 + \frac{1}{8}\,NH_4^+ + \frac{1}{8}\,H_2O \tag{3}$$
Formation of soluble Mn(II) by reducing Mn(III,IV)-oxides
$$\frac{1}{4}\,CH_2O + \frac{1}{2}\,MnO_2(c) + H^+ = \frac{1}{4}\,CO_2 + \frac{1}{2}\,Mn^{+2} + \frac{1}{8}\,H_2O \tag{4}$$
Fermentation reactions
$$\frac{3}{4}\,CH_2O + \frac{1}{4}\,H_2O = \frac{1}{4}\,CO_2 + \frac{1}{2}\,CH_3OH \tag{5}$$
Formation of soluble Fe(II) by reducing Fe(III)-oxides
$$\frac{1}{4}\,CH_2O + FeOOH(c) + 2\,H^+ = \frac{1}{4}\,CO_2 + \frac{7}{4}\,H_2O + Fe^{+2} \tag{6}$$
Sulfate reduction
$$\frac{1}{4}\,CH_2O + \frac{1}{8}\,SO_4^{2-} + \frac{1}{8}\,H^+ = \frac{1}{8}\,HS^- + \frac{1}{4}\,CO_2 + \frac{1}{4}\,H_2O \tag{7}$$
Methane formation
$$\frac{1}{4}\,CH_2O = \frac{1}{8}\,CH_4 + \frac{1}{8}\,CO_2 \tag{8}$$

[a]Sequence of processes leading to progressively lower redox intensity.

electron acceptors available in the deeper portions of the lake and its sediments (Table 5). The incipient reduction of oxygen is followed by reduction of NO_3^- and NO_2^-. Reduction of MnO_2 should occur at about the same $p\epsilon$ levels as that of NO_3^- reduction, followed by reduction of FeOOH(s) to Fe^{2+}. When sufficiently negative $p\epsilon$ levels have been reached, fermentation reactions and reduction of SO_4^{2-} and of CO_2 may occur. Typically, there is mediation (by different enzymes) of redox processes in both directions. The reaction $NO_3^- \rightarrow N_2$ is an exception, because no enzyme catalyzes the reverse reaction, the breaking of the strong bonding of the N_2 molecules. The fact that $N_2(g)$ has not been converted largely into NO_3^- indicates a lack of efficient biological mediation of the reverse reaction also, for the mediating catalysis must operate equally well for reactions in both directions. Denitrification may occur by an indirect mechanism such as reduction of NO_3^- to NO_2^- followed by reaction of NO_2^- with NH_4^+ to produce N_2 and H_2O. Reaction path calculation has been used by Thorstenson (1970) to predict the compositional changes in the aqueous phase as a function of the organic matter decomposed.

Figure 8 gives free energy values (ΔG^0 at pH = 7) for the important biologically mediated redox processes, a proportion of which is exploited by the organisms for synthesis of new cells. A yield proportional to ΔG of the redox reaction is found experimentally (McCarty, 1971).

For the reactions which include O_2, ΔG is calculated assuming that the four electron reductions of O_2 to H_2O ($O_2 + 4H^+ + 4e^- \rightleftarrows 2H_2O$; log K = 83.1 [25°C]) are the "operative" redox couple in biologically mediated redox reactions and not the two electron reductions ($O_2 + 2H^+ + 2e \rightleftarrows H_2O_2$; log K = 23.1 [25°C]) which often occur as a rate determining step in the reduction of O_2 in an electrodic system (Stumm, 1977).

As the stoichiometric equation [Eq. (10)] predicts, phosphate and nitrate are eliminated from the water in a fixed ratio during photosynthesis. During algal respiration, and as a result of mineralization of algae, occurring predominantly in the deeper water layers and in the sediments, phosphate and nitrate are liberated in the same fixed ratio. The influence of photosynthetic and respiratory processes on the composition of lake waters is frequently reflected in a correlation of concentration of soluble phosphate and nitrate (Figure 9). In lakes, ratios may differ from those of Eq. (10). Because oxygen participates in this reaction, a similar correlation exists between phosphate or nitrate and oxygen. As shown subsequently, a complex series of interrelated biological, geological, and physical long-term processes lead to the evolution of lakes with constant proportions of mean annual C:N:P concentrations (cf. Figure 13).

Need for chemical speciation

Historically, limnologists were primarily interested in determining collective parameters and the elemental composition. This information alone is often inadequate for identifying the mechanisms that control the composition of natural waters and for understanding their perturbation. The limnologist needs to know the form of the species in which the element is present, in order to gain some insight into the role of the elements in the sedimentary cycles, into the physical chemistry of lake waters, and into the nature of pollutant interactions as well as into the complexities of the biochemical cycle. It is especially important to recall that biological availability and physiological and toxicological effects depend on the specific structure of the individual substances; e.g., $CuCO_3(aq)$ affects the growth of algae in a different way than $Cu^{2+}(aq)$; organic isomers usually differ in their toxicologic effects.

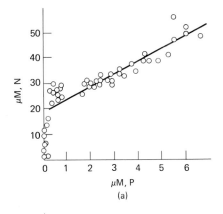

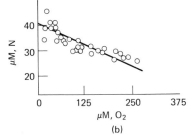

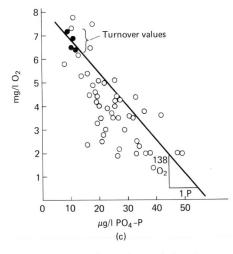

FIGURE 9. Stoichiometric correlations between concentrations of nitrate, phosphate, and oxygen. (a) and (b) Lake Zürich (from Stumm and Morgan, 1970), and (c) Lake Gersau (from Ambühl, 1975). For (b) and (c) results only from the deeper water layers were considered.

Interaction of organic substances with trace metals. Despite the biochemical importance of many of the trace metals, the chemical forms of these compounds are seldom known. Complexation by organic material needs to be considered in addition to inorganic complex formation. Thermodynamically one may approach the problem by extending the chemical model for the equilibrium distribution of the major species to minor components (Morel and Morgan, 1972; Stumm and Brauner, 1975).

In lakes, one typically encounters organic matter corresponding to 1–10 mg/liter of total organic carbon. This material is present in three categories:

(1) Low molecular weight organic substances in true solutions. Individual organic substances are usually present in concentrations seldom exceeding 10^{-6} M. Wuhrmann and Riniker (Wuhrmann, 1976) have determined individual amino acids, sugars, and a few carboxylic acids in Lake Zurich water. Amino acids are typically present in concentrations between 10^{-10} M (methionine) and $1-4 \times 10^{-8}$ M (valine, alanine, glycine, lysine, serine). Acetate and pyruvate are also present in the concentration range of $1-3 \times 10^{-8}$ M.

(2) Polymeric organic substances which contain a sufficient number of hydrophilic functional groups ($-COO^-$, $-NH_2$, $-R_2NH$, $-RS^-$, ROH, RO^-) remain in solution despite their molecular size. Polypeptides, certain lipids, polysaccharides, and many of the substances classified as humic acids, fulvic acids, and Gelbstoffe belong to this category.

(3) Colloidal organic material either as high-molecular weight compounds or as organic substances sorbed or chemically bound to inorganic colloids. We know very little about the composition and constitution of these substances. Many inorganic colloids are coated with organic substances.

All three categories of organic material may interact chemically with and play important roles in the transformations of metal ions. Although some exudation products of biota may have special steric arrangements or donor atoms which make them relatively selective toward individual trace metals, most organic matter may not be present in the form of selective complex formers; the organic functional groups compete for association with inorganic cations and protons; cations and protons can satisfy their coordinative requirements with inorganic anions including OH^- as well as with organic ligands. Most organic ligands in natural waters appear to have, at best, complex forming tendencies similar to acetate, citrate, amino acids, phthalate, salicylate, and quinoline-carboxylate. An inspection of *Stability Constants* (Sillén and Martell, 1964, 1971) shows that these classes of compounds are able to form moderately stable complexes with most multivalent cations.

In order to gain some insight into the interaction of common organic material with metal ions, we hypothetically "titrate" a representative inorganic solution of lake water with organic material. Total concentrations of trace metals are taken to be similar to those typically reported for lake waters. Organic matter of the approximate composition $C_9H_{11}O_8N$ is made up by mixing equal molar quantities of acetic acid, citric acid, tartaric acid, glycine, glutamic acid, and phthalic acid, thus containing these functional groups (hydroxy, carboxylic, amino) which are believed to be principally responsible for the complex and chelate-forming properties of organic seawater constituents. A few representative results of the calculations are given in Table 6. [This model is patterned after that described in detail by Stumm and Brauner (1975) for sea water. For help with the calculation we are indebted to John C. Westall.]

Some significant implications can be derived from the results of these calculations as displayed in Table 6. (1) "Conventional" complex forming organic ligands at concentrations much larger than those typically encountered in lake waters affect the distribution of many metal species to limited extent only. (2) In the case of Cu(II) however, organic ligands are able to complex the Cu(II) atom even at relatively low concentrations. Because algal growth is strongly dependent upon free Cu^{2+} (Sunda and Guillard, 1976), organic matter, either incipiently present in the lake or formed from exudates of algae, may indeed exert a pronounced influence on the physiological response of algae by regulating most sensitively free Cu. Furthermore, Cu(II), by tying up organic ligands, may also coregulate the chelation of other metals. Metals and ligands form a complicated network of interactions; because each metal ties with all ligands and each ligand ties with all metals, the free concentrations of metal ions as well as the distribution of any metal or ligand depend on the total concentrations of the other constituents of the system (Morel *et al.*, 1974).

Regulation of metal ions by interactions at the solid–solution interface.   In lakes and rivers, heavy metals are removed from solutions and rapidly transferred into the sediments although these solutions are undersaturated with respect to possible solid metal ion precipitates. Most surfaces of suspended matter—either hydrous oxides of Al(III), Si(IV), Fe(III), Mn(III, IV), or organic matter, or oxides coated with organic matter, contain inorganic surface groups, $\equiv$MeOH, or functional organic groups, $\equiv$ROH, that contain O-donor atoms capable of forming surface complexes with metal cations (Hohl and Stumm, 1976; Stumm *et al.*, 1976; Schindler *et al.*, 1976; Schindler, 1976; Murray, 1975), e.g.,

$$\equiv ROH + Me^{2+} \rightleftarrows \equiv ROMe^+ + H^+ \qquad (12)$$
$$2\equiv ROH + Me^{2+} \rightleftarrows (\equiv RO)_2Me + 2H^+. \qquad (13)$$

As these equations suggest, the binding of metal ions to the surfaces is strongly pH dependent, i.e., the pH dependence can be explained with the basicity of the RO^- group and the affinity of this group to the metal ion. Figure 10 gives the pH-dependence of "adsorption" of some metal ions on amorphous silica (Schindler *et al.*, 1976). A few distribution coefficients, experimentally determined are given in Figure 5.

Because of the strong tendency of heavy metal ions to bind to surfaces of suspended matter, the settling material acts like an efficient conveyor belt scavenging heavy metal ions and transporting them into the sediments (Figures 5, 19). It is for this reason that sediments give excellent memory storage of the historic development of the loading of a lake with metals.

TABLE 6.   Equilibrium Model: Effect of Complex Formation on Speciation of Metals[a]

Inorganic fresh water, pH = 7.0, 25°C; free ligands: p_{SO_4}, 3.4; p_{HCO_3} 3.1; p_{CO_3}, 6.1; p_{Cl}, 3.3 | *Inorganic fresh water + 7 × 10⁻⁶ mol/liter of each of the following organic ligands: acetate, citrate, tartrate, glycinate, glutamate, and phtalate, corresponding to 2.3 mg/liter of soluble organic carbon.[b] Inorganic ligands remain unchanged*

M	M_T	Free M	Major species		Free M	Major inorg. species		Free ligand	Organic complexes[c]					
									Acet. 7.55	Citr. 6.91	Tartr. 8.02	Glyc. 5.16	Glut. 5.16	Phtal. 6.99
Ca	2.7	2.72	CaHCO₃	4.6	2.72	CaHCO₃	4.6		7.0	5.2	5.6	9.1	8.6	5.7
Mg	3.7	3.72	MgSO₄	5.1	3.72	MgSO₄	5.1		8.0	7.0	7.1	8.0	9.1	—[e]
Fe(III)	Satd[d]	17.70	Fe(OH)₂	8.7	17.73	Fe(OH)₂	8.7		19.0	7.2	—	15.1	—	—
Mn(II)	7.0	7.04	MnSO₄	8.5	7.04	MnSO₄	8.5		11.3	9.7	—	11.5	11.1	—
Cu(II)	7.0	7.46	CuCO₃	7.2	9.93	CuCO₃	9.7		13.1	7.0	11.3	9.4	9.4	11.4
Zn(II)	6.7	6.72	ZnSO₄	8.2	6.72	ZnSO₄	8.2		10.3	10.5	8.9	9.6	8.6	9.1
Cd(II)	7.7	7.73	CdSO₄	9.2	7.76	CdSO₄	9.2		11.5	9.2	9.6	11.5	10.3	9.7
Pb(II)	7.0	8.02	PbCO₃	7.1	8.04	PbCO₃	7.1		11.0	8.9	8.8	10.1	—	9.2
Ag(I)	9.0	9.19	AgCl	9.5	9.19	AgCl	9.5		13.8	17.5	—	13.3	—	—
								%[f]	1.5	98.2	35.2	0.3	0.4	29.0

[a]All concentrations are given as $-\log(mol/liter)$; charges of species are omitted.
[b]Organic matter of approx. composition $C_{13}H_{17}O_{12}N$.
[c]The concentrations refer to the sum of all complexes, e.g., CuCit, CuHCit, CuCit₂.
[d]Solution is in equilibrium with Fe(OH)₃(s).
[e]No stability constants are available for such complexes.
[f]Percentage of total ligand bound to metal ions.

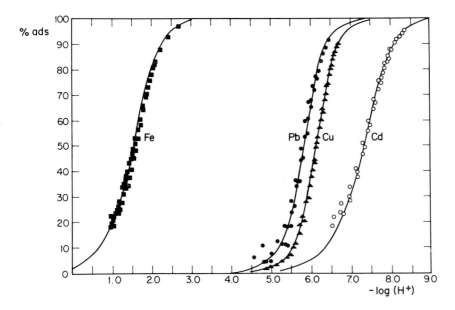

FIGURE 10.   Adsorption of metal ions on amorphous silica as a function of -log (H^+). From Schindler *et al.* (1976).

Disturbance of balance between photosynthesis and respiration

Sensitivity of aquatic systems to chemical impact

In a lake ecosystem, a large number of components interact in a variety of complex ways. It is this interaction that makes it so dangerous to study in a fragmental way an isolated part of the lake ecosystem. In order to examine *the sensitivity* of lake systems to chemical perturbation, we need to know which fluxes or which interconnections are particularly significant.

In an aquatic ecosystem, all its members are interlocked by various feedback loops (homeostasis) and thus adapted for mutual advantage. In a qualitative sense we may consider Le Chatelier's principle which may be expressed as follows: A system tends to change so as to minimize the external stress.

Buffer intensities.   For equilibrium systems, buffer intensities, buffer factors, and interaction intensities have been put forward (Morel *et al.*, 1973) as sensitivity parameters for each component i in the face of variation in any other components j: $\delta' = \delta pX_i/\delta\Sigma X_j$. It can be shown that the buffer intensities of heterogeneous systems (water + sediment phases + atmosphere) are much larger than those of a homogeneous solution (Stumm and Morgan, 1970; Stumm and Stumm-Zollinger, 1971). For example, the buffer intensity, $\beta = dC_B/d\text{pH}$ (C_B = concentration of strong base) at pH = 8 of a Na-feldspar–kaolinite and of a CaCO$_3$(c)–CO$_2$ (3×10^{-4} atm) suspension are, respectively, 3000 and 30 times greater than that of a 10^{-3} M HCO$_3^-$ solution. The simple equilibrium system CaCO$_3$, H$_2$O, CO$_2$ with three phases has an infinite buffer intensity with regard to dilution (H$_2$O) and to the addition of the base Ca(OH)$_2$ or the acid CO$_2$; i.e., the system (as long as the three phases coexist in equilibrium) resists attempts to perturbation caused by the addition (or withdrawal) of components of the system. According to the phase rule, any increase in the number of components and phases, i.e., increasing the chemical diversity, makes the hypothetical equilibrium system more resistant toward a larger number of external influences imposed on the system and hence less subject to perturbations resulting from external stresses.

Homeostasis.   Anyone who tries to regulate a chemical reaction system by a multitude of valves or switches soon becomes frustrated with the instability of the experimental system and appreciative of automatic control devices (servo systems). Feedback is an essential feature of such a control system (Figure 4c).

The same kind of cybernetic mechanism prevails at the level of the individual organism as well as in groups of organisms and in entire ecological systems. Because of the involved network of checks and balances and the complicated food web, each species has multiple relationships with other species in the community. Even in a moderately complex network of species and nutrients the effects of a change in any pathway will spread through the system and feedback on the variables initially involved in ways quite different from the first one-step effects (Lane and Levins, 1977). The word "homeostatic" has been used to indicate constancy maintained by negative feedback. A living species adapts to diverse and various environments by two methods: genetic specialization and adaptive plasticity of the phenotype (Dobzhansky, 1955). This latter type of adaptation, whereby a species adjusts successfully to a spectrum of environments, occurs by homeostatic mode. Information concerning the effects of an organism's own actions on a variable of the system is perceived and fed back to the organism, thereby altering its subsequent performance. Population homeostasis requires a similar feedback of information on whether the system is in balance and, if not, how far it is away from the balance point (Stumm and Stumm-Zollinger, 1971).

Comparison between terrestrial and aquatic ecosystems. Terrestrial and aquatic ecosystems differ in the organization of their food chain. Terrestrial ecosystems which have productivities similar to aquatic systems typically contain a large biomass with only few trophic levels. Aquatic systems on the other hand are characterized by a relatively small biomass and a more complicated foodweb. Plant biomass dominates on land, while in lake waters animal biomass is of nearly similar magnitude as plant biomass. Primary production is consumed to a much larger extent in aquatic systems than in terrestrial systems; in the latter most of the biomass is decomposed by microorganisms. The delicate balance between photosynthetic and heterotrophic organisms is controlled to a large extent by herbivores (Steele, 1974); phytoplankton is being eaten as fast as it is produced. The products of photosynthesis become extremely diluted in aquatic systems.

The microbial transformations of a diversity of substrates distributed more or less uniformly through the water masses have to occur at concentrations that are typically at the level of below 10^{-6} M. The resorption of a substrate, V, by aquatic microorganisms (algae, bacteria)—typically by a mixed biocoenosis—occurs according to the equation

$$V = \frac{V_{max} S}{K_S + S} \qquad (14)$$

where V and V_{max} are, respectively, observed rate of resorption and maximum rate of resorption; S, concentration of substrate; and K_S, concentration of substrate where $V = \frac{1}{2} V_{max}$ (Hobbie and Wright, 1965; Jannasch, 1967; Stumm and Stumm-Zollinger, 1971; Wuhrmann, 1972).

The half-rate concentration, K_S, is for many substrates, such as orthophosphate, aminoacids, carbohydrates, below 10^{-9} M. The great capabilities of

physiological regulatory mechanisms are reflected within the great spectrum of ecological conditions (temperature, pressure, pH, redox intensity) under which bacteria and blue–green algae occur in the aquatic habitats (Wuhrmann, 1972).

Pollution by algal nutrients

As we have seen [Eq. (10)], solar energy recirculates C, N, P, S and other elements in approximately fixed proportions, thereby maintaining the biogeochemical parity of the biomass. The rates of cycling have to be synchronized to preserve the relative proportions representative of the biota (e.g., approximate atomic ratios of carbon, nitrogen, and phosphorus in aquatic systems as 106:16:1). Deviation from these requirements of ecosystem inputs and outputs, or the acceleration of the cycling of one element, may produce ecological maladjustments, globally, regionally, and locally.

The delicate balance between photosynthesis and respiration in a lake may be perturbed by adding either an excess of organic compounds or an excess of inorganic algal nutrients (e.g., phosphorus, nitrogen). In the first case, heterotrophic processes (decomposition) tend to dominate and dissolved oxygen may become exhausted (biochemical oxygen demand). In the second case, the immediate result is progressive accumulation of algae and plants. In either case the initial perturbation will be followed by a readjustment that ultimately will lead to a new balance.

In a stratified lake an excessive production of algae and oxygen in the upper layers ($P >> R$) may be paralleled by anaerobic conditions at the bottom ($R >> P$), because most of the photosynthetic oxygen escapes to the atmosphere and does not become available to the deeper water layers (Figure 6).

Limiting nutrients. For most inland waters phosphorus is the limiting nutrient in determining productivity. In some estuaries and in many marine coastal waters, nitrogen appears to be more limiting to algal growth than phosphorus. Deficiency in trace elements usually occurs only as a temporal or spatial transient.

Because of the complex functional interactions in lake ecosystems the limiting factor concept needs to be applied with caution: The limiting nutrient determines, in a stoichiometric sense [Eq. (10)], the maximum possible biomass standing crop.

Schindler (1974, 1977) used evidence from whole-lake experiments to show convincingly the phosphorus limitation in lakes; he also demonstrated that natural mechanisms compensate for deficiency of nitrogen and carbon in eutrophic lakes. In experimentally fertilized lakes, invasion of atmospheric carbon dioxide supplied enough carbon to support and maintain phy-

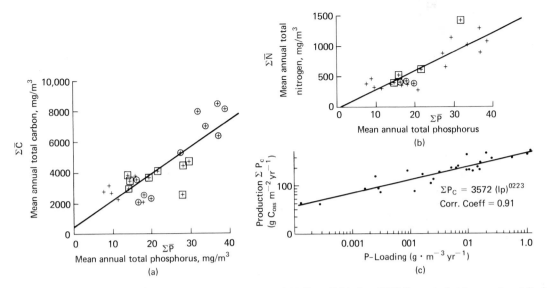

FIGURE 11.   Phosphorus limitations in lakes. Figures (a) and (b) (from Schindler, 1977) illustrate that in experimentally fertilized lakes of the Experimental Lakes area of the Fresh Water Institute in Winnipeg (Environment Canada), ratios of mean annual concentrations C/P and N/P tend to become constant. Figure (a) shows that the C-content increases as a consequence of P-addition to the lakes, while Figure (b) illustrates that the N-content of a lake increases when P-input is increased, even when little or no nitrogen is added with fertilizer. Every point represents the results of a different lake. For details see Schindler (1977). Figure (c) gives the primary production as a function of P-loading per unit volume for some North American and European lakes. From Imboden and Gächter (1975).

toplankton populations that are proportional to P-concentrations over a wide range of values. There was a strong tendency in every case for lakes to correct carbon deficiencies—obviously the rate of CO_2 supply from the atmosphere is sufficiently fast (Emerson, 1975), maintaining concentrations of both chlorophyll and carbon that were proportional to the P-concentration (Figure 11).

Schindler also demonstrated that biological mechanisms are in many cases capable of correcting algal deficiencies of nitrogen. While a sudden increase in the P-input may cause algae to exhibit symptoms of limitation by either N or C or both, there are long-term processes at work which appear to correct the deficiencies eventually, once again leaving phytoplankton growth proportional to the concentration of P. As Schindler (1977) points out, this "evolution" of appropriate nutrient ratios in fresh waters involves a complex series of interrelated biological, geological, and physical processes, including photosynthesis, the se-

lection of species of algae that can fix atmospheric nitrogen, alkalinity, nutrient supplies and concentrations, rates of water renewal, and turbulence. Various authors have observed shifts in algal species with changing N/P ratios; low N/P ratios appear to favor N-fixing blue-green algae, whereas high N/P ratios, as they are achieved by controlling P-input by extensive waste treatment, cause a shift from the bloom of blue-green algae to forms that are less objectionable. Shapiro (1973) concludes that a lower pH (or increased CO_2) gives green algae a competitive advantage over blue-greens.

Table 7 illustrates the change in N/P ratios typically encountered in passing from the land to the sea. The data given and their comparison with the average ratio in phytoplankton illustrate plausibly that fresh waters typically receive an excess of N over that needed. Agricultural drainage contains relatively large concentrations of bound nitrogen because nitrogen is washed out more readily from fertilized soil than phosphorus.

TABLE 7.   Variation in N:P Ratios in Passing from the Land to the Sea

N:P (by atoms). Most commonly encountered values:

Municipal sewage	Inland waters	Coastal waters	Ocean	Phytoplankton
6–14	15–40	2–25	15	10–17

Change in ratio caused by:	Agricultural drainage	Denitrification	(N-fixation) P-sedimentation N in rain	

In estuaries denitrification is frequently encountered because NO_3-bearing waters may come into contact with organically enriched water layers; the N/P ratio can also be shifted by differences in the circulation rate of these two nutrients.

O_2 consumption in hypolimnion resulting from increased productivity. The deeper portions of a lake receive phosphorus in two forms: (1) the preformed P, i.e., the P that enters the deeper waters as such (or adsorbed on clays); (2) phosphorus in the form of biogenic debris. Most of the latter is being oxidized to form phosphate of oxidative origin, P_{ox}. For every atom of P of oxidative origin found, a stoichiometric equivalent of oxygen atoms—276 oxygen atoms per atom of P, or 140 g of oxygen per g of P [cf. Eq. (10)]—have been consumed. Accordingly, a flux of P_{ox} is paralleled by a flux of O_2 utilization, as indicated schematically in Figure 12. The tolerable phosphorus loading of a lake may be related to the hypolimnetic oxygen consumption. The annual P-loading per lake surface, L_t (mg of P m^{-2} $year^{-1}$), causes (under the simplifying assumption that all L_t becomes phosphorus of oxidative origin, P_{ox}), during the stagnation period, T_{st} (days), an approximate oxygen consumption, $\Delta[O_2]$ (mg m^{-3}), of the hypolimnion, assumed to be homogeneously mixed, of depth z_H (m) (Imboden, 1973):

$$\Delta[O_2] = 140 \frac{T_{st} L_t}{365 z_H}, \qquad (15)$$

Correspondingly, a maximum P-loading, L_{max}, could be estimated for a tolerable oxygen consumption, $\Delta[O_2]_{max}$:

$$L_{max} = \Delta[O_2]_{max} \cdot 7 \times 10^{-3} \cdot \frac{365}{T_{st}} z_H. \qquad (16)$$

Many complicating factors must not be overlooked. The simple stoichiometric relations may be too schematic; they may change from lake to lake.

The acceleration of the cycling of phosphorus

The mining of phosphate and its application in agriculture, industry, and the household have increased nearly exponentially over the last few decades (Figure 13). The flow of P from land to water has increased because of various technological measures (clearing land, deforestation, establishing monocultures, municipal waste disposal, and urban drainage); the consequences are reflected in the progressively increased concentrations of P in rivers and lakes (Figure 13a).

Chapra has generated a historical simulation from variables indicative of human development (population density, land use, etc.) which compares favorably with present measurements. The historical profiles

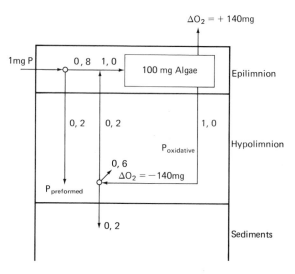

FIGURE 12.   Scheme on the limnological transformation of phosphorus in a stratified lake. One milligram of phosphorus introduced into a lake may lead to the synthesis of 100 mg of algae (dry mass) which upon mineralization causes an oxygen consumption in the hypolimnion of 140 mg of O_2.

(Figure 13b) indicate that the lakes have been subject to two major periods of increased phosphorus loads; first during the latter part of the nineteenth century, the time of change from forested to agricultural land use, and second, since 1945, with increased sewering, population growth, and the introduction of phosphate detergents.

Our present drainage systems for sewage, industrial wastes, and storm water runoff accelerate the transport of nutrients and other pollutants to the rivers and the sea; waste treatment plants are remarkably inefficient in mitigating this civilizational flux. Present-day aerobic biological waste treatment mineralizes substantial fractions of bacterially oxidizable organic substances but is usually not capable of eliminating more than 30 to 50% of phosphate components, because most municipal waters are nutritionally unbalanced (deficient in organic carbon) for a heterotrophic enrichment process. Phosphates may be removed in a supplementary chemical precipitation step with Al(III), Fe(III), or Ca^{2+} (Figure 14).

The calculation illustrated in Figure 12 indicates that the organic material that is introduced into the lake with domestic wastes (20–100 mg of organic matter/liter) may be small in comparison to the organic material that will be biosynthesized from fertilizing constituents (3–8 mg of P/liter which can yield 300–800 mg of organic matter/liter).

Phosphate exchange with sediments. The distribution of phosphate between the sediments and the overlying water is of considerable importance for the productivity of the lake. According to Hayes and Phillips

(1958), the "dynamic equilibrium" of phosphorus in a surface water may be represented by

phosphorus in aqueous phase
(small fraction of total)
$$\rightleftharpoons \text{phosphorus in solid phase.} \quad (17)$$
(large fraction of total)

Significant quantities of phosphate are usually found in the sediments of surface waters, especially in the sediments of eutrophic lakes and estuaries. Inorganic solid P phases may be found either by direct precipitation of phosphate with Ca, Al, and Fe compounds in the water column or by chemical reactions in the sediments. Clays may also act as scavengers for phosphate.

Heterogeneous solubility equilibria represent a buffer system for orthophosphate. As Figure 14 predicts, a solution in the pH range of natural waters and in equilibrium with the solid phases typically encountered in sediments maintains soluble orthophosphate ($H_2PO_4^-$, HPO_4^{-2}) at a molar concentration of $-\log P = 5.5 \pm 1.0$. The concentration of total soluble phosphorus, however, can be higher because of the presence of soluble organic phosphorus. This is illustrated by the transfer cycle:

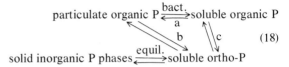

solid inorganic P phases $\underset{\text{equil.}}{\rightleftharpoons}$ soluble ortho-P

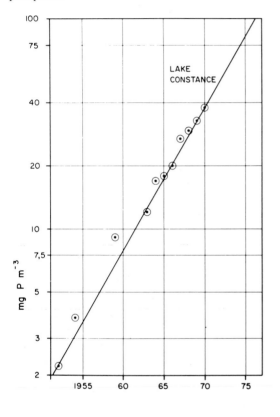

(a)

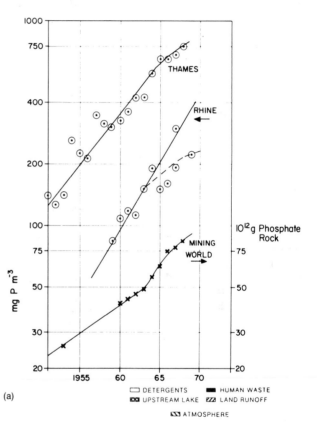

FIGURE 13.   Historical loadings of total phosphorus to some Great Lakes. From Chapra (1977). (a) Total P in Lake Constance during the circulation period in spring. Total P in the Rhine (border Netherlands/Germany) and in the Thames (at Salcham). (b) The mining of phosphate and the increase of its concentration in inland waters.

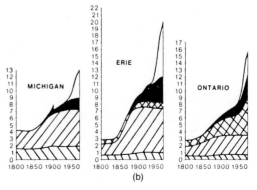

(b)

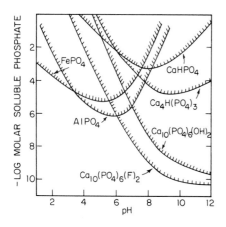

FIGURE 14.   Solubility diagrams for solid phosphate phases. The diagrams have been calculated by considering the solubility equilibria together with the appropriate acidity and complex formation constants. The calcium phosphate phases were calculated assuming that 1×10^{-3} M free Ca^{2+} is maintained and that F^- is controlled by $CaF_2(s)$. The aluminum and iron phosphate phases were computed assuming that Al^{3+} and Fe^{3+} are controlled by the respective hydroxide solids.

While the concentration of soluble inorganic phosphate remains defined by the solubility equilibrium, the turnover rates of reactions a and c determine the concentration of soluble organic P; that is, by incorporating phosphorus into organic compounds that do not participate directly in the solubility equilibria with solid phases, bacteria tend to increase the concentration of soluble P. The buffering action of the sediments prevents the accumulation of excess quantities of phosphorus readily available for assimilation in the overlying waters, and supplies phosphorus to the water when it becomes depleted.

In an aerobic lake P is retained much more efficiently than in an anaerobic lake. Most likely the iron(III) oxides in the sediments provide negative feedback control in regulating the P-concentrations in the lake water. As soon as a lake turns anaerobic and reducing conditions develop at the sediment–water boundary, the sediments release P to the overlying waters (positive feedback control). Williams *et al.* (1976) have shown that inorganic phosphorus not associated with apatite was possibly associated with amorphous hydrated ferric oxide in the oxidized microzone, but was present as vivianite ($Fe_3(PO_4)_2 \cdot 8H_2O$) and possibly other forms in the reduced zone.

Cores from Lake Erie sediments show (Williams *et al.*, 1976) that detrital apatite–phosphorus input has been approximately constant over the last few hundred years relative to the total sedimentation rate. Apatite is not a significant source of soluble phosphorus for Lake Erie. By contrast, rate of sedimentation of non-apatite inorganic phosphorus and organic phos-

phorus has steadily increased in accordance with increased loadings in recent years of the source material, namely P of anthropogenic origin. It was concluded that the sediments of Lake Erie contain sufficient P-retaining sites to prevent major remobilization of phosphate under any conceivable condition provided the overlying water remains oxygenated.

Phosphorus models of lake eutrophication

Empirical models.   Vollenweider (1968) related external sources of nutrients such as natural and agricultural runoff and municipal and industrial contributions to the enrichment of lakes. He has shown convincingly on the basis of data of 20 lakes that a valid correlation can be established between areal limiting nutrient loading (g m^{-2} yr^{-1}) and mean lake depth on one hand and the degree of enrichment on the other (Figure 15a). The demarcation line indicated in Figure 15 gives a relevant reference value on permissive P-loadings. Numerous models in which productivity is related to certain lake variables have been reviewed by Shannon and Brezonik (1972).

Source functions.   Obviously the quantity of nutrients introduced into a surface water from a given drainage area is dependent on density of population and livestock, on the methods and intensity of fertilization, on the type of cultivation (e.g., forests, grassland, cropland), on the pedological characteristics of the soil, on topography, and on the type of waste treatment system involved. It has been expressed by Imboden and Gächter (1975) as

$$N = A_D[(1 - a)C + a \cdot n + p \cdot s(1 - \eta)] \quad (19)$$

where N is total nutrient supply to the lake; A_D, area of the drainage basin without lake surface area; a, the fraction of noncultivated land within A_D (forests, rocks, and urban areas); C and n are the areal nutrient export from cultivated and noncultivated land, respectively; p, the population density; s, the per caput supply to the sewer system; and η, the removal efficiency of the waste treatment plant for the specific nutrient under discussion. Absolute values for these parameters have been estimated by Gächter and Furrer (1972) for European conditions and by Chapra (1977) (phosphorus only) for the Great Lakes area (Table 8).

Conceptual models.   Conceptual models attempt to explain interactions between different system components and thus are potentially capable of providing a sensitivity analysis and insight into the dynamics of the response of the system. Vollenweider (1975) has summarized one-box nutrient mass balance models. More refined models have considered (1) physical partitioning in lakes (e.g., division into epilimnion and

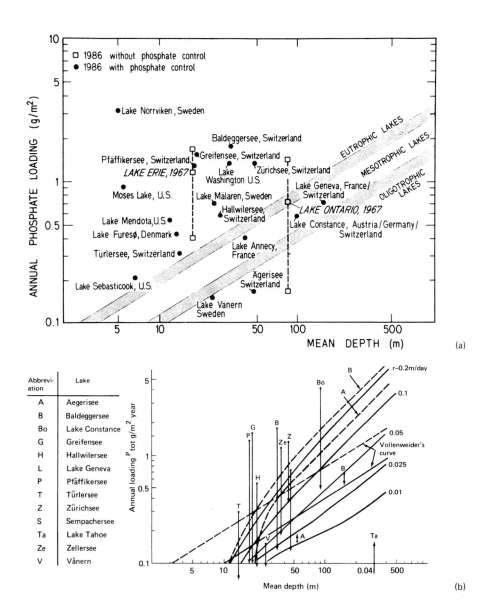

FIGURE 15.   Critical phosphorus loading as a function of depth. (a) From Vollenweider (1969). The loading given for the various lakes is based on information available in 1967. For most of these lakes, the loading has increased markedly within the last years. (b) After Imboden (1974). Tolerable annual phosphorus loading per lake area. $L_{t.max}$ as a function of mean depth z for different hydraulic loading factors r.

hypolimnion or into trophogenic and tropholytic zones) and (2) chemical–biological transformations (e.g., uptake of nutrients by biota and its mineralization).

Imboden (1973, 1974) presented a two-box model in which the total phosphorus concentration is separated into two components, the soluble P and the particulate P. Rates of mineralization and of photosynthesis were represented by first order rate laws. The model results in a system of four coupled differential equations because solvable numerical expressions can be derived for $d[P]_{soluble}/dt$ and $d[P]_{part}/dt$ in the epilimnetic as well as hypolimnic compartment. For example the variation of $d[P]_{soluble}/dt$ in the epilimnion is given by

$$d[P]_{soluble}/dt = \text{lake input} - \text{lake output}$$
$$+ \text{transport gain from hypolimnion}$$
$$- \text{transport loss into hypolimnion}$$
$$+ \text{mineralization} - \text{photosynthesis.} \quad (20)$$

The model estimates the mean hypolimnetic O_2 consumption as a function of P-loading; critical P-loads are given for varying mean lake depth and hydraulic loading. The model is able to describe a large class of lakes with a few common parameters (Figure 15B).

Imboden and Gächter (1977) refined this model in many regards, especially by (1) selecting primary production as a measure of the extent of eutrophy, and (2) by describing productivity as a nonlinear function of orthophosphate and particulate phosphate, and by considering lake morphometry, hydraulic loading, respiration rate, sedimentation, vertical eddy diffusion, depth of thermoclines, and exchange of P at the sediment–water interface. Many lake-specific parameters are needed in this model. Application of the model to specific lakes shows a good agreement between observation and calculation of the P-variation as a function of time and depth (Figure 16) and can be used to predict the effectiveness of different eutrophication control measures such as reduction of P-loading, discharge of hypolimnetic water, aeration of the hypolimnion, and destratification.

Impact of xenobiotic substances on aquatic ecosystems

The number of synthesized chemicals now totals 1.8 million and is growing at a rate of 250,000 new formulations annually, of which 300–500 reach the stage of commercial production (Gilette, 1974). Globally 100–200 million tons are produced. It is estimated that up to one-third of the total production of these synthetic organic chemicals finds its way into the environment.

Refractory substances

Many of these synthetic chemicals survive long enough in the environment—most often because they are not readily biodegradable—to accumulate in the water; in the biosphere, concentrations at higher trophic levels may often exceed the relatively low levels in solution. A compound has been defined as refractory in a particular environment if it maintains its identity in that environment for more than an arbitrary length of time, say for example 2 days (Wuhrmann, 1972). Not all refractory compounds found in the environment are of synthetic origin. Alexander (1975) has surveyed the long-lived natural organics

occurring in the environment including components of humus, kerogens, petroleum hydrocarbons, lignins, tannins, and the like. Many substances are altered readily to the extent that they lose their original structural entity, but the metabolites so formed are non- or slowly degradable. For example, the so-called biodegradable detergents yield refractory degradation intermediates that may persist much longer than the parent compound (Leidner et al., 1976). Because the half-rate concentrations for the uptake of organic substrates by microorganisms [Eq. (14)] lie in the range of 10^{-6} to 10^{-9} M, the rate of uptake and biodegradation at lower concentrations can be very slow.

Figure 17 gives gas chromatographic results of the analysis of volatile substances in water of Lake Zurich (Grob and Grob, 1973). Gasoline-hydrocarbons—introduced mostly through the atmosphere—are the most dominant substances. The efficient washout of hydrocarbons from the atmosphere is evident from the analysis of the surface water collected immediately after a rain thunderstorm. Samples collected from a depth of 30 m contain gasoline-hydrocarbons at a concentration ca. 20 times smaller than in the surface layer. The comparison between samples of the surface water and those of the depth give some insight into the degradability of some of the organic substances. There are some substances (Nos. 4, 25, 48, 76, 98, 105) that are more concentrated in the deep water than in the surface water. The substances concentrated in the deep waters are with the exception of naphthalene all chloro compounds which are obviously remarkably persistent.

The tendency for accumulating refractory substances in the food chain is much larger in aquatic ecosystems than in terrestrial ecosystems. Biological uptake, lipophilic storage and biomagnification and adsorption tendency may be related to the n-octanol–water partition coefficient (Chiou et al., 1977)

$$K = a_o/a_w \cong c_o/c_w \qquad (21)$$

where a and c refer to activity and concentration, respectively: o and w refer to the octanol and water phase. Chiou et al. (1977) have shown that the octanol–water partition coefficient of a wide variety of chemicals is inversely related to the aqueous solubility

TABLE 8.   Estimated Coefficients for Eq. (19)

Coefficient	Morphology	Runoff (m year^{-1})	Nitrogen (kg of N km^{-2} year^{-1})	Phosphorus (kg of P km^{-2} year^{-1})
c	Steep slopes	1.0	1635	69
n	Steep slopes	1.0	82	0–4
c	Plain areas	0.6	2100	35
n	Plain areas	0.6	960	0–4
s			4.4[a]	1.1[a]
η			0.3–0.9	0.2–0.9

[a]Dimension of kg caput^{-1} yr^{-1}. From Imboden and Gächter (1975).

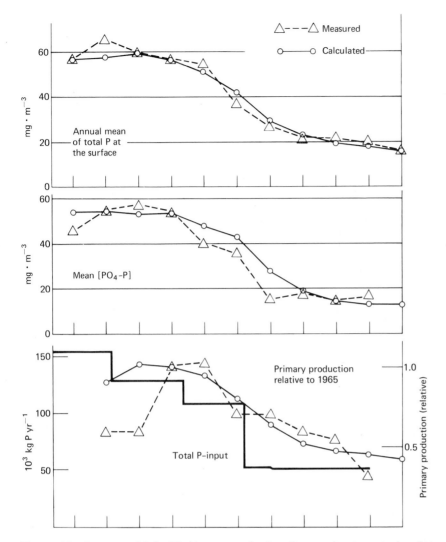

FIGURE 16.   Response of Lake Washington to reduction of sewage input: comparison between observation and model calculation. Values for observed primary production are taken from Edmondson (1972), Figure 4 by graphical integration. From Imboden and Gächter (1977).

and that a correlation is observed between the bioconcentration factors in rainbow trout and the aqueous solubility (Figure 18).

The environmental and toxicological evaluation of many of these refractory substances is extremely difficult; little is known about their toxicity or their harmlessness. The harmfulness of a substance depends on its interaction with organisms or entire communities. The intensity of this interaction depends on the specific structure and on the activity of the substance under consideration; but other factors such as temperature, turbulence, and presence of other substances are also important.

In evaluating the toxicity, we need to distinguish between (1) substances which endanger animals and man—i.e., impair their health—or poison water organisms. One often speaks of acute toxicity especially

if effects are observed within short time periods (≤ days); and (2) substances which affect primarily the organization and structure of aquatic ecosystems. In this interaction contaminants may impair the self-regulatory functions of the system even if no acutely damaging effects on individual organisms are observed.

Many xenobiotic substances are known to be hygienically objectionable in drinking water; their toxicological effects in man have been reviewed recently (Page *et al.* 1976; WHO, 1976).

Chemical ecology

Chemicals which exhibit neither acute nor chronic toxicity with regard to individual organisms may nevertheless disturb selectively the self-regulation of

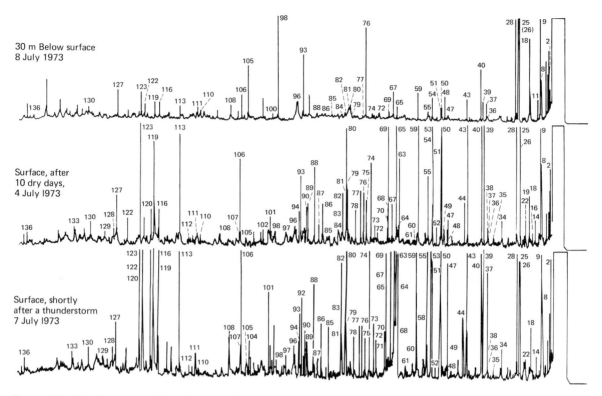

FIGURE 17.   Gas chromatographic analysis of volatile organic substances in water of Lake Zürich. From Grob and Grob (1973). Identified substances: 2, heptane; 8, octane; 9, benzene; 11, isononane; 14, carbon tetrachloride; 18, trichlorethylene; 19, nonane (alkane C_9); 22, isodecane; 25, tetrachlorethene; 26, toluene; 28, dimethyldisulfide; 34, isodecane; 35, aminomethylpyridine; 36, decane (alkane C_{10}); 37, ethylbenzene; 38, 2-methylpentanol-2; 39, 1,4-dimethylbenzene; 40, 1,3-dimethylbenzene; 43, 1,2-dimethylbenzene; 44, isoundecane; 47, propylbenzene; 48, chlorbenzene; 49, undecane (alkane C_{11}); 50, 4-ethyltoluene; 51, 3-ethyltoluene; 52, limonene; 53, cineol; 54, 1,3,5-trimethylbenzene; 55, 2-ethyltoluene; 59, 1,2,4-trimethylbenzene; 60, isopropyltoluene; 61, isododecane; 63, dimethyltrisulfide; 64, propyltoluene; 65, 1,2,3-trimethylbenzene; 67, isobutylbenzene; 68, dodecane (alkane C_{12}); 69, dimethylethylbenzene; 70, methylpropylbenzene; 72, dimethylethylbenzene; 73, methylisopropylbenzene; 74, methylisopropylbenzene; 75, C_4-benzene; 76, dichlorbenzene; 77, terpene $C_{10}H_{16}O$; 78, dimethylethylbenzene; 79, C_5-benzene; 80, 1,2,4,5-tetramethylbenzene; 81, C_5-benzene; 82, 1,2,3,5-tetramethylbenzene; 83, terpene $C_{10}H_{14}O$; 84, alkane C_{13}; 85, terpene $C_{10}H_{16}O$; 86, C_4-benzene; 87, terpene $C_{10}H_{14}O$; 88, campher; 89, C_5-benzene; 90, C_5-benzene; 93, 1-chlordecane (inner standard); 94, C_5-benzene; 97, alkane C_{14}; 98, trichlorbenzene; 101, cyclocitral; 102, caran-4-ol; 105, naphthaline; 106, alkane C_{15}; 107, 1-phenyl-2-thiapropane; 108, alkane C_{11}; 110, 2-methylnaphthaline; 111, alkane C_{16}; 112, 1-methylnaphthaline; 113, molecular weight 182; 116, dimethylnaphthaline; 119, alkane C_{17}; 120, diphenyl; 122, alkane C_{17}; 123, diphenylether; 127, tri-n-butylphosphate; 128, alkane C_{18}; 129, acenaphthene; 130, $tert$-butylacetophenon; 133, alkane C_{19}; 136, alkane C_{20}.

aquatic ecosystems. All organisms produce chemicals; some of these become dispersed in the aquatic environment, e.g., humic acids, hydrocarbons, alkaloids, terpenes, vitamines, hormones, antibiotics, and insecticides. These substances may cause various inter- and intraspecific effects (Table 9) (Sondheimer and Simeone, 1970). These substances are usually produced to enhance the dominance of some organisms in their competition with other organisms. Insecticides and antibiotics are excreted by organisms to protect them from other organisms. Thus, many substances exuded by algae or other organisms are chemotactically active. Behavioral patterns such as food finding, avoidance of injury, choosing of a habitat or

host, social communications, sexual behavior, and migration or recognition of territory appear to be controlled sensitively and specifically by chemical clues. The production and exudation of chemicals is of adaptive value for the species and the community (enhancement of information transfer).

Man too competes with other species for food; he enhances his dominance by destroying pathogens and pests. Industrial production of chemicals may be considered to be part of man's biological activity. There is however a significant difference in the tolerance toward interspecific chemicals between man and organisms. Man has learned in a long evolution to tolerate or to avoid most toxins of the organisms. Organisms

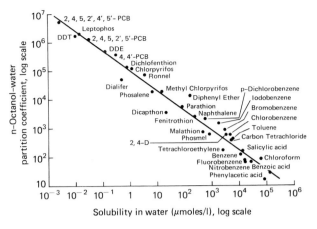
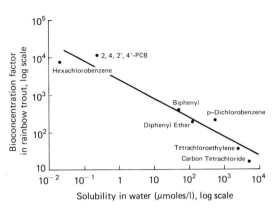

FIGURE 18.   Lipophility and bioaccumulation. Both n- octanol–water partition coefficient and bioconcentration factor in rainbow trout are inversely proportional to aqueous solubility. From Chiou *et al.* (1977).

and ecosystems on the other hand had little time to adapt to the synthetic chemicals of man.

Contaminants that differ structurally from these signaling substances (pheromones, allelochemical substances, telemediators) may blur chemotactical stimuli or may mislead by mimicking signals and thus cause sociological changes. They are also effective at very low concentrations. For example 10^{-10} M morpholine (10^{-5} mg/liter) in river water can influence the homing of salmons (Scholz *et al.*, 1976).

Figure 19 gives an example of how a community of organisms may become perturbed as a result of pollution (Patrick *et al.*, 1954); the frequency distribution of diatoms is modified: the number of species that occur with low frequency (few individuals per species) is reduced while few species become very abundant. As a consequence of the presence of many microhabitats in a "healthy" water, many species can survive. Because of interspecies competition, most species are present in low population density. Pollution destroys microhabitats, diminishes the chance of survival for some of the species, and thus in turn reduces the competition; the more tolerant species become more numerous.

This shift in the frequency distribution of species—also observed typically with other organisms—is a general consequence of the chemical impact on waters by substances nonindigenous to nature.

Aquatic ecosystems may be perturbed in different ways (immissions of degradable or nondegradable chemicals, effect of toxins, heat shocks, etc). Some of the gross changes in the communities resulting from many different types of disturbances are similar and predictable: the structure of the ecosystem is simplified, e.g., by elimination of some of the organisms either through toxic or inhibitory effects or through competitive displacement by more tolerant organisms, by perturbation of regulatory factors, such as masking or disturbing chemotactic signals, and by acceleration of nutrient cycles.

TABLE 9.   Interorganismic Chemical Effects (Functions)

Intraspecific effects	Interspecific effects
Toxic or inhibitory repellents (autotoxins or autoinhibitors)	Repellents, suppressants
	Inductants, counteractants
Pheromones—chemical messages	Venoms
Signals for	Attractants chemical lures
Reproductive behavior	Stimulants (hormones)
Social regulation	Olfactants
Alarm and defense	
Territory and trail marking	
Food location	
Roles Adaptation of species and organization of communities	
Niche differentiation	
Succession of communities	
Chemical evolution to increase information and rate of information	
Transfer in chemical signaling	

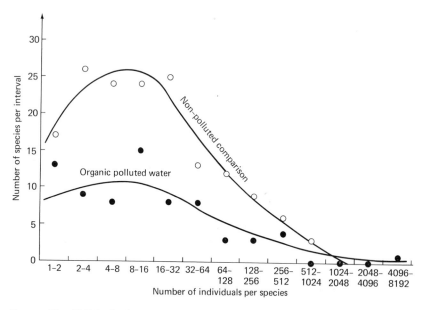

FIGURE 19.   Shift in the frequency distribution of diatoms as a result of subtle organic pollution. From Patrick *et al.* (1954).

Heavy metals and acidity

Phenomenology of heavy metal pollution of lakes

Heavy metals form the largest group among the chemical elements. Although many of them occur only in trifling amounts in the global lithosphere, man can mobilize them by extracting fossil fuels and mines in which heavy metals are more or less concentrated. Man's agricultural and industrial activities lead to a distribution of metals to the atmosphere and the hydrosphere. The man-made fluxes exceed sometimes the natural ones. The resulting higher concentrations in surface waters cannot be easily detected because of two main problems in analytical chemistry: (1) Dilution of heavy metals, such as Cr, Co, Ni, Cu, Zn, Cd, Pb, and Hg lead to relatively low concentration levels ($\leqslant \mu g$/liter). In many cases time-consuming preconcentration methods have to be employed in order to determine the content of these elements. Smaller but biologically important fluctuations as function of time and depth can hardly be observed. (2) Heavy metals are not well buffered. During sampling and processing steps concentrations are lowered through losses to interfaces or increased through contamination.

It is very difficult to establish dependable reference or background values for metal concentrations in lake water (Turekian, 1969). Geochemical and man-made inputs overlap because in most regions of the world atmospheric fallout is already influenced by man's activity although some catchment areas of lakes are not disturbed by man.

Sediments as indicators.   Sediment cores contain information about the events that occurred in precultural times in the lake and in its catchment area. Sediment analysis in which the above mentioned analytical problems are strongly reduced, can therefore provide the necessary background values and the historic development of metal pollution. The vertical distribution of heavy metals in core profiles indicates man's impact since the beginning of industrialization, as illustrated for example in Lake Ontario (Thomas, 1972) or Lake Windermere (Aston *et al.*, 1973) with Hg, and in Greifensee (Tschopp, 1977) with Cu, Zn, Cd, and Pb (Figure 20). The observed maximum values in the upper layers are two to five times as high as the background values. Domestic discharges provide additional indicators, such as nitrogen, phosphorus, and organic carbon. Foerstner *et al.* (1974) compared heavy metal contents (Zn, Pb) with nitrogen and phosphorus contents in sediment cores of Lake Constance. It was concluded that the observed increase of these four elements in the lake sediment is a result of the simultaneous impact by municipal wastewaters and disposal of industry and agriculture. These latter sources can very often be traced with the aid of horizontal distribution patterns in lake and river sediments, e.g., with Hg in Lake Geneva (Vernet, 1972) and Lake Maggiore (Damiani and Thomas, 1974). As Foerstner (1976) indicated, acute cases of mercury pollution in lakes and rivers originate mainly from direct industrial emissions (Table 10).

Concentration ranges in lake water.   Recent studies of three Swiss lakes with similar geochemical back-

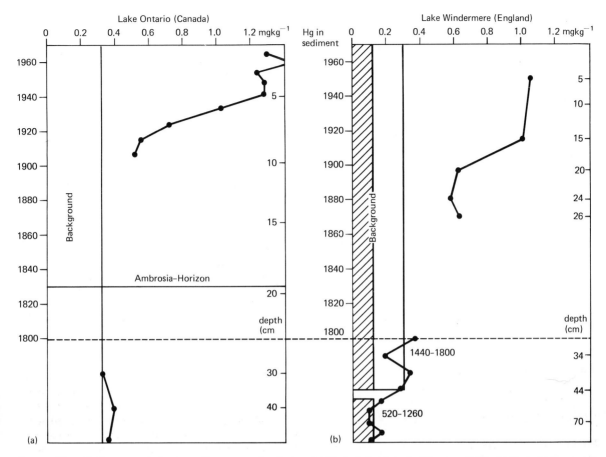

FIGURE 20a.   Sediments as indicators of heavy metal pollution. (a) Hg in Lake Ontario (Thomas, 1972). (b) Hg in Lake Windermere (Aston, 1973). Figure (a) and (b) from Förstner and Müller (1974).

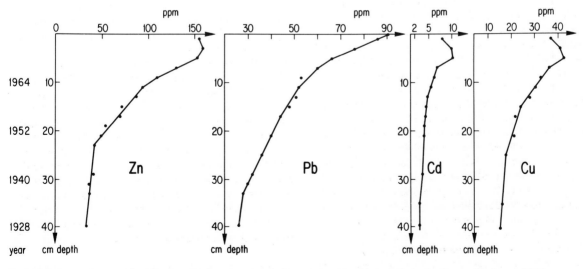

FIGURE 20b.   Sediments as indicators of heavy metal pollution. (c) Zn, Pb, Cd, and Cu in Greifensee (Tschopp, 1977).

TABLE 10.   Maximum Concentrations and Sources of Mercury in Lake Sediments (Examples)

Lake/river	Country	Max. conc. (mg kg⁻¹)	Source
Lake Saoseo	Switzerland	2.2	Atmospheric fallout
Lake Trummen	Sweden	3.1	Municipal waste water
Lake Vänern	Sweden	10.4	Chlor-alkali industry
Lake Björken	Sweden	11.2	Wood-pulp mill
Clay Lake	Canada	8.4	Chlor-alkali industry
St. Clair River	USA/Canada	60 (2000)	Chlor-alkali industry (Dow Chemical, Sarnia)
Detroit River	USA/Canada	86	Chlor-alkali industry (Wyandotte Chem., Mich.)

Data from Foerstner (1976).

ground, namely, the Lake of Alpnach (Baccini, 1976), the Lake of Biel (Santschi, 1975), and the Greifensee (Tschopp, 1977), permit a comparison of man's influence on heavy metal impacts (Table 11).

Besides the differences in their orographic and hydraulic properties the three lakes differ mainly in the population density in the effective drainage area. The observed mean annual concentrations in the tributaries increase, as a result of domestic sewages, for copper and zinc, but not for iron. A comparison of annual concentration ranges of elements in different lakes can be misleading since it does not take into account (a) the influence of the *physical state* of the metal species on their residence time. In the chosen example Fe is dominantly in the particular form (>0.45 μm), whereas Cu and Zn are found mainly in the dissolved phase (<0.45 μm), (b) influence of the hydraulic, orographic, and biotic properties on the *sedimentation rate;* or (c) direct *input* by rains.

Mass balances.   In order to establish a lake's role as a sink, one has to determine its retention ability for incoming material. With known sedimentation rates and metal contents of sediments one can estimate the quantity per time that is retained by a lake. Flux diagrams (Figure 21) of the three lakes (Table 11) illustrate the retention abilities for iron and copper. Iron is almost completely sedimented which can be explained by the dominantly particulate form of the incoming species. The distinctly anaerobic conditions in the hypolimnion of Greifensee during the stagnation period permit the reduction of Fe(III) to Fe(II) which leads to an increase in total hypolimnetic concentration, because the dissolved species become dominating. Nevertheless, the lake cannot export this dissolved form during winter circulation. As soon as oxygen is redelivered through hydrodynamic mixing processes, Fe(II) is oxidized and reprecipitated. In contrast to iron, the copper input is dominantly in the dissolved form. The retention value for the Greifensee (85%) in comparison to the two other lakes seems very high. A high organic production combined with low

hydraulic loading (Table 11) and an anaerobic H₂S-bearing hypolimnion may account for this phenomenon. However the stoichiometric approach of a mass balance cannot provide direct information about lake internal processes induced or modified by the biosphere.

Estimation of man's contribution to the heavy metal loading

The metal loads to a municipal sewage plant and its ability to eliminate metals were investigated by Roberts et al. (1977) and others (Table 12). The anthropo-

TABLE 11.   Comparison of Mean Annual Heavy Metal Concentration (Fe, Cu, Zn) in the Tributaries of Three Swiss Lakes

	Lake of Alpnach	Lake of Biel	Greifensee
Surface area (km²)	4.76	39.3	8.56
Average depth (m)	21	31	19
Hydraulic loading (m/year)	76	200	12
Theoretical residence time t_{H_2O} (years)	0.3	0.2	1.6
Effective drainage area[a] (km²)	150	4100	120
Population density in the effective area (capita/km²)	100	180	500
Water runoff per capita (10^7 liter/caput/year)	2.4	1.0	0.2
Mean annual concentration in tributaries (M) of total			
Iron	14×10^{-6}	13×10^{-6}	12×10^{-6}
Copper	2×10^{-8}	7×10^{-8}	9×10^{-8}
Zinc	7×10^{-8}	14×10^{-8}	31×10^{-8}

[a]Considering other lakes in the tributary system which serve as sinks.
Data from Krummenacher, Baccini, Santschi, Tschopp, Imboden.

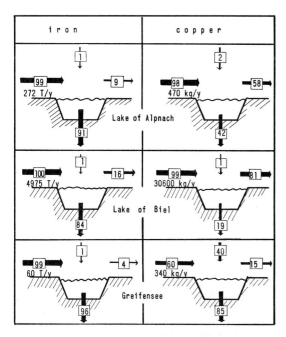

FIGURE 21.   Iron and copper balances of three Swiss lakes. T/y, tons/year; ◀▢▶ , fraction of total input in %.

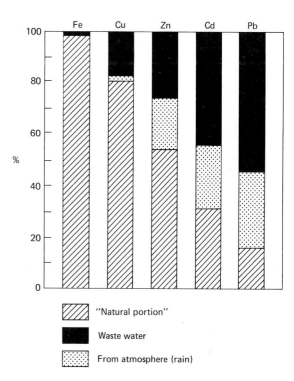

FIGURE 22.   Anthropogenic portions in the heavy metal load of a prealpine lake (Lake of Alpnach, Switzerland).

genic contribution to the lake of Alpnach having little industry in its catchment area is already significant for Cu, Zn, Cd, and Pb (Figure 22). If one considers the fact that the atmospheric fallout of these elements (except iron) is already dominated by man's activity (Imboden and Stumm, 1973), one can speak of a dominating man-made flux in the case of Zn, Cd, and Pb. These fluxes overlap with discharges of phosphorus leading to eutrophication. Studies of Lake Michigan (Winchester and Nifong, 1971) and Greifensee (Figure 21) show clearly that in highly industrialized catchment areas the atmospheric contribution becomes a

more and more significant contribution in the trace metal balance of lakes.

Chemical speciation and biological availability.   Total heavy metal concentrations in water and sediments or the rough distinction between particulate and dissolved forms do not give sufficient information for an evaluation of the influence of these elements on the balance between photosynthesis and respiration. The chemical perturbation by increased heavy metal fluxes is essentially a question of the concentration of all these species which are biologically available and may lead to a toxic or even lethal level in aquatic organisms. At the present time there are no detailed experimental data on the chemical nature of heavy metals in lake water. Many laboratory and some field observations indicate that some phytoplankton species can decrease the availability of heavy metals, especially $Cu(II)$, by exudation of organic ligands. Organic pollutants from domestic sewage may have similar effects. Specific mechanisms of mercury speciation could be elucidated by Jernelöv (1972) and Wood (1975) who studied the formation of methylated mercury in aquatic systems. Because methylmercury may be produced at a rate faster than it is degraded by other organisms, it may accumulate in fish. It is one of the few examples which demonstrate an increase of biological availability of a nonessential element in toxic concentrations through a chemical transformation by

TABLE 12.   Specific Heavy Metal Discharges in Waste Water (g/caput/year)

	Cr	Zn	Cu	Cd	Pb	Ni
USA						
Input to a municipal						
sewage plant						
New York	50	220	80	7	—	40
Pittsburgh	15	90	20	3	16	6
Muncie	40	200	50	—	160	25
Los Angeles	150	300	100	3	40	40
Residence area						
New York	13	35	30	2,6	—	13
Pittsburgh	3	28	16	1,8	10	2
Muncie	1,2	35	16	1,0	16	3
Switzerland						
Input to a municipal						
sewage plant	16	110	22	0,9	25	14
Residence area	2	40	8	0,7	25	2

Data from Roberts (1976).

the system. Other metals, e.g., Sn, Pt, Au, Tl, and Pb and metalloids such as As, Se, and Te can be converted to volatile methylated products. The latter group is of extreme toxicity. For a recent review on biomethylation of toxic elements see Ridley *et al.* (1977).

Models of metal distribution in lakes

In order to evaluate the significance of heavy metal impacts on lakes one has to develop models which can predict the distribution of these elements between particulate matter that is sedimented and dissolved species which are partly available to the aquatic organisms.

The inorganic approach. If one assumes a steady state condition for the heavy metal balance in a perfectly mixed lake, one can postulate a constant distribution of metals between the particulate and dissolved phase (see Figure 5). The rate of sedimentation and consequently the residence time of the metal is also a function of the distribution parameter D. Based on numerous laboratory experiments one can apply an adsorption model which can define the distribution coefficient as a function of stability constants of surface complexes with dissolved ligands and the proton concentration (see "Need for chemical speciation," p. 100). The comparison with field data of different lakes indicates that the natural material has an adsorption ability between SiO_2 and TiO_2 (Figure 23). According to the proposed model, additional domestic and industrial metal discharges, which are not necessarily accompanied by adsorbing particulate matter, can primarily increase the concentration of dissolved ligands. The effect would be an increase of the dissolved fraction which in turn leads to a higher relative residence time of the metal in the lake.

The role of biomass. It is evident that the internal production of biomass extends the quantity of particulate matter adsorbing and sedimenting heavy metals. In addition, contrary to most allochthonous suspended particles, a considerable fraction of the biomass produced is mineralized before reaching the sediment. As a consequence, heavy metals which are transferred onto or into biogenic particulate matter in the epilimnion reappear partially in the dissolved phase of the hypolimnion (Baccini, 1976). According to this observation the biomass can significantly influence the lake internal Cu and Zn distribution, even in a mesotrophic lake. Such a description implies a state of equilibrium for the subsystems of a lake. If one assigns to each phase a conditional formation constant for metal complexes and a corresponding ligand activity (Table 13) (Bundi 1977; Baccini *et al.,* 1977), one can predict the metal distribution for higher total concen-

trations (Table 13). According to this model an increase of total Cu concentration in Lake of Alpnach by a factor of 3 (without changing the other parameters) would result in a concentration increase in the biomass (phytoplankton) of a factor of approximately 4. It is obvious that the biomass is a main factor in any feed-back mechanism controlling the heavy metal balance in lakes. If the increase of the total metal impact leads to a toxic concentration in the biomass, the latter would be reduced thus increasing the residence time of the incoming metal. Such a positive feed-back could influence decisively the ecological balance in a lake.

The influence of eutrophication. Man-made heavy metal discharges coincide mostly with loadings of nutrients, such as phosphorus, and organic ligands for heavy metal complexation. According to the models discussed, the synchronal increases of ligand activity in the dissolved phase could prevent partially or even completely an increased absorption by the biomass. Consequently the master variable phosphorus would still determine the balance between photosynthesis and respiration. However one has to consider the fact that a strongly eutrophic lake has a seasonally or permanently reduced hypolimnion offering high concentrations of sulfides. The formation of heavy metal sulfides can in turn accelerate the sedimentation rate of some metals, such as Cu_2S, CuS, ZnS, CdS, PbS,

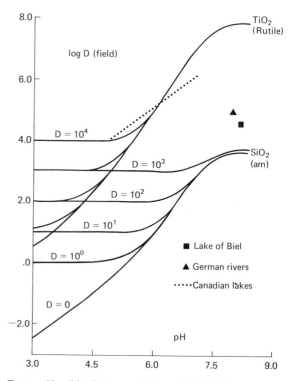

FIGURE 23.   Distribution coefficient *D* for Cu(II) as a function of pH. Model sediments: TiO_2 (rutile), upper curve; SiO_2 (amorph), lower curve. From Schindler (1976).

TABLE 13.   Cu(II) Distribution in Lake Waters: Comparison of Calculated and Observed Copper Distribution in the "Three-Phase Approach"[a,c,d]

	$Cu_T = 1.6 \times 10^{-8}$ mol/liter (Lake of Alpnach)		$Cu_T = 5 \times 10^{-8}$ mol/liter (Lake of Biel)	
	Model	Field data	Model	Field data[b]
Dissolved species	85	81	81	70–90
Allochthonous particles	6	8	7 }	10–30
Algae	9	11	12 }	
Copper content of plankton (ppm)	40	38	168	79

[a]Cu-distribution (%).
[b]With ligand parameter values of Lake of Alpnach.
[c]Data from Santschi (1975).
[d]For this computation of Cu(II) distribution, the following equilibrium parameters have been used (data from Bundi, 1977, and Baccini et al., 1977).

		Stability constants	
Ligand	Activity (mol/liter)	log β_1	log β_2
CO_3^{2-}	1.3×10^{-5} (pH = 8.1)	6.9	10.4
OH^-	1.3×10^{-6}	6.0	14.3
D	1.0×10^{-7}	11.0	—
A	3.0×10^{-7}	9.5	—
P	1.5×10^{-7}	9.6	—

D: Dissolved ligands (parameter for ligands chemically not defined).
A: Algae (activity corresponds to 200 μg/liter of particulate organic nitrogen).
P: Allochthonous particulate ligands (activity corresponds to 3 mg/liter of dry matter).

HgS, which have very low solubility products. Such a process could explain the observed high retention of Cu by the Greifensee (Figure 21).

However the same reduced conditions promote the formation of alkylated species, such as CH_3Hg^+, leading to a new mobilization in the lake internal cycles. Therefore in a well eutrophic lake Hg uptake [in the form of CH_3Hg^+, CH_3SHgCH_3, or $(CH_3)_2Hg$] by fish may exceed the uptake in a less eutrophic lake even if the latter should contain a larger total Hg concentration. It is postulated by different authors that iron and manganese offer another transport path for heavy metals in a chemically reduced hypolimnion. Both elements are dominantly in the dissolved phase and experience an oxidation process at the oxidizing upper interface leading to the formation of new particulate oxide surfaces for trace metal absorption. While sedimenting they become redissolved during reduction of the carrier material. Tessenow (1975) indicated clearly that such processes can also induce lateral movements of Fe and Mn in lakes, a mechanism which would also influence trace metal transports.

Ecological consequences

If a lake is primarily considered as reservoir for drinking water and food (fish and mollusks), the tolerable concentrations are still above the average values observed in most lakes. The accumulation of heavy met-
als in the food chain have been studied in more detail for methyl-mercury by various authors. Drastic effects are known from heavily polluted sections of the Rhine river (Foerstner and Müller, 1974). In order to preserve ecological diversity and to minimize sociological adaptation, criteria for heavy metal impacts have to include tolerable concentration limits for the plankton. Various authors (Hynes, 1960; Wuhrmann and Eichenberger, 1975; Winner et al., 1975) have shown that increased heavy metal loads can induce transformations in quality and quantity of the aquatic biocoenoses. In most cases pollution combines several elements. Therefore the possibility of synergistic effects must be considered. The primary producers, which are confronted directly with the chemistry of the lake, are most sensitive organisms for changes in heavy metal concentrations. Gächter (1976) measured the seasonal effects of Cu, Zn, Cd, Pb, and Hg on the photosynthetic activity of phytoplankton in two prealpine lakes (Figure 24). Several metals give not just an additive effect on toxicity but show clearly a synergistic one. The observed seasonal variations could not be related to changes in chemical parameters such as pH, hardness, dissolved organic nitrogen, and allochthonous particulate matter. This and similar experiments indicate that increased metal loading would primarily change the phytoplankton composition in lakes which in turn could influence the balance between photosynthesis and respiration.

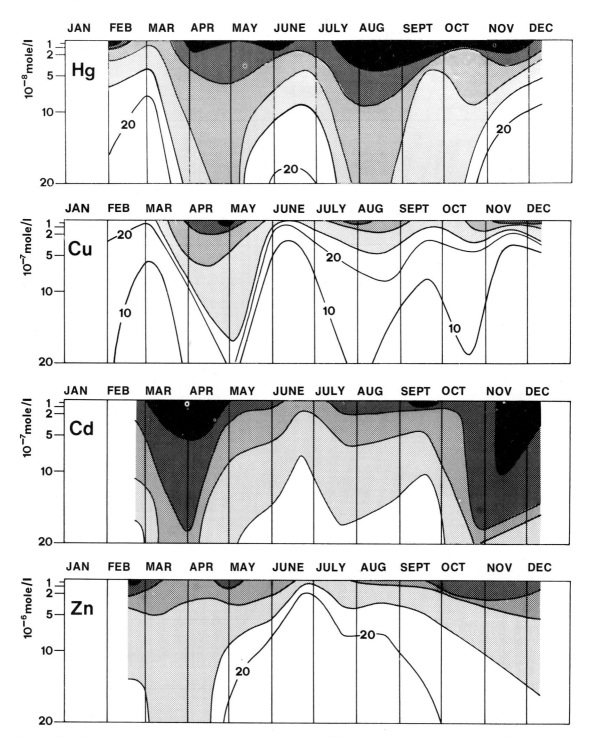

FIGURE 24.   Seasonal variation of relative photosynthesis (control = 100%) in Lake of Alpnach as a function of increased heavy metal concentration. The darker the area between lines of equal relative photosynthetic activity, the smaller the reduction. The scale on the ordinate gives the units of concentration increase, i.e., for Hg, 10^{-8} M/liter; Cu and Cd, 10^{-7} M/liter; Zn and Pb, 10^{-6} M/liter. In the combined experiment (Hg, Cu, Cd, Zn, and Pb), the units of concentration increase for each metal are 10 times lower than in the single metal experiments. From Gächter (1976).

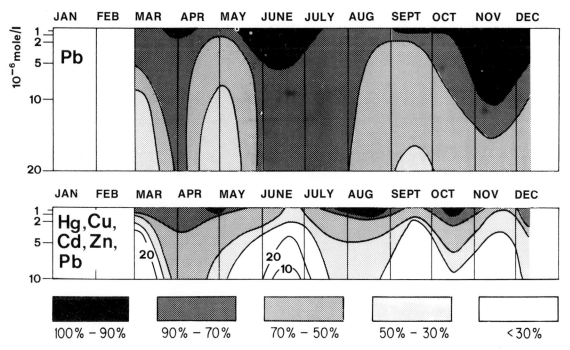

FIGURE 24 continued.

Perturbations by acid precipitation

The pH of rain water in equilibrium with the CO_2 of the atmosphere is approximately 5.5. Fuel combustion products contain sulfur dioxide and nitrogen oxides which react with water and oxygen to sulfuric and nitric acids. As a result the pH of rain and snow has been lowered to between 3 and 5 in eastern USA and in Scandinavia during the past decades (Likens and Bormann, 1974; Cogbill, 1975; Odén and Ahl, 1970). Since the carrier of additional acids is the atmosphere the sources of pH lowering substances may lay far outside of the precipitation area. For Sweden it was estimated (Rodhe, 1972) that more than 70% of the sulfur in the atmosphere stems from industrial activities. Almost 80% of this impact is thought to be "imported" from industrial centers in Germany and England.

It is evident from the section "Factors regulating the chemical composition of lake water systems" (see p. 93) that the buffering capacity of a lake, which is a result of the geochemical composition of the drainage area, is the decisive factor in the response to increased acid impacts. The lithosphere of the northern USA, Canada, and Scandinavia consists mostly of granitic rocks which give poorly buffered surface waters. Acid precipitation in these regions has caused the pH decline in rivers and lakes (Figure 25). The resulting biological effect on fish population is very drastic. Increased acidity has resulted in a decimation or elimi-

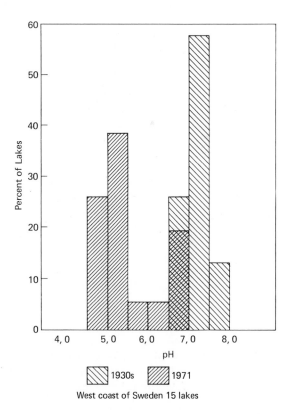

FIGURE 25. Frequency distribution of pH in 15 lakes near the Swedish west coast sampled in the 1930s and 1971. From Wright and Gjessing (1976).

nation of several fish species. In addition there is a tendency to fewer plankton species causing major alterations in the food chain (Hendrey and Wright, 1976).

From a chemical point of view one has to consider secondary effects of increased acidity in lakes and their catchment area. As indicated in Figure 23, a lowering of pH can alter drastically the distribution of heavy metals, namely, accelerate geochemical weathering processes and raise the dissolved and biologically available fraction. In addition the emissions of sulfur and nitrogen oxides from combustion of fossil fuels are accompanied by heavy metals and pesticides (Hagen and Langeland, 1973). Beamish and Van Loon (1977) and others interpret observed high concentrations of Mn and Zn in acid lakes as a possible result from increased mobilization from the lake sediments and catchment area.

Acid rain may also mobilize phosphates and indirectly increase eutrophication of inland and coastal waters. In extreme cases, however, high acidity may reduce productivity.

Conclusions

Every lake is a little cosmos; solar energy is extracted by the phytoplankton and used to support a biological community, to organize the ecosystem and to drive the cycles of nutrients and other elements. Every lake is also a mirror of its environment. Although man interfers primarily with terrestrial ecosystems, man's impact on the ecology finds—because of the interdependence of terrestrial and aquatic ecosystems—its most sensitive response in inland waters, especially in lakes. The rapid changes that have been observed in the last decades in chemical and biological properties of many lakes reflect the human influence on the environment and are a byproduct of progressive energy dissipation. Of particular importance is that, in order to expand the food output for an increasing population, in many drainage areas of lakes more energy flow has to be diverted by agriculture (by deforestation, conversion of grass land into crop land, applying excessively fertilizers, herbicides and pesticides), to the benefit of fewer species, thus shifting the communities in the direction of monocultures. This promotes the transport of fertilizers and xenobiotic substances to lakes and enhances the rates of erosion and chemical denudation, causing a disturbance of the ecological balance of lakes.

The side effects of technology are felt over increasingly larger distances even at times becoming global in character. Thus lakes reflect not solely the activities

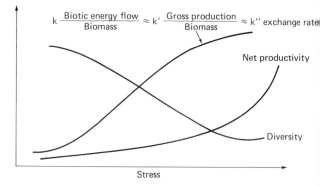

FIGURE 26.   Effect of stress upon an ecosystem. Stress is interpreted as a nonpredictive change in chemical and physical variables. Every stress causes a simplification of the organization of the ecosystem and an acceleration of its nutrient cycles.

within their drainage area, but also the impact of emissions carried over large distances by the atmosphere. Here the burning of fossil fuel, resulting in the release of oxides of N, H, and S, and of trace metals constitutes an especially relevant influence.

Figure 26 generalizes in a concise way how chemical and physical perturbations affect an ecosystem in general. A lake ecosystem (lake plus drainage area) can be characterized by a flow of energy and nutrients through a network of interlocking cycles. Every stress, that is, a nonpredictive change of chemical and physical variables—resulting as a byproduct of direct or indirect technological energy inputs into the system—increases, macroscopically speaking, the ratio of biotic energy flux to biomass (Margalef, 1973). Correspondingly, nature simplifies its ecosystem structure; by impairing negative feedback mechanisms and by accelerating nutrient cycles, the randomness of the system is increased. This model permits in a gross way to generalize many aspects of man's actions on lakes.

A number of scholars, especially H. T. Odum, E. Odum, Margalef, and Woodwell, have tried to abstract from a large number of observations and to generalize the temporal development of ecological communities. Building on the ideas of Lotka (1924), the bioenergetic basis of succession of ecosystems has been recognized. As every other closed (but energy transparent) system, an ecosystem has a tendency to develop toward a macroscopic steady state. Actually, natural nonperturbed ecosystems exposed to a solar input tend to change into a climax community. Such a climax community can maintain a macroscopically constant composition if cybernetic regulatory and symbiotic functions prevail. At steady state an optimum in metabolic efficiency is attained. The changes schematically depicted in Figure 26 that occur with increasing stress are the reversal of the ecological succession.

The interdependence between the acceleration of nutrient cycles (e.g., as indicated by an increase in the specific growth rate of certain organisms) and simplification of ecosystem structure is typically observed as a consequence of lake pollution with organic or inorganic substances (metals). Similar reductions in diversity are observed with chemical or petrochemical substances. The disturbance of the ecological balance between photosynthesis, P, and respiration, R, ($P \leqq R$), caused either by organic pollution or pollution by fertilizing nutrients, leads to an increase of the specific growth rate of heterotrophic or phototrophic organisms, i.e., to an increase in the ratio energy flux/biomass (corresponding to the metabolic rate per heterotrophic cell or rate of energy fixation). This increase is accompanied by a decrease in the organization of the ecosystem, e.g., a narrowing of food chain and decrease in the number of trophic levels.

Lake eutrophication exemplifies the dramatic change of the entire community of a lake as a consequence of the supply to the lake of a fertilizing nutrient: the phytoplankton increases and changes its composition; despite a corresponding increase in zooplankton density, a significant part of the phytoplankton biomass settles into the deeper water layers where the resulting oxygen consumption and ultimate anaerobiosis change drastically the fauna at the sediment–water interface. As long as the phosphorus loading of the lake is small, and as long as dissolved oxygen prevails at the sediment–water interface, sediments are a sink for phosphates [which become bound to iron(III) oxides]. As soon as the loading exceeds a critical limit, a significant lowering of the redox intensity at the sediment–water interface results in a change of sign in the feedback mechanism of the P-regulation; under anaerobic conditions, sediments release P accumulated in earlier years. As a further consequence of eutrophication, dramatic changes in the species distribution occur at all trophic levels; pronounced shifts in the fish populations have been observed (Beeton, 1969). Obviously an increase in primary production affects an aquatic ecosystem and its food web to a much larger extent than a terrestrial system.

Our present drainage systems for sewage, industrial wastes, and storm water runoff often accelerate the transport of nutrients and other pollutants to the lakes. Waste treatment plants, although necessary, remain technological fixes. Ecological (and social) considerations must codetermine the technological development in the drainage areas of lakes. It is important to maintain lakes as diversified life support ecosystems and as a source and reservoir for evolutionary diversity.

References

Alexander, M. (1975). Environmental and microbiological problems arising from recalcitrant molecules. *Microbial. Ecol.*, **2**:17–27.

Ambühl, H. (1975). Versuch der Quantifizierung der Beeinflussung des Oekosystems durch chemische Faktoren: Stehende Gewässer. *Schweiz. Z. Hydrol.*, **37**:35–52.

Aston, S. R., *et al.* (1973). Mercury in lake sediments: A possible indicator of technological growth. *Nature*, **241**:450–451.

Baccini, P. (1976). Untersuchungen über den Schwermetallhaushalt in Seen. *Schweiz. Z. Hydrol.*, **38**:121–158.

Baccini, P., H. Hohl, and Th. Bundi. (1977). Phenomenology and modelling of heavy metal distribution in lakes. *Verh. Int. Verein. Limnol.* (In preparation).

Baccini, P., and P. V. Roberts. (1976). Die Belastung der Gewässer durch Metalle. Eine akute oder künftige Gefahr? Neue Zürcher Zeitung No. 40, 18 February 1976.

Beamish, R. J., and J. C. Van Loon. (1977). Precipitation loading of acid and heavy metals to a small acid lake near Sudbury, Ontario. *J. Fish. Res. Board Can.*, **34**:649–658.

Beeton, A. M. (1969). Changes in the environment and biota of the Great Lakes. Pp. 150–187. In: *Eutrophication: Causes, Consequences, Correctives*. Natl. Acad. Sci., Washington, D.C.

Bundi, Th. (1977). Untersuchungen zur Aufnahme von Kupfer durch Chlorella pyrenoidosa in Abhängigkeit der Kupferspeziierung. Thesis Swiss Fed. Inst. Technol., Zurich.

Chapra, St. C. (1977). Total phosphorus model for the Great Lakes. *J. Env. Engr. Div. Am. Soc. Civil Eng.*, **103**:147–161.

Chiou, C. T., V. H. Freed, D. W. Schmedding, and R. L. Kohnert. (1977). Partition coefficient and bioaccumulation of selected organic chemicals. *Envir. Sci. Technol.*, **11**:475–478.

Cogbill, C. V. (1975). Thesis, Cornell University, Ithaca, N.Y.

Damiani, V., and R. L. Thomas. (1974). Mercury in the sediments of the Pallanza Basin. *Nature*, **251**:696–697.

Degens, E. T., A. Paluska, and E. Eriksson. (1976). Rates of soil erosion. Pp. 185–191. In: B. H. Svensson and R. Söderlund (eds.), *Nitrogen, Phosphorus and Sulfur—Global Cycles*. SCOPE Report 7, Ecol. Bull., Stockholm, Sweden.

Dobzhansky, T. (1957). *Evolution, Genetics and Man*. Wiley, New York, NY.

Emerson, St. (1975). Chemically enhanced CO_2 gas exchange in a eutrophic lake: A general model. *Limnol. Oceanogr.*, **20**:743–753.

Feth, J. H., C. E. Roberson, and W. L. Polzer. (1964). Sources of mineral constituents in water from granitic rocks, Sierra Nevada, California and Nevada. U.S. Geol. Surv. Water-Supply Paper 1535-I, 170.

Förstner, U. (1976). Lake sediments as indicators of heavy-metal pollution. *Naturwissenschaften*, **63**:465.

Förstner, U., and G. Müller. (1974). *Schwermetalle in Flüssen und Seen*. Springer-Verlag.

Förstner, U., G. Müller, and G. Wagner. (1974). Schwermetalle in den Sedimenten des Bodensees. *Naturwissenschaften*, **61**:270–272.

Gächter, R. (1976). Untersuchungen über die Beeinflussung der planktischen Photosynthese durch anorganische Metallsalze im eutrophen Alpnachersee und der mesotrophen Horwer Bucht. *Schweiz. Z. Hydrol.*, **38**:97–119.

Gächter, R., and O. J. Furrer. (1972). Der Beitrag der Landwirtschaft zur Eutrophierung der Gewässer in der Schweiz. I. Ergebnisse von direkten Messungen im Einzugsgebiet verschiedener Vorfluter. *Schweiz. Z. Hydrol.*, **34**:41–70.

Garrels, R. M., and F. T. MacKenzie. (1967). Origin of the chemical compositions of some springs and lakes. Pp. 222–242. In: W. Stumm (ed.), *Equilibrium Concepts of Natural Water Systems*. Adv. Chem. Series 67.

Garrels, R. M., and F. T. MacKenzie. (1971). *Evolution of Sedimentary Rocks*. W. W. Norton, New York, NY.

Gillette, R. (1974). Cancer and the environment (II): Groping for new remedies. *Science,* **186**:242.

Goldberg, E. D. (1972). Man's role in the major sedimentary cycle. Pp. 267–288. In: D. Dyrssen and D. Jagner (eds.), *The Changing Chemistry of the Oceans*. Almqvist & Wiksell, Stockholm.

Goldberg, E. D. (1976). *The Health of the Oceans*. Unesco Press, Paris.

Grob, K., and G. Grob. (1973). Organische Stoffe in Zürichs Wasser. Neue Zürcher Zeitung, 10 September 1973.

Hagen, A., and A. Langeland. (1973). Polluted snow in southern Norway and the effect of the meltwater on freshwater and aquatic organisms. *Envir. Poll.*, **5**:45–57.

Hayes, F. R., and J. E. Phillips. (1958). Lake water and sediment. IV. Radiophosphorus equilibrium with mud, plants, and bacteria under oxidized and reduced conditions. *Limnol. Oceanogr.*, **3**:459–475.

Hendrey, G. R., and R. F. Wright. (1976). Acid precipitation in Norway: Effects on aquatic fauna. *J. Great Lakes Res.*, **2**:192 (Suppl. 1).

Hobbie, J. E., and R. T. Wright. (1965). Bioassay with bacterial uptake kinetics: Glucose in freshwater. *Limnol. Oceanogr.*, **10**:471–474.

Hohl, H., and W. Stumm. (1976). Interaction of Pb^{2+} with hydrous γ-Al_2O_3. *J. Colloid Interface Sci.*, **55**:281–288.

Hynes, H. B. N. (1960). *The Biology of Polluted Waters*. Liverpool Univ. Press., Liverpool.

Imboden, D. M. (1973). Limnologische Transport- und Nährstoff-modelle. *Schweiz. Z. Hydrol.*, **35**:29–68.

Imboden, D. M. (1974). Phosphorus model of lake eutrophication. *Limnol. Oceanogr.*, **19**:297–304.

Imboden, D. M., and R. Gächter. (1975). Modelling and control of lake eutrophication. *Proc. 6th Triennial World Congress Int. Fed. Automatic Control*, August 1975. Part 3, Contribution No. 61.1.

Imboden, D. M., and R. Gächter. (1977). A dynamic lake model for trophic state prediction. *Int. J. Ecolog. Modelling*. (In press).

Imboden, D. M., and W. Stumm. (1973). Der Einfluss des Menschen auf die geochemischen Kreisläufe in der Atmopshäre. *Chimia*, **27**:155–165.

Jannasch, H. W. (1967). Growth of marine bacteria at limiting concentrations of organic carbon in seawater. *Limnol. Oceanogr.*, **12**:264–271.

Jernelöv, A. (1972). Factors in the transformation of mercury to methylmercury. Pp. 167–172. Mercury and food chains. Pp. 174–177. In: R. Hartung and B. D. Dinman (eds.), *Environmental Mercury Contamination*. Ann Arbor Science, Ann Arbor, MI.

Kramer, J. (1967). Equilibrium models and composition of the Great Lakes. Pp. 243–254. In: W. Stumm (ed.), *Equilibrium Concepts of Natural Water Systems*. Adv. Chem. Ser. 67.

Krummenacher, Th. (1976). Die Nährstoffbilanz des Alpnachersees. Thesis, Swiss Fed. Inst. Technol., Zurich.

Lane, P., and R. Levins. (1977). The dynamics of aquatic systems. 2. The effects of nutrient enrichment on model plankton communities. *Limnol. Oceanogr.*, **22**:454–471.

Leidner, H., R. Gloor, and K. Wuhrmann. (1976). Abbaukinetik linearer Alkylbenzolsulfonate. *Tenside Deter.*, **13**:122–130.

Lerman, A. (1974). Eutrophication and water quality of lakes: Control by water residence time and transport to sediments. *Hydrol. Sci. Bull.*, **19**:25–34.

Lerman, A., and G. J. Brunskill. (1971). Migration of major constituents from lake sediments into lake water and its bearing on lake water composition. *Limnol. Oceanogr.*, **16**:880–890.

Lerman, A., and R. R. Weiler. (1971). Diffusion of chloride and sodium in Lake Ontario sediment: 1. Ionic interactions and 2. accumulated amount of a reacting species. *Earth Planet. Sci. Let.*, **13**:220–221.

Li, Y. H. (1976). Population growth and environmental problems in Taiwan (Formosa): A case-study. *Envir. Conserv.*, **3**:171–177.

Likens, G. E., and F. H. Bormann. (1974). Acid rain: A serious regional environmental problem. *Science,* **184**:1176–1179.

Lotka, A. J. (1924). *Elements of Physical Biology*. Corrected reprint by Dover Publications Inc., New York, NY, in 1956; new title: *Elements of Mathematical Biology*.

Margalef, R. (1973). Ecological theory and prediction in the study of interaction between man and the rest of the biosphere. Pp. 307–353. In: H. Sioli (ed.), *Oekologie und Lebensschutz in internationaler Sicht (Ecology and Bioprotection: International Conclusions)*. Verlag Rombach, Freiburg/Germany.

McCarty, P. L. (1971). Energetics and bacterial growth. Pp. 495–531. In: S. J. Faust and J. V. Hunter (eds.), *Organic Compounds in Aquatic Environments*. M. Dekker, New York, NY.

Morel, F., R. E. McDuff, and J. H. Morgan. (1973). Interactions and chemostasis in aquatic chemical systems: Role of pH, pE, solubility, and complexation. Pp. 157–200. In: P. R. Singer (ed.), *Trace Metals and Metal-Organic Interactions in Natural Waters*. Ann Arbor Science, Ann Arbor, MI.

Morel, F., and J. J. Morgan. (1972). A numerical method for computing equilibria in aqueous chemical systems. *Environ. Sci. Technol.*, **6**:58–67.

Morgan, J. J. (1967). Applications and limitations of chemical thermodynamics in water systems. Pp. 1–29. In: W.

Stumm (ed.), *Equilibrium Concepts of Natural Water Systems*. Adv. Chem. Ser. 67.

Mortimer, C. H. (1971). Chemical exchanges between sediments and water in the Great Lakes—speculations on probable regulatory mechanisms. *Limnol. Oceanogr.*, **16**:387–404.

Murray, J. W. (1975). The interaction of metal ions at the manganese dioxide-solution interface. *Geochim. Cosmochim. Acta*, **39**:505–519.

Odén, S., and T. Ahl. (1970). Ymer Årsbok 103.

Page, T., R. H. Harris, and S. S. Epstein. (1976). Drinking water and cancer mortality in Louisiana. *Science*, **193**:55–57.

Patrick, R., M. H. Hohn, and J. H. Wallace. (1954). A new method for determining the pattern of the diatom flora. *Proc. Nat. Acad. Sci. USA*, **259**:1–12.

Ridley, W. P., L. J. Dizikes, and J. M. Wood. (1977). Biomethylation of toxic elements in the environment. *Science*, **197**:329–339.

Roberts, P. V., H. R. Hegi, A. Weber, and H. R. Krähenbühl. (1977). Metals in municipal wastewater and their elimination in sewage treatment. IAWPR Workshop, Vienna, 1975. (In press).

Rodhe, H. (1972). A study of the sulfur budget for the atmosphere over Northern Europe. *Tellus*, **24**:128–138.

Santschi, P. (1975). Chemische Prozesse im Bielersee. Thesis, University of Berne.

Schindler, P. W. (1967). Heterogeneous equilibria involving oxides, hydroxides, carbonates, and hydroxide carbonates. Pp. 196–221. In: W. Stumm (ed.), *Equilibrium Concepts in Natural Water Systems*. Adv. Chem. Ser. 67.

Schindler, D. W. (1974). Eutrophication and recovery in experimental lakes: Implications for lake management. *Science*, **184**:897–899.

Schindler, P. W. (1976). The regulation of trace metal concentrations in natural water systems: A chemical approach. *J. Great Lakes Res.*, **2**:132–145 (Suppl. 1).

Schindler, D. W. (1977). Evolution of phosphorus limitation in lakes. *Science*, **195**:260–262.

Schindler, P. W., B. Fürst, R. Dick, and P. U. Wolf. (1976). Ligand properties of surface silanol groups. I. Surface complex formation with Fe^{3+}, Cu^{2+}, Cd^{2+} and Pb^{2+}. *J. Colloid Interface Sci.*, **55**:469–475.

Scholz, A. T., R. M. Horrall, J. C. Cooper, and A. D. Hasler. (1976). Imprinting to chemical cues: The basis for home stream selection in salmon. *Science*, **192**:1247–1249.

Shannon, E. E., and P. L. Brezonik. (1972). Relationship between lake trophic state and nitrogen and phosphorus loading rates. *Environ. Sci. Technol.*, **6**:719–725.

Shapiro, J. (1973). Blue–green algae: Why they become dominant. *Science*, **179**:382–384.

Sillén, L. G., and A. E. Martell. (1964, 1971). *Stability Constants of Metal–Ion Complexes*. Chem. Soc. London, Special Publ. No. 17 and No. 25.

Sondheimer, E., and J. B. Simeone. (eds.). (1970). *Chemical Ecology*. Academic Press, New York, NY.

Steele, J. H. (1974). *The Structure of Marine Ecosystems*. Harvard Univ. Press, Cambridge, MA.

Stumm, W. (1977). What is the Pε of the Sea? *Thalassia Jugoslavica*. (In press).

Stumm, W., and P. A. Brauner. (1975). Chemical speciation. In: J. P. Riley and G. Skirrow (eds.), *Chemical Ocean-ography*. Vol. I, 2nd edition. Academic Press, New York, NY.

Stumm, W., H. Hohl, and F. Dalang. (1976). Interaction of metal ions with hydrous oxide surfaces. *Croatica Chem. Acta*, **48**:491–504.

Stumm, W., and J. J. Morgan. (1970). *Aquatic Chemistry*. Wiley-Interscience, New York, NY.

Stumm, W., and E. Stumm-Zollinger. (1971). Chemostasis and homeostasis in aquatic ecosystems; principles of water pollution control. In: J. D. Hem (ed.), *Non-Equilibrium Systems in Natural Waters*. Adv. Chem. Series 106.

Sunda, W., and R. R. L. Guillard. (1976). The relationship between cupric ion activity and the toxicity of copper to phytoplankton. *J. Marine Res.*, **34**:511–529.

Tessenow, U. (1974). Lösungs-, Diffusions- und Sorptionsprozesse in der Oberschicht von Seesedimenten. IV. Reaktionsmechanismen und Gleichgewichte im System Eisen-Mangan-Phosphat im Hinblick auf die Vivianitakkumulation im Ursee. *Arch. Hydrobiol.*, **47**:1–79 (Suppl.).

Tessenow, U. (1975). Akkumulationsprozesse in der Maximaltiefe von Seen durch postsedimentäre Konzentrationswanderung. *Verh. Int. Verein. Limnol.*, **19**:1251–1262.

Thomas, R. L. (1972). The distribution of mercury in the sediments of Lake Ontario. *Can. J. Earth Sci.*, **9**:636–651.

Thorstenson, D. C. (1970). Equilibrium distribution of small organic molecules in natural waters. *Geochim. Cosmochim. Acta*, **34**:745–770.

Tschopp, J. (1977). Thesis, Swiss Fed. Inst. Technol., Zurich (to be published).

Turekian, K. K. (1969). The oceans, streams, and atmosphere. Pp. 297–323. In: K. H. Wedepohl (ed.), *Handbook of Geochemistry*. Vol. I. Springer-Verlag.

Vernet, J. P. (1972). Levels of mercury in the sediments of some Swiss lakes including Lake Geneva and the Rhone River. *Eclogae Geol. Helv.*, **65**:293.

Vollenweider, R. A. (1968). *Scientific Fundamentals of the Eutrophication of Lakes and Flowing Waters, with Particular Reference to Nitrogen and Phosphorus as Factors in Eutrophication*. Technical Report DAS/CSI/68.27 OECD, Paris.

Vollenweider, R. A. (1969). Möglichkeiten und Grenzen elementarer Modelle der Stoffbilanz von Seen. *Arch. Hydrobiol.*, **66**:1–36.

White, D. E., J. D. Hem, and G. A. Waring. (1963). Chemical composition of subsurface waters. U.S. Geol. Survey Profess. Paper 440 F, 14.

Williams, J. D. H., J.-M. Jacquet, and R. L. Thomas. (1976). Forms of phosphorus in the surficial sediments of Lake Erie. *J. Fish. Res. Can.*, **33**:413–429.

Winchester, J. W., and G. D. Nifong. (1971). Water pollution in Lake Michigan by trace elements from pollution aerosol fallout. *Water, Air Soil Poll.*, **1**:50–64.

Winner, R. W., J. Scott van Dyke, N. Caris, and M. P. Farrel. (1974). Response of the macroinvertebrate fauna to a copper gradient in an experimentally-polluted stream. *Verh. Int. Verein. Limnol.*, **19**:2121–2127.

Wood, J. M. (1975). Biological cycles for elements in the environment. *Naturwissenschaften*, **62**:357–364.

World Health Organization (1976). *Health Hazards from*

New Environmental Pollutants. Technical Report Series 586, Geneva.

Wright, R. F., and E. T. Gjessing. (1976). Changes in the chemical composition of lakes. *Ambio,* **5**:219–223.

Wuhrmann, K. (1972). Stream purification. In: R. Mitchell (ed.), *Water Pollution Microbiology*. Wiley-Interscience, New York, NY.

Wuhrmann, K. (1973). Bedeutung der Mikroorganismen für aquatische Stoffkreisläufe. *Pathol. Microbiol.,* **39**:55–70.

Wuhrmann, K. (1976a). Chemical impact on inland aquatic ecosystems. *Pure Appl. Chem.,* **45**:193–198.

Wuhrmann, K. (1976b). Grenzen der mikrobiellen Selbstreinigung der Oberflächengewässer und ihre Konsequenzen für die Trinkwasseraufbereitung. *Gas-Wasser-Abwasser,* **57**:184–193.

Wuhrmann, K., and E. Eichenberger. (1975). Experiments on the effects of inorganic enrichment of rivers on periphyton primary production. *Verh. Int. Verein. Limnol.,* **19**:2028–2034.

Chapter 5

Organic Compounds in Lake Sediments

M. A. Barnes and W. C. Barnes

Introduction

Although broad classes of natural organic compounds have been isolated from lake sediments for several decades, the identification of specific compounds is largely a product of the past 15 years and has paralleled the development of modern analytical techniques such as combined gas chromatography–mass spectrometry. Although the identification of optical and geometric isomers needs more study, much progress has already been made in relating sediment compounds to precursor organisms and to microbial processes in the water column and the sediment. The mechanisms and rates of microbial lysis and decomposition of phytoplankton and higher plants are now well known. Chemoheterotrophic microorganisms normally decompose algae and extracellular organic compounds as sources of required elements and energy but seldom use the compounds themselves in unaltered form (Golterman, 1975). Thus, with the exceptions of the vitamins and some nitrogenous bases, sediment organic compounds are largely either of microbial origin or have been derived from phytoplankton and zooplankton remains and feces which have survived microbial attack, or from littoral and terrestrial sources. The relative proportions of organic matter derived from these sources is largely a function of lake morphology and productivity. Small, shallow lakes may have much of their organic matter derived from littoral sources (Wetzel, 1975), whereas larger and deeper lakes, especially fjord lakes, have a much larger input of autochthonous planktonic organisms. Less productive lakes appear to have much of their sediment organic matter derived from allochthonous sources (Mackereth, 1966; Brunskill et al., 1971), whereas lakes of high productivity have sediment organic matter derived largely from within the lakes themselves (Gorham, 1960; Gorham, et al. 1974). Sanger and Gorham (1970) and Gorham and Sanger (1975)

concluded from their studies of pigments that productive Minnesota lakes have sediment organic matter which is largely autochthonous.

Complex relationships may exist between plankton and microorganisms in lakes. Daft et al. (1975) studied the lysis of cyanophytes by aerobic gram-negative myxobacteria from freshwater lakes, reservoirs, and soils. These bacteria were motile by gliding and utilize the algae as sources of attachment as well as sources of nutrients. They are mesophiles and appeared to thrive under the same conditions required for blooms of the cyanophytes. However, the numbers of the lytic bacteria appeared to be too small to completely lyse a bloom. Some evidence exists that algal blooms can control microbial populations in lakes. Chróst (1975) found that algae blooming in eutrophic lakes released antibacterial substances which inhibited the growth and respiration of gram-positive bacteria but not of gram-negative rods. Algae with resistant cells walls may have a relatively high probability of being incorporated in sediments with their cellular organic compounds intact. Kudryavtsev (1975) studied the rates of decomposition of *Chlorella, Melosira,* and *Asterionella* by both gram-positive and gram-negative bacteria; the diatoms were attacked more slowly than the chlorophyte, especially in cultures inoculated with natural water from a reservoir.

The morphology, trophic state, stratification, and oxygen content of lakes also have strong influences on the preservation and interconversions of organic matter. Seasonal density stratification partially or completely depletes hypolimnetic oxygen, leading to changes in the distribution of aerobic, microaerophilic, and anaerobic decomposers in the water column and to changes in the benthic animals which are mainly responsible for the oxygenation of surficial sediments. Thus, an understanding of the physical, chemical and, biological conditions within a lake is required before the history of sediment organic compounds can be interpreted.

The scope of this review is limited to naturally occurring specific organic compounds, which we attempt to relate to precursor organisms and to physical, chemical, and biological processes which modify original compounds during and after their sedimentation in lakes. Similar reviews have been undertaken in the recent past by Cranwell (1975, 1976a) and by Philp et al. (1976); the present chapter expands upon and updates these studies. General concepts of organic geochemistry, including the use of biological markers, are found in recent books (Eglinton and Murphy, 1969; Swain, 1970) and review articles (Maxwell et al., 1971; Eglinton, 1973). The organic components of soils, which share many similarities with those of lake sediments, are discussed in a recent book edited by Gieseking (1975). Humic acids, complex macromolecular polyelectrolytes which comprise a large proportion of soil and lake sediment organic matter and which are involved in reactions with inorganic species, are not covered here, as they were reviewed by Gjessing (1976) and were the subject of a recent symposium (Povoledo and Golterman, 1975). Inorganic–organic relationships are discussed in works edited by Singer (1973) and Nriagu (1976). We have not attempted to review the large field of organic pollutants in aquatic sediments, as this subject is covered in annual reviews (Powers et al., 1976).

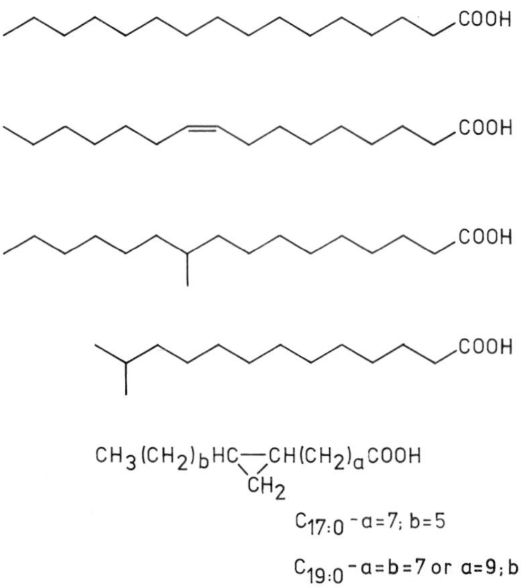

Fatty acids

Because of their relative ease of isolation and identification, and their stability and widespread distribution in lakes, fatty acids and hydrocarbons have been examined extensively. A variety of parameters based on these studies have been proposed as indicators of precursor organisms, of the relative importance of autochthonous versus allochthonous sources, of the effects of lake environment, geochemistry, and trophic state, and of the locations of redox boundaries in the water and sediment.

Total monocarboxylic acids (Figure 1 [1] as an example) isolated from small nonproductive lakes in temperate regions range from 0.02 to 0.08% of the dry sediment (Cranwell, 1974) as compared to 0.1% for small productive lakes (Eglinton et al., 1968). Total fatty acids isolated from the surficial sediments of Lake Huron, a large oligotrophic lake, represent 0.014% of the dry sediment (Meyers et al., 1976); total acids decrease to 40 μg/g at 20 cm depth in the sediment, with relatively small further decrease from 20 to 50 cm.

Distribution and recovery of sediment lipids depend on the extraction method used. Solvent extraction of acidified sediments releases 50 to 75% of the total acids from the sediment of productive lakes, with the

FIGURE 1. Fatty acids: saturated, mono-unsaturated, branched.

remainder being released after subsequent acid or alkaline hydrolysis (Brooks et al., 1976; Matsuda and Koyama, 1977). The effect of the extraction method seems less marked in the sediments of nonproductive lakes. Cranwell (1974) isolated 88% of the total sediment fatty acids by soxhlet extraction of acidified oligotrophic lake sediments. The wide variety of extraction procedures used makes direct comparisons between the results obtained by different workers difficult. In this review, comparisons are made only between samples isolated in a similar manner.

Saturated straight-chain (normal) monocarboxylic acids isolated by solvent extraction of productive lake sediments comprise 60 to 80% of the total mono acids present; they range from C_{14} to C_{32}, with major modes at n-C_{16} (Figure 1 [1]) and at n-C_{24}, n-C_{26}, or n-C_{28} (Cranwell, 1974; Brooks et al., 1976; Eglinton and Hunneman, 1968; Matsuda and Koyama, 1977; Barnes and Barnes, 1978). The same range and bimodal distribution of normal fatty acids were obtained by solvent extraction and subsequent acid hydrolysis of sediments from Esthwaite Water (Brooks et al., 1976), by alkaline hydrolysis of sediments from Lake Biwa (Ishiwatari and Hanya, 1973), and by solvent extraction and subsequent alkaline hydrolysis of sapropelic sediments from Powell Lake, a deep meromictic fjord lake with saline bottom waters (Barnes and Barnes, 1978). In all of these studies the distribution appeared to be unaffected by the extraction method used.

In contrast, the bimodal distribution observed for acids isolated by solvent extraction of sediments from Rostherne Mere, a highly productive lake, shifted to a monomodal distribution of acids ranging from n-C_{14} to n-C_{32}, with n-C_{16} dominant, in the posthydrolysis extract of the sediment (Brooks et al., 1976). In the sediments of Grasmere, the least productive of the productive English lakes studied by Brooks et al. (1976), the acids extracted by both methods have the monomodal distribution more commonly observed in nonproductive lakes, with n-C_{26} and, to a lesser extent, n-C_{24} and n-C_{28} as the dominant acids. In the Grasmere sediments, the range of acids isolated by solvent extraction was from n-C_{15} to n-C_{32}; after subsequent acid hydrolysis the shorter chain acids were absent, with the range being from n-C_{22} to n-C_{32}. The English lakes studied by Brooks et al. (1976) are small (1 to 2 km^2), shallow (15 to 30 m), and cool, with temperature at the sediment–water interface ranging from 6 to 10°C. The lakes are productive and have sediment organic carbon contents ranging from 7 to 9%; the total normal saturated acids isolated by solvent extraction followed by acid hydrolysis range from 31 to 330 μg/g of dry sediment.

For comparison, sediment fatty acids were extracted by Brooks et al. (1976) from three subtropical productive environments—a lagoon, a tidal flat, and a brackish coastal swamp—with mean annual air temperatures ranging from 25 to 30°C. Despite the apparent high productivity of the environments, the preservation of organic matter in the sediment (1.2 to 3% organic C) and the saturated normal acids extracted (12 to 40 μg/g of dry sediment) were low. The effect of the extraction method used is evident in this study: solvent-extracted acids have longer chain lengths (n-C_{24} or n-C_{26} mode) compared with those released by subsequent acid hydrolysis of the sediment (n-C_{16} mode). Brooks et al. (1976) attributed this shift to the hydrolytic release of acids associated with resistant microbial cell walls. Cho and Salton (1966) reported short chain acids (n-C_{12} to n-C_{18}) with n-C_{16} comprising 50% of the total acids and with a strong even-carbon preference in lipids released from resistant gram-negative bacterial cell walls.

Despite very low values for total fatty acids isolated by solvent extraction of oxidizing and reducing sediments from the Dead Sea (4 to 16 μg/g of dry sediment), the pattern of occurrence is similar to that observed in productive lakes (Nissenbaum et al., 1972). Both free and esterified acids have a bimodal distribution, with modes at n-C_{16} and at n-C_{22}, n-C_{24}, or n-C_{26}; odd-carbon acids (n-C_{21} to n-C_{27}) were observed only in the free acids isolated from the deepest (330 m), most reducing sediments in the lake.

In the fatty acids (total range n-C_{14} to n-C_{32}) reported by Brooks et al. (1976) from productive lakes, three patterns are apparent: monomodal with n-C_{16} dominant, monomodal with n-C_{24} or n-C_{26} dominant, and bimodal with both of these modes present. A variety of processes give rise to these patterns. Short chain acids have been attributed to autochthonous

planktonic sources and long chain acids to allochthonous (terrestrial) sources (Cranwell, 1976a). Solvent-soluble acids isolated from both gram-negative bacteria (Cho and Salton, 1966; Oliver and Colwell, 1973) and algae (Schneider et al., 1970; Erwin, 1973) range from n-C_{12} to n-C_{18}, have n-C_{16}, n-$C_{16:1}$ (Figure 1 [2]), or n-$C_{18:1}$ dominant, and show a strong even-carbon preference. In contrast, gram-positive bacteria also have acids ranging from n-C_{12} to n-C_{18}, but have C_{15} or C_{17} branched acids dominant (Cho and Salton, 1966; Kaneda, 1967). Solvent-soluble surficial waxes isolated from aquatic and terrestrial plants (leaves, pollen, flowers, fruit) and insects contribute long chain acids (C_{20} to C_{34}) with a high even-carbon preference (Eglinton and Hamilton, 1967; Mazliak, 1968; Jackson and Baker, 1970). Fungal acids range from n-C_{10} through n-C_{24}, with the dominant acids tending to be n-$C_{16:1}$, n-$C_{18:1}$, and n-$C_{18:2}$ (Weete, 1974). Welch and Burlingame (1973) report acids ranging from n-C_{10} through n-C_{32} for a yeast (Saccharomyces cerevisiae); although the dominant acids are n-$C_{16:1}$ > n-$C_{18:1}$ > n-$C_{16:0}$, 2% of the total acids range from n-C_{20} to n-C_{32}, with n-$C_{26:0}$ as a secondary mode.

Bird and Molton (1972) reviewed fatty acids synthesized by microorganisms using glucose, acetate, or hydrocarbons as a carbon source. While bacteria cultured on glucose or acetate produced primarily short chain acids, those cultured on hydrocarbons produced longer chain acids reflecting the chain length of the source when the amount of hydrocarbon source was limited. The range of acids and the low even-carbon preference commonly observed for microbially degraded sediment lipids in nature probably reflect the relative proportions of gram-positive bacteria, gram-negative bacteria, and fungi, the range of available substrates, the effect of limiting nutrients in the environment (Berkaloff and Kader, 1975), and the effect of extracellular components produced by plankton on the evolving bacterial population. Algal blooms have been shown to produce bactericides which inhibit the growth and respiration of gram-positive bacteria (Chróst, 1975). Parasitism of phytoplankton as great as 70% has been reported for both healthy, rapidly growing cells and senescent algae in the English lakes; the best known organisms are the chytridiaceous or biflagellated phycomycetous fungi, which infect diatoms, desmids, and blue–green algae (Canter and Lund, 1948, 1969; Wetzel, 1975). Weete (1974) reports mono-, di-, and tri-unsaturated fatty acids in the range n-C_{13} through n-C_{20}, and in some species branched C_{14}, C_{15} and C_{16} acids, from aquatic fungi. Because of the difference in fatty acid content in the various precursor organisms, parameters such as the ratio of short to long chain acids (Σn-C_{16} to n-C_{18}/Σn-C_{20} to n-C_{32}) and the even-carbon preference (CPI) have been used by a number of writers as a measure of microbial degradation and of the relative contributions of autochthonous and allochthonous organisms (Ishiwatari and Hanya, 1975; Cranwell, 1976b).

Lipids released by sediment hydrolysis appear to arise from a variety of sources and to be bound by a number of mechanisms. Short chain acids (n-$C_{16:0}$ and n-$C_{16:1}$ in bacteria; n-$C_{16:1}$ in yeasts) bound to microbial membranes or cell walls through ester or amide links are released by acid hydrolysis (Cho and Salton, 1966; Weete, 1974; Boon et al., 1975, 1976). Intact diatoms and some algae are more resistant to microbial decay (Kudryavtsev, 1975) and can survive solvent extraction with sonication (Barnes and Barnes, 1978); however, cell contents can be released by alkaline hydrolysis with accompanying solution of siliceous frustules or by acid hydrolysis of lipopolysaccharide cell walls (Barnes and Barnes, 1978). Longer chain acids are released by hydrolysis of resistant phytopolymers such as cutin, suberin, pollen, and fungus and lycopod spores (Eglinton and Hunneman, 1968; Hunneman and Eglinton, 1972; Mazliak, 1968; Hamilton and Hamilton, 1972; Barbier, 1970; Weete, 1974; Lytle and Sever, 1973). Hydrolysis releases acids sorbed to clays (Meyers and Quinn, 1973) or bonded by occlusion and by ester or amide links to humates and fulvates (Farrington et al., 1977; Schnitzer, 1975).

Povoledo et al. (1975) isolated short chain fatty acids in the range n-C_{12} to n-C_{18} by solvent extraction of sediment humic acids from lakes of the Precambrian Shield of Canada. The even-carbon preference was high (CPI = 20) for the normal acids, the dominant components of which were n-$C_{14:0}$, n-$C_{16:0}$, and n-$C_{16:1}$, present in approximately equal amounts; 28% of the acids were branched. The authors suggested that the acids were derived from microorganisms rather than from terrestrial rooted plants.

Ishiwatari (1975) isolated long chain acids (range n-C_{11} to n-C_{34}) associated with humic acid isolated from Lake Haruna, a small (1.23 km²), shallow (13 m) mesotrophic lake in Japan. Prior to the separation of the humic acids, the sediments were extracted with benzene–methanol to remove loosely bound lipids. The humic acids were methylated following their alkaline extraction from the sediment, and the methylated humic acids were then extracted with benzene to separate the strongly bound fatty acids. Although long chain acids were found in small quantities, the dominant acids were n-$C_{16:0}$ > n-$C_{16:1}$ > n-$C_{14:0}$ > n-$C_{18:1}$, with small amounts of branched acids in the range br-C_{11} through br-C_{17} and longer unsaturated acids to n-$C_{24:1}$. The primary source of the organic matter in the lake sediments is phytoplankton. Fatty acids strongly bound to the sediment humic acids represented 0.2 to 0.3% of the total weight of humic acids; Ishiwatari (1975) estimated that approximately 10% of these fatty acids were accessible to direct extraction of the sediments with benzene–methanol.

Schnitzer (1975) reported less than 10% of hydrocarbons and fatty acids associated with soil humates and fulvates are removed by solvent extraction. Normal fatty acids (104 μg/g of humic acid) comprised 16% of total monocarboxylic acids isolated by solvent extraction of unmethylated humic acid. The normal acids ranged from n-C_{12} to n-C_{32}, with n-C_{12} and n-C_{16} dominant; the even-carbon preference was 12. Branched and cyclic acids (545 μg/g of humic acid) comprised 84% of the solvent-extractable acids; thus, the ratio of n-saturated acids to branched plus cyclic acids is a low value of 0.19. Schnitzer (1975) used thin-layer chromatography or column chromatography to separate the strongly bound fatty acids (1380 μg/g of humic acid) by percolation of solvent through methylated humic acids adsorbed onto Al_2O_3. The even-carbon preference for these strongly bound fatty acids is much lower (CPI = 2.6), and branched acids were absent. Schnitzer suggested that the humic acids have a sponge-like structure made up of phenolic and benzenecarboxylic acids which limit interior dimensions. Normal acids and alkanes are strongly sorbed to interior sites and are thus inaccessible to solvent extraction; the more bulky branched acids and alkanes are adsorbed onto outer surfaces of the humic and fulvic acids. Schnitzer attributes fatty acids accessible to solvent extraction to microbial sources and the strongly bound normal acids to plant waxes. However, the low even-carbon preference of the strongly bound normal acids suggests some microbial modification of plant wax acids, which tend to be even-carbon acids (Eglinton and Hamilton, 1967), has occurred during the formation of the soil humates (Braids and Miller, 1975). Thus, although lipids strongly bound to soil and lake sediment humates are a source of small amounts of long chain acids, the dominant acids in the shallow and mesotrophic lakes studied are saturated and unsaturated short chain acids (Ishiwatari 1975; Povoledo et al. 1975; Schnitzer 1975).

In their study of productive English lakes, Brooks et al. (1976) found a significant increase in even-carbon preference (CPI) for acids isolated by a subsequent sediment hydrolysis relative to those isolated by a preliminary solvent extraction (Rostherne mere, CPI 24.3 vs 13.9; Esthwaite Water, CPI 9.8 vs. 6.5; Grasmere, CPI 8.4 vs 4.5). The high CPI and abundance of n-C_{16} suggest a significant contribution of cell wall lipids from algae and gram-negative bacteria in sediments from Rostherne mere and Esthwaite Water; on the other hand, the high CPI and longer chain acids are consistent with a significant contribution from the hydrolysis of allochthonous fresh plant material, humic compounds, or resistant phytopolymers in the sediments of Esthwaite Water and Grasmere.

Less productive lakes such as Grasmere, oligotrophic lakes such as Ennerdale Water and Seathwaite Tarn, and older peats have approximately 90% of their monobasic fatty acids as n-alkanoic acids in the range n-C_{14} through n-C_{30}, with n-C_{24} or n-C_{26} dominant (Cranwell, 1974). In his study of productive lakes, oligotrophic lakes, and potential contributors of allochthonous materials, such as peats, deciduous humus, and coniferous humus, from areas surrounding these lakes, Cranwell reported even-carbon preference for solvent-extracted normal carboxylic acids from spruce humus (H-layer; CPI = 27) and recent peats (CPI = 13); on the average, productive lakes exhibited similar or higher even-carbon preference (Blelham Tarn, CPI = 9.6) than oligotrophic lakes (Ennerdale Water, CPI = 5.9; Seathwaite Tarn, CPI = 6.5).

Branched and cyclic acids accessible to solvent extraction comprise 84% of those acids associated with soil humates (Schnitzer, 1975), 28% of those from lake sediment humates (Ishiwatari, 1975; Povoledo *et al.*, 1975), 12% of the total monocarboxylic acids from productive lake sediments, and 3–8% of those from oligotrophic lakes (Cranwell, 1973a, 1974). Analysis of Cranwell's data suggests several potential chemical markers which may serve to discriminate between productive and nonproductive lakes and their different contributions from autochthonous and allochthonous sources; combined with paleobotanical evidence, the use of chemical markers permits identification of earlier trophic states in lakes. Potential parameters include: (1) the ratio of n-saturated acids to branched and cyclic acids; (2) the contribution of branched odd-carbon acids such as br-C_{13}, b-C_{15}, br-C_{17}, and br-C_{19} to the total branched and cyclic acids; (3) the contribution of iso-branched even-carbon acids (Figure 1 [4]); (4) cyclopropanoic acids (Figure 1 [5]); (5) isoprenoid acids; and (6) branched acids with a mid-chain methyl group (Figure 1 [3]). Productive lakes have more branched and cyclic acids (n-sat/br + cyclic = 11.1 to 31.7) than deciduous humus (n-sat/br + cyclic = 9.4), spruce humus (n-sat/br + cyclic = 11), or acid peat (n-sat/br + cyclic = 12 to 18.2). Productive lakes in Cranwell's study have 40 to 56% of their branched and cyclic acids as odd-carbon iso and anteiso acids (br-C_{13} to br-C_{19}, with br-C_{15} dominant) as compared to 16 to 27% in oligotrophic lakes. The even-carbon acid, iso-C_{14} (Figure 1 [4]); contributes 8 to 12% of the branched and cyclic acids in productive lakes but 1% or less in oligotrophic lakes or in acid and mull humus. Cyclopropanoic acids (Figure 1 [5]) are more common in productive lakes, in the surface sediments of oligotrophic lakes, in recent peats, and in mull humus (6 to 12% of the total branched and cyclic acids). By contrast, phytanic acid (Figure 2 [6]), the most common of the isoprenoid acids (C_{16}, C_{17}, C_{19}, and C_{20}), contributed 20 to 28% of the branched + cyclic acids of oligotrophic lakes and lesser amounts to productive lakes (4 to 7%) and to acid or mull humus and peat (7 to 8%). Like the isoprenoid acids, 10-methyl hexade-

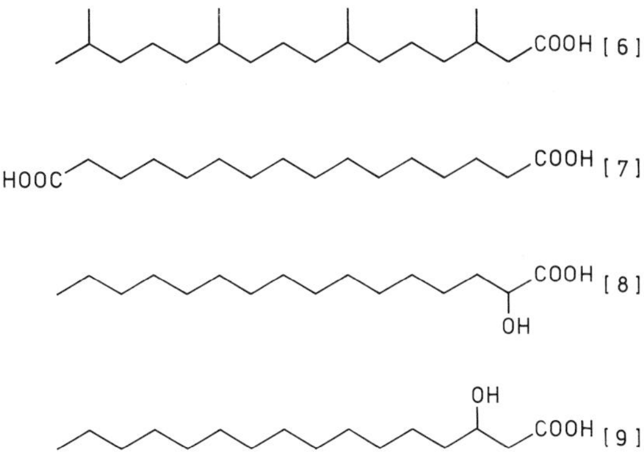

FIGURE 2.   Isoprenoid, dicarboxylic, and hydroxy fatty acids.

canoic acid (Figure 1 [3]) and 10-methyl octadecanoic acid are more common in nonproductive than in productive lakes (Cranwell, 1974). Cranwell (1973a) reported small or negligible changes in the amounts and distribution of the branched + cyclic acids with depth to 60 cm in the sediments of Blelham Tarn; as a result he concluded that the 10-methyl acids did not arise from the corresponding cyclopropanoic acids as a reduction product in anaerobic sediments.

In Cranwell's (1976b) study of aerobic and anaerobic decay of a bloom of the dinoflagellate *Ceratium hirundinella*, collected from Blelham Tarn, trends in the branched + cyclic acid fraction after anaerobic decay matched those observed for the sediments of this and other productive lakes which develop periodic oxygen depletion in their hypolimnions. The branched + cyclic acids after aerobic decay tended to follow trends observed in oligotrophic lakes with oxygenated bottom waters. Whereas branched odd-carbon acids (br-C_{13}, br-C_{15}, and br-C_{17}) were the dominant branched + cyclic acids resulting from anaerobic decomposition, those arising from aerobic decay were equally distributed between the odd-carbon branched acids, isoprenoid acids, and cyclopropanoid acids. Algae decomposed under aerobic conditions showed marked increases in the isoprenoid C_{16}, C_{19}, and C_{20} acids and the cyclopropanoid C_{17} and C_{19} acids relative to both the fresh algae and the products of anaerobic decomposition. Isoprenoid and cyclopropanoid acids may serve as markers of aerobic microbial decomposition.

Cranwell's (1973a, 1974) studies of saturated, unsaturated, branched, and cyclic acids isolated from small productive and nonproductive lakes in a temperate climate show significant correlations between sediment lipids and those isolated from planktonic sources and from peats, deciduous humus, and coniferous humus from the surrounding environments. In addition, changes in the lipid patterns were shown to correlate with pollen horizons in lake sediment cores, indicating their relationships with changes in climate, trophic state, and amount and type of allochthonous contributions.

In summary, bimodal distributions of acids tend to characterize productive lakes with significant contributions both from algae and bacteria and from higher plants. However, the input of organic compounds from acid peats, deciduous humus, and littoral plants and the subsequent microbial decomposition in the water column and sediment can shift the overall distribution to monomodal favoring the longer chain acids more commonly characteristic of oligotrophic lakes. Branched odd-carbon acids, cyclopropanoic C_{17} and C_{19} acids, and 10-methyl C_{16} and C_{18} acids are all associated with bacterial sources (Polacheck et al., 1966; Christie, 1970) and aquatic fungi (Ballio and Barcellona, 1971; Weete, 1974).

In general, the unsaturated acids show similar distributions to those observed for the saturated acids in recent lake sediments. Short chain unsaturated acids are associated with autochthonous algal and bacterial sources, whereas longer chain acids are derived from allochthonous higher plants (Cranwell, 1974). Total mono-unsaturated (one double bond) alkenoic acids (e.g., Figure 1 [2]) range from 72 to 285 $\mu g/g$ of dry sediment in productive lakes (Brooks et al., 1976; Matsuda and Koyama, 1977), with 2 to 10 times more mono-unsaturated acids being extracted by the initial solvent extraction of acidified sediments than by subsequent acid or alkaline hydrolysis. Young sediments from productive lakes have the largest contributions of solvent extractable mono-unsaturated acids and a correspondingly low ratio of n-saturated to mono-unsaturated acids (0.13 to 2.9). Despite the low values for total unsaturated acids isolated by solvent extraction of oxidizing and reducing Dead Sea sediments (1.12 to 4.22 $\mu g/g$) (Nissenbaum et al., 1972), the ratio of n-saturated to unsaturated acids (2.63 to 5.23) is more similar to that for productive lakes than to that for oligotrophic lakes (30 to 91) (Cranwell, 1974; Brooks et al., 1976; Matsuda and Koyama, 1977).

Values of the ratio of n-saturated to mono-unsaturated acids similar to those of productive lakes are found in gram-negative bacteria (0.61 to 4.3) (Cho and Salton, 1966), green algae (0.36 to 1.23) and blue-green algae (0.86 to 2.6) (Schneider et al., 1970), and in loosely bound fatty acids associated with lake sediment humic acids (2.37) (Povoledo et al., 1975). Fewer unsaturated acids, and the larger ratios of n-saturated to mono-unsaturated acids found in non-productive lakes, are observed in recent spruce humus (4.8), deciduous humus (14), and acid peats (11 to 30) (Cranwell, 1974).

Brooks et al. (1976) and Matsuda and Koyama (1977) observed the largest contributions of mono-unsaturated acids in small, shallow eutrophic lakes with 5.5 to 9.1% organic carbon in their sediments, such as Esthwaite Water and Lake Suwa. In a study of aerobic and anaerobic decay of *Ceratium hirundinella*, the principal source of autochthonous organic matter in Blelham Tarn, Cranwell (1976b) observed a progressive loss of mono-unsaturated acids during decay. In the fresh dinoflagellate bloom, the ratio was found to be 1.32, whereas it was 3.7 in the aerobically decayed alga and 2.9 in the recent (<30 years) sediments of the Tarn. Larger ratios were found for the products of anaerobic decay of the alga (6.4) and in older (100 to 150 years) Tarn sediments (8.5) (Cranwell, 1974, 1976b). Thus, high sediment concentrations of mono-unsaturated acids appear to be favored by high algal productivity and by low oxygen concentrations, but not by completely anaerobic conditions. In the biochemical synthesis of unsaturated acids, molecular oxygen is required directly for the aerobic processes which desaturate saturated acids. Eubacteria use an anaerobic process which dehydrates β-hydroxy acids (Erwin, 1973). Oxygen-depleted conditions may also favor the preservation of mono-unsaturated acids, whether derived directly from algae or produced by bacterial and fungal degradation of algal blooms (Erwin, 1973; Weete, 1974).

Unsaturated acids from productive environments show two patterns of distribution. Significant amounts of long chain acids were isolated by Matsuda and Koyama (1977) by solvent extraction and subsequent hydrolysis of the sediments of Lake Suwa. The range of unsaturated acids found was from n-$C_{15:1}$ to n-$C_{26:1}$, with a single mode at n-$C_{16:1}$ for the solvent extract and at n-$C_{18:1}$ after the hydrolysis. In Grasmere, Brooks et al. (1976) found a range from n-$C_{16:1}$ to n-$C_{30:1}$ and a bimodal distribution with modes at n-$C_{18:1}$ and n-$C_{24:1}$ for the solvent extract, shifting to a monomodal distribution with n-$C_{18:1}$ dominant after hydrolysis. In highly productive Rostherne mere, the distribution of unsaturated acids is monomodal, with n-$C_{16:1}$ > n-$C_{18:1}$ for the solvent extract, shifting to n-$C_{16:1}$ ≈ n-$C_{18:1}$ after hydrolysis. In Esthwaite Water the pattern is similar, with n-$C_{18:1}$ dominant in the solvent extract and n-$C_{22:1}$ most abundant after subsequent hydrolysis. Mono-unsaturated acids isolated from subtropical swamp, lagoon, and tidal flat sediments are primarily short, with n-$C_{16:1}$ dominant in solvent extracts and n-$C_{18:1}$ dominant after sediment hydrolysis (Brooks et al., 1976). Nissenbaum et al. (1972) reported short chain unsaturated acids with n-$C_{18:1}$ > n-$C_{16:1}$ dominant in both shallow oxidizing and deep reducing sediments from the Dead Sea. They concluded that both acids were rapidly utilized regardless of the environment; however, the decrease in n-$C_{16:1}$ relative to n-$C_{18:1}$ is more marked in the solvent-soluble free acids from the reducing environments than in acids released by hydrolysis of acids esterified to sediment lipids.

While n-$C_{16:0}$, n-$C_{16:1}$, and n-$C_{18:1}$, in order of abundance, tend to be the dominant acids in gram-negative bacteria (Cho and Salton, 1966) and blue-green algae (Schneider *et al.*, 1970; Erwin, 1973), n-$C_{18:1}$ and polyunsaturated acids tend to be dominant in green algae (Schneider *et al.*, 1970; Erwin 1973); n-$C_{16:1}$ and polyunsaturated C_{16} and C_{20} acids are reported for freshwater diatoms (Kates and Volcani, 1966; Erwin, 1973). Lower temperatures, increased oxygen concentrations, and increased salinity (e.g., the Dead Sea) tend to favor the formation of unsaturated acids by algae and bacteria (Erwin, 1973; Oliver and Colwell, 1973). In a review of the sources of unsaturated acids, Matsuda and Koyama (1977) noted that hexadec-9-enoic acid (Δ^9-$C_{16:1}$) and octadec-9-enoic acid (Δ^9-$C_{18:1}$) are the most common mono-unsaturated acids in phytoplankton, zooplankton, fungi, mycobacteria, and higher plants; however, these acids differ in their stereoisomerism with respect to the double bond in different organisms.

Brooks *et al.* (1976) attributed the abundance of n-$C_{16:1}$ isolated by solvent extraction of sediments from Rostherne mere and the subtropical environments they studied to algal sources. A blue-green alga, *Microcystis aeruginosa*, is a major planktonic source in Rostherne mere, while mixed green and blue-green algae contribute to the subtropical sediments. The shift to n-$C_{18:1}$ with sediment hydrolysis in the subtropical samples was attributed to bacterial degradation. Brooks *et al.* (1976) concluded that identification of the stereochemistry and site of unsaturation was necessary if unsaturated acids are to be used as biological markers.

In a study of mono-unsaturated acids isolated from the surficial sediments of Lake Suwa, Matsuda and Koyama (1977) identified the position of the double bond in acids ranging from n-$C_{15:1}$ to n-$C_{26:1}$ using combined gas chromatography–mass spectrometry of the methoxylated derivatives. The ratio of octadec-9-enoic acid to *cis*-octadec-11-enoic acid was suggested as a measure of the relative importance of algal and higher plant to bacterial sources. The mono-unsaturated acids isolated by solvent extraction (240 μg/g of dry sediment) and by subsequent alkaline hydrolysis of the sediment (46 μg/g) were converted to their methoxy esters:

$$\ce{>C=C< ->[Hg(OAc)_2][CH_3OH] -\underset{CH_3O}{\overset{|}{C}}-\underset{HgOAc}{\overset{|}{C}}- ->[NaBH_4] -\underset{CH_3O}{\overset{|}{C}}-\underset{H}{\overset{|}{C}}-}$$

The relative proportions of the isomers were estimated and the position of double bonds identified from the ion intensity and mass spectral fragmentation patterns of the methoxy esters. Matsuda and Koyama (1977) observed no significant difference in the patterns for the unsaturated acids isolated by solvent extraction from those released by sediment hydrolysis. In both extracts the Δ^9 isomer (double bond at C_9, numbered from the carboxyl group) was dominant in

the n-$C_{15:1}$ to n-$C_{19:1}$ acids and the ω^9 isomer (double bond at C_9, numbered from the terminal carbon) was dominant in n-$C_{20:1}$ through n-$C_{24:1}$. Positional isomers for n-$C_{24:1}$ ranged from Δ^7 to Δ^{21}. The principal planktonic sources in the lake are diatoms *(Melosira, Cyclotella, Fragilaria)* and blue-green algae *(Microcystis)*. The ratio of octadec-9-enoic acids to *cis*-octadec-11-enoic acid shifts from 0.87 for acids isolated by solvent extraction to 1.91 for those released by hydrolysis of the sediment. Matsuda and Koyama (1977) concluded the greater abundance of *cis*-octadec-11-enoic acid in the solvent-extracted free acids is consistent with a larger bacterial contribution. The free acids had a lower even-carbon preference (CPI = 7) compared to that of the bound unsaturated acids (CPI = 31.8); this low CPI is also consistent with microbial alteration of the unsaturated free acids. The higher CPI of the bound acids may relate to their derivation from diatoms whose frustules were dissolved by the alkaline hydrolysis, releasing cell contents which had been protected from microbial attack.

Although both mono- and polyunsaturated acids are common constituents of phytoplankton, zooplankton, higher plants, and animals, only the mono-unsaturated acids have been studied in lake sediments. Cranwell (1974) observed significant amounts of mono-unsaturated acids in older sediments of eutrophic lakes; however, the concentration decreased with depth. There is some evidence that lake sediment humates contain loosely bound lipids which include short chain mono- and di-unsaturated acids (Povoledo *et al.*, 1975), but strongly bound lipids in lake sediment humates (Ishiwatari, 1975) and soil humates (Schnitzer, 1975) preserve only mono-unsaturated acids. If lake sediment humates have the sponge-like structure proposed by Schnitzer for soil humates, polyunsaturated acids are probably excluded by their size and conformation to exterior surfaces where they are more available for oxidation and for incorporation into crosslinks in the humic acid structure itself (Philp and Calvin, 1976). Relative to the fresh bloom, Cranwell (1976b) noted substantial losses in the mono- and tetra-unsaturated acids in both the aerobic and anaerobic decomposition of *Ceratium hirundinella;* however, there were significant increases in the di- and tri-unsaturated acids during the anaerobic decay of the bloom. Cranwell attributed the absence of polyunsaturates in the sediments of Blelham Tarn to oxidation during the aerobic conditions which prevail during the winter.

Rhead *et al.* (1971, 1972) studied the fate of labeled oleic acid (n-$C_{18:1}$) ([9,10-^{3}H]oleic acid and [1-^{14}C]oleic acid) injected into sediments near the high tide level of the Severn Estuary. While only 5% or less of the labeled oleic acid was recovered after 9 days incubation, 2% of the label was incorporated into free saturated normal acids and about 0.2% into branched acids (br-C_{15} and br-C_{17}). Ten percent of the label was found to be in polar compounds, including hydroxy acids. The majority of these acids were bound acids which were isolated by hydrolysis of the sediment. Most of the label was incorporated into nonlipid cellular components and acetyl CoA or lost as $^{14}CO_2$ and ^3H_2O. On the basis of the ratio of ^3H to ^{14}C in the newly produced saturated acids, Rhead et al. (1972) concluded that short chain acids (n-C_{12} to n-C_{14}) were produced by hydrogenation and subsequent β-oxidation with loss of C_2 units from the original labeled oleic acid (the degradative path), and that n-C_{16} acid was produced in about equal amounts by both the degradative path and complete synthesis from labeled acetyl CoA, the end-product of the degradative path; n-C_{18} acid was found to have more label than the original substrates and was suggested to be both a product of the hydrogenation of oleic acid and of recycling of labeled n-$C_{16:0}$. Thus, unsaturated acids, once freed from organic matter, appear to be rapidly degraded in sediments and converted to other products.

Hydroxy acids were the most abundant fatty acids found by Eglinton et al. (1968) in 5000-year-old sediments from a depth of 336 to 382 cm in a core collected from Esthwaite Water. Saturated monocarboxylic acids (0.1% dry sediment), dicarboxylic acids (e.g., Figure 2 [7]) (0.05%) and hydroxy acids (0.6%) were isolated after HCl–HF demineralization and alkaline hydrolysis of the sediment. Pollen analysis on the same sample suggested that the principal allochthonous sources of organic matter included deciduous trees (alder, oak, birch, and small amounts of hazel, elm, and willow), grasses, and minor conifers (pines) and sedges. α-Hydroxy (e.g., Figure 2 [8]) and β-hydroxy (e.g., Figure 2 [9]) acids made up 29.4% of the total hydroxy acids; they ranged from C_{10} to C_{24} and had an even-carbon preference of 2.4. Although the α and β isomers were not separated by gas chromatography, the mass spectral fragmentation pattern was consistent with the α isomer being dominant in the longer chain and the β isomer dominant in the shorter chain acids. The distribution of the α- and β-hydroxy acids parallels that of the saturated monocarboxylic acids and the branched C_{15} and C_{17} acids. ω-Hydroxy acids (34.9%) were even-carbon acids ranging from C_{16} to C_{24}, with C_{22} dominant. The α,ω-dicarboxylic acids (e.g., Figure 2 [7]) were found to parallel the ω-monohydroxy acids, both in their dominant acid and in their even-carbon character. Eglinton et al. (1968) attributed the α- and β-hydroxy acids and the dicarboxylic acids to bacterial oxidation of saturated monocarboxylic acids and ω-hydroxy acids, respectively. The 10,16-dihydroxyhexadecanoic acid (18.8% of the hydroxy acids) and the short chain (C_{16} and C_{18}) ω-hydroxy acids were attributed to cutin; longer chain (C_{20} to C_{26}) ω-hydroxy acids were present in relative amounts similar to those observed in sub-

erin, a constituent of cork from the woody parts of plants. p-Hydroxybenzoic acid (Figure 3 [10]) was the only component identified in a mixture of aromatic acids isolated by exhaustive alkaline hydrolysis of the sediment; it was attributed to lignin.

The principal cutin acid in angiosperms and most gymnosperms is 10,16-dihydroxyhexadecanoic acid (Figure 3 [11]); 9,16-dihydroxyhexadecanoic acid is prominent in many gymnosperms and is the dominant cutin acid in Pinus sylvestris. The dominant cutin acid in lower plants such as ferns and lycopods is the 16-monohydroxy C_{16} acid; however, the main cutin acids in higher plants such as the apple are di- and trihydroxy acids such as 10,16-dihydroxy C_{16} and erythro-9,10,18-trihydroxy C_{18} (Eglinton and Hunneman, 1968; Hunneman and Eglinton, 1972). Short chain ω-monohydroxy acids from C_{12} to C_{18} with the hydroxyl group on the terminal carbon are common in all gymnosperms. Long chain even-carbon ω-monohydroxy acids and α,ω-dicarboxylic acids are common in plant epicuticular waxes (Eglinton and Hamilton, 1967).

Bird and Molton (1972) reported the ability of a wide variety of bacteria, yeasts, and molds to utilize hydrocarbons, alcohols, and acids as substrates by introducing a hydroxyl group at the terminal carbon (ω-) or one carbon from the terminal carbon (ω-1); products include short chain dicarboxylic acids, 3-hydroxy acids, and the ω- and (ω-1)-monohydroxy acids. Boon et al. (1975b) reviewed bacterial sources for 2- and 3-monohydroxy acids (the α- and β-isomers) for even-, odd-, and branched-carbon acids from C_{12} to C_{18}. In their study of hydroxy acids isolated from a diatomaceous ooze at a water depth of 183 m in a marine environment, they attributed the α-, ω-, and (ω-1)-monohydroxy acids to the modifications of algal source material by aerobic microbial processes occurring in the water column during sedimentation. 3-Hydroxy acids were interpreted as a measure of microbial alteration in the sediment.

Cranwell (1976b), in his study of the products of aerobic and anaerobic decay of a bloom of Ceratium hirundinella collected from Blelham Tarn, reported 2- and 3-hydroxy acids ranging from C_{14} to C_{20} whose distribution paralleled that of the saturated normal acids. The presence of branched hydroxy C_{15} and C_{17}

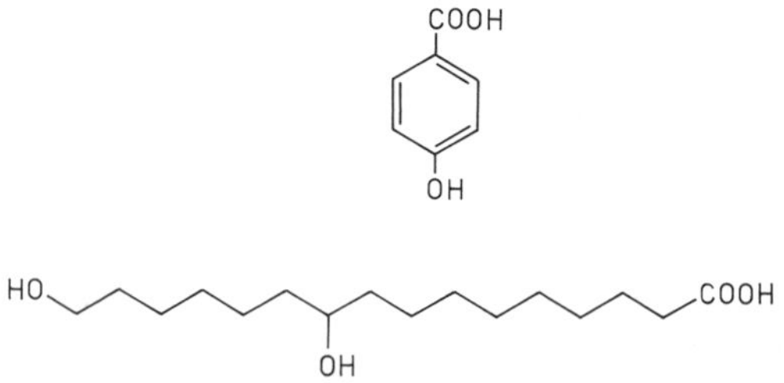

FIGURE 3.   p-Hydroxybenzoic acid and a dihydroxy fatty acid.

acids is consistent with bacterial oxidation of the normal and branched saturated acids. Anaerobic microbial hydration of the cis-C_9 double bond in the $C_{16:1}$ and $C_{18:1}$ monoenoic acids was suggested as the source of the 10-hydroxy C_{16} and C_{18} acids which were isolated.

Dicarboxylic acids ranging from n-C_{15} to n-C_{32}, with modes at C_{16} and in the region of n-C_{24} to n-C_{28}, were isolated from the 200-m core taken from Lake Biwa (Ishiwatari and Hanya, 1973; Ishiwatari and Hanya, 1975). At most depths in the core, the distribution of dicarboxylic acids parallels that of the monocarboxylic acids. The pheopigments and monocarboxylic acids show a maximum concentration, and the dicarboxylic acids a large concentration, at 85 m in the core, within a zone corresponding to an extended warm climate period, as estimated from pollen analyses (Ishiwatari and Hanya, 1975; Fuji, 1974). The n-C_{16} diacid is the principal acid in this zone, and the even-carbon preference of the long chain acids decreases; both factors are consistent with a significant input of short chain planktonic acids which, along with allochthonous sources, are microbially altered to the dicarboxylic acids. Long chain even-carbon monocarboxylic acids with a large CPI are present throughout the core, suggesting that a contribution of stable allochthonous organic matter was present during the entire depositional history of the lake sediments penetrated by the core. At core depths greater than 130 m, the absolute concentration of diacids decreases with depth and the n-C_{16} diacid becomes dominant; the total contribution of long chain monoacids remains high. It is not clear whether microbial conditions at the time of deposition favored the production of the n-C_{16} diacid or whether the longer chain diacids degrade at a greater rate than the monoacids with time and depth of burial.

Johns and Onder (1975) identified 10,16-dihydroxy-hexadecanoic acid as the dominant acid in mangrove leaves and twigs from northern Queensland, with lesser amounts of the mono- and dicarboxylic n-$C_{16:0}$, n-$C_{18:1}$, and n-$C_{18:0}$ acids. Although significant amounts of the dihydroxy acid were found in estuarine tidal-flat sediments colonized by mangroves, this acid was absent from samples from other environments. Even-carbon dicarboxylic acids ranging from n-C_{16} to n-C_{24}, with n-C_{16} dominant, and smaller amounts of octadecenedioic acid, were isolated from the tidal-flat sample. While the monocarboxylic n-$C_{18:1}$ acid appeared to be rapidly utilized by microorganisms, the dicarboxylic n-$C_{18:1}$ acid was used at a slower rate and accumulated in the younger surficial sediments.

The absence of the 10,16-dihydroxy C_{16} acid was interpreted by Johns and Onder (1975) as an indicator of the small contribution from mangroves and other higher plants to a shallow fresh-water lagoon which drained a surrounding agricultural area in Victoria, Australia. Although mangroves were absent from the environment, grasses and aquatic plants were present. Even-carbon dicarboxylic acids ranging from n-C_{16} to n-C_{24}, with n-C_{16} dominant, were attributed to *in situ* production by microorganisms from the organic matter available. The diacid distribution pattern, with a high ratio of long chain diacids to monocarboxylic acids, was similar to the pattern found by Johns and Onder in the sediments of S.E. Victoria tidal flats colonized by *Zostera* sp., with no mangroves. Although the n-$C_{18:1}$ mono- and dicarboxylic acids were dominant in mangrove leaves, the n-C_{16} dicarboxylic acid was the major diacid isolated from all of the sediments studied, even those with abundant mangroves in the environment.

Isoprenoid compounds

Chlorophyll (Figure 4 [12]) is considered to be the most common precursor of phytol (Figure 5 [13]) and other isoprenoid compounds arising during diagenesis in lake sediments (Cox *et al.*, 1970; Maxwell *et al.*, 1973; Simoneit *et al.*, 1975; de Leeuw *et al.*, 1975). In saline lakes such as the Dead Sea, aerobic halophilic bacteria contribute dihydrophytol (Figure 5 [17]) to the sediment as the diether of phosphatidyl glycerylphosphate (Figure 5 [18]). As a result, exceptionally high values for the ratio dihydrophytol:phytol ($\approx$3:1) and for the ratio dihydrophytol:phytanic acid:phytane (45:29:1) are observed (Nissenbaum *et al.*, 1972; Kaplan and Friedman, 1970; Kaplan and Baedecker, 1970; Kates *et al.*, 1965).

Using combined gas chromatography–mass spectrometry of the methyl esters and gas chromatography of the menthyl esters, Maxwell *et al.* (1973) established the absolute configurations of the free isoprenoid acids from C_{14} to C_{19}, including phytanic acid

FIGURE 4. Chlorophyll. ⧏ = group below plane of ring.

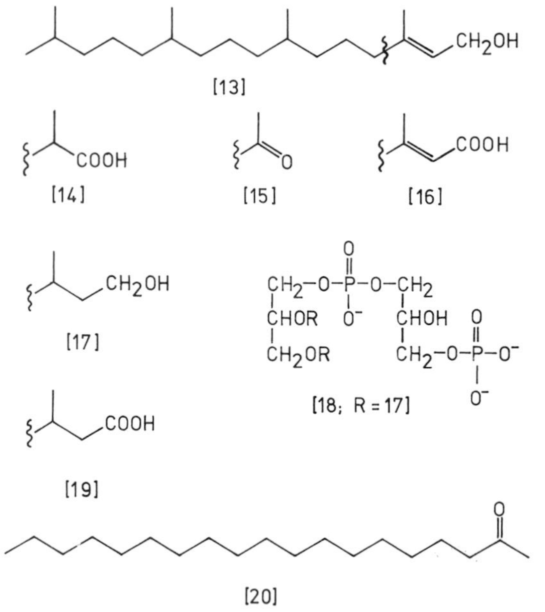

FIGURE 5. Phytol [13]; terminations of phytol derivatives shown to right of ξ in [13] through [17] and [19]. [18] is the dihydrophytol diether of phosphatidyl glycerylphosphate. Methyl ketone is shown in [20].

(Figure 5 [19]), isolated by solvent extraction from the lacustrine Green River oil shale of Eocene age; their stereochemistry was found to be compatible with derivation from the phytol side chain of chlorophyll. Using similar techniques, Simoneit et al. (1975) established the absolute configurations of the C_{14} to C_{16} isoprenoid acids and the relative configurations of phytone (Figure 5 [15]) and C_{19} and C_{20} isoprenoid acids isolated after oxidation of kerogen from the same shale. Similarities in stereochemistry support phytol as the direct or indirect precursor of isoprenoid compounds in lake sediments.

Boon et al. (1975c) report the presence of (E)Δ^2-phytenic acid (Figure 5 [16]) and the absence of dihydrophytol in degraded detritus of Fontinalis antipyretica collected from Lonnekermeer, a small nonpolluted oligotrophic lake at Twente, Holland. Both dihydrophytol (Brooks and Maxwell, 1974) and phytenic acid have been postulated as intermediates in the diagenesis of phytol in sediments (Ikan et al., 1975a; de Leeuw et al., 1975). Two mechanisms have been proposed for the biosynthetic conversion of phytol to phytanic acid: via dihydrophytol or via phytenic aldehyde and phytenic acid (Lough, 1973). In tracer experiments with mice, Mize et al. (1969) found that [^{14}C]phytol was converted to labeled phytenic acid, and that [^{14}C]phytanic acid was altered to labeled 2-hydroxyphytanic acid and to the C_{19}-, C_{16}-, and C_{14}-isoprenoid acids. Phytol, dihydrophytol, and phytanic acid have been identified in cow rumen lipids; tracer experiments using [U-^{14}C]phytol (Patton and Benson,

1966) showed the conversion of phytol to dihydrophytol and phytanic acid by microorganisms inhabiting the rumen. As rumen and anaerobic sediment microflora are similar, such processes may also occur in lake sediments below the aerobic zone. Since dihydrophytol and phytenic acid appear to be mutually exclusive, both in sediments and as biosynthetic intermediates, dihydrophytol has been proposed as an indicator compound for phytol diagenesis in oxygen-poor environments, and phytenic acid as an indicator of oxygen-rich environments (Boon et al., 1975c; de Leeuw et al., 1975).

In addition to (E)Δ^2-phytenic acid and phytanic acid, de Leeuw et al. (1975) isolated C_{15} to C_{17} and C_{19} isoprenoid acids as free lipids, and phytone and phytol as bound lipids, from the degraded plant debris of Lonnekermeer cores. In tracer studies, labeled phytol was injected at the boundaries between moss and algal detritus and sand, and between mud and sand layers in the core. The principal labeled products from incubation studies were phytanic acid, phytone, and phytadienes. Both phytenic acid and dihydrophytol were absent. In simulation experiments, phytol was heated with montmorillonite at 60°C for 2 to 28 days, both in the presence and the absence of oxygen and water. A complex array of isoprenoid hydrocarbons, ketones, aldehydes, acids, alcohols, and di- and trimeric compounds were isolated. In one experiment with oxygen, phytenic acid was produced, but it was not found in the products of any of the oxygen-poor experiments. Regardless of whether phytol alteration is biogenic or abiogenic, dihydrophytol was postulated as an indicator of alteration under anoxic conditions and phytenic acid as an indicator of oxygenated conditions (de Leeuw et al., 1974; de Leeuw et al., 1975; Boon et al., 1975c).

Phytanic acid (Figure 5 [19]), phytone (Figure 5 [15]), and phytadienes were isolated as labeled products arising from incubation in lake sediments of [U-^{14}C]phytol at 20°C for 2 to 8 weeks (Brooks and Maxwell, 1974; de Leeuw et al., 1974). In addition, Brooks and Maxwell (1974) isolated labeled dihydrophytol and pristanic acid (Figure 5 [14]) as incubation products from Esthwaite Water sediments. Labeled phytol was reesterified during incubation; chlorophyll, pheophytin, carboxylic acids, and sediment-bound acids were proposed as potential esterifying groups. With the exception of phytadienes, all the compounds labeled in the incubation studies were present in the sediment prior to incubation. As phytol was observed to dehydrate to phytadienes during thin-layer chromatography, the labeled phytadienes were assumed to be artifacts of the clean-up procedure used in the incubation studies. Pristane and phytane were not labeled during the short incubation periods used; however, their presence as unlabeled components of sediments estimated as <5 years old by the ^{137}Cs method suggests rapid diagenesis of phytol to phytane and pristane does occur. Phytanic acid and phytone were reported as alteration products synthesized by phytol-utilizing bacteria isolated from Esthwaite Water sediments (Brooks and Maxwell, 1974). The conversion of phytol to dihydrophytol, phytanic acid, and pristanic acid was attributed to microbial processes, including reduction under anaerobic conditions. Several authors have noted that both phytol and phytenic acid can be overlooked. Rijpstra *et al.* (1976) report the conversion of phytol to the methyl ethers of phytol and isophytol by BF$_3$-methanol, a reagent commonly used to esterify and transesterify carboxylic acids. In sediments extracted using alkaline benzene–methanol, phytenic acid is converted to the methyl ester during the extraction process; in the subsequent clean-up procedures, methyl phytenate chromatographs with the hydrocarbon fraction rather than with the acids (Boon *et al.*, 1975c; de Leeuw *et al.*, 1975).

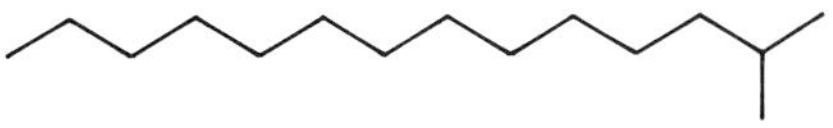

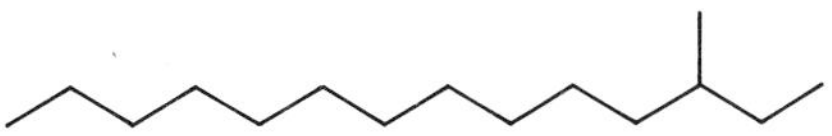

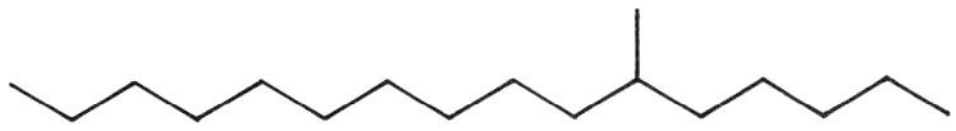

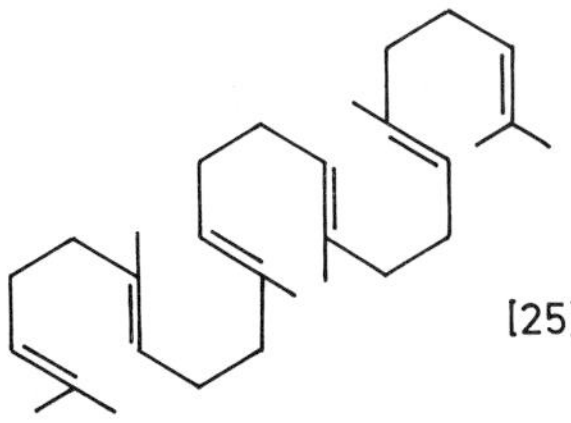

Alcohols and ketones

Plant cuticular waxes include long chain even-carbon alcohols and aldehydes ranging from C$_{12}$ to C$_{36}$, with C$_{26}$, C$_{28}$, or C$_{30}$ as major components. Odd-carbon long chain mono-ketones of waxes range from C$_{24}$ to C$_{33}$, with C$_{29}$ and C$_{31}$ as principal constituents (Kolattukudy and Walton, 1972). Although long chain alcohols, ketones and methyl ketones have been isolated from peats and soils (Morrison, 1969; Braids and Miller, 1975), they have not yet been studied in detail in lake sediments. Ikan *et al.* (1975b) reported 0.25 μg/g of n-C$_{22}$ and n-C$_{24}$ saturated and mono-unsaturated alcohols in marine sediments. Cranwell (1976b) found C$_{15}$, C$_{17}$, and C$_{19}$ methyl ketones (Figure 5 [20]) and phytone (Figure 5 [15]) as alteration products of the anaerobic and aerobic decay of a dinoflagellate collected from Blelham Tarn. He also reported methyl n-alkyl ketones ranging from n-C$_{19}$ to n-C$_{33}$, with a strong odd-carbon preference, and even-carbon alcohols ranging from C$_{18}$ to C$_{30}$ in lake sediments (Cranwell, 1976a).

Pentacyclic triterpenoid acids

Pentacyclic triterpenoid acids with a hopane structure are quite common in lacustrine sediments (Eglinton *et al.*, 1974). A C$_{32}$ hopanoic acid (Figure 7 [28b]) is the most abundant free acid in Rostherne mere and Grasmere sediments (van Dorsselaer *et al.*, 1974). Cranwell (1976a) reports that a 17β H,21β H-C$_{32}$ (Figure 7 [28b]) hopanoic acid is the most common constituent of the branched and cyclic alkanoic acid fraction in

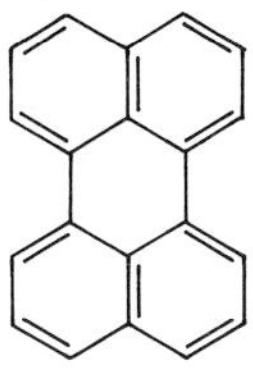

FIGURE 6. Normal [21], iso- [22], and anteiso-branched [23] hydrocarbons, a mid-chain methyl hydrocarbon [24], and squalene [25].

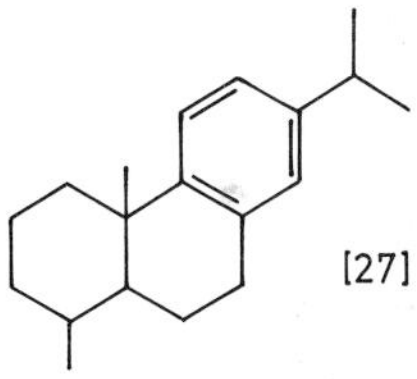

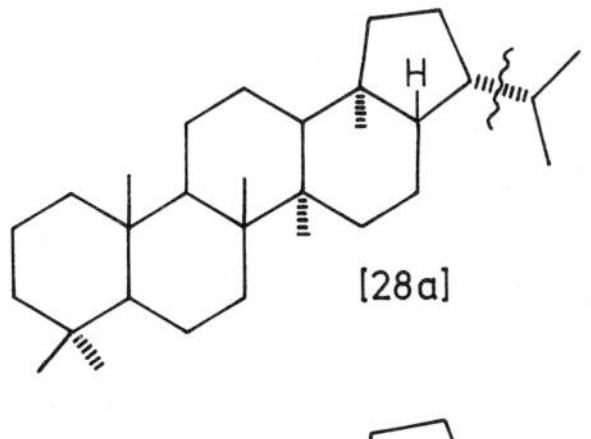

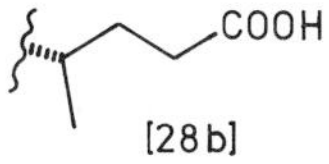

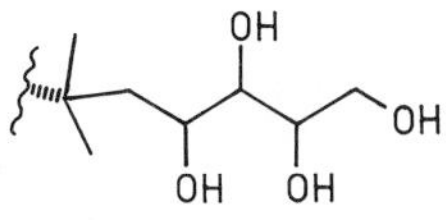

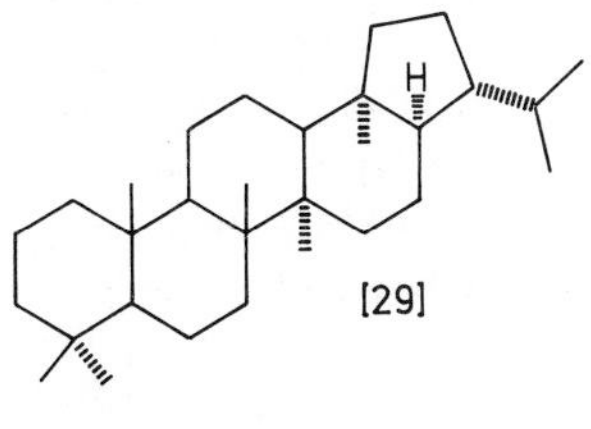

FIGURE 7. Perylene [26], dehydroabietin [27], some members of the hopane series [28], and 17α H-hopane [29].

five sediment horizons from a Scottish loch and suggests that the tetrahydroxy C_{35} hopane derivative (Figure 7 [28c]) isolated from *Acetobacter xylinum* by Förster *et al.* (1973) may be its precursor.

Steranes and triterpanes

Although much work has been accomplished on the steranes and triterpanes of ancient rocks and petroleums (e.g., Ensminger *et al.*, 1974; van Dorsselaer *et al.*, 1974), comparatively little work has been done to date on their occurrence in modern lacustrine sediments. However, the pentacyclic triterpanes of the hopane series are widespread and abundant (Eglinton *et al.*, 1974; van Dorsselaer *et al.*, 1974; Cranwell, 1976a). Many of the triterpenoids with the hopane (Figure 7 [28a]) skeleton have been found in prokaryotes (Bird *et al.*, 1971a), ferns, mosses, and lichens; however, the sediments of Rostherne mere, Grasmere, and Esthwaite Water contain the $(17\alpha H,21\beta H)$-hopane series (Figure 7 [29]) which is not known in living organisms (van Dorsselaer *et al.*, 1974) but may arise from the activities of microorganisms during sedimentation.

Hydrocarbons

Total hydrocarbons range from 5 to 180 μg/g in unpolluted lake sediments (Meyers *et al.*, 1976; Brooks *et al.*, 1976) to 860 to 1600 μg/g in polluted sediments from Lake Zug, Switzerland (Giger *et al.*, 1974) and Lake Washington, U.S.A. (Wakeham and Carpenter, 1976). As a rule, lake sediment saturated normal hydrocarbons range in chain length from n-C_{15} to n-C_{35}. However, in Lake Kivu, a rift-valley lake in East Africa, the dominant hydrocarbons are methane and heptadecane (n-C_{17}), with small amounts of short chain hydrocarbons to n-C_6; primary sources in the lake are plankton (dominantly *Nitzschia* sp.) and methane-generating and methane-oxidizing bacteria (Degens *et al.*, 1973). A bimodal distribution, with dominant hydrocarbons at n-C_{17} and n-C_{27}, n-C_{29} or n-C_{31}, is observed in Rostherne mere, Powell Lake, Lake Washington, Lake Zug, and nearshore shallow sediments of the Dead Sea; these lakes are characterized by both a planktonic contribution and an allochthonous contribution from terrestrial sources.

Cranwell (1973b) reports that hydrocarbons in the surrounding plant cover correlate with sediment hydrocarbons in oligotrophic lakes. A monomodal distribution, with n-C_{31} dominant and approximately equal to the sum of n-C_{27} + n-C_{29}, was observed for hydrocarbons both in sediments from Burnmoor Tarn,

Seathwaite Tarn, and Ennerdale Water, and in the surrounding acid peats and coniferous wood humus. On this basis, Cranwell proposed that a strongly dominant n-C_{31} alkane pattern is an indicator of acid peats or coniferous humus as allochthonous sources in oligotrophic lakes. Cranwell noted a shift to a broadly monomodal distribution, with approximately equal amounts of n-C_{27}, n-C_{29}, and n-C_{31}, in older sediments from Burnmoor and Seathwaite Tarns, where the dominant pollen is from deciduous trees; this pattern is found in productive lakes, in mull humus from deciduous trees, and as products of anaerobic decay of the dinoflagellate *Ceratium hirundinella*. The change in pollen type and hydrocarbon pattern correlates with the clearing of the forests in the Middle Ages (Cranwell, 1973b). Hydrocarbons from both fresh samples of *Ceratium hirundinella* and the products of its aerobic decay show the n-C_{31} > (n-C_{27} + n-C_{29}) pattern in contrast to that observed with anaerobic decay.

Heptadecane (Figure 6 [21]) is a major component in the products of both aerobic and anaerobic decay of *Ceratium hirundinella;* however, it is absent in both the fresh alga and in sediments from Blelham Tarn, where the dinoflagellate was collected (Cranwell, 1976b). As n-C_{17} is a dominant hydrocarbon in most photosynthetic algae and bacteria, it has been used as an indicator of autochthonous sources (Han *et al.*, 1968). While the presence of n-C_{17} indicates a significant contribution from algae or bacteria, its absence may also reflect removal by competitive microbial processes in productive environments such as Mud Lake, Blelham Tarn, and Grasmere, and in shallow-water subtropical sediments (Han *et al.*, 1968; Cranwell, 1973b, 1976b; Brooks *et al.*, 1976).

The strong odd-carbon preference in hydrocarbons from fresh algae approaches unity in hydrocarbons altered by the aerobic and anaerobic decay of *Ceratium hirundinella*. Cranwell (1976b) suggested that an increase in hydrocarbons in the region of n-C_{18} to n-C_{26} and a CPI near unity are indicators of microbial alteration. Increases in the n-C_{18} through n-C_{20} and longer chain hydrocarbons have been observed in nonphotosynthetic bacteria and yeasts (Han *et al.*, 1968; Bird and Lynch, 1974).

Bound hydrocarbons, released by acid hydrolysis of sediments, represented 10 to 24% of the total hydrocarbons in productive lakes analyzed by Brooks *et al.* (1976); they were probably bound to clays and humates. A significant difference in distribution of free and bound hydrocarbons was observed only in Grasmere; the free hydrocarbons had a large odd-carbon preference and a pattern consistent with drainage from surrounding peats. Bound hydrocarbons showed a marked decrease in odd-carbon preference and an increase in the n-C_{25}, n-C_{27}, and n-C_{29} hydrocarbons similar to increases observed from microbial alteration of hydrocarbons in productive environments (Brooks et al., 1976; Cranwell, 1976b) and in hydrocarbons bound to soil humates (Schnitzer, 1975).

In productive lakes such as Grasmere, Esthwaite Water, and Rostherne mere, mono-unsaturated hydrocarbons in amounts from 0.1 to 10 μg/g of dry sediment were isolated with a range similar to that of the saturated hydrocarbons but with a lower odd-carbon preference (Brooks et al., 1976).

The 7- and 8-methyl heptadecanes were isolated from Rostherne mere, where the blue-green alga *Microcystis* sp. is the dominant phytoplankter; a similar compound with a shorter elution time was isolated from Grasmere (Eglinton et al., 1974). The 6-methyl hexadecane (Figure 6 [24]) was isolated from Powell Lake, Canada (Barnes and Barnes, 1978); 6- and 7-methyl hexadecanes have been identified in *Chroococcus* sp. (Bird and Lynch, 1974), a blue-green alga identified in the lake plankton. Branched hydrocarbons from br-C_{17} to br-C_{20} with a mid-chain methyl group on carbon 4, 6, 7, or 8 are diagnostic of blue-green algae and comprise up to 75% of the total hydrocarbons in *Lyngbya majuscula* (Bird and Lynch, 1974; Oehler, 1976).

Gas-liquid chromatograms of aliphatic hydrocarbons extracted by Wakeham and Carpenter (1976) from surficial sediments of Lake Washington, U.S.A. showed hydrocarbons ranging from n-C_{17} to n-C_{33} superimposed on an unresolved complex mixture typical of petroleum contamination in marine and estuarine sediments (Blumer and Sass, 1972; Farrington and Meyers, 1975; Yen, 1975). While n-alkanes make up 17% of the total aliphatic hydrocarbons in sediments deposited prior to the development of metropolitan Seattle, adjacent to Lake Washington, after 1880, they comprise only about 1% of the hydrocarbons of the surficial sediments. The odd-carbon preference for the n-C_{14} to n-C_{20} hydrocarbons changes from 3 to 4 in the older sediments to 1 in the modern sediments, while that for the n-C_{20} through n-C_{36} hydrocarbons changes from 4 to 2. On the basis of radiocarbon dating of the total organic matter in the surficial sediments and a date of 18,000 years B.P. for the extractable hydrocarbons, Wakeham and Carpenter (1976) estimated that 90% of the hydrocarbons were of fossil origin. No major oil spill has occurred in Lake Washington, and sewage has been diverted from the lake since 1963. As normal and branched alkanes make a very small contribution to the surficial sediment hydrocarbons, Wakeham and Carpenter concluded that lubricating oils, which have the normal and branched alkanes removed during the refining process, rather than fuel oils were the primary source of the contamination and arise from urban storm run-off. Normal alkanes extracted from sediments deposited prior to 1880 ranged from n-C_{14} to n-C_{36}, with n-C_{27} or n-C_{29} dominant. Higher plants were considered the major

source of organic matter in the lake prior to that time. Pristane ranged from 1 μg/g in surficial sediments to 0.1 μg/g in the older sediments, while phytane ranged from 0.06 to 0.02 μg/g. Pristane and phytane levels in the nonpolluted sediments from the Dead Sea are 0.05 and 0.02 to 0.03 μg/g, respectively (Nissenbaum et al., 1972).

Wakeham (1977) used synchronous fluorescence spectroscopy to distinguish the aromatic hydrocarbons of Lake Washington sediments. Surficial sediments have naphthalenes and 3- and 4-ring compounds as their dominant aromatic hydrocarbons; these were suggested to be derived from stormwater run-off carrying petroleum-derived pollutants. Samples of older sediments, deposited about 1850 and 1900, from the same core contained perylene (Figure 7 [26]) in amounts from 1.0 to 1.4 μg/g of dry sediment, in addition to the naphthalenes and 3- and 4-ring compounds. Perylene was proposed as a by-product of processes in reducing sediments. Ishiwatari and Hanya (1975) found perylene in amounts ranging up to 1.6 μg/g of dry sediment in samples from the 200-m core from Lake Biwa. In an earlier paper, they found a wide range of aromatic hydrocarbons, including small amounts of perylene, in the waters of a highly polluted river draining into Tokyo Bay (Ishiwatari and Hanya, 1974).

Alkylated phenanthrenes and anthracenes have been reported in one example of plant waxes (Kolattukudy and Walton, 1972). Diterpenes make up 20 to 95% of the hydrocarbons in some species of the gymnosperm family Podocarpaceae (del Castillo et al., 1967). Maxwell et al. (1971) reviewed the conversion of mono- and diterpenes in fossil pine stumps buried in peats to alkylated benzenes and phenanthrenes. *Flavobacterium resinovarum* isolated from pine forest soil can utilize diterpenes from pine trees as a sole source of carbon, and dehydroabietin (Figure 7 [27]) is found in pine forest soil. Maxwell et al. (1971) suggested that microorganisms may convert terpenoid compounds to the alkylated aromatics observed in soil and sediments.

Hydrocarbons from cuticular lipids in higher plants usually show a strong odd-carbon preference, range from n-C_{23} to n-C_{35}, and have n-C_{29} or n-C_{31} dominant (Kolattukudy, 1975; Kolattukudy and Walton, 1972; del Castillo et al., 1967). Some emergent monocotyledones in fresh waters, such as *Juncus effusus*, show a higher plant pattern, while others, including those with floating leaves, show a low odd-carbon preference and have a broad carbon range (n-C_{13} to n-C_{37}), with n-C_{25} or n-C_{27} dominant (Nishimoto, 1974). Submerged freshwater plants have a high odd-carbon preference, have a broad carbon range, and have n-C_{19} or n-C_{21} dominant.

Ferns, lycopods, fungi, yeasts, and bacteria commonly have a broad carbon range and a low odd-carbon preference. Ferns and lycopods, which lie phylogenetiially beneath the flowering plants, but above algae, fungi, and bacteria, have a bimodal distribution with dominant hydrocarbons at n-C_{17} and n-C_{29}, and at n-C_{17} or n-C_{18} and at n-C_{25}, n-C_{27}, or n-C_{29}, respectively (Lytle and Sever, 1973; Lytle *et al.*, 1976). Algae commonly have major components at n-C_{17}, n-$C_{17:1}$, n-C_{15}, or n-C_{13}; some green and blue-green algae have a second mode at n-C_{23}, n-C_{25}, or n-$C_{27:1}$. Fungi have n-C_{29} dominant, while yeasts and bacteria show both monomodal and bimodal distributions with n-C_{18} and n-C_{27} dominant (Gelpi *et al.*, 1970; Bird and Lynch, 1974; Han *et al.*, 1968; Weete, 1974).

Botryococcus braunii, a widespread freshwater alga, has three distinct physiological states: 20% of the dry weight of the green active colonies have n-$C_{17:1}$, the dienes at n-$C_{27:2}$, n-$C_{29:2}$, and n-$C_{31:2}$, and a triene at n-$C_{29:3}$ as major components; 70% of the dry weight of the brown resting stage have the tetramethyl acyclic triterpene botryococcene and isobotryococcene ($C_{34:6}$) as major components in the ratio 9:1 (Knights *et al.*, 1970).

Of the isoprenoid hydrocarbons, pristane, but not phytane, has been isolated from flowering plants and evergreen gymnosperms of the family Podocarpaceae (Kolattukudy and Walton, 1972; Lytle and Sever, 1973) and occurs as a product of the conversion of phytol by zooplankton (Farrington and Meyers, 1975). Pristane and phytane comprise as much as 27% of saturated hydrocarbons in ferns (Lytle *et al.*, 1976) and occur in lesser amounts in diatoms (Tornabene *et al.*, 1974), lycopods (Lytle and Sever, 1973), algae, and bacteria (Han *et al.*, 1968; Farrington and Meyers, 1975). Lytle and Sever (1973) suggest, on the basis of gas–liquid chromatography retention times, that pristane and phytane are present in spleenworts, liverworts, and mosses. Squalene (Figure 6 [25]) makes up 0.5% of the dry weight of the methane oxidizer *Methylococcus* sp. (Bird *et al.*, 1971b). More squalene is produced by yeast under anaerobic than aerobic conditions (Weete, 1974). Squalene, dehydro-, and tetrahydrosqualene are synthesized by some bacteria, including *Halobacterium cutirubrum* (Bird and Lynch, 1974).

In a study of the diagenesis of fatty acids and hydrocarbons of *Spartina alterniflora* and *Juncus romerianus* in sandy sediments of a salt marsh, Johnson and Calder (1973) concluded that *in situ* microbial activity rapidly altered fatty acids with an increase in branched acids, characteristic of bacteria, and a loss of unsaturated acids. Hydrocarbons were more stable, but altered hydrocarbons at the base of 60-cm cores had a broader range in carbon number and an odd-carbon preference of 1; n-C_{27} and n-C_{29}, which were dominant in the fresh or dormant plants, decreased, and dominant hydrocarbons shifted to n-C_{18} and approximately equal amounts of n-C_{23}, n-C_{24}, and n-C_{25}, a pattern characteristic of bacteria. Swetland and Wehmiller (1975) observed less rapid alteration of lipids in marsh sediments with a large clay content. Fatty acids were more extensively altered than hydrocarbons, which were a better index of original marsh grasses contributing to the sediment over a period of 2500 years.

Sterols

Sterols are useful in determining the nature of precursor organisms for sediment organic matter, as well as the conditions of diagenesis, but their occurrence and depth distribution in recent lacustrine sediments have only recently been investigated. Schwendinger and Erdman (1964) determined the concentrations of total sterols in bogs and swamps but did not attempt to identify the individual sterols present. Henderson *et al.* (1972) isolated the sterols from an 87-m stratigraphic section of Pleistocene Mono Lake sediments from east-central California and from recent sediments from the same lake. The recent sediments contain major amounts of cholesterol (Figure 8 [30]), brassicasterol (Figure 8 [34]), and campesterol (Figure 8 [31]), with lesser amounts of stigmasterol (Figure 8 [35]), β-sitosterol (Figure 8 [32]), and ergostanol (Figure 9 [37]). The most abundant zooplankton of the modern lake are brine shrimp, which were found to contain cholesterol as the only steroid. Diatoms from the lake contain no steroids, but other algae were found to contain cholesterol, campesterol, ergost-7-en-3β-ol (Figure 9 [41]), and, tentatively, 24-ethylcholest-7-en-3β-ol (Figure 9 [42]), as well as minor brassicasterol. The trace of ergostanol represents the only saturated steroid found in the recent sediment. The Pleistocene lake sediments, however, contain abundant hydrogenated steroids such as cholestanol (Fig-

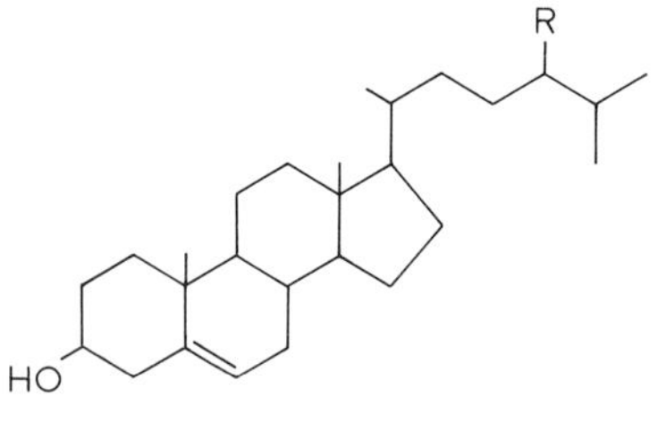

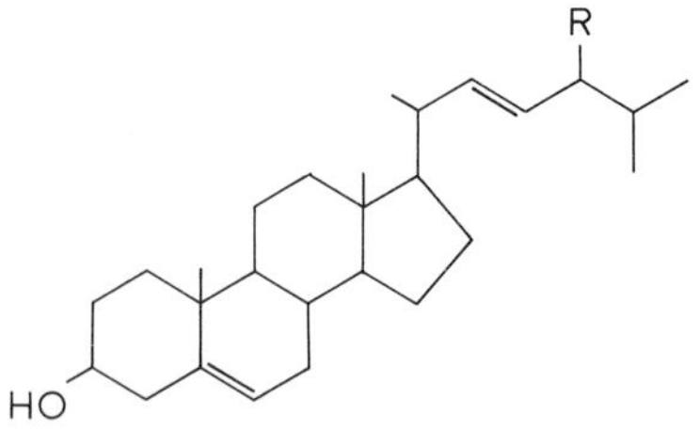

FIGURE 8.   Sterols.

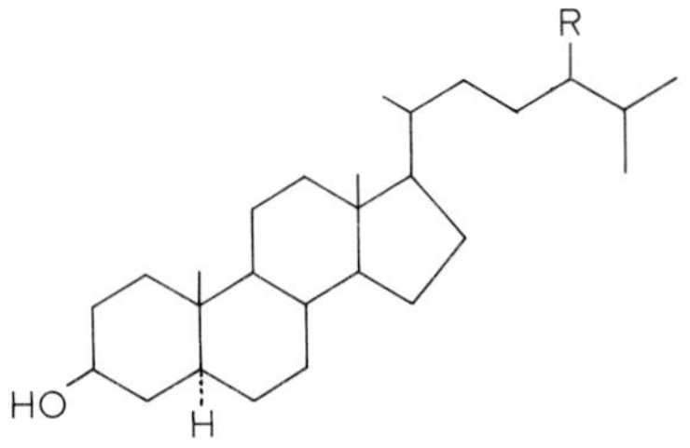

FIGURE 9. 5α-Stanols ([36] through [38]), 5β-stanols ([39] and [40]), fungisterol [41], and 24-ethylcholest-7en-3β-ol [42].

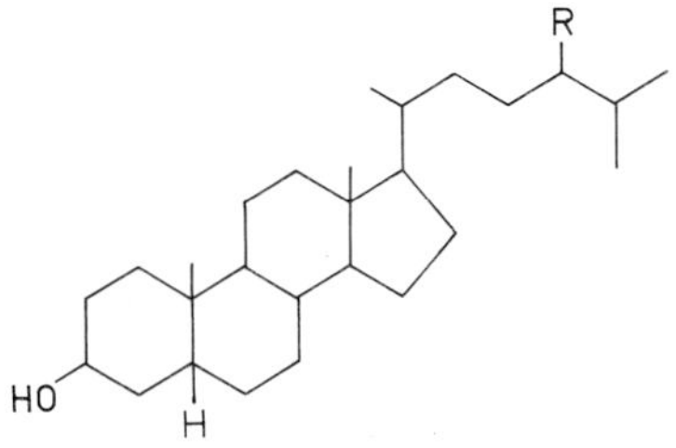

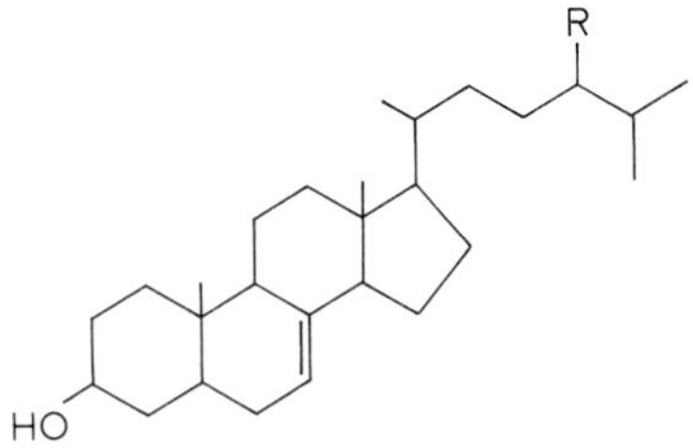

ure 9 [36]) and stigmastanol (Figure 9 [38]). Although a slow process of hydrogenation of the sediment sterols may be inferred, no linear increase in the stanol:sterol ratio was found in the older sediments.

Ogura (1974) and Ogura and Hanya (1973) examined sterols from the 200-m core obtained from Lake Biwa, Japan. The earliest sediments sampled have an age, based on ^{14}C and fission-track methods, of between 5 × 10^5 and 1 × 10^6 years (Yamamoto et al., 1974). A progressive increase in the stanol:sterol ratio with sediment age was found (Ogura and Hanya, 1973), but significant stanols also exist in the surface sediment. Hydrogenation of sterols in the surface sediments of other Japanese lakes was observed by Ogura (1974). Ogura also demonstrated the progressive hydrogenation of sterols in anaerobic cultures of Lake Yuno-ko surface sediments over a 40-day period at 37°C. In the Lake Biwa sediments, the hydrogenation rate appears to decrease exponentially with depth, suggesting that the process is dominantly, if not wholly, microbial. Thermal processes are unlikely in the sediments, and Ishiwatari and Hanya (1975) found no progressive change in even-carbon preference (CPI) of monocarboxylic acids with depth in the same core.

Gaskell and Eglinton (1974, 1975) showed that hydrogenation of [^{14}C]cholesterol to [^{14}C]cholestanol took place in cores of sediments from Rostherne mere,

England under laboratory conditions and after return of a labeled core to the lake, although the amounts of 5α-[^{14}C]cholestanol and 5β-[^{14}C]cholestanol produced were quite small. Rostherne mere is highly eutrophic and has a large input of bird feces. In further work, Gaskell and Eglinton (1976) identified the major sterol constituents of the lake sediments. Of the Δ^5-sterols, cholest-5-en-3β-ol (= cholesterol) is most abundant, followed by 24-ethylcholest-5-en-3β-ol (Figure 8 [32]) and 24-methylcholest-5-en-3β-ol (Figure 8 [31]). 24-Methylcholesta-5,22-dien-3β-ol (Figure 8 [34]), 24-ethylcholesta-5,22-dien-3β-ol (Figure 8 [35]), and cholesta-5,22-dien-3β-ol (Figure 8 [33]) make up lesser amounts. The 5α-stanols, in order of abundance, comprise 24-ethyl-5α-cholestan-3β-ol (Figure 9 [38]), 5α-cholestan-3β-ol (Figure 9 [36]), 24-methyl-5α-cholestan-3β-ol (Figure 9 [37]), and a C$_{26}$ stanol. 5α-Cholestan-3β-ol is, however, the most abundant stanol in the upper 7 cm of the sediment core. 5β-Stanols are rare and consist of 5β-cholestan-3β-ol (Figure 9 [39]) and 24-ethyl-5β-cholestan-3β-ol (Figure 9 [40]). The total stanol:Δ^5-sterol ratio in prehydrolysis extracts ranged from 0.3 for the upper 7 cm to 5.0 for the lower 12 cm of the 30-cm core. Extractions without prior hydrolysis are thought to release "free" lipids which are not bound into cell walls. Gaskell and Eglinton (1976) found a close parallelism in the sediment Δ^5-sterols and 5α-stanols with respect to the proportions of compounds with a hydrogen-, methyl-, or ethyl-branch at the C-24 position, suggesting that the microbial hydrogenation process is unaffected by the alkyl group.

Nishimura and Koyama (1976) found an exponential decrease in the rate of decrease of the total sterol:total stanol ratio with depth in a 155-cm core from eutrophic Lake Suwa, Japan. At the surface the stanol:sterol ratio is about 0.025, whereas it is nearly constant at about 0.53 in the lower 50 cm of the core. A plankton sample was also collected from the lake, with 99% of the sample consisting of the diatom Melosira granulata. The stanol:sterol ratio of the plankton was found to be 0.0125. The principal sterols in the diatoms comprised cholesterol (Figure 8 [30]) and campesterol (Figure 8 [31]), whereas brassicasterol (Figure 8 [34]), β-sitosterol (Figure 8 [32]), and stigmasterol (Figure 8 [35]) were less abundant. In the sediments, cholesterol, campesterol, and β-sitosterol are most abundant at the surface, with somewhat lesser amounts of brassicasterol and stigmasterol. Cholesterol and brassicasterol decrease markedly in relative and, especially, actual amounts with depth in the core, whereas stigmasterol and β-sitosterol increase in relative amounts, but decrease in actual amounts. The minor stanols of the diatom extract consisted mainly of cholestanol (Figure 9 [36]), with lesser amounts of stigmastanol (Figure 9 [38]) and ergostanol (Figure 9 [37]). Cholestanol made up nearly half of the surface sediment stanols, with ergostanol and stigmastanol in nearly equal proportions making up the remainder, but decreased in relative abundance with depth. Stigmastanol is the principal stanol in the lower part of the core. Although the data permit the assumption that stanols are microbially produced from the corresponding sterol throughout the 1.5-m-depth interval covered by the core, the actual amounts of sterols and stanols at a depth of 1.5 m were only 3.6 and 10%, respectively, of the amounts at the sediment surface. Thus, as Nishimura and Koyama (1976) were careful to point out, the alternative possibility that microbial degradation of sediment sterols at a more rapid rate than that of the corresponding stanols could lead to the observed increase in the stanol:sterol ratio with depth also. The presence of stanols in the Lake Suwa *Melosira* extract may result from bacteria, or more probably fungi, living on dead diatom cells. Nishimura and Koyama (1976) do not report the proportions of living *Melosira* cells in their plankton sample, but microbial degradation of plankton is common during blooms within the euphotic zone. Fungisterol [= ergost-7-en-3β-ol (Figure 9 [41])] was found by Henderson *et al.* (1972) in Mono Lake algae, and the slime mold *Physarum polycephalum* contains stigmastanol (Figure 9 [38]) and campestanol (Figure 9 [37]), according to Lenfant *et al.* (1970). The lack of sufficient work on the lipids of lacustrine fungi and bacteria precludes any firm suggestions as to the origin of planktonic stanols. Bird *et al.* (1971b) found significant amounts of sterols in *Methylococcus capsulatus,* but bacteria and blue-green algae in general are thought to lack sterols.

Algal sterols have recently been reviewed by Goodwin (1973, 1974). It is difficult to determine the relative importance of allochthonous and littoral higher plant contributions versus those of autochthonous algal sources, as many of the sterols from algae and higher plants are identical or differ only in the configuration about C-24, not commonly reported in studies of sediment sterols. Because of the lack of information, sterols which differ only in their absolute configuration about C-24 are not distinguished here; thus, poriferasterol (24R-ethylcholesta-5,22-dien-3β-ol) is grouped with stigmasterol (24S-ethylcholesta-5,22-dien-3β-ol). Sterols with an ethyl group at C-24 are more common in higher plants (Gaskell and Eglinton, 1976) but are also found in fresh-water algae (Goodwin, 1974). Gaskell and Eglinton (1974, 1976) interpreted the increased abundance of cholesterol in the upper 7 cm of Rostherne mere sediments, as compared with C_{29} sterols at depth, as indicating an increased algal input. However, the principal alga of the lake at present is a blue-green, so the cholesterol may be derived from another source, perhaps bird feces. Cranwell (1976a) found that the abundance of cholesterol and 5α-cholestanol in soils and sediments is directly related to the

algal input, with eutropic lakes having larger amounts of these C_{27} sterols than oligotrophic lakes.

Although sediment sterols appear to carry much information about the relative importance of algal and higher plant inputs to lakes, and about the nature and amount of diagenetic modification of organic materials within the sediment, insufficient data are commonly available on bacterial and fungal populations both in the water column and in the sediment to permit the proper interpretation of the information at present. Without a comprehensive understanding of the biology and ecology of a lake, interpretations based mainly on chemical data may be misleading.

Pigments

Gorham (1960) examined chlorophyll-related pigments in the sediments of five lakes of the English Lake District. The lakes ranged in productivity from Wastwater and Ennerdale Water, which have oxygenated hypolimnions throughout the year, to Priest Pot, a small, highly productive pond. Total carbon contents ranged from 7.2 to 18.9% on a dry weight basis, while chlorophyll derivatives, measured on the 667 nm absorbance peak of pheophytin *a,* ranged from 0.2 to 6.9 units/g dry weight of sediment, a 33-fold increase. Swain (1970) suggested that sediment chlorophyll derivatives may be a more sensitive index of past productivity than the organic carbon content. Nineteen lakes in the Lake District were studied by Gorham *et al.* (1974), who found a close correlation between algal standing crop, chlorophyll (Figure 4 [12] = chlorophyll *a*) content of the epilimnion and sediment pigments. They also suggested the use of sedimentary pigments as indicators of past productivity but did not believe that the pigment diversity could be used as a sensitive productivity index. Preservation of pigments appears to be related to the burial of pigment-containing organic matter in anaerobic sediments (Vallentyne, 1955). In lakes with thermal mixing the stirring of surficial sediments by benthic organisms may permit aerobic pigment diagenesis to go on for a long period of time after sedimentation. Stockner and Lund (1970) found that 50% of diatom cells at the sediment surface contained intact chloroplasts, whereas this proportion had dropped to 10% at a 2.5 cm depth. Barnes and Barnes (unpublished data) found intact chloroplasts in green algae to depths of 80 cm in sediment cores from a meromictic fjord lake in British Columbia.

Daley and Brown (1973) found that senescent cultures of green and blue-green algae undergo photochemical destruction of the tetrapyrrole ring, with chlorophyll *a* being destroyed more rapidly than chlorophyll *b* in one culture. This suggests that the ratios of the chlorophylls may not always indicate changes in phytoplankton populations in paleolimnological studies. Chlorophyll derivatives were not found to form photochemically, but pheophytin *a* and pheophorbide *a* were metabolically produced in a dark-incubated culture of one blue-green alga. In a related study, Daley (1973) found that cultures of a blue-green alga infected with a myxobacterium or a cyanophage experienced chlorophyll destruction only in the light and concluded that the bacterium and virus aided the degradation process only by lysing the cell wall, permitting the tetrapyrrole ring to be oxidized photochemically. Thus, the chlorophyll component may not be mineralized at the same rate as the majority of organic matter, and a higher proportion may survive to become incorporated in sediments where it is protected from photochemical destruction. Daley (1973) also fed the green alga *Scenedesmus quadricauda* and the blue-green *Anacystis nidulans* to the cladoceran *Daphnia pulex*. Chlorophyll was readily destroyed, and pheophytins and, to a lesser extent, pheophorbides accumulated in the feces.

Handa (1975) analyzed chlorophyll derivatives and carotenoids in the 200-m Lake Biwa core, and found close correlations between the two and with the ratio of the sum of carbon contained in carbohydrates, amino acids, proteins, and lipids to the total organic carbon in the sediments. Handa suggested that this ratio reflected the relative importance of autochthonous input. High sediment pigment concentrations were found at similar depths to those reported by Mori (1974) as having high concentrations of diatom remains, with the exception of one major pigment peak at 85 to 105 m depth, which is not represented by a diatom concentration and which may have been derived from algae lacking resistant cell walls.

Gorham and Sanger (1976) used pigment concentrations as indicators of culturally induced eutrophication in Shagawa Lake, Minnesota. The lake lies in a region of generally unproductive lakes, but was disturbed through the introduction of iron mine wastes and sewage effluent beginning in the late 1880s, leading to the formation of spring diatom and summer blue-green algae blooms. Initiation of human disturbance is readily observable in sediment cores due to the abrupt increase in the content of hematite grains from the mine effluent and correlates well with an equally abrupt increase in pigment concentration. The concentration of chlorophyll derivatives in relation to both epiphasic (containing no oxygen) and hypophasic (oxygen-containing) carotenoids is considerably higher than in other holomictic Minnesota lakes, and higher than in even the most productive group of English Lake District lakes analyzed by Gorham *et al.* (1974). Gorham and Sanger (1976) suggested that sedi-

mentary pigments are a more sensitive indicator of eutrophication than are the diatoms and cladocerans, but if qualitative as well as quantitative indications are desired, then the individual pigments must be analyzed rather than simply separating the pigments into groups.

Griffiths and Edmondson (1975) separated the carotenoid oscillaxanthin, found only in certain blue-green algae, from the sediments of Lake Washington. By comparing the changes in depth of oscillaxanthin maxima in cores collected 5 to 6 years apart, they were able to determine the amount of sedimentation during the intervening time and to estimate early compaction. Their work indicates that careful separation and quantification of individual carotenoids may provide an important tool for the determination of past changes in plankton populations. Brown (1969) reviewed the use of specific carotenoid pigments as indicators of precursor organisms.

Carbohydrates

The methods used for the extraction of total carbohydrates and for the identification of individual sugar monomers exert a strong influence on the results obtained (Handa, 1972). Total carbohydrates are usually determined by the phenol–sulfuric acid method, which gives larger results than other methods which have been used. Individual sugars are released from sediments by acid hydrolysis and identified by paper chromatography with known standards or by gas-liquid chromatography. Because of the diversity of mono-, di-, oligo-, and polysaccharides found in nature, total carbohydrate contents are difficult to interpret (Lowe, 1978). Carbohydrate contents are commonly reported in terms of dry weight of sediment or of volume of wet sediment. If carbohydrate contents are to be related to the trophic state of lakes, it would be useful if the proportions of the total organic carbon of sediments accounted for by carbohydrates were given. Carbohydrate carbon constitutes $9.5 \pm 2.0\%$ of the total organic carbon contents of the soil "A" horizons tabulated by Lowe (1978).

Although the major part of sediment monosaccharides is bound into high molecular weight polymers such as cellulose and hemicellulose, some sugar monomers and polymers may be bonded to or occluded in humic materials or adsorbed onto mineral grains. Although the carbohydrate contents of humic acids are commonly low, Clark and Tan (1969) found that the ethanol-soluble portions of soil humic acids are bound to polysaccharides through ester linkages and that the remaining ethanol-insoluble humic acids contain little carbohydrate. Thus, carbohydrates released from sediments by ethanol extraction without prior hydrolysis, which are commonly termed "free" carbohydrates, may be in part bound to humic materials.

Total carbohydrates in the 200-m core from Lake Biwa, Japan were reported by Handa (1972, 1974). Carbohydrates decrease in a general manner with depth in the core according to $N = 1.18e^{-0.0056Z}$, where N is in mg of carbohydrate per g of dry sediment and Z is depth in m, although fluctuations were observed which correlate well with the climatic profile of the lake sediments (Fuji and Horie, 1972; Fuji, 1974). Total carbohydrates as determined by the phenol–sulfuric acid method ranged from 5 to 44 mg/g of dry sediment in samples from sediments of eutrophic Clear and Blue Lakes, Minnesota (Rogers, 1965). An average of 34% of the total carbohydrates was released by acid hydrolysis of the sediments. A sharp peak in total carbohydrate content at a depth of 6 m in a core from Hall Lake, Minnesota was attributed to a high level of bacterial activity by Swain (1970) because of a greatly increased ribose (Figure 10 [43]) content at that depth. Handa and Mizuno (1973) found glucose (Figure 10 [46]), galactose (Figure 10 [47]), mannose (Figure 10 [48]), arabinose (Figure 10 [44]), xylose (Figure 10 [45]), rhamnose (Figure 10 [51]), fucose (Figure 10 [50]), and ribose, in order of decreasing abundance, in the surface sediments of Lake Suwa, Japan. With the exception of fucose, these are the same sugars found by Rogers (1965) in the Minnesota lakes. In Lake Suwa, glucose, galactose, mannose, and fucose decrease markedly with depth in the upper 24 cm of the sediment, whereas the other sugars remain more or less constant. Handa and Mizuno (1973) suggested that the Lake Suwa carbohydrates were derived dominantly from phytoplankton on the basis of the similarity in monosaccharide composition between the sediments and the diatoms and blue–green algae of the lake. Matsuyama (1973) analyzed the carbohydrate content of settling seston collected in sediment traps attached to a fixed vertical line in meromictic Lake Suigetsu, Japan. At the collecting site the water depth was 22 m, with the chemocline occurring at 7 m. A progressive decrease in particulate carbohydrates occurs with depth, with a slight increase at the chemocline due to the decreased rate of settling and to the biomass of purple sulfur bacteria (*Chromatium* sp.) which thrive at that depth. Dissolved carbohydrates show the opposite relationship, being greatest at the lake bottom where they are released by decomposition and decreasing upward. A sharp decrease at the chemocline was suggested by Matsuyama to result from the utilization of carbohydrates by bacteria.

The carbohydrate contents of the surface sediments of Lake Trummen and 13 other lakes in Sweden, Norway, and Iceland can be related to the productivity of the lakes (Fleischer, 1972). Ethanol-soluble "free" sugars occur only in trace amounts in oligotrophic lakes, whereas glucose and to a lesser extent maltose (a disaccharide composed of two glucose monomers) and sucrose (a glucose-fructose (Figure 10 [49]) dimer) are found in eutrophic lake sediments. Rogers (1965) found glucose, galactose, xylose, and mannose, but only trace amounts of maltose and sucrose, in the free sugars of eutrophic Blue and Clear Lakes. Lactose, a glucose–galactose dimer which is common in domestic sewage, was found in trace amounts in only one sample by Rogers, and not at all by Fleischer, suggesting that it is readily degraded. Galactose, glucose, arabinose, xylose, and mannose are abundant in the hydrolysates of both the oligotrophic and eutrophic lake sediments investigated by Fleischer (1972), with the amounts of the individual sugars ranging from about 80 to 800 mg/liter of wet sediment. The productivity of the lakes seems to have little effect on either the total amounts or the relative proportions of the hydrolyzable sugars.

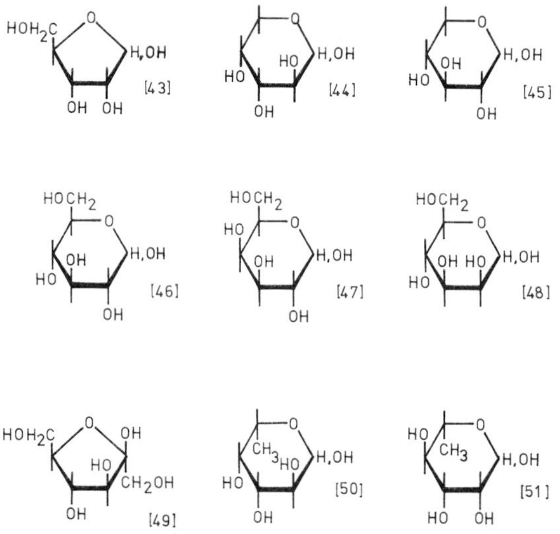

FIGURE 10.   Carbohydrates.

Amino acids and amino sugars

Nissenbaum *et al.* (1972) found that amino acids make up a much larger part of the organic contents of deepwater reducing sediments than of shallow-water oxidizing sediments in the Dead Sea, which suggests that amino acid degradation is accomplished largely through the activities of aerobic microorganisms. In the deeper water sediments, amino acids constitute 16 to 24% of the nonhumic and fulvic organic matter. Nissenbaum *et al.* (1972) suggested that the high concentrations of amino acids, including the unstable amino acids proline (Figure 11 [55]) and tyrosine (Fig-

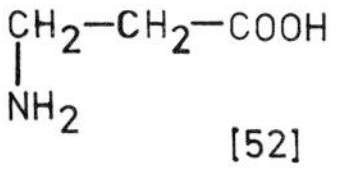

CH2—CH2—COOH
|
NH2   [52]

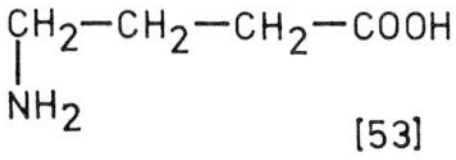

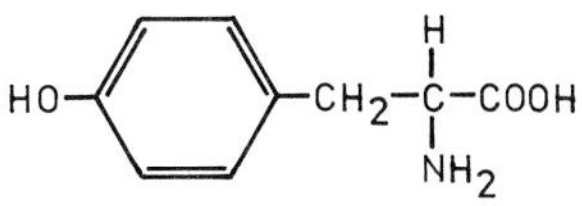

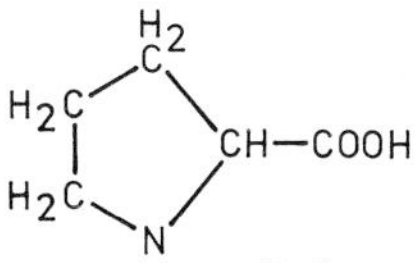

CH2—CH2—CH2—COOH
|
NH2   [53]

HO—⟨benzene ring⟩—CH2—C(H)(NH2)—COOH   [54]

[pyrrolidine structure with CH—COOH]   [55]

[N-acetylglucosamine structure]   [56]

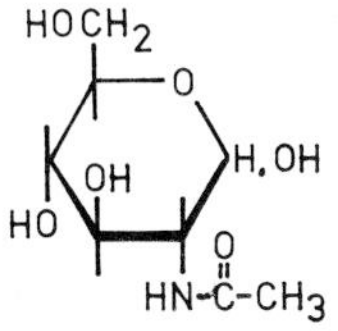

FIGURE 11.   Amino acids ([52] through [55]) and *N*-acetylglucosamine [56].

ure 11 [54]), in these sediments indicated that degradation of cellular materials has not been extensive. This result seems to contradict the common assumption that most of the planktonic organic matter of lakes is degraded during sedimentation. The microorganisms of the Dead Sea were discussed by Nissenbaum (1975).

Amino acids and amino sugars were extracted from the 200-m sediment core taken from Lake Biwa, Japan by Terashima and Mizuno (1974). Total amino acid content decreased from about 2600 μg/g at a depth of 11 m in the sediment to 130 μg/g at 170 m; all of the major groups of protein-derived amino acids decreased at approximately the same rate. The rate of decrease of the nonprotein amino acids β-alanine (Figure 11 [52]) and γ-aminobutyric acid (Figure 11 [53]) is much less than that of the protein-derived acids. Tyrosine (Figure 11 [54]) and proline (Figure 11 [55]) decrease at about the same rate as the other protein-derived amino acids.

The surface sediments of Lake Ontario contain an average of 5300 μg of N/g of dry sediment, with more than 90% of the total nitrogen bound in organic forms. Insoluble combined amino acids account for 45 to 51% of the total nitrogen (Kemp and Mudrochova, 1973). Most of the remaining sediment nitrogen occurs in unknown compounds; soluble free and combined amino acids make up only a small proportion of the total nitrogen. Samples were taken from five widely separated locations in this large lake. The distribution of the various amino acids was found to be similar at all sites, indicating that much of the organic matter in the sediments is derived from autochthonous sources. In addition, the amino acid compositions of suspended sediments, zooplankton, and humic acids resemble those of the insoluble fraction of the sediment organic matter, suggesting that the humic acids and the sediment organic matter share common precursors.

Total amino sugar content of Lake Ontario sediments averages 2.80 mg/g of dry sediment, or about 0.16 of the average amount of the total amino acids. This high ratio suggests that the amino sugars may be derived largely from the chitinous exoskeletons of zooplankton, mainly *Daphnia,* which are relatively more resistant to degradation than are the protein and peptide sources of the amino acids. Such an explanation may also account in part for the greater concentrations of the hexosamines in oligotrophic than in eutrophic Wisconsin lakes (Keeney *et al.,* 1970). Amino sugars are generally absent from the upper part of the Lake Biwa sediment core (Terashima and Mizuno, 1974) but occur in samples taken at 95 m and deeper. This distribution may be explained by the abundance of cladocerans and insects, whose exoskeletons contain chitin, in the lake. Chitin is a polymer of *N*-acetylglucosamine (Figure 11 [56]).

Purines and pyrimidines

Relatively little information is as yet available on the nitrogenous base contents of recent lacustrine sediments. Van der Velden and Schwartz (1974) and van der Velden *et al.* (1974) reported a rapid decrease in the content of purine and pyrimidine derivatives with depth in sediment cores from Lake Erie, as well as a general underabundance of uracil (Figure 12 [62]).

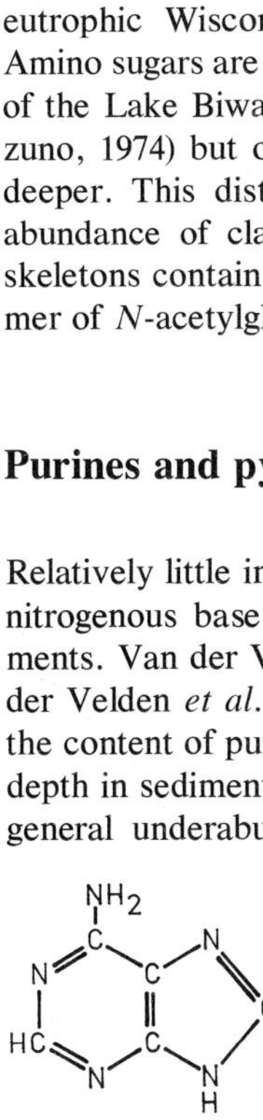

[purine structure with NH2]   [57]

[purine structure with O and H2N—C]   [58]

[purine structure with OH]   [59]

[pyrimidine structure with NH2]   [60]

[pyrimidine structure with O and C—CH3]   [61]

[pyrimidine structure with O]   [62]

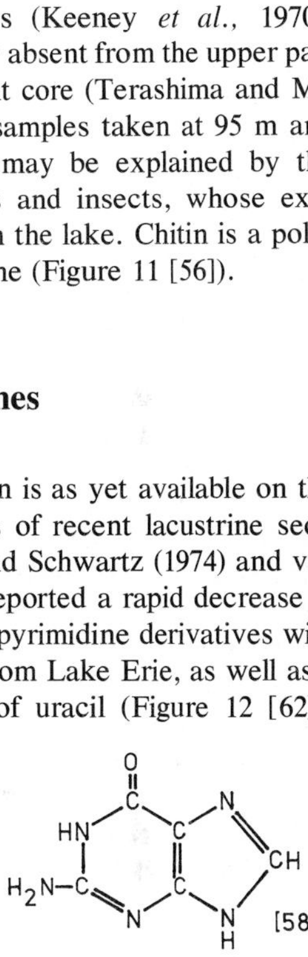

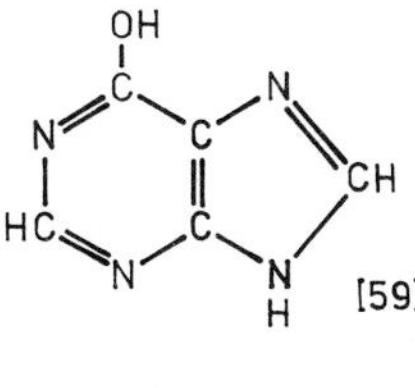

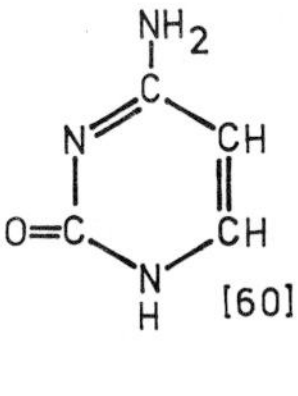

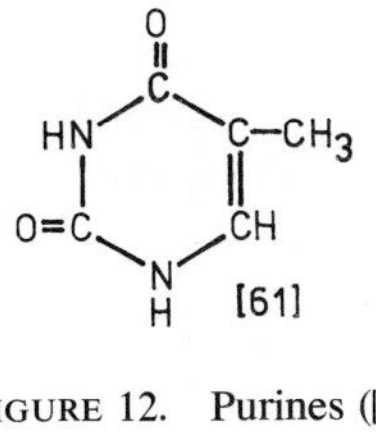

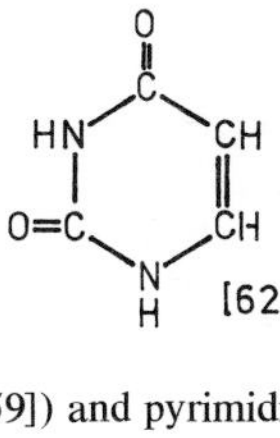

FIGURE 12.   Purines ([57] through [59]) and pyrimidines ([60] through [62]).

Their data agree with the general decrease in total nitrogen content in these sediments reported by Kemp et al. (1972). The most abundant bases include guanine (Figure 12 [58]), adenine (Figure 12 [57]), cytosine (Figure 12 [60]), and thymine (Figure 12 [61]), with hypoxanthine (Figure 12 [59]) and uracil (Figure 12 [62]) being less common. The total content of purine and pyrimidine derivatives in the surface sediments was 108 and 123 $\mu g/g$ in the two cores analyzed, representing about 1–2% of the total sediment nitrogen content. The general absence of uracil from sediments was suggested by Cranwell (1976a) to be the result of preferential degradation during sedimentation of RNA, which contains uracil, over DNA, which does not. A rapid increase in the concentrations of the purines and pyrimidines in Lake Erie sediments deposited since 1950 was suggested to indicate increasing rates of cultural eutrophication (van der Velden and Schwartz, 1974). In further work on Lake Erie and on Lakes Ontario and Huron, van der Velden and Schwartz (1976) found that the rates of decrease of total purine and pyrimidine derivatives, as a proportion of organic carbon contents, were different in each of the three lakes. In each lake, however, the total purines and pyrimidines was a constant value of 0.1% of sediment organic carbon content below depths representing deposition at 120 years B.P., the time of forest clearance for agriculture in the region.

Summary

Research in lacustrine organic geochemistry has focused on identification of specific organic compounds isolated from a variety of sedimentary environments, and their correlation both with contributing biota and subsequent microbial alterations and with the effects of lake morphology, geochemistry, trophic state, and oxygen content on their preservation or alteration. Although lipids, proteins, and carbohydrates are broadly distributed in living organisms and subsequently in sediments, some individual compounds and patterns of distribution of classes have been identified which appear to characterize individual taxa (e.g., Hunneman and Eglinton, 1972; Erwin, 1973; Bird and Lynch, 1974; Goodwin, 1974; Weete, 1974; Kolattukudy, 1975). The α,ϵ-diaminopimelic acid (Kemp and Mudrochova, 1973), cyclopropanoic acids, 10-methyl C_{16} and C_{18} acids (Cranwell, 1973a), and squalene, dehydrosqualene, and tetrahydrosqualene (Bird et al., 1971b), all of which are components of bacteria, yeast, or fungi, have been proposed as markers of microbial sources. The C_{17-20} hydrocarbons with a mid-chain methyl on carbon 4, 6, 7, or 8 are specific to blue–green algae (Oehler, 1976; Bird and Lynch, 1974). The ω-hydroxy C_{16} acid is the major cutin acid in ferns and lycopods; the 9,16- or 10,16-dihydroxy C_{16} acids are dominant in gymnosperm cutin acids; the dihydroxy C_{16} and trihydroxy C_{18} acids are dominant in angiosperms (Hunneman and Eglinton, 1972; Eglinton and Hamilton, 1967).

Unique skeletal structures associated with isoprenoids, triterpenoids, and their stereoisomers are frequently preserved despite changes in functional groups arising from oxidative or reductive processes occurring during or after sedimentation. On this basis a link has been established between phytol derivatives and chlorophyll (Maxwell et al., 1973; de Leeuw et al., 1975), and between sterane and stanol derivatives and sterols (Gaskell and Eglinton, 1974, 1975). Hopane-derived acids and hydrocarbons have been attributed, respectively, to the microbial alteration of a bacterial C_{35} tetrahydroxy hopane and hopenes found in prokaryotes, ferns, mosses, and lichens (Eglinton et al., 1974; van Dorsselaer et al., 1974; Cranwell, 1976a; Bird et al., 1971a).

Although individual compounds serve as useful markers, the patterns of distribution of different classes in the same sample provide a more reliable measure of the relationship of sediment organic matter to precursor compounds and their alteration products. In the study of the 200-m core from Lake Biwa, the lipids, proteins, and carbohydrates were correlated with palynology, micropaleontology, geochemistry, and sedimentology (Horie, 1974; Ishiwatari and Hanya, 1973, 1975). Long chain hydrocarbons and monoketones with a high odd-carbon preference and long chain saturated, unsaturated, ω-hydroxy, and dicarboxylic acids, alcohols, and aldehydes with high even-carbon preferences are common components of waxes, cutin, and suberin from higher plants (Eglinton and Hamilton, 1967; Kollattukudy, 1975) and are widely distributed in soils, peats, and humus (Cranwell, 1973b, 1974). A narrow range of short chain acids and hydrocarbons with a high even- and odd-carbon preference, respectively, are characteristic of photosynthetic bacteria and algae (Han et al., 1968; Oliver and Colwell, 1973; Erwin, 1973); while short chain acids are predominant, a broader carbon range is found in nonphotosynthetic microorganisms (Weete, 1974; Welch and Burlingame, 1973). Both monomodal and bimodal distributions with a broad carbon range and low odd-carbon preference are commonly found in hydrocarbons from nonphotosynthetic microorganisms (Weete, 1974; Gelpi et al., 1970; Bird and Lynch, 1974) and lower plants (Lytle et al., 1976). Hydrocarbons from emergent fresh-water monocotyledons show a higher plant pattern; submerged plants show a broad range, high odd-carbon preference, and a maximum at n-$C_{19 \text{ or } 21}$; those with floating leaves have a low odd-carbon preference and a maximum at n-$C_{25,27}$ (Nishimoto, 1974).

Productive lakes commonly show increased concentrations in surficial sediments of free sugars (Fleischer, 1972; Rogers, 1965), hydrolyzable amino acids (Swain, 1970), pigments (Gorham et al., 1974), and branched and cyclic acids (Cranwell, 1973a, 1974). Solvent-extractable straight chain acids and hydrocarbons show acid maxima at n-C_{16} and n-$C_{22,24,}$ $_{or\ 26}$ and hydrocarbon maxima at n-C_{17} and n-$C_{27\ or\ 29}$ (Brooks et al., 1976).

Nonproductive lakes show an increased abundance of amino sugars (Kemp and Mudrochova, 1973), with lesser amounts of branched and cyclic acids and only traces of free carbohydrates. Acids show a maximum at n-$C_{26,24,\ or\ 28}$ and hydrocarbons a maximum at n-$C_{27,29,31}$ or at n-C_{31} (Brooks et al., 1976; Cranwell, 1973b). The monomodal distribution of lipids in oligotrophic lakes reflects terrestrial plants and soils as primary sources of organic matter; the bimodal distribution in productive environments reflects both an autochthonous contribution from planktonic sources and microbial alteration products and an allochthonous contribution from terrestrial sources.

Ratios of short to long chain acids and hydrocarbons, of C_{27} to C_{29} sterols, and the sum of carbohydrate, protein, and lipid carbon relative to the total organic carbon (Handa, 1975) have been used as measures of the relative contributions of autochthonous and allochthonous sources. The accumulation of pheophytins and pheophorbides has been suggested as a measure of chlorophyll derivatization through zooplankton grazing (Daley, 1973); the ratio of the octadec-9-enoic acid to cis-octadec-11-enoic acid was suggested as a measure of the relative importance of higher plant and algal sources compared to bacterial alteration products (Matsuda and Koyama, 1977).

Microbial alteration products show a broader distribution of acids and hydrocarbons with a low carbon preference. Potential markers are the n-C_{18-26} hydrocarbons (Cranwell, 1976b), branched and cyclic acids, short chain dicarboxylic acids, and the 2-, 3-, ω-, and (ω-1)-hydroxy acids. Parallel distributions of 2- and 3-hydroxy acids with monocarboxylic acids, of dicarboxyic acids with the mono acids or ω-hydroxy cutin acids (Eglinton and Hunneman, 1968; Ishiwatari and Hanya, 1975), and of the 5α-stanols with the $\Delta^5 C_{27,28,\ and\ 29}$ sterols (Gaskell and Eglinton, 1974, 1975) have been attributed to microbial alteration of planktonic and higher plant sources. Incubation of lake sediments with [^{14}C]cholesterol (Gaskell and Eglinton, 1974, 1975), [^{14}C]phytol (de Leeuw et al., 1975; Boon and Rijpstra et al., 1975; Brooks and Maxwell 1974), and [^{14}C] oleic acid (Rhead et al., 1971, 1972) has demonstrated that reduction, oxidation, and mineralization by microbial processes can occur within days or weeks.

In contrast to the oxygen-rich waters of oligotrophic lakes, the development in productive lakes of the seasonal density stratification partially depletes hypolimnetic oxygen, leading to changes in the distribution of aerobic, microaerophilic, and anaerobic decomposers in the water column and to changes in the benthic animals which are mainly responsible for the oxygenation of surficial sediments. Increases in the concentration of compounds sensitive to oxidation, such as amino acids (Nissenbaum et al., 1972), polyunsaturated acids, and chlorophyll (Daley and Brown, 1973), and the occurrence of the C_{16} and C_{18} 10-hydroxy acids (Cranwell, 1976b), dihydrophytol (Boon et al., 1975c; de Leeuw et al., 1975), 3-hydroxy acids, and 5β-stanols (Reed, 1977), are observed in, and potential markers of, oxygen-poor environments and anaerobic decay. In meromictic lakes, carbohydrate contents of seston and water have been correlated with bacterial activity above and below the chemocline (Matsuyama, 1973). Distributions of the branched and cyclic acids in productive and oligotrophic lakes parallel those observed in anaerobic and aerobic decay of phytoplankton (Cranwell, 1974, 1976b). Increases in the concentrations of the amino sugars (Kemp and Mudrochova, 1973), of nonprotein amino acids (Terashima and Mizuno, 1974), of the 2-, ω-, (ω-1)-hydroxy acids (Boon et al., 1975b), of phytenic acid (Boon et al., 1975c), and of 5α-stanols (Reed, 1977) are associated with oxygen-rich conditions and/or aerobic microbial processes.

Increases in the concentration in surficial sediments of purines and pyrimidines (van der Velden and Schwartz, 1976), of cholesterol and the ratio of C_{27} to C_{29} sterols (Cranwell, 1976a), of lactose, a common component in domestic sewage (Rogers, 1965; Fleischer, 1972), and of the carotenoid oscillaxanthin (Griffiths and Edmondson, 1975) correlate with increased algal productivity arising through cultural eutrophication. Straight chain hydrocarbons superimposed on an unresolved complex mixture, an old radiocarbon age for extractable paraffins, a low odd-carbon preference, and high concentrations of pristane, phytane, and aromatics in surficial sediments relative to the normal hydrocarbons have been used as indicators of pollution of lake sediments by fossil fuels (Wakeham and Carpenter, 1976; Wakeham, 1977).

References

Ballio, A., and S. Barcellona. (1971). Identification of 10-methyl branched fatty acids in Microbispora parva by combined gas chromatography–mass spectrometry. Gazz. Chim. Ital., **101**:635–636.

Barbier, M. (1970). Chemistry and biochemistry of pollens. Pp. 1–34. In: L. Reinhold and Y. Liwschitz (eds.), Progress in Phytochemistry. Vol. 2. Interscience, London.

Barnes, M. A., and W. C. Barnes. (1978). Manuscript in preparation.

Berkaloff, C., and J. C. Kader. (1975). Variations of the lipid composition during the formation of cysts in the green alga *Protosiphon botryoides*. *Phytochemistry,* **14**:2353–2355.

Bird, C. W., and J. M. Lynch. (1974). Formation of hydrocarbons by micro-organisms. *Chem. Soc. Rev.,* **3**:309–328.

Bird, C. W., and P. M. Molton. (1972). The production of fatty acids from hydrocarbons by micro-organisms. Pp. 125–169. In: F. D. Gunstone (ed.), *Topics in Lipid Chemistry.* Vol. 3. Paul Elek, London.

Bird, C. W., J. M. Lynch, S. J. Pirt, and W. W. Reid. (1971a). The identification of hop-22(29)-ene in prokaryotic organisms. *Tetrahedron Lett.,* **34**:3189–3190.

Bird, C. W., J. M. Lynch, S. J. Pirt, W. W. Reid, C. J. W. Brooks, and B. S. Middleditch. (1971b). Steroids and squalene in *Methylococcus capsulatus* grown on methane. *Nature,* **230**:473–474.

Blumer, M., and J. Sass. (1972). Oil pollution: persistence and degradation of spilled fuel oil. *Science,* **176**:1120–1122.

Boon, J. J., J. W. de Leeuw, and P. A. Schenck. (1975a). Organic geochemistry of Walvis Bay diatomaceous ooze—I. Occurrence and significance of the fatty acids. *Geochim. Cosmochim. Acta,* **39**:1559–1565.

Boon, J. J., F. de Lange, P. J. W. Schuyl, J. W. de Leeuw, and P. A. Schenck. (1975b). Organic geochemistry of Walvis Bay diatomaceous ooze—II. Occurrence and significance of the hydroxy fatty acids. Preprint of paper presented at 7th Meeting on Organic Geochemistry, Madrid.

Boon, J. J., W. I. C. Rijpstra, J. W. de Leeuw, and P. A. Schenck. (1975c). Phytenic acid in sediments. *Nature,* **258**:414–416.

Braids, O. C., and R. H. Miller. (1975). Fats, waxes, and resins in soil. Pp. 343–368. In: J. Gieseking (ed.), *Soil Components.* Vol. 1. Springer-Verlag, New York, NY.

Brooks, P. W., and J. R. Maxwell. (1974). Early stage fate of phytol in a recently-deposited lacustrine sediment. Pp. 977–991. In: B. Tissot and F. Bienner (eds.), *Advances in Organic Geochemistry, 1973.* Éditions Technip, Paris.

Brooks, P. W., G. Eglinton, S. J. Gaskell, D. J. McHugh, J. R. Maxwell, and R. P. Philp. (1976). Lipids of Recent sediments, part I: Straight-chain hydrocarbons and carboxylic acids of some temperate lacustrine and subtropical lagoonal/tidal flat sediments. *Chem. Geol.,* **18**:21–38.

Brown, S. R. (1969). Paleolimnological evidence from fossil pigments. *Mitt. Int. Verein. Theor. Angew. Limnol.,* **17**:95–103.

Brunskill, G. J., D. Povoledo, B. W. Graham, and M. P. Stainton. (1971). Chemistry of surficial sediments of sixteen lakes in the Experimental Lakes Area, northwestern Ontario. *J. Fish. Res. Board Can.,* **28**:277–294.

Canter, H. M., and J. W. G. Lund. (1948). Studies on plankton parasites. I. Fluctuations in the numbers of *Asterionella formosa* Hass. in relation to fungal epidemics. *New Phytol.,* **47**:238–261.

Canter, H. M., and J. W. G. Lund. (1969). The parasitism of planktonic desmids by fungi. *Osterr. Bot. Z.,* **116**:351–377.

Castillo, J. B. del, C. J. W. Brooks, R. C. Cambie, G. Eglinton, R. J. Hamilton, and P. Pellitt. (1967). The taxonomic distribution of some hydrocarbons in gymnosperms. *Phytochemistry,* **6**:391–398.

Cho, K. Y., and M. R. J. Salton. (1966). Fatty acid composition of bacterial membrane and wall lipids. *Biochim. Biophys. Acta,* **116**:73–79.

Christie, W. W. (1970). Cyclopropane and cyclopropene fatty acids. Pp. 1–49. In: F. D. Gunstone (ed.), *Topics in Lipid Chemistry.* Logos, London.

Chróst, R. J. (1975). Inhibitors produced by algae as an ecological factor affecting bacteria in water. II. Antibacterial activity of algae during blooms. *Acta Microbiol. Pol. (B),* **7**:167–176.

Clark, F. E., and K. H. Tan. (1969). Identification of a polysaccharide ester linkage in humic acid. *Soil Biol. Biochem.,* **1**:75–81.

Cox, R. E., J. R. Maxwell, G. Eglinton, C. T. Pillinger, R. G. Ackman, and S. N. Hooper. (1970). The geological fate of chlorophyll: the absolute stereochemistries of a series of acyclic isoprenoid acids in a 50 million year old lacustrine sediment. *Chem. Commun.,* 1639–1641.

Cranwell, P. A. (1973a). Branched chain and cyclopropanoid acids in a recent sediment. *Chem. Geol.,* **11**:307–313.

Cranwell, P. A. (1973b). Chain-length distribution of n-alkanes from lake sediments in relation to post-glacial environmental change. *Freshwater Biol.,* **3**:259–265.

Cranwell, P. A. (1974). Monocarboxylic acids in lake sediments: indicators, derived from terrestrial and aquatic biota, of paleoenvironmental trophic levels. *Chem. Geol.,* **14**:1–14.

Cranwell, P. A. (1975). Environmental organic chemistry of rivers and lakes, both water and sediment. Pp. 22–54. In: G. Eglinton (ed.), *Environmental Chemistry.* Vol. 1. Chemical Society, London.

Cranwell, P. A. (1976a). Organic geochemistry of lake sediments. Pp. 75–88. In: J. O. Nriagu (ed.), *Environmental Biogeochemistry.* Vol. 1. Ann Arbor Science Publishers, Ann Arbor, MI.

Cranwell, P. A. (1976b). Decomposition of aquatic biota and sediment formation: organic compounds in detritus resulting from microbial attact on the alga *Ceratium hirundinella. Freshwater Biol.,* **6**:41–48.

Daft, M. J., S. B. McCord, and W. D. P. Stewart. (1975). Ecological studies on algal-lysing bacteria in fresh waters. *Freshwater Biol.,* **5**:577–596.

Daley, R. J. (1973). Experimental characterization of lacustrine chlorophyll diagenesis. II. Bacterial, viral and herbivore grazing effects. *Arch. Hydrobiol.,* **72**:409–439.

Daley, R. J., and S. R. Brown. (1973). Experimental characterization of lacustrine chlorophyll diagenesis. I. Physiological and environmental effects. *Arch. Hydrobiol.,* **72**:277–304.

Degens, E. T., R. P. von Herzen, H.-K. Wong, W. G. Deuser, and H. W. Jannasch. (1973). Lake Kivu: Structure, chemistry and biology of an East African rift lake. *Geol. Rundsch.,* **62**:245–277.

Dorsselaer, A. van, A. Ensminger, C. Spyckerelle, M. Dastillung, O. Sieskind, P. Arpino, P. Albrecht, G. Ourisson, P. W. Brooks, S. J. Gaskell, B. J. Kimble, R. P.

Philp, J. R. Maxwell, and G. Eglinton. (1974). Degraded and extended hopane derivatives (C_{27} to C_{35}) as ubiquitous geochemical markers. *Tetrahedron Lett.,* **14**:1349–1352.

Eglinton, G. (1973). Chemical fossils: a combined organic geochemical and environmental approach. *Pure Appl. Chem.* **34**:611–631.

Eglinton, G., and R. J. Hamilton. (1967). Leaf epicuticular waxes. *Science,* **156**:1322–1335.

Eglinton, G., and D. H. Hunneman. (1968). Gas chromatographic–mass spectrometric studies of long chain hydroxy acids—I. The constituent cutin acids of apple cuticle. *Phytochemistry,* **7**:313–322.

Eglinton, G., and M. T. J. Murphy. (1969). *Organic Geochemistry: Methods and Results.* Springer-Verlag, New York, NY.

Eglinton, G., D. H. Hunneman, and K. Douraghi-Zadeh. (1968). Gas chromatographic–mass spectrometric studies of long chain hydroxy acids—II. The hydroxy acids and fatty acids of a 500-year-old lacustrine sediment. *Tetrahedron,* **24**:5929–5941.

Eglinton, G., J. R. Maxwell, and R. P. Philp. (1974). Organic geochemistry of sediments from contemporary aquatic environments. Pp. 941–961. In: B. Tissot and F. Bienner (eds.), *Advances in Organic Geochemistry, 1973.* Éditions Technip, Paris.

Ensminger, A., A. van Dorsselaer, C. Spyckerelle, P. Albrecht, and G. Ourisson. (1974). Pentacyclic triterpenes of the hopane type as ubiquitous geochemical markers: origin and significance. Pp. 245–260. In: B. Tissot and F. Bienner (eds.), *Advances in Organic Geochemistry, 1973.* Éditions Technip, Paris.

Erwin, J. (1973). Comparative biochemistry of fatty acids in eukaryotic microorganisms. Pp. 41–143. In: J. A. Erwin (ed.), *Lipids and Biomembranes of Eukaryotic Microorganisms.* Academic Press, New York, NY.

Farrington, J. W., and P. A. Meyers. (1975). Hydrocarbons in the marine environment. Pp. 109–136. In: G. Eglinton (ed.), *Environmental Chemistry.* Vol. 1. Chemical Society, London.

Farrington, J. W., S. M. Henrichs, and R. Anderson. (1977). Fatty acids and Pb-210 geochronology of a sediment core from Buzzards Bay, Massachusetts. *Geochim. Cosmochim. Acta,* **41**:289–296.

Fleischer, S. (1972). Sugars in the sediments of Lake Trummen and reference lakes. *Arch. Hydrobiol.,* **70**:392–412.

Förster, H. J., K. Biemann, W. G. Haigh, N. H. Tattrie, and J. R. Colvin. (1973). The structure of novel C_{35} pentacyclic terpenes from *Acetobacter xylinum. Biochem. J.,* **135**:133–143.

Fuji, N. (1974). Palynological investigations on 12-meter and 200-meter core samples of Lake Biwa in central Japan. Pp. 227–235. In: S. Horie (ed.), *Paleolimnology of Lake Biwa and the Japanese Pleistocene.* Otsu Hydrobiol. Station, Kyoto Univ., Otsu, Japan.

Fuji, N., and S. Horie. (1972). Palynological study on 200 meters core sample of Lake Biwa in Japan. *Proc. Japan Acad.,* **48**:500–504.

Gaskell, S. J., and G. Eglinton. (1974). Short-term diagenesis of sterols. Pp. 963–976. In: B. Tissot and F. Bienner (eds.), *Advances in Organic Geochemistry, 1973,* Éditions Technip, Paris.

Gaskell, S. J., and G. Eglinton. (1975). Rapid hydrogenation of sterols in a contemporary lacustrine sediment. *Nature,* **254**:209–211.

Gaskell, S. J., and G. Eglinton. (1976). Sterols of a contemporary lacustrine sediment. *Geochim. Gosmochim. Acta,* **40**:1221–1228.

Gelpi, E., H. Schneider, J. Mann, and J. Oró. (1970). Hydrocarbons of geochemical significance in microscopic algae. *Phytochemistry,* **9**:603–612.

Gieseking, J. (ed.). (1975). *Soil Components.* Vol. 1. Springer-Verlag, New York, NY.

Giger, W., M. Reinhard, C. Schaffner, and W. Stumm. (1974). Petroleum-derived and indigenous hydrocarbons in recent sediments of Lake Zug, Switzerland. *Envir. Sci. Technol.,* **8**:454–455.

Gjessing, E. T. (1976). *Physical and Chemical Characteristics of Aquatic Humus.* Ann Arbor Science Publishers, Ann Arbor, MI.

Golterman, H. L. (1975). *Physiological Limnology.* Elsevier, Amsterdam.

Goodwin, T. W. (1973). Comparative biochemistry of sterols in eukaryotic microorganisms. Pp. 1–40. In: J. A. Erwin (ed.), *Lipids and Biomembranes of Eukaryotic Microorganisms.* Academic Press, New York, NY.

Goodwin, T. W. (1974). Sterols. Pp. 266–280. In: W. D. P. Stewart (ed.), *Algal Physiology and Biochemistry* (Bot. Monogr., Vol. 10). Univ. of California Press, Berkeley, CA.

Gorham, E. (1960). Chlorophyll derivatives in surface muds from the English Lakes. *Limnol. Oceanogr.,* **5**:29–33.

Gorham, E., and J. E. Sanger. (1975). Fossil pigments in Minnesota lake sediments and their bearing upon the balance between terrestrial and aquatic inputs to sedimentary organic matter. *Verh. Int. Verein. Theor. Angew. Limnol.,* **19**:2267–2273.

Gorham, E., and J. E. Sanger. (1976) Fossilized pigments as stratigraphic indicators of cultural eutrophication in Shagawa Lake, northeastern Minnesota. *Geol. Soc. Am. Bull.,* **87**:1638–1642.

Gorham, E., J. W. G. Lund, J. E. Sanger, and W. E. Dean, Jr. (1974). Some relationships between algal standing crop, water chemistry, and sediment chemistry in the English Lakes. *Limnol. Oceanogr.,* **19**:601–617.

Griffiths, M., and W. T. Edmondson. (1975). Burial of oscillaxanthin in the sediment of Lake Washington. *Limnol. Oceanogr.,* **20**:945–952.

Hamilton, S., and R. J. Hamilton. (1972). Plant waxes. Pp. 199–269. In: F. D. Gunstone (ed.), *Topics in Lipid Chemistry.* Vol. 3. Wiley, New York, NY.

Han, J., E. D. McCarthy, W. van Hoeven, M. Calvin, and W. H. Bradley. (1968). Organic geochemical studies, II. A preliminary report on the distribution of aliphatic hydrocarbons in algae, in bacteria, and in a recent lake sediment. *Proc. Nat. Acad. Sci. USA,* **59**:29–33.

Handa, N. (1972). Organogeochemical studies of a 200 meters core sample from Lake Biwa: The determination of carbohydrate and organic carbon. *Proc. Japan Acad.,* **48**:510–515.

Handa, N. (1974). Geochemical studies on organic materials in a 200-meter core from Lake Biwa. Pp. 184–193. In: S. Horie (ed.), *Paleolimnology of Lake Biwa and the Japa-*

nese Pleistocene. Otsu Hydrobiol. Station, Kyoto Univ., Otsu, Japan.

Handa, N. (1975). Organogeochemical studies of a 200-meter core sample from Lake Biwa. III. The determination of chlorophyll derivatives and carotenoids. *Proc. Japan Acad.,* **51**:442–446.

Handa, N., and K. Mizuno. (1973). Carbohydrates from lake sediments. Geochem. J., 7:215–230.

Henderson, W., W. E. Reed, and G. Steel. (1972). The origin and incorporation of organic molecules in sediments as elucidated by studies of the sedimentary sequence from a residual Pleistocene lake. Pp. 335–352. In: H. R. von Gaertner and H. Wehner (eds.), *Advances in Organic Geochemistry, 1971.* Pergamon, Oxford.

Horie, S. (1974). *Paleolimnology of Lake Biwa and the Japanese Pleistocene.* Otsu Hydrobiol. Station, Kyoto Univ., Otsu, Japan.

Hunneman, D. H., and G. Eglinton. (1972). The constituent acids of gymnosperm cutins. *Phytochemistry,* **11**:1989–2001.

Ikan, R., M. J. Baedecker, and I. R. Kaplan. (1975a). Thermal alteration experiments on organic matter in recent marine sediment—II. Isoprenoids. *Geochim. Cosmochim. Acta,* **39**:187–194.

Ikan, R., M. J. Baedecker, and I. R. Kaplan. (1975b). Thermal alteration experiments on organic matter in recent marine sediment—III. Aliphatic and steroidal alcohols. *Geochim. Cosmochim. Acta,* **39**:195–203.

Ishiwatari, R. (1975). Chemical nature of sedimentary humic acids. Pp. 87–107. In: D. Povoledo and H. L. Golterman (eds.), *Humic Substances: Their Structure and Function in the Biosphere.* Centre for Agricultural Publishing and Documentation, Wageningen.

Ishiwatari, R., and T. Hanya. (1973). Organic geochemistry of a 200-meter core sample from Lake Biwa. I. Identification of fatty acids by combined gas chromatography–mass spectrometry. *Proc. Japan Acad.,* **49**:731–736.

Ishiwatari, R., and T. Hanya. (1974). Gas chromatographic–mass spectrometric identification of organic compounds in a river water. Pp. 1051–1065. In: B. Tissot and F. Bienner (eds.), *Advances in Organic Geochemistry, 1973.* Éditions Technip, Paris.

Ishiwatari, R., and T. Hanya. (1975). Organic geochemistry of a 200-meter core sample from Lake Biwa. II. Vertical distribution of mono- and di-carboxylic acids and polynuclear aromatic hydrocarbons. *Proc. Japan Acad.,* **51**:436–441.

Jackson, L. L., and G. L. Baker, (1970). Cuticular lipids of insects. *Lipids,* **5**:239–246.

Johns, R. B. and O. M. Onder. (1975). Biological diagenesis: dicarboxylic acids in recent sediments. *Geochim. Cosmochim. Acta,* **39**:129–136.

Johnson, R. W., and J. A. Calder. (1973). Early diagenesis of fatty acids and hydrocarbons in a salt marsh environment. *Geochim. Cosmochim. Acta,* 37:1943–1955.

Kaneda, T. (1967). Fatty acids in the genus *Bacillus.* I. Iso- and anteiso-fatty acids as characteristic constituents of lipids in 10 species. *J. Bacteriol.,* **93**:894–903.

Kaplan, I. R., and M. J. Baedecker. (1970). Biological productivity in the Dead Sea. Part II: Evidence for phosphatidyl glycerophosphate lipid in sediment. *Israel J. Chem.,* **8**:529–533.

Kaplan, I. R., and A. Friedman. (1970). Biological productivity in the Dead Sea. Part I: Microorganisms in the water column. *Israel J. Chem.,* **8**:513–528.

Kates, M., and B. E. Volcani. (1966). Lipid components of diatoms. *Biochim. Biophys. Acta,* **116**:264–278.

Kates, M., L. S. Yengoyan, and P. S. Sastry. (1965). A diether analog of phosphatidyl glycerophosphate in *Halobacterium cutirubrum. Biochim. Biophys. Acta,* **98**:252–268.

Keeney, D. R., J. G. Konrad, and G. Chesters. (1970). Nitrogen distribution in some Wisconsin lake sediments *J. Water Poll. Control Fed.,* **42**:411–417.

Kemp, A. L. W., and A. Mudrochova. (1973). The distribution and nature of amino acids and other nitrogen-containing compounds in Lake Ontario surface sediments. *Geochim. Cosmochim. Acta,* 37:2191–2206.

Kemp, A. L. W., C. B. J. Gray, and A. Mudrochova. (1972). Changes in C, N, P, and S in the last 140 years in three cores from Lakes Ontario, Erie, and Huron. Pp. 251–279. In: H. E. Allen and J. R. Kramer (eds.), *Nutrients in Natural Waters.* Wiley, New York, NY.

Knights, B. A., A. C. Brown, and E. Conway. (1970). Hydrocarbons from the green form of the freshwater alga *Botryococcus braunii. Phytochemistry,* **9**:1317–1324.

Kolattukudy, P. E. (1975). Biochemistry of cutin, suberin and waxes, the lipid barriers on plants. Pp. 203–246. In: T. Galliard and E. I. Mercer (eds.), *Recent Advances in the Chemistry and Biochemistry of Plant Lipids.* Academic Press, New York, NY.

Kolattukudy, P. E., and T. J. Walton. (1972). The biochemistry of plant cuticular lipids. Pp. 121–175. In: R. T. Holman (ed.), *Progress in the Chemistry of Fats and Other Lipids.* Vol. 13. Pergamon, Oxford.

Kudryavtsev, V. M. (1975). Dynamics of the decomposition of tagged algae by bacteria. *Microbiology,* **43**:767–771.

Leeuw, J. W. de, V. A. Correia, and P. A. Schenck. (1974). On the decomposition of phytol under simulated geological conditions and in the top-layer of natural sediments. Pp. 993–1004. In: B. Tissot and F. Bienner (eds.), *Advances in Organic Geochemistry, 1973.* Éditions Technip, Paris.

Leeuw, J. W. de, B. R. Simoneit, J. J. Boon, W. I. C. Rijpstra, F. de Lange, J. C. W. van der Leeden, V. A. Correia, A. L. Burlingame, and P. A. Schenck. (1975). Phytol derived compounds in the geosphere. Preprint of paper presented at 7th Meeting on Organic Geochemistry, Madrid.

Lenfant, M., M. F. Lecompte, and G. Farrugia. (1970). Identification des stérols de *Physarum polycephalum. Phytochemistry,* **9**:2529–2535.

Lough, A. K. (1973). The chemistry and biochemistry of phytanic, pristanic and related acids. Pp. 5–48. In: R. T. Holman (ed.), *Progress in the Chemistry of Fats and other Lipids.* Vol. 14. Pergamon, London.

Lowe, L. E. (1978). Carbohydrates in soil. Pp. 65–93. In: M. Schnitzer and S. U. Kahn (eds.), *Soil Organic Matter.* Elsevier, Amsterdam.

Lytle, T. F., and J. R. Sever. (1973). Hydrocarbons and fatty acids of *Lycopodium. Phytochemistry,* **12**:623–629.

Lytle, T. F., J. S. Lytle, and A. Caruso. (1976). Hydrocarbons and fatty acids of ferns. *Phytochemistry,* **15**:965–970.

Mackereth, F. J. H. (1966). Some chemical observations on post-glacial lake sediments. *Phil. Trans. Roy. Soc. London (Ser. B)*, **250**:165–213.

Matsuda, H., and T. Koyama. (1977). Positional isomer composition of monounsaturated fatty acids from a lacustrine sediment. *Geochim. Cosmochim. Acta*, **41**:341–345.

Matsuyama, M. (1973). Organic substances in sediment and settling matter during Spring in a meromictic Lake Suigetsu. *J. Oceanogr. Soc. Japan*, **29**:53–60.

Maxwell, J. R., R. E. Cox, G. Eglinton, C. T. Pillinger, R. G. Ackman, and S. N. Hooper. (1973). Stereochemical studies of acyclic isoprenoid compounds—II. The role of chlorophyll in the derivation of isoprenoid-type acids in a lacustrine sediment. *Geochim. Cosmochim. Acta*, **37**:297–313.

Maxwell, J. R., C. T. Pillinger, and G. Eglinton. (1971). Organic geochemistry. *Quart. Rev.*, **25**:571–628.

Mazliak, P. (1968). Chemistry of plant cuticles. Pp. 49–111. In: L. Reinhold and Y. Liwschitz (eds.), *Progress in Phytochemistry*. Vol. 1. Interscience, London.

Meyers, P. A., and J. G. Quinn. (1973). Factors affecting the association of fatty acids with mineral particles in seawater. *Geochim. Cosmochim. Acta*, **37**:1745–1759.

Meyers, P. A., N. Takeuchi, and R. A. Bourbonniere. (1976). Fatty acids and hydrocarbons in Lake Huron sediments. *Geol. Soc. Am. Absts.*, **8**:1010–1011.

Mize, C. E., J. Avigan, D. Steinberg, R. C. Pittman, H. M. Fales, and G. W. A. Milne. (1969). A major pathway for the mammalian oxidative degradation of phytanic acid. *Biochim. Biophys. Acta*, **176**:720–739.

Mori, S. (1974). Diatom succession in a core from Lake Biwa. Pp. 247–254. In: S. Horie (ed.), *Paleolimnology of Lake Biwa and the Japanese Pleistocene*. Otsu Hydrobiol. Station, Kyoto Univ., Otsu, Japan.

Morrison, R. I. (1969). Soil lipids. Pp. 558–575. In: G. Eglinton and R. T. J. Murphy (eds.), *Organic Geochemistry: Methods and Results*. Springer-Verlag, New York, NY.

Nishimoto, S. (1974). A chemotaxonomic study of n-alkanes in aquatic plants. *J. Sci. Hiroshima Univ. Ser. A*, **38**:159–163.

Nishimura, M., and T. Koyama. (1976). Stenols and stanols in lake sediments and diatoms. *Chem. Geol.*, **17**:229–239.

Nissenbaum, A. (1975). The microbiology and biogeochemistry of the Dead Sea. *Microbial Ecol.*, **2**:139–161.

Nissenbaum, A., M. J. Baedecker, and I. R. Kaplan. (1972). Organic geochemistry of Dead Sea sediments. *Geochim. Cosmochim. Acta*, **36**:709–727.

Nriagu, J. O. (ed.). (1976). *Environmental Biogeochemistry*. Ann Arbor Science Publishers, Ann Arbor, MI.

Oehler, J. H. (1976). Experimental studies in Precambrian paleontology: structural and chemical changes in blue–green algae during simulated fossilization in synthetic chert. *Geol. Soc. Am. Bull.*, **87**:117–129.

Ogura, K. (1974). Information of sterols in a core sample. Pp. 194–201. In: S. Horie (ed.), *Paleolimnology of Lake Biwa and the Japanese Pleistocene*.

Ogura, K., and T. Hanya. (1973). The cholestanol–cholesterol ratio in a 200-meter core sample of Lake Biwa. *Proc. Japan Acad.*, **49**:201–204.

Oliver, J. D., and R. R. Colwell. (1973). Extractable lipids of

gram-negative marine bacteria: fatty-acid composition. *Int. J. Sys. Bacteriol.*, **23**:442–458.

Patton, S., and A. A. Benson. (1966). Phytol metabolism in the bovine. *Biochim. Biophys. Acta*, **125**:22–32.

Philp, R. P., and M. Calvin. (1976). Possible origin for insoluble organic (kerogen) debris in sediments from insoluble cell-wall materials of algae and bacteria. *Nature*, **262**:134–136.

Philp, R. P., J. R. Maxwell, and G. Eglinton. (1976). Environmental organic geochemistry of aquatic sediments. *Sci. Prog.*, **63**:521–545.

Polacheck, J. W., B. E. Tropp, J. H. Law, and J. A. McCloskey. (1966). Biosynthesis of cyclopropane compounds. VIII. The conversion of oleate to dihydrosterculate. *J. Biol. Chem.*, **241**:3362–3364.

Povoledo, D., and H. L. Golterman. (eds.). (1975). *Humic Substances: Their Structure and Function in the Biosphere*. Centre for Agricultural Publishing and Documentation, Wageningen.

Povoledo, D., D. Murray, and M. Pitze. (1975). Pigments and lipids in the humic acids of some Canadian lake sediments. Pp. 233–258. In: D. Povoledo and H. L. Golterman (eds.), *Humic Substances: Their Structure and Function in the Biosphere*. Centre for Agricultural Publishing and Documentation, Wageningen.

Powers, C. F., W. D. Sanville, and F. S. Stay. (1976). Aquatic sediments. *J. Water Poll. Control Fed.*, **48**:1433–1439.

Reed, W. (1977). Biogeochemistry of Mono Lake, California. *Geochim. Cosmochim. Acta*, **41**:1231–1245.

Rhead, M. M., G. Eglinton, G. H. Draffan, and P. J. England. (1971). Conversion of oleic acid to saturated fatty acids in Severn Estuary sediments. *Nature (London)*, **232**:327–330.

Rhead, M. M., G. Eglinton, and P. J. England. (1972). Products of the short-term diagenesis of oleic acid in an estuarine sediment. Pp. 323–333. In: H. R. von Gaertner and H. Wehner (eds.), *Advances in Organic Geochemistry, 1971*. Pergamon, Oxford.

Rijpstra, W. I. C., J. W. de Leeuw, and P. A. Schenck. (1976). The action of borontrifluoride-methanol on isoprenoid alcohols. *Geochim. Cosmochim. Acta*, **40**:1289–1290.

Rogers, M. A. (1965). Carbohydrates in aquatic plants and associated sediments from two Minnesota lakes. *Geochim. Cosmochim. Acta*, **29**:183–200.

Sanger, J. E., and E. Gorham. (1970). The diversity of pigments in lake sediments and its ecological significance. *Limnol. Oceanogr.*, **15**:59–69.

Schneider, H., E. Gelpi, E. O. Bennett, J. Oró (1970). Fatty acids of geochemical significance in microscopic algae, *Phytochemistry*, **9**:613–617.

Schnitzer, M. (1975). Chemical, spectroscopic, and thermal methods for the classification and characterization of humic substances. Pp. 293–310. In: D. Povoledo and H. L. Golterman (eds.), *Humic Substances: Their Structure and Function in the Biosphere*. Centre for Agricultural Publishing and Documentation, Wageningen.

Schwendinger, R. B., and J. G. Erdman. (1964). Sterols in recent aquatic sediments. *Science*, **144**:1575–1576.

Simoneit, B. R. T., L. A. Clews, C. D. Watts, and J. R. Maxwell. (1975). Stereochemical studies of acyclic isoprenoid compounds—V. Oxidation products of Green River Formation oil shale kerogen. *Geochim. Cosmochim. Acta,* **39**:1143–1145.

Singer, P. C. (ed.). (1973). *Trace Metals and Metal-Organic Interactions in Natural Waters.* Ann Arbor Science Publishers, Ann Arbor, MI.

Stockner, J. G., and J. W. G. Lund. (1970). Live algae in postglacial lake deposits. *Limnol. Oceanogr.,* **15**:41–58.

Swain, F. M. (1970). *Non-marine Organic Geochemistry.* Cambridge Univ. Press, Cambridge.

Swetland, P. J., and J. F. Wehmiller. (1975). Lipid geochemistry of recent sediments from Great Marsh, Lewes, Delaware. Pp. 285–303, In: T. M. Church (ed.), *Marine Chemistry in the Coastal Environment.* Symp. Ser. 18. Am. Chem. Soc., Washington.

Terashima, M., and A. Mizuno. (1974). Preliminary results of amino acid and amino-sugar determination on a 200-meter core sample from Lake Biwa. Pp. 219–224. In: S. Horie (ed.), *Paleolimnology of Lake Biwa and the Japanese Pleistocene.* Otsu Hydrobiol. Station, Kyoto Univ., Otsu, Jdapan.

Tornabene, T. G., M. Kates, and B. E. Volcani. (1974). Sterols, aliphatic hydrocarbons, and fatty acids of a nonphotosynthetic diatom, *Nitzschia alba. Lipids,* **9**:279–284.

Vallentyne, J. R. (1955). Sedimentary chlorophyll determination as a paleobotanical method. *Can. J. Botany,* **33**:304–313.

Velden, W. van der, and A. W. Schwartz. (1974). Purines and pyrimidines in sediments from Lake Erie. *Science,* **185**:691–693.

Velden, W. van der, and A. W. Schwartz. (1976). Nucleic acid base contents as indicators of biological activity in sediments. Pp. 175–183. In: J. O. Nriagu (ed.), *Environmental Biogeochemistry.* Vol. 1. Ann Arbor Science Publishers, Ann Arbor, MI.

Velden, W. van der, G. J. F. Chittenden, and A. W. Schwartz. (1974). Studies on the geochemistry of purines and pyrimidines. Pp. 293–304. In: B. Tissot and F. Bienner (eds.), *Advances in Organic Geochemistry, 1973.* Éditions Technip, Paris.

Wakeham, S. G. (1977). Synchronous fluorescence spectroscopy and its application to indigenous and petroleum-derived hydrocarbons in lacustrine sediments. *Envir. Sci. Technol.,* **11**:272–276.

Wakeham, S. G., and R. Carpenter. (1976). Aliphatic hydrocarbons in sediments of Lake Washington. *Limnol. Oceanogr.,* **21**:711–723.

Weete, J. D. (1974). *Fungal Lipid Biochemistry.* Plenum, New York, NY.

Welch, J. W., and A. L. Burlingame. (1973). Very long-chain fatty acids in yeast. *J. Bacteriol.,* **115**:464–466.

Wetzel, R. G. (1975). *Limnology.* Saunders, Philadelphia. PA.

Yamamoto, A., S. Kanari, Y. Fukuo, and S. Horie. (1974). Consolidation and dating of the sediments in core samples from Lake Biwa. Pp. 135–144. In: S. Horie (ed.), *Paleolimnology of Lake Biwa and the Japanese Pleistocene.* Otsu Hydrobiol. Station, Kyoto Univ., Otsu, Japan.

Yen, T. F. (1975). Genesis and degradation of petroleum hydrocarbons in marine environments. Pp. 231–266. In: T. M. Church (ed.), *Marine Chemistry in the Coastal Environment.* Symp. Ser. 18. Am. Chem. Soc., Washington.

Chapter 6

Radionuclide Limnochronology

S. Krishnaswami and D. Lal

Introduction

Radioactive nuclides present in the environment have proved very valuable for the introduction of time parameter in a variety of earth science problems. Their utility in the field of oceanography, meteorology, hydrology, and related fields has been well documented (Eriksson, 1962; Lal, 1963; Sheppard, 1963; Broecker, 1963, 1965; Lal and Suess, 1968; Lal, 1969; Machta, 1974; Fitch et al., 1974; Goldberg and Bruland, 1974; Oeschger and Gugelmann, 1974; Burton, 1976; Ku, 1976; Turekian and Cochran, 1977). The application of radionuclides for deciphering the time element in limnological processes is still in its infancy. The past decade has witnessed a surge of activity in this field, especially in limnochronology and gas exchange across the water–air interface. In this chapter we will discuss the application of radionuclides for determining the chronology of sediments and other deposits forming from contemporary lakes and those collected from glacial and "fossil" lakes. The sedimentary record of contemporary lakes contains information on the recent past of the environment, whereas those from the glacial and "fossil" lakes can be used to reconstruct the long-term history of the earth's past, especially its climatic changes.

The radioactivities which are present on the earth's surface can be broadly classified into three categories, based on their origin:

Primordial

These are nuclides which were present during the formation of earth and are still present on the earth's surface because of their very long half-lives, $>10^8$ years. The isotopes ^{40}K, ^{87}Rb, ^{232}Th, ^{235}U, and ^{238}U belong to this group. Also included in this category are the radioactive daughter nuclides produced continuously from ^{232}Th, ^{235}U, and ^{238}U. The major fraction of the inventory of these nuclides is contained in the earth's crust. Figure 1 shows the U–Th series nuclides which are of interest in limnological processes.

Cosmic ray produced

These nuclides are produced continuously, directly in the earth's atmosphere and in the lithosphere as a result of interactions of primary and secondary components of the cosmic radiation. Several nuclides with half-lives ranging between a few minutes to millions of years are produced in this manner. Table 1 lists the cosmic ray isotopes with half-lives > 1 day, in order of decreasing half-life.

Man-made

These nuclides have been injected into the earth's environment during the past 2–3 decades, due to testing of nuclear weapons. Until 1969 about 200 megaton equivalent of fission products had been injected into the earth's environment, the peak period of testing being 1961–1962 (Joseph et al., 1971). Several radioactivities are produced during the weapon testing; their quantities and relative proportions depend on the size, nature, and material of the weapon. The principal man-made nuclides are given in Table 2. In addition to nuclear explosives, nuclear reactors also contribute to man-made radioactivities; however, the contribution to artificial radioactivity due to operation of nuclear reactors is usually localized and small compared to that due to testing of nuclear weapons.

Delivery of radionuclides to lakes

Lakes receive most of their radioactivity through two sources.

Land-derived

Several of the isotopes belonging to the U–Th series (Figure 1) are introduced into the lakes by rivers and ground water through weathering of crustal rocks and soil layers. The concentrations of radionuclides in rivers vary by orders of magnitude and seem to depend on the nature of the bedrock and the chemical composition of river water. In general, waters draining sedimentary rocks appear to have more U and Ra, compared to those draining granites and basalts (Bhat and Krishnaswami, 1969). Table 3 lists the range of concentration of some of the U–Th series nuclides in rivers. Ground waters can contribute radionuclides to lakes through their direct seepage into the lake basins. In addition to the dissolved load of radionuclides to lakes, there is a considerable input of nuclides in the particulate phase through the physical erosion of soil

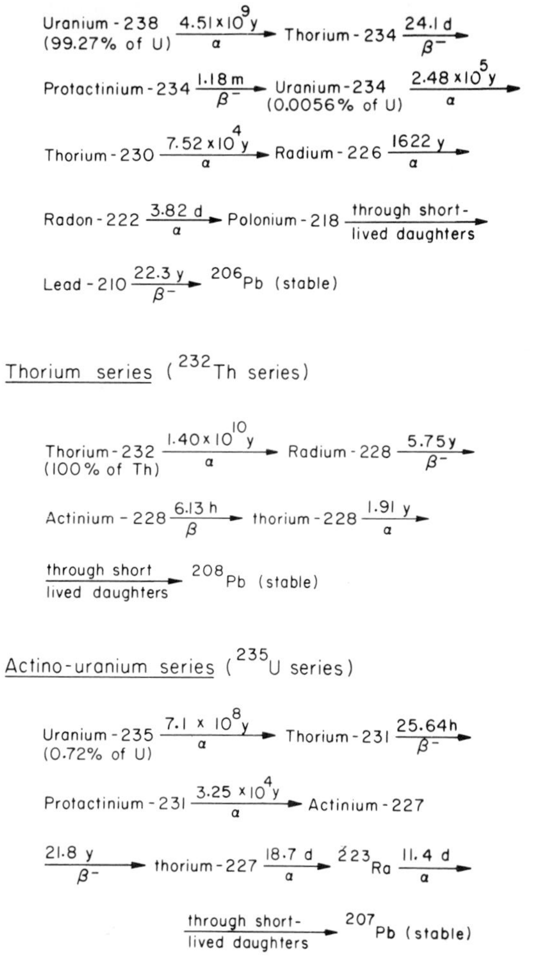

FIGURE 1.   The three natural U–Th series radioactive nuclides, their half-lives and mode of decay. Only those isotopes which are useful from a chronological point of view are given.

TABLE 1   Isotopes (half-life > 1 day) Produced by Cosmic Rays in the Atmosphere

Isotope	Half-life	Main radiation	Main target nuclide(s)
^{3}He	Stable	—	N,O
^{10}Be	1.5×10^6 years	β^-—550 KeV	N,O
^{26}Al	7.2×10^5 years	β^+—1.17 MeV	Ar
^{36}Cl	3.0×10^5 years	β^-—714 KeV	Ar
^{81}Kr	2.1×10^5 years	K—X ray	Kr
^{14}C	5730 years	β^-—156 KeV	N,O
^{32}Si	~ 300 years	β^-—100 KeV	Ar
^{39}Ar	270 years	β^-—565 KeV	Ar
^{3}H	12.3 years	β^-—18 KeV	N,O
^{22}Na	2.6 years	β^+—540 KeV / γ—1.3 MeV	Ar
^{35}S	87.5 days	β^-—167 KeV	Ar
^{7}Be	53.4 days	γ—480 KeV	N,O
^{37}Ar	35 days	K—X ray	Ar
^{33}P	25.3 days	β^-—250 KeV	Ar
^{32}P	14.3 days	β^-—1.7 MeV	Ar

horizons which are rich in organic matter and U–Th series nuclides.

Atmospheric

All the isotopes produced or injected into the atmosphere, e.g., cosmic ray produced and man-made nuclides and ^{210}Pb (produced from decay of ^{222}Rn in the atmosphere), are brought down to the earth's surface by wet precipitation and dry fallout processes. The deposition pattern of nuclides from the atmosphere depends on their source function. Nuclides produced/injected in the troposphere are deposited relatively uniformly over the earth's surface. The average resi-

TABLE 2.   Principal Artifical Radionuclides

(a) Fission products		
Nuclide	Half-life	Fission yield from ^{235}U (%)
^{89}Sr	50.4 days	4.8
^{90}Sr	28.5 years	5.8
^{95}Zr	63.3 days	6.3
^{106}Ru	1 year	0.4
^{137}Cs	30 years	6.0
^{141}Ce	32.5 days	6.0
^{144}Ce	285 days	5.7
^{147}Pm	2.5 years	2.4

(b) Induced Activities			
Nuclide	Half-life	Nuclide	Half-life
^{3}H	12.3 years	^{55}Fe	2.7 years
^{14}C	5730 years	^{57}Co	270 days
^{35}S	87.5 days	^{58}Co	72 days
^{51}Cr	27.8 days	^{60}Co	5.3 years
^{54}Mn	312 days	^{65}Zn	244 days
		^{239}Pu	2.43×10^4 years
		^{241}Pu	14.9 years

TABLE 3.   Concentrations of [238]U, [232]Th, and [226]Ra in River Waters

River	Concentration (dpm/liter)			Reference
	[238]U	[232]Th	[226]Ra	
Major rivers				
Amazon	0.03	0.021	0.02	Moore (1967)
Mississippi	0.75	0.011	0.07	Moore (1967)
Congo	0.09	—	—	Bertine et al. (1970)
Ganges	1.2–4.9	—	0.20	Bhat and Krishnaswami (1969)
Mackenzie	0.38–0.6	—	—	Turekian and Chan (1971)
St. Lawrence	~ 0.02	—	0.06	Rona and Urry (1952)
Minor rivers				
Two European rivers	0.12–0.48	—	—	Bertine et al. (1970)
Six Indian rivers	~ 0.01–2.7	—	0.05–0.20	Bhat and Krishnaswami (1969)
				Borole et al. (1977)
Several North American rivers	~ 0.01–1.7	—	—	Sackett et al. (1973)

dence time of nuclides in the troposphere is only few days (Poet et al., 1972; Moore et al., 1973; Turekian et al., 1977). The activities formed in the stratosphere exhibit a latitudinal dependence in their fallout pattern with maximum deposition in the mid-latitudes and minimum near the poles and the equator. The deposition pattern of ^{90}Sr, an artificial nuclide primarily of stratospheric origin, is shown in Figure 2 (Joseph et al., 1971). The low ^{90}Sr deposition in the southern latitudes is due to the fact that the tests were carried out in the northern hemisphere, and interhemispheric stratosphere mixing is much slower compared to stratosphere–troposphere exchange times (Martell, 1970; Machta, 1974). The residence time of nuclides (other than the gaseous [14]CO$_2$ and noble gases) in the stratosphere is estimated to be ~ 1 year based on the study of natural and artificial nuclides (Junge, 1963; Bhandari et al., 1966; Lal and Rama, 1966; Martell, 1970). The fallout pattern of long-lived cosmic ray isotopes, ^{3}H, [32]Si, and [10]Be, is also expected to exhibit a latitudinal variation, since, for these isotopes, the stratospheric contributions to the total fallout is significant (Lal and Peters, 1967). However, unlike the artificial nuclides, the cosmic ray isotopes have a hemispherically symmetrical source function and hence are expected to have identical deposition in both hemispheres. Figure 3 shows the calculated fallout pattern for a long-lived cosmic ray isotope [other than for nuclides which exist in gaseous form in the atmosphere (Lal and Peters, 1967)]. Additionally, in the case of cosmic ray-produced nuclides, since production from the troposphere also contributes to fallout, the mid-latitude peak in the deposition is less pronounced compared to that for ^{90}Sr, which deposits mainly from the stratosphere.

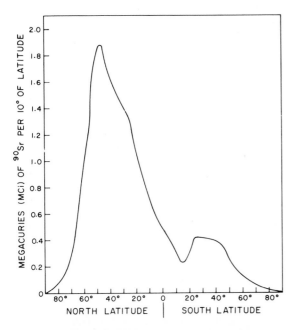

FIGURE 2.   Latitudinal distribution of ^{90}Sr fallout for the period 1958–1967 (from Joseph et al., 1971). The mid-latitude peak in the ^{90}Sr deposition is clearly evident. There are two reasons for the relatively lower deposition in the southern latitudes: (i) weapon tests were conducted in the northern hemisphere and (ii) the interhemispheric–stratospheric exchange is much slower compared to the stratosphere–troposphere exchange.

Limnochronology

Radioactive chronologies are generally based on either (i) the decay of a radioactive nuclide, or (ii) the build-up (ingrowth) of a daughter nuclide to attain secular equilibrium with its parent.

In addition, if the nuclide has a sporadic source function, e.g., the artificial nuclides, then a correlation of the pattern of its distribution in the depository with the pattern of injection can also be used as a chronometer.

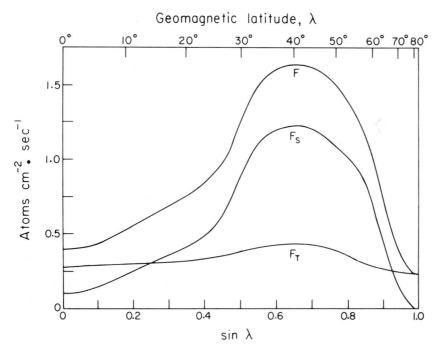

FIGURE 3.   Calculated deposition pattern of a long-lived cosmic ray-produced nuclide (e.g., ^{3}H, ^{32}Si, ^{10}Be) having an average global production rate of 1 atom · cm^{-2} sec^{-1}. The tropospheric fallout pattern (F_T) is almost independent of latitude, whereas the stratospheric fallout (F_S) exhibits mid-latitude maximum. The total fallout (F) also exhibits a mid-latitude peak but is less pronounced compared to that for ^{90}Sr (Figure 2), which is primarily of stratospheric origin. Figure from Lal and Peters (1967).

Case (i)

When a technique is based on the decay of a nuclide with depth in the sediment, then the basic requirements are: (i) the flux of the radionuclide to the sediment–water interface has remained constant and (ii) no migration of the radionuclide has occurred over the dating interval, i.e., the change in the concentration of the nuclide in the system is only due to its radioactive decay. If these assumptions are valid, then the activity of the nuclide in the sediment at any depth, z, from the sediment water interface is given by:

$$A(z) = A_0 e^{-\lambda t} \tag{1}$$

where A_0 is the activity of the nuclide (disintegrations per minute per gram of sediment, dpm/g) in a freshly deposited sediment at time $t = 0$, i.e., at the sediment–water interface, and λ is its radioactive decay constant. The value of A_0 is the ratio of the deposition rate of the nuclide (dpm/cm^2/time) to the deposition rate of sediment (g/cm^2/time) at the interface. Also if the sediment accumulation rate S (cm/time) is constant over the interval t, then $t = z/S$. Substituting for A_0 and t in Eq. (1),

$$A(z) = \frac{\phi\lambda}{S\rho(z)}e^{-\lambda z/S} \tag{2}$$

where ϕ is the flux of the nuclide, atoms/cm^2/time, and $\rho(z)$ is the *in situ* density at depth z. A plot of log $A(z)$ vs depth (z) should be a straight line if both the deposition rates of the isotope and sediment (i.e., ϕ and S) and $\rho(z)$ have remained constant during the dating interval. This model may be called the constant flux, constant sediment accumulation model.

However, if the sedimentation rate has changed during the dating interval, the ages of different strata in the sediment column can be deduced from the integrated activity of the isotope in the core (Goldberg, 1963; McCaffrey, 1977). The time t taken to deposit a sediment layer of thickness z in a continuously depositing sediment with a constant radionuclide flux is

$$t = \left(\frac{1}{\lambda}\right) \ln\left[Q_0/Q(z)\right] \tag{2a}$$

where Q_0 is the standing crop (activity/unit area) of the nuclide below the sediment–water interface and $Q(z)$ is the standing crop remaining below depth z from the surface. [In Eq. (2a) it is assumed that in the sediment column steady state exists between supply and decay of the radionuclide and that the removal of the radionuclide occurs only through its radioactive decay]. Since a new value of $Q(z)$ is available for various depths in the core, it is possible to calculate their ages and hence the sedimentation rates between the depth intervals.

Case (ii)

When the chronology relies on the ingrowth of a daughter from its parent, then the ratio of the daughter to parent activity at any time, t, is,

$$\frac{A_d}{A_p} = \frac{\lambda_d}{\lambda_d - \lambda_p}[1 - e^{(\lambda_p - \lambda_d)t}] \qquad (3)$$

where A is activity, λ is the decay constant, and the subscripts d and p refer to daughter and parent nuclides, respectively. In Eq. (3) it is assumed that the activity of the daughter, A_d, $= 0$ at $t = 0$, i.e., the time of formation of the deposit. If $A_d \neq 0$ at $t = 0$, then it is essential to have a precise knowledge of A_d/A_p at the time of formation. In this method also, the assumption of validity of a no-migration system as required in case (i) is necessary for both the parent and daughter nuclides.

The assumptions and activity–time relation discussed above hold for highly simplified models. For example, generally one does not take into consideration the variation of *in situ* density, ρ, with depth in a core. This variation is mainly brought about by compaction and could be very significant in the top ~ 1 m of the core. The effect of compaction would be to decrease the sediment accumulation rate compared to original value. Emery and Rittenberg (1952) have related sediment accumulation rate (cm/time) and porosity by the relation:

$$S_z(1 - P_z) = S_i(1 - P_i) \qquad (4)$$

where S is the sediment accumulation rate (cm/time), P is the porosity (percentage water by volume), and the subscripts z and i are the two depths in the core. The *in situ* density, ρ, is related to porosity as:

$$\rho = d(1 - P) \qquad (5)$$

where d is the density of the dry solid. Thus knowing the water content and sediment accumulation rate at one depth, it is possible to correct for changes in sediment accumulation rate brought about by compaction. Detailed mathematical models relating porosity and sedimentation rates for lake sediments are discussed by Robbins and Edgington (1975) and Robbins (1977). The effect of compaction can automatically be taken care of if one expresses the sedimentation rate in mass units, g/cm²/time; in this case the depth, z, in Eq. (2) has to be expressed in units of g/cm².

The common requirement of the closed system assumption could be violated if (i) the nuclides undergo postdepositional migration independent of the sediments and (ii) if there is mixing of the sediments with

the associated nuclides of interest due to physical and biological processes. Both processes would result in the redistribution of the radionuclides in the sediments. These effects are expected to be greatest near the sediment–water interface and hence short-term chronologies (based on short-lived natural isotopes and fallout nuclides) which depend on the distribution of nuclides near the sediment–water interface are highly susceptible to these modifications.

All three of the U and Th series nuclides (Figure 1) include daughter products which have widely different chemical and nuclear properties and hence are separated from one another during weathering, transportation, and deposition. This separation creates radioactive disequilibrium among the members of the series, which forms the fundamental basis of all U and Th dating techniques. This disequilibrium is of two types: (a) enrichment of daughter nuclide over the parent, in which case the decay of the excess or unsupported daughter activity is used for dating, and (b) the preferential incorporation of the parent over the daughter in a sedimentary deposit, in which case the growth of daughter activity is used as the time indicator.

For cosmic ray isotopes, dating methods rely on the decay of the nuclide after its burial on the sediment. The correlation chronology applies to artificial nuclides, whose deposition on the earth's surface has exhibited significant time variations, due to their sporadic injections in the atmosphere. The peak in the atmospheric fallout occurred in 1963, and this peak, if discernible in a given sediment, can be used as a time marker.

Dating methods

U-Th series nuclides

[210]Pb. [210]Pb with a half-life of 22.3 years (Hohndorf, 1969) is ideal for dating lake sediments deposited during the last century, a period of time during which appreciable geochemical changes have occurred due to industrialization. [210]Pb is introduced into lakes through several pathways.

DIRECT DEPOSITION FROM THE ATMOSPHERE THROUGH WET PRECIPITATION AND DRY FALLOUT (SETTLING OF AEROSOLS BY GRAVITATIONAL AND ELECTROSTATIC FORCES). Most of the ^{210}Pb in the atmosphere results from the radioactive decay of [222]Rn escaping from the earth's crust (Israel, 1958; Jaworowski, 1969). [222]Rn is produced in the crust from [226]Ra (Figure 1). The mean exhalation rate of [222]Rn from land is ~ 45 atoms/cm²/min (Wilkening *et al.*, 1975). Turekian *et al.* (1977), however, based on the

^{210}Pb flux estimate, suggested a higher value of about 1.5 times this amount. Significant variations from the mean value exist since the ^{222}Rn escape rate depends primarily on the nature of the soil (porosity, grain size, etc.) and environmental conditions (wind pattern, pressure). The ^{222}Rn flux from the ocean to the atmosphere is about two orders of magnitude lower compared to that from the land since ^{226}Ra concentration in sea water is much less than that in the earth's crust (Broecker *et al.*, 1967). A small amount of ^{210}Pb is also contributed to the atmosphere through the enhanced use of radium-rich phosphate fertilizers. The ^{210}Pb flux from this source is estimated to be (Jaworowski *et al.*, 1972; Moore *et al.*, 1976a) in the range of 2.2×10^{14} – 1.3×10^{15} dpm per year, compared to the annual production of $\sim 1.3 \times 10^{18}$ dpm from ^{222}Rn escaping from land.

In addition to these sources, ^{210}Pb could also be injected into the atmosphere through the reaction ^{208}Pb (2 n, γ) ^{210}Pb (Stebbins, 1961; Peirson *et al.*, 1966) from nuclear explosives containing Pb as a structural material. It is likely that some of the nuclear tests carried out could have introduced ^{210}Pb in the environment; if so the magnitude and the locations of injections are unknown. Evidence both for and against the artificial injection of ^{210}Pb through weapon testings exists. For a detailed review on this, reference is made to Bhandari *et al.* (1966), Robbins (1977), and Turekian *et al.* (1977).

Whatever may be the mechanism of production, ^{210}Pb is removed from the atmosphere to the earth's surface by wet precipitation and dry fallout on a time scale much shorter than its radioactive half-life. The mean residence time of ^{210}Pb in the atmosphere is of the order of 5 to 10 days (Burton and Stewart, 1960;

Francis *et al.*, 1970; Poet *et al.*, 1972; Moore *et al.*, 1973; Turekian *et al.*, 1977). The available data on the ^{210}Pb deposition flux at any given location seem to exhibit a positive correlation with local rainfall, with correlation coefficients ranging between 0.3 and 0.7 (Turekian *et al.*, 1977). Figure 4 shows the monthly ^{210}Pb deposition and rainfall for Hokkaido, Japan, where a significant seasonal variation in the ^{210}Pb concentration in rain water has been observed (Fukuda and Tsunogai, 1975) probably due to the influence of northwest monsoon. Such marked seasonal trends in the ^{210}Pb concentration in rain water have not been observed for several other stations for which data are available. If the linear relation between ^{210}Pb deposition and wet precipitation are valid, then the intercept at zero rainfall should be a measure of the dry fallout. Estimates made in this manner (Turekian *et al.*, 1977) indicate that for several stations a significant fraction, $\sim$ 30–60% of the total ^{210}Pb deposition is due to dry fallout.

The annual deposition rate of ^{210}Pb on the earth's surface is of the order of 1 dpm/cm^2/year and it shows significant geographical variations. The mean and ranges of annual deposition of ^{210}Pb for several stations are listed in Table 4. The data in Table 4 show that the annual ^{210}Pb flux varies considerably, the standard deviation in the yearly^{210}Pb flux (for a period of $\sim$ 5 years) being $\sim$ 30% of the mean.

^{210}Pb FROM STREAMS AND RIVERS.   The major source of ^{210}Pb in surface water is rainfall. ^{210}Pb can also be introduced into rivers through weathering of soil and effluent discharge from ground water. Quantitative data on different sources of ^{210}Pb in rivers are not available; however, it can be inferred from the behav-

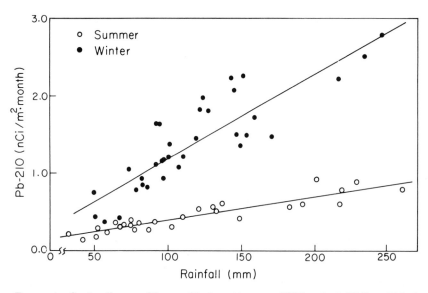

FIGURE 4.   Scatter diagram of the monthly deposition rate of ^{210}Pb and rainfall (from Fukuda and Tsunagai, 1975). The data show a significant correlation between rainfall and the ^{210}Pb deposition rate.

TABLE 4.   Variations in Total Annual Deposition of ^{210}Pb (via Precipitation and Dry Fallout)

Location	Period of observation	Number of observations	^{210}Pb deposition rate Range (dpm/cm²/year)	Mean	Reference
New Zealand (18° S–46° S)					
Kaitala	1968–74	4	0.27–0.50	0.37	Turekian *et al.* (1977)
Auckland	1968–72	3	0.22–0.36	0.30	
New Plymouth	1968–73	3	0.34–0.50	0.44	
Havelock	1968–74	4	0.17–0.19	0.18	
Wellington	1968–73	3	0.26–0.41	0.34	
Greymouth	1968–73	5	0.68–0.87	0.75	
Christchurch	1968–70	3	0.12–0.14	0.14	
Dunedin	1968–74	6	0.15–0.27	0.18	
Invercargill	1968–73	4	0.13–0.28	0.21	
India (11° N–34° N)					
Srinagar	1962–66	5	0.65–1.40	1.09	Joshi *et al.* (1969)
Delhi	1962–66	5	0.48–1.10	0.80	
Calcutta	1962–66	4	0.29–0.85	0.61	
Nagpur	1962–66	4	0.50–0.85	0.61	
Bombay	1962–66	5	1.10–1.90	1.50	
Bangalore	1962–66	5	0.23–0.67	0.49	
Ootacamund	1962–66	5	0.39–0.70	0.52	
Australia (12° S–42° S)					
Sydney	1964–70	7	0.17–0.44	0.32	Bonnyman and Molina-Ramos (1971)
Berry	1965–70	6	0.28–0.53	0.42	
Melbourne	1964–70	7	0.19–0.40	0.30	
Warragul	1964–70	7	0.33–0.55	0.40	
Adelaide	1964–70	7	0.22–0.45	0.32	
Meadows	1965–70	6	0.29–0.49	0.35	
Hobart	1964–70	7	0.15–0.21	0.18	
Hadspen	1965–70	6	0.25–0.38	0.32	
Perth	1964–70	7	0.15–0.32	0.26	
Wokalup	1965–70	6	0.14–0.30	0.28	
Brisbane	1964–70	7	0.30–0.43	0.39	
Samford	1965–70	6	0.28–0.47	0.37	
Townsville	1964–70	7	0.12–0.33	0.23	
Darwin	1964–70	7	0.36–0.73	0.57	
Alice Springs	1965–70	6	0.24–0.46	0.34	
Port Hedland	1965–70	6	0.13–0.26	0.19	
United Kingdom (51° 44′ N, 5° 02′ W)					
Milford Haven	1962–64	3	0.42–0.58	0.51	Peirson *et al.* (1966)
Japan (41° 50′ N, 140° 25′ E)					
Hokkaido	1970–71	2	1.6–1.8	1.7	Fukuda and Tsunagoi (1975)
Hokkaido	1970–71	2	2.8–2.5	2.6	
Hokkaido	1970–71	2	2.8–2.7	2.7	
Hokkaido	1970–71	2	1.6–1.4	1.5	

ior of ^{210}Pb in freshwater systems that the amount of ^{210}Pb contributed to streams by the weathering and ground water discharge should be small.

The first study of ^{210}Pb in rivers was reported by Rama *et al.* (1961) who measured ^{210}Pb concentrations in three locations along the Colorado River, which is contaminated by waste liquids from uranium mining operations. They observed that the ^{210}Pb concentrations decreased dramatically, from 14 dpm/liter at the source to ~ 0.3 dpm/liter within short distances down-stream. Based on this variation, Goldberg (1963) estimated the removal time of dissolved ^{210}Pb in Colorado and Sacramento rivers to be of the order of weeks. Recently Benninger *et al.* (1975) and Lewis (1976) have carried out extensive studies on the fate of ^{210}Pb in the Susquehanna River system. Their results also indicate a quick removal of dissolved ^{210}Pb from streams, similar to the results of Rama *et al.* (1961), with a residence time of < 1.5 days (Lewis, 1976). Additionally, based on material balance calculations,

Benninger *et al.* (1975) have estimated that most of the atmospheric ^{210}Pb (>99%) is trapped in the soil layers, and only < 0.8% leaves the terrain as attached to stream-borne particles. These studies clearly demonstrate that the contribution of dissolved ^{210}Pb via stream and rivers to lakes should be small.

^{210}Pb PRODUCED IN SITU IN THE LAKE WATER COLUMN THROUGH THE DECAY OF ^{226}Ra.   The contribution of this source may vary from lake to lake depending on the ^{226}Ra concentration of the lake water. In Tansa, Tulsi, and Powai lakes in Bombay, India, the ^{210}Pb production from ^{226}Ra in the water column is of the order of 0.01 dpm/cm^2/year (using a ^{226}Ra concentration of 0.1 dpm/liter similar to that in rivers flowing through nearby regions, and a mean water depth of 20 m), two orders of magnitude lower than the atmospheric flux of ~ 1.5 dpm/cm^2/year. However, this source may contribute significantly to ^{210}Pb in deep lakes having high dissolved ^{226}Ra in water and receiving relatively low atmospheric ^{210}Pb flux, e.g., Lake Tanganyika. The recent results (Craig, 1974) of ^{210}Pb–^{226}Ra measurements in Lake Tanganyika water column have shown that ^{210}Pb is highly deficient with respect to its parent ^{226}Ra, indicating its continuous removal to the sediments. Based on the extent of ^{210}Pb deficiency, a scavenging residence time of ~ 5 years has been estimated for ^{210}Pb and stable Pb from this lake water. In this lake the *in situ* production rate of ^{210}Pb from ^{226}Ra in water is comparable to its atmospheric flux.

PARTICULATE ^{210}Pb FROM THE CATCHMENT AREA. The particulate ^{210}Pb introduced into lakes along with suspended materials draining from the catchment area, is contributed from two sources: (i) *in situ* production from ^{226}Ra contained in soil layers and (ii) adsorbed ^{210}Pb from stream water, which, as mentioned earlier, receives most of its ^{210}Pb from atmospheric input. The data on the concentrations of ^{210}Pb and ^{226}Ra in stream-borne particles are sparse; the results of Lewis (1976) indicate that the particulate activity ratio of ^{210}Pb/^{226}Ra for the Susquehanna River system is ~ 2. The excess ^{210}Pb (i.e., which is over and above that expected from radioactive secular equilibrium with its parent ^{226}Ra) in these particulate phases probably originates from atmospheric input.

The total ^{210}Pb flux, ϕ, into the lake is given by:

$$\phi = \phi_a + \phi_d + \phi_i + \phi_p \qquad (6)$$

where ϕ is the flux (atoms/cm^2/year) and the subscripts *a, d, i,* and *p* refer to atmospheric, riverine dissolved, *in situ* production in water column, and particulate riverine source, respectively.

The "dissolved" ^{210}Pb introduced into lakes is quickly removed to sediments by the adsorption/scav-

enging process on particles. The residence time of ^{210}Pb in fresh water systems is only of the order of few weeks (Schell, 1974). the ^{210}Pb introduced via the riverine particles also settles on the sediment, its residence time being governed by particle size. Incorporation of ^{210}Pb into lake sediments from the above sources results in excess ^{210}Pb activity in these deposits over and above the activity arising from the decay of its parent ^{226}Ra. Geochronology of lake sediments is based on the decay of this excess ^{210}Pb, commonly designated as ^{210}Pb$_{exc}$. Its value is estimated from the total measured ^{210}Pb activity (^{210}Pb$_{tot}$) using the relation:

$$^{210}\text{Pb}_{exc} = {}^{210}\text{Pb}_{tot} - {}^{210}\text{Pb}_{supp} \qquad (7)$$

where ^{210}Pb$_{supp}$ is the ^{210}Pb activity in radioactive secular equilibrium with ^{226}Ra contained in the sample. The first successful attempts to date lake sediments using ^{210}Pb$_{exc}$ were carried out by Krishnaswami *et al.* (1971).

Once the ^{210}Pb$_{exc}$ deposits in the lake sediments, its depth distribution should be governed by Eqs. (1) and (2), as long as the assumptions mentioned in "Limnochronology" (see p. 155) are valid. The large scatter

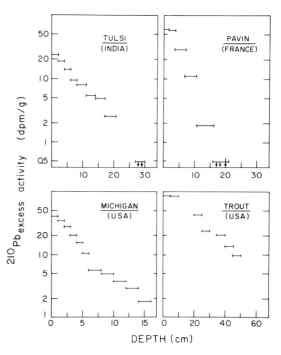

FIGURE 5.   Observed depth distribution of ^{210}Pb activity in lake sediments. Results for lakes Pavin and Tulsi (adapted from Krishnaswami *et al.,* 1971 and Krishnaswami, 1973) represent the first successful attempts to date lake sediments by the ^{210}Pb method. Data for Lake Michigan (Robbins and Edgington, 1975) and Trout Lake (Koide *et al.,* 1973) are also shown. The deduced sedimentation rates in these cores are a few mm/year.

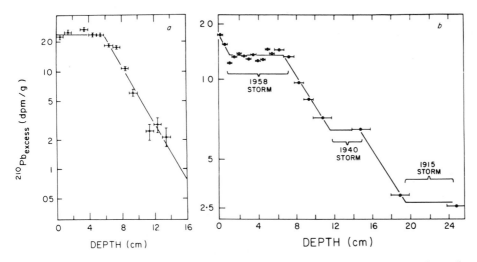

FIGURE 6. ^{210}Pb distribution in Huron and Michigan lake sediments. (a) ^{210}Pb$_{exc}$ distribution in a sediment core from Lake Huron (adapted from Robbins *et al.*, 1977). The uniform concentration of ^{210}Pb$_{exc}$ in the top ~ 6 cm of the core is due to mixing effects at the sediment–water interface. (b) ^{210}Pb$_{exc}$ distribution in a sediment core from Lake Michigan (adapted from Edgington and Robbins, 1976a). The breaks in sedimentation rates caused by storms during various years is clearly discernable in the depth profile of ^{210}Pb.

observed in the yearly ^{210}Pb atmospheric fallout (Table 4) casts doubt on the "constant flux" assumption, though it has been shown to be valid for glaciers (Goldberg, 1963; Crozaz *et al.*, 1964; Nezami *et al.*, 1964; Ambach and Eisner, 1968; Picciotto *et al.*, 1968; Windom, 1969). The scatter in the atmospheric ^{210}Pb flux would be reflected in the ^{210}Pb depth distribution of the sediments, if annual layers of lake cores are analyzed for their ^{210}Pb content. However, the scatter would probably be smoothed out considerably if the ^{210}Pb flux is averaged over a few years. The ^{210}Pb analysis in lake sediments are carried out generally on 1- to 2-cm-thick layers, which in most cases represent several years of deposition, and hence the scatter in the data should be much less. This is supported by the observation that in many lake sediment cores, ^{210}Pb$_{exc}$ exhibits smooth exponential decay with depth, as expected from Eqs. (1) and (2). Some examples of observed depth distribution of ^{210}Pb$_{exc}$ activities in lake sediments are given in Figures 5 and 6.

The disturbing observation of constant ^{210}Pb activity in the top several centimeters of some lake cores questions the validity of the no-migration assumption; for example, see results for Lakes Pavin and Huron in Figures 5 and 6, respectively. In addition to radioactive decay two other important mechanisms which can modify the ^{210}Pb distribution in lake sediments are biological mixing ("bioturbation," brought about by deposit feeding organisms) and physical disturbances. This mixing can blur the stratigraphic record stored in sediments, especially near the sediment–water interface. The significance of this process on the depth distribution of radionuclides in lake sediments is dis-

cussed in "Particle reworking processes in lake sediments" (see p. 170).

The reliability of the ^{210}Pb method to study lacustrine chronology has been demonstrated in several cases. For Lake Mendota, Wisconsin, the estimated ^{210}Pb rate of 0.6 cm/year (Koide *et al.*, 1973) is identical to the rate of 0.62 cm/year (Bortleson and Lee, 1972) obtained on the same core from palynological studies. For Linsley Pond, Connecticut, the pollen and ^{210}Pb rates were compatible (Brugam, 1975). The recent results of Edgington *et al.* (1977) indicate that in two cores from Lake Erie the estimated sediment accumulation rates from ^{210}Pb, ^{137}Cs, and pollen analysis are in excellent agreement. However, in two other cores the ^{210}Pb rates were significantly higher than those inferred from *Ambrosia* pollen profiles. Similarly, attempts to compare ^{210}Pb rates with pollen stratigraphy have met with only limited success for Lake Michigan (Robbins and Edgington, 1975) and Lake Superior (Bruland *et al.*, 1975), possibly because of difficulties associated with pollen stratigraphy, which is very sensitive to complete retrieval of sediment and assignment of correct dates to different pollen horizons. ^{210}Pb and paleomagnetic measurements gave consistent rates for Lake Windermere, England (Eakins and Morrison, 1974). Intercomparison of sediment accumulation rates estimated using different radiometric techniques has been carried out to check on the validity of the ^{210}Pb method by Krishnaswami (1974), Robbins and Edgington (1975), and Edgington and Robbins (1976). These authors have studied fallout nuclides, ^{55}Fe, ^{137}Cs, and ^{239}Pu, along with ^{210}Pb to date sediments from the Indian, French

TABLE 5. ^{210}Pb Studies in Some Lakes: Sedimentation Rates and ^{210}Pb Flux

Lake	^{210}Pb sedimentation rate		^{210}Pb flux	Purpose of study	Reference(s)
	(mm/year)	(mg/cm²/year)	(dpm/cm²/year)		
India					
Tansa	~ 40	~ 2800	—	Geochronology	Krishnaswami et al. (1971); Krishnaswami (1973)
Tulsi	2.6	160	1.6	Geochronology	Krishnaswami et al. (1971); Krishnaswami (1973)
France					
Pavin	1.3	13	1.3	Geochronology	Krishnaswami et al. (1971)
Leman	1.2	72	0.4	Geochronology	Krishnaswami et al. (1971)
Montcynere	1.5	21	0.9	Geochronology and geo-chemical studies	Krishnaswami (1973); Meybeck et al. (1975)
Lagodiville	0.7	13	—	Geochronology and geo-chemical studies	Krishnaswami (1973); Meybeck et al. (1975)
United States					
Mendota	6.0	18	3.2	Geochronology	Koide et al. (1972, 1973)
Trout	6.3	60	6.4	Geochronology	Koide et al. (1972, 1973)
Tahoe	1.0	21	0.5	Geochronology	Koide et al. (1972, 1973)
Michigan	0.1–4.0	12–94	0.4–1.5	Geochronology, surface mixing	Robbins and Edgington (1975); Edgington and Robbins (1976a)
Superior	0.1	—	—	Geochronology, inter-comparison of ^{210}Pb and palynological dates	Bruland et al. (1975)
Washington	3.8	—	—	Comparative geochemis-try of ^{210}Pb and Pb	Schell (1974)
Huron	1.0–1.1	21, 51	~ 2	Surface mixing of lake sediments	Robbins et al. (1977)
United Kingdom					
Windermere	2.4	60	3.1	Geochronology, pollu-tion effects	Krishnaswami (1973);
Windermere	2.1	—	—	Geochronology	Eakins and Morrison (1974)
Loweswater	2.0	—	—	Geochronology	Eakins and Morrison (1974)
Blelham Tarn	2.0–3.6	—	—	Geochronology and in-tercomparison of ^{137}Cs and ^{210}Pb dates	Pennington et al. (1976)
Japan					
Biwa	0.8–9.0	—	—	Geochronology	Matsumoto (1975a)
Shinji	1.2–2.7	13–71	0.9–2.2	Geochronology	Matsumoto (1975b)
Belgium					
Mirwart	1.5–1.8	64–104	~ 0.5	Comparative geochemis-try of Pb isotopes	Petit (1974)

(Krishnaswami, 1974), and American (Robbins and Edgington, 1975; Edgington and Robbins, 1976) lakes. Their results indicated that in most cases the short-term rates (for the last two decades) derived from fallout nuclides were invariably high, compared to the long-term (last century) rates deduced from ^{210}Pb. This discrepancy is primarily due to mixing effects in the near surface regions of the sediments, which would seriously affect the distribution of fallout nuclides. Robbins and Edgington (1975) found that if the surface mixing effects are considered, then the short- and long-term sedimentation rates are identical, lending additional support to the ^{210}Pb dating technique.

The $^{210}Pb_{exc}$ dating method has been successfully used to decipher the chronology of lake and near shore sediments deposited during the last century, with ac-cumulation rates ranging between 0.1 and > 40 mm/ year. Table 5 summarizes most of the work carried out to date using the ^{210}Pb method of dating lacustrine sediments. In addition to estimation of sediment accumulation rates and documentation of major environmental changes like storms (Figure 6b), ^{210}Pb dating finds extensive application in geochemical and pollution studies. Robbins and Callender (1975) have used ^{210}Pb dates to quantitatively estimate reaction rates, Bortleson and Lee (1972) have deduced the time of eutrophication of Lake Mendota by studying the time variation in the chemical composition of sediments, and Edgington and Robbins (1976b) and Goldberg *et al.* (1976) have used the time variation of minor element content of lake sediments as an indicator of pollution history. It must be mentioned here that though ^{210}Pb dating has been successfully used to derive recent environmental changes recorded in lake sediments, the interpretation of data stored in the top few centimeters, especially near the sediment–water interface, should be made with caution. This is because in several lakes this interfacial region is characterized by intense biological and chemical interactions, which could result in the obliteration of the original pattern of distribution of tracers and other stratigraphic markers.

[226]Ra. The dissolved [226]Ra (half-life = 1622 years) in lakes originates from streams, which in turn derive their [226]Ra supply from weathering. The [226]Ra content of streams varies considerably and seems to depend on the nature of the bedrock and the chemical composition of the stream water. Typically, the [226]Ra concentrations of stream (and river) waters center around 0.1 dpm/liter (Moore, 1967; Bhat and Krishnaswami, 1969). In addition, [226]Ra can also enter the lakes in particulate form through streams. In natural waters, [226]Ra is less reactive compared to ^{210}Pb and hence is likely to have a longer residence time in the lake waters before being removed to sediments.

The decay of [226]Ra excess [$^{226}Ra_{exc} = (^{226}Ra_{total} - ^{226}Ra_{supp})$. $^{226}Ra_{supp}$ is the [226]Ra activity in secular equilibrium with its parent [230]Th] within a sedimentary column has been suggested as a potential dating tool for lake sediments (Koide *et al.*, 1976); however, no results have been reported using this technique. This method has been used successfully to date a near shore marine sediment (Koide *et al.*, 1976) and is based on the decay of unsupported [226]Ra incorporated in the sediments probably through specific biological species. Hence, it is likely that the application of the [226]Ra method would be restricted to those lake sediments which contain abundant [226]Ra enriching organisms.

Though the application of [226]Ra to lake sediments has not been established, this isotope has been successfully employed to measure accumulation rates of fresh water ferromanganese concretions (Krishnaswami and Moore, 1973; Dean *et al.*, 1973; Moore *et al.*, 1976b; Johansen and Robbins, 1977). Prior to the work of Krishnaswami and Moore (1973) freshwater

ferromanganese deposits were assigned growth rates ranging between 0.1 and 3000 mm/10[3] year (Manheim, 1964; Harris and Troup, 1970), depending on the model used for their formation. Krishnaswami and Moore (1973) explored the possibility of dating these nuclides using [210]Pb. During their analysis they observed very large excess of [226]Ra, ~ 100–200 dpm/g, in the near surface regions of these deposits, which exhibit exponential decrease with depth in the nodule (Figure 7). Assuming that the variation of [226]Ra with depth is caused by radioactive decay, the accretion rate of the nodule was estimated to be ~ 2 mm/10[3] years, about 2–3 orders of magnitude slower than the deposition rates of lake sediments commonly observed (Table 5). Similarly, Johansen and Robbins (1977) have estimated the growth rates of ferromanganese nodules from Lake Michigan to be 0.9 – 3.7 mm/10[3] years based on the variation of the Ra/Ba ratio in them.

Another lacustrine mineral in which [226]Ra measurements could yield interesting results is barite. If barites are formed authigenically from the lake waters, they might contain easily measurable amounts of [226]Ra and [230]Th. Then as proposed recently (Lal and Somayajulu, 1975), it should be possible to date the sediments and/or other deposits in which they get incorporated on the assumption that the [226]Ra/[230]Th activity ratio has remained constant at deposition. It would of course be necessary to ascertain whether the isolated barite is authigenic or continental, and this can proba-

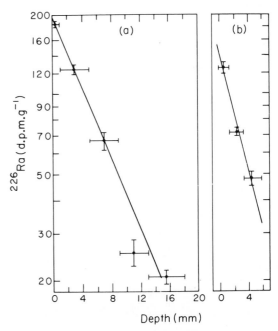

FIGURE 7. [226]Ra concentration depth profile in two freshwater ferromanganese nodules (from Krishnaswami and Moore, 1973). The data yield accumulation rates of few mm/10[3] year for the nodules.

bly be done using criteria similar to those put forward by Goldberg *et al.* (1969) for distinguishing marine and continental barites.

The concentrations of ^{226}Ra and the ^{226}Ra/^{230}Th activity ratio have been used as indicators to check on the validity of the closed system assumptions for dating lacustrine carbonates (Kaufman, 1964; Kaufman and Broecker, 1965). ^{226}Ra is relatively more soluble and mobile compared to ^{230}Th and hence any disturbances of the system resulting from environmental effects could change the ^{226}Ra/^{230}Th activity ratio from the expected value. However, because of the short half-life of ^{226}Ra (1622 years), only those disturbances which occurred during the last few thousand years will be registered in the system, and the effects of earlier disturbances (> 5000 years) would have been erased. The expected ^{226}Ra/^{230}Th ratio in a system (Kaufman, 1964; Kaufman and Broecker, 1965) which has an initial ^{234}U/^{238}U ratio = 1 is given by:

$$^{226}\text{Ra}/^{230}\text{Th} = 1 - \frac{\lambda_0}{\lambda_6 - \lambda_0}\left[\frac{1}{1 + e^{\lambda_0 t}} - \frac{e^{-\lambda_6 t}}{1 - e^{-\lambda_0 t}}\right] \quad (8)$$

If the initial ^{234}U/^{238}U ratio is $\neq 1$, as observed in several of the freshwater systems, then

$$^{226}\text{Ra}/^{238}\text{U} = 1 - \frac{\lambda_6 e^{-\lambda_0 t}}{\lambda_6 - \lambda_0} + \frac{\lambda_0 e^{-\lambda_6 t}}{\lambda_6 - \lambda_0}$$
$$+ (R - 1)\,\lambda_0\lambda_6\left[\frac{1}{(\lambda_4 - \lambda_0)\,(\lambda_4 - \lambda_6)} + \frac{e^{-(\lambda_0 - \lambda_4)t}}{(\lambda_0 - \lambda_4)\,(\lambda_0 - \lambda_6)}\right.$$
$$\left. + \frac{e^{-(\lambda_6 - \lambda_0)t}}{(\lambda_6 - \lambda_4)\,(\lambda_6 - \lambda_0)}\right] \quad (9)$$

where R = measured ^{234}U/^{238}U ratio, λ = decay constant, and the subscripts, 4, 0, and 6 refer to ^{234}U, ^{230}Th, and ^{226}Ra, respectively.

Kaufman (1964) measured the ^{226}Ra/^{230}Th ratios of several samples and concluded that even if ^{226}Ra concentrations indicate a closed system, the intercomparison of ^{230}Th ages with ^{14}C should be used as a check on the reliability of the estimated ages.

^{230}**Th.** ^{230}Th, a daughter nuclide of the ^{238}U decay series, has been used extensively to date marine corals (Barnes *et al.*, 1956; Tatsumoto and Goldberg, 1959; Blanchard, 1963; Thurber *et al.*, 1965; Veeh, 1966; Broecker and Van Donk, 1970). These carbonates, during their growth, incorporate in their skeleton the uranium isotopes from the water column with very little ^{230}Th. Therefore the time-dependent growth of ^{230}Th to attain radioactive secular equilibrium following synchronous deposition of ^{234}U can be used to estimate the age of the sample, if the assumptions outlined in "Limnochronology" (see p. 155) hold.

The expected ^{230}Th/^{238}U activity ratio in a sample having initial ^{234}U/^{238}U = 1 and ^{230}Th = 0 at time of formation is given by:

$$^{230}\text{Th}/^{238}\text{U} = (1 - e^{-\lambda_0 t}). \quad (10)$$

However, in most of the natural water systems the ^{234}U/^{238}U activity ratios are > 1 (see "^{234}U/^{238}U," p. 000) due to preferential leaching of ^{234}U during the weathering process. In this case the ^{230}Th/^{238}U activity ratio would be:

$$^{230}\text{Th}/^{238}\text{U} = (1 - e^{-\lambda_0 t})$$
$$+ (R - 1)\frac{\lambda_0}{\lambda_0 - \lambda_4}(1 - e^{(\lambda_4 - \lambda_0)t}). \quad (11)$$

The assumptions given in "Limnochronology" (see p.155) have been shown to be valid for marine corals. Kaufman (1964) and Kaufman and Broecker (1965) have tried to extend the ^{230}Th/^{234}U dating technique to lacustrine carbonates using the same assumptions. Their results based on $\sim$ 50 samples of gastropods, calcareous algae, tufa, and marl from Lakes Lahontan and Bonneville indicate that in general ^{230}Th ages are in agreement with ^{14}C and, for samples beyond the ^{14}C range, the ^{230}Th ages are consistent with stratigraphic information. However, unlike the marine corals, several of the lacustrine deposits seem to incorporate ^{230}Th in them during their growth, as evidenced by the presence of measurable ^{232}Th in them. Hence a correction for the initial ^{230}Th content would be necessary to get reliable age estimates of the lacustrine carbonates. This problem was overcome by estimating the initial or nonradiogenic ^{230}Th content of the samples using the relationship:

$$^{230}\text{Th (initial)} = {}^{230}\text{Th (observed)}$$
$$- {}^{230}\text{Th (expected)} \quad (12)$$

where ^{230}Th (observed) is the measured ^{230}Th content of the sample and ^{230}Th (expected) is the calculated ^{230}Th abundance in samples of known ^{14}C age. Using samples < 20,000 years old they estimated that the initial ^{230}Th/^{232}Th ratios in the Lake Lahontan and Bonneville samples should be $\sim$ 1.7. Also this correction involves the assumption that the initial ^{230}Th was incorporated at the time of formation of the carbonate and not at a later date.

The ^{230}Th/^{234}U method has also been used successfully to obtain absolute ages of saline deposits from pluvial lakes (Goddard, 1970). Analogous to that in lacustrine carbonates, part of the ^{230}Th contained in these salt deposits is of nonradiogenic origin. When the measured ^{230}Th/^{234}U activity ratios are corrected for the nonradiogenic components, in a manner similar to that used for the carbonates, excellent agreement between ^{230}Th/^{234}U ages and ^{14}C ages have been reported (Goddard, 1970).

In spite of the uncertainty in the nonradiogenic ^{230}Th correction, the ^{230}Th/^{238}U method has proved to be a very valuable dating tool for lacustrine carbonate and salt deposit samples up to $\sim$ 300,000 years old, where no other dating method is applicable. Using this technique it has been possible to study the fluctuations in the size of pluvial lakes back to $\sim$ 200,000 years and implications thereof to global climatic changes (Broecker, 1965).

^{234}U/^{238}U. The discovery of anomalously high ^{234}U/^{238}U activity ratios in natural waters (Cherdyntsev and Chalov, 1955; Cherdyntsev et al., 1961; Thurber, 1962, 1963) opened the possibility of using this radioactive disequilibrium between the two uranium isotopes as a dating tool for deposits forming from such waters. The fractionation or disequilibrium between these uranium isotopes has been attributed to recoil effects during the transformation of ^{238}U to ^{234}U involving α and β particle emissions (Figure 1). The recoil energy imparted to the daughter nucleus seems to be large enough to occasionally rupture chemical bonds, thereby releasing the ^{234}U atom or leaving it in a metastable lattice position (Starik et al., 1958; Cherdyntsev et al., 1961), or to oxidize it to a +6 valence state (Rosholt et al., 1963; Dooley et al., 1966). Because of these effects ^{234}U is more susceptible to leaching compared to ^{238}U from rocks and soil, resulting in an excess ^{234}U in natural waters. The extent of ^{234}U/^{238}U disequilibrium in the waters seems to depend both on the type of soil or rock being weathered and the chemical composition of the water (Thurber, 1963; Bhat and Krishnaswami, 1969). In addition, a certain fraction of ^{234}U can be formed in the water because of the preferential dissolution of α recoil ^{234}Th (Kigoshi, 1971).

Any solids forming from these waters would have a ^{234}U/^{238}U activity ratio the same as in the water. This excess ^{234}U can be used as a measure of the age of the system, if (i) the ^{234}U/^{238}U ratio at the time of its formation is known and if (ii) the system has remained "closed" over the dating interval. If these assumptions hold, then the age–activity ratio relation is given by:

$$\left[\left(\frac{A_{234}}{A_{238}} \right)_t - 1 \right] = \left[\left(\frac{A_{234}}{A_{238}} \right)_0 - 1 \right] e^{-\lambda_4 t} \quad (13)$$

where A_{234}/A_{238} is the ^{234}U/^{238}U activity ratio, λ_4 is the decay constant of ^{234}U, and the subscripts t and 0 refer to time t and zero, respectively. Thurber (1963) and Veeh (1966) have successfully used this method to date marine corals, assuming $[A_{234}/A_{238}]_0$ to be the same as that in modern corals. Since ^{234}U has a half-life of 250,000 years, in principle this method should be applicable to date samples formed up to $\sim 10^6$ years ago. However, analytical uncertainties in the precise estimation of ^{234}U/^{238}U activity ratios is the major limiting factor in its application.

Thurber (1963) and Kaufman (1964) have explored the possibility of using this method to date lacustrine carbonates from pluvial lakes. In these samples, the major problem is to ascertain the ^{234}U/^{238}U activity ratios at the time of the carbonate deposition. Based on the analyses of several samples, Kaufman (1964) observed that the ^{234}U/^{238}U activity ratios in old samples were too high to be consistent with the assumption that these samples formed with the same ^{234}U/^{238}U activity ratio as those observed in samples $< 20,000$ years old. This variation could be attributed to changes in the ^{234}U/^{238}U ratios of lake water, caused by climate variations or because the lacustrine carbonates are "open" systems and the presently measured activity ratios are due to secondary effects caused by ground-water interactions with the carbonates. Because of these uncertainties the ^{234}U/^{238}U dating method has met only with limited success for dating lacustrine carbonates.

Another important application of ^{234}U/^{238} disequilibrium is to date the time of formation of closed-basin lakes (i.e., lakes without outflow). Chalov et al. (1964), using the assumptions of constant influx of uranium with a fixed ^{234}U/^{238}U activity ratio to the lakes, were able to date two Alpine lakes. The ^{234}U/^{238}U activity ratio at any time t, is given by:

$$\left[\left(\frac{A_{234}}{A_{238}} \right)_t - 1 \right]$$
$$= \left[\left(\frac{A_{234}}{A_{238}} \right)_0 - 1 \right] \left[1 - e^{-\lambda_4 t} \right] \Big/ \lambda_4 t \quad (14)$$

where $(A_{234}/A_{238})_0$ is the ^{234}U/^{238}U activity ratio in the feed waters and $(A_{234}/A_{238})_t$ is the activity ratio in the lake water measured at time t. Though Chalov et al. (1964) obtained reliable age estimates for two Alpine lakes, this method involves the assumption of constant ^{234}U/^{238}U activity ratios in the feed water over the entire dating interval, which is hard to test.

^{228}Th/^{232}Th. Koide et al. (1973) observed that there is an excess of ^{228}Th over its grandparent ^{232}Th in the acid leaches of lacustrine and near-coastal sediments. The authors suggested that this ^{228}Th excess can be used to date sediments deposited during the last decade; it can also be used as a permissive evidence that the core tops have been preserved during coring operations. No results have yet been reported using this technique for lake sediments.

Though this method has been shown to yield sedimentation rates in agreement with those deduced using other techniques for nearshore sediments (Koide et al., 1973; Krishnaswami et al., 1973) because of the short radioactive half-life of ^{228}Th (1.9 years; Figure 1), this method would be restricted to samples near the sediment–water interface, a region dominated by physical and biological mixing. Hence, as discussed later, the ^{228}Th excess distribution in the sediments should be more useful to study the mixing processes in surface sediments rather than geochronology.

Cosmic ray produced nuclides

The various cosmic ray-produced nuclides having half-lives exceeding 1 day are listed in Table 1. Among these, nine have half-lives exceeding 1 year. Only four of these are chemically suitable for dating sediments: ^{10}Be, ^{26}Al, ^{14}C, and ^{32}Si. The extremely small production rates of the first two, ^{10}Be and ^{26}Al (Lal and Peters, 1967), coupled with relatively large sedimentation rates as encountered in lakes (Table 5) make them useful only in very special circumstances. The remaining two cosmic ray-produced nuclides, ^{14}C and ^{32}Si, are indeed suitable for limnochronological studies. Their half-lives lie on either side of the half-life of ^{226}Ra, and they thus extend the time bracket which can be studied properly in a very complementary manner. Most studies in lake sediments are, however, as yet confined to ^{14}C.

^{14}C.   Radiocarbon (^{14}C) is primarily produced in the atmosphere by the capture of thermal neutrons with nitrogen. The global average production rate of ^{14}C in the atmosphere is ~ 2 atoms/cm^2/sec (Lal and Peters, 1967). The ^{14}C produced is quickly oxidized to $^{14}CO_2$, mixes with atmospheric CO_2 ($^{12}CO_2$), and enters into all chemical and biochemical reactions of CO_2, like air–ocean exchange, photosynthesis, etc. Once a material is separated from the reservoir where it continually receives fresh supply of ^{14}C and is in equilibrium, the concentration of ^{14}C in it decreases due to radioactive decay. The ^{14}C age of a sample, t, is calculated from the relation:

$$t = (1/\lambda) \quad \ln \frac{(^{14}C/^{12}C)_0}{(^{14}C/^{12}C)_t} \tag{15}$$

where λ is the decay constant of ^{14}C, $(^{14}C/^{12}C)_0$ is the radiocarbon specific activity of the sample when it formed, and $(^{14}C/^{12}C)_t$ is the measured value at time t. Thus, the absolute age of the sample can be estimated by simple comparison of its radiocarbon specific activity at the time of its formation with its present value, provided the change in the $^{14}C/^{12}C$ activity in the sample is only due to radioactive decay. The specific activity of radiocarbon in the sample at the time of its formation is unknown, but in the ^{14}C dating method it is assumed to be identical to that of its modern counterpart, i.e., in a sample of similar species collected at the present time. The validity of this assumption necessitates constancy of the $^{14}C/^{12}C$ ratio in the atmosphere during the dating interval.

The ^{14}C specific activity in the atmosphere can change because of several causes: variation in the ^{14}C production rate due to changes in cosmic ray flux and/ or earth's magnetic field, changes in the CO_2 partial pressure in the atmosphere, and effects from changes in the oceanic circulation pattern. The $^{14}C/^{12}C$ variations in the atmosphere for the past $\sim 10,000$ years

have been well documented through the measurement of ^{14}C in wood samples of known age (Suess, 1965). Figures 8 and 9 show the deduced fluctuations in the atmospheric ^{14}C level. Two types of fluctuations are evident, short-term variations which occur on a time scale of ~ 100 years (Figure 8) and long-term oscillations with a period of $\sim 10,000$ years (Figure 9). It appears from the available data that the short-time variations are caused by changes in ^{14}C production caused by solar modulation of cosmic ray flux (Lingenfelter and Ramaty, 1970; Damon, 1970; Lingenfelter, 1976). In addition to this, radiocarbon specific activity in the atmosphere has registered a monotonous decrease of about 2% during the last century due to dilution of ^{14}C by "fossil" CO_2 from industrial fuel combustion (Suess, 1955, 1965). The long-term variation in the ^{14}C specific activity is $\sim 9\%$ (Figure 9), much larger compared to 2–3% fluctuations occurring during the 100-year periods (Figure 8). The causes for the long-term oscillations are not well understood (Suess, 1965, 1967, 1968, 1970; Lal and Suess, 1968; Damon, 1970) but could be due to the after effect of a very quiet sun during ice ages and/or changes in the magnetic field of the earth (Bucha, 1970) and/or variations in the atmospheric P_{CO_2} caused by climate changes (Lal and Venkatavaradan, 1970). The P_{CO_2} decreases by 4.5% per degree drop in temperature (Kanwisher, 1960). Thus the low temperatures during ice ages could have resulted in a low P_{CO_2} in the atmosphere, with a corresponding increase in $^{14}C/^{12}C$ specific activity. Kaufman (1964) has estimated that the maximum increase in the atmospheric radiocarbon activity is 4% for a temperature drop of 6°C in the

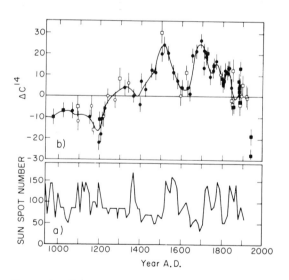

FIGURE 8.   Short-term variations in the radiocarbon specific activity ($^{14}C/^{12}C$) in the atmosphere (from Lal and Suess, 1968). The lower part of the figure shows the changes in sunspot numbers during the same period. The data show an inverse correlation between the $\Delta^{14}C$ and sunspot numbers.

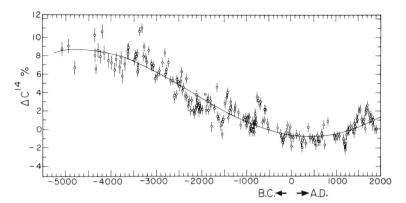

FIGURE 9. Deviations in ^{14}C activity in the atmosphere as measured in tree ring-dated wood from that expected using a value of 5730 years for ^{14}C half-life. Figure from Lal and Suess, 1968. The curve drawn is a best-fit sine wave with a period of 10,320 years and amplitude of 9.5%.

surface ocean. However, an opposite effect, i.e., decrease in the $^{14}C/^{12}C$ specific activity, would result if the oceanic mixing rates were faster during the glacial periods.

In addition to the above variations in the $^{14}C/^{12}C$ ratios in the atmosphere, there has been an abrupt increase, in the last two decades, by more than 50% in the $^{14}C/^{12}C$ ratio in the atmosphere due to nuclear weapon tests (Gulliksen et al., 1972; Rafter and O'Brien, 1972). Because of this, the ^{14}C specific activity of recent lake deposits will be relatively enhanced, compared to the prebomb era. However, the increase will be only gradual, spreading over a period of ~ 5 years or so, due to the slow exchange between atmospheric CO_2 and the dissolved bicarbonate/carbonate in lake water. Detailed studies of the pattern of increase in the radiocarbon specific activity in lake deposits due to nuclear weapon testing have not yet been reported.

The uncertainties discussed above in the atmospheric $^{14}C/^{12}C$ activity are caused by global events and are applicable to samples which derive their carbon from well-mixed large reservoirs like the atmosphere and the oceans. For samples which extract their carbon from small independent bodies like lakes, there could be additional uncertainties in ascertaining the initial $^{14}C/^{12}C$ ratio. The radiocarbon specific activity in lake waters depends on the $^{14}C/^{12}C$ ratio of water draining into the lake, the exchange of CO_2 between lake water and the atmosphere, and the residence time of water in the lake. Following Broecker and Walton (1959) and Thurber and Broecker (1970), the variation of ^{14}C specific activity with time in lake is given by:

$$\frac{dN}{dt} = A_r K_{rl} + A_a K_{al} - A_l K_{ls} - A_l K_{la} - \lambda N \quad (16)$$

where N is the ^{14}C activity in the lake, A is the specific activity $^{14}C/^{12}C$, and K_{ij} is the rate of carbon input/output from reservoir i to j. The subscripts a, r, l, and s refer to atmosphere, river, lake, and sediment. Thus to get an idea of the time variation of ^{14}C in lake waters in the past it is essential to know the specific activity and concentration of bicarbonate in the inflowing rivers and the exchange rate of CO_2 across the water–air interface. The values of several of these parameters and their secular variations are not known. Their values in the past could be significantly different from the present values due to climatic changes, variations in the drainage area and pattern of rivers flowing into lake, etc. However, an idea of the variation of ^{14}C specific activity in the past can be obtained by changing the parametric values to reasonable extremes.

The $^{14}C/^{12}C$ ratios of lake carbonates and organic carbon are often less than those in terrestrial plants formed at the same time. This ^{14}C deficiency results from the utilization of lake water CO_2 which originates mainly from carbonate rocks. Because of this, the ^{14}C ages of even freshly forming lacustrine deposits could be several hundreds of years.

In spite of these uncertainties, ^{14}C dating of lake deposits has proved valuable toward the study of several interesting problems, e.g., the establishment of absolute chronology for climatic fluctuations during the last ~ 40,000 years, causes and extent of ^{14}C variations in the atmosphere, and the chronology of changes in the earth's magnetic field directions.

The ^{14}C chronology of lake deposits has probably contributed much more to the understanding of ancient climates compared to the studies of any other landscape elements since lakes preserve in their sediments and strand line morphology sensitive records of changes which permit detailed analysis and interpretation. Since the first attempt by Libby (1955) to date deposits from Great Basin lakes, considerable work has been reported in this field, especially to correlate climatic fluctuations during the last ~ 50,000 years (Broecker, 1965; Broecker and Kaufman, 1965; Flint and Gale, 1958; Stuiver, 1964; Horie, 1968; Smith, 1968; Bowler, 1970).

Another important application of radiocarbon in lake sediments is to evaluate the variation of ^{14}C specific activity in the atmosphere during the past and its possible causes (Stuiver, 1967, 1970, 1971). Changes in the ^{14}C chronology of lake sediments can arise due to any of the global causes discussed above which lead to changes in the atmospheric ^{14}C specific

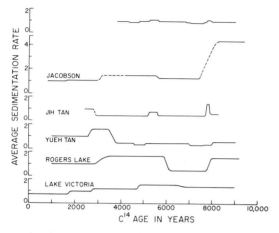

FIGURE 10.   Relative ^{14}C sedimentation rates for five lakes as a function of ^{14}C age. (The sedimentation rates have been normalized by equating the recent rate for the last few thousand years to one.) Changes in sedimentation rates common to all the lakes occurred only during ~ 2500 years B.P. reflecting a global effect. Figure from Stuiver, 1971.

activity or due to local phenomenon. It is possible to deduce information specifically on the long-term global changes by studying the ^{14}C distribution in lake sediments from widely different latitudes. Results of such studies (Stuiver, 1967, 1970) have shown that the sedimentation rates ~ 2500 years ago in several widely separated lakes were high by a factor of ~ 1.5 compared to the present value, but that there were no global changes in sedimentation rates during 2500–9000 years B.P. (Figure 10). The fairly rapid apparent

increase in sedimentation rate about 2500 years ago is probably due to change in the ^{14}C time scale. Similar changes in the ^{14}C/^{12}C ratios have been observed for tree rings and are attributable to change in the atmospheric ^{14}C/^{12}C ratios (Figure 9). The constancy of sedimentation rate during 2500–9000 years B.P. implies the absence of variations due to global effects. The ^{14}C variation in the atmosphere, as deduced from lake sediment data, is shown in Figure 11, which shows a rising trend as far back as 10,000 years.

The ^{14}C sediment chronology has proved very useful toward delineation of secular variations in the directions of earth's magnetic field during the last ~ 50,000 years (Denham and Cox, 1971; Creer et al., 1972; Barbetti and McElhinny, 1972).

^{32}Si.   This nuclide is produced in the atmosphere by spallation of argon by high-energy cosmic ray particles. The average production rate of ^{32}Si in the atmosphere is estimated to be ~ 1.6×10^{-4} atoms/cm^2/sec (Lal and Peters, 1967). Its half-life is not known accurately but is estimated to be about 300 years (Honda and Lal, 1964; Jantsch, 1967; Clausen, 1973).

The latitudinal deposition pattern of ^{32}Si from the atmosphere has not been well established due to paucity of data. The available results on the ^{32}Si deposition rate via wet precipitations are restricted to the Indian (8–25° N) and Scandinavian (~ 65° N) subcontinents (Dansgaard et al., 1966; Kharkar et al., 1966; Nijampurkar, 1975) and are in satisfactory agreement with the predicted value. The fallout of ^{32}Si during 1962–1965 was observed to be relatively higher compared to

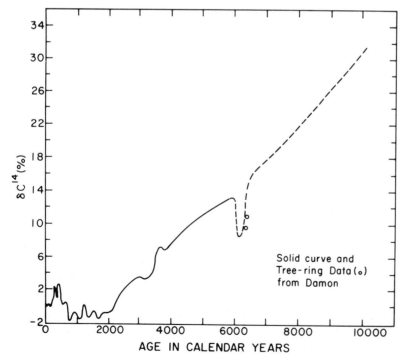

FIGURE 11.   Variation in the radiocarbon specific activity in the atmosphere, for the past ~ 10,000 years as deduced from ^{14}C activity in wood and lake sediments (from Stuiver, 1967). The data indicate a rising trend in the ^{14}C activity for the past ~ 10,000 years.

its deposition prior to 1962 and post-1965 (Dansgaard *et al.*, 1966; Nijampurkar, 1975; Lal *et al.*, 1977), which should be attributed to its injection in the atmosphere from nuclear weapons testing.

^{32}Si in lakes originates through its direct deposition on the lake surface from the atmosphere by wet and dry fallout processes and from streams which derive their water from wet precipitations. The concentrations of ^{32}Si in lakes and rivers can vary significantly; besides differences arising due to variations in the concentrations of ^{32}Si in source waters, its concentration is expected to be controlled by biological productivity and interactions between the dissolved and particulate silicates present in the drainage basins. Results of ^{32}Si measurements along the path of several Indian rivers (Nijampurkar *et al.*, 1966) indicate that ^{32}Si concentrations can change by a factor of two within a few hundred miles.

The ^{32}Si activity introduced in lake waters is expected to be removed to sediments mainly through siliceous organisms produced in the water, with a ^{32}Si/Si specific activity identical to that in lake water. Analogous to the case of ^{14}C, once these tests are deposited as sediments, their specific activity would decrease due to radioactive decay and can be used as a measure of the age of sediments incorporating these tests. However, unlike the simple situation in the case of the radiocarbon method, where most of the carbon in sediments originates from the water, a significant fraction of the silica present in sediments could be from clay and other minerals transported from the drainage basin. Because of this, the specific activity of ^{32}Si in the total silica present in sediments would be considerably less than that in the overlying lake water. To use the specific activity as an index of age, one would have to selectively extract the biogenic or the authigenic phases, which seems feasible on the basis of some laboratory tests and studies with marine sediments (Kharkar *et al.*, 1963). Otherwise, the age of sediments has to be based on simplified assumptions such as consistency of rate of sedimentation and rate of introduction of ^{32}Si in the lake.

To date no chronological studies have been reported for lake sediments using ^{32}Si, although its utility for this purpose has been demonstrated by Krishnaswami *et al.* (1971) and Nijampurkar (1975). The chief attraction of using ^{32}Si for dating lake sediments is of course its useful half-life of $\sim$ 300 years which nicely dovetails with ^{210}Pb.

Artificial radionuclides

Since the early 1950s, environmental radioactivity has increased considerably, primarily because of nuclear weapon tests conducted in the atmosphere. The large injections during the Castle tests of 1954, 1958, and those conducted by the USSR and USA during 1961–

1962 resulted in an increase of the natural radiation levels by orders of magnitude. The atmospheric radioactivity was at its peak during 1962–1963 and is on the decrease since then, though there had been small increases due to a few French and Chinese weapon tests conducted during the late 1960s and early 1970s. The time variation in the annual fallout of ^{90}Sr, a typical bomb nuclide, is shown in Figure 12. As discussed earlier in "Delivery of radionuclides to lakes" (see p. 000), most of the artificial nuclides have been injected in the stratosphere from where they are removed to the troposphere with a mean residence time of $\sim$ 1 year (Bhandari *et al.*, 1966; Lal and Rama, 1966; Martell, 1970). From the troposphere, these nuclides deposit on the earth's surface mainly through wet precipitations, with a mean residence time of the order of few days.

The principal artificially injected nuclides are given in Table 2. Of these ^{90}Sr, ^{137}Cs, ^{3}H, ^{55}Fe, and Pu isotopes ^{239,240}Pu have been measured in several lake waters and sediments. These measurements have been made:

(i) To obtain information on sediment accumulation

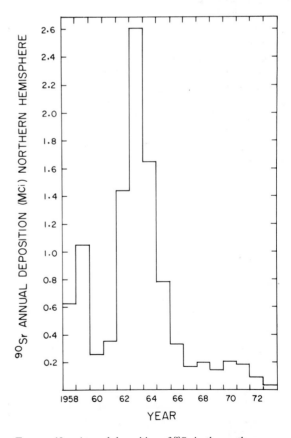

FIGURE 12.   Annual deposition of ^{90}Sr in the northern hemisphere. The peak in the fallout was in 1963. This peak if discernable, in lake sediments, can be used as a time marker. Data compiled from Volchok (1973).

rates in lakes. The pattern of delivery of bomb-produced nuclides from the atmosphere has exhibited complex temporal variations, because of their sporadic injection. These time variations in the source function are expected to be recorded and preserved in a continuously accumulating, undisturbed sediment. Thus by correlating the distribution pattern of these nuclides in sediments with their delivery pattern from the atmosphere it is possible to derive sediment accumulation rates for the past two decades. ^{137}Cs is the most extensively used nuclide for such studies (Martin, 1971; Krishnaswami et al., 1971; Pennington et al., 1973, 1976; Ritchie et al., 1973). Figure 13 illustrates an example of the method. One of the major problems in obtaining reliable sediment accumulation rates based on the distribution of bomb-produced nuclides is the postdepositional mixing, erosion, and redeposition processes, which obliterate the original delivery pattern to the sediments. These postdepositional disturbances have restricted the application of artificially injected nuclides as a time marker in lake sediments. However, their study in such disturbed sediments has provided useful information on the particle reworking processes (Robbins and Edgington, 1975; Edgington and Robbins, 1976a; Robbins et al., 1977).

(ii) To study the nature and quantity of fallout over aqueous surfaces and their possible implications to the observed greater cumulative deposition of ^{90}Sr over the oceans (Machta et al., 1970; Volchok et al., 1970; Volchok, 1974). One of the possible causes for the measured greater deposition of ^{90}Sr over the oceans relative to adjacent land areas has been attributed to dry fallout, the aqueous surface being more retentive for the dry particles striking it. However, results of experiments conducted in Crater Lake, Oregon (Volchok et al., 1970) disproved this idea.

(iii) To use them as tracers for studying vertical mixing of lake waters (Nelson et al., 1970; Imboden et al., 1977; Tongersen et al., 1977). Of the few studies reported in this direction, the application of ^{3}H and ^{3}H–^{3}He holds promise as tracers for estimating eddy diffusivities and turnover times.

(iv) To study the uptake and migration of radionuclides in lake systems (Wahlgren and Nelson, 1973; Cushing, 1975; Edgington and Robbins, 1975; Lerman and Leitzke, 1975).

Particle reworking processes in lake sediments

Biological and physical activities occurring near the sediment-water interface result in lateral and vertical redistribution and displacement of sediments. In lakes, these processes can markedly alter the concentration profiles of stratigraphic markers (e.g., pollen grains) and other chemical and radioactive tracers up to several centimeters below the sediment–water interface (Davis, 1974). However, since these particle reworking processes are more predominant near the interface, the distribution of recent stratigraphic markers (e.g., artificially injected radionuclides) and short-lived radioactive isotopes is expected to be relatively more influenced by mixing than by net sedimentation. Hence study of such tracers in lake sediments becomes more important for obtaining information on the interfacial particle reworking processes than documenting sedimentation rates.

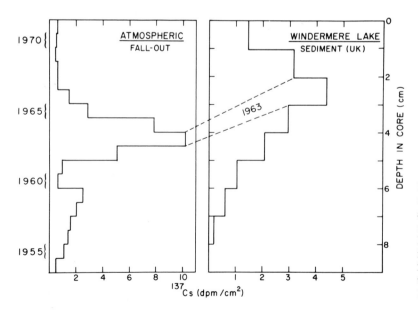

FIGURE 13. ^{137}Cs depth profile in sediments of Lake Windermere and its atmospheric fallout at the same location (data from Pennington et al., 1973). The peak in the ^{137}Cs concentration between 2 and 3 cm is attributed to peak in the atmospheric deposition during 1963.

Both in lake and marine sediments detailed studies of particle reworking processes, their rates, and their effects on the preserved records in the sediments have just begun. Hence the mathematical models which can truly represent the effects of deposit feeders and the subsequent evolution of depth profiles of tracers have not yet been fully developed. Several different approaches have been considered to represent the effects of particle reworking in sediments, such as, pseudodiffusion model, discrete layer model, and the signal theory approach (Goldberg and Koide, 1962; Berger and Heath, 1968; Bruland, 1974; Guinasso and Schink, 1975; Aller, 1977; Goreau, 1977; Nozaki, 1977; Turekian and Cochran, 1977). Of these, the more widely used model is a diffusion model, in which the particle reworking process is treated as a diffusion analogue. The major justification for treating the particle reworking process as a diffusion analogue stems from the idea that the particle transport by mixing is a random process and that the sample size integrates both spatially and temporally several of these mixing events. Though the diffusive model developed seems to satisfactorily represent the state of art, it is likely that this simple model could be considerably modified into a complex one as the effects of biology on sedimentary records come into sharper focus. In this section, we will discuss this model in some detail.

The concentration of any radioactive nuclide within a sediment stratum is expected to be governed by three major processes: radioactive decay, sedimentation, and mixing. In the diffusive-type model (which treats mixing like a diffusive process) the time variation in the concentration of a given nuclide at depth z below the moving sediment–water interface is given by:

$$\frac{\partial}{\partial z}\left(K \frac{\partial}{\partial z} \rho A \right) - S \frac{\partial}{\partial z} \rho A - \lambda \rho A = \frac{\partial}{\partial t} \rho A \quad (17)$$

where K is the mixing coefficient (cm^2/time), S is the sediment accumulation rate (cm/time), λ is the decay constant, A is the nuclide concentration (dpm/g) at depth z from the interface, and ρ is the *in situ* density of the sediment (g/cm^3). [In Eq. (17) the *in situ* production of nuclide from its parent in the sediment is not included. For nuclides having *in situ* production (e.g., ^{210}Pb), Eq. 17 has to include a production term.] Assuming steady state, i.e., $\partial A/\partial t = 0$, and K, S, and ρ to be constant with time and depth, the depth distribution of activity can be obtained by solving Eq. (17) with the boundary conditions $A(z) = A^*_0$ for $z = 0$ and $A(z) = 0$ for $z \to \infty$.

$$A(z) = A^*_0 \exp(\alpha z) \quad (18)$$

where

$$\alpha = \frac{S - (S^2 + 4K\lambda)^{1/2}}{2K} \quad (19)$$

[The assumptions of constant K and ρ used for solving Eq. (17) are both questionable. The rapid drop off in the abundance of organisms with depth requires that biogenic reworking rates must be depth dependent. Similarly, the decrease in water content with depth in core necessitates an increase in bulk density, invalidating the assumption of constant ρ. These variations can be taken into consideration by expressing both K and ρ as a function of depth, z. In this chapter, however, we deal only with the case of constant K and ρ, which though highly oversimplified provides a handle to probe into particle reworking processes and their rates.]

Eq. (18) describes the activity at any depth for a general case of mixing, sedimentation, and decay. Two particular cases of Eq. (17) are:

(i) $K = 0$, i.e., no mixing. The equation reduces to the standard sedimentation equation:

$$-S \frac{dA}{dz} = \lambda A$$

Solving the above equation for constant S and the boundary condition $A(z) = A_0$ at $z = 0$ yield:

$$A(z) = A_0 \exp\left(-\frac{\lambda z}{S} \right). \quad (20)$$

(ii) Radionuclide distribution is governed predominantly by mixing [i.e., $S^2 \ll 4K\lambda$ in Eq. (19)]. In this case the equation for the depth distribution of the nuclide is given by:

$$K \frac{d^2 A}{dz^2} = \lambda A$$
$$A(z) = A^+_0 \exp\left[-\left(\frac{\lambda}{K} \right)^{1/2} z \right]. \quad (21)$$

In lake sediments, which accumulate at a rate of a few mm/year (Table 5), the depth distribution of isotopes like ^{234}Th ($t_{1/2} = 24.1$ days) and ^{7}Be ($t_{1/2} = 53.4$ days) is expected to be governed primarily by particle reworking processes, analogous to ^{210}Pb in deep sea sediments (Nozaki *et al.*, 1977) and ^{234}Th in nearshore marine sediments (Aller and Cochran, 1976). Thus the study of these short-lived nuclides in lake sediments should give an idea about mixing processes.

The activity of the nuclide at the sediment–water interface A_0^*, A_0, and A_0^+ in Eqs. (19)–(21) will be governed by mixing, sedimentation, and decay. The interrelation between these intercepts (Table 6) can be deduced from the condition of conservation of total amount of activity deposited per unit area (Σdpm/cm^2) in a long column of the core. The quantity:

$$\int_0^\infty A(z)\, dz = \Sigma(\text{dpm/cm}^2) \quad (22)$$

should be the same for all models considered, if there is no loss of activity of nuclide due to physical pro-

TABLE 6.   Some Models for the Distribution of Radionuclides in Lake Sediments

Model	Equations governing the model	Activity of nuclide at sediment–water interface (dpm/g)	Slope[a]	Total amount of nuclide deposited $\Sigma(dpm/cm^2)$
Undistributed sedimentation ($K = 0$)	$-S\dfrac{dA}{dz} = \lambda A$ $A(z) = A_0 e^{-\lambda z/S}$	A_0	$-(\lambda/S)$	$A_0 \rho S/\lambda$
Negligible sedimentation over the dating interval ($S \sim 0$)	$K\dfrac{d^2A}{dz^2} = \lambda A$ $A(z) = A_0^+ e^{-z(\lambda/K)^{1/2}}$	A_0^+	$-\left(\dfrac{\lambda}{K}\right)^{1/2}$	$A_0^+ \rho \left(\dfrac{K}{\lambda}\right)^{1/2}$
Mixing and sedimentation significant	$K\dfrac{d^2A}{dz^2} - S\dfrac{dA}{dz} = \lambda A$ $A(z) = A_0^* e^{\alpha z}$ $\alpha = \dfrac{S - (S^2+4K\lambda)^{1/2}}{2K}$	A_0^*	$\dfrac{S - (S^2 + 4K\lambda)^{1/2}}{2K}$	$-A_0^* \rho \dfrac{2K}{S - (S^2+4K\lambda)^{1/2}}$

[a]For log $A(z)$ vs z plot.

cesses like erosion and redeposition by bottom currents.

The form of Eqs. (18), (20), and (21) are similar suggesting that even in a core which undergoes diffusive type of mixing, the depth distribution of nuclide will still be exponential in nature. Thus the straight line nature in the log activity, $A(z)$, vs depth plot does not necessarily imply an undisturbed sedimentation history for the core. However, the activity of the radionuclide at the sediment–water interface, A_0, A_0^*, and A_0^+ and the slopes of the log $A(z)$ vs z plots will be quite different for different cases.

The above models are for continuous mixing operative throughout the sediment column. However, it is more likely that in most cases the mixing is restricted to the top few centimeters near the sediment–water interface (Figure 6b), where the abundance of deposit feeding organisms are maximum (Davis, 1974; Robbins et al., 1977). Detailed mathematical models, confining mixing to a top layer of certain thickness, have been carried out by Guinasso and Schink (1975), Robbins and Edgington (1975), and Robbins (1977).

To date, the mixing studies have been largely confined to marine sediments. The data on the distribution of microtektites, man-made ^{239}Pu and ^{210}Pb excess in deep sea sediments indicate mixing depths of $\sim$ 10 cm, with mixing coefficients of the order of 0.1 cm²/year (Guinasso and Schink, 1975; Nozaki et al., 1977) orders of magnitude lower than that observed for nearshore and lake sediments, 1.0–5000 cm²/year (Davis, 1974; Guinasso and Schink, 1975; Aller and Cochran, 1976; Robbins et al., 1977). The availability of a number of radionuclides of different half-lives and source functions holds promise that the character of mixing can be deduced from a simultaneous study of their distribution. In particular, nuclides like ^{7}Be, fallout isotopes, and short-lived Th isotopes (^{234}Th, ^{228}Th) are

useful for such studies. Of particular interest is ^{7}Be, a cosmic ray-produced nuclide with a 53-day half-life. This nuclide, because of its short half-life, provides a means of looking at seasonal variations in mixing rates, analogous to ^{234}Th in nearshore sediments (Aller and Cochran, 1976). However, its flux to the sediment–water interface is likely to exhibit time variations and hence, for quantitative modelling purposes, it is essential to know its source function. In spite of this, ^{7}Be might be more useful than ^{234}Th, since the application of ^{234}Th would be restricted to lakes having a relatively high concentration of ^{238}U in the water column (a few micrograms/liter, which is uncommon). The first successful attempts to use ^{7}Be for estimating short-term particle mixing rates have been reported by Krishnaswami et al. (1978). Their results on a box core collected from Lake Whitney, New Haven indicate that ^{7}Be is present in unambiguously measurable concentrations up to $\sim$ 3 cm below the interface, yielding a particle mixing coefficient of $\sim$ 3 cm²/year. The more significant observation made by these investigators was that the standing crop of ^{7}Be in lake sediment was almost equal to its atmospheric deposition at New Haven. This suggests that in fresh-water environments ^{7}Be is removed to sediments within a short time after its injection and hence should prove to be a very valuable tracer for evaluating short-term particle reworking rates in lakes.

Summary

Recently, the attention of scientists from a number of fields has been focused on the chronology of lake deposits because they are easily accessible and contain valuable information on the recent history of the local environment. After the first attempt by Libby to date lake sediments by the radiocarbon method, nearly two decades ago, several new methods based on both natural and artificial nuclides have been developed and are being developed to decipher the chronology of lake deposits and the information stored in them. The aim of this chapter has been to present an overall view of the present status of the various dating techniques and a compilation of the recent investigations.

Radionuclide limnochronology is a relatively new and expanding field and offers challenges to scientists working in different fields to develop new methods, to improve the existing ones, and to discover new datable materials. One aspect of limnochronology which is nascent and which requires particular attention is the sedimentary mixing processes and their rates. Until its role in the distribution of radionuclides in sediments is well understood, the simplistic closed system assumption for dating recently deposited sediments should be viewed with caution. The availability of several radionuclides (^{7}Be, fallout isotopes) and techniques like X-radiography should allow a detailed evaluation of the nature of bioturbation and other mixing processes and their effects on the stored records.

ACKNOWLEDGMENTS.   Our thanks are due to Drs. K. K. Turekian, B. L. K. Somayajulu, Y. Nozaki, and J. A. Robbins for critical reading of the manuscript. Discussions with members of the geochemistry group at Yale were helpful. We record our thanks to Mr. M. Sarin for valuable technical assistance.

One of us (SKS) was a member of the Department of Geology and Geophysics, Yale University, and was supported by a grant (EY-76-S-02-3573) from ERDA during the preparation of the chapter.

References

Aller, R. C. (1977). The influence of micro benthos on chemical diagenesis of marine sediments. Ph.D. thesis, Yale Univ. 600 pp.

Aller, R. C., and J. K. Cochran. (1976). ^{234}Th/^{238}U disequilibrium in nearshore sediment: particle reworking and diagentic time scales. *Earth Planet Sci. Lett.*, **29**:37–50.

Ambach, W., and H. Eisner. (1968). Pb-210 methode zur von eis eines alpinen gletschers. *Acta Phys. Aust.*, **27**:271–274.

Barbetti, M., and M. McElhinny. (1972). Evidence of a geomagnetic excursion 30,000 yr BP, *Nature (London)*, **239**:327–330.

Barnes, J. W., E. J. Lang, and H. A. Potratz. (1956). Ratio of ionium to uranium in coral limestone. *Science*, **124**:175–176.

Benninger, L. K., D. M. Lewis, and K. K. Turekian. (1975). The use of natural ^{210}Pb as a heavy metal tracer in river–

estuarine system. pp. 201–210. In: T. M. Church (ed.), *Marine Chemistry in the Coastal Environment.* Am. Chem. Soc. Symp. Ser. Vol. 18.

Berger, W. H., and G. R. Heath. (1968). Vertical mixing in pelagic sediments. *J. Mar. Res.*, **26**(2):134–143.

Bertine, K. K., L. H. Chan, and K. K. Turekian. (1970). Uranium determination in deep sea sediments and natural waters using fission-tracks. *Geochim. Cosmochim. Acta*, **34**:641–648.

Bhandari, N., D. Lal, and Rama. (1966). Stratospheric circulation studies based on natural and artificial radioactive tracer elements. *Tellus*, **XVIII**:391–406.

Bhat, S. G., and S. Krishnaswami. (1969). Isotopes of U and Ra in Indian rivers. *Proc. Ind. Acad. Sci.*, **70A**:1–17.

Blanchard, R. L. (1963). Uranium decay series disequilibrium in age determination of marine calcium carbonates. Ph.D. Thesis, Washington University. 175 pp.

Bonnyman, J., and J. Molina-Ramos. (1971). *Concentrations of ^{210}Pb in Rainwater in Australia during the Years 1964–70.* Tech. Rep. CXRL/7, Commonwealth X-ray and Radium Laboratory, Melbourne, Australia.

Borole, D. V., S. Krishnaswami, and B. L. K. Somayajulu. (1977). Investigations on dissolved uranium, silicon and on particulate trace elements in estuaries. *Estuarine Coastal Mar. Sci.*, **5**:743–754.

Bortleson, G. C., and G. F. Lee. (1972). Recent sedimentary history of Lake Mendota, Winsonsin. *Environ. Sci. Technol.*, **6**:799–808.

Bowler, J. M. (1970). Late Quarternary environments—A study of lakes and associated sediments in South Eastern Australia. Ph.D. Thesis, Australian National University. 340 pp.

Broecker, W. S. (1963). Radioisotopes and large-scale oceanic mixing. Pp. 88–108. In: M. N. Hill (ed.), *The Sea, Ideas and Observations on Progress in the Study of the Sea.* Vol. 2. Interscience Publishers.

Broecker, W. S. (1965). Isotope geochemistry and the Pleistocene climactic record. Pp. 737–753. In: H. E. Wright, Jr., and D. G. Grey (eds.), *The Quarternary of the United States.* Princeton University Press, Princeton, NJ.

Broecker, W. S., and A. Kaufman. (1965). Radiocarbon chronology of Lake Lahontan and Lake Bonneville II. *Bull. Geol. Soc. Amer.*, **76**:537–566.

Broecker, W. S., and A. Walton. (1959). The geochemistry of C-14 in freshwater systems. *Geochim. Cosmochim. Acta*, **16**:15–38.

Broecker, W. S., and J. Van Donk. (1970). Isolation changes, ice volumes and ^{18}0 record in deep sea cores. *Rev. Geophys. Space Phys.*, **8**:169–198.

Broecker, W. S., Y. H. Li, and J. Cromwell. (1967). Radium-226 and radon-222 concentrations in the Atlantic and Pacific Oceans. *Science*, **158**:1307–1310.

Brugam, R. B. (1975). The human disturbance history of Linsley Pond, North Branford, Connecticut. Ph.D. Thesis, Yale University. 184pp.

Bruland, K. W. (1974). Pb-210 geochronology in the coastal marine environment. Ph.D. Thesis, Univ. Calif. San Diego, La Jolla, CA. 106 pp.

Bruland, K. W., M. Koide, C. Bowser, J. Maher, and E. D. Goldberg. (1975). ^{210}Pb and pollen geochronologies on Lake Superior sediments. *Quat. Res.*, **5**:89–98.

Burton, W. M., and N. G. Stewart. (1960). Use of long lived

natural radioactivity as an atmospheric tracer. *Nature*, **186**:584–589.

Burton, J. D. (1976). Radioactivity in marine environment. Pp. 91–191. In: J. P. Riley and G. Skirrow (eds.), *Chemical Oceanography*. Vol. 3. Academic Press, London.

Bucha, V. (1970). Influence of the Earth's magnetic field on radiocarbon dating. Pp. 501–511. In: I. U. Olsson (ed.), *Radiocarbon Variations and Absolute Chronology. Almqvist and Wiksell, Stockholm*.

Chalov, P. I., T. V. Tuzova, and Y. A. Musin. (1964). The ^{234}U/^{238}U ratio in natural waters and its use in nuclear geochronology. *Geochem. Int.*, **3**:402–408.

Cherdyntsev, V. V., and P. I. Chalov. (1955). Ob izotopnom sostave radioelementov—V privodnykh obyektakh V sviazi S voprosami geokronologii. Pp. 175–233. In: *Trudy III Sessii Komissi Opredelenkyu Absolyutnogo. Izd. Akad. Nauk. SSSR*.

Cherdyntsev, V. V., D. P. Orlov, E. A. Isabaev, and V. I. Ivanov. (1961). Isotopic composition of uranium in minerals. *Geochemistry*, **10**:927–936.

Clausen, H. B. (1973). Dating of polar ice by ^{32}Si. *J. Glaciol.*, **23**(66):411–416.

Craig, H. (1974). Lake Tanganyika Geochemical and Hydrographic Study, 1973 Expedition Scripps Institution of Oceanography Report. SIO Reference series 75-5.

Creer, K. M., R. Thompson, L. Molyneux, and F. J. Mackereth. (1972). Geomagnetic secular variations recorded in the stable magnetic remanence of recent sediments. *Earth. Planet. Sci. Lett.*, **14**:115–127.

Crozaz, G., E. Picciotto, and W. DeBreuck. (1964). Antarctic snow chronology with ^{210}Pb. *J. Geophys. Res.*, **69**:2594–2604.

Cushing, C. E. (ed.). (1975). *Radioecology and Energy Resources*. Ecological Soc. Amer. Dowden, Hutchinson and Ross Inc.

Damon, P. E. (1970). Climatic versus magnetic perturbation of the atmospheric ^{14}C reservoir. Pp. 571–593. In: I. U. Olsson (ed.), *Radiocarbon Variations and Absolute Cheonology*. Almqvist and Wiksell, Stockholm.

Dansgaard, W., H. B. Clausen, and A. Aarkrog. (1966). Evidence for bomb produced ^{32}Si. *J. Geophys. Res.*, **71**:5474–5477.

Davis, R. B. (1974). Stratigraphic effects of tubifiuds in profundal lake sediments. *Limnol. Oceanogr.*, **19**:466–488.

Dean, W. E., S. K. Ghosh, S. Krishnaswami, and W. S. Moore. (1973). Geochemistry and accretion rates of freshwater ferromanganese nodules. Pp. 13–18. In: M. Morgenstein (ed.), *The Origin and Distribution of Manganese Nodules in the Pacific and Prospects for Exploration*. NSF-IDOE.

Denham, C. R., and A. Cox. (1971). Evidence that the Laschamp polarity event did not occur 13,300–30,400 years ago. *Earth Planet. Sci. Lett.*, **13**:181–190.

Dooley, J. R., H. C. Granger, and J. N. Rosholt. (1966). U-234 fractionation in the sandstone type uranium deposits of the Ambrosia Lake District. *New Mexico Econ. Geol.*, **61**:1362–1368.

Eakins, J. D., and R. T. Morrison. (1974). Dating lake sediments by the determination of Pb-210. AERE-PR/EMS (United Kingdom Authority Research Group). **1**:10–12.

Edgington, D. N., and J. A. Robbins. (1975). The behaviour of plutonium and other long lived radionuclides in Lake Michigan, II. Patterns of deposition in sediments. Pp. 245–260. In: *Impacts of Nuclear Release into the Aquatic Environment*. International Atomic Energy Agency, Vienna.

Edgington, D. N., and J. A. Robbins. (1976a). Pattern of deposition of natural and fall-out radionuclides in the sediments of Lake Michigan and their relation to Limnological processes. Pp. 705–729. In: J. O. Nriagu (ed.), *Environmental Biogeochemistry*. Vol. 2. Ann Arbor Science, MI.

Edgington, D. N., and J. A. Robbins. (1976b). Records of lead deposition in Lake Michigan sediments since 1800. *Environ. Sci. Technol.* **10**:266–274.

Edgington, D. N., J. A. Robbins, and A. W. L. Kemp. (1977). Comparitive ^{210}Pb, ^{137}Cs and pollen geochronologies of sediments from Lakes Erie and Ontario. Abstract. Am. Soc. Limnol. Oceanogr. 40th Annual Meeting.

Eriksson, E. (1962). Radioactivity in hydrology. Pp. 47–60. In: H. Irasel and A. Krebs (eds.), *Nuclear Radiation in Geophysics*. Academic Press, New York, NY.

Emery, K. O., and S. C. Rittenberg. (1952). Early diagenesis of California basin sediments in relation to origin of oil. *Am. Assoc. Petrol. Geol. Bull.*, **36**:735–806.

Fitch, F. J., S. C. Forster, and J. A. Miller. (1974). Geological time scale. *Reports Prog. Phys.*, **37**:1433–1496.

Flint, R. F., and W. A. Gale. (1958). Stratigraphy and radiocarbon dates at Searles Lake, California. *Am. J. Sci.*, **256**:689–714.

Francis, C. W., G. Chester, and L. A. Haskin. (1970). Determination of the ^{210}Pb mean residence time in the atmosphere. *Environ. Sci. Technol.*, **4**:587–589.

Fukuda, K., and S. Tsunogai. (1975). Pb-210 in precipitation in Japan and its implication for the transport of continental aerosols across the ocean. *Tellus*, **27**:514–521.

Goddard, J. (1970). ^{230}Th/^{234}U dating of saline deposits from Searles Lake, California. MS thesis, Queens College, New York, NY. 50 pp.

Goldberg, E. D. (1963). Geochronology with ^{210}Pb. Pp. 121–131. In: *Radioactive Dating*. International Atomic Energy Agency, Vienna.

Goldberg, E. D., and K. Bruland. (1974). Radioactive geochronologies. Pp. 451–489. In: *The Sea*, Vol. 5. *Marine Chemistry*. John Wiley, New York, NY.

Goldberg, E. D., and M. Koide. (1962). Geochronological studies of deep sea sediments by the ionium–thorium method. *Geochim. Cosmochim. Acta*, **26**:417–445.

Goldberg, E. D., B. L. K. Somayajulu, J. Galloway, I. R. Kaplan, and G. Faure. (1969). Differences between barite of marine and continental origins. *Geochim. Cosmochim. Acta*, **33**:287–289.

Goldberg, E. D., V. Hodge, M. Koide, and J. J. Griffin. (1976). Metal Pollution in Tokyo as recorded in sediments of the Palace Moat. *Geochem. J.*, **10**:165–174.

Goreau, T. J. (1977). Quantitative effects of sediment mixing on stratigraphy and geochemistry: a signal theory approach. *Nature*, **265**:525–526.

Guinasso, N. L., Jr., and D. R. Schink. (1975). Quantitative estimates of biological mixing rates in abyssal sediments. *J. Geophys. Res.*, **80**:3032–3043.

Gulliksen, S., R. Nydal, and K. Lovseth. (1972). Further calculations on the ^{14}C exchange between the ocean and the atmosphere. In: *Proc. 8th Intl. Conf. Radiocarbon Dating*. Wellington, New Zealand (1972). C64-C73.

Hariss, R. C., and A. G. Troup. (1970). Chemistry and origin of freshwater ferromanganese nodules. *Limnol. Oceanor.*, **15**:702–712.

Hohndorf, A. (1969). Bestimmug der halbwertz eit von ^{210}Pb. *Z. phys.*, **24a**:612–615.

Honda, M., and D. Lal. (1964). Spallation cross-sections for long-lived nuclides in iron and light nuclei. *Nucl. Phys.*, **51**:363–368.

Horie, S. (1968). Late Pleistocene climatic changes inferred from stratigraphic sequences of Japanese lake sediments. Pp. 177–188. In: B. Morrison and H. E. Wright (eds.), *Means of Correlation of Quarternary Successions*. Univ. of Utah Press.

Imboden, D. M., R. F. Weiss, H. Craig, R. L. Michel, and C. R. Goldman. (1977). Lake Tahoe geochemical study. 1. Lake chemistry and tritium mixing study. *Limnol. Oceanogr.*, **22**:1039–1051.

Israel, H., (1958). Du Natur liche radio-aktivatat in boden, wasser und luft. *Beitr. Phys. Atmos.*, **30**:177–188.

Jantsch, K. (1967). Kernreaktionen mit Tritonen beim ^{30}Si. *Kernenergie,* **10**(3):89–91.

Jaworowski, Z. (1969). Radioactive lead in the environment and in the human body. *Atom. Energy. Rev.*, **7**:3–45.

Jaworowski, Z., J. Bilkrewicz, Kownacka, and S. Wlodek. (1972). Artificial sources of natural radionuclides in environment. Pp. 809–818. In: J. A. S. Adams, W. M. Lowder, and T. F. Gessell (eds.), *in: Natural Radiation Environment II*. Vol. 2.

Johansen, K. A., and J. A. Robbins. (1977). Growth rates of ferromanganese nodules from Lake Michigan. Abstract. Am. Soc. Limnol. Oceanogr. 40th Annual Meeting.

Joseph, A. B., P. F. Gustafson, I. R. Russell, E. A. Schuert, H. L. Volchok, and A. Tamplin. (1971). Sources of radioactivity and their characteristics. Pp. 6–41. In: *Radioactivity in the Marine Environment*. U.S. National Academy of Sciences, Washington, D.C.

Joshi, L. V., C. Rangarajan, and S. Gopalkrishnan. (1969). Measurement of ^{210}Pb in surface air and precipitation. *Tellus,* **21**:107–112.

Junge, C. E. (1963). *Air Chemistry and Radioactivity*. Academic Press, New York, NY.

Kanwisher, J. (1960). pCO_2 in seawater and its effect on the movement of CO_2 in nature. *Tellus,* **12**:209–215.

Kaufman, A. (1964). ^{230}Th-^{234}U dating of carbonates from Lakes Lahontan and Bonneville. Ph.D. Thesis, Columbia University.

Kaufman, A., and W. S. Broecker. (1965). Comparison of ^{230}Th and ^{14}C ages for carbonate materials from Lakes Lahontan and Bonneville. *J. Geophys. Res.,* **70**:4039–4054.

Kharkar, D. P., D. Lal, and B. L. K. Somayajulu. (1963). Investigations in marine environments using radioisotopes produced by cosmic rays. Pp. 175–187. In: *Radioactive Dating*. International Atomic Energy Agency, Vienna.

Kharkar, D. P., V. N. Nijampurkar, and D. Lal. (1966). Global fall-out of ^{32}Si. *Geochim. Cosmochim. Acta,* **30**:621–631.

Kigoshi, K. (1971). Alpha-recoil Th-234: dissolution into water and the U-234/U-238 disequilibrium in nature. *Science,* **173**:47–48.

Koide, M., K. W. Bruland, and E. D. Goldberg. (1973). Th-228/Th-232 and Pb-210 geochronologies in marine and lake sediments. *Geochim. Cosmochim. Acta,* **37**:1171–1187.

Koide, M., K. Bruland, and E. D. Goldberg. (1976). ^{226}Ra geochronology of a coastal marine sediment. *Earth Planet. Sci. Lett.,* **31**:31–36.

Krishnaswami, S. (1973). Geochemistry of transition elements and radioisotopes in marine and fresh-water environments. Ph.D. Thesis, Bombay Univ. 224 pp.

Krishnaswami, S. (1974). Man-made plutonium in fresh-water and marine environments. *Proc. Ind. Acad. Sci.,* **80**:116–123.

Krishnaswami, S., D. Lal, J. M. Martin, and M. Meybeck. (1971). Geochronology of lake sediments. *Earth Planet. Sci. Lett.,* **11**:407–414.

Krishnaswami, S., D. Lal, B. S. Amin, and A. Soutar. (1973). Geochronological studies in Santa Barbara basin: ^{55}Fe as a unique tracer for particulate settling. *Limnol. Oceanogr.,* **18**:763–770.

Krishnaswami, S., and W. S. Moore. (1973). Accretion rates of fresh-water ferromanganese deposits. *Nature* **243**:114–116.

Krishnaswami, S., L. K. Benninger, R. C. Aller, and K. L. Von Damm. (1978). Application of Be-7 for estimating particle reworking rates in near shore and lake sediments, abstract 065, AGU Spring Meeting.

Ku, T-L. (1976). The uranium-series methods of age determination. *Ann. Rev. Earth Planet. Sci.,* **4**:347–379.

Lal, D. (1963). On the investigations of geophysical processes using cosmic ray produced radioactivity. Pp. 115–142. In: J. Geiss and E. D. Goldberg (eds.), *Earth Sciences and Meteoritics*. North-Holland Publishing Co.

Lal, D. (1969). Characteristics of the large scale oceanic circulation as derived from the distribution of radioactive elements. Pp. 29–48. *Morning Review Lectures.* 2nd International Oceanographic Congress, Moscow, 30 May–9 June 1966. (Unesco pub.).

Lal, D., and B. Peters. (1967), Cosmic ray produced radioactivity of the earth. Pp. 551–612. In: *Handbuch der Physik*. Vol. 46. Springer Verlag, Berlin.

Lal, D., and Rama. (1966). Characteristics of global tropospheric mixing based on man-made ^{14}C, ^{3}H and ^{90}Sr. *J. Geophys. Res.,* **71**:2865–2874.

Lal, D., and H. Suess. (1968). Radioactivity of atmosphere and hydrosphere, *Ann. Rev. Nucl. Sci.,* **18**:407–434.

Lal, D., and B. L. K. Somayajulu. (1975). On the importance of studying magnetic susceptibility stratigraphy and geochronology of Lake Biwa sediments. Pp. 530–535. In: S. Horie, (ed.), *Paleolimnology and the Japanese Pleistocene.* Vol. 3. Kyoto University. Kyoto.

Lal, D., and V. S. Venkatavaradan. (1970). Analysis of the causes of ^{14}C variations in the atmosphere. Pp. 549–569. In: I. U. Olsson (ed.), *Radiocarbon Variations and Absolute Chronology*. Almqvist and Wiksell, Stockholm.

Lal, D., V. N. Nijampurkar, G. Rajagopalan, and B. L. K. Somayajulu. (1978). Annual fall-out of ^{7}Be, ^{32}P, ^{35}S, ^{22}Na, ^{210}Pb, ^{32}Si in Indian rains. Sub. Proc. Ind. Acad. Sci.

Lerman, A., and T. A. Lietzke. (1975). Uptake and migration of tracers in lake sediments. *Limnol. Oceanogr.,* **20**:497–510.

Lewis, D. M. (1976). The geochemistry of manganese, iron, uranium, Pb-210 and major ions in the Susquehanna River. Ph.D. Thesis, Yale University. 272 pp.

Libby, W. F. (1955). *Radiocarbon Dating.* University of Chicago Press, Chicago, IL. 124 pp.

Lingenfelter, R. E. (1976). Cosmic ray produced neutrons and nuclides in the Earth's atmosphere. Pp. 193–205. In: B. S. P. Shen and M. Merker (eds.), *Spallation and Nuclear Reactions and Their Applications.* D. Reidel Publishing Co., Dordrecht, Holland.

Lingenfelter, R. E., and R. Ramaty. (1970). Astrophysical and geophysical variations in ^{14}C production. Pp. 513–537. In: I. U. Olsson (eds.), *Radiocarbon Variations and Absolute Chronology.* Almqvist and Wiksell, Stockholm.

Machta, L. (1974). Global scale atmospheric mixing. *Advan. Geophys.,* **18B**:33–56.

Machta, L., K. Telegadas, and D. L. Harris. (1970). ^{90}Sr fallout over Lake Michigan. *J. Geophys. Res.,* **75**:1092–1096.

Manheim, F. T. (1964). Manganese-iron accumulations in shallow marine environment. Pp. 217–276. In: D. Schink and J. Corliss (eds.), *Proc. Symposium on Marine Geochemistry.*

Martell, E. A. (1970). Transport patterns and residence times for atmospheric trace constituents vs. altitude. Pp. 138–157. Advances in Chemistry Series, No. 93, *Radionuclides in the Environment.*

Martin, J. M. (1971). Contribution a l'etude des apports terrigenes d'oligoelements stables et radioactifs a l'océan. Ph.D. Thesis, Univ. Paris. 156 pp.

Matsumoto, E. (1975a). Accumulation rate of Lake Biwa Sediments by ^{210}Pb method. *J. Geol. Soc. Japan,* **81**:301–306.

Matsumoto, E. (1975b). ^{210}Pb geochronology of sediments from Lake Shinji. *Geochem. J.,* **9**:167–172.

McCaffrey, R. J. (1977). A record of the accumulation of the sediment and trace metals in a Connecticut, USA, salt marsh. Ph.D. thesis, Yale Univ. 156 pp.

Meybeck, M., J. M. Martin, and P. Oliver. (1975). Geochimie des eaus et des sediments de queleques lacs volcaniques du massif central francaise. *Veh. Int. Verein. Limnol.,* **19**:1150–1164.

Moore, W. S. (1967). Amazon and Mississippi River concentrations of U, Th and Ra isotopes. *Earth Planet. Sci. Lett.,* **2**:231–234.

Moore, H. E., S. E. Poet, and E. A. Martell. (1973). ^{222}Rn, ^{210}Pb, ^{210}Bi, and ^{210}Po profiles and aerosol residence times versus altitude. *J. Geophys. Res.,* **78**:7065–7075.

Moore, W. S., W. Dean, and S. Krishnaswami. (1976b). Episodic growth of ferromanganese nodules in Oneida Lake, New York. Pp. 1017–1018. Geol. Soc. Amer. Abstract Denver, CO.

Moore, H. E., E. A. Martell, and S. E. Poet. (1976a). Sources of ^{210}Pb in the atmosphere. *Environ. Sci. Tech.,* **10**:586–591.

Nelson, D. M., P. F. Gustafson, and J. Sedlet. (1970). Fallout radionuclides as a tracers of lake mixing. Pp. 490–494. In: *Proc. 13th Conf.,* Great Lakes Res.

Nezami, M., G. Lambert, C. Lorius, and S. Laberyrie. (1964). Mesure de taux d' accumulation de la neige au bord de continet antarctique par la method du plomb-210. *C.R. Acad. Sci. Paris,* **259**:3319–3322.

Nijampurkar, V. N. (1975). Applications of cosmic ray produced isotope Si-32 to hydrology with special reference to dating groundwaters. Ph.D. Thesis, Bombay Univ. 165 pp.

Nijampurkar, V. N., B. S. Amin, D. P. Kharkar, and D. Lal. (1966). "Dating" ground waters of ages younger than 1000–1500 years using natural ^{32}Si. *Nature,* **210**:478–480.

Nozaki, Y. (1977). Distribution of natural radionuclides in sediments influenced by bioturbation. *Jour. Geol. Soc. Japan.* **8**: 699–706.

Nozaki, Y., J. K. Cochran, K. K. Turekian, and G. Keller. (1977). Radiocarbon and ^{210}Pb distribution in submersible-taken deep-sea cores from Project FAMOUS. *Earth Planet. Sci. Lett.,* **34**:167–173.

Oeschger, H., and A. Gugelmann. (1974). Das geophysikalisches Verhalten der Umweltisotope als Basis fur Modellrechnungen in der Isofopenhydrologie. *Osterreisch. Wasserwirst.,* **26**:43–49.

Peirson, D. H., R. S. Cambray, and G. S. Spicer. (1966). Lead-210 and polonium-210 in the atmosphere. *Tellus,* **18**:427–433.

Pennington, W., R. S. Cambray, and E. M. Fisher. (1973). Observations on lake sediments using fall-out ^{137}Cs as a tracer. *Nature,* **242**:324–326.

Pennington, W., R. S. Cambray, J. D. Eakins, and D. D. Harkness. (1975). Radionuclide dating of the recent sediments of Blelham Tarn. *Freshwater Biol.,* **6**:317–331.

Petit, D. (1974). Pb-210 et isotopes stables du plomb dans des sediments lacustres. *Earth Planet. Sci. Lett.,* **23**:199–205.

Picciotto, E., R. Cameron, G. Crozaz, S. Deutsch, and S. Wilgin. (1968), Determination of rate of snow accumulation at the pole of relative inaccessibility, eastern Antarctica. *J. Glaciol.,* **7**:273–287.

Poet, S. E., H. E. Moore, and E. A. Martell. (1972). ^{210}Pb, ^{210}Bi and ^{210}Po in the atmosphere: Accurate measurement and application to aerosol residence time determination. *J. Geophys. Res.,* **77**:6515–6527.

Rafter, T. A., and B. J. O'Brien. (1972). ^{14}C measurements in the atmosphere and in the South Pacific Ocean. A recalculation of exchange rates between the atmosphere and the ocean. In. *Proc. 8th Intl. Conf. Radiocarbon Dating.* Wellington, New Zealand (1972). C17-C42.

Rama, M. Koide, and E. D. Goldberg. (1961). Pb-210 in natural waters. *Science,* **134**:98–99.

Ritchie, J. C., J. R. McHenry, and A. C. Gill. (1973). Dating recent reservoir sediments. *Limnol. Oceanogr.,* **18**:254–263.

Robbins, J. A., and E. Callender. (1975). Diagenesis of manganese in Lake Michigan sediments. *Am. J. Sci.,* **275**:512–533.

Robbins, J. A., and D. N. Eddington. (1975). Determination of recent sedimentation rates in Lake Michigan using ^{210}Pb and Cs-137. *Geochim. Cosmochim. Acta,* **39**:285–304.

Robbins, J. A. (1977). Geochemical and Geophysical Applications of Radioactive Lead. In: J. O. Nriagu (ed.), *Biogeochemistry of Lead.* Elsevier Scientific Publishers, Netherlands. (In press).

Robbins, J. A., J. R. Krezoski, and S. C. Mozley. (1977). Radioactivity in sediments of Great Lakes: Post depositional redistribution by deposit feeding organisms. *Earth Planet. Sci. Lett.* **36**:325–333.

Rona, E., and W. D. Urry. (1952). Radioactivity of ocean sediments: VIII. Radium and uranium content of ocean and river water, *Am. J. Sci.,* **250**:241–262.

Rosholt, J. N., W. R. Shields, and E. L. Garner. (1963). Isotopic fractionation of uranium in sandstone. *Science,* **139**:224–226.

Sackett, W. M., T. Mo, R. F. Spalding, and M. E. Exner. (1973). A revaluation of the marine geochemistry of Uranium. Pp. 757–769. In: *Proc. Symp. on "Radioactive Contamination of the Marine Environment."* International Atomic Energy Agency, Vienna.

Schell, W. R. (1974). Sedimentation rates and mean residence times of stable Pb and Pb-210 in Lake Washington, Puget Sound estuaries and a coastal region. USAEC Rep. RLO-2225-T14-6.

Sheppard, P. A. (1963). Atmospheric tracers and the study of the general circulation of the atmosphere. *Rep. Prog. Phys.,* **XXVI**:213–267.

Smith, G. I. (1968). Late quarternary geologic and climatic history of Searles Lake, Southeastern California. Pp. 293–310. In: R. B. Morrison and H. E. Wright (eds.), *Means of Correlation of Quarternary Successions.* University of Utah Press.

Starik, I. Y., F. E. Starik, and B. A. Mikhailov. (1958). Shifts of isotopic ratios in natural materials. *Geochemistry,* 587–590.

Stebbins, A. K. (1961). Second special report on the high altitude sampling program. Pp. 127–133. U.S. Dept. Def. Repl. DASA 539-B.

Stuiver, M. (1964). Carbon isotopic distribution and correlated chronology of Searles Lake sediments. *Am. J. Sci.,* **262**:377–392.

Stuiver, M. (1967). Origin and extent of atmospheric C14 variations during the past 10,000 years. Pp. 27–40. In: *Radioactive Dating and Methods of Low level counting.* International Atomic Energy Agency, Vienna.

Stuiver, M. (1970). Long-term C14 variations. Pp. 197–213. In: I. U. Olsson (ed.), *Radiocarbon Variations and Absolute Chronology.* Almqvist and Wiksell, Stockholm.

Stuiver, M. (1971). Evidence for the variation of atmospheric ^{14}C content in the late Quarternary. Pp. 57–70. In: K. K. Turekian (ed.), *Late Cenozoic Glacial Ages.* Yale Univ. Press.

Suess, H. E. (1955). Radiocarbon concentration in modern wood. *Science,* **122**:415–417.

Suess, H. E. (1965). Secular variations of the cosmic-ray-produced carbon-14 in the atmosphere and their interpretations. *J. Geophys. Res.,* **70**:5937–5952.

Suess, H. E. (1967). Bristlecone-pine calibration of the radiocarbon time scale from 4100 B.C. to 1500 B.C. Pp. 143–151. In: *Radioactive Dating and Low level counting.* International Atomic Energy Agency, Vienna.

Suess, H. E. (1968). Climatic changes, solar activity, and the cosmic-ray production rate of natural radiocarbon. *Meteorol. Monogr.,* **8**:146–150.

Suess, H. E. (1970). The three causes of the secular C^{14} fluctuations, their amplitudes and time constants. Pp.

595–605. In: I. U. Olsson (ed.), *Radiocarbon Variations and Absolute Chronology.* Almqvist and Wiksell, Stockholm.

Tatsumoto, M., and E. D. Goldberg. (1959). Some aspects of the marine geochemistry of uranium. *Geochim. Cosmochim. Acta,* **17**:201–208.

Thurber, D. L. (1962). Anomalous ^{234}U/^{238}U in nature. *J. Geophys. Res.,* **67**:4518–4520.

Thurber, D. L. (1963). Anomalous ^{234}U/^{238}U and an investigation of the potential of ^{234}U for Pleistocene chronology. Ph.D. Thesis, Columbia, Univ., New York, NY.

Thurber, D. L., and W. S. Broecker. (1970). The behaviour of radiocarbon in the surface waters of Great Basin. Pp. 379–400. In: I. U. Olsson (ed.), *Radiocarbon Variations and Absolute Chronology,* Proc. 12th Nobel Symp.

Thurber, D. L., W. S. Broecker, R. L. Blanchard, and H. A. Portraz. (1965). Uranium series ages of Pacific atoll coral. *Science,* **149**:55–58.

Torgersen, T., Z. Top, W. B. Clarke, W. J. Jenkins, and W. S. Broecker. (1977). A new method for physical limnology—tritium–helium–3 ages—results for Lakes Erie, Huron, and Ontario. *Limnol. Oceanogr.,* **22**:181–193.

Turekian, K. K., and L. H. Chan. (1971). The marine geochemistry of uranium isotopes, ^{230}Th and ^{231}Pa. In: A. O. Brunfelt and E. Steines (eds.), *Activation Analysis in Geochemistry and Cosmochemistry.* Universitetsforlaget, Oslo.

Turekian, K. K., and J. K. Cochran. (1977). Marine chronologies with natural radionuclides. In: J. P. Riley and G. Skirrow (eds.), *Chemical Oceanography.* Academic Press, London. (In press).

Turekian, K. K., Y. Nozaki, and L. K. Benninger. (1977). Geochemistry of atmospheric radon and radon products. *Ann. Rev. Earth Planet. Sci.,* **5**:227–255.

Veeh, H. H. (1966). ^{230}Th/^{238}U ages of Pleistocene high sea level stands. *J. Geophys. Res.,* **71**:3379–3386.

Volchok, H. L. (1973). World wide deposition of ^{90}Sr through 1972. USAEC, HASL-276, I-3-18.

Volchok, H. L. (1974). Is there excess ^{90}Sr fall-out in the oceans? Health and Safety Laboratory, USAEC, HASL-296, I-82-89.

Volchok, H. L., M. Feiner, H. J. Simpson, W. S. Broecker, V. E. Noshkin, V. T. Bowen, and E. Willis. (1970). Ocean Fall-out—The Crater Lake Experiment. *J. Geophys. Res.,* **75**:1084–1091.

Wahlgren, M. A., and D. M. Nelson. (1973). Residence times for ^{239}Pu and ^{137}Cs in Lake Michigan water. Pp. 85–89. In: *Annual report.* Argonne National Lab, Argonne, IL., ANL-8060 (Part III, Ecology).

Wilkening, M. H., W. E. Clements, and D. Stanley. (1975). Radon-222 flux measurements in widely separated regions. Pp. 717–730. In: J. A. S. Adams, W. M. Lowder, and T. F. Gessel (eds.), *Natural Radiation Environment II.*

Windom, H. (1969). Atmospheric dust records in permanent snowfields: Implications to marine sedimentation. *Geol. Soc. Am. Bull.,* **80**:761–782.

Chapter 7

The Mineralogy and Related Chemistry of Lake Sediments

Blair F. Jones[1] and Carl J. Bowser

Introduction

The sediment reservoir of a lake plays an important role in helping to elucidate the many processes occurring within the total lake system, including its surrounding surface and ground water drainage basins. Of course, lake bottoms have long been recognized as the depositional site of both mineral and organic matter that is transported to the lake from the drainage basin, as well as matter which forms and settles from within the water body proper. However, early studies of lakes tended to treat the sediments as simply a repository having little or no additional reaction with the lake once deposited. The sediments were viewed primarily as a record of the lake history.

In more recent years, however, there has been a growing awareness of the role sediments play in the dynamics of lake systems. Recycling of mineralized organic matter, especially the nutrients, in sediments by organic decay and pore fluid transfer processes are now recognized as essential components of models that attempt to describe the nutrient dynamics of lake and reservoir systems (see for example, Allen and Kramer, 1972; Gahler, 1969; Lerman and Brunskill, 1971; Mackereth, 1965, 1966; Middlebrooks *et al.*, 1974; and Mortimer, 1941, 1971). In addition, the active role lake sediments play in regulating cycles of trace metals, radionuclides, and synthetic organic chemicals (pesticides, soaps, industrial effluents, etc.) is gaining increasing attention, particularly from students of lake systems in culturally developed areas of the world (for example, Jenne, 1968, 1977; Schnitzer and Kahn, 1972; Stumm and Morgan, 1970; see also Chapter 4).

Thus, the interactive role of sediments and lake water has come to be appreciated as fundamental in

lake processes. On the other hand, the *mineralogical composition* of lake sediments and its importance in helping to understand lake processes is generally *not* fully appreciated in the field of aquatic chemistry. The separation of sediments into "organic" and "inorganic" phases is at least conceptually understood in limnology; however, even then, much literature reflects no critical use of such "phase" distinctions. The reasons for neglecting sediment mineralogy are several, but probably are related mostly to two factors. First, mineralogy is a field generally peripheral to the training of many students of lakes. Second, and perhaps much more importantly, separation and identification of mineral phases and study of their areal variations in lake systems is generally difficult and time consuming.

Bulk and extractive chemical techniques have been used in attempts to characterize the "mineral" fraction of sediments without mineralogic separation and identification. Such chemical procedures may be useful for some types of problems, but, in the past, such approaches have met with only limited success, and the reasons for this will be discussed throughout the chapter. It is important to note here only that bulk and extractive chemical analyses do not recognize that sediments are, in fact, complex mixtures of discrete mineral phases and organic compounds, the study of which can provide important insights into lake chemistry and dynamics.

From a review of the literature on lake sediments it is clear that restriction of the discussion to lake sediment *mineralogy* alone would not be adequate. To properly elucidate the relationship between the constituent inorganic and organic phases of lake sediments and lake sedimentation processes, the mineralogical *and* chemical aspects of lake sediments must be discussed. In fact, it is not always possible to separate mineralogical and chemical evidence in lake sediment studies. It must be appreciated that some uses of bulk

[1]Publication approved by the Director, U.S. Geological Survey.

and extractive chemical analyses represent a valuable technique of "chemical mineralogy." For certain sediments, especially fine-grained and/or organic rich sediments, extractive chemical analyses represent the only way possible with present techniques to distinguish chemically dissimilar "phases."

It is important to understand, however, that without specific phase characterization of sediments, whether by direct examination (optical microscope, scanning or transmission electron microscopy, X-ray diffraction) or indirectly (by extractive chemical techniques "specific" for certain phases), studies of lake sediment chemistry will lack transfer value. Attempts to extend empirically established interactive relationships between sediments, pore fluids, and overlying lake waters require detailed knowledge of the *processes* involved, which, in turn, will eventually require characterization of the critical *phases* within the sediment.

The sections of this chapter have been arranged to consider first the major sources and processes affecting the distribution of lake sediment phases, and then factors of importance in analysis of the sediment mass. Representative examples of lake sediment chemical composition and a listing of important mineral phases in sediments are included as background. The chapter presents a summary of the *tools* of sediment analysis (mineralogical and chemical techniques), the *phases* of sediments (the minerals associated with each major chemical type of sediment), and finally a listing of the important *principles* involved in the interpretation and application of sediment mineralogy to fresh water lakes.

Mineral sources

One of the prime goals of studying the quantitative mineralogy and chemistry of sediments is the evaluation of the sources of sediment phases and the relative importance of each source. It is useful to distinguish: (1) the minerals brought into the lake by surface water (streams and overland flow), shore erosion, glacial transport, and aeolean processes (allogenic fraction); (2) the minerals originating from processes occurring within the water column (endogenic fraction); and (3) the minerals resulting from processes that occur within the sediments once deposited (authigenic fraction). Such imposition of order on nature inevitably leads to cases where distinction of origin is almost impossible (as, for example, a carbonate-precipitating lake in a limestone terrain). However, we feel that distinction among these three types of sediment helps to elucidate the important types of interactions between lakes and sediments.

Allogenic fraction

Particulate mineral matter depositing in or moving through the freshwater environment plays an important role in helping to understand the physical and chemical character of lakes and the evolution of the lake through time. Physical processes (waves, currents) act to transport and sort minerals, and, therefore, studies of the size and mineralogic distribution of particulate sedimentary matter yields a time-integrated picture of major transport systems within the lake (see Chapter 3). Studies of the mineralogical and chemical makeup of sediment particles supplied to the lake by streams, shore erosion, atmospheric fallout, and cultural sources can yield important information about the bedrock and surficial geology of the drainage basin, weathering, the relative importance of the various inputs, and quantitative estimates of cultural loadings on the lake systems. Sedimentary material derived from outside the lake proper can be referred to as *allogenic,* a term that will be used throughout this chapter.

Endogenic fraction

Numerous chemical processes occur within the lake water mass that lead to chemical precipitation or absorptive uptake of metals from aquatic solutions. Removal of these *endogenic,* or water column-derived, particulates by settling, filtering organisms, or flocculation represents an important transport mechanism for chemical elements to the lake sediments. The mineralogy and chemistry of such endogenic matter preserved in lake sediments can then be an important indicator of the processes of mineral precipitation within the lake. Moreover, from the quantitative mineralogy of the sediments, the relative importance of endogenic and allogenic processes might be estimated.

Because of the highly temporal character of typical lacustrine endogenic processes (organic productivity, carbonate precipitation, etc.), quantititative assessment of endogenic mineral production in lake systems from studies of the water column proper is hampered by the fact that observations on lakes are generally made only a few times during the year, and not necessarily at the time the rates of such processes are at their maxima. Moreover, year to year variations in climate and/or elemental inputs make it difficult to assess the average rate and intensity of such processes. In contrast, however, studies of the quantitative mineralogy and chemistry of endogenic material in lake sediments can provide an integrated picture of the importance of such processes over tens to tens of thousands of years.

To the extent that the mineralogy of lake sediments is little altered by postdepositional reactions (diagenesis) and that physical and biological mixing depths in sediments are small relative to the total amount of sediments deposited in the lake, the mineralogy and chemical variations of the sediments with depth can provide information on the physical and chemical changes that have occurred in the life of the lake. Such information can be useful in evaluating long-term climatic changes of the region and in helping to assess the effects of cultural activities on the lake.

Authigenic fraction

Lake sediments derived from either allogenic or endogenic processes are usually subjected to a changed physical/chemical environment once deposited as a result of decomposition of buried organic matter and/or physical and chemical mixing caused by bottom-dwelling organisms. Such environments are important in lakes and can lead to significant changes in the mineralogy and bulk chemistry of the sediments.

Knowledge of the processes and products of lake sediment alteration (diagenesis) is important to properly understand lake–sediment systems for a variety of reasons. The diagenetically derived, or authigenic, phases represent a mineralogic imprint on the preserved sediments that can replace otherwise recognizable allogenic and endogenic phases. Perhaps more importantly, though, diagenetic processes involve substantial changes in the composition of sediment-associated pore fluids. Diffusion- and/or advection-controlled transfer of solutes between the sediment and overlying water is important in determining whether the major fraction of labile particulate matter (generally endogenic) arriving at the sediment–water interface will be trapped and preserved within the sediment or whether a significant fraction of that matter is returned to the lake water. Such processes are especially important in determining the diagenetic flux of nutrients (phosphate and nitrate) and silica to the overlying water because of the importance of these nutrients in stimulating continued growth of organic matter within the lake. Such processes have been recognized as important in both oceanic and lake systems, but, because of the generally higher productivity levels of lakes as compared to the open ocean, lacustrine sediments usually exhibit significantly higher pore-fluid concentrations and fluxes between sediments and overlying water.

Driving forces

The fact that many older published sediment analyses attempted to distinguish only between the "inorganic" and "organic" fractions of samples reflects the simple fact that the source of such sediment can be considered as either external to the lake (allogenic) or internal (endogenic *and* authigenic).[2] The relative importance of the two major sediment sources is largely determined by the capacity of the lake waters to support organic growth and the resultant biomass as compared to the supply of material from streams and, to an extent, shore erosion.

The concept of lake "life cycles," ranging from youthful, with largely allogenic sediments, to mature and old age, with mostly endogenic (commonly) organic sediments (Hutchinson, 1957), has been useful when applied to freshwater bodies (defined herein as less than 5000 mg/liter total dissolved solids), because it recognizes the importance of nutrient supported organic productivity in lakes. Attempts to classify lakes according to relative levels of organic productivity ultimately led to the concept of trophic state. Early related to the vertical oxygen distribution within the water column (Thienemann, 1925), trophic state has since been redefined by Hutchinson (1969) and Mortimer (1969) on hypolimnetic oxygen consumption rates, by Hooper (1969) on organic carbon productivity, again by nutrient supply (Beeton and Edmondson, 1972), and most recently using algal biomass (Carlson, 1977). The terms commonly used are *eutrophic* for highly productive lakes, *oligotrophic* for low productivity lakes, and *mesotrophic* for intermediate productivity lakes. With few modifications (Hutchinson, 1969) or exceptions (Richardson and Richardson, 1972), such concepts have been applied to numerous lake systems throughout the world, although quantification remains a problem.

The importance of the effects of organic productivity on lake sediments cannot be neglected. Photosynthetic fixation of carbon and nutrient utilization is a *prime driving force* for precipitation of "inorganic" mineral phases of endogenic origin in freshwater lakes. Equally important, sedimentation of organic matter on the lake floor and its subsequent oxidation are *primary driving forces* for sediment oxygen consumption and the subsequent effects of reduction on mobilization of elements such as iron, phosphorus, manganese, and sulfur.

In essence, then, the allogenic fraction of lake sediments can be considered as reflecting primarily physical factors in lake systems (erosion and transport), whereas the endogenic and authigenic fractions reflect principally chemical factors in lake systems. The importance of organic productivity in lakes is merely underscored here; the *effects* of such processes will be elaborated on in the ensuing pages of this chapter.

[2]Both endogenic and authigenic fractions are combined here because, as will be shown in the following text, the two fractions can generally be related to variations in lake productivity.

Factors of importance in sediment–water interaction

To this point in the discussion we have emphasized the three major sources of lake sediments (allogenic, endogenic, and authigenic) and the importance of these sources in helping to understand the character of lake sedimentation processes. Moreover, one can recognize that lake sediments play an active role in regulating the composition of lake systems. To understand the *kinetics* of mass transfer of substances across the sediment–water interface, and the *processes* that regulate interfacial transport of important solutes in lakes, several additional factors involved in lake–sediment interaction must be considered. Of particular importance are the effects of sediment grain size, pore fluid processes, the effects of biological mixing and sediment resuspension, and variations in rates of sedimentation.

Grain size

One of the most important factors in determining mechanisms and rates of transfer of solutes between lake water and sediments is grain size. The role of silicate and oxide surfaces in regulating the aquatic chemistry of trace metals, organic compounds, and nutrient elements was set out clearly by Jenne (1968) and expanded on more recently (Jenne, 1977). The associated principles of surface chemistry have been detailed by Parks (1967, 1975). The concepts have been applied by Gibbs (1977) to Amazon and Yukon river transport of transition metals and by various authors (Krenkel, 1975; Singer, 1973) to aquatic chemistry and limnology in general.

Because of the importance of surface reactions in lake sediments, it is clear that fine-grained materials have the most potential for interaction with lake water. Surface areas of typical clay-size sediment are measured in square *meters* per gram (Grim, 1968), whereas sandsize sediment areas are measured in tens of square *centimeters* per gram. As pointed out by Jenne (1968), because amorphous and crystalline ferric oxides most commonly occur as surface coatings on grains, they are able "to exert chemical activity which is far out of proportion to their [mass] concentration."

More recently, Gibbs (1977) provided data suggesting that thickest coatings of iron and mangenese oxides on river-transported particles occur not on the smallest grains but on silt-size particles. He postulated that the oxide coatings are inherited in the weathering zone and, therefore, are not the result of river-transport processes. He suggested that in the weathering zone the rate of supply of metals to the grains is the controlling factor. This, in turn, can be related to the higher permeability of coarser grained soils.

The detrital organic matter resulting from lake productivity is relatively fine grained and low in density, thus tending to accumulate with the fine-grained silicate fraction. Because oxidation of organic matter is an essential factor in most sediment diagenesis (or authigenesis), such sediments are generally the most chemically reactive parts of the lake system.

Porosity of lake muds typically range from 70 to 95% (Robbins and Callender, 1975) as compared to values generally less than 40% for sands (Blatt *et al.*, 1972). The relatively greater capacity of muds for compaction, then, means that the total advective transport of solutes to the lake by compaction will be greater for muds than for sands. Moreover, the fact that surface area to solid mass ratios of fine sediments is much higher than that for sands means that relatively small diagenetic changes in the solid phases will be reflected in relatively greater pore fluid concentration changes in the fine-grained sediments. Advective and diffusive transport of solutes diagenetically regenerated from fine-grained sediments is clearly more important than for coarser sediments.

Mineralogic differences in clays are also important in regulating solute transfer to lake waters because of the variations in surface area for different minerals of equivalent grain size and the significant differences in ion-exchange and sorptive capacity of various clay mineral species encountered in lakes (see, for example, Table 1).

The more recent work of Jenne (1977) emphasizes several features of clay minerals in sediments that are important to processes and kinetics of solute transfer between lake waters and sediments. Briefly summarized they are:

(1) For trace metal and organic sorption in fine-grained sediments the clay mineral phase can be viewed simply as a mechanical substrate upon which organics and secondary minerals are precipitated.

(2) Mechanistically the processes of precipitation and sorption on mineral substrates are not distinguishable. Conceptually, adsorption is analagous to precipitation of solid solutions of variable composition.

(3) The specific adsorption capacity of metals on surfaces can be limited. Because of the ability of layer silicate surfaces to catalyze reactions, or to promote hydrolysis, cleavage, and decomposition, reaction mechanisms may be different for the same element in trace versus macro-concentrations in sediments.

(4) The more important trace metal sinks in sediments are thermodynamically unstable species that tend to be amorphous or poorly crystalline and exhibit extensive isomorphic substitution.

(5) "Armoring" of the substrate with metal oxide and organic coatings is common, "slowing rates of

TABLE 1.   Cation Exchange Capacity and Surface Areas of Typical Clay Minerals

	Kaolinite	Illite	Chlorite	Smectite	Vermiculite	Source/ technique
Cation exchange capacity (meq/100 g)	3–15	10–40	10–40	80–150	100–150	a
Surface area (m²/g)	16	56		38		b
	12	52–82		203–250		c
	114		92	234	75	d
	57		97	221	87	e
	19	127		778		f
	20	139		775	237	g
				760	548	h

[a]Grim (1968): typical range of values listed.
[b]Grim (1968): nitrogen adsorption (BET).
[c]Grim (1968): water vapor adsorption.
[d]Bower and Hatcher (1966): ethylene glycol adsorption.
[e]Bower and Hatcher (1966): Cl⁻ repulsion (negative adsorption).
[f]Bower (1963): Langmuir O-phenanthroline method.
[g]Bower (1963): ethylene glycol adsorption.
[h]Milford and Jackson (1962): glycerol adsorption.

reaction of substrates with associated water." This latter observation of Jenne's (1977) should be tempered by consideration of recent experimental work by Petrović (1976), Petrović et al., (1976), and Berner and Holdren (1977) on the dissolution of alkali-feldspars, and on the studies of potassium uptake kinetics in Brazilian soils by Goedert (1973), which indicate that dissolution reactions alone do not lead to uniform and continuous coatings on mineral grains.

(6) Specific adsorption of metals may be more important for some metal–clay or metal–oxide systems (Kinniburgh, 1974.)

(7) Ion-exchange capacity of the clay mineral substrate is generally inadequate to explain total metal adsorption capacity in lake–sediment systems.

The essence of the substrate and coating concepts for the interaction of other sediment phases with clays is schematically illustrated in Figure 1 (taken from Jenne, 1977). A simple change of scale replacing the clay particle with an entire lacustrine sediment mass demonstrates the applicability of the conceptual model.

Pore fluids

Chemical reaction between the organic and inorganic phases of lake sediments and fluids trapped within (or moving slowly through) the sediments is a significant process in most lake systems. The chemical gradients existing between the sediments and overlying lake water and the largely physical processes of sediment compaction and bioturbation cause the transfer of water and solutes across the sediment–water interface. Thus, chemical interaction between lakes and sediments is largely regulated through solute transfer associated with pore fluid processes. This interrela-

tionship between sediments and lakes is of critical importance especially with regard to the dynamics of nutrient elements.

The essential aspects of sediment/water interaction in lakes are illustrated in Figure 2, modified from Lerman (1977). Pathways to the sediment are through allogenic and endogenic particulate transport and burial of pore fluids. Fluxes from the sediment are largely dissolved solutes and arise from: molecular diffusion, compaction, bioturbation, and groundwater discharge in coarser-grained porous sediment. A brief recap of recent progress on pore fluid studies, especially as it applies to freshwater lakes, is presented below to underscore several essential elements of lake water–sediment interaction that are important factors in the mineralogy and chemistry of lake sediments:

(1) Authigenic phases form in sediments from specific reactions between unstable or metastable solid phases and the pore fluids, and, thus, pore fluid compositions are reflections of these processes.

(2) Barely detectable changes in the composition of the solid sediment phases (precipitation/dissolution, sorption/desorption, ion exchange, etc.) are reflected in substantial changes in the composition of pore fluids. These fluids are readily separated from the sediments and are more amenable to direct analysis than are the critical individual solid phases.

(3) Profiles of pore fluid compositional changes through the sediment–water interface indicate whether aqueous solutes are being taken up or released by solid–liquid reactions in the sediment, and, therefore, are indicators of the direction of reactions. Such information can be used to evaluate the relative stability of detected or presumed authigenic sediment phases.

(4) Deeper in the sediments where pore fluid profiles

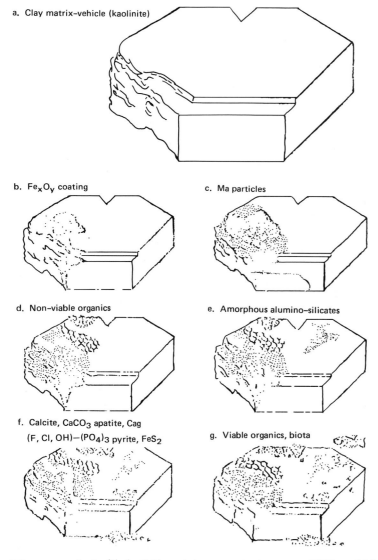

a. Clay matrix–vehicle (kaolinite)

b. Fe$_x$O$_y$ coating

c. Ma particles

d. Non-viable organics

e. Amorphous alumino–silicates

f. Calcite, CaCO$_3$ apatite, Cag
(F, Cl, OH)–(PO$_4$)$_3$ pyrite, FeS$_2$

g. Viable organics, biota

FIGURE 1.   Diagrammatic representation of trace-metal sinks on clay surface (from Jenne, 1977).

are near constant with depth the solute concentrations can be used to evaluate whether specific phases are controlling the fluid composition.

(5) Depth profiles of specific solute concentrations in pore fluids across the sediment–water interface, combined with information on sediment accumulation and bioturbation rates, allow quantitative estimates of the *flux* of solutes into or from the sediments.

To date, extension of Fick's laws of diffusion to models of marine and lacustrine sediments has involved: (1) inclusion of sedimentation rate, compaction, and solid mixing processes in describing advective transport of fluids; (2) modification of diffusion coefficients for tortuosity, or the increased path length a solute ion must traverse by following the interconnected pore spaces in sediments; and (3) inclusion of first-order chemical reaction terms for solutes. Recently considerable attention has been given to the effects of sediment adsorption (Berner, 1976a, 1976b,

1977) and bioturbation (Schink and Guinasso, 1977; Goldhaber *et al.*, 1977) on diffusional transport of solids and fluids in sediments. Such processes are especially important in lake systems.

Dynamic interactions between lake waters and sediments are generally important over distances ranging from a few centimeters to a few tens of centimeters, a distance over which porosity changes with depth are not generally important. Schink and Guinasso (1977) proposed a steady-state (i.e., $\partial c/\partial Z = 0$) model for the distribution of silica in sediments which takes into account bioturbation, adsorption, and dissolution. They recognized the need to describe separately the solid and fluid phases of the sediment and proposed model equations of the form:

$$0 = \phi D_c(\partial^2 c/\partial Z^2) - \nu(\phi + K^*_D)\partial c/\partial Z$$
$$+ K_B B(c_f - c)/c_f \quad \text{(fluid phase)}$$

and

$$0 = D_B(\partial^2 B/\partial Z^2) - \nu(\partial B/\partial Z)$$
$$- K_B B(c_f - c)/c_f \quad \text{(solid phase)}$$

where: ϕ = porosity,

D_c = diffusion coefficient of aqueous species (corrected for tortuosity),

c = concentration of dissolved species in aqueous phase,

Z = depth in sediment relative to the sediment–water interface,

ν = sedimentation rate of solid and fluid phase,

K^*_D = effective adsorption coefficient of dissolved species on solid phases,

K_B = dissolution rate (first order) of solid phase reacting to form the aqueous species in interstitial water,

B = concentration of dissolvable particulate material in bulk sediment (solids and fluids),

c_f = concentration of the species at saturation in fluid phase, and

D_B = rate of vertical mixing of sediment solid phases (bioturbation).

From left to right the three terms in each equation represent diffusion, advection by sedimentation, and chemical reaction, respectively.

Appropriate to lake studies in situations where the sedimentation rate is moderately high (approx. 3 mm/year and greater), and where sediment adsorption of ions is rapid and strong, Berner (1976a) demonstrated that advective transport (because of deposition and compaction) can become more important than diffusional transport, thus illustrating that disequilibrium pore fluid profiles can be preserved more readily in lake systems. Similarly Lasaga and Holland (1976) evaluated a model of diffusion for non-steady-state sedimentation conditions ($dc/dt \neq 0$) and showed that nonequilibrium pore fluid profiles can be produced in rapidly depositing sediments (approximately 3 mm/year or more) in response to irregular distribution of oxidizable organic carbon in the sediment.

Actual measurements of pore fluid profiles for a number of aqueous solutes in coastal estuaries have shown that temporal variations with periods of a year or less are readily observed (Goldhaber *et al.*, 1977; Matisoff *et al.*, 1975). In Chesapeake Bay strong temporal variations in chloride and sulfate concentrations were observed to depths of 20 and 50 cm, respectively, with a periodicity of less than 1 year (Matisoff *et al.*, 1975). Similar rapid variations of chloride were detected down to 20 cm in Lake Wingra sediments by Paddock (1975).

The chloride data from Matisoff *et al.* (1975) were modelled by Holdren *et al.* (1975). A best fit to the data was found for an annual periodic variation super-

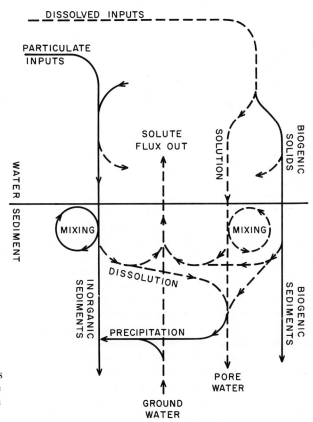

FIGURE 2.   Transport and reaction paths between sediments and lake water (modified from Lerman, 1977). Solid phase routes indicated by solid lines; solute phase routes shown by dashed lines.

imposed on a long-term (approx. 25-year cycle) decrease in average chloride content. More recent work
on Long Island Sound (Goldhaber et al., 1977) has
shown that successful models of sulfate distribution
must include consideration of the mechanisms of bioturbation as well as temporal effects.

Temporal variations in pore fluid chemistry are particularly important in lake systems, especially in the
upper 10–20 cm of the sediment. This is the critical
zone for transfer of solutes between the sediment and
overlying water, and, therefore temporal changes
must be accounted for in quantitative studies of nutrient and trace metal fluxes between lake sediments
and waters. Short-term periodic variations in lake
water properties associated with, for example, seasonal temperature changes, lake overturn, productivity, storm runoff (e.g., chloride in northern U.S. lakes
where NaCl is used for snow removal), and long-term
variations such as might be related to climatic or
cultural development factors, all have direct effects on
temporal variations in lake sediment pore fluid
chemistry.

In fresh water lake systems the effects of ion–ion
interaction can probably be safely ignored for major
ions. However, metal complexation by organic ligands
in lacustrine pore fluids is important (Rashid, 1974;
Lerman and Childs, 1973) and may have to be considered in estimating transport of these pore fluid species
in lake systems.

Several investigators have used pore fluid chemistry
to evaluate authigenic phase changes occurring in sediments. Though shallow pore fluid gradients are controlled by several kinetic processes, pore fluid profiles
deeper in the sediment column tend to show less depth
variation, implying possible equilibrium control on
pore fluid concentrations.

In proposing a steady-state model for manganese
diagenesis in Lake Michigan, Robbins and Callender
(1975) demonstrated that decreasing concentration of
extractable manganese in the solid sediment with
depth was caused by diagenetic remobilization of
manganese with subsequent diffusion out of the sediment and reuptake of manganese deeper in the sedi-
ment. Estimation of the ion activities of Mn^{2+} (0.65×10^{-5}) and CO_3^{2-} (0.48×10^{-5}) at depth in the sediment
yielded an activity product of 3.12×10^{-11} which is
close to that estimated for rhodochrosite ($MnCO_3$) at
$10°C$ ($K_{sp} = 3 \times 10^{-11}$) and, thus, led them to conclude
that rhodochrosite solubility was controlling the Mn^{2+}
concentration in the pore fluids deeper in the core.
Direct evidence for the occurrence rhodochrosite was
not found, although this is not too surprising, considering the fine-grained character of the sediment. Rhodochrosite has, however, been obtained directly from
cores in nearby Green Bay (Callender et al., 1974).
Similar studies by Holdren et al. (1975) conclude that
rhodochrosite solubility is controlling the concentra-

tion of Mn^{2+} in the deeper pore fluids in Chesapeake
Bay sediments.

In a study of cores from the eutrophic Greifensee in
Switzerland Emerson (1976) attempted to evaluate
controls on the composition of phosphorus, iron, and
manganese using pore fluid data combined from several cores. From straightforward ion activity product
calculations he concluded that: (1) calcite is undersaturated in the upper few centimeters of the core, but is
at saturation deeper in the core; (2) phosphate concentrations are controlled by equilibrium with respect to
vivianite; (3) pore fluids are 10-fold supersaturated
with respect to siderite; (4) generally, rhodochrosite is
undersaturated in the sediments; and (5) the presence
of orthorhombic sulfur is possible as a reactant in the
formation of pyrite from iron monosulfides. Several
considerations make it difficult to unequivocally prove
mineral equilibrium control in the study, including:
uncertainty about the uncomplexed fraction of iron in
pore fluids, the form of iron sulfides present in the
sediment, and the possible existence of solid solution
in carbonate phases such as calcic-rhodochrosite (Callender et al., 1974) and manganosiderite. E. Jenne
(personal communication) has evaluated Emerson's
calculations using a modified version of the WATEQ
computer model of Truesdell and Jones (1974) and
concurs that Emerson's conclusions are largely war-
ranted within the possible error in his measurements.
However, in addition, Jenne has been able to show
that the full range of Emerson's data is not inconsistent with saturation with respect to rhodochrosite.
Presumably because of the fine-grained character of
the sediments Emerson (1976) made no attempt to
verify his conclusions by examining the solid phases
from the sediments. His study must be regarded, however, as one of the most complete of its kind to date,
and, hopefully, will stimulate further studies of a similar kind on lake sediments.

Significant improvements of our understanding of
sediment diagenetic processes and their role in influencing the composition of lakes must include study of
both the solid phases and associated fluid phases and
their changes with depth in the sediment. Virtually
every publication on pore fluid processes is notably
lacking in parallel studies of the mineralogy or chemistry of the solid phases. Second, trends in application
of pore fluid studies to lake sediments will be toward
measurement of more chemical parameters than have
been measured in the past. Redundance of measurements will allow more confidence in the conclusions
drawn from models of solid–fluid phase interactions.
For example, although the measurement of any two of
the four parameters pH, alkalinity, p_{CO_2}, or ΣCO_2 will
enable complete description of aqueous carbonate
equilibria in freshwater lakes, measurements of three
of the parameters will serve as a better check on the
results. Third, more concern must be shown for col-

lection of lake sediment pore fluid data over several periods of time. Only limited conclusions can be drawn from one-time only studies, especially if such studies are directed toward understanding and quantifying the dynamics of interchange between sediments and lake waters. Finally, further attention should be given to the effect of hydraulic head gradients across the sediment. The chemical profile cannot be confidently evaluated without establishing the direction of the gradient and rate of water movement, even in very fine-grained materials.

Biologic mixing (bioturbation) and sediment resuspension

Inasmuch as diffusional transport and advective transport by deposition were considered to be the major pathways of transport of various solutes between lake water and sediments (Berner, 1971; Lerman and Brunskill, 1971; Mortimer, 1971; Moore and Silver, 1975; Manheim, 1976), modeling of sediment pore fluid transport processes has generally emphasized the roles of sediment compaction, rapid sedimentation, and groundwater as the important advective or mass transfer processes in solute transport (Berner, 1971, 1974, 1976a; Lasaga and Holland, 1976). In the past few years, however, the important role of biological mixing, or bioturbation, and/or sediment resuspension has come to be appreciated as a major solute transfer process in bottom sediments of organically productive waters such as lakes and coastal marine sediments (for example, Schink and Guinasso, 1977; Goldhaber *et al.*, 1977; Bruland *et al.*, 1975; Benninger *et al.*, 1977). Significant infaunal populations of. burrowing and ingesting organisms are present in a wide variety of lake sediment environments and can efficiently mix sediments over dimensions of several centimeters over relatively short periods of time (Wetzel, 1975). In addition, nektonic organisms, such as sculpin and *Pontoporeia,* can significantly stir the sediment surface by their feeding habits. Tubificid oligochaetes can even enhance the *deposition* of phosphorous (Davis *et al.*, 1975). It seems clear that the processes connected with benthic zoofauna of lakes are effective in the transport of fluids and solid sediments near the sediment–water interface, and, therefore, must be considered in lake sedimentation processes.

Transport of solid phases by advective mixing (eddy diffusion) has recently been modeled by Guinasso and Schink (1977) and Goldhaber *et al.* (1977). The one-layer mixing model of Guinasso and Schink (1977) illustrates the importance of the ratio of the mixing rate (D_B) to the rate of sedimentation (ν). Assuming a bioturbate mixed layer of depth L overlying sediment with no biological (or physical) mixing they illustrated how variations in the sedimentation rate and biologic mixing rates could modify the depth distribution of a

transient impulse of sedimentation (the factor: $G \equiv D_B/L\nu$). Intuitively it can be seen that if biologic mixing rates are slow relative to sedimentation rates ($G < 0.02$) transient solid phase variations will be little modified by bioturbation and, thus, well preserved in the sediment record. If, on the other hand, biologic mixing rates are rapid relative to sedimentation rates ($G > 3$) the mixing process will effectively smooth out short-term sedimentation rate variations over the mixing depth (L).

Bioturbation rates of many sediments are typically lower than fluid diffusion rates. Hence, pore fluid profiles are generally little affected by such mixing processes (that is, equilibrium is established in short times relative to disturbance by mixing). Estimates of sediment mixing rates vary from 1.65×10^{-11} to 1.8×10^{-7} cm²/sec (Guinasso and Schink, 1975; Nozaki *et al.*, 1977; Robbins *et al.*, 1977) compared to typical pore fluid diffusion rates of 10^{-6} cm²/sec (Manheim, 1976). Exceptions occur in some coastal marine waters and in lake sediments with abundant benthic faunal communities. Thus, bioturbation may be a more important process in modifying depth variations of solid phases than in disturbing pore fluid profiles in all but the most rapidly mixed sediments. These models, however, have been applied mainly to marine water. The generally higher sedimentation rates and greater organic productivity of many lakes would indicate that mixing models should be particularly useful in lake sediment studies.

At this point two essential features of bioturbation and sediment resuspension processes emerge in terms of their importance in lake–sediment solute interaction.

(1) Advective mixing must be evaluated to be able to accurately calculate mass fluxes of solutes to and from the sediments in cases where mixing rates are high relative to sedimentation rates and rates of diffusion of dissolved species.

(2) The effect of mixing processes on the mineral phases of sediments is important in most lake systems and, therefore, must be better evaluated.

Sedimentation rates

Systematic studies of sedimentation rate variations are fundamental to interpretation of a variety of lake–sediment interaction processes, and, just as important, to analysis of the kinetics of transfer between the lake–sediment reservoirs. Mass accumulation rates of not only minerals, but also organic debris, nutrient elements, and trace metals in sediments and their temporal variations require accurate and meaningful sedimentation rate determinations. Calculation of regenerative fluxes from sediments requires knowledge of diffusive fluxes of elements from the sediments *and* mass accumulation rates. Estimates of the relative importance of lake sediment sources (river inputs, shore erosion, endogenic precipitation) incorporate sedimentation rate data in the calculations. And, finally, studies of temporal variations in lacustrine sedimentation and the relation of such variations to climatic and/or anthropogenically induced changes in lakes, again, require knowledge of sedimentation rates and their temporal variations over time scales generally ranging from a few years to a few tens of thousands of years.

Estimates of lake sedimentation rates have used a variety of methods (see also Chapter 6). Single event dates, such as a low-level lake stand in Lake Michigan using a radiocarbon dated, shell-rich horizon (Hough, 1963), and the accumulation of sediments since the last glaciation in Lake Superior (Dell, 1974; Bruland *et al.,* 1975; Maher, 1977) yield rates of sedimentation averaged over the total time period.

Perhaps the most common technique used in sedimentation rate determinations in the U.S. is based on the rapid rise of ragweed pollen *(Ambrosia)* following extensive forest clear-cutting and soil cultivation by man in the latter part of the last century (see for example, Bortleson and Lee, 1972; Craig, 1972; Davis, 1968; Kemp *et al.,* 1974; and Maher, 1977). Similarly, Nriagu and Bowser (1969) found a rise in the fly-ash content of sediments following initiation of coal burning in south central Wisconsin; similar patterns for lead in Lake Michigan were found by Edgington *et al.* (1974). Coincidence of the fly-ash and ragweed pollen distributions in Lake Mendota sediments was verified by Bortleson and Lee (1972).

The most recent dating techniques have used the natural radioisotope lead-210 (Krishniswami *et al.,* 1971; Koide *et al.,* 1973) and the bomb fallout nuclide cesium-137 (Pennington *et al.,* 1973). The relatively short lived isotopes (22.3 years for ^{210}Pb and 30 years for ^{137}Cs) are ideally suited for lake sediments whose rates of sedimentation are on the order of a few millimeters per year.

Bioturbation effects on postdepositional mobility of the nuclides are important. Bruland *et al.* (1975), Robbins and Edgington (1975), Robbins *et al.* (in press), and Nozaki *et al.* (1977) have all, for example, interpreted nonlinear log ^{210}Pb activity versus depth plots as simple one-layer mixed zones of a relatively constant activity (a few centimeters in thickness) overlying a nonmixed lower zone extending to below the zone of excess ^{210}Pb activity in the core. Mixing depths of the relatively short-lived radionuclide ^{137}Cs ($t_{1/2}$ = 30 years) in Lake Michigan were reported to depths of 8 cm (Robbins and Edgington, 1975) and to depths near 50 cm in Lake Ontario (Bowen and Noshkin, 1973). Similar arguments using ^{210}Pb profiles in Lake Superior suggest an approximately 2-cm-thick bioturbation zone (Bruland *et al.,* 1975). Typical plots are shown in Figure 3.

From Fick's first law of diffusion for steady-state diffusion of a radionuclide strongly adsorbed to the solid sediment fraction, in a sediment of constant porosity (ϕ), and undergoing decay by first-order reaction kinetics,

$$\frac{\partial B}{\partial t} = D_B(\partial^2 B/\partial Z^2) - \nu(\partial B/\partial Z) - \lambda B = 0$$

where B = concentration of radionuclide in bulk phase of sediment,

D_B = rate of vertical mixing,

Z = depth from sediment water interface,

ν = sedimentation rate, and

λ = decay constant of radionuclide,

where, as shown earlier, the three terms left to right represent eddy diffusion, advection due to deposition, and chemical reaction (decay), respectively. With no mixing the deposition and decay terms dominate the expression, giving a typical radionuclide activity vs depth curve, as in Figure 3a. If bioturbate mixing is rapid relative to sedimentation and decay a zone of constant radionuclide activity (apparent infinite sedimentation rate) is produced; below the zone of bioturbation a normal nuclide decay pattern is produced, as in Figure 3b. If the mixing rate term and the sum of the deposition rate and decay rate terms are nearly equal, however, the radionuclide activity vs depth profile will appear as a break in the sedimentation rate, and thus indistinguishable from a case with an actual change in sedimentation rate.

The steepening of radionuclide activity depth curves due to sediment mixing gives the *effect* of a greater sedimentation rate in the upper sediment column. Such effects can be erroneously interpreted as increased sedimentation rates, possibly due to the effects of man on the lake and its surroundings, when, in fact, they are merely steady-state profiles. Such profiles require in addition careful examination of the quantitative mineral composition and chemistry of the sediment as a function of depth to help test whether or not such profiles are the result of changes in sedimentation rates of any sediment fraction. Note here that constancy in the mineralogical and solid phase chemical composition are neither necessary nor sufficient conditions to prove steady-state deposition. Mineralogic and chemical *variability* with depth is, however, indicative of non-steady-state sedimentation (for example, Bruland *et al.,* 1975).

Transient appearance of some sedimentological event (as, for example, a rapid rise in ragweed pollen deposition) is effectively mixed downward into older sediment, thus increasing the *apparent* depth of sediment deposited since onset of the event. The depth concentration characteristics of such transient events were described by Schink and Guinasso (1977). The effect of bioturbation in tending to cause *overestimation* of sedimentation following recognizable transient

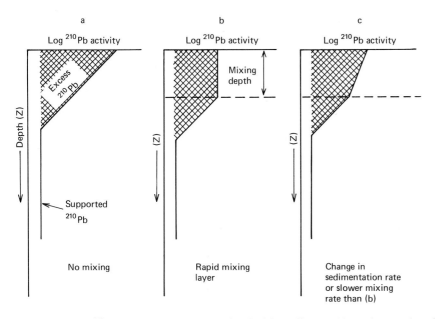

FIGURE 3.   Log ^{210}Pb concentration vs depth plots for lake sediments: (a) steady state deposition, no mixing; (b) steady state deposition, rapid mixed upper sediment layer; (c) steady state deposition, slower mixing of upper sediment layer *or* non-steady-state deposition.

events in the lake sediment records means that interpretation of, for example, pollen records should be used with great caution.

Several examples of high mixing rates have been published recently from the Great Lakes region. Mixing depths of up to 7.0 cm were found by Edgington and Robbins (1976) in Lake Michigan, for example. In a whole-lake fertilization experiment Schindler (1976) found that the layer of nutrient-enriched sedimentary detritus was rapidly (less than 1 year) mixed down to an average depth of 6 cm by the zoobenthos in a small lake on the Canadian Shield. Johansen and Robbins (1977) have reported ^{210}Pb and ^{137}Cs evidence for biological mixing to depths of 10 cm in Southern Lake Huron; Krezoski and Robbins (1977) and Robbins *et al.* (1977) demonstrated nearly the same depth distribution for zoobenthic oligochaetes and *Pontoporeia*. Evanko (1977) found significant populations of benthic crutaceans (up to 100,000 organisms/m²) at depths of 5 cm in Lake Erie sediments, including one species which burrowed to depths of 30 cm. In a controlled laboratory study McCall and Fisher (1977) showed that typical sediment population densities of the oligochaete *Tubifex* (5–100 × 10³ individuals/m²) were capable of completely reworking the top 5 cm of sediment every 2 weeks.

Sedimentation rates were determined using the rise in ragweed *(Ambrosia)* pollen and the decline in chestnut *(Castanea)* pollen in lakes Erie, Huron, and Ontario by Kemp *et al.* (1974). Average sedimentation rates for each lake were listed as 6.1 ± 4.3, 1.0 ± 0.4, and 2.5 ± 1.7 mm/year, respectively, without consid-

ering bioturbation. With a fixed depth of biologic mixing, the *apparent* depth of sediment deposited since a given time is approximately equal to the *actual* thickness of sediment deposited *plus* the depth of rapid biologic mixing. Thus, the error in sediment rate estimate due to bioturbation is greater the shorter the time interval over which sedimentation rates are measured. For example, the *differences* in post-1930 and pre-1930 sedimentation rates calculated by Kemp *et al.* (1974) for Lake Ontario cores could be eliminated by having bioturbate mixing depths ranging from 0.4 to 10 cm. Moreover, since feeding activity of the zoobenthic burrowing communities is regulated by available nutrients and carbon sources, one would expect biologic mixing depths *and* rates to be greater in more productive lakes. The importance of anthropogenic trace metal, nutrient, and pollutant loadings on sediments can be judged only from knowledge of recent sedimentation rates (for example, Kemp and Thomas, 1976). Biologic mixing rates and depths must be considered before accurate assessment of potential cultural effects can be evaluated.

To consider elements that are carried to lake sediments and partly remobilized diagenetically and diffused into the overlying water, one must identify the fraction that is remobilized compared to the fraction that remains in the sediment. For example, Callender (personal communication) has estimated that the average regenerative flux of phosphorus from White Lake, Michigan, sediments is nearly 12% of that which is deposited by lake sedimentation.

To estimate the fraction of diagenetically remobilized metals, nutrients, etc., from sediments requires knowledge of the mass accumulation rates. Mass accumulation rates of a sediment component are calculated directly from bulk sedimentation rates by converting total sedimentation rate to total mass accumulation rate (correcting for porosity and sediment density) and multiplying the total mass accumulation rate by the analyzed mass fraction of the component. Coupled with quantitative mineralogic (or chemical) data mass accumulation rate maps for specific mineral (or chemical) components can be generated. This would overcome the problem in proper interpretation of percentage maps caused by the superposition of differences in sedimentation rates for each of the phases. Percentage variation alone does not allow the sedimentation pattern for any one mineral (or, for that matter, any element in a sample analysis) to be uniquely determined. The limitations of mineral or chemical *percentage* maps seem obvious enough, especially as such maps are used to analyze source directions for specific phases; however, use of such plots is common in the literature.

Chemical composition of lake sediments

Major and minor element chemical analyses of lake sediments from a variety of environments and geographical localities are tabulated in Table 2. No attempt is made to provide an unbiased sample of the range of compositions that lacustrine sediments exhibit but merely to illustrate some typical lake analyses.

A review of the analyses presented here reveals considerable compositional variation, yet a number of factors prevents one from drawing any generalizations about lake sediment compositions from the data. First, complete chemical analyses of sediments are surprisingly rare in the literature; the most complete analyses seemingly are more common in the older literature. The trend in sediment analyses seems to be toward specific analyses for the few elements of interest relative to the specific problem addressed by the author. While certainly most economic in terms of objectives of the specific study, it does limit the utility of such data for other kinds of studies. Second, there is little, if any, agreement on standard procedures for these analyses. Some, for example Rossmann (1973), used acid-peroxide extracts of sediments, while others have used techniques ranging from emission spectographic analysis (Degens and Kulbicki, 1973) to classical wet chemistry (Twenhofel, 1933) to HF-HNO₃-perchloric acid fusion and atomic absorption analysis (Bortleson, 1970). As will be shown in the ensuing discussion, knowledge of the specific phase distribu-

tion of each element is critical for many studies, and, therefore, total analyses are of more limited value. The forms of iron in sediments, for example, include several silicate phases (various amphiboles, pyroxenes, clays) magnetite, ferric oxide coatings, sulfides, carbonate, and iron-organic matter.

A few general observations can be drawn from such data. The high calcium values (Lakes Kivu, Michigan, Mendota, for example) normally reflect a significant sediment carbonate fraction. The analyses of sediments high in calcite ($CaCO_3$) and low in Mg can reflect either allogenic or endogenic sources; analyses with both high calcium *and* magnesium, plus balancing carbonate (rarely reported), such as the diatom facies of Lake Kivu, or surficial sediments from Lakes Erie and Michigan, suggest, but do not prove, dolomite, $CaMg(CO_3)_2$, as a component phase (Callender, 1969). In southern Green Bay (Callender, personal communication) the Ca/Mg ratios of sediments are close to stoichiometric dolomite, presumably reflecting actual detrital dolomite input. Allogenic lake sediments containing a reasonably high fraction of relatively unweathered, basaltic silicate matter might also have high Ca and Mg contents. The problems of using nothing but whole sediment analyses for interpretations requiring information on chemical reactivity of specific elements should be obvious.

Silicon to aluminum ratios vary from low values near 2 (Lake Albert) to nearly 15 in Lake Monona sludge. If clastic (allogenic) sediments are predominant, such values would generally reflect variations in the quartz to feldspar ratio. Feldspathic sediments would have Si/Al ratios of approximately 2 or 3, and, of course, more quartzose sediments can have much larger Si/Al ratios. The Si/Al ratios for the several analyses in Hutchinson and Wollack (1940) are highly correlated (correlation coefficient = 0.95) suggesting that both elements reflect the allogenic (clastic) fraction of the sediment with little contribution from endogenic phases. In addition, and perhaps more significantly, considerable amorphous silica (diatoms) is contributed to lake sediments in productive lakes. High Si/Al values in Lakes Kivu, Mendota, Monona, and Crystal undoubtedly reflect this latter productivity effect, whereas the Lake Superior ratio, even though relatively high, probably reflects quartz/feldspar ratios of the sediments.

Similar kinds of sediment grouping using *total* chemical analyses are no doubt possible; however, to draw conclusions from such data can be misleading. Knowledge of the major constituent mineral phases or the combination of total analysis data with analyses that chemically distinguish among major phases is important in understanding the dominant factors which control the lake sediment chemistry (allogenic vs endogenic vs authigenic).

TABLE 2.   Chemical Analyses of Lake Sediments

African Lakes

	L. Kivu							L. Tanganyika	L. Edward	L. Albert
	Organic facies	Carbonate facies	Sulfide facies	Diatom facies	Manganese facies	Aluminum facies	Average analysis			
Source	a									
Si	18.9	18.5	21.3	26.0	24.5	26.3	18.6	26.3	29.2	24.9
Al	4.71	2.65	2.81	3.86	6.14	6.51	4.97	9.95	4.29	12.1
Fe	5.11	5.46	9.93	5.74	6.92	5.53	5.32	5.04	2.38	6.22
Ca	6.00	12.8	3.36	1.36	1.14	0.93	9.51	1.21	3.00	1.36
Mg	0.78	0.60	0.66	0.96	0.96	0.84	1.15	1.21	1.21	1.39
Na	—	—	—	—	—	—	—	—	—	—
K	—	—	—	—	—	—	—	—	—	—
Mn	0.05	0.04	0.03	0.04	0.35	0.13	0.09	0.03	0.03	0.19
P	—	—	—	—	—	—	—	—	—	—
S	—	—	—	—	—	—	—	—	—	—
N	—	—	—	—	—	—	—	—	—	—
CO_2	—	—	—	—	—	—	—	—	—	—
Org C	—	—	—	—	—	—	—	—	—	—
L.O.I.	—	—	—	—	—	—	—	—	—	—
Si/Al	4.01	6.98	7.58	6.74	3.99	4.04	3.74	2.64	6.81	2.06
No. anal.	(31)	(36)	(27)	(44)	(28)	(92)	(381)	(31)	(51)	(92)

Great Lakes

	L. Ontario	L. Erie	L. Michigan		L. Superior	Silver Bay
			Core 115	SE		
Source	b		c	d	e	f
Si	23.9	25.9	25.4	—	24.3	24.98
Al	5.05	4.79	2.75	—	2.38	7.76
Fe	3.74	2.76	1.48	1.24	2.45	9.33
Ca	0.40	0.35	10.8	3.22	1.22	2.41
Mg	1.28	1.28	4.08	1.66	—	2.32
Na	0.53	0.41	0.27	0.03	0.50	1.25
K	2.27	2.17	1.19	0.16	0.05	2.39
Mn	0.06	0.06	0.08	—	—	0.18
P	0.07	0.06	0.13	0.02	—	0.14
S	0.04	0.03	0.08	—	—	0.04
N	—	—	—	—	—	—
CO_2	—	—	—	—	—	—
Org C	—	—	—	2.01	2.30	—
L.O.I.	—	—	—	—	—	6.39
Si/Al	4.73	5.41	9.24	—	10.21	3.22
No. anal.	(1)	(1)	(1)	(1)	(1)	(11)

TABLE 2 *(Continued)*

Source	Minnesota Lakes (46)					Connecticut
	Low organic group	High organic group	Intermediate group	High carbonate group	Low carbonate high organic group	Linsley Pond
			g			h
Si	—	—	—	—	—	22.11
Al	—	—	—	—	—	2.91
Fe	5.01	3.80	2.86	2.21	2.46	8.46
Ca	0.90	1.95	6.35	15.2	6.76	0.86
Mg	0.73	0.43	1.02	0.85	1.67	0.60
Na	0.75	0.40	0.45	0.26	0.73	—
K	1.17	0.66	1.02	0.49	1.23	—
Mn	0.62	0.10	0.19	0.15	0.37	—
P	0.13	0.17	0.21	0.14	0.08	—
S	0.24	0.48	0.47	0.63	1.09	—
N	0.79	2.37	1.06	1.16	0.64	—
CO_2	1.43	2.20	7.66	16.96	9.16	—
Org C	7.59	21.00	9.20	9.85	6.10	—
L.O.I.	17.96	41.92	18.19	19.84	12.40	28.8
Si/Al	—	—	—	—	—	7.60
No. anal.	(8)	(13)	(10)	(10)	(5)	(1)

Source	Wisconsin Lakes					
	L. Mendota (calcareous)				L. Monona (calcareous)	
	Core top	Core bottom	Precultural	Postcultural	Sludge	Core bottom
	i		j		j	k
Si	6.60	9.01	—	—	13.9	4.07
Al	1.95	0.31	2.11	4.59	0.95	2.17
Fe	0.54	0.49	1.09	2.12	2.03	0.48
Ca	24.5	20.9	22.8	22.8	14.9	19.65
Mg	1.60	1.14	1.63	1.68	—	—
Na	—	—	—	1.84	—	—
K	—	—	0.54	1.15	—	—
Mn	—	—	0.05	0.12	—	—
P	—	—	0.10	0.19	—	—
S	—	—	—	—	—	—
N	—	—	—	—	—	—
CO_2	26.7	27.0	—	—	—	—
Org C	—	—	9.46	9.87	9.71	—
L.O.I.	—	—	—	—	34.8	43.7
Si/Al	3.38	29.1	—	—	14.6	1.88
No. anal.	(1)	(1)	(1)	(1)	(1)	(1)

Wisconsin Lakes

	L. Wingra (Calcareous)	Devils Lake (Noncalcareous)	Crystal Lake — Sludge	Crystal Lake — Core "middle"	Little St. Germain L.	Trout Lake	L. Minocqua
					Noncalcareous glacial lakes		
Source	j	l	m		j	j	j
Si	—	24.7	19.26	30.03	—	—	—
Al	0.86	6.39	1.40	8.56	1.61	2.92	3.56
Fe	0.22	2.69	1.31	3.07	9.62	5.72	5.86
Ca	23.8	0.46	0.24	1.69	0.12	0.37	0.26
Mg	0.61	1.39	0.01	0.87	0.24	0.37	0.37
Na	—	Tr	—	—	—	—	—
K	0.07	Tr	—	—	0.36	0.50	0.91
Mn	0.03	0.91	—	—	0.23	0.27	0.16
P	0.05	—	—	—	1.41	0.57	0.73
S	—	—	—	—	—	—	—
N	—	—	—	—	—	—	—
CO_2	—	—	—	—	—	—	—
Org C	6.89	—	—	—	23.5	22.3	18.1
L.O.I.	—	—	53.37	9.42	—	—	—
Si/Al	—	3.87	13.8	3.51	—	—	—
No. anal.	(1)	(1)	(1)	(1)	(1)	(1)	(1)

Wisconsin Lakes

	Weber L.	Little John L.	Devils Lake
	Noncalcareous glacial lakes		
Source		j	
Si	—	—	—
Al	2.84	2.59	7.42
Fe	1.13	3.57	2.48
Ca	0.09	0.31	0.18
Mg	0.22	0.43	0.38
Na	—	—	—
K	0.60	0.52	0.91
Mn	0.03	0.05	0.03
P	0.32	0.17	0.10
S	—	—	—
N	—	—	—
CO_2	—	—	—
Org C	31.7	33.3	12.9
L.O.I.	—	—	—
Si/Al	—	—	—
No. anal.	(1)	(1)	(1)

[a]Degens and Kulbicki (1973).
[b]Kemp and Dell (1975).
[c]Frye and Shimp (1973).
[d]Rossmann (1973).
[e]Nussmann (1965).
[f]Swain and Prokopovich (1957).
[g]Dean and Gorham (1976a).
[h]Hutchison and Wollack (1940).
[i]Twenhofel (1933).
[j]Bortleson (1970).
[k]Twenhofel (1937).
[l]Twenhofel and McKelvey (1939).
[m]Twenhofel and Broughton (1939).

Mineral composition of lake sediments

A summary list of minerals found in lake sediments is presented in Table 3, based almost entirely on field studies in North America, central Europe, and East Africa (principal specific references are given in Table 8). Inasmuch as very little quantitative mineralogy has been done on lacustrine materials, especially on bulk samples, or outside the St. Lawrence Great Lakes, variations in print size are shown in an attempt to estimate the *frequency* of occurrence of lacustrine mineral phases more than the relative amounts.

Examination of the mineral list brings out a few important points. First, the total number of mineral phases that have been identified in lacustrine sediments is small. A list of less than 20 minerals would include the components of all but a tiny fraction of the total mass of freshwater lake sediments. An assemblage including quartz, feldspar, calcite, dolomite, illite, smectite, apatite, and iron sulfides or iron oxides could be offered as representative of all lacustrine materials. Second, it is apparent the three major source types tend to be dominated by certain chemical classes of minerals. Thus, the bulk of the allogenic minerals are the rock-forming aluminosilicates, the endogenic species are dominated at least in quantity by carbonate (calcite), and the most commonly cited examples of mineral authigenesis in lacustrine sediments are oxides, phosphates, and sulfides. Finally, it should be remembered that most of the mineralogic work has been done on the best crystallized material. Better characterization of amorphous or cryptocrystalline material, as, for example, the multiple metal phosphates or mixed layer clays, might well change some impressions about relative importance. Mineral phases that exist in small percentages in sediments may be most useful in terms of what they tell us about some of the critical processes going on within lake systems. The ability to detect and identify these low-concentration phases is one of the most important areas of lake sediment research.

Modern techniques for mineralogic and chemical study of lacustrine sediments

The sampling and analysis of lake sediments are obviously an essential part of chemical and mineralogic study. Recent investigations of lake sediments have indicated that some of the more traditional approaches are either incorrect or at least misleading in the type of results that they can produce. For example, characterization of trace metal chemistry in sediments from sample grabs ignores the fact that such metals typically show strong gradients near the sediment–water interface, and that proper understanding of the process governing the distribution of these metals in sediments must be derived from studies of thin sample intervals from undisturbed cores.

A discussion of the mineralogic and chemical aspects of lake sediments would be incomplete without some exposition of more recent methods for sampling and analysis. Hopefully, some of these techniques will be utilized by a broader group of limnologists and geochemists and employed in future studies of lakes. In part, our purpose here is to expose the reader to some of the varied approaches that are possible.

Sampling

It is obvious that the mineralogy of a lake sediment will be dependent on physiographic environments within the lake and its immediate surrounding area. Runoff from terrain of high relief may supply coarse material with abundant and sometimes mineralogically complex lithic fragments. The mineralogic and compositional maturity of the clastic sediment will be a function of the continued mechanical energy input to that specific portion of the lake. Thus, beaches and sand bars or other areas subject to strong current action favor the resistate minerals, chiefly quartz, whereas the accumulation of organic material, clay, or precipitate minerals takes place under relatively static conditions. Thus, the mineralogic nature of a given lake sediment is characterized by where samples are collected. The sediments from the deepest "hole" of the lake can be taken for mineralogic indications of the trophic level of the lake, or perhaps to assess diagenesis of lake bottom materials, but they are probably not representative of the lake sediment as a whole, nor are they likely to be definitive about sediment source.

Similarly, the mineral composition in lacustrine sediment is likely to vary both with water depth as well as area of the lake. This variation will depend not only on the processes of distribution of sediment over the lake area, but also on rates of sediment accumulation at any given point. Furthermore, it is unlikely that this rate will be uniform, as the input fluctuates with seasonal or climatic change (Anderson, 1977). Temporal changes in materials available for sedimentation, such as clastic sediment associated with spring runoff or organic remains accumulating after a period of high biological productivity, cause variations in the sediment mineral composition over scales ranging from fractions of a millimeter to several centimeters. If burrowing or bottom stirring zoobenthos are absent from the sediment such temporal variations can be preserved as laminated sediment (varves, if the period of obvious compositional variation is 1 year). The

TABLE 3. Minerals Reported from Freshwater Lake Sediments[a]

Mineral	Allogenic	Endogenic	Authigenic
Non-Clay Silicates			
QUARTZ—SiO_2	X		
POTASH FELDSPAR—$KAlSi_3O_8$	X		
PLAGIOCLASE—$(Na,Ca)(Al,Si)Si_2O_8$	X		
Mica—$K(Mg,Fe,Al)_3AlSi_3O_{10}(OH)_2$	X		
Amphibole—$(Ca,Mg,Fe,Al)_{3.5}Si_4O_{11}(OH)$	X		
pyroxene—$(Ca,Mg,Fe)_2Si_2O_6$	X		
(other heavy minerals, $\rho > 3.0$)	X		
OPALINE SILICA (diatoms)		X	
Clays			
ILLITE—$K_{.8}Mg_{.35}Al_{2.26}Si_{3.43}O_{10}(OH)_2$	X		
SMECTITE—$X_{.3}Mg_{.2}Al_{1.9}Si_{3.9}O_{10}(OH)_2$	X		
Chlorite—$Mg_5Al_2Si_3O_{10}(OH)_8$	X		
Kaolinite—$Al_2Si_2O_5(OH)_4$	X		
mixed-layer clays, vermiculite—intermediate	X		?
palygorskite—$(Ca,Mg,Al)_{2.5}Si_4O_{10}(OH)\cdot4H_2O$	X		?
nontronite—$X_{.5}Fe_2Al_{.5}Si_{3.5}O_{10}(OH)_2$	X		X
Carbonates			
CALCITE—$CaCo_3$	X	X	x
DOLOMITE—$CaMg(CO_3)_2$	X		?
Aragonite—$CaCO_3$	x	X	
Mg-Calcite—intermediate		x	X
rhodochrosite—$MnCO_3$			X
monohydrocalcite—$CaCO_3\cdot H_2O$		X	?
siderite—$FeCO_3$	?		?
Fe-Mn Oxides			
GOETHITE, Lepidocrocite—$FeOOH$	X	x	X
MAGNETITE—Fe_3O_4	X		
Hematite, maghemite—Fe_2O_3	X		?
birnessite—$(Na,Ca)Mn_7O_{14}\cdot3H_2O$	?		X
todorokite—$(Na,Ca,K,Ba,Mn)_2Mn_5O_{12}\cdot3H_2O$	?		X
psilomelane—$(Ba,K)(MnO_2)_{2.5}\cdot H_2O$			X
ilmenite—$FeTiO_3$	X		
Phosphates			
APATITE—$Ca_5(PO_4)_3(OH,F)$	X		x
Vivianite—$Fe_3(PO_4)_2\cdot8H_2O$			X
ludlamite—$(Fe,Mn,Mg)_3(PO_4)_2\cdot4H_2O$			X
(?) lipscombite—$Fe_3(PO_4)_2(OH)_2$			X
(?) phosphoferrite—$(Mn,Fe)_3(PO_4)_2\cdot3H_2O$			X
(?) anapaite—$Ca_3Fe(PO_4)_3\cdot4H_2O$			X
Sulfides			
MACKINAWITE—$FeS_{.9}$		x	X
pyrite—FeS_2	X		x
griegite—Fe_3S_4			X
sphalerite—ZnS		x	
Fluoride			
fluorite—CaF_2			X

[a]Print size is varied to illustrate the frequency of occurrence. Illite and smectite formulas are taken from Perry (1971); palygorskite and nontronite formulas are derived from Weaver and Pollard (1973). X in formulas refers to monovalent cation exchange.

secondary homogenization by organisms can go unrecognized when grab samples of surficial bottom sediment are used in lieu of cores.

With increasing concern about changing patterns of lake sedimentation in response to anthropogenic influences, and need to measure steady-state element profiles in the upper several centimeters of sediment where such gradients are significant, or where careful estimates of sedimentation rates require undisturbed upper sediment profiles, it is clear that sediment grab samples are totally inadequate. Moreover the shock wave produced by coring devices which force water and sediment through the core tube is sufficient to blow away the top several millimeters to centimeters of sediment during core entry. Certain kinds of piston corers, gravity corers (for example, Bruland *et al.*, 1975), a special sediment–water interface corer, the Jenkin corer (Mortimer, 1971), and the recently developed box corers (Reineck, 1963; Bouma and Marshall, 1964) can be used to collect virtually undistrubed sediment–water interface samples.

The principal consequence of sampling and handling of lacustrine sediments comes from changes in temperature, moisture content, or oxidation state. The first two seldom affect the actual mineral species present in any but saline lake sediments, but both may significantly influence the distribution of solute species between solution and solid phases, especially in terms of sorption. Of course, calcium carbonate in pore fluids close to saturation may be precipitated by an increase in temperature and concomitant loss of CO_2, and temperature-related effects on the exchange complex of some clay minerals can significantly alter their properties. However, the most profound changes are related to redox potential, especially with respect to carbon, sulfur, phosphate, nitrogen, and transition metals. Introduction of atmospheric oxygen to reduced sediments can bring about precipitation of ferromanganese oxy-hydroxides and associated reactions involving the other constituents (Bray *et al.*, 1973).

Laboratory procedures for mineralogic analysis

Beyond simple sample description and examination with the binocular microscope, particle-size separation is usually the first step in the mineralogic analysis of lacustrine sediments. Major classes of minerals in sedimentary materials are commonly grouped by size. Thus multimineralic aggregates (including fecal pellets) or rock fragments are typical of coarsest fractions. Quartz, feldspar, and heavy minerals (principally silicates and oxides) normally dominate the sand sizes, but diatom frustules may be abundant also. Mica, volcanic glass, or carbonates are most likely found in the silt-size ranges, whereas clay minerals

and oxy-hydroxides are the most common constituents of clay-size lacustrine deposits. A number of lacustrine studies have shown a general correlation between grain size and mineralogy (e.g., Mann, 1951; Nelson, 1967; Court *et al.*, 1972). The most obvious relationship to be expected is the increased percentage of clay minerals with greater depth of water (as in Lake Ontario; Thomas, 1969a) or the larger percentage of crystalline rock phenocryst minerals in littoral zones (as in Lake Elsinore; Mann, 1951). Such simple associations can be severely complicated by prior glacio-fluvial and related lacustrine sedimentation in the basin, such as with Lake Superior (Dell, 1971). Influential factors outside the immediate lake area include the inherent size distribution of soil and bedrock source material, selective transport by streams of varying competence, and local weathering and soil development processes (Gibbs, 1967, 1977).

Particle-size analysis of lacustrine materials done coincidentally with mineralogic study has most frequently employed standard sieve and pipette methods (see Thomas, 1969a, or Gross *et al.*, 1972). Special size separations are usually made for mineralogic purposes; some part of the sand fraction is used for microscopic work (e.g., Court *et al.*, 1972). Clay mineral analysis has typically been done on < 2 μm fractions obtained by settling or centrifugation (Moore, 1961; Dean and Gorham, 1976a); the most detailed work on the alpine lake clays was done on < 1 μm cuts (Quakernaat, 1968). Because of their importance in reflecting minor silicate authigenesis, more attention should be paid to the ultrafine (< 0.5 μm) fractions of lake sediments, which can be separated by high-speed centrifuge just as from soils (Jackson, 1974) or marine sediments (Scafe and Kunze, 1971). At the same time, applying the limits of particle size analysis to mineralogic separations may give an unrepresentative picture. For example, to avoid missing fine silt-size clay mineral particles or aggregates, Potter *et al.* (1975) examined material ranging up to 10 μm in diameter. To date, little use has been made of density gradient or zonal centrifuge methods, though techniques for analysis of fine-grained sediment have been described in detail (Halma, 1969a, 1969b; Bonner *et al.*, 1970; Francis and Tamura, 1972; Francis *et al.*, 1976).

Physical and chemical preparation of samples prior to X-ray diffraction analysis involve a number of important considerations. Washing of the samples is sometimes followed by treatment with some sort of dispersant to ensure uniform settling of finer materials, but the effects of such an agent as sodium hexametaphosphate on dissolution or dispersion of natural colloidal oxy-hydroxide coatings (Cook *et al.*, 1975) and/or of alkali carbonate or dilute ammonium hydroxide on dissolution of amorphous silica (Quakernaat, 1968) are poorly defined. Ultrasonic treatment is the most widely used physical means of disaggregation and dispersal (Thomas, 1969a), but other mechanical means, such as blending, have also been employed (Cook *et al.*, 1975).

Size separation of the inorganic fraction of sediments, especially the finest grained materials, is made difficult because of the presence of significant amounts of organic matter. The most common method used for destruction of organic material prior to mineralogic examination is hydrogen peroxide (e.g., Court *et al.*, 1972; Singer *et al.*, 1972; Dean and Gorham, 1976a). Douglas and Fiessinger (1971) warn that simple peroxide treatment of sediments to oxidize and remove organic matter can bring about rather acid conditions leading to degradation of clay minerals in the sample. They recommend addition of a suitable buffer to maintain the pH in neutral or alkaline ranges. Furthermore, peroxide may oxidize the structural iron of minerals and solubilize Mn oxides under mildly acid conditions, increasing total mineral surface area (Jenne and Luoma, 1977). It is also apparent that peroxide oxidation of sulfides will lower the pH in the same way as formation of oxides from organic acids. This reaction has been utilized as a trace element extractor (Gad and LeRiche, 1966).

Destruction of organic matter by sodium hypochlorite (commercial bleaching agent Chlorox) has been recommended by Anderson (1963). The high pH prevents acid attack, but it is likely to cause oxy-hydroxide precipitation of metals released from organic complexes. Removal of more than 90% of a sample's organic carbon by 0.1 M sodium pyrophosphate has been reported (McKeague, 1967) in the course of extraction of organically complexed Fe and Al from podzolic soils, and this reagent has also been used in lake sediments (Quakernaat, 1968; Thomas, 1969a). On tests with reference clays, hypochlorite was deemed ineffective as a minor metal extractant, whereas pyrophosphate was considered reasonably good (Lahann, 1976); neither treatment had deleterious effects on X-ray diffraction properties of remaining solids.

The relatively small amount of mineralogic microscopy on lake sediments has usually been in connection with density separations of sand fractions for heavy mineral analysis (e.g., Nelson, 1967). The most commonly used heavy liquid has been tetrabromethane (e.g., Moore, 1961; Dell, 1971); light fractions have been slide mounted and stained for differentiation of potash feldspar, plagioclase, and quartz, also (Moore, 1961; Court *et al.*, 1972; Dean and Gorham, 1976a).

Study of the fine-grained aluminosilicate minerals in lacustrine sediments by X-ray diffractometry is normally facilitated by removal of the more soluble or amorphous phases. For carbonate, removal and the

determination of inorganic carbon can be combined, if a buffer is used to prevent dissolution of the phases of interest; for example, Quakernaat (1968) added 0.25 N HCl to a pH of 4.5. For removal of calcite and aragonite, but not dolomite, Dean and Gorham (1976a) treated their samples with molar ammonium acetate at a pH of 5.2 while samples from the Deep Sea Drilling program have been processed with sodium acetate-buffered acetic acid (Cook *et al.*, 1975). A more comprehensive technique has been recommended by Bodine and Fernalld (1973) for removal of sulfate and carbonate minerals from silicate assemblages without undue alteration of clays that may be affected by even mild acid conditions. The method involves boiling in 0.2 M EDTA at a pH of 10. Presumably, ferromagnesian chelation at this pH does not result in disruption of octahedral bonding in sheet silicates.

Besides organics and carbonates, amorphous oxy-hydroxides can cause significant interference in X-ray diffraction analysis of lake sediment. The methods developed for extraction of these materials from soils (e.g., Mehra and Jackson, 1960; McKeague *et al.*, 1971; Jackson, 1974) or pelagic sediments (e.g., Chester and Hughes, 1967) can be applied in the fluvial or lacustrine environment as well (Quakernaat, 1968). The effectiveness of the sodium citrate-dithionite procedure for removal of Fe and Mn oxy-hydroxides was demonstrated on reference clays by Anderson and Jenne (1970), and the dissolution of both amorphous and cryptocrystalline forms was indicated by two different rates. However, structural alteration of clays, particularly interlayer complexes, may result from such treatment (Dudas and Harward, 1971), and the 0.2 M acid ammonium oxalate treatment of Schwertmann (1959, 1964) seems preferable for removal of the amorphous iron oxides (McKeague and Day, 1966). Recently Ugolini and Jackson (1977) have shown that oxalate-leached iron can exceed citrate-dithionite-leached iron in soil samples from Antarctica. Since the amorphous iron fraction (oxalate) should be *less than* the amorphous plus crystalline oxide fraction (citrate-dithionite), they have interpreted their data as indicating structural removal of iron from silicate micas by the oxalate extraction procedure. This was also the conclusion of Subramanian (1975) based on Mössbauer data for citrate-dithionite-treated marine clays.

Manganese oxides can be extracted separately from iron oxides through use of relatively dilute hydroxylamine hydrochloride (Chao, 1972). For removal of amorphous silica and alumina, the sample can apparently be subjected to 2.5 min boiling 0.5 N KOH treatment with minimum dissolution of crystalline components (Dudas and Harward, 1971). Molar hydroxylamine hydrochloride plus 25% acetic acid (Chester and Hughes, 1967), however, will apparently extract the bulk of the carbonate, Mn oxides, and colloidal iron oxy-hydroxide in a single 4-hr treatment with very little structural effect on reference clays (Lahann, 1976).

For the X-ray diffraction analysis of lacustrine or fluvial clays most workers have made oriented mounts on glass slides, filters, or ceramic tiles after saturation of exchange sites with molar salt solutions and washing salt free. Identification was assisted by exposing replicate mounts to vapor of glycerol (Quakernaat, 1968; Dell, 1971; Court *et al.*, 1972) and/or ethylene glycol from 8 hr (Potter *et al.*, 1975) to 1 week (Gross *et al.*, 1972) for expandable phases and heating from 450°C (Moore, 1961) to 550°C (Potter *et al.*, 1975) for differentiation of chlorite.

By and large, few attempts have been made to separate kaolinite from chlorite, or definitively characterize expandable or mixed-layer clay species in lacustrine materials. As exceptions, Singer *et al.* (1972) examined the distribution of kaolinite by means of the 550°C endothermic peak area on differential thermal analysis curves, and Court *et al.* (1972) attempted some differentiation of expandable clays of Lake Tahoe by using Mg saturation plus glycerol, K saturation, and 500°C heating in sequence. Vermiculite has been distinguished from smectite by its lack of expansion with glycerol (as opposed to glycol) and its collapse to 10 Å on K saturation at moderate humidities (Harward *et al.*, 1969), and chlorite has been identified by persistance of the 14-Å peak on heating.

A summary of the procedures recommended for sample preparation and X-ray diffraction examination of fine-grained sediments are listed in Figure 4. If the extraction solutions are to be chemically analyzed to evaluate specific labile or dissolved phases, then procedures specific to those phases should be chosen (see following text).

Some effort has usually been made to at least semi-quantify the X-ray diffraction results obtained on lake sediment samples. The sources of error in all attempts at quantitative X-ray diffraction analysis are mainly threefold, according to Cubitt (1975): instrumental variation, actual differences between replicate samples (including preferred orientation), and inhomogeneity within each individual sample. He found that peak area is more accurate than peak height, and that the best standardization technique was a combination method whereby a calibration curve was made from standard additions of one of the components being determined to samples representing the full range of compositions. Use of MoS_2 as an internal standard added to powdered and pressed (8000 psi) pellets originally proposed by Quakernaat (1970) has been recommended for quantitative diffraction work by Cody and Thompson (1976).

Many of the attempts to present semiquantitative results from X-ray diffraction data on fine-grained lacustrine sediments are based simply on peak area measurement of relative intensities, such as for the

---

SUGGESTED SEQUENCE FOR MINERALOGIC ANALYSIS
OF FINE GRAINED LACUSTRINE SEDIMENTS*

1. Wash with pure H_2O to Ω <300 μmhos/cm^2

2. Disperse ultrasonically

3. Extract organic matter with 0.1M $Na_4P_2O_7$

4. Extract carbonates and amorphous oxides with
   25% v/v acetic acid & 1M $NH_2OH \cdot HCL$

5. Separate size fractions by gravity settling (sedimention or centrifuge)
   examine fractions >10 μm e.s.d.$^+$ with optical microscope

6. Saturate subsamples of all fractions <20 μm e.s.d.$^+$ with 0.5N NaCl, KCl, $MgCl_2$
   wash salt free by high speed centrifuge, dialysis or ultrafine filter

7. Orient mount for x-ray with paste smear, thick suspension, membrane filter,
   or pressed pellet for dried, non or partially treated fraction

8. X-ray diffraction examination
   a) pre-treat Mg saturated subsample with glycerol prior to run
   b) run Na saturated sample untreated and after treatment with ethylene glycol
   c) run K saturated sample untreated
   d) run untreated or Na saturated sample after heating at 550°C

*For chemical analysis of the fluid phase, or association of specific chemical constituents, duplicate samples and other methods are recommended

$^+$ e.s.d. = equivalent spherical diameter

FIGURE 4.   Flow chart of suggested methods of sample preparation for mineralogic studies of fine-grained lake sediments.

profundal sediments of 46 lakes in Minnesota (Dean and Gorham, 1976a), or for the large number of samples obtained from southern Lake Michigan (Gross *et al.*, 1972).

Some estimates of clay species percentage have been based on modifications of the calculation techniques of Johns *et al.* (1954). This method employs the 10-Å illite peak as an internal standard. The relative amounts of other clay minerals are weighted with respect to illite, summed, and equated to 100%. The weighting factors of Johns *et al.* (1954) have either been adopted directly (Moore, 1961; Knebel *et al.*, 1968) or were taken from Schultz (1960, 1964), such as was done by Callender (1969) and Dell (1971). Pierce and Siegel (1969) tried five different calculation schemes based on this approach to get clay mineral percentage from the same diffractograms and, except for the dominance of smectite in their cores, found little uniformity in results. It has been shown elsewhere that even when the greatest care is taken to prepare identical samples for X-ray diffraction examination, considerable variation can be expected in 10-Å peak intensity (Austin and Leininger, 1976). But, the principal problem in the method of Johns *et al.* (1954) could be that the constant weighting factors do not take into account the effects of different matrices on counting rates. Devine *et al.* (1972) have calculated interaction coefficients from peak intensity ratios (which account for inconsistencies in sample preparation and instrumental response) and mass absorption coefficients (which allow for the effects of percentage variations of all minerals on peak intensity from any one species). These effects can also be ascertained through use of a system of reference intensities (Chung, 1974a, 1974b, 1975). Problems may arise from indiscriminate application of the method to only the principal low-angle reflections of clay mineral assemblages that include mixed-layer species, but the potential for refinement recognized by Devine *et al.* (1972) suggests strongly that the technique could provide significant improvement in quantitative data on fine-grained lacustrine sediment mineralogy.

Because of their crystallinity and, as a result, their well-defined reflections, sediments composed of quartz and carbonate minerals have been least subject to the errors incurred in quantitative X-ray diffraction analysis. In some cases, special techniques supplemental to X-ray diffraction have been developed for quantitative analysis of other mineral species. For the differentiation of diatomaceous opal from volcanic glass, which both provide diffuse diffraction interference to X-ray examination of lake sediments from the East African Rift, Richardson and Richardson (1972) heated the sample to 900°C for 4 hr, thereby converting the opaline silica to cristobalite.

The problems of quantitative X-ray techniques can be avoided altogether through "chemical mineralogy," though one might suspect that one set of analytical uncertainties is simply being replaced by another. Thus, quartz and feldspar contents of Great Lakes sediments have been determined by potassium pyrosulfate fusion (Thomas, 1969b); feldspar was differentiated by analysis of Na, K, and Ca on acid dissolution of the fusion residue, with due allowance for composition, cation exchange, adsorption, and grain size effects through comparison with standards.

Carbonate minerals are typically determined as total carbonate through some type of destructive analysis. The most nonspecific technique is that of ignition loss between 550 and 1000°C as utilized by Dean and Gorham (1976a) for carbonate contents greater than 10%. The most common carbonate analysis has been by weight loss or gasometric measurement on addition of HCl (e.g., Moore, 1961; Callender, 1969; Richardson and Richardson, 1972; Singer *et al.* 1972) or sulfurous acid (Thomas, 1969a). A comparison of two methods was afforded by Kennedy and Smith (1977) in the determination of the relative proportions of dolomite and calcite in the alpine Bow and Hector lakes of southwestern Alberta.

The determination of iron oxy-hydroxide phases in sediments is notoriously complex and X-ray diffraction techniques have sometimes proven insensitive even to crystalline forms. A comprehensive evaluation of methodology for the characterization of iron oxides in soils, including chemical, X-ray, Mössbauer spectroscopy, infrared absorption, and differential thermal analysis, has been given by Kodama *et al.* (1977). A fractionation sequence worked out by McKeague (1967, 1968) and colleagues proposed extraction by $0.1\ M\ Na_4P_2O_7$ for organic iron, by $0.2\ M$ acid ammonium oxalate for amorphous iron oxides, and by sodium citrate-dithionite for crystalline iron oxides. Kodama *et al.* (1977) verified the dithionite minus oxalate measure of crystalline oxides, but also Schwertmann's (1973) precautions on excessively restrictive interpretation. The earlier cited results of Ugolini and Jackson (1977), showing oxalate–dithionite extracted iron ratios greater than 1, throw renewed doubt on the use of such techniques to accurately distinguish crystalline from amorphous iron oxide ratios in sediments. The usefulness of the Mössbauer method for identification of small amounts of iron oxide phases which are far lower than X-ray detection limits, and for information on grain size or Fe^{3+}/Fe^{2+} ratios, is also emphasized by Kodama *et al.* (1977).

The association of phosphate with amorphous, cryptocrystalline, or compositionally highly variable phases has led to reliance on extraction techniques to differentiate the forms and amounts of phosphorus present in soils and sediments (Williams and Mayer,

1972). The most extensively tested phosphate fractionation scheme is that of Williams *et al.* (1971a, 1971b); the procedures have been summarized by Syers *et al.* (1973) and, though certainly not free of ambiguity, are probably the best available. The objective is to separate phosphorus sorbed on amorphous (or short-range ordered) iron and/or aluminum oxyhydroxides, or that occluded within crystalline oxides and calcite, from apatite-associated phosphate. The scheme is based on successive extractions with NaOH, sodium citrate-dithionite, and HCl. The sum of the extractable phosphorus in the first steps provides a measure of the iron plus aluminum-associated phosphate, whereas the phosphate removed by the succeeding HCl treatment is considered apatite.

The selective dissolution and chemical allocation schemes devised by Jackson (1974) for the total mineralogic analysis of soils can be applied to lake sediments as well. These techniques must be supplemented by direct phase determinations and interpreted with suitable caution.

New techniques that have recently been utilized for direct examination of very fine-grained material and reactive mineral surfaces include scanning electron microscopy (SEM) and X-ray photoelectron spectroscopy (XPS) (Petrović *et al.*, 1976; Berner and Holdren, 1977). Clastic sediment samples from the Great Lakes have been examined with a combination of transmission electron microscopy (TEM) and X-ray energy dispersive spectroscopy (XES) by Mudroch *et al.* (1977).

Pore fluid analysis

The extraction and analysis of pore fluids from sediments is the principal technique used for evaluating sediment–water interaction processes involving solute species. Techniques for the recovery and analysis of pore fluids have improved considerably over the past 10 years, through discovery of experimental factors that can modify fluid composition during sampling (temperature and pressure changes, atmospheric contamination, etc.) and through improvement in microanalytical techniques for typical pore fluid constituents. In principle, the concept of extracting fluids from sediments is relatively simple. Generally the fluid is extracted from the sediment by a piston "squeezer" (Manheim, 1965; Kalil and Goldhaber, 1973; Siever, 1962) or gas membrane squeezer (Reeburgh, 1967; Martens, 1974; Robbins and Gustinis, 1976). Other techniques used have involved centrifugation (Holdren, 1974), simple sample dispersion and dilution followed by centrifugation or filtration (Rittenberg *et al.*, 1955), and gas displacement (Lusczynski, 1961), although they generally have not yet gained wide acceptance. Loading of sample into squeezers can involve a simple mechanical transfer of core sections to squeezers; however, recognition of atmospheric contamination effects has led to development of techniques using nitrogen-purged glove boxes (Bray *et al.*, 1973) or involving more elaborate mechanical sample transfer systems (Martens, 1974; Bowser, 1974).

Consequences of squeezing techniques that have been documented recently basically stem from the problem of maintaining samples in an *in situ* condition through the squeezing process (Manheim, 1976). Pressure effects on the composition of fluids extracted during the squeezing process were evaluated by Manheim (1966). Such effects are not significant in marine sediments at squeezing pressures below 1400 kg/cm² (20,000 psi), but lower threshold pressures were indicated for freshwater sediments. Theoretical considerations of an enlarged double layer for particles in contact with more dilute pore fluids (Van Olphen, 1963) plus experimental work (Lagerwerff, 1964; Rosenbaum, 1976) suggest that ion exclusion effects will increase with pressure on squeezing of fine-grained freshwater sediments; but most current techniques recover nearly all pore fluids at pressures below 35 kg/cm² (500 psi), which should be no problem.

Effects of temperature changes in cores before squeezing were described by Mangelsdorf *et al.* (1969), Fanning and Pilson (1971), and Sayles *et al.* (1973) who showed that concentration changes up to 60% occurred in changing temperatures from 2°C to ambient temperature. Evidence cited from Leg 15 of the Deep Sea Drilling Project (Heezen *et al.*, 1973) suggested that the temperature effects may be reversible; however, this has yet to be demonstrated.

The effects of long-term core storage before squeezing were demonstrated by Manheim (1967), and indicate that pore fluid extraction studies must be made within as short a time as possible after collection. *In situ* probes recently described by Barnes (1973) and Sayles *et al.* (1976) attempt to overcome both known temperature and potential pressure effects by extracting pore fluids while in the sediment. To date neither system has been used in freshwater lakes.

An interesting *in situ* probe utilizing dialysis membrane chambers described by Hesslein (1976) has been used in freshwater and marine environments, but without calibration. The known cation exclusion properties of such membranes (Dean, 1969) have yet to be evaluated in natural water systems.

Sample contamination is a serious problem with pore fluid studies of low-level trace metal, nutrient, and dissolved gas profiles. Several designs have been described recently that attempt to overcome such problems (Martens, 1974; Bowser, 1974; Mattisoff *et al.*, 1975). The systems all effectively use inert plastics for sample handling and squeezing and provide for sample handling in an inert atmosphere of nitrogen or helium.

Statistical analysis

The collection of mineral and/or chemical data on lake sediments, of course, is used primarily to explain the processes controlling chemical variations in the water body itself. If there is insufficient direct cause and effect information, the use of statistics may be an important part of this evaluation process.

Statistical tools applicable to lacustrine sediment studies include:

(1) Design of statistically valid sampling strategies.

(2) Description of sample attributes as estimates of sample populations (mean, standard deviation, skewness, kurtosis, etc.)

(3) Hypothesis testing to evaluate differences or similarities among samples (inference).

(4) Evaluation of precision and accuracy of data measurements.

(5) *Lacking prior knowledge of variable correlations,* to seek interrelationships by use of simple correction or, with large multivariate data sets, by some form of factor or cluster analysis.

(6) Development of mathematical relationships among variables (multiple regression), including description of uncertainty or error.

Examples of applications to lacustrine studies follow.

Randomized replicate sampling to evaluate the statistical uncertainty of samples and the spacing of points in a sample net to distinguish the scale of variability of measured sediment parameters are essential elements in valid sampling design (Griffiths, 1967). Simply put, the scale of the sample variation and the local variability in sample properties must be established for the samples to be interpreted properly. Effectively "blind" sampling of lake sediments from floating platforms is potentially an ideal means of taking random samples. However, such sampling procedures are not commonly used in lake sediment studies. It is more common practice to obtain sediment samples from the "deep hole" of smaller lakes (for example, Dean and Gorham, 1976a, or Hornbrook and Garrett, 1976). This approach is of limited value, requiring the assumption that such samples are best integrated and reflect the sum of both allogenic and endogenic processes in the lake. Such assumptions must be tested before valid inferences can be drawn from the data.

On the other hand, statistically valid sampling strategies can often require a number of samples and sample tests that are either prohibitively expensive, or time consuming, or both. Under such circumstances it is perhaps better to design the "best possible" sampling strategy, imperfect as it may be, and to ask the statistician to help in assessing the *limits* to which such data can be used. In either case, it is fundamental to understand the uncertainty in such data and the extent to which it can meaningfully be used to evaluate interrelationships among samples.

Description of the statistical variability or uncertainty of measured sample parameters is important in estimating both the quantitative mineralogy and chemical composition of sediments. Good estimates of the true or population distribution can be made only with sufficient samples of measurements of sample properties. The number of measurements or samples must be chosen such that the *estimated* population distribution falls within some predetermined range of the "true" value. Considerable use of such statistics has been made for grain size analyses of sediments to elucidate differences in physical transport processes (see, for example, Chapter 3; Moore, 1961; and Thomas *et al.,* 1972, 1973, on Great Lakes applications) and for pollen analysis to evaluate historical changes in the flora of lake environments (for example, Maher, 1977; Kemp *et al.,* 1974). Statistical uncertainties in the estimation of mineral percentages by grain-counting techniques are determined largely by the total number of grains counted and the fractional percentage each mineral phase makes up of the total sample. A useful discussion of such problems was by van der Plas and Tobi (1965). To measure mineral percentages to a standard deviation of ± 4 to 10% (95% confidence level) requires a minimum of about 400 measured grains (see, for example, Mann, 1951, for heavy minerals in Lake Elsinore, Calif.). In contrast, the reported sand fraction measurements of Dean and Gorham (1976a) on a minimum of 100 grains per sample yield standard deviations (95% confidence level) ranging from 10 to 20% which would justify reporting their values to only one significant figure.

Simple correlation analysis is perhaps most widely used to analyze interrelationships of variables. Examples of its use in lake sediment analysis are to be found in Cronan (1969), Dean and Gorham (1976a), Thomas *et al.* (1972), and Rossmann *et al.* (1972). An example drawn from the latter article is shown in Table 4. The samples are sediments from Green Bay (Lake Michigan) and are composed largely of iron and manganese oxide nodules. By using chemical extraction of only the oxides, carbonates (minor), and part of the organic fraction, the contribution of insoluble clastic silicates to the analyses is eliminated. Since iron and manganese are the two major elements in the samples and since they form separate phases in the samples, they show, as expected, strong negative correlations with one another. Other elements tend to partition with either the iron or manganese phases and their correlation coefficients are close to one for significant associations. One can safely conclude from these data that silicon and phosphate are related to the iron oxide phase(s) and that Ba, Ni, Co, Mo, Sr, and Mg are associated with the manganese phase(s).

Inasmuch as most mineralogical and chemical basic

data on lake sediments are expressed on a percentage basis, such ratio data are constrained by the fact that it is a "closed" set or a constant sum. The effects of closure are well known to students of geological statistics (Chayes, 1971; Miesch, 1969) but little recognized in the literature on lake sediments.

If, as in the case of ferromanganese nodule analyses from Rossmann et al. (1972), Table 4, the sample is principally a two-phase mixture, then correlations of minor and trace elements with the major metals (Mn and Fe in this case) give reasonably clear associations that can be interpreted with some confidence (also see, Cronan, 1969). However, in complex mineralogical mixtures typically found in lake sediments, such analysis can produce misleading results. The correlation table listed in Dean and Gorham (1976a), for example, claiming that correlations greater than ± 0.37 are "significant" at the 99% level not only completely ignores the problem of data closure, but also makes the invalid assumption of an equal level of significance to all data.

An instructive example is drawn from the work of Bortleson (1970), summarized in Bortleson and Lee (1972). A partial analysis of one of his sediment samples from Lake Monona (WC-46) is shown in Table 5 for total phosphorus, iron, and manganese. Simple correlation coefficients between Fe–Mn, Fe–P, and Mn–P are also shown. The data show significant positive correlations in all three cases and seem adequate to warrant the conclusion that the iron, manganese, and phosphorus are all related to the same "fraction"

of the sediment. In sediments dominated by iron and manganese oxides, phosphorus is associated with iron phases and not with manganese (Williams et al., 1971a, 1971b, 1971c; Rossmann et al., 1972; Syers et al., 1973; Nriagu and Dell, 1974). Most of the Fe, Mn, and P are presumably related to the oxide portion of the sediment and, therefore, by implication are inversely related to the sum of the non-oxide phases (carbonate plus silicate plus organic matter). Thus the interrelationships between Fe, Mn, and P analyses can be recast so that the sum of the three oxides equals 100%. These results are shown in Table 5 along with a new correlation matrix for the three elements. The inverse correlation of iron with manganese is consistant with earlier work, but the *inverse* phosphorus–iron association is not expected. One is tempted to conclude that both phosphorus and manganese are associated with the carbonate fraction of the sediment, as did Bortleson and Lee (1972); however, the example is used here simply to illustrate how the same data can show both positive and negative correlations between variables, and that knowledge of mineral–element associations is important to the evaluation of correlation matrices.

Bortleson and Lee (1974) attempted to rationalize the apparent Fe–P–Mn correlations in lakes ranging from oligotrophic to eutrophic in northern Wisconsin. They argued that, in spite of the fact that total P–Mn correlations were generally "better" than total P–Fe correlations, the phosphorus was related to iron compounds and that no Mn–P associations should be

TABLE 4. Correlation Matrix for (a) Ferromanganese Nodules and (b) Nodule-Rich Sediments from Green Bay, Lake Michigan

				(a) Electron probe analyses			
Element	Fe	Mn	Ba	Ca	K	Si	P
Fe	1.00						
Mn	−1.00	1.00					
Ba	−0.93	0.93	1.00				
Ca	−0.52	0.51	0.23	1.00			
K	−0.20	0.19	0.32	−0.09	1.00		
Si	0.93	−0.94	−0.86	−0.34	−0.17	1.00	
P	0.68	−0.69	−0.64	−0.05	−0.17	0.88	1.00

					(b) Acid and peroxide extracts							
Element	Fe	Mn	Ni	Cu	Co	Ba	Mo	Sr	Mg	Zn	Na	K	Cr
Fe	1.00												
Mn	−0.83	1.00											
Ni	−0.87	0.74	1.00										
Cu	−0.68	0.54	0.56	1.00									
Co	−0.88	0.98	0.76	0.55	1.00								
Ba	−0.81	0.96	0.62	0.46	0.97	1.00							
Mo	−0.73	0.93	0.73	0.32	0.90	0.87	1.00						
Sr	−0.88	0.98	0.77	0.48	0.98	0.96	0.92	1.00					
Mg	−0.90	0.89	0.88	0.68	0.87	0.80	0.84	0.88	1.00				
Zn	−0.47	0.14	0.72	0.38	0.15	−0.03	0.20	0.20	0.47	1.00			
Na	−0.78	0.61	0.72	0.87	0.61	0.51	0.44	0.58	0.83	0.48	1.00		
K	−0.91	0.75	0.81	0.75	0.77	0.68	0.63	0.76	0.89	0.49	0.91	1.00	
Cr	0.30	−0.47	−0.08	−0.15	−0.51	−0.54	−0.42	−0.42	−0.26	−0.48	−0.18	0.26	1.00

TABLE 5.   Statistical Analysis of Phosphorus, Iron, and Manganese Data for Total Analyses of Lake Monona (Wisconsin), Sample WC-46

Section number	Total concentration[a] (mg/g)			$\dfrac{Element}{(P + Fe + Mn)} \times 100$[b]		
	P	Fe	Mn	P	Fe	Mn
1	1.83	18.5	0.760	8.68	87.7	3.60
2	1.71	17.0	0.717	8.80	87.5	3.69
3	1.51	17.4	0.673	7.71	88.8	3.44
4	1.60	20.3	0.720	7.07	89.7	3.18
5	1.66	20.0	0.740	7.41	89.3	3.30
6	1.77	20.1	0.812	7.80	88.6	3.58
7	1.92	19.3	0.882	8.69	87.3	3.99
8	1.44	16.5	0.784	7.69	88.1	4.19
9	1.34	13.2	0.695	8.80	86.6	4.56
10	1.33	12.0	0.707	9.47	85.5	5.04
11	1.17	10.9	0.494	9.31	86.8	3.93
12	1.17	10.0	0.477	10.0	85.9	4.10
13	1.22	7.70	0.458	13.0	82.1	4.88
14	1.23	7.80	0.433	13.0	82.4	4.58
15	1.12	7.33	0.418	12.6	82.7	4.71
16	1.06	7.23	0.383	12.2	83.4	4.42
17	0.910	6.50	0.376	11.7	83.5	4.83
18	0.785	5.30	0.364	12.2	82.2	5.64
19	0.756	5.53	0.377	11.7	82.5	5.83
20	0.744	5.20	0.372	11.8	82.3	5.89
21	0.764	5.73	0.376	11.1	83.4	5.47

Correlation coefficients

P-Fe	+0.94		−0.98
Fe-Mn	+0.95		−0.87
P-Mn	+0.93		+0.78

[a]Data expressed as fraction of total sediment (dry wt.).
[b]Data recast to Fe + Mn + P = 100%.

implied. By using *total* element analyses for Fe, Mn, and P (i.e., treating the sediment as if it were a single "phase"), data were lost that would have permitted better evaluation of element associations. Ferromagnesian silicates from relatively unweathered Quaternary glacial deposits and Precambrian igneous and metamorphic rocks constitute a significant fraction of the sediments of northern Wisconsin lakes; and, hence, silicate iron (not associated with *either* phosphorus *or* manganese) is included in the analysis. Thus, lower correlations of phosphorus with iron than with manganese were to be expected. Extractive chemistry that would distinguish between allogenic silicate iron and "labile" oxyhydroxides coating the grains would provide data for more explicit evaluation of the iron, phosphorus, and manganese associations.

A related technique for discovering variable relationships is the use of factor analysis. With the advent of high-speed computers the application of factor analysis is gaining wider use, and there are numerous examples of its use in lake sediment studies (Thomas *et al.*, 1972; Potter *et al.*, 1975; Dean and Gorham, 1976a, 1976b). Used to sort out "commonality" among samples, especially where the number of sam-

ples and types of measurements are relatively large, factor analysis is used in both R-mode (associations among sample *variables*) and Q-mode (associations among samples) (Harbaugh and Merriam, 1968). Such data analysis is subject to the same constraints as closed data sets discussed in connection with correlation analysis, making interpretation of factor analysis tables involving percentage data (especially R-mode) more difficult than heretofore appreciated.

The greatest difficulty arising in the interpretation of the factor analysis results is in determining what is a "significant" factor loading. The closed data set problem and data of variable precision have already been mentioned as fundamental limitations. Just as important, however, is the fact that data interpretation must be made in the knowledge of real processes and relationships among variables. For example, Dean and Gorham (1976a) discuss "anomalous" correlations among the clastic (allogenic) silicate minerals, and are led to suggest that, because they cannot rationalize the differences in terms of *bedrock mineralogy,* the variability is due to climatic differences across the state. The role of erodibility of bedrock or glacial cover and regional differences in the mineral composition of glacial deposits (Wright, 1972; Arneman and Wright, 1959), also reflected in the groundwater chemistry (Winter, 1977), is not considered. Moreover, interpretation of the inverse relation of silt percentage and X-ray diffraction peak height of feldspar solely as a weathering effect does not recognize the well-known fact that feldspars are enriched in the coarser fraction of sediments, whereas clay minerals are more prevalent in silt and finer fractions (Cuthbert, 1941; Gibbs, 1977). The diluting effect of the finer grained nonfeldspar minerals on the mixtures results in negative correlations between the two factors *because* the data are subject to the restriction of closure (Chayes, 1971).

Linear regression techniques have been applied to lake sediment data to *quantify* the relationships among variables. Simple, two-variable, linear regression equations will differ depending on which of the two variables is chosen as independent and which is dependent. The "reduced major axis" line is sometimes calculated where distinction of dependence and independence of variables is not evident (Till, 1974). Confidence limit curves should be shown on regression plots to help emphasize the uncertainties in using such fitted equations for extrapolation outside the range of the data on which it is based.

Multiple regression techniques are essentially similar to two-variable linear regression extended to multivariate data. Gibbs (1967, 1977) used multiple regression to evaluate the major "controlling" factors on suspended sediment and total solute variations in the Amazon River. Linear regression may also be extended to nonlinear relationships through transforming the variables or generation of complex computer-fitted polynomials.

In summary, applied statistics is essentially an *empirical* tool used to discover and evaluate *unknown* relationships among variables. Where previous studies have demonstrated interrelationships, either through statistical modelling, or by experiment, it serves no purpose to apply correlation or factor analysis to such data other than to reaffirm such established relationships. All too often such analysis has contributed nothing new to already known correlations. That such tools can be used to seek new and perhaps significant relationships among the important variables should not be denied; only that one should make judgments about such empirically established variable relationships in the light of previously discovered processes and correlations.

Origin of major mineral groups

Several mineral phases in lake sediments can be derived from either allogenic, endogenic, or authigenic processes (calcite, for example). Discussion of the relative importance of the three sediment sources for each specific mineral group and evaluation of the important factors controlling the origin and distribution of these phases requires a discussion by mineral group (see Table 3).

Non-clay clastic minerals

The clastic components of most lake sediments are dominated by silt and/or sand-size materials consisting principally of quartz and feldspar with or without some ferromagnesian minerals and detrital carbonate. The well crystallized, wholly allogenic silicate and oxide phases commonly reflect sediment source and transport and are evidently little altered in the lacustrine environment. These minerals are particularly useful for the determination of source and the evaluation of physical processes taking place within a lake.

The most common mineral species in lacustrine sediments as a whole is quartz, though it may be completely absent in volcanic, carbonate, or tropical terranes. Thomas has demonstrated a strong positive correlation of quartz plus feldspar with median grain size (Thomas, 1969a) in Lakes Erie and Ontario sediments and a positive correlation of quartz with feldspar contents (Thomas, 1969b). Without the influence of mechanical separation factors, quartz is normally recognized as ubiquitous in sediments derived from quartzose lithologies, as, for example, the granitic rocks around Lake Tahoe (Court et al., 1972) or from glacial and bedrock controlled sedimentation in the Great Lakes. Trends in the quartz/feldspar ratio noted by Dean and Gorham (1976a) in sediments from 46

Minnesota Lakes reflect bedrock and surficial cover mineral abundance.

A specific study of feldspar distribution in Lake Ontario sediments by Thomas (1969b) demonstrated a partial loss of plagioclase and a relative increase of potash feldspar away from shore. This is interpreted as due to chemical weathering resulting from greater transport time for offshore sediments and agrees with the stoichiometric dissolution reaction sequence worked out by Garrels and Mackenzie (1967). Kemp and Dell (1976) have referred to "subaqueous weathering" in comparing offshore sediments in Lakes Erie and Ontario with shoreline bluff source materials, but they suggest that the observed decrease of plagioclase also could be due to finer grain size and selective sorting during transport and deposition.

Generally, the silicate minerals of the Great Lakes follow trends to be expected from the controls exerted by water depth on mechanical (largely wind) energy dissipation and lacustrine sedimentation. In Lakes Huron and Michigan, where the simple transition from shelf to offshore basin characteristic of Lakes Erie and Ontario is largely lacking, quartz decreases away from escarpments and sills toward intervening trough-shaped deeps (Thomas et al., 1973; Moore, 1961). In part, quartz is more abundant in southern Lake Huron, Lake Michigan, and parts of Lake Erie because of shallower water and more pronounced effects of turbulent mixing on fine sediment winnowing.

In a few studies of lacustrine sediments investigators have tried to use heavy mineral analysis of sand fractions to obtain more information on sediment source and transport. This involves careful evaluation of small variations in the overall heavy mineral assemblage, which may be statistically dangerous, and requires considerable basic knowledge of the lake–drainage basin system.

An example of such an investigation is that of Mann (1951) on Lake Elsinore, California. The study of Lake Elsinore sediments featured an attempt to use heavy mineral frequency, together with grain-size distribution, to delineate provenance of lacustrine sediments in a shallow fault-block lake basin. Mann correlated mechanical analyses of the nearshore sediments with three zones recognized in the heavy mineral suites and the three distinctive lithologic groupings seen in the bedrock of the drainage area: intermediate plutonic rocks, metamorphics, and pegmatites. Hornblende alone makes up more than 50% of each zonal average, and, together with biotite, opaques and pyroxene constitute nearly 97% of representative heavy mineral suites. The intermediate plutonic rocks can be characterized by relatively abundant chlorite and well-sorted sand, the metamorphics by kyanite and coarse but poorly sorted sediment, and pegmatitic sources by monazite, tourmaline, and cassiterite associated with the deltaic sediments of the inflow of the San Jacinto

River. The bottom sediments of the lake were, as to be expected, uniformly finer grained than the littoral deposits. Generally, despite the shallow nature of the lake and the evidence of mixing by the wind, the diagnostic mineralogic phases indicated that transportation of detritus along shore was not important.

A statistically valid differentiation of heavy mineral variation would appear to be most useful in lake systems where less homogenization of the sediments is evident. Moore (1961), for example, found no difference between the silicate-oxide mineral suite in the sediments of a restricted part of northeastern Lake Michigan and the glacial tills of adjacent land areas. In a broader perspective, Dell (1971) was able to show a regional trend in cores of Lake Superior sediments from dominant pyroxene in the west to hornblende in the east (despite stratigraphic variations in five postglacial units) reflecting control by general bedrock lithologies. In Lake Ontario a decrease in the hornblende to pyroxene ratio from north to south and west to east was noted by Kemp and Dell (1976). In contrast clinopyroxene and amphibole variations showed no simple pattern in the sediments of Lake Tahoe (Court et al., 1972), although hypersthene and basaltic hornblende were shown to be associated with inputs of volcanic rock fragments.

Bradbury and Megard (1972) used the distribution of hematite and limonite with depth in the sediments of Shagawa Lake, Minnesota, to document the mining history of Ely. At the same time, they used the distribution of chlorite and tourmaline as references. They reasoned that the influx of tourmaline to shallower areas was constant and relatively permanent, as its greater density precluded transport to greater depths by lake currents. From the tourmaline distribution they deduced changes in the rate of sedimentation in the lake. These changes were correlated with mining and lumbering activities and other indications of human settlement effects in the lake area.

In summary, variations in the non-clay clastic fraction of most lake sediments is generally reflective of variations in drainage area geology (e.g., Larkin, 1964). Superimposed on these primary input factors are the processes acting within the lake of selective settling and current winnowing of finer grained sediment fractions. These latter effects are more important in shallower parts of lakes and thus generally are more effective in the shoreline areas than in the deeper offshore basins. Selective destruction of silicate clastic phases by weathering is probably more important in the lake drainage area than in the lake proper.

Clay minerals

A large number of studies have now indicated that, like the detrital mineralogy of coarser size fractions in lake sediments, the clay minerals primarily reflect source lithologies, at least in the climates of the higher latitudes where weathering is not so intense as to obliterate the effect of compositional differences in parent materials. Thus, in the Amazon Basin, Gibbs (1967) found that the chlorite and illite obtained in the high relief, incompletely weathered Andean portion of the drainage basin persisted in the suspended sediment of the lower Amazon itself, despite the kaolinite and gibbsite dominance in the highly weathered material from the lowland tributaries. In contrast, the paucity of even clay minerals, much less other aluminosilicates (as in Lake Tanganyika or the northern basin of Lake Kivu; Degens et al., 1971, 1972) can be cited as an example of the lack of significant detrital input to some of the large lakes of the East African rift valleys.

Relative to the abundance of minerals in lacustrine environments in the central U.S., Potter et al. (1975) considered the importance of source rocks and climate on the clay mineralogy of alluvial muds of the Mississippi River Basin. They found two major clay mineral associations: smectite dominant eastward from the Rocky Mountains to Indiana, and an illite–chlorite–kaolinite association characteristic of the eastern part of the basin. The association of high smectite sediments with the western, more arid areas was argued by Potter et al. (1975) to be related to the clay mineralogy of Cretaceous, Tertiary, and Pleistocene sediments that underlie much of that region and not to weathering. The eastern facies is principally the result of erosion of middle and lower Paleozoic sediments that are rich in illite–chlorite and notably lacking in smectite. These authors also argue that Pleistocene glaciation, through drainage diversion and the aerosol transport of loess, has resulted in smectite being more widespread than bedrock distribution would suggest.

Studies of clay mineral distribution in the sediments of the Great Lakes support the concept of source as the dominant control on species abundance. The early work of Cuthbert (1944) suggested that the dominant clay mineral in Lake Erie deposits is illite. Similarly, Moore (1961) indicated that in the sediments of northeastern Lake Michigan half the clay fraction consists of illite, 30% is comprised of what he termed mixed-layer minerals, and 20% is chlorite. These results were identical with the average clay mineral composition given for 16 till samples considered to be the primary source material. His data also indicated that there is little variation in the northeastern Lake Michigan sediment clay suite with water depth, distance from source, or depth of sediment burial.

Summary of the work by Gross et al. (1972) on numerous samples from cores in southern Lake Michigan covering the entire postglacial sediment section shows that mean values for seven stratigraphic units range from 26 to 49% illite (generally increasing in older sediments), from 29 to 38% chlorite (decreasing in older sediments), and from 22 to 28% expandable layer clays (the latter include vermiculite, smectite, and true mixed-layer clays). Gross *et al.* (1972) note that there are close mineral compositional affinites of the lacustrine stratigraphic units with the till deposits of the surrounding area.

The dependence of the clay mineralogy from the entire thickness of Lake Superior sediments on the clay composition of the unweathered tills in the drainage basin has been demonstrated by Dell (1971). Mixed-layer clays are more common than in other Great Lakes sediments, and together with illite they comprise over 60% of the total clay. Kaolinite, chlorite, vermiculite, and other expandable layer clays are also present, but generally in amounts less than 15% each. In contrast, studies by investigators on the surficial sediments in Lake Ontario (Thomas *et al.*, 1972), Lake Huron (Thomas *et al.*, 1973), and Lake Erie (Thomas *et al.*, 1976) have identified a consistent suite of clay minerals composed of illite (everywhere clearly dominant), chlorite, and kaolinite. They observed no smectite or mixed-layer minerals, although the techniques on which their observations are based are not spelled out in much detail.

The importance of sediment source is also evident in studies of the clay mineralogy of the reservoir sediments on the Columbia River. Knebel *et al.* (1968) showed that the ratio of smectite to illite increases progressively downstream. The clay mineral distribution is attributed to the inputs of illite from plutonic and metamorphic bedrock in the upper basin and to the west of the middle river reaches, and smectite from basaltic rocks to the south and east, including the lower Snake River drainage.

The relation of lacustrine clays to source in the Alpine Lakes of Switzerland has been mentioned by Serruya (1969) for Lake Geneva and demonstrated in some detail by Müller and Quakernaat (1969) for Lake Constance. Mica and chlorite characterize the alpine crystalline rocks, whereas the Tertiary formations, especially local outcrops of volcanic tuff, contribute smectite to the sediments. Schöttle (1969) attributed the very low smectite content of the Gnadensee (a small part of the southwest arm of Lake Constance) to reworked glacial deposits.

In sediments from a permanently ice-covered lake of arctic Canada, Coakley and Rust (1968) pointed out the minimal amount of chemical weathering of the clay minerals. They attributed kaolinite, illite, and lesser amounts of chlorite–smectite to Cretaceous–Tertiary shales in the drainage and noted that both quartz and feldspar persisted down into the clay-size fraction, a fact that indicates little if any chemical weathering of the glacially derived source material.

Dean and Gorham (1976a) attempted a semiquantitative mineralogic analysis of the clay-size fraction in their examination of sediments from 46 Minnesota lakes. They concluded that there were no marked

regional differences in clay suites, though better crystallinity characterized the clays from lake sediments in the southwestern part of the state as compared to the northeastern part. Dean and Gorham (1976a) noted that bedrock lithology appears to be the dominant control on silt-size mineralogy, and that chlorite distribution in the clay fraction is related to micaceous metamorphic and some sedimentary rocks, including tills derived locally from these areas. Other interpretations were discussed earlier in the statistics section.

Lakes Maurepas and Pontchartrain, Louisiana, receive an appreciable amount of saline water as a result of winds and tides generated by currents from the Gulf of Mexico. Brooks and Ferrell (1970) found that smectite and illite contents of surficial sediments increase with increasing salinity (chloride ranging from 500 to 4500 mg/liter), whereas kaolinite decreases with increasing salinity. Such a distribution was explained by differential settling as kaolinite being flocculated more rapidly than illite and smectite. Alternatively such effects could be explained by different sources for the kaolin and illite/smectite, perhaps comparable to that indicated by Griffin (1962) for Gulf of Mexico sediments. As discussed earlier, mass accumulation rate data for the specific clay minerals would allow differentiation of such effects. Recent studies by Hahn and Stumm (1970) demonstrate significant differential flocculation between illite and smectite but not between illite and kaolinite. Thus, the Lake Pontchartrain and Maurepas results suggest a potential avenue for future sediment research. Salinity gradients could provide a

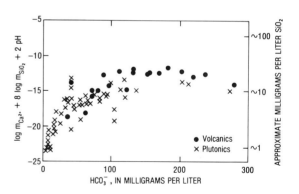

FIGURE 5. Diagram illustrating the trend of compositional change in waters from crystalline rocks (adapted from Garrels 1967). The axes of the plot are taken to conform with the constituent variables for calcium aluminosilicate hydrolysis as discussed in the text. The ratio (in logarithmic form) of dissolved calcium and silica concentrations to hydrogen ion for the approach to equilibrium of kaolinite and Ca-smectite is plotted against the bicarbonate concentration of spring waters from the Sierra Nevada range. The approach to constant stoichiometric ratio suggests solute control by clay phase equilibria. However, the dominant role of SiO_2 and the possible effects of other limits on silica concentration are alluded to on the right side of the plot.

significant mechanism for mineral separation in mer-omictic lake systems.

No *definitive* evidence has been offered for the authigenesis of major clay mineral species in freshwater lacustrine environments [except, perhaps, for the iron smectite, nontronite (see p. 210)] in contrast to some saline lake systems (see Eugster and Hardie, Chapter 8). Not only are the surface energies of disordered particles important and the kinetics of nucleation slow and poorly known in detail, but the basic thermochemical properties of even well-crystallized natural sheet silicates are the subject of significant controversy (Zen, 1972). In his summary of the application of equilibrium concepts and activity diagrams such as used by Kramer (1967) to silicate mineral stability in the Great Lakes systems, Sutherland (1970) recognized limitations imposed by uncertainty in thermochemical data, variable composition and crystallinity, or metastability of mineral phases, but insisted that trends in solution composition were consistent with an approach to equilibrium, especially with respect to kaolinite and calcium smectite. The latter was suggested by slope limits appropriate to the stoichiometry for the reaction,

$$6Ca_{0.17}Al_{2.33}Si_{3.67}O_{10}(OH)_2 + 2CO_2 + 9H_2O \rightarrow$$
$$\text{smectite}$$
$$7Al_2Si_2O_5(OH)_4 + Ca^{2+} + 2HCO_3^- + 8SiO_2,$$
$$\text{kaolinite}$$

on an activity–activity diagram of 2 pH–pCa versus pSiO$_2$ (aq) for analyses of lake waters and sediment pore fluids from the lower Great Lakes. Approach to constancy for the activity product of such a reaction was interpreted in the extensive study of Sierra Nevada springs by Garrels and Mackenzie (1967) not to

"mean that the controlling solids are well-crystallized, clearly distinguishable substances, but that there is definitely an interplay between the waters and solid aluminosilicates. Further, the aluminosilicates apparently differ from each other in important compositional steps, and are not simply continuous gradations resulting from progressive adsorption and alteration as water compositions change." (p. 231).

The trend of aqueous compositional change associated with hydrolysis reactions of calcium aluminosilicate such as plagioclase feldspar is shown in Figures 5 and 6 (adapted from Garrels, 1967). The compositional reaction paths shown are for the dissolution of plagioclase with the system open or closed to CO$_2$ and encompass nearly all the groundwaters from igneous rocks originally considered by Garrels (1967). These considerations are most appropriate, for example, to the selective dissolution of plagioclase from inshore to offshore in Lakes Ontario and Erie first proposed by Thomas (1969b).

The use of this and related activity diagrams is made

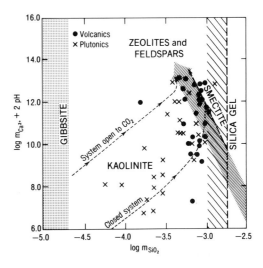

FIGURE 6. Diagram illustrating compositional trends associated with the dissolution of plagioclase under dissolved CO$_2$ conditions of equilibrium with the atmosphere (p_{CO_2} = 10$^{-3.5}$) or soil air (p_{CO_2} = 10$^{-1.5}$). The range represented by the two reaction paths includes nearly all analyses originally considered by Garrels (1967). The large patterned arrow suggests a general large composition shift dictated by formation of a smectite phase. Indefinite gibbsite and gel limits on SiO$_2$ concentrations for the stability field of kaolinite are indicative of uncertainties in appropriate thermochemical data; also for this reason no attempt has been made to indicate stability boundaries for the zeolite or feldspar phases which would be the end result of further geochemical evolution accompanying added solute concentration.

difficult by the fact that the stoichiometric smectite–kaolinite reaction product is dominated by the pSiO$_2$ term. Large pSiO$_2$ variations with pH could be related to uncoupled factors, such as diatom production or dissolution, and thus give a false indication of "equilibrium" with respect to some silicate phases. Inasmuch as such diagrams may be more useful to recognize *lack* of equilibrium among phases rather than proof thereof, perhaps they are best described as disequilibrium diagrams.

Although trends in the solute composition of natural lake water may appear constrained by aluminosilicate equilibria, the difficulties in actual formation of an authigenic clay phase have been demonstrated by Kittrick (1970), who precipitated kaolinite from aluminosilicate suspension only after a period of 3 to 4 years, and then only in solutions slightly supersaturated with respect to kaolinite, but clearly undersaturated with respect to any other aluminosilicate. The difficulty of clay mineral synthesis in aqueous systems was ascribed by Hem and Lind (1974) to the energy required for deprotonation of AlOH and SiOH to form Al–O–Si bonds. Despite this, metastable, cryptocrystalline precipitates or surface states may exert some stoichiometrically comparable influence on lake water compositions. Thus, Sutherland (1969) interpreted the calcium versus sodium behavior in waters from the Great Lakes and Lake Onandaga, New York, in terms of solution composition and cation–clay interaction involving kaolinite and a smectite phase without consideration of compositional detail for the solids. The scatter in his fluid activity–activity diagrams suggests long-term trends and general limits, especially in silica concentrations, rather than any exact controls on lake water chemistry. This is certainly to be expected where seasonal fluctuations and residence times are commonly shorter than Kittrick's (1970) laboratory aluminosilicate synthesis rates, as, for example, in Sutherland's (1970) data for Lakes Erie and Ontario. Thus, it seemed inappropriate that Brookins' (1972) consideration of clay mineral alteration in a recently constructed Kansas reservoir was based on plotting of a few water analyses on a pH minus pMg vs log silica activity diagram around an unspecified kaolinite–smectite boundary. It was not surprising there was complete lack of evidence for authigenic reaction in the clay mineral distribution and their Rb–Sr isotope ratios. Singer et al. (1972) employed a similar activity plot for Lake Kinneret and its saline spring inflow to evaluate an authigenic origin for the palygorskite (5 to 15% of the sediment clay fraction), but their reference was to a sepiolite stability boundary obtained in synthesis experiments by Wollast et al. (1968). Even so, Singer et al. (1972) provided evidence that all the clay mineral species were derived from soils and sediments within the drainage basin. The association of high kaolinite concentrations (composing from 10 to 30% of the < 2 μm fraction) with the Jordan River delta and currents within the lake indicated that kaolinite deposition is related to more rapid settling associated with its larger particle size and perhaps flocculation resulting from the higher salinity of the lake than the river. Smectite comprised the majority of the remaining clay fraction (50 to 80%) of Lake Kinneret; illite was absent.

One of the most thorough examinations of surficial lacustrine sediment mineralogy in all size ranges was done on Lake Tahoe by Court et al. (1972). They identified two principal sediment types in the lake, organic ooze and mineral detritus. Intergrades of chlorite–smectite and chlorite–vermiculite (operationally defined as the clay fraction showing incomplete expansion with glycerin and incomplete collapse on potassium saturation) are widely distributed, but restricted with only rare exceptions to organic oozes. Smectite and vermiculite, the other principal clay minerals, vary inversely with the chlorite content. The authors suggested that this results in part from differences in grain size of the various clay minerals. Court et al. (1972) maintained that " . . . no evidence was found of diagenetic change through time . . .", attributing the chloritic fraction as well as vermiculite to the

weathering of granitic rocks, and the smectite to the weathering of volcanic rocks. On the other hand, the correlation could indicate the development of interlayer complexes in the finest fractions of soils in the surrounding watershed, or intergrade-forming reactions between fine clay and colloidal materials after deposition in organic oozes of the lake. They have explained the changes in the relative amounts of clay-size mica, smectite, and vermiculite by variations in the type of weathering and deposition in the basin. Vermiculite was considered typical of postglacial chemical weathering and soil development, whereas abundant clay-size mica was apparently derived from the more intense physical processes accompanying glaciation. The paradoxical abundance of smectite, considering the dominance of granite in the drainage basin, could be explained by the fact that most of the glaciation was in the areas underlain by volcanic rocks. The mineralogy of the sand and silt-size fractions generally supported the clay mineral evidence.

The study of Court et al. (1972) illustrates a few points that are broadly applicable to studies of other lake sediments and deserve emphasis. The first, and perhaps most obvious, is that in dealing with percentage data (closed data sets) the inverse correlations of the major clay mineral percentages are to be expected. The problem would be more readily addressed if information on the bulk sedimentation rate of specific phases had been calculated (see discussion in the sedimentation rate section).

Second, Court et al. (1972) employed the normal practice of using an arbitrarily defined 2-μm cutoff for the clay-size fraction. Chlorite typically occurs in the coarsest part of the clay mineral fraction, and, if the size–abundance maximum for that mineral ranges near the 2-μm cutoff for different samples, the resultant percentage data can be affected by variations in mean size of the chlorite near the 2-μm cutoff. Under such circumstances it is possible to see a "variation" in the percentage of the phase even when the percentage of that phase was a *constant* fraction of the total sediment.

Finally, the study of Court et al. (1972) is one of the few to *attempt* distinction between interlayered clays and simple clay mixtures or, for that matter, even identification of vermiculite in modern lake sediments. The reported presence or absence of many phases, especially clay minerals, in lake sediments may be more a matter of investigative methodology than any other factor.

Pyroclastic minerals

Lakes in volcanic regions (active and inactive) generally have bottom sediments of more complex compositions. Commonly the clay mineralogy of such material is dominated by smectite derived from the devitrification of volcanic glass. A noteworthy example of this situation is Crater Lake of Oregon, whose sediments have been studied in considerable textural and mineralogic detail by Nelson (1967). The enclosed, steep-sided lake basin derives its sediment entirely from surrounding lavas, ash, pumice, scoria, breccia, tuff, and agglomerate containing plagioclase, hypersthene, augite, and hornblende as their principal mineral constituents. In addition, smectite occurs in both the clay and sand fractions of the sediment, apparently derived from the alteration of ash (Nelson, 1967). The silt fraction is generally made up almost entirely of feldspar, whereas the mafic minerals are found mostly in the sands. Quartz is very rare. Specific rock sources can be identified for different sand layers at the same location by mineralogy. Nelson (1967) has used heavy minerals and rock fragments of distinctive textural and/or mineralogic composition to identify sediment sources, e.g., wind-blown pumice surrounding Mt. Mazama, rock fall, and debris slides, or slowly creeping moss sediment mats. Similarly, Deike and Jones (unpublished manuscript) have utilized the distinctive textures of "lithic matrix fragments" to identify sediment sources in the saline Lake Abert basin of south central Oregon.

The largest examples of lakes in volcanic terrane in the western hemisphere are relatively shallow Lake Nicaragua and its smaller satellite, Lake Managua, Guatamala. The bulk of the sediments were described by Swain (1966) as copropelic, richly diatomaceous clay and silt containing X-ray and microscopically identifiable volcanic glass, quartz, plagioclase, smectite, chlorite, and illite. The smectite was referred to as "organic complexed dioctahedral montmorillonite." The diffractograms (Swain, 1966, Figure 9) offered were not very definitive for identification of clay minerals, but suggest the presence of mixed-layer species, as well as amorphous silica. Better characterization of such materials would be useful, but, because of the abundance of glass and semiamorphous devitrification products, it remains a difficult problem.

In East Africa Richardson and Richardson (1972) concluded that the crystalline clay minerals at many levels from a Lake Naivasha core and in more saline Lake Rukwa had been altered or destroyed in the highly alkaline environment. They noted that X-ray diffraction data on the clay fraction were very poor with only a general "doming" in the region of the principal clay mineral (smectite) relfections. Conditions leading to the "alteration" of the silicate clay fraction while a feldspar fraction persists are inconsistent with the relative stability of such minerals under lacustrine conditions. Probably either the high percentage of organic matter and diatom (opaline) silica in the sediments has interfered with examination of the cryptocrystalline silicate fractions, or very little of such material is present.

The conversion of amorphous opal to cristobalite at 900°C was utilized by Richardson and Richardson (1972) to distinguish variably abundant, volcanic glass from endogenic opaline silica. In contrast, sediments which they examined from Pilkington Bay, Lake Victoria, or from Lake Chila, contained readily defined kaolinite, quartz, and chlorite, reflecting the nonvolcanic setting of these areas. Also in East Africa, Lake Tanganyika, in a region of both volcanic and crystalline rocks, has deep basin turbidite units (Degens et al. 1971) made up of nonvolcanic silt-sized quartz, feldspar, and mica, whereas some finer grained sediments are almost entirely composed of the skeletal remains of diatoms and organic matter, as in the noncarbonate sapropelic volcanic sediments of Lake Kivu to the north (Degens et al., 1973). The shallow sill deposits between the major basins of Lake Tanganyika lack turbidite deposits and contain smectite and even traces of sepiolite (Degens et al., 1971). Though the latter two species suggest a preponderance of volcanic inputs, the deep basin sediments of Lake Tanganyika contain essentially only well-crystallized mica and chlorite. It is apparent that the silica derived from dissolution of primary silicates is stimulatory to the production of significant diatom populations, and the remains of these organisms are ubiquitous components of lacustrine sediments in volcanic or crystalline terrains.

Opaline silica

Commonly the largest fraction of silica in lake sediments is from the detrital contribution of quartz sand. However, in many lakes significant amounts of SiO_2 can be accumulated in lake deposits through largely endogenic processes. Evidence for direct *inorganic* precipitation of a silica from lakes is rare and has been related to cooling of geothermal solutions or to the dilution of alkaline brines (Jones et al., 1967). On the other hand, sedimentation of *organically* derived diatom frustules is the most important endogenic contribution of SiO_2 to the sediments of lakes. Silicified structures are not uncommon in many aquatic organisms, but, compared to diatoms, they contribute only a small quantity of silica to sediments of most lakes (Wetzel, 1975). Remains of diatoms in sediments are often difficult to recognize in highly turbulent shallows where the frustules are subject to damage (Hecky and Kilham, 1973), in undersaturated environments where dissolution and the diagenetic remobilization rate of silica approaches its accumulation rate (Parker and Edgington, 1976), or where the solubility of the frustules has been enhanced by meromixis (Merilainen, 1969). In contrast, diatom remains in highly productive lakes can constitute the dominant component of rapidly accumulating lacustrine deposits as, for example, in Lake Naivasha (Richardson and Richardson,

1972) and eutrophic Minnesota lakes (Bradbury, 1975).

Although the dissolution of solid phases and biological activity are important controls on silica concentrations in lakes, they cannot always explain the low temporal and spatial variations found for dissolved silica in fresh waters. Sorption reactions between dissolved silica and solid phases have been suggested as a more likely buffer mechanism for dissolved silica concentrations in rivers and soils (Edwards and Liss, 1973).

The ultimate source of most silica in solution is silicate mineral dissolution; furthermore, as was noted in the discussion of clay minerals, silicate hydrolysis reactions are typically incongruent, producing not only dissolved species but also secondary solids, such as hydrated metal oxides (chiefly of aluminum and iron) or clay minerals. These materials, plus organic degradation products, have the essential attributes of an excellent substrate for sorption and desorption, i.e., extensive surface area and high charge density. Iron oxy-hydroxides and high molecular weight organic matter can be effective sorbers of anionic ligands such as silica or phosphate under normal or acid conditions because their zero point of charge (pH at which the net surface charge is zero) is more alkaline than associated freshwater sedimentary materials and, thus, they behave as cationic surfaces. At the same time the very fine particle size of the clay minerals provides large amounts of surface area, commonly with oxy-hydroxide coatings (Jenne, 1968, 1977). Thus, weathering reactions, which make most of the SiO_2 available to natural waters, also provide mechanisms to regulate its concentration through sorption on residual products.

Silica concentrations in some lake waters could be related to simple solubility control by solid silicate phases; however, to prove such controls would not be easy. The fact that some lake water SiO_2 concentrations fall in the concentration range appropriate for quartz (6 mg/liter) or chalcedony (17 mg/liter; Fournier, 1973) is only suggestive of such controls. Response to such influences must be slow, however. Interstitial waters from Lake Michigan sediment ranged from 29 to 38 mg/liter of silica according to Callender (1969), whereas bottom waters in the open lake are well *below* 6 mg/liter. Silica contents of stream, spring, and lake waters have been referred to the stability of clay minerals, as discussed earlier (Garrels and Mackenzie, 1967; Kramer, 1967; Sutherland, 1970; also see references summarized in Jones et al., 1974, and Fritz, 1975), but the actual authigenic development of even cryptocrystalline alumino-silicates in normal surface waters has not been adequately documented. On the other hand, the coprecipitation of silica from lake waters with hydrated oxides of iron and manganese has been demonstrated by Mortimer

(1941) and by Kato (1969), who was thus able to explain the correlation of some lacustrine silica levels with the redox cycle in lakes. Higher silica concentrations were attained under reducing conditions as ferrous iron remained in solution. Significant concentrations of silica (up to 12 wt %) have been determined by electron probe analysis in the amorphous iron oxide fraction of freshwater ferromanganese nodules in Lake Tomahawk and Green Lake in Wisconsin (Bowser, unpublished data).

Silica and iron-rich sediments are evidently forming presently in the shallower (< 250 m depth) parts of Lake Malawi in southern East Africa (Müller and Förstner, 1973). The principal sediment clay mineralogy is dominated by the presence of the iron smectite, nontronite, directly overlying diatomite deposits and close to the sediment–water interface. Some of the material contains a significant amount of amorphous hydrous ferric oxide ("limonite") admixed with opaline silica (commonly displaying an oolitic texture) and vivianite. The nontronite-rich sediments are found in relatively shallow oxic waters as a distinct "facies." Similar enriched facies of "limonite" and vivianite also occur in the shallower water sediments. Müller and Förstner (1973) argue that the nontronite is formed authigenically within the lake by reaction of silica-enriched hydrothermal waters and ferrous iron derived by interaction of the hydrothermal waters with the sediments. Nontronite has also been reported by Shapiro et al. (1971) from the bottom sediments of Lake Washington, where there is no evidence of hydrothermal activity.

The cited nontronite occurrences are unusual for freshwater lake sediments, having in common an abundance of diatom remains, minor detrital sediment, and development of anoxic hypolimnia resulting from organic productivity with consequent mobility of silica and iron. Perhaps nontronite authigenesis has gone unrecognized because of dilution by significant allogenic material. Additional locations to look for nontronite formation could be possibly in the organic carbon and diatom-rich sediment of some lakes in Minnesota.

Diatom frustules have long been noted as conspicuous components of some lacustrine sediments (e.g., Swain, 1970), especially in the very fine-grained profundal sediments of large noncalcareous lakes, where they are undiluted by influx of allogenic detritus or endogenic carbonate precipitates (e.g., Lake Baikal; Kozhov, 1963; or Tanganyika; Degens et al., 1971). Diatom species distribution and frequency with depth in sediment has been extensively utilized (see Bradbury, 1975, and references therein) to delineate the hydrologic history (Winter and Wright, 1977) and effects of human settlement, especially eutrophication (Bradbury and Winter, 1976). Assessment of nutrient loadings from diatom studies has been combined with mineralogy as an indicator of anthropogenically de-rived sediment, such as with hematite from iron ore in Lake Shagawa, Minnesota (Bradbury and Megard, 1972).

Perhaps the most concerted efforts to relate diatom remains to the natural geochemistry of associated waters and mineralogy of lacustrine sediments have been made in East Africa (Richardson, 1968; Kilham, 1971; Hecky, 1971; Richardson and Richardson, 1972; Hecky and Kilham, 1973). These authors not only worked out diatom species stratigraphies for many lakes, but correlated diatom abundances with aspects of water chemistry, such as salinity, nutrients, tem-perature, and climatic conditions. Kilham (1971) es-tablished key species as indicators of the range in silica concentration in African lake waters and Ri-chardson and Richardson (1972) utilized these species variations to evaluate stratification of water masses. Diatoms effectively limit silica concentrations in many Rift Valley lakes and cause significant undersaturation in some highly alkaline waters (Kilham and Hecky, 1973). Further, evidence for the effective role of inhib-itors (trace elements and organic compounds) on the dissolution of the amorphous silica from frustules was provided. The evidence supports indications of the importance of inhibitors from the laboratory experi-ments of Lewin (1961).

In contrast to the extensive preservation of diatoms at depth in the African lake cores, the slow dissolution of diatom remains in Lake Michigan sediments has been documented by Parker and Edgington (1976). These authors indicate that partial degradation of dia-toms occurs by zooplankton grazing or disintegration during settling in the water column. From both ob-served pore fluid profiles of silica and microscopic examination of diatom abundances, they were able to show that diagenetic remobilization of silica is essen-tially complete within the top 10 cm of sediment and, therefore, suggested that Lake Michigan sediments are not important sinks of diatom silica. Corroded diatom frustules are also common in nearby Green Bay sediments (Bowser, unpublished data). An exam-ple of such effects is illustrated in Figure 7.

The contrasting conditions between East African lakes and the Great Lakes may be due to larger silica transport in rivers and springs from more readily weathered volcanic rocks in the Rift Valleys, to differ-ences in the character of the associated organic mate-rial, or to the existence of more continuous productiv-ity in the tropical waters of the African lakes. Many of the still unresolved aspects of this question have been debated for some time (Round, 1964). Lewin (1961) summarized the observational evidence and provided experimental data suggesting a definitive role for col-loidal oxy-hydroxide coatings. Considering the impor-tant role played by diatoms in both rapid uptake and release of silica, and the relatively slow interaction of

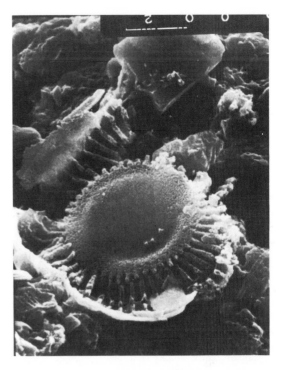

FIGURE 7.   Corroded diatom (*Cyclotella meneghiniana*) from Green Bay sediments. Field of view is 38 × 30 μm.

silicates with dissolved silica in natural waters, kinetic controls appear most important in lakes. Additional insights may be gained from the recent efforts of Kastner *et al.* (1977) to define the controls on marine diatomaceous silica recrystallization.

Carbonate minerals

Carbonate minerals constitute an important fraction of many lake sediments. They are essentially unique in that they can be derived in significant quantities from all three sediment sources (allogenic, endogenic, au-thigenic). Examples of carbonate input from each of the major sources are drawn here from field studies of specific lakes or lake regions. General development of carbonate equilibria in natural water systems is given by Garrels and Christ (1965), Stumm and Morgan (1970), Berner (1971), and Skirrow (1975).

Graf (1960) noted, in an extensive review of the mineralogy and geochemistry of fluvial and lacustrine carbonate deposits, that both calcite and dolomite in some lake sediments are related primarily to the con-tribution of fluvial detritus eroded from carbonate rocks in the surrounding source areas. For example, limestone and dolomite detritus in Alpine alluvial fans and in the Molasse beds of adjacent regions in France, Switzerland, and Germany can account in large part for the carbonate sediments common to the lakes of the area, i.e., Geneva (Serruya, 1969) and Constance (Müller, 1966). Similarly, many calcareous lake deposits in Sweden, British Columbia, or the midwestern U.S. are derived from outcrops of carbonate bedrock and/or associated glacial deposits. Based on the similarity of morphology and size distribution of dolomite and quartz, Coakley and Rust (1968) argue that the dolomite found at depth in the sediments of an arctic Canadian Lake is detrital in origin. Kennedy and Smith (1977) showed that two similar, glacier-fed lakes of Canada decrease in total carbonate and relative proportion of dolomite to calcite with grain size. They suggested that such variations are likely related to hydrodynamic sorting of the carbonate phases rather than solution or precipitation processes acting within the lake. Both density differences and differential size produced by comminution through glacial erosion were thought to contribute to this process.

Calcareous or marly lake deposits commonly occur in karstic terranes. Swain (1970) cites Stankovic (1960) on Lake Ohrid, Yugoslavia, a basin of karst origin representing coalesced solution depressions, the bottom sediments of which are comprised of fine calcareous sands and silts in shallow waters, and calcareous clays at depth.

Although many calcite-rich lake sediments may have largely allogenic sources of carbonate, many other lacustrine carbonate sediments are truly endogenic, their principal constituents having been precipitated directly from the water column both organically and inorganically. Dissolved calcium and inorganic carbon can, of course, be supplied through dissolution of older carbonate rocks in the drainage area, as:

$$CaCO_3 + H_2O + CO_2 \rightarrow Ca^{2+} + 2HCO_3^-$$

or

$$CaMg(CO_3)_2 + 2H_2O + 2CO_2 \rightarrow$$
$$Ca^{2+} + Mg^{2+} + 4HCO_3^-$$

or by hydrolysis/carbonation reactions with calcium-bearing silicates, as, for example:

$$CaAl_2Si_2O_8 + 3H_2O + 2CO_2$$
calcic plagioclase
$$= Al_2Si_2O_5(OH)_4 + Ca^{2+} + 2HCO_3^-.$$
kaolinite

Besides requiring a source of sufficient calcium and dissolved carbonate for precipitation, numerous factors within the lake can affect the solubility and, thus, precipitation of carbonates in lakes. Both organic and inorganic mechanisms are believed responsible for carbonate precipitation.

Inorganically the effect of temperature and p_{CO_2} on the solubility of calcite has been recognized as important to the distribution of lacustrine marls (Kindle, 1929). Higher water temperatures characteristic of shallow water depths favor precipitation through decreased solubility of both $CaCO_3$ and CO_2. Thus, for example, thick marl deposits are found in the shallow

waters of Lake Neuchatel (Portner, 1951). Carbonate deposition associated with the CO_2 loss accompanying emergent springs was convincingly demonstrated by Terlecky (1974) near Rochester, New York.

In the same way, the fixation of inorganic carbon in the photic zone of lakes by photosynthetic organisms results in significant lowering of p_{CO_2}. The subsequent effect is to exceed the solubility of calcite and aragonite in surface waters of productive lakes. Eutrophic, hard water lakes commonly exhibit covariance of calcite, organic carbon, and diatom concentrations in the sediments.

At greater depths in lakes, particularly deep or productive lakes, lower temperature and decay of organic matter can significantly alter carbonate solubility. Deep, cold waters of lakes can hold more inorganic carbon, and thereby promote the dissolution of carbonate. For example the p_{CO_2} at a 100 m depth in Flaming Gorge reservoir, Utah, has a concentration over 10 times atmospheric levels (B. F. Jones and E. Bolke, unpublished data). Dean and Gorham (1976a) indicate that decomposition of organic matter in the profundal zone of high organic carbon (> 39%) lake sediments in central Minnesota generates sufficient CO_2 to dissolve any calcium carbonate that may have formed endogenically, whereas lake sediments having lower contents of organic carbon contain calcite.

A number of studies on specific lakes or lake regions in which carbonate sediments are found are of interest as examples of specific controls on carbonate deposition.

Soft argillaceous marls, locally rich in shells, are generally common in postglacial freshwater sediments throughout the midwestern U.S. The origin of the dissolved carbonate in the associated lake waters of these lakes is apparently largely from the leaching of calcite-bearing glacial deposits (Graf, 1960). Swain (1970) discusses a number of Minnesota lakes as examples of "alkalitrophic" basins. These lakes are marl forming and lie in carbonate-rich late Pleistocene glacial drift.

Microscopic calcite, found in gastropod shells, diatom tests, terrigenous detritus, and a wide variety of organic materials derived from plants were reported in Wisconsin lakes by Twenhofel and McKelvey (1941). The calcareous lake sediments of the southeastern part of the state, especially lakes Mendota and Monona, typically contain a black "sludge" or gyttja overlying a much thicker deposit of light-colored marl. At the sharp interface between the layers an increase in the percentage of clastic silicates in the upper layer occurs (Murray, 1956). The average carbonate content drops from 67% in the marl to 33% in the sludge. The black color in the upper sludge results in part from authigenic sulfide. Though the supply of calcareous material from glacial deposits has surely been decreased by leaching over time, the sharp transition in

Lake Mendota sediments was attributed by Murray (1956) to input of clastics related to cultivation and urbanization in the surrounding area. The interpretation was supported by Nriagu and Bowser (1969) on the basis of fly-ash distribution in the sediments and by Bortleson and Lee (1972) on the basis of the ragweed (Ambrosia) pollen distribution.

The distribution of carbonate minerals in the Great Lakes sediments is highly variable, reflecting in part the range of lithologies contributed directly to the lakes and to the glacial deposits through which much of the material now composing the lake sediment has been cycled. Reported calcite plus dolomite concentrations range from over 30% at more than 1 m depth in Lake Michigan sediments (Callender, 1969; Gross et al., 1972), or over 40% at even greater depths in Lake Superior cores (Dell, 1971), to near zero in the surficial sediments of the central basin of Lake Erie (Thomas et al., 1976) and Lake Superior (Dell, 1971). Carbonate is low in the surficial sediments of Lake Huron overall (up to 4% as CO_3), with the higher values in the eastern part of the lake attributed to proximity of the carbonate bedrock of the Bruce peninsula (Thomas et al., 1973). Lake Ontario sediments at depth are also relatively low in carbonate (Thomas et al., 1972), but some very high concentrations in surficial materials are associated with calcite abundance only in the fine silt fraction. The dolomite which might be expected from the erosion of regional Silurian and Ordovician carbonate rocks is missing. Kemp and Thomas (1976) have suggested that this is the result of dissolution of detrital carbonate rock fragments and precipitation of authigenic calcite. Kemp and Dell (1976) have cited some sand-size, clear, euhedral calcite crystals from the Kingston basin and Hamilton Harbor sediments which they believe to be recent precipitates. In southern Green Bay (R. Rossmann, unpublished data) stoichiometric Ca/Mg ratios are very close to one in acid extracts of organic sediments, which argues strongly for dominance of the carbonate fraction by detrital dolomite, most of which presumably is transported into the southern part of the Bay by the Fox River.

The lack of carbonate in large sections of postglacial lacustrine sediments associated with the Great Lakes has been attributed to the variable dissolution of these glacially contributed components by lake waters following deposition. This mechanism was first discussed by Moore (1961) to explain the laminated sediment in the vicinity of Little Traverse Bay, Lake Michigan. He noted an inverse relationship between sediment size and detrital carbonate content modified only by a darker clay which contained dolomite, but not calcite like its lighter counterpart. He attributed the loss of calcite to dissolution brought about by organic decay, although he suggested that some of the difference might be due to differential transport. The dissolution

concept was subsequently invoked by Dell (1971, 1973a) to account for a decrease of 50% in the winter layers of varves in Lake Superior; however, in the light of Kennedy and Smith's (1967) findings, it is possible that at least part of the effect is due to hydrodynamics.

The Gnadensee, a part of the western reaches of Lake Constance which has been subject to significant anthropogenic influences, was studied by Schöttle (1969; Shöttle and Müller, 1968). Carbonates are dominant components of the sediments, except in the near shore areas, and include calcite, dolomite, and aragonite. The dolomite is entirely detrital, the aragonite is fragmental but completely biogenic in origin, whereas the calcite may be either detrital or endogenic. Much of the calcite is apparently produced by plants such as macrophyta, by algae, or by molluscs. Special attention was paid to the carbonate lumps (called "onkoids") produced by the blue–green algae. In these, the calcite content was shown to average 92% and form around a nucleus. The area of occurrence of these forms has enlarged considerably since 1911.

Schöttle (1969) divided the bottom of the Gnadensee into three zones which increase in carbonate content from near shore to the slope, but then decrease toward the central deep water zone where the finest sediments occur, and where organic decay promotes carbonate dissolution. The total carbonate content and calcite to dolomite ratio of the nearshore area is similar to the surrounding bedrock and is detrital, but most of the other carbonate lake sediment is endogenic. Schöttle (1969) estimated that the annual biogenic production of carbonates is 10 times larger than the clastic (allogenic) contribution.

Based on gasometric determinations Serruya (1971) contrasted the distribution of carbonates at Lake Kinneret and Lake Constance. From this she suggested that $CaCO_3$ precipitation at Lake Kinneret is controlled by photosynthesis and deposition is continuous. Reactions of calcium sulfate with ammonia, which has the highest concentrations in areas of maximum $CaCO_3$, were cited as the source of calcium for precipitation. Bicarbonate produced as a result of sulfate reduction (Berner, 1971) might also accomplish the same thing.

Evidence for the formation of dolomite in the low-temperature environment is sparse. In the Coorong area of South Australia, von der Borch et al. (1975, 1976) have documented the formation of stoichiometric ordered dolomite in the sediments of ephemeral alkaline lakes which results from groundwater seepage discharge into the interdunal lagoons of a regressive seacoast. Aragonite, Mg-calcite, and protodolomite assemblages form from a marine or mixed seawater–groundwater reservoir. The mean salinity of these waters is 3.5 g/liter and the mean molal Mg/Ca ratio is 1.67, though monomineralic dolomite is associated with waters as dilute as 1.4 g/liter and an Mg/Ca ratio as low as one. Indeed von der Borch (1976) indicates that groundwaters play the dominant role in Coorong-type dolomite formation. Though Müller et al. (1972) suggest that aspects of the water chemistry other than Mg/Ca ratio do not seem to affect the formation of Mg carbonates on a large scale, the data indicate that dolomite formation in the lacustrine environment requires a certain salinity and low levels of dissolved or cryptocrystalline silica in inflowing waters. Further, low sulfate concentrations seem to be necessary to prevent large scale Mg complexing in solution. This may be accomplished by the coincident precipitation of gypsum, as in the Mg-salinization mechanism suggested by Sherman et al. (1962), and the subsequent flushing of the evaporite phase (von der Borch, 1976).

Dolomite formation in truly freshwater lakes has been suggested by Dean and Gorham (1967a) and Müller et al. (1972). In the profundal sediments of the 46 Minnesota lakes examined by Dean and Gorham (1976a), the mean carbonate content (calculated from loss on ignition) in 27 carbonate lakes was 26%, and varied up to a maximum of 46%. X-ray diffraction results indicated that most of the carbonate was in the form of low magnesium calcite, although minor amounts of high-Mg calcite, dolomite, and aragonite were detected. According to the authors, dolomite is confined to lake sediments from the southern and western part of the state. They suggest the dolomite could be derived either detritally from nearby Paleozoic age carbonate rocks or from high-Mg calcite in the manner proposed by Müller et al. (1972). More dolomite was found in the sediments of Elk Lake than any other. It is the only one cited by Dean and Gorham (1976a) with a molal Mg/Ca ratio exceeding 7, the level favored by Müller et al. (1972) for the formation of dolomite from precursor high-Mg calcite. The lack of more detail on order reflections in the x-ray data, such as given by Barnes and O'Neil (1971) for metastable magnesium carbonates from California stream deposits, and the criteria for identification of dolomite employed by Dean and Gorham (1976a), as well as Müller et al. (1972), do not permit more exact definition of dolomite origin, or of the transformation from variable Ca and Mg to a fixed carbonate composition.

Besides calcite and aragonite, two other phases of $CaCO_3$ have been reported as precipitates from lacustrine waters of high alkalinity, vaterite (γ-$CaCO_3$) and monohydrocalcite ($CaCO_3 \cdot H_2O$). Vaterite has been identified by X-ray and electron diffraction as a precipitate formed in Holkham Lake, Norfolk, U.K., by Rowlands and Webster (1971). This unique occurrence is attributed to photosynthetic activity raising the pH to over 9 near the point of input of springs from underlying chalk bedrock. Other than a high calcium content, no further details of the solution chemistry

were given. The proximity of the small lake to the sea does suggest the higher concentration of other solutes as well. Duedall and Buckley (1971) suggested that the solute matrix determines the specific phase of calcium carbonate precipitated from aqueous solution. They cite experimental evidence for the effect of the Mg/Ca ratio and sodium carbonate concentration of the fluid on the polymorph of $CaCO_3$ precipitated. Sodium carbonate concentration also appears to influence the occurrence of the other phase of $CaCO_3$, monohydrocalcite at Lake Issyk-Kul (Sapozhnikov and Tsvetkov, 1959) or Lake Kivu (Stoffers and Fischbeck, 1974). Based on experimental studies the latter authors suggested that the monohydrocalcite formed under water, in part from a carbonate gel resulting from explosive diatom blooms in the surface waters of the lake. They further proposed that the phase was stabilized by magnesium and phosphate.

The relative roles of organic and inorganic processes in determining the nature of lacustrine carbonate mineralogy has not been entirely sorted out. Plants and planktonic algae are well known for their ability to extract CO_2, raise pH, and thus promote precipitation of carbonate. Phytoplankton production can be a major factor in the precipitation of $CaCO_3$. Among others, Wetzel (1966) referred to colloidal carbonate precipitation resulting from organic productivity. Chara is the plant species most frequently cited for its contribution of calcitic fragments to lacustrine marls. Aragonitic gastropod shells are commonly noted in such deposits also. Despite the presence of these organisms and algal "bioherms" in Fayetteville Green Lake, New York, Brunskill (1969) attributed the bulk of the carbonate in the laminated deposits of the lake to the accumulation of euhedral calcite which had been precipitated in response to increased water temperature in the summer. In part he based his conclusions on examination of actual collections of the crystal "rain" of calcite. Green and Round Lakes range from 1.8 to 2.6 g/liter in concentration, are meromictic, and approach gypsum saturation in the more concentrated waters. According to Brunskill's (1969) calculations, supersaturation up to eight times is achieved in surficial waters in midsummer, with values two to four times calcite saturation above the chemocline and one to two times below it being maintained through the winter. The annual $CaCO_3$ sedimentation rate obtained by Brunskill (1969) from sediment trap data was 240 g/m^2, with no increase in crystal precipitation rates nearer shore.

In Lake Balaton, Hungary, as described by Müller (1970, 1971), high-Mg calcite is precipitated during phytoplankton blooms and aragonite encrusts the leaves of water plants. Müller (1971) notes that though lake water salinity is less than 500 mg/liter, the metastable carbonate assemblage is similar to that commonly found in the marine environment. Indeed, the molal Mg/Ca ratio approaches the oceanic value (molal Mg/Ca is 5 for sea water), whereas much higher ratios in saline lakes studied by Müller *et al.* (1972) elsewhere are associated only with aragonite as a primary precipitate.

Both high-Mg calcite and aragonite are found in sediment cores from Lake Kivu in the western Rift Valley of East Africa (Degens *et al.*, 1973), which presently ranges in salinity from 0.75 g/liter at the surface to greater than 5 g/liter in bottom waters. Molar Mg/Ca ratios decrease from a surface value of 30 to about 6 at depth. Aragonite appears to be dominant where carbonate exceeds about 12% of the sediment and the pore fluid salinity is higher. In the sapropelic layers with more than 7.5% organic carbon, carbonate is lacking. Degens *et al.* (1973) believe that the occurrence of high-Mg calcite is an indication of hydrothermal discharges in the lake bottom.

In the U.S., magnesium calcite is found in association not only with western Minnesota lakes (Dean and Gorham, 1976a), but also with the sulfate Devils Lake system in North Dakota (Callender, 1968) and throughout the same region in soils associated with the deposits of glacial Lake Aggaziz (Sherman, *et al.* 1962). Lacustrine Mg-calcite is also peripheral to the high sulfate Basque Lakes, British Columbia (Nesbitt, 1974).

The occurrence of Mg-calcite is illustrative of the uncertainties surrounding the relative roles of organic and inorganic processes in the formation of aqueous carbonates. Although biogenic factors appear to be the dominant influence on marine carbonate mineralogy (Milliman, 1976), inorganic factors may be more important in lacustrine environs.

Iron and manganese

As discussed earlier, oxide coatings on sediments, especially iron, are ubiquitous in the oxygenated environments of most lakes (Jenne, 1968, 1977). In addition, thick oxidate coatings on sand and gravel nuclei are abundant in many lakes of the world. Modern freshwater ferromanganese deposits have been reviewed by Callender and Bowser (1976); similar shallow marine deposits have been reviewed by Manheim (1965) and Calvert and Price (1977), and the mineralogy of both marine and freshwater nodules was recently reviewed by Burns and Burns (1977).

Deposits of ferromanganese oxides are especially abundant in many lakes in the glaciated regions of North America and Europe. Iron and manganese is readily derived from weathering of mechanically ground, largely crystalline rock debris which is permeable and readily weathered under the humid cold–temperate climate and abundant vegetation. The chemically complex humus derived from decay of the abundant plant litter is an effective ligand former for iron and greatly aids in its solubilization and transport in surface and groundwaters.

Iron and manganese can be transported to the site of nodule and crust formation by several means. In dissolved form it may enter the lake from discharge of surface and groundwater, probably largely as humic/fulvic acid complexes, and in particulate form it is either transported as inorganic oxides or oxide coatings on stream sediment or it may be sedimented by particulate organic matter formed endogenically.

The ferromanganese deposits occur mainly in lakes where sedimentation rates are low, waters are well oxygenated, and there is little or no fine-grained, organic-rich matter in the surface sediment. These oxides occur as grain and rock outcrop coatings, surface crusts, concretions, or nodules and are dispersed within the sediment. As with marine nodules, the deposits are found principally at or very near the sediment–water interface. Nodules, especially those whose dimensions are on the order of centimeters, are most noticeable, but, overall, they are not as abundant as coatings and oxidate crusts. The most widespread occurrences of Fe–Mn oxide coatings and small nodules in North America are in northern Lake Ontario (Cronan and Thomas, 1972) and Green Bay, Lake Michigan (Rossmann and Callender, 1969; Callender and Bowser, 1976), but they are also found in all of the St. Lawrence Great Lakes. Crusts around pebbles and cobbles constitute much of the most concentrated lacustrine ferromanganese deposits yet reported: Oneida Lake, New York, and Lake Tomahawk, Wisconsin (see Callender and Bowser, 1976). In addition, crustal masses occur as fragments on the muds of Lake Windermere in the English Lake district (Gorham and Swaine, 1965) or cementing sands beneath nodules in northern Lake Michigan (Callender *et al.*, 1973). True nodular shapes range from as small as 1 mm in Green Bay, Lake Michigan, to several centimeters in Lake Champlain or Lake George, New York. Nearly all nodules have some sort of nucleus, but there appears to be no compositional preference; rock fragments, quartz sand, clay chips, or a fragment of a preexisting nodule are all likely.

Much of the material in lacustrine ferromanganese deposits is very fine-grained, poorly crystalline to amorphous, or an admixture of phases on a micron scale, and consequently mineralogic characterization is very difficult. Coey *et al.* (1974) have argued that most of the iron in lake sediments exists as amorphous ferric hydroxide (as determined by X-ray diffraction and Mössbauer spectroscopy), but this is not generally true of manganese–iron nodules and crusts. The basic oxide mineralogy appears to be similar to marine ferromanganese nodules (Burns and Burns, 1977).

Goethite is the dominant iron phase, whereas the manganese oxides include todorokite, birnessite, and psilomelane (Callender and Bowser, 1976; Bowser *et al.* 1970).

Recently, Anthony (1977) reported siderite ($FeCO_3$) from Lake of the Clouds, Minnesota; however, the diagnostic data were not given. If true, this would be the only documented occurrence of siderite from a freshwater lake, and would be important, considering the fact that manganese should be more subject than iron to authigenic recrystallization in such environments, and that rhodochrosite (noted in several freshwater localities; Callender *et al.*, 1974) was *not* reported.

Freshwater phases tend to be less crystalline than their marine counterparts, possibly a result of faster accretion rates and thus having less time for recrystallization. Goethite and amorphous $Fe(OH)_3$ are generally more abundant than the manganese minerals in both freshwater and shallow marine deposits, just the opposite of their relative abundances in deepwater marine nodules. As noted earlier in Lake Malawi, Müller and Förstner (1973) described iron oxide pellets and crusts with associated "opal" and nontronite; however, they offered no X-ray identification of the oxide phases.

Electron probe analyses of iron and manganese phases from two nodules from Lake Tomahawk are shown in Table 6. Of interest are the high phosphorus and silica contents of the goethite and the high barium in the manganese phase. Such observations are supported by the correlation matrices shown in Table 4.

A summary of X-ray diffraction experiments on three Wisconsin nodule localities is shown in Figure 8. Samples were X-rayed (untreated), then treated for approximately 1 hr in 25% w/v hydroxylamine hydrochloride ($NH_2OH \cdot HCl$) which selectively removes the manganese oxide phases. Manganese mineral diffraction lines were confirmed by their disappearance in X-rayed subsamples that had been treated with hydroxylamine.

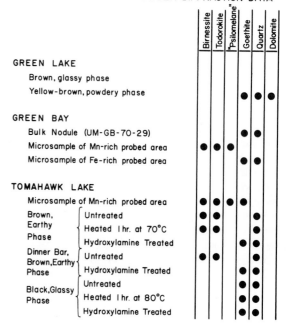

FIGURE 8.   Summary X-ray diffraction data for ferromanganese nodules from three Wisconsin localities. Results are shown for untreated, heated, and hydroxylamine hydrochloride-treated samples.

Unique to freshwater deposits is psilomelane (Bowser *et al.*, 1970). Psilomelane is less abundant than todorokite and birnessite in freshwater environments. Its cited occurrences in the marine environment are questionable. Evidently, the lack of sulfate to form barite, as in marine sediments, permits barium to coprecipitate with manganese (Rossmann and Bowser, unpublished manuscript).

The manganese carbonate rhodochrosite has been reported from several freshwater environments. Centimeter-dimension nodular masses were reported by Callender *et al.* (1974) from Green Bay (Lake Michigan), where the rhodochrosite forms by the diagenetic remobilization of manganese from buried ferromanganese oxide nodules. Manganosiderite was noted in the brackish anaerobic bottom waters of Lake Kivu (Degens and Kulbicki, 1973).

The majority of freshwater nodules display concentric bands of alternating Fe-rich (lighter) and Mn-rich (darker) laminations, which are presumably precipitated during growth of the nodules. Minor transition metal cations, such as Cu, Co, Ni, and Zn as well as barium, are associated with the Mn phase (though at lower concentrations than in marine nodules). Elements with aqueous anionic charge such as silica, phosphate, and arsenic are related to the iron lamina (Callender and Bowser, 1976). Some of these elemental associations are apparent in electron probe scans of nodules such as shown in Figure 9. The manganese–

TABLE 6.   Electron Microprobe Analyses of Ferromanganese Nodules from Tomahawk Lake, Wisconsin

| | Dinner bar | | Hershey bar | |
	Fe rich	Mn rich	Fe rich	Mn rich
Fe_2O_3	77.84	0.71	78.44	2.93
MnO_2	1.80	83.68	1.80	65.18
CaO	0.32	1.52	0.91	3.66
P_2O_5	3.27	0.20	2.88	0.24
SiO_2	8.02	0.27	7.40	0.00
K_2O	0.07	0.56	0.08	0.42
BaO	0.00	8.07	0.00	2.77
Total	91.30	95.01	91.49	75.20
		100.10[a]		100.36[a]

[a]Sum after converting Fe_2O_3 to goethite.

TABLE 7.   Chemical Composition of Freshwater, Shallow Marine, and Oceanic Ferromanganese Nodules

	Element	Green Bay	Northern Lake Michigan	Lake Ontario	Lake Oneida	Black Sea	Marginal Pacific Ocean	Average Deep Sea
wt. %	Fe	27.3	12.4	20.5	23.0	26.7	7.3	11.7
	Mn	12.8	9.8	17.1	14.4	6.9	23.9	19.0
	C_{org}	0.83	0.15	—	—	0.60	—	0.10
ppm	Co	160	234	650	70	8	96	2800
	Cu	41	63	360	80	4	305	4000
	Ni	458	1195	725	40	28	543	5800
	Zn	460	926	2020	150	—	—	400–4000
	As	578	311	50	—	750	—	—
	Pb	79	—	1890	140	—	65	1000
$(\times 10^{-4})$	Cu/Mn	3.2	6.4	21.0	5.6	5.8	127.	210.
	Co/Mn	12.5	23.8	38.0	4.9	11.6	40.2	147.
	Ni/Mn	35.8	121.	42.4	2.8	40.6	227.	305.
	Zn/Mn	35.9	94.	118.	10.4	—	—	—

barium and iron–silicon associations are clearly evident.

The iron to manganese ratio is commonly higher in freshwater than in marine ferromanganese deposits, though these ratios are also more highly variable in lacustrine materials. The oceanic mean Fe/Mn ratio is 0.47, whereas northern Lake Michigan and Green Bay average 2.2 (Rossman, 1973). Representative chemical analyses of nodules from several freshwater environments are compared with shallow and deep-sea nodule averages in Table 7 (condensed from Callender and Bowser, 1976). The complete Fe/Mn range for marine

nodules is from 160 to 0.02 and for Green Bay from 111 to 0.21, so much overlap is apparent. The widespread deposit of Lake Ontario increases regularly in Fe/Mn from 0.4 in the north to 11 in the south, evidently the result of differential solubility accompanying a decreasing trend in redox levels for relatively oxidizing conditions. This is related to the fact that ferrous iron is more readily oxidized than manganous manganese and the iron oxy-hydroxides are uniformly less soluble than the Mn oxides (see Figure 10). In Green Bay Fe/Mn ratios range from greater than 100 at river mouths to less than 1 at greatest distance from

GREEN BAY

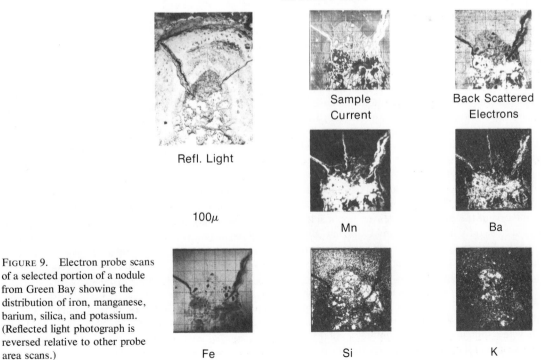

FIGURE 9.   Electron probe scans of a selected portion of a nodule from Green Bay showing the distribution of iron, manganese, barium, silica, and potassium. (Reflected light photograph is reversed relative to other probe area scans.)

Refl. Light

100μ

Sample Current

Back Scattered Electrons

Mn

Ba

Fe

Si

K

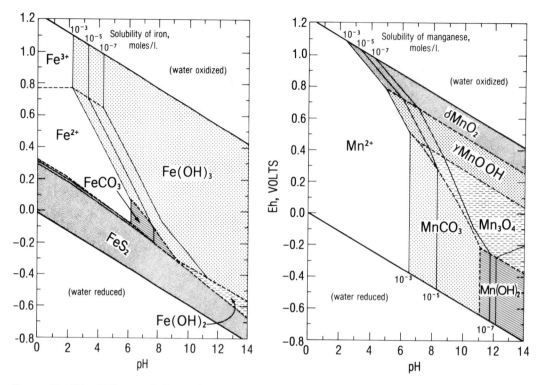

FIGURE 10.   Eh–pH diagrams for iron and manganese phases in lake systems (modified from Hem, 1977). Diagrams are drawn for 25°C, 1 atm, and solute concentrations of 10^{-3} molal total carbon dioxide species (~ 60 mg/liter of HCO_3^-) and of 10^{-4} molal total sulfur species (~ 10 mg/liter of SO_4).

stream inflow. This results from selective precipitation of iron from the river waters on mixing and settling with the suspended load as a separate or sorbed phase.

Transport of iron and manganese by lacustrine inflow is enhanced by organic and inorganic complexes of iron and manganese and by the slow rate of oxidation of these complexes. Both elements are rendered more mobile in freshwater than in seawater by more common acidic, anoxic, or organic-rich environments. Recent work by Burns and Nriagu (1976) indicated that the largest fraction of both iron and manganese in Lake Erie waters occurs as inorganic suspended particulate matter. Alternately, Koenings (1976) demonstrated that cation binding by colloidal and dissolved organic matter is an effective iron ligand in lake systems.

As inflow enters a freshwater lake, mixing tends to break down complexes so that simple solubility and redox equilibria of the oxy-hydroxides are applicable. The neutral to slightly alkaline pH and oxidizing conditions of the lake waters favor oxide precipitation, with higher values necessary for manganese precipitation than for iron. Reduced manganese is generally more mobile than iron, i.e., manganese oxides exhibit a reduced field on an Eh–pH plot with respect to iron minerals (Figure 10). Variable amounts of organic matter in lake sediments can lead to greater solubilization of manganese relative to iron; therefore, it can be

more readily transported by continued solubilization and precipitation that occurs in response to bottom water oxygen variations throughout the year. The direct decrease of iron/manganese ratios away from major source rivers in Green Bay as well as the sharp variations in Fe/Mn ratios vertically in cores are excellent testimony to the relative mobility of iron and manganese in the lake environment (Callender and Bowser, 1976). The differential solubility of oxides of iron versus manganese is the essence of the geochemical separation mechanism first proposed by Krauskopf (1957).

Under some lower redox conditions ferromanganese oxy-hydroxides and carbonates might be expected to coexist. Callender and Bowser (1976) note that the redox conditions in the muds of Lake Michigan and Ontario suggest that control of iron concentrations by amorphous $Fe(OH)_3$ and siderite is possible, but to date has not been proven. The carbonate may be present in an amount (1%) sufficient to buffer the iron in solution but not enough to detect by X-ray (3%). The discontinuous masses of rhodochrosite in the organic muds of Green Bay postdate the formation of nodules and reflect diagenesis during burial by finer sediment. The oxidation of organic matter and the diagenetic mobilization of Mn from oxy-hydroxides lead to the formation of $MnCO_3$ and result in an increase of nodule Fe/Mn with depth. The iron remains immobilized in the oxides of the associated nodules.

Callender and Bowser (1976) point out that while lake waters can be the original source of metals for ferromanganese deposits, relatively little nodule growth occurs by direct precipitation of metals from these waters. The major fraction of iron and manganese reaching the lake floor is as organic and inorganic particulate matter. However, the *direct* source of aqueous iron and manganese for nodule growth comes from sediment pore fluids; the enriched iron and manganese in the pore fluids result from diagenetic reactions (largely oxidation of organic matter) which release the metals from the sediment particulate matter. Robbins and Callender (1975) modelled the manganese distribution in a core from southern Lake Michigan according to one-dimensional diffusion based on remobilization of Mn under reducing conditions established by organic diagenesis. In southern Green Bay the pore waters of organic muds may be a source of metals to bottom waters which carry them to deposition on oxidized sands by current action. In other areas, e.g., the New York lakes, shapes of deposits argue forcefully for an underlying interstitial water source; dissolved metals appear to be fluxed to the sediment–water interface by diffusion gradients or metal-rich groundwaters.

Another factor of importance often overlooked in evaluating the major sources of dissolved iron and manganese to nodule environments is direct discharge of groundwater into the lake. The association of 2- to 3-cm-thick crusts of iron–manganese oxides in Lakes Tomahawk and Trout (Wisconsin) with coarse glacial gravels and sands and patchy distribution of the deposits in discharge lakes indicates the importance of groundwater transport of metals to lakes. Discharge of groundwater along stream beds and precipitation of oxide crusts have also been noted in some Swedish lake areas (Callender and Bowser, 1976). In contrast, Sozanski and Cronan (1976) suggest that the botryoidal form on the surface of nodules in the Shebandowan Lakes of Ontario is indicative of colloidal accretion from superjacent waters and note that poor development of the nodule underside could result from re-solution in more reducing muds.

Phosphorus

Some of the most important authigenic processes in lake sediments involve phosphorus. Phosphate concentrations in lacustrine sediment may get as high as 0.75% (by weight), but most values are less than 0.25%. Though the element can never be considered more than a minor constituent of total lake chemistry, the phosphorus nutrient function has made its distribution and complex mineralogy of considerable interest in connection with the entrophication concerns of the last decade. Initially an increase of p abundance with deeper water in small l clearly demonstrated, and was associated with fine particle settling (Livingstone and Boykin, 1962; Frink, 1967; Delfino et al., 1969). This association was then specifically correlated with colloidal oxy-hydroxides (Frink, 1969; Bortleson and Lee, 1972). Comprehensive reviews of phosphorus associations in lacustrine sediments have been presented by Williams and Mayer (1972) and Syers et al. (1973).

Williams et al. (1971c) subdivided the phosphorus of lake sediment into four categories: (1) surface sorbed, (2) coprecipitate or minor component of an amorphous phase, (3) constituent of an organic ester, or (4) component of a discrete mineral, such as apatite or vivianite. (In subsequent work Williams et al., 1976, combined the first two types.) Their studies of a range of calcareous and noncalcareous surficial sediments from 14 Wisconsin lakes indicated that most of the phosphorus was covalently bonded to an amorphous or short-range order complex related in composition to some form of hydrated iron oxide; the Fe/P ratio for the complex was at least between 5 and 10, and, where associated with active iron oxide precipitation, ranged even higher. Extensive investigation of the effects and results of extractive techniques for characterization of phosphate bound to the solid in sediments and soils allowed Williams et al. (1971c) to rule out the presence of significant siderite, sulfide, goethite, or hematite. They did not consider that calcite could account for any significant amount of phosphate not associated with iron. Furthermore, their analysis suggested that organic phosphorus was tied up in humic and fulvic fractions with the clay minerals, particularly smectites. Although closely associated with sedimented organic matter (such as in Lake Erie; Williams et al., 1976), organic phosphorus showed no obvious relationship to lake trophic levels (Sommers et al., 1972). The studies of Shukla et al. (1971) indicated that goethite and hematite can take up significant phosphate, but less than the noncrystalline fraction. The form of hydrated iron oxide responsible for phosphorus retention is most likely $Fe_2O_3 \cdot nH_2O$ (Towe and Bradley, 1967) or colloidal $Fe(OH)_3$. The degree of short-range order in the amorphous Fe–P complex, and probably the oxidation state of the Fe, can apparently be related to water depth or duration of lake stratification (Williams et al., 1971c, 1976). Koenings and Hooper (1976) demonstrated the role of an anaerobic hypolimnion and colloidal organic matter in retarding the precipitation of ferric oxy-hydroxide and concomitantly preventing phosphate sorption in an acid bog lake.

Williams and Mayer (1972) and Syers et al. (1973) pointed out that no mineralogic evidence exists for discrete phase ferric or aluminum phosphates such as strengite ($FePO_4 \cdot 2H_2O$), variscite ($AlPO_4 \cdot 2H_2O$), or wavellite $(Al_3(OH)_3(PO_4)_2)$ in modern lacustrine sediments. Sutherland *et al.* (1966) and Kramer (1967) have considered hydroxyapatite solubility control on the dissolved inorganic phosphorus concentration in pore fluids from the Great Lakes, and this has been supported by Williams and Mayer (1972). However, Syers *et al.* (1973) have pointed out that solute super-saturation does not mean that hydroxyapatite will pre-cipitate; substantial supersaturation in some of the lakes studied by Williams *et al.* (1971a) was associated with very small amounts of apatite, probably detrital, in surficial sediments. The large body of work re-viewed by Syers *et al.* (1973) has made it clear that the forms of inorganic phosphorus deduced from selective dissolution and fractionation techniques could not have been predicted using the solubility product ap-proach alone.

From mineral occurrences and thermodynamic con-siderations Nriagu and Dell (1974) argued that lacus-trine sediment diagenesis leads to the formation of complex, but at least cryptocrystalline, Ca, Al, Fe, and Mn hydroxyphosphates. Specifically, they have suggested that these minerals form from reaction of an iron oxy-hydroxide precipitate with solute phosphorus in surficial lake sediments near the mud–water inter-face where the ferrosoferric (mixed valence Fe) com-pounds might be most stable. Presumably, further iron reduction after burial in somewhat anaerobic sedi-ments can lead to formation of vivianite or related phases, with some incongruent dissolution yielding an upward flux of phosphate. Dell (1971) described authi-genic vivianite from the reduced postglacial clays of Lakes Superior, Erie, and Ontario, and Kjensmo (1968) noted it in a limited layer of a core from Lake Svinsjøen, Norway. Winter (personal communication) indicates that vivianite is not at all uncommon in lake sediment cores from Minnesota, usually in late-glacial silts and clays at the base of the sediment sequence. Müller and Förstner (1973) have explained the forma-tion of banded fibrous vivianite crusts, coatings, and crack fillings in uppermost sediment layers at Lake Malawi, East Africa, by dissolution of phosphatic fish debris and redeposition as ferrous phosphate under reducing alkaline conditions. Nriagu and Dell (1974) looked in detail at phosphatic nodules from Lake Erie and the composition of associated pore fluids. Calcula-tion of ion activity products for vivianite from the upper layers of sediment compared favorably with vivianite stability constant data; values were even higher at depth. Low redox values may have aided release of iron from ferrous silicate (clay) for further interaction with phosphate. In contrast, oxidizing con-ditions may have inhibited the decomposition of clay minerals but provided colloidal iron hydroxide for phosphate uptake. Warry and Kramer (1976) demon-strated experimentally the rapid removal of phosphate from solutions simulating Lake Erie hypolimnetic

waters by amorphous iron oxide, which was readily altered to cryptocrystalline strengite and/or phospho-siderite at 90°C.

At dissolved oxygen levels below about 1 ppm, the iron oxide–phosphate complex becomes unstable and dissolves. A layer of oxidized mud at the sediment–water interface may act as a barrier keeping soluble ferrous phosphate from diffusing out of deeper anoxic layers, but Williams and Mayer (1972) question whether the barrier is effective if the sediments are unconsolidated and contain a high water content.

Mixed metal phosphate phases seem to be associ-ated with intermediate redox conditions. Nriagu and Dell (1974) indicate that iron and calcium concentra-tions appropriate for the sediment–water interface $(10^{-4}$ and 10^{-3} M, respectively) favor anapaite $(Ca_3Fe(PO_4)_3 \cdot 4H_2O)$ over the hydroxyapatite consid-ered in the equilibrium model of Sutherland *et al.* (1966). The nodules from Lake Erie contain some ludlamite $(Fe, Mn, Mg)_3(PO_4)_2 \cdot 4H_2O$, as well as Mn-bearing vivianite. Similarly, apatites are found with more than 5% Fe plus Mn in the lake sediments. From consistent solubility trends and essentially constant ratio of cations to phosphate, Norvell (1974) demon-strated experimentally the precipitation of Ca, Fe, and Mn phosphate, probably as cryptocrystalline apatite, in wholly anoxic lake sediment. Nriagu and Dell (1974) indicate that partial oxidation of vivianite should produce ferrosoferric minerals like lipscombite $(Fe_3(PO_4)_2(OH)_2)$, and point to the poorly character-ized yellowish grains in some Lake Erie sediments and to the amorphous "crystals," or probably phosphofer-rite $[(Mn,Fe)_3(PO_4)_2 \cdot 3H_2O]$ spheres, that Shapiro *et al.* (1971) described from Lake Washington. Further attempts at mineralogic specification will be needed to develop quantitative reaction models and to improve on the efforts of Bortelson and Lee (1974), where the association of P with Fe was argued, but lack of any mineralogic information precluded evaluation of phase distribution or the relative mobility of phosphate.

In the absence of sufficient iron at typical concen-trations of other cations (e.g., 10^{-3} M), the computa-tions of Nriagu (1976) indicate that the mineral con-trols on inorganic phosphate will be apatite and clay minerals. If silica is low, a common association is kaolinite–apatite. Nriagu (1976) notes that the stability of apatite will be extended by the substitution of fluo-rine for hydroxyl in the structure. According to D'Anglejan (1967), carbonate hydroxyapatite can re-sult from diagenesis of carbonate sediment.

The coprecipitation of phosphate with calcite in a marl lake has been documented by Otsuki and Wetzel (1972). Their work indicated that phosphate is mainly incorporated into particulate carbonate with the rapid growth of crystals; the precipitation was attributed to the rise in pH accompanying photosynthetic utiliza-tion of CO_2, which is well known in marl lakes. Leckie

(1969) showed experimentally that phosphate uptake can occur readily by epitaxial growth of carbonate-substituted apatite on calcite surfaces. He suggested that in an eutrophic lake $CaCO_3$ may be formed in the epilimnion as a result of algal activity, and then settle to the bottom where reaction with phosphorus released by reduction of iron oxy-hydroxides takes place. However, Williams *et al.* (1971c) and Norvell (1974) demonstrated the uptake of phosphorus by amorphous iron fractions in lake sediments even under anoxic conditions. In fact, Shukla *et al.* (1971) found no relation of phosphate uptake to $CaCO_3$ content in calcareous lake sediments of Wisconsin.

Williams and Mayer (1972) emphasized that apatite in its many varieties is the most common phosphate mineral in sedimentary environments. Williams *et al.* (1976), in their study of the forms of phosphorus in the surficial sediments of Lake Erie, found that detrital apatite commonly contained the bulk of the sedimentary phosphorus, particularly in nearshore areas where the single most important source was the bluffs lining the northern shore of the central basin. By contrast, nonapatite inorganic and organic phosphorus was predominant mainly in fine-grained sediments accumulating in offshore depositional areas. According to Williams *et al.* (1976), the nonapatite inorganic phosphorus was closely related to the reactive iron content of the sediments, whereas organic phosphorus content was closely related to organic carbon. The approximate atomic ratio of iron to phosphorus in the resulting "ferric oxide–orthophosphate complex" is about 3:1. In the reduced zone this complex does not survive, but the same ratio is passed on to products of diagenetic reaction, such as vivianite and other combinations with ferrous iron. Organic phosphorus exists as an integral part of sediment organic matter associated with clay minerals and ferric oxide, and these components remain in relative constant ratio even under reducing conditions where the iron is recombined. Only part of the iron is available to react with phosphate, the unreactive portion being associated with chlorite and other primary minerals. Burns *et al.* (1976) attribute an eastward movement of nonapatite phosphorus in Lake Erie to a resuspended organic floc moving within 2 m of the sediment water interface.

Williams and Mayer (1972) studied a deep core from the Mississauga basin of Lake Ontario and concluded that an increase in apatite with depth was not related to shift in provenance but to diagenesis of other forms of phosphorus to apatite with time. This transformation is depicted schematically in Figure 11, taken from Williams and Mayer (1972). The processes of mineralization of organic phosphorus and release of sorbed phosphorus under reducing conditions in lacustrine sediment can provide regenerated solute phosphate through diffusion from pore fluids, but this will be counterbalanced by apatite formation. Callender (per-

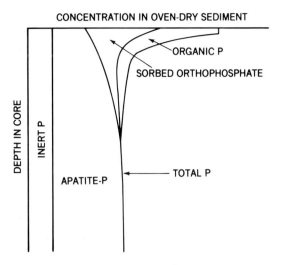

FIGURE 11. Distribution of phosphorus in a sediment profile from Lake Erie (from Willaims and Mayer, 1972) hypothetically depicted, and illustrating the diagenesis of mineral phosphate from amorphous to crystalline form. Percentage of each form is given by area fields.

sonal communication) has estimated that sediment regeneration has contributed about 40% of the phosphorus loading to White Lake, Michigan. This was deduced from analysis of pore fluids and associated solids, and attributed to dissolution of ferric hydroxide-associated phosphorus in response to diagenetic decomposition of organic matter. The amount of phosphorus regeneration is only slightly less than the 45% estimated by Livingstone and Boykin (1962) for Linsley Pond, Connecticut, on the assumption that variations of total phosphorus content of sediment bands were the result of a constant rate of phosphorus deposition with a variable rate of subsequent regeneration.

From the mineralogic reactions considered for Lakes Erie and Ontario, Williams and Mayer (1972) conclude that regeneration of solute phosphorus from sediment is an important control on the rate at which sedimentation and mineralization remove phosphorus from the lake waters.

Sulfide

Although the development of iron sulfides in lake sediments has long been recognized, precise definition of its mineralogic form has frequently not been accomplished. Vallentyne (1961) cited the quantitative determination of sulfur phases in some Japanese fresh and brackish water sediments, including the chemical and X-ray identification of pyrite making up from 10 to 80% of the total sulfur in the deposits. Identification of pyrite in Lake Michigan cores by Moore (1961) was contrasted with its absence in onshore tills that are otherwise mineralogically identical. Further work by

Vallentyne (1963) treated sulfide materials in lacustrine sediments in some detail and revealed an abundance of pyrite spherules in nearly all fine-grained deposits containing organic matter and reduced sulfur compounds. They have been specifically mentioned by Richardson and Richardson (1972) at Lake Naivasha, Kenya, and their occurrence was included along with the diatom stratigraphy. Vallentyne (1963) separated enough pyrite from Little Round Lake, Ontario, for complete analyses and thereby demonstrated its purity. Vallentyne also reviewed the possible forms of sulfide and theories of origin, concluding that the role of microorganisms and mineral species other than pyrite was poorly known. Subsequently, the mechanisms of pyrite formation by sulfurization of an initially amorphous precipitate of FeS, or mackinawite ($FeS_{0.9}$), with intermediate formation of greigite (Fe_3S_4), have been outlined by Berner (1971) and documented with election microscopy and isotopic data by Sweeney and Kaplan (1973) (Figure 12). Reaction mechanisms have been detailed by Rickard (1975). Apparently, the transformation of iron monosulfides to pyrite will not occur in the absence of sulfur. These studies appear to rule out an essential role for organisms, except in the sulfate reduction process itself. It is also apparent that the lack of sufficient solute sulfur in many freshwater environments will limit iron sulfide formation to cryptocrystalline FeS or greigite (Fe_3S_4). An abundance of organically complexed iron inflow to lakes stratified by shelter, long ice cover, and great depth compared to surface area can lead to high sulfide in sediment, low levels of solute sulfur, and so-called "iron meromixis" (Kjensmo, 1967). Of course, the occurrence of amorphous FeS is strongly suggested in those lake sediments where a correlation does exist between sulfide sulfur and excess acid solu-

ble iron, such as at Lake Mendota (Nriagu, 1968), but optical or X-ray data for a sulfide phase cannot be obtained. Dell (1971) has identified both FeS (as "hydrotroilite") and greigite at depth in cores from Lake Superior.

The development of the H_2S or solute bisulfide required to form lacustrine metal sulfide minerals is most commonly associated with anaerobic conditions accompanying organic decay, which promotes iron reduction as well. Moore (1961) attributed the pyrite, which he proved was not detrital in northeastern Lake Michigan sediments, to association with organic decay in shelly material. In cases where anoxic decay does not develop in the presence of high organic matter, as in the bottom sediments of Lake Victoria (Beauchamp, 1964), sulfur can be entirely organically bound. In other cases, hydrogen sulfide may be derived from sources extraneous to the lake sediments. In at least two locations in California, Lake Elsinore (Mann, 1951) and O'Neill Forebay Reservoir (Prokopovich, 1973), sulfide formation has been related to H_2S introduction from active fault zones.

Perhaps the most striking occurrence, however, is the microcrystalline sphalerite on resin globules suspended in Lake Kivu, East Africa, as reported by Degens et al. (1972). These micron-sized spheres are apparently formed through the scavenging of organic material by tiny bubbles produced in the degassing of waters from the anoxic depths of the stratified lake. The resinous membrane is described as acting as a template for the growth of sphalerite, and metal uptake is so selective that the ZnS is quite pure. Degens et al. (1972) assert that the zinc and dissolved gases (CO_2, CH_4, H_2S) in the waters below 60 m are from volcanically associated hydrothermal springs seeping into the lake bottom. Pyrite framboids a few microns in size are commonly found as suspended material in the bottom waters as well. Suspended sulfide spherules have been carried to Lake Tanganyika via the Ruzizi River outflow from Lake Kivu, perhaps especially at times of most intense hydrothermal activity (Degens et al., 1973). Pyrite, in the form of fine layers composed of framboids, is abundant in the upper two stratigraphic units of Lake Tanganyika sediments (Degens et al., 1971).

In many limnological studies, the identification of sulfides in sediment is made from acid solubilization and release of H_2S, or some other inference, so that mineralogic form and elemental association are unspecified. For example, Swain (1965) has simply suggested that the iron in the organic anoxic sediments of Linsley Pond, Connecticut, has largely been removed as FeS and may be associated with manganese. Swain (1965) cited a correlation in bulk sediment Fe_2O_3, SO_3, and ignition loss as caused by iron sulfide formation in the presence of abundant organic matter in Nisswa

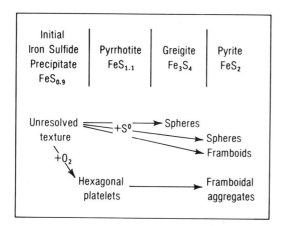

FIGURE 12.   Forms of iron sulfides in sediments (modified from Sweeney and Kaplan, 1973). Pyrrhotite has been reported only from marine environs. Schematic sequence suggests textures developed during sulfurization reactions.

Lake of Central Minnesota. Ludlam (1967) suggested the occurrence of tetragonal FeS in the dark lamina of Cayuga Lake, New York, from the mode of coloration alone. More specific identification of the sulfide phases might assist in placing an upper limit on fluxes of ferrous iron from the sediment.

Fluoride

The highest fluoride solution contents are found in waters associated with volcanic terrains. This is most readily explained by the rise in pH accompanying relatively rapid silicate hydrolysis of pyroclastics (Jones, 1966) and the resulting decrease in solubility of calcite and hydroxyapatite which precipitates calcium from solution. Kilham and Hecky (1973) demonstrated that this phenomenon is most pronounced in areas such as East Africa, where fluoride is richer in the volcanic rocks initially and there is a relative paucity of calcium. They pointed out that the highest fluoride levels are found in the saline lakes of the eastern Rift Valley, and studied the fluoride balance in most detail in the Momela Lakes on the slopes of Mt. Meru, Tanzania. Here they documented the loss of fluoride from solution through the decrease of the F/Cl ratio from surface waters to pore fluids in surficial sediments. In contrast, this ratio remains constant in lake waters undergoing evaporative concentration. Authigenic development of fluorite, CaF_2, or fluorapatite, $Ca_5(PO_4)_3F$, is suggested through secondary reaction with previously precipitated calcite. Such a mode of formation perhaps is more likely because of prior precipitation of calcite and removal of Ca resulting from the more rapid increase of carbonate species than F on weathering and evaporative concentration, rather than because of kinetic inhibition as alluded to by Kilham and Hecky (1973, p. 939). Favorable thermodynamic conditions have been identified for the replacement of calcite by fluorite in the subsurface of the saline Lake Magadi system, Kenya (Jones *et al.,* 1977). Nriagu (1976) gives an equilibrium constant for the conversion of hydroxyapatite to the fluoride form, but this cannot be evaluated for Kilham and Hecky's (1973) waters because of a lack of pH data. Under neutral conditions, however, this transformation should be favored by less than 1 mg/liter of fluoride in solution.

Summary

A number of different aspects of the mineralogy and chemistry of lake sediments have been discussed in some detail in this chapter. In addition, specific lakes cited, along with their major mineral categories,

source types, and main references, are given in Table 8. The following list summarizes briefly the most important points of the discussion:

(1) Understanding and quantification of processes controlling lake water and sediment chemistry require precise definition of the mineral phases as well as the bulk chemical composition of lacustrine deposits.

(2) Identification of mineral sources is useful to elucidate important interactions between sediments and overlying lake waters. Minerals may be classified according to source as *allogenic,* if transported to the lake; *endogenic,* if formed through processes taking place within the water column; and *authigenic,* if resulting from reactions within the sediment after deposition.

(3) The allogenic fraction of lake sediments reflects primarily the physical factors in lake systems. The endogenic and authigenic fractions reflect principally chemical factors. The latter are commonly related to variations in lake productivity.

(4) Mechanisms and rates of transfer of solutes between lake water and sediment are a function of mineral surface area, which, in turn, is closely related to grain size. The finest grained, commonly cryptocrystalline, metal oxides usually occurring as coatings on clay minerals apparently exert an influence on lake chemistry out of proportion to their total mass.

(5) Pore fluid chemistry reflects authigenic reactions in lake sediments. Often barely detectable diagenetic changes in solid phases can be recognized in the pore fluid chemistry and thus used to evaluate diagenetic changes in sediments as well as whether the precipitation or dissolution of specific solid phases is controlling fluid composition. Future pore fluid studies must be expanded to the study of temporal variations and coupled with more detailed mineralogic investigation of associated solid phases to further delineate long-term chemical changes. Combined with information on sediment accumulation and bioturbation rates, fluxes of solutes into and from sediments can be quantitatively estimated.

(6) Biologic mixing and sediment resuspension have important effects on mineral phase distribution and chemistry. Such effects are potentially more important in lake deposits than in the marine sediments where they have been most studied.

(7) Distribution and mass accumulation rates of minerals and estimates of the relative importance of sediment sources depend on meaningful sedimentation rate data. Coupled with quantitative mineralogic information, sedimentation rate knowledge will permit evaluation of accumulation rates for specific mineral or related chemical components and avoid misconceptions arising from percentage constituent data alone.

(8) Bulk chemical analyses of lacustrine sediments are of limited value without information on specific

TABLE 8. Summary of Lakes and Associated Mineralo-chemical References Used in Text

Region–lake	Mineralogy cited	Source type	References[a]
Europe			
Constance	Clastics; quartz, feldspar, clays	Allogenic	Müller (1966); Müller and Quaker-naat (1969)
(Gnadensee)	Carbonates	Endogenic	Schöttle (1969); Schöttle & Müller (1968)
Geneva	Clastics	Allogenic	Serruya (1969)
	Carbonates	Endogenic	
Neuchatel	Carbonates	Endogenic	Portner (1951)
Greifensee	Carbonates, Phosphate, sulfide	Endogenic Authigenic	Emerson (1976)
Balaton	Carbonate	Endogenic	Müller (1970, 1971)
Ohrid	Carbonate	Allo., endo.	Swain (1970)
Svinsjøen	Clays, sulfide, vivianite	Allo., endo.	Kjensmo (1967, 1968)
Windermere, Esthwaite	Fe–Mn oxides	Authigenic	Gorham and Swaine (1965)
Holkham Lake	Carbonate	Endogenic	Rowlands and Webster (1971)
Israel			
Kinneret	Clays	Allogenic	Singer et al. (1972)
	Carbonate	Endogenic	Serruya (1971)
Central Asia			
Baikal	Clastic silicates Diatoms	Allogenic	Kozhov (1963)
Issyk-Kul	Carbonate	Endogenic	Sapozhnikov and Tsvetkov (1959)
Australia			
Coorong lakes	Carbonate	Authigenic	von der Borch (1975); von der Borch et al. (1976)
E. Africa			
Victoria	Quartz, clays, feldspar	Allogenic	Richardson and Richardson (1972)
	Organic sulfur	Endogenic	Beauchamp (1964)
Albert	Clastic silicates	Allogenic	Degens et al. (1973)
Kivu	Pyroclastics	Allogenic	Degens et al. (1973)
	Diatom silica	Endogenic	Degens et al. (1973)
	Carbonates (including Mn)	Endo., auth.	Degens et al. (1973); Stoffers & Fischbeck (1974)
	Sulfides (including Zn)	Endo., auth.	Degens et al. (1972)
Tanganyika	Clays, clastic silicates	Allogenic	Degens et al. (1971)
	Diatom silica	Endogenic	Degens et al. (1971)
Malawi	Diatom silica	Endogenic	Müller and Förstner (1973)
	Iron silicate, Fe-oxide, sulfide	Authigenic	Müller and Förstner (1973)
	Vivianite	Authigenic	Müller and Förstner (1973)
Naivasha	Pyroclastics, feldspar, clays	Allogenic	Richardson and Richardson (1972)
	Diatom silica	Endogenic	Richardson and Richardson (1972)
Chila	Clastics	Allogenic	Richardson and Richardson (1972)
Momela lakes	Fluorite	Authigenic	Hecky and Kilham (1973)
Canadian Shield			
Great Slave, Great Bear	Clastic silicates	Allogenic	Larkin (1964)
Winnepeg	Clastic silicates	Allogenic	Larkin (1964)
	Diatoms	Endogenic	
	Fe–Mn oxides	Allo., endo.	Coey et al. (1974)
Experimental lakes area	Clastics	Allogenic	Brunskill et al. (1971); Schindler (1976)
	Fe–Mn oxides	Endogenic	Coey et al. (1974)
Shebandowan lakes	Fe–Mn oxides	Authigenic	Sozanski and Cronan (1976)
Little Round	Sulfide	Authigenic	Vallentyne (1963)
British Columbia, Alberta Bow, Hector	Carbonates	Allo., endo.	Kennedy and Smith (1977)
Basque	Carbonates	Endogenic	Nesbitt (1974)

TABLE 8   (*continued*)

Region–lake	Mineralogy cited	Source type	References[a]
St. Lawrence Great Lakes			
Superior	Clastics; quartz, feldspar, clays	Allogenic	Dell (1971)
	Carbonates	Allogenic	Dell (1971)
	Vivianite, sulfide	Endo., auth.	Dell (1971)
	Fe–Mn oxides	Allo., auth.	Callender & Bowser (1976)
(Silver Bay)	Clastics	Allogenic	Swain and Prokopovich (1957)
Michigan	Clays, carbonates	Allogenic	Moore (1961); Gross *et al.* (1972)
	Diatom silica	Endogenic	Parker and Edgington (1976)
(Green Bay)	Carbonates, Fe–Mn oxides	Authigenic	Callender *et al.* (1973) Callender and Bowser (1976)
Huron	Quartz, clays, carbonate	Allogenic	Thomas *et al.* (1973)
Erie	Clastics	Allogenic	Thomas *et al.* (1976); Kemp and Dell (1976)
	Fe–Mn oxides	Endogenic	Burns and Nriagu (1976)
Ontario	Quartz, clays, carbonates	Allogenic	Thomas (1969a); Thomas *et al.* (1972)
	Feldspar		Thomas (1969b); Kemp and Dell (1976)
	Phosphates, Fe–Mn oxides	Authigenic	Cronan and Thomas (1972); Nriagu and Dell (1974)
Conterminous U.S.			
California			
Tahoe	Clastics; quartz, feldspar, clays	Allogenic	Court *et al.* (1972)
Elsinore	Clastic silicates, oxides, sulfide	Allo., auth.	Mann (1951)
Connecticut			
Linsley Pond	Quartz, feldspar, sulfide	Allo., endo.	Hutchinson and Wollack (1940); Swain (1965)
	Phosphate	Authigenic	Livingstone and Boykin (1962)
Bantam	Clastics, phosphate	Allo., auth.	Frink (1967, 1969)
Louisiana			
Pontchartrain, Maurepas	Clays	Allogenic	Brooks and Ferrell (1970)
Catahoula	Clastics, clays	Allogenic	Swain (1961)
Michigan			
Lawrence	Carbonate, phosphate	Endogenic	Otsuki and Wetzel (1972)
Minnesota			
Statewide (46)	Quartz, feldspar, clays Carbonate	Allogenic Endogenic	Dean and Gorham (1976a)
Kabekona, Leech Nisswa, Cedar Bog	Clastics, carbonate	Allo., endo.	Swain (1961, 1965, 1970)
Shagawa, Sallie, Elk, Minnetonka, Pickeral	Diatoms, clastics	Endo., allo.	Bradbury and Megard (1972); Bradbury and Winter (1976); Bradbury (1975)
Lake of the Clouds	Fe–Mn oxides, vivianite, siderite	Endogenic	Anthony (1977)
Montana			
Flathead	Clastic silicates, diatoms	Allo., endo.	Swain (1961)
New York			
Oneida, George, Champlain	Fe–Mn oxides	Authigenic	Callender and Bowser (1976)
Cayuga	Carbonate, sulfide	Endo., auth.	Ludlam (1967)
Fayetteville Green, Round	Carbonate, sulfide	Endo., auth.	Brunskill (1969)
Oregon			
Crater	Pyroclastics, clays	Allogenic	Nelson (1967)

TABLE 8   (*continued*)

Region–lake	Mineralogy cited	Source type	References[a]
Washington			
L. Washington	Clastics	Allogenic	Swain (1965)
	Phosphate, Fe–Mn oxides	Authigenic	Shapiro *et al.* (1971)
Wisconsin			
Mendota, Monona	Carbonate, clastics	Endo., allo.	Twenhofel and McKelvey (1941); Murray (1956)
Wingra	Sulfide, phosphate	Authigenic	Nriagu and Bowser (1969); Bortleson and Lee (1972); Williams *et al.* (1971a, 1971c)
Trout, Tomahawk	Fe–Mn oxides	Authigenic	Callender and Bowser (1976)
Crystal	Fe–Mn oxides	Authigenic	Twenhofel and Broughton (1939)
Central America			
Nicaragua and Managua	Pyroclastics, clays	Allogenic	Swain (1966)
	Diatom silica	Endogenic	

[a]Source references in which locality is mentioned or discussed; earlier references are contained therein.

mineral distribution. Individual elements may be associated with a number of different phases.

(9) Not counting trace quantities of heavy minerals (density > 3.0 g cm^{-3}), the total number of mineral phases that have been identified in freshwater lake sediments is small. Quartz, feldspar, calcite, dolomite, illite, smectite, apatite, iron sulfides, or iron oxides account for the vast majority of lacustrine minerals. Trace amounts of endogenic or authigenic phases may be highly significant indicators of important chemical processes and, thus, warrant more detailed study.

(10) Sampling and laboratory procedures for study of lacustrine sediment mineralogy and related chemistry have been adapted from procedures developed for investigation of marine sediments or soils. Very fine-grained material requires the use of complex analytical equipment and procedures, especially centrifugal separation and X-ray diffractometry, but optical methods should not be neglected. Sequential extraction techniques have been very useful for supplementary information on amorphous or cryptocrystalline phases. Carefully obtained pore fluid analyses should be most helpful as well.

(11) Statistical analysis has frequently been misused in the investigation of lacustrine sediments. Inadequate sample data have been subjected to involved treatment such as factor analysis, which either complicated or simply reaffirmed relationships established by direct observation, experiment, or straightforward correlation methods. Insufficient recognition has been given to the problem of closed data sets in constituent chemical analysis and quantitative mineralogy.

(12) Most lake sediments are dominated by non-clay clastic minerals, which are positively correlated with the sand or silt-size fraction. The most important minerals are quartz and feldspar, with or without heavy minerals and detrital carbonate. These allogenic materials are subjected to selective sorting and winnowing,

but remain effectively unaltered in the lacustrine environment, except for a minor amount of dissolution or "subaqueous weathering."

(13) Studies of clay mineralogy in freshwater lakes suggest that little clay mineral authigenesis occurs, and that these phases, like the minerals of coarser grained fractions, primarily reflect source lithologies. However, investigation of intergrades and mixed-layer clays has been inadequate to indicate possible lake water interactions with these materials; the possible association of nontronite with reducing, siliceous, iron-rich conditions needs such further study. Use of activity–activity diagrams for evaluation of silicate "stability" in lake environments has so far resulted in ambiguous conclusions, insufficiently supported by mineralogic detail.

(14) Pyroclastic sediments are subject to greater dissolution or alteration than more common sedimentary silicates. Lakes dominated by volcanogenic material are commonly associated with high diatom productivity.

(15) The principal short-term controls on silica concentrations in freshwater lakes are diatoms and silicate sorption. Clay mineral diagenesis may eventually limit silica solubility, but this has yet to be conclusively demonstrated.

(16) Calcite is the dominant carbonate mineral and the principal endogenic phase in lacustrine sediments. The relative roles of organic and inorganic processes in determining the nature and amount of lacustrine carbonate is controversial, but the importance of both is clear. Evidence for the origin of magnesium-bearing carbonate in freshwater lakes is ambiguous, and dolomite formation is unlikely in the freshwater lacustrine environment. Rhodochrosite is the only other carbonate which is well documented, though rare, in lake sediments.

(17) The ubiquitous presence of iron and manganese

oxides in lake sediments, as grain coatings or as distinct crusts and nodular masses, underscores the mobility of these metals in oxidizing–reducing conditions of lake systems. The ability of the Fe–Mn oxides to selectively sorb other transition metal elements and the diagenetic interaction of iron with both phosphorous and silica mean that the ferromanganese oxides play a key role in the exchange of trace transition metals and nutrients between sediments and the overlying water column.

(18) The phosphate mineralogy of lake sediments is dominated by authigenic processes. Though detrital apatite is little altered in the lacustrine environment, solute or organic phosphate is sorbed by iron oxides and eventually incorporated either into vivianite or more complex mixed valence metal phosphates in the sediment. This material may eventually be further transformed into diagenetic apatite and essentially removed from further water–sediment interaction. Regeneration of solute phosphorus by reduction of amorphous iron oxides in lake sediments is an important control on the rate at which sedimentation and mineral diagenesis remove phosphorus from lake waters.

(19) Amorphous or cryptocrystalline iron monosulfide is common in reduced lacustrine sediments, but transformation to pyrite has only rarely been documented, probably because of the lack of time and added elemental sulfur to complete the reaction. Other sulfides are rare.

(20) Authigenic fluorite or fluorapatite is probably more common in lake sediments than has heretofore been appreciated. The transformation of calcite or apatite to these phases may be accomplished readily in the diagenetic lacustrine environment, but it is probably of such small quantitative magnitude as to go undetected in all but high fluoride lithologic provinces.

For nearly all of the major mineral groups discussed in this chapter, there is some controversy about interpretations of origin. Nowhere is this better illustrated than in the case of authigenic versus allogenic origin for lacustrine clay minerals. Much of the controversy could be avoided if these studies had been designed and carried out to actually *test* between alternate hypotheses. To simply state that observations are consistent with one or another idea alone is not adequate, and all too often merely perpetuates eroneous concepts. Numerous papers reviewed in the preparation of this chapter, while professing a particular origin for minerals in various lake environments, simply did not consider that their data were inadequate to rule out alternative explanations. Future studies aimed at true *tests* of alternate hypotheses of mineral origin need to be made before many lake sediment controversies can be put to rest.

Future application of detailed mineralogic and chemical extraction techniques to lake sediments offers potentially new and useful insight into both chemical and physical lake processes. Bottom sediments play a significant role in controlling the dynamics of many metals and nutrients in lakes. More vigorous mineralogic studies of critical sediment phases will be required before some of these processes will be fully understood. Treatment of sediments as a chemically homogenous "phase" has severely limited the recognition of these sediments as complex mixtures from numerous different sources, each capable of specific reactions with entrapped pore fluids and overlying waters. Ultimately, better knowledge of the origin and distribution of these sediment mineral phases will allow us to better interpret the evolution of the lake system through time, and thus to better evaluate the influence of changing conditions on the lake processes, such as those resulting from the cultural activities of man.

ACKNOWLEDGMENTS.   We wish to thank T. C. Winter, H. P. Eugster, E. A. Jenne, D. A. Livingstone, D. K. Nordstrom, and particularly E. Callender for helpful comments. We also thank Brenda Lawson, Gloria Boehm, and Betty Hudner for clerical assistance, and Carolyn Moss and Paul Dombrowski for help with the illustrations. We are especially grateful for extended encouragement and aid to our efforts given by Judy Bowser and Betty Jones. Special inspiration was provided by C. Saint-Saens, J. Coltrane, and friends.

References

Allen, H. E., and J. R. Kramer. (1972). *Nutrients in Natural Waters*. Wiley-Interscience, New York, NY.

Anderson, B. J., and E. A. Jenne. (1970). Free-iron and manganese oxide content of reference clays. *Soil Sci.*, **109**:163–169.

Anderson, J. U. (1963). An improved pretreatment for mineralogical analysis of samples containing organic matter. *Clays Clay Min.*, **10**:380–388.

Anderson, R. Y. (1977). Short term sedimentation response in lakes in western United States as measured by automated sampling. *Limnol. Oceanogr.*, **22**:423–433.

Anthony, R. S. (1977). Iron-rich rhythmically laminated sediments in Lake of the Clouds, northeastern Minn. *Limnol. Oceanogr.*, **22**:45–54.

Arneman, H. F., and H. E. Wright, Jr. (1959). Petrography of some Minnesota tills. *J. Sed. Petrol.* **29**:540–554.

Austin, G. S., and R. K. Leininger. (1976). The effect of heat-treating sedimented mixed-layer illite-smectite as related to quantitative clay mineral determinations. *J. Sed. Petrol.*, **46**:206–216.

Barnes, I., and J. R. O'Neil. (1971). Calcium-magnesium carbonate solid solutions from Holocene conglomerate cements and travertines in the Coast Range of California. *Geochim. Cosmochim. Acta.* **35**:699–718.

Barnes, R. O. (1973). An *in situ* interstitial water sampler for use in unconsolidated sediments. *Deep Sea Res.*, **20**:1125–1128.

Beauchamp, R. S. A. (1964). The Rift Valley lakes of Africa. *Verh. Int. Verein. Limnol.,* **15**:91–99.

Beeton, A. M., and W. T. Edmondson. (1972). The eutrophication problem. *J. Fish. Res. Board Can.,* **29**:673–682.

Benninger, L. K., R. C. Aller, E. P. Dion, and K. K. Turekian. (1977). Pb-210 distribution in sediments of Long Island Sound. *Trans. Am. Geophys. Union,* **58**:422.

Berner, R. A. (1971). *Principles of Chemical Sedimentology.* McGraw–Hill, New York, NY.

Berner, R. A. (1974). Kinetic models for the early diagenesis of nitrogen, sulfur, phosphorus, and silicon in anoxic marine sediments. Pp. 427–450. In: E. D. Goldberg (ed.), *The Sea.* vol. 5.

Berner, R. A. (1976a). The benthic boundary layer from the point of view of a geochemist. In: N. McCave (ed.), *The Benthic Boundary Layer.* Plenum Press, New York, NY.

Berner, R. A. (1976b). Inclusion of adsorption in the modelling of early diagenesis. *Earth Plan. Sci. Lett.,* **29**:333–340.

Berner, R. A. (1977). Stoichiometric models for nutrient regeneration in anoxic sediments. *Limnol. Oceanogr.,* **22**:781–786.

Berner, R. A., and G. R. Holdren, Jr. (1977). Mechanism of feldspar weathering. Some observational evidence. *Geology,* **5**:369–372.

Blatt, H., G. Middleton, and R. Murray. (1972). *Origin of Sedimentary Rocks.* Prentice–Hall, Englewood Cliffs, NJ.

Bodine, M. W., Jr., and T. H. Fernalld. (1973). EDTA dissolution of gypsum, anhydrite, and Ca–Mg carbonates. *J. Sed. Petrol.* **43**:1152–1156.

Bonner, W. P., T. Tamura, C. W. Francis, and J. W. Amburgey, Jr. (1970). Zonal centrifugation—a tool for environmental studies. *Env. Sci. Technol.* **4**:821–825.

Bortleson, G. C. (1970). The chemical investigation of recent lake sediments from Wisconsin lakes and their interpretation. Ph.D. Thesis, Univ. Wisconsin.

Bortleson, G. C., and G. F. Lee. (1972). Recent sedimentary history of Lake Mendota, Wis. *Environ. Sci. Tech.,* **9**:799–808.

Bortleson, G. C., and G. Lee. (1974). Phosphorus, iron, manganese distribution in sediment cores of six Wisconsin lakes. *Limnol. Oceanogr.,* **19**:794–801.

Bouma, A. H., and N. F. Marshall. (1964). A method for obtaining and analyzing oceanic sediment samples. *Marine Geol.,* **2**:81–99.

Bower, C. A. (1963). Adsorption of *O*-phenanthroline by clay minerals and soils. *Soil Sci.,* **95**:192–195.

Bower, C. A., and J. T. Hatcher. (1966). Simultaneous determination of surface area and cation-exchange capacity. *Soil Sci. Soc. Am. Proc.,* **30**:525–527.

Bowser, C. J. (1974). Core and pore fluid studies. In: Cruise Report Mn74-01, R/V Moana Wave, Univ. Hawaii. Publ. HIG-74-9:177–183.

Bowser, C. J., E. Callender, and R. Rossman. (1970). Electron-probe and x-ray studies of freshwater ferromanganese nodules from Wisconsin and Michigan. *Geol. Soc. Am. Abs.,* **2**:500–501.

Bradbury, J. P. (1975). Diatom stratigraphy and human settlement in Minnesota. *Geol. Soc. Am. Spec. Paper,* **171**:1–74.

Bradbury, J. P., and R. O. Megard. (1972). Stratigraphic record of pollution in Shagawa Lake, Northeastern Minnesota. *Geol. Soc. Am. Bull.,* **83**:2639–2648.

Bradbury, J. P., and T. C. Winter. (1976). Areal distribution and stratigraphy of diatoms in the sediments of Lake Sallie, Minnesota. *Ecology,* **57**:1005–1014.

Bray, J. T., O. P. Bricker, and B. N. Troup. (1973). Phosphate in interstitial waters of anoxic sediments: oxidation effects during sampling procedure. *Science,* **180**:1362–1364.

Brooks, R. A., and R. E. Ferrell, Jr. (1970). The lateral distribution of clay minerals in Lakes Pontchartrain and Maurepas, Louisiana. *J. Sed. Petrol.,* **40**:855–863.

Brookins, D. G. (1972). Possible accumulation of authigenic, expandable-type clay minerals in the substructure of Tuttle Creek Dam, Kansas, U.S.A. *Eng. Geol.,* **6**:251–259.

Bruland, K. W., M. Koide, C. Bowser, L. J. Maher, and E. D. Goldberg. (1975). Lead-210 and pollen geochronologies on Lake Superior sediments. *Quat. Res.,* **5**:89–98.

Brunskill, G. J. (1969). Fayetteville Green Lake, New York. II. Precipitation and sedimentation of calcite in a meromictic lake with laminated sediments. *Limnol. Oceanogr.,* **14**:830–847.

Brunskill, G. J., D. Povoledo, B. W. Graham, and M. P. Stainton. (1971). Chemistry of surface sediments of sixteen lakes in the experimental lakes area, Northwestern Ontario. *J. Fish. Res. Board Can.,* **28**:277–294.

Burns, N. M., and J. O. Nriagu. (1976). Forms of iron and manganese in Lake Erie waters. *J. Fish. Res. Board Can.,* **33**:463–470.

Burns, N. M., J. D. H. Williams, J. M. Jaquet, A. L. W. Kemp, and D. C. L. Lam. (1976). A phosphorus budget for Lake Erie. *J. Fish. Res. Board Can.,* **33**:564–573.

Burns, R. G., and V. M. Burns. (1977). Mineralogy of ferromanganese nodules. In: G. P. Glasby (ed.), *Marine Manganese Deposits.* Elsevier, New York, NY.

Callender, E. (1968). The postglacial sedimentology of Devils Lake, North Dakota. Ph.D. thesis, Univ. of North Dakota.

Callender, E. (1969). Geochemical characteristics of Lakes Michigan and Superior sediments. Pp. 124–160. *Proc. 12th Conf. Great Lakes Res.*

Callender, E., and C. J. Bowser. (1976). Freshwater ferromanganese deposits. Pp. 343–394. In: K. H. Wolf (ed.), *Handbook of Strata-Bound and Stratiform Ore Deposits.* Vol. 7, Elsevier, New York, N.Y.

Callender, E., C. J. Bowser, and R. Rossman. (1974). Geochemistry of ferromanganese and manganese carbonate crusts from Green Bay, Lake Michigan. *Trans. Am. Geophys. Union,* **54**:340.

Calvert, S. E., and N. B. Price. (1977). Shallow water, continent margin deposits: distribution and geochemistry. In: G. P. Glasby (ed.), *Marine Manganese Deposits.* Elsevier, New York, NY.

Carlson, R. E. (1977). A trophic state index for lakes. *Limnol. Oceanogr.,* **22**:361–369.

Chao, T. T. (1972). Selective dissolution of manganese oxides from soils and sediments with acidified hydroxylamine hydrochloride. *Soil Sci. Soc. Am. Proc.,* **36**:764–678.

Chayes, F. (1971). *Ratio Correlation.* Univ. Chicago Press, Chicago, IL.

Chester, R., and M. J. Hughes. (1967). A chemical technique for the separation of ferromanganese minerals, carbonate minerals, and adsorbed trace elements from pelagic sediments. *Chem. Geol.*, **2**:249–262.

Chung, F. H. (1974a). Quantitative interpretation of x-ray diffraction patterns of mixtures. I. Matrix-flushing method for quantitative multicomponent analysis. *J. Appl. Cryst.*, **7**:519–525.

Chung, F. H. (1974b). Quantitative interpretation of x-ray diffraction patterns of mixtures. II. Adiabatic principal of x-ray diffraction analysis of mixtures. *J. Appl. Cryst.*, **7**:526–531.

Chung, F. H. (1975). Quantitative interpretation of x-ray diffraction patterns of mixtures. III. Simultaneous determination of a set of reference intensities. *J. Appl. Cryst.*, **8**:17–19.

Coakley, J. P., and B. R. Rust. (1968). Sedimentation in an Arctic Lake. *J. Sed. Petrol.*, **38**:1290–1300.

Cody, R. D., and G. L. Thompson. (1976). Quantitative x-ray powder diffraction analyses of clays using an orienting internal standard and pressed disks of bulk shale samples. *Clays Clay Min.*, **24**:224–231.

Coey, J. M. D., D. W. Schindler, and F. Weber. (1974). Iron compounds in lake sediments. *Can. J. Earth Sci.*, **11**:1489–1493.

Cook, H. E., P. D. Johnson, J. C. Matti, and I. Zemmels. (1975). Methods of sample preparation and x-ray diffraction data analysis. *Initial Repts. Deep Sea Drilling Project,* Natl. Sci. Foundation, **38**:999–1007.

Court, J. E., C. R. Goldman, and N. J. Hyne. (1972) Surface sediments in Lake Tahoe, California–Nevada. *J. Sed. Petrol.*, **42**:359–377.

Craig, R. J. (1972). Pollen influx to laminated sediments: a pollen diagram from northeastern Minnesota. *Ecology*, **53**:46–57.

Cronan, D. S. (1969). Inter-element associations in some pelagic deposits. *Chem. Geol.*, **5**:99–106.

Cronan, D. S., and R. L. Thomas. (1972). Geochemistry of ferromanganese oxide concentrations and associated deposits in Lake Ontario. *Geol. Soc. Am. Bull.*, **83**:1493–1502.

Cubitt, J. M. (1975). A regression technique for the analysis of shales by x-ray diffractometry. *J. Sed. Petrol.*, **45**:546–553.

Cuthbert, F. L. (1944). Clay minerals in Lake Erie sediments. *Am. Mineral.*, **29**:378–388.

D'Anglejan, B. F. (1967). Origin of marine phosphorites off Baja California, Mexico. *Marine Geol.*, **5**:15–44.

Davis, M. B. (1968). Pollen grains in lake sediments: redeposition caused by seasonal water recirculation. *Science*, **162**:796–799.

Davis, R. B., D. L. Thurlow and F. E. Brewster. (1975). Effects of burrowing tubificid worms on the exchange of phosphorous between lake sediments and overlying water. *Verh. Int. Verein. Limnol.*, **19**:382–394.

Dean, J. A. (1969). *Chemical Separation Methods*. Van Nostrand Reinhold, New York, NY.

Dean, W. E., and E. Gorham. (1976a). Major chemical and mineralogical components of profundal surface sediments in Minnesota Lakes. *Limnol. Oceanogr.*, **21**:259–284.

Dean, W. E., and E. Gorham. (1976b). Classification of Minnesota Lakes by Q- and R-mode factor analysis of sediment mineralogy and geochemistry. In: D. F. Meriam (ed.), *Quantitative Techniques for the Analysis of Sediments*. Pergamon Press, New York, NY.

Degens, E. T., and G. Kulbicki. (1973). Hydrothermal origin of metals in some East African Rift Lakes. *Mineral. Deposita*, **8**:388–404.

Degens, E. T., R. P. von Herzen, and H. K. Wong. (1971). Lake Tanganyika: water chemistry, sediments, geological structure. *Naturwissenschaften*, **58**:229–241.

Degens, E. T., H. Okada, S. Honjo, and J. C. Hathaway. (1972). Microcrystalline sphalerite in resin globules suspended in Lake Kivu, East Africa. *Mineral. Deposita*, **7**:1–12.

Degens, E. T., R. P. von Herzen, H-K. Wong, W. G. Deuser, and H. W. Jannasch. (1973). Lake Kivu: structure, chemistry and biology of an East African Rift Lake. *Geol. Rundschau.*, **62**:245–277.

Delfino, J. J., G. C. Bortleson, and G. F. Lee. (1969). Distribution of Mn, Fe, P, Mg, K, Na, and Ca in the surface sediments of Lake Mendota, Wisconsin. *Environ. Sci. Technol.*, **3**:1189–1192.

Dell, C. I. (1971). Late Quaternary sedimentation in Lake Superior. PhD. Thesis, Univ. of Michigan.

Dell, C. I. (1973a). A special mechanism for varve formation in a glacial lake. *J. Sed. Petrol.* **43**:838–840.

Dell, C. I. (1973b). Vivianite: an authigenic phosphate mineral in Great Lake sediments. Pp. 1027–1028. *Proc. 16th Conf. Great Lakes Res.*

Dell, C. I. (1974). The stratigraphy of northern Lake Superior late-glacial and post-glacial sediments. Pp. 179–192. *Proc. 17th Conf. Great Lakes Res.*, Pt. 1.

Deudall, I. W., and D. E. Buckley. (1971). Calcium carbonate monohydrate in seawater. *Nature, Phys. Sci.*, **234**:39–30.

Devine, S. B., R. E. Ferrell, and G. K. Billings. (1972). A quantitative x-ray diffraction technique applied to fine-grained sediments of the deep Gulf of Mexico. *J. Sed. Petrol.*, **42**:468–475.

Douglas, L. A., and F. Fiessinger. (1971). Degradation of clay minerals by H_2O_2 treatments to oxidize organic matter. *Clays Clay Min.*, **19**:67–68.

Dudas, M. J., and M. E. Harward. (1971). Effect of dissolution treatment on standard and soil clays. *Soil Sci. Soc. Am. Proc.*, **35**:134–140.

Edgington, D. N., J. A. Robbins, and Carttunen. (1974). The distribution of Pb-210 and stable lead in Lake Michigan sediments. *Argonne Natl. Lab. Rept.*, ANL-8060, **3**:63–76.

Edgington, D. H., and J. A. Robbins. (1976). Patterns of deposition of natural and fallout radionuclides in the sediments of Lake Michigan and their relation to limnological processes. Pp. 705–730. In: J. O. Nriagu (ed.), *Environmental Biogeochemistry* Vol. 2. Ann Arbor Sci. Publ., Ann Arbor, MI.

Edwards, A. M. C., and P. S. Liss. (1973). Evidence for buffering of dissolved silicon in fresh waters. *Nature*, **243**:341–342.

Emerson, S. (1976). Early diagenesis in anaerobic lake sediments: chemical equilibria in interstitial waters. *Geochim. Cosmochim. Acta*, **40**:925–934.

Evanko, M. A. (1977). Vertical sediment distribution of meiobenthic crustaceans in Lake Erie–Ashtabula, Ohio. (abst.) *Proc. 20th Conf. Great Lakes Res.*

Fanning, K. A., and M. E. Q. Pilson. (1971). Interstitial silica and pH in marine sediments: some effects of sampling procedure. *Science,* **173**:1228–1231.

Fournier, R. O. (1973). Silica in thermal waters: laboratory and field investigations. Pp. 122–139. *Proc. Int. Symp. Hydrochem. Biochem.,* Japan, 1970, Washington, D.C.

Francis, C. W., and T. Tamura. (1972). An evaluation of zonal centrifugation as a research tool in soil science. II. Characterization of soil clays. *Soil Sci. Soc. Am. Proc.,* **36**:372–376.

Francis, C. W., F. S. Brinkley, and E. A. Bondietti. (1976). Large-scale zonal rotors in soil science. *Soil Sci. Soc. Am. Proc.,* **40**:785–792.

Frink, C. R. (1967). Nutrient budget: rational analysis of eutrophication in a Connecticut lake. *Environ. Sci. Tech.,* **1**:425–428.

Frink, C. R. (1969). Chemical and mineralogical characteristics of eutrophic lake sediments. *Soil Sci. Soc. Am. Proc.,* **33**:369–372.

Fritz, B. (1975). Etude thermodynamique et simulation des reactions entre mineraux et solutions application a la geochimie des alterations et des eux continentales. Universite Louis Pasteur de Strasbourg, *Sciences Geologiques Memoire N°41.*

Frye, J. C., and N. F. Shimp. (1973). Major, minor, and trace elements in sediments of Late Pleistocene Lake Saline compared to those in Lake Michigan sediments. *Ill. Geol. Survey Environ. Geol. Notes,* **60**:14.

Gad, M., and H. Le Riche. (1966). A method for separating detrital and nondetrital trace elements in reduced sediments. *Geochim. Cosmochim. Acta,* **30**:841–846.

Gahler, A. R. (1969). Sediment–water nutrient interchange. In: *Eutrophication Biostimulation Assessment Workshop.* U. of California, Berkeley, CA.

Garrels, R. M. (1967). Genesis of some ground waters from igneous rocks. In: P. H. Abelson (ed.), *Researches in Geochemistry.* John Wiley, New York, NY.

Garrels, R. M., and C. L. Christ. (1965). *Solutions, Minerals and Equilibria.* Harper and Row, New York, NY.

Garrels, R. M., and F. T. Mackenzie. (1967). Origin of the chemical compositions of some springs and lakes. In: R. F. Gould (ed.), *Equilibrium Concepts in Natural Water Systems.* Am. Chem. Soc., Adv. in Chem. Ser. **67**:222–242.

Gibbs, R. J. (1967). The Geochemistry of the Amazon River System: Part I. The factors that control the salinity and composition and concentration of the suspended solids. *Geol. Soc. Am. Bull.,* **78**:1203–1232.

Gibbs, R. J. (1977). Transport phases of transition metals in the Amazon and Yukon Rivers. *Geol. Soc. Am. Bull.,* **88**:829–843.

Goedert, W. J. (1973). Cation equilibria in soils of Rio Grand do Sul, Brazil. Ph.D. Thesis, Univ. Wisconsin.

Goldhaber, M. B., R. C. Aller, J. K. Cochran, J. K. Rosenfeld, C. S. Martens, and R. A. Berner. (1977). Sulfate reduction, diffusion, and bioturbation in Long Island Sound sediments: report of the FOAM group. *Am. J. Sci.,* **277**:193–237.

Gorham, E., and D. J. Swaine. (1965). The influence of oxidizing and reducing conditions upon the distribution of some elements in lake sediments. *Limnol. Oceanogr.,* **10**:268–279.

Graf, D. L. (1960). Geochemistry of carbonate sediments and sedimentary carbonate rocks; part I. Carbonate mineralogy–carbonate sediments. *Ill. Geol. Surv. Circ.,* **39**:297.

Griffin, G. M. (1962). Regional clay-mineral facies: products of weathering intensity and current distribution in the northeastern Gulf of Mexico. *Geol. Soc. Am. Bull.,* **73**:737–767.

Griffiths, J. C. (1967). *Scientific Method of Analysis of Sediments.* McGraw–Hill, New York, NY.

Grim, R. E. (1968). *Clay Mineralogy.* 2nd ed. McGraw–Hill, New York, NY.

Gross, D. L., J. A. Lineback, N. F. Shimp, and W. A. White. (1972). Composition of Pleistocene sediments in southern Lake Michigan, U.S.A. *24th Int. Geol. Cong.,* **8**:215–222.

Guinasso, N. J., Jr., and D. R. Shink. (1975). Quantitative estimates of biological mixing rates in abyssal sediments. *J. Geophys. Res.,* **80**:3032–3043.

Hahn, H. H., and W. Stumm. (1970). The role of coagulation in natural waters. *Am. J. Sci.,* **268**:354–368.

Halma, G. (1969a). A simple and rapid method to obtain a linear density gradient. *Clay Min.,* **8**:47–57.

Halma, G. (1969b). The separation of clay mineral fractions with linear heavy liquid density gradient columns. *Clay Min.,* **8**:59–69.

Harbaugh, J. W., and D. F. Merriam. (1968). *Computer Applications in Stratigraphic Analysis.* John Wiley, New York, NY.

Harward, M. E., D. D. Carstea, and A. H. Sayegh. (1969). Properties of vermiculites and smectites: expansion and collapse. *Clays Clay Min.,* **16**:437–447.

Hecky, R. E. (1971). The paleolimnology of the alkaline, saline lakes on the Mount Meru lahar. Ph.D. Thesis, Duke University.

Hecky, R. E., and P. Kilham. (1973). Diatoms in alkaline, saline lakes: ecology and geochemical implications. *Limnol. Oceanogr.,* **18**:53–71.

Heezen, B. C., *et al.* (1973). *Initial Reports of the Deep Sea Drilling Project.* Washington (U.S. Govt. Printing Office), 20. 958 pp.

Hem, J. D. (1977). Reactions of metal ions at surfaces of hydrous iron oxide. *Geochim. Cosmochim. Acta,* **41**:527–538.

Hem, J. D., and C. J. Lind. (1974). Kaolinite synthesis at 25°C. *Science,* **184**:1171–1173.

Hesslein, R. H. (1976). An *in situ* sampler for close interval pore water studies. *Limnol. Oceanogr.,* **21**:912–914.

Holdren, G. C. (1974). Measurement of sediment interstitial phosphorus release from intact sediment cores. M.S. Thesis, Univ. of Wisconsin.

Holdren, G. R., Jr., O. P. Bricker, III, and G. Matisoff. (1975). A model for the control of dissolved manganese in the interstitial waters of Chesapeake Bay. In: T. M. Church (ed.), *Marine Chemistry in the Coastal Environment.* Am. Chem. Soc., Symposium Ser., **18**:364–381.

Hornbrook, E. H. W., and R. G. Garrett. (1976). Regional geochemical lake sediment survey, east-central Saskatchewan. *Geol. Survey Canada Paper* 75-41. 20 pp.

Hough, J. L. (1963). The prehistoric Great Lakes of North America. *Am. Sci.,* **51**:84–109.

Hutchinson, G. E. (1957). *A Treatise on Limnology. Vol. I. Geography, Physics, and Chemistry.* John Wiley, New York, NY.

Hutchinson, G. E. (1969). Eutrophication, past and present. Pp. 17–28. In: *Eutrophication: Causes, Consequences, Correctives*. Natl. Acad. Sci. Symposium.

Hutchinson, G. E., and A. Wollack. (1940). Studies on Connecticut lake sediments: II. Chemical analysis of a core from Linsley Pond, North Branford. *Am. J. Sci.*, **238**:493–517.

Jackson, M. L. (1974). *Soil Chemical Analysis–Advanced Course*. 2nd ed. Madison, WI (published by the author). 895 pp.

Jenne, E. A. (1968). Controls on Mn, Fe, Co, Ni, Cu, and Zn concentrations in soils and water: the significant role of hydrous Mn and Fe Oxides. In: *Trace Inorganics in Water*. Am. Chem. Soc., Adv. in Chem. Ser., **73**:337–387.

Jenne, E. A. (1977). Trace element sorption by sediments and soils—sites and processes. Pp. 425–553. In: W. Chappell and K. Peterson (eds.), *Molybdenum in the Environment*. Marcel-Dekker, New York, NY.

Jenne, E. A., and S. N. Luoma. (1977). Forms of trace elements in soils, sediments, and associated waters: an overview of their determination and biological availability. *Biological Implications of Metals in the Environment*. 15th Life Sciences Symposium, Hanford, WA. 74 pp.

Johansen, K. A., and J. A. Robbins. (1977). Fallout cesium-137 in sediments of southern Lake Huron and Saginaw Bay. (abst.) *Proc. 20th Conf. Great Lakes Res.*

Johns, W. D., R. E. Grim, and W. F. Bradley. (1954). Quantitative estimations of clay minerals by diffraction methods. *J. Sed. Petrol.*, **24**:242–251.

Jones, B. F., (1966). Geochemical evolution of closed basin water in the western Great Basin. In: J. L. Rau (ed.), *Second Symposium on Salt*. Northern Ohio Geological Society, **1**:181–200.

Jones, B. F., S. L. Rettig, and H. P. Eugster. (1967). Silica in alkaline brines. *Science*, **158**:1310–1314.

Jones, B. F., V. C. Kennedy, and G. W. Zellweger. (1974). Comparison of observed and calculated concentrations of dissolved Al and Fe in stream water. *Water Resour. Res.*, **10**:791–793.

Jones, B. F., H. P. Eugster, and S. L. Rettig. (1977). Hydrochemistry of the Lake Magadi basin, Kenya. *Geochim. Cosmochim. Acta*, **41**:53–72.

Kalil, E. K., and M. Goldhaber. (1973). A sediment squeezer for removal of pore waters without air contact. *J. Sed. Petrol.*, **43**:553–557.

Kastner, M., J. B. Keene, and J. M. Gieskes. (1977). Diagenesis of siliceous oozes. I. Chemical controls on the rate of opal-A to opal-CT transformation—an experimental study. *Geochim. Cosmochim. Acta*, **41**:1041–1060.

Kato, K. (1969). Behavior of dissolved silica in connection with oxidation–reduction cycle in lake water. *Geochem. J.*, **3**:87–97.

Kemp, A. L. W., T. W. Anderson, R. L. Thomas, and A. Mudrochova. (1974). Sedimentation rates and recent sediment history of Lakes Ontario, Erie and Huron. *J. Sed. Petrol.*, **44**:207–218.

Kemp, A. L. W., and C. I. Dell. (1975). The geochemistry and mineralogy of Lakes Ontario and Erie bluffs, sediments. Pp. 50–58. In: *Proc. 3rd Ann. Conf. Environ. Earth Sci. Res. Rept. Ser. 20*. Dept. Geol. Sci. Brock Univ., St. Catherines, Ont.

Kemp, A. L. W., and C. I. Dell. (1976). A preliminary comparison of the composition of bluffs and sediments from Lakes Ontario and Erie. *Can. J. Earth Sci.*, **13**:1070–1081.

Kemp, A. L. W., and R. L. Thomas. (1976). Cultural impact on the geochemistry of the sediments of Lakes Ontario, Erie and Huron. *Geosci. Can.*, **3**:191–207.

Kennedy, S. K., and N. D. Smith. (1977). The relationship between carbonate mineralogy and grain size in two alpine lakes. *J. Sed. Petrol.*, **47**:411–418.

Kilham, P. (1971). A hypothesis concerning silica and freshwater planktonic diatoms. *Limnol. Oceanogr.*, **16**:10–18.

Kilham, P., and R. E. Hecky. (1973). Fluoride: geochemical and ecological significance in East African waters and sediments. *Limnol. Oceanogr.*, **6**:932–945.

Kindle, E. M. (1929). A comparative study of different types of thermal stratification in lakes and their influence on the formation of marl. *J. Geol.*, **37**:150–157.

Kinniburgh, D. G. (1974). Cation adsorption by hydrous metal oxides. Ph.D. thesis, Univ. Wisconsin.

Kittrick, J. A. (1970). Precipitation of kaolinite at 25°C and 1 atm. *Clays Clay Min.*, **18**:261–267.

Kjensmo, J. (1967). The development and some main features of "iron-meromictic" soft water lakes. *Arch. Hydrobiol.*, Suppl. Bd., **32**:137–312.

Kjensmo, J. (1968). Late and post-glacial sediments in the small meromictic Lake Svinsjoen. *Arch. Hydrobiol.*, **65**:125–141.

Knebel, H. J., J. C. Kelly, and J. T. Whetten. (1968). Clay minerals of the Columbia River. A qualitative, quantitative, and statistical evaluation. *J. Sed. Petrol.*, **38**:600–611.

Kodama, H., J. A. McKeague, R. J. Tremblay, J. R. Gosselin, and M. G. Townsend. (1977). Characterization of iron oxide compounds in soils by Mossbauer and other methods. *Can. J. Earth Sci.*, **14**:1–15.

Koenings, J. P. (1976). *In situ* experiments on the dissolved and colloidal state of iron in an acid bog lake. *Limnol. Oceanogr.*, **21**:674–683.

Koenings, J. P., and F. F. Hooper. (1976). The influence of colloidal organic matter on iron and iron-phosphorus cycling in an acid bog lake. *Limnol. Oceanogr.*, **21**:684–696.

Koide, M., K. W. Bruland, and E. D. Goldberg. (1973). Th-228/Th-232 and Pb-210 geochronologies in marine and lake sediments. *Geochim. Cosmochim. Acta*, **37**:1171–1184.

Kozhov, M. (1963). *Lake Baikal and its Life*. Biol. Mon. XI. Junk Publications, The Hague.

Kramer, J. R. (1967). Equilibrium models and composition of the Great Lakes. In: R. F. Gould (ed.), *Equilibrium Concepts in Natural Water Systems*. Am. Chem. Soc. Adv. in Chem. Ser. **67**:243–254.

Krauskopf, K. B. (1957). Separation of manganese from iron in sedimentary processes. *Geochim. Cosmochim. Acta*, **12**:61–84.

Krenkel, P. A. (ed.). (1975). *Heavy Metals in the Aquatic Environment*. Pergamon Press, New York, NY.

Krezoski, J. R., and J. A. Robbins. (1977). Radioactivity in sediments of the Great Lakes: post-depositional redistribution by deposit-feeding organisms. (abst.) *Proc. 20th Conf. Great Lakes Res.*

Krishniswami, L. D., J. M. Martin, and M. Meybeck. (1971). Geochronology of lake sediments. *Earth Planet. Sci. Lett.,* **11**:407–411.

Lagerwerff, J. V. (1964). Extraction of clay-water systems. *Soil Sci. Soc. Am. Proc.,* **28**:502–506.

Lahann, R. W. (1976). The effect of trace metal extraction procedures on clay minerals. *J. Environ. Sci. Health,* **11**:639–662.

Larkin, P. A. (1964). Canadian Lakes. *Verh. Int. Verein. Limnol.,* **15**:76–90.

Lasaga, A. C. (1977). The modelling of kinetics and transport phenomena in early diagenesis. *Trans. Am. Geophys. Union,* **58**:516.

Lasaga, A. C., and H. D. Holland. (1976). Mathematical aspects of non-steady-state diagenesis. *Geochim. Cosmochim. Acta,* **40**:257–266.

Leckie, J. O. (1969). Interaction of calcium phosphate at calcite surfaces. Ph.D. thesis, Harvard Univ.

Lerman, A. (1977). Migrational processes and chemical reactions in interstitial waters. In: E. D. Goldberg, I. N. McCave, J. J. O'Brien, and J. H. Steel (eds.), *The Sea,* **6**:695–738.

Lerman, A., and G. J. Brunskill. (1971). Migration of major constituents from lake sediments into lake water and its bearing on lake water composition. *Limnol. Oceanogr.,* **16**:880–890.

Lerman, A., and C. W. Childs. (1973). Metal-organic complexes in natural waters: control of distribution by thermodynamic, kinetic, and physical factors. Pp. 201–236. In: P. C. Singer (ed.), *Trace Metals and Metal-Organic Interactions in Natural Waters.* Ann Arbor Science Publ., Ann Arbor, MI.

Lewin, J. C. (1969). The dissolution of silica from diatom walls. *Geochim. Cosmochim. Acta,* **21**:182–192.

Livingstone, D. A., and J. C. Boykin. (1962). Distribution of phosphorus in Linsley Pond mud. *Limnol. Oceanogr.,* **7**:57–62.

Ludlam, S. (1967). Sedimentation in Cayuga Lake, New York. *Limnol. Oceanogr.,* **12**:618–632.

Lusczynski, N. J. (1961). Filter-press method of extracting water samples for chloride analysis. *U.S.G.S. Water Supply Paper 1544-A.* 8 pp.

Mackereth, F. J. H. (1965). Chemical investigations of lake sediments and their interpretations. *Proc. Royal Soc.,* **161**:295–309.

Mackereth, F. J. H. (1966). Some chemical observations on postglacial lake sediments. *Phil. Trans. Roy. Soc. London,* **258**:165–213.

Maher, L. J., Jr. (1977). Palynological studies in the western arm of Lake Superior: *Quat. Res.,* **7**:14–44.

Mangelsdorf, P. C., Jr., T. R. S. Wilson and E. Daniell. (1969). Potassium enrichments in interstitial waters of marine sediments. *Science.* **165**:171.

Manheim, F. T. (1965). *Manganese-Iron Accumulations in the Shallow Marine Environment.* Univ. Rhode Island: Narragansett Mar. Lab. Occ. Publ.

Manheim, F. T. (1966). A hydraulic squeezer for obtaining interstitial water from consolidated and unconsolidated sediments. *U.S.G.S. Prof. Paper 550-C* C256-C261.

Manheim, F. T. (1967). Evidence for submarine discharge of water on the Atlantic continental slope of the southern United States, and suggestions for further research. *Trans. New York Acad. Sci.,* Ser. II. **29**:839–853.

Manheim, F. T. (1976). Interstitial waters of marine sediments. Pp. 115–186. In: J. P. Riley and R. Chester (eds.), *Chemical Oceanography.* 2nd ed., Vol. 6.

Mann, J. R., Jr. (1951). The sediments of Lake Elsinore, Riverside County, California. *J. Sed. Petrol.,* **21**:151–161.

Martens, C. S. (1974). A method for measuring dissolved gases in pore waters. *Limnol. Oceanogr.,* **19**:525–530.

Matisoff, G., O. P. Bricker, III, G. R. Holdren, Jr., and P. Kaerk. (1975). Spatial and temporal variations in the interstitial water chemistry of Chesapeake Bay sediments. In: T. M. Church (ed.), *Marine Chemistry in the Coastal Environment.* Am. Chem. Soc., Symposium Ser. **18**:343–363.

McCall, P. L., and J. B. Fisher. (1977). Vertical transport of sediment solids by *Tubifex tubifex* (Oligochaeta). (abst.) *Proc. 20th Conf. Great Lakes Res.*

McKeague, J. A. (1967). An evaluation of 0.1M phyrophosphate and phrophosphate-dithionite in comparison with oxalate as extractants of the accumulation products in podzols and some other soils. *Can. J. Soil Sci.,* **47**:95–99.

McKeague, J. A. (1968). Humic-fulvic acid ratio, Al, Fe, and C in pyrophosphate extracts as criteria of A and B horizons. *Can. J. Soil Sci.,* **48**:27–35.

McKeague, J. A., and J. H. Day. (1966). Dithionite and oxalate-extractable Fe and Al as aids in differentiating various classes of soils. *Can. J. Soil Sci.,* **46**:13–22.

McKeague, J. A., J. E. Brydon, and N. M. Miles. (1971). Differentiation of forms of extractable iron and aluminum in soils. *Soil Sci. Soc. Am. Proc.,* **35**:33–38.

Mehra, O. P., and M. L. Jackson. (1960). Iron oxide removal from soils and clays by a dithionite-citrate system buffered with sodium-bicarbonate. *Clays Clay Min.,* **7**:317–327.

Merilainen, J. (1969). Distribution of diatom frustules in recent sediments of some meromictic lakes. *Mitt. Int. Ver. Theor. Agnew. Limnol.,* **17**:186–192.

Middlebrooks, E. J., D. H. Falkenberg, and T. E. Maloney. (eds.). (1974). *Modelling the Eutrophication Process.* Ann Arbor Science Publ., Ann Arbor, MI.

Miesch, A. T. (1969). The constant sum problem in geochemistry. In: D. F. Meriam (ed.), *Computer Applications in the Earth Sciences.* Plenum Press, London.

Milford, H. H., and M. L. Jackson. (1962). Specific surface determination of expansible layer silicates. *Science,* **135**:929–930.

Milliman, J. D. (1976). *Marine Carbonates.* Springer-Verlag, New York, NY.

Moore, C. A., and M. L. Silver. (1975). Nutrient transport by sediment–water interaction. *Proc. Int. Clay Conf.,* **1975**:495–504.

Moore, J. E. (1961). Petrography of northeastern Lake Michigan bottom sediments. *J. Sed. Petrol.,* **3**:402–436.

Mortimer, C. H. (1941). The exchange of dissolved substances between mud and water in lakes. *J. Ecol.,* **29**:280–329.

Mortimer, C. H. (1969). Physical factors with bearing on eutrophication in lakes in general and in large lakes in particular. Pp. 340–370. In: *Eutrophication: Causes, Consequences, Correcives.* Nat'l. Acad. Sci. Symposium.

Mortimer, C. H. (1971). Chemical exchanges between sediments and water in the Great Lakes—speculations on probable regulatory mechanisms. *Limnol. Oceanogr.*, **16**:387–404.

Mudroch, A., A. J. Zeman, and Sandilands, R. (1977). Identification of mineral particles in fine grained lacustrine sediments with transmission electron microscope and x-ray dispersive spectroscopy. *J. Sed. Petrol.*, **47**:244–250.

Müller, G. (1966). Die Sedimentbildung im Bodensee. *Naturwissenschaften*, **53**:237–247.

Müller, G. (1970). High-magnesian calcite and protodolomite in Lake Balaton (Hungary) sediments. *Nature Phys. Sci.*, **226**:749–750.

Müller, G. (1971). Aragonite: inorganic precipitation in a freshwater lake. *Nature Phys. Sci.*, **229**:18.

Müller, G., and U. Forstner. (1973). Recent iron ore formation in Lake Malawi, Africa. *Mineral. Deposita.*, **8**:278–290.

Müller, G., and J. Quakernaat. (1969). Diffractometric clay mineral analysis of recent sediments of Lake Constance (central Europe). *Contr. Mineral. Petrol.*, **22**:268–275.

Müller, G., G. Irion, and U. Forstner. (1972). Formation and diagenesis of inorganic Ca–Mg carbonates in the lacustrine environment. *Naturwissenschaften*, **59**:158–164.

Murray, R. C. (1956). Recent sediments of three Wisconsin lakes. *Geol Soc. Am. Bull.*, **67**:883–910.

Nelson, C. H. (1967). Sediments of Crater Lake, Oregon. *Geol. Soc. Am. Bull.*, **78**:833–848.

Nesbitt, H. W. (1974). The study of some mineral-aqueous solution interactions. Ph.D. Thesis, Johns Hopkins Univ.

Norvell, W. A. (1974). Insolubilization of inorganic phosphate by anoxic lake sediment. *Soil Sci. Soc. Am. Proc.*, **38**:441–445.

Nozaki, Y., J. K. Cochran, K. K. Turekian, and G. Keller. (1977). Radiocarbon and ^{210}Pb distribution in submersible-taken deep-sea cores from project FAMOUS. *Earth Planet. Sci. Lett.*, **34**:167–173.

Nriagu, J. O. (1968). The distribution of iron in lake sediments. *Trans. Wis. Acad. Arts Sci.*, **56**:153–164.

Nriagu, J. O. (1976). Phosphate–clay mineral relations in soils and sediments. *Can. J. Earth Sci.*, **13**:717–736.

Nriagu, J. O., and C. J. Bowser. (1969). The magnetic spherules in sediments of Lake Mendota, Wisconsin. *Water Res.*, **3**:833–842.

Nriagu, J. O., and C. I. Dell. (1974). Diagenetic formation of iron phosphates in recent lake sediments. *Am. Mineral.*, **59**:934–946.

Nussmann, D. G. (1965). Trace elements in the sediments of Lake Superior. Ph.D. thesis, Univ. of Michigan.

Otsuki, A., and R. G. Wetzel. (1972). Coprecipitation of phosphate with carbonates in a marl lake. *Limnol. Oceanogr.*, **17**:763–767.

Paddock, R. W. (1975). Chloride transport between sediment and water in Lake Wingra. M. S. Thesis, Univ. Wisconsin.

Parker, J. I., and D. N. Edgington. (1976). Concentration of diatom frustules in Lake Michigan sediment cores. *Limnol. Oceanogr.*, **21**:887–893.

Parks, G. A. (1967). Aqueous surface chemistry of oxides and complex oxide minerals. Isoelectric point and zero point of charge. In: R. F. Gould (ed.), *Equilibrium Concepts in Natural Water Systems*. Am. Chem. Soc., Adv. in Chem. Ser. **67**:121–161.

Parks, G. A. (1975). Adsorption in the marine environment. Pp. 241–308. In: J. P. Riley and Skirrow (eds.), *Chemical Oceanography*. 2nd ed., Vol 1.

Pennington, W., R. S. Cambray, and E. M. Fisher. (1973). Observations on lake sediments using fallout ^{137}Cs as a tracer. *Nature*, **242**:324–326.

Perry, E. A., Jr. (1971). Silicate–sea water equilibria in the ocean system: a discussion. *Deep Sea Res.*, **18**:921–924.

Petrovic, R. (1976). Rate control in felspar dissolution—II. The protective effect of precipitates: *Geochim. Cosmochim. Acta*, **40**:1509–1522.

Petrovic, R., R. A. Berner, and M. B. Goldhaber. (1976). Rate control in dissolution of alkali feldspars—I. Study of residual feldspar grains by x-ray photoelectron spectroscopy. *Geochim. Cosmochim. Acta*, **40**:537–548.

Pierce, J. W., and F. R. Siegel. (1969). Quantification in clay mineral studies of sediments and sedimentary rocks. *J. Sed. Petrol.*, **39**:187–193.

Plas, L. van der, and A. C. Tobi. (1965). A chart for judging the reliability of point counting results. *Am. J. Sci.*, **263**:87–90.

Portner, C. (1951). Le mecanisme de la precipitation du $CaCO_3$ et la determination de lepaisseur du depot annuel de la vase dans le lac de Neutchatel. *Geol. Rundschau.*, **39**:212–216.

Potter, P. E., D. Heling, N. F. Shimp, and W. Van Wie. (1975). Clay mineralogy of modern alluvial muds of the Mississippi River basin. *Bull. Centre Reche. Pau-SNPA.*, **2**:353–389.

Prokopovich, N. P. (1973). Iron sulfide concretions from Tulare formation at O'Neill Forebay reservoir, western Merced County, California, *Am. Assn. Petrol. Geol.*, **57**:12.

Quakernaat, J. (1968). X-ray analyses of clay minerals in some recent fluviatile sediments along the coasts of Central Italy. *Publ. Fys-geog. Lab. Univ. Amsterdam*, **12**:105.

Quakernaat, J. (1970). Direct diffractometric quantitative analysis of synthetic clay mineral mixtures with molybdenite as orientation-indicator. *J. Sed. Petrol.*, **40**:506–513.

Rashid, M. A. (1974). Adsorption of metals on sedimentary and peat humic acids. *Chem. Geol.*, **13**:115–123.

Reeburgh, W. S. (1967). An improved interstitial water sampler. *Limnol. Oceanogr.*, **12**:163–165.

Reineck, H. E. (1963). Der Kastengreifer. *Natur. Mus.*, **93**:103–108.

Richardson, J. L. (1968). Diatoms and lake typology in East and Central Africa. *Int. Rev. Geo. Hydrobiol.*, **53**:229–338.

Richardson, J. L., and A. E. Richardson. (1972). History of an African Rift Lake and its climatic implications. *Ecol. Mon.*, **42**:499–534.

Rickard, D. T. (1975). Kinetics and mechanism of pyrite formation at low temperatures. *Am. J. Sci.*, **275**:636–652.

Rittenberg, S. C., K. O. Emery, and W. L. Orr. (1955). Regeneration of nutrients in sediments of marine basins. *Deep Sea Res.*, **3**:23–45.

Robbins, J. A., and E. Callender. (1975). Diagenesis of manganese in Lake Michigan sediments. *Am. J. Sci.,* **275**:512–533.

Robbins, J. A., and D. N. Edgington. (1975). Determination of recent sedimentation rates in Lake Michigan using Pb-210 and Cs-137. *Geochim. Cosmochim Acta,* **39**:285–304.

Robbins, J. A., and J. Gustinis. (1976). A squeezer for efficient extraction of pore water from small volumes of anoxic sediment. *Limnol. Oceanogr.,* **21**:905–909.

Robbins, J. A., J. R. Krezoski, and S. C. Moxley. (1977). Radioactivity in sediments of the Great Lakes: postdepositional redistribution by deposit feeding organisms. *Earth Planet. Sci. Lett.* **36**:325–333.

Rosenbaum, M. S. (1976). Effect of compaction on the pore fluid chemistry of montmorillonite. *Clays Clay Min.,* **24**:118–121.

Rossman, R. (1973). Lake Michigan ferromanganese nodules: Ph.D. Thesis, Univ. of Michigan.

Rossman, R., and E. Callender. (1969). Geochemistry of Lake Michigan manganese nodules. *Proc. Conf. Great Lakes Res.,* **12**:306–316.

Rossman, R., E. Callender, C. J. Bowser. (1972). Interelement geochemistry of Lake Michigan ferromanganese nodules. *Proc. 24th Intl. Geol. Congr.,* Montreal, Sec., **10**:336–341.

Round, F. E. (1964). The diatom sequence in lake deposits: some problems of interpretation: *Verh. Int. Verein. Limnol.,* **15**:1012–1020.

Rowlands, D. L. G., and R. K. Webster. (1971). Precipitation of vaterite in lake water. *Nature Phys. Sci.,* **229**:158.

Sapozhnikov, D. G., and A. I. Tsvetkov. (1959). Precipitation of hydrous calcium carbonate on the bottom of Lake Issyk-Kul. (In Russian). *Doklady Akad. Nauk. SSSR* **124**:402–405.

Sayles, F. L., T. R. S. Wilson, D. N. Hume and P. C. Mangelsdorf, Jr. (1973). In situ sampler for marine sedimentary pore waters: evidence for potassium depletion and calcium enrichment. *Science,* **181**:154–156.

Sayles, F. L., P. C. Mangelsdorf, Jr., T. R. S. Wilson, and D. N. Hume. (1976). A sampler for the *in situ* collection of marine sedimentary pore waters. *Deep Sea Res.,* **23**:259–264.

Scafe, D. W., and G. W. Kunze. (1971). A clay mineral investigation of six cores from the Gulf of Mexico. *Marine Geol.,* **10**:69–85.

Schindler, D. W. (1976). Biogeochemical evolution of phosphorus limitation in nutrient-enriched lakes of the Precambrian Shield. In: J. Nriagu (ed.), *Environmental Biogeochemistry.* Ann Arbor Sci. Publ., Ann Arbor, MI.

Schink, D. R., and N. L. Guinasso, Jr. (1977). Effects of bioturbation on sediment–seawater interaction. *Marine Geol.,* **23**:133–154.

Schöttle, M. (1969). The sediments of the Gnadensee. *Arch. Hydrobiol.,* Suppl Bd., **35**:255–308.

Schöttle, M., and G. Müller. (1968). Recent carbonate sedimentation in the Gnadensee (Lake Constance) Germany. In: G. Müller and G. M. Friedman (eds.), *Recent Developments in Carbonate Sedimentology in Central Europe.* Springer-Verlag, Berlin.

Sommers, L. E., R. F. Harris, J. D. H. Williams, D. E. Armstrong, and J. K. Syers. (1972). Fractionation of organic phosphorus in lake sediments. *Soil Sci. Soc. Am. Proc.,* **36**:51–54.

Sozanski, A. G., and D. S. Cronan. (1976). Environmental differentiation of morphology of ferromanganese oxide concretion in Shebandowan Lakes, Ontario. *Limnol. Oceanogr.,* **21**:894–898.

Stankovic, S. (1960). The Balkan Lake Ohrid and its Living World. Biol. Mon. IV. Junk, The Hague.

Stoffers, P., and R. Fischbeck. (1974). Monohydrocalcite in the sediments of Lake Kivu (East Africa). *Sedimentology,* **21**:163–170.

Stumm, W., and J. J. Morgan, (1970). *Aquatic Chemistry.* Wiley-Interscience, New York, NY.

Subramanian, V. (1975). A note on the effect of chemical treatments in mineralogical studies of sediments. *Experienta,* **31**:12–13.

Sutherland, J. C. (1969). Geochemical systems in Onondaga Lake (central New York state) compared with the Great Lakes. Pp. 357–363. *Proc. 12th Conf. Great Lakes Res.*

Sutherland, J. C. (1970). Silicate mineral stability and mineral equilibria in the Great Lakes. *Environ. Sci. Technol.,* **4**:826–833.

Sutherland, J. C., J. R. Kramer, L. Nichols, and T. Kurtz. (1966). Mineral-water equilibria, Great Lakes: silica and phosphorus. Univ. of Michigan Pub. **15**:439–445.

Swain, F. M. (1965). Geochemistry of some quaternary lake sediments of North America. Pp. 765–781. In: H. E. Wright and D. G. Frey (eds.), *The Quaternary of the United States.* Princeton Univ. Press, Princeton, NJ.

Swain, F. M. (1966). Bottom sediments of Lake Nicaragua and Lake Managua, Western Nicaragua. *J. Sed. Petrol.* **36**:522–540.

Swain, F. M. (1970). *Non-Marine Organic Geochemistry.* Cambridge Univ. Press, Cambridge.

Swain, F. M., and N. Prokopovich. (1957). Stratigraphy of upper part of sediments of Silver Bay area, Lake Superior. *Geol. Soc. Am. Bull.,* **68**:527–542.

Sweeney, R. E., and I. R. Kaplan. (1973). Pyrite framboid formation. Laboratory synthesis and marine sediments. *Econ. Geol.,* **68**:618–634.

Syers, J. K., R. F. Harris, and D. E. Armstrong. (1973). Phosphate chemistry in lake sediments. *J. Environ. Qual.,* **2**:1–14.

Terlecky, P. M., Jr. (1974). The origin of a late Pleistocene and Holocene marl deposit. *J. Sed. Petrol.,* **44**:456–465.

Thienemann, A. (1925). *Die Binnengewasser mitteleuropas.* Binnengewasser I.E. Schweizerbartsche Verlagsbuchhandlung, Stuttgart.

Thomas, R. L. (1969a). A note on the relationship of grain size, clay content, quartz and organic carbon in some Lake Erie and Lake Ontario sediments. *J. Sed. Petrol.,* **42**:66–84.

Thomas, R. L. (1969b). The qualitative distribution of feldspars in surficial bottom sediments from Lake Ontario. Pp. 364–379. *Proc. 12th Conf. Great Lakes Res.*

Thomas, R. L., A. L. W. Kemp, and C. F. M. Lewis. (1972). Distribution, composition, and characteristics of the surficial sediments of Lake Ontario. *J. Sed. Petrol.,* **42**:66–84.

Thomas, R. L., A. L. W. Kemp, and C. F. M. Lewis. (1973). The surficial sediments of Lake Huron. *Can. J. Earth Sci.,* **10**:226–271.

Thomas, R. L., L. M. Jaquet, A. L. W. Kemp, and C. F. M. Lewis. (1976). The surficial sediments of Lake Erie. *J. Fish. Res. Board Can.,* **33**:385–403.

Till, R. (1974). *Statistical Methods for the Earth Scientist.* John Wiley, New York, NY.

Towe, K., and W. Bradley. (1967). Mineralogical constitution of colloidal "hydrous ferric oxides." *J. Colloid. Sci.,* **24**:384–392.

Truesdell, A. H., and B. F. Jones. (1974). WATEQ, A computer program for calculating chemical equilibria of natural waters. *U.S.G.S. J. Res.,* **2**:238–248.

Twenhofel, W. H. (1933). The physical and chemical characteristics of the sediments of Lake Mendota, a fresh water lake of Wisconsin. *J. Sed. Petrol.,* **3**:68–76.

Twenhofel, W. H. (1937). The bottom sediments of Lake Monona, a fresh-water lake of southern Wisconsin. *J. Sed. Petrol.,* **7**:67–77.

Twenhofel, W. H., and W. A. Broughton. (1939). The sediments of Crystal Lake, an oligotrophic lake in Vilas County, Wisconsin. *Am. J. Sci.,* **237**:231–252.

Twenhofel, W. H., and V. E. McKelvey. (1939). The sediments of Devils Lake, a eutrophic–oligotrophic lake of southern Wisconsin. *J. Sed. Petrol.,* **9**:105–121.

Twenhofel, W. H., and V. E. McKelvey. (1941). Sediments of fresh water lakes. *Am. Assn. Petrol. Geol.,* **25**:826–849.

Ugolini, F. C., and M. L. Jackson. (1977). Weathering and mineral synthesis in antarctic soils. *Proc. Internat. Sympos. on Antarctic Geol. Geophys..* Madison, WI.

Vallentyne, J. R. (1961). On the rate of formation of black spheres in recent sediments. *Verh. Int. Verein. Limnol.,* **14**:291–295.

Vallentyne, J. R. (1963). Isolation of pyrite spherules from recent sediments. *Limnol. Oceanogr.,* **8**:16–30.

Van Olphen, H. (1963). *An Introduction to Colloid Chemistry.* Wiley-Interscience, New York, NY.

Von der Borch, C. C., D. E. Lock, and D. Schwebel. (1975). Ground-water formation of dolomite in the Coorong region of South Australia. *Geology,* **3**:283–285.

Von der Borch, C. C. (1976). Stratigraphy and formation of Holocene dolomitic carbonate deposits of the Coorong area, South Australia. *J. Sed. Petrol.,* **46**:952–966.

Warry, N. D., and J. R. Kramer. (1976). Some factors affecting the synthesis of cryptocrystalline strengite from an amorphous phosphate complex. *Can. Min.,* **14**:40–46.

Weaver, C. E., and L. D. Pollard. (1973). *The Chemistry of Clay Minerals.* Elsevier, New York, NY.

Wetzel, R. G. (1966). Productivity and nutrient relationships in marl lakes of northern Indiana. *Verh. Int. Verein. Limnol.,* **16**:321–332.

Wetzel, R. G. (1975). *Limnology.* W. B. Saunders, Philadelphia, PA.

Williams, J. D. H., and T. Mayer. (1972). Effects of sediment diagenesis and regeneration of phosphorus with special reference to Lakes Erie and Ontario. In: H. E. Allen and J. R. Kramer (eds.), *Nutrients in Natural Waters.* Wiley Interscience, New York, NY.

Williams, J. D. H., J. K. Syers, R. F. Harris, and D. E. Armstrong. (1971a). Fractionation of inorganic phosphate in calcareous lake sediments. *Soil Sci. Soc. Am. Proc.,* **35**:250–255.

Williams, J. D. H., J. K. Syers, D. E. Armstrong, and R. F. Harris. (1971b). Characterization of inorganic phosphate in noncalcareous lake sediments. *Soil Sci. Soc. Am. Proc.,* **35**:556–561.

Williams, J. D. H., J. K. Syers, S. S. Shukla, R. F. Harris, and D. E. Armstrong. (1971c). Levels of inorganic and total phosphorus in lake sediments as related to other sediment parameters. *Environ. Sci. Tech.* **5**:1113–1120.

Williams, J. D. H., T. P. Murphy, and T. Mayer. (1976). Rates of accumulation of phosphorus forms in Lake Erie sediments. *J. Fish. Res. Board Can.,* **33**:430–439.

Winter, T. C. (1977). Classification of the hydrologic settings of lakes in the north central United States. *Water Res. Res.,* **13**:753–767.

Winter, T. C., and H. E. Wright, Jr. (1977). Paleohydrologic phenomena recorded by lake sediments. *Trans. Am. Geophys. Union,* **58**:188–196.

Wollast, R., F. T. Mackenzie, and O. P. Bricker. (1968). Experimental precipitation and genesis of sepiolite at earth-surface conditions. *Am. Mineral.,* **35**:1645–1662.

Wright, H. E., Jr. (1972). Quaternary history of Minnesota. In: P. K. Sims and G. B. Moore (eds.), *Geology of Minnesota.* Minnesota Geol. Survey 515–547.

Zen, E-an. (1972). Gibbs free energy, enthalpy, and entropy of ten rock forming minerals: calculations, discrepancies, implications. *Am. Mineral.,* **57**:524–553.

Chapter 8
Saline Lakes

Hans P. Eugster and Lawrence A. Hardie

Introduction

Most lakes are well flushed and the chemical constituents of their waters do not accumulate beyond the potable range. In unusual circumstances, however, the solute load may be increased and the lake then becomes saline. This is caused either by evaporation exceeding inflow or by the inflow being saline or both. Saline lakes are quite common in certain parts of the earth, but they have neither the size nor abundance of normal lakes. For this reason, few extensive studies have been made of such lakes and consequently their hydrologic, geochemical, sedimentological, and biological environments remain little explored. This is a pity, for saline lakes have much to teach us about processes under extreme conditions and, once we understand them, we will have greatly improved our understanding also of normal lakes. This paucity of studies is also surprising because saline lakes not only are of economic significance but are important in the geologic record as sensitive indicators of past tectonic and climatic events.

Saline lakes range from small ephemeral ponds, such as that of Saline Valley, California (Hardie, 1968), to deep perennial stratified brine bodies like the Dead Sea (Neev and Emery, 1967). They may be surrounded by huge mountains fringed by coalescing alluvial fans, such as Deep Springs Lake, California (Jones, 1965), or they may be isolated depressions in an immense desert plain like the Ubari Sand Sea in the Libyan desert (Glennie, 1970, pp. 58–59).

Saline lakes present a bewildering variety of compositions and concentration ranges. The lower concentration boundary is not easy to define. Beadle (1974) discussed possible criteria for distinguishing fresh from saline waters and has chosen the boundary at about 5‰ dissolved solids, based principally on biological tolerance. The upper boundary is determined by the solubility of the most soluble minerals in equilibrium with the residual brines. These brines may reach concentrations of close to 400,000 ppm total dissolved solids and they can be alkaline $Na-CO_3$ concentrates precipitating trona ($NaHCO_3 \cdot Na_2CO_3 \cdot 2H_2O$) as at Lake Magadi, Kenya (Eugster, 1970), or $Mg-Na-SO_4$ bitterns depositing epsomite ($MgSO_4 \cdot 7H_2O$) and bloedite ($Na_2SO_4 \cdot MgSO_4 \cdot 4H_2O$) as in the Basque Lakes, British Columbia (Goudge, 1924), or $Na-SO_4-Cl$ waters from which mirabilite ($Na_2SO_4 \cdot 10H_2O$) and halite ($NaCl$) are crystallizing as from Great Salt Lake, Utah (Whelan, 1973).

Saline lakes may contain a variety of salt-tolerant plants from blue–green algae to sedges, and a variety of unusual animals like the fish *Tilapia* and shrimp *Artemia* (see Beadle, 1974) that have extraordinary tolerances to high salt concentrations.

Finally, saline lakes are sources of economically important chemicals such as lithium, borax, potassium, nitrates, sodium carbonates, zeolites, and others.

In this chapter we will concentrate on chemical and mineralogical aspects of saline lakes. We have discussed the sedimentological aspects of saline lakes in a separate paper (Hardie *et al.,* in press). First we will outline the environmental setting of saline lakes and their chemical variability. Next we discuss the processes by which the lake waters initially acquire their solutes and how the water compositions evolve as a consequence of precipitation of salts and mineral–brine interactions. These general principles are then illustrated by a number of case studies of modern and ancient saline lakes and their deposits. We have relied primarily on first-hand experience and have not attempted to cover the literature on saline lakes systematically.

Conditions for saline lake formation

Three basic conditions must be met for a saline lake to form and persist: (1) outflow of water must be re-

FIGURE 1.   Oblique aerial view of Saline Valley, California, looking north. The white area is the dry salt-encrusted playa with its small ephemeral lake at the western edge. Note the huge coalescing alluvial fans that encircle the playa. These fans are 4–8 km from apex to toe and rise to some 500–700 m above the playa at their apices. The mountain wall is part of the Inyo Mountains that reach 3000 m above the playa. Note the straight truncations of the dissected spurs at the base of the mountains that spectacularly mark the faulted edge of the basin. The snow-covered peaks in the far background are part of the Sierra Nevada which are separated from the Inyos by Owens Valley.

stricted, such as it is in a hydrologically closed basin; (2) evaporation must exceed inflow; and (3) the inflow must be sufficient to sustain a standing body of water. Hydrologically closed basins can be produced by a variety of processes, such as by tectonic rifting, by block faulting or thrusting, by volcanic cratering or lava flow damming, by glacial scour, by damming with vegetation or sediments such as land slides or barrier bars, and by wind deflation. The condition for evaporation to exceed inflow is met in the high-pressure desert belts of the subtropical and polar regions, as well as in local orographic (rain shadow) deserts which are independent of latitude.

Neither closed basins nor evaporative conditions are uncommon, but, taken in combination and then coupled with a plentiful inflow of water from springs, ground water, or rivers, the occurrences of saline lakes become greatly limited.

The most favorable conditions for the formation of saline lakes, we think, are to be found in rain shadow basins. Such basins provide the unique combination of high mountains acting as a precipitation trap but with arid valley floors (see Figure 1). Good examples are the many saline lakes located east of the crest of the Andes and Cordillerans of South and North America. The least favorable arid areas are deserts with low relief, such as the Sahara or Gobi deserts.

It is this sensitive response of saline lakes to their environmental setting that makes them useful indicators of climatic and tectonic events in the geologic past.

Compositional variability of saline lake waters

A substantial number of chemical analyses of brines from saline lakes in many parts of the world have been published. Two of the more comprehensive sources of such analyses from all continents are those of Clarke (1924) and Livingstone (1963). Representative compilations of brine analyses from particular areas are those of Ver Planck (1958, p. 123), Whitehead and Feth (1961), Jones (1966), and Phillips and van Denburgh (1971) for the western U.S.; of Cummings (1940), Rawson and Moore (1944), and Tomkins (1954) for western Canada; of Beadle (1932) and Talling and Talling (1965) for Africa; of Löffler (1956) for Iran; of Hutchinson (1937) for Tibet; and of Bonython (1955) for Australia. Valyashko (1972) gives some data on Lake Inder, Russia (references to other Russian saline lakes are given in this paper).

Saline lake brines, like river and spring waters around the world, are dominated by a relatively few major solutes, namely, SiO_2, Ca, Mg, Na, K, HCO_3, CO_3, SO_4, and Cl. Table 1 presents some typical analyses of saline lake brines from the western U.S. The relative proportions of the major solutes vary remarkably from one saline lake to the next. This is illustrated in Figure 2, which is a plot of brine analyses from many parts of the world, and in Figure 3, which shows how saline lakes of different compositions (see Table 1) within the Great Basin of the western U.S. are distributed geographically. It is clear from Figure 2 that the major anion compositions of saline lakes are very diverse, but the vast bulk of the brines are dominated by a single cation, Na. Lake brines rich in Ca and/or Mg are uncommon while there are none known to us in which K is the major cation. Inspection of hundreds of analyses also shows that several cation–anion incompatibilities exist in concentrated brines. High $HCO_3 + CO_3$ concentrations are coupled with very low to only trace amounts of Ca and Mg. Likewise high SO_4 concentrations are coupled to low Ca values. For brines in which Ca is a major anion (such as Bristol Dry Lake, the Dead Sea) the only significant anion is Cl ($\pm$Br). For brines in which Mg is a major component either Cl (e.g., the Dead Sea) or $Cl + SO_4$ (e.g., Basque Lakes, Hot Lake, Gulf of Karabogaz) dominates the anion composition. Therefore, a few particular major brine types exist in saline lakes. These are (a) $Na–CO_3–Cl–SO_4$ brines, (b) $Na–Cl–SO_4$, (c) $Na–Mg–Cl–SO_4$, and (d) $Ca–Mg–Na–Cl$. Of course, these major types can be subdivided to give subtypes such as $Na–CO_3–Cl$, $Na–CO_3–SO_4$, $Ca–Na–Cl$, $Mg–Na–Cl$, etc. In order to compare and contrast brine subtypes we will adopt an arbitrary scheme of nomenclature in this review. Our scheme is shown in Figure 4. Major ions present in less than 5 mol % of the total anions or cations are not used in the chemical label; ions present in >5 but <25 mol % are shown in parentheses; ions present in >25 mol % are

FIGURE 3.   Saline Lakes of western North America. The numbers in parentheses refer to the brine types of Figure 4, the first number referring to the cation field, the second to the anion field.

shown in order of abundance. Anions and cations are plotted separately and then combined for the final label, with cations listed first. For example, Soap Lake, Washington, brine has Na >95% of the cations and $HCO_3 + CO_3 > 50$, Cl between 25 and 50, SO_4 between 5 and 25% of the ions; therefore, it was classified as a $Na–CO_3–Cl–(SO_4)$ brine. Each field in Figure 4 has a number so that a numerical version of this scheme can be used with convenience in diagrams like Figure 3, where we have shown the distribution of saline lakes in the western U.S. In this numerical version the Soap Lake brine would be labeled 1-7, cation field being listed before the anion field. In the following section on brine evolution we attempt to show the mechanisms and processes that can account for the development of these different major brine types and subtypes.

Finally, we must mention that there exist a few saline lakes in which solutes normally present only in trace amounts become significant components. Some examples are Br in the Dead Sea (5000–7000 ppm), Sr in Great Salt Lake (2000 ppm), PO_4 in Searles Lake, California (900 ppm), and B in Borax Lake, California

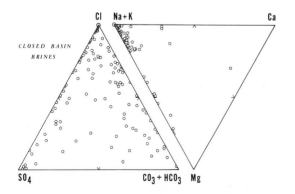

FIGURE 2.   Compositions of closed-basin brines in the system $Ca–Mg–Na–K–(HCO_3 + CO_3)–SO_4–Cl$. In mol%. From Hardie and Eugster (1970).

TABLE 1.   Analyses of Brines from Saline Lakes of Western North America[a]

	1[b]	2	3	4	5	6	7	8	9	10	11	12	13	14
	Kamloops Lake No. 7, B.C.	Basque Lake No. 1, B.C.	Hot Lake, Wash.	Lenore Lake, Wash.	Soap Lake, Wash.	Harney Lake, Ore.	Summer Lake, Ore.	Alkali Valley, Ore.	Abert Lake, Ore.	Surprise Valley, Calif.	Great Salt Lake, Utah	Honey Lake, Calif.	Pyramid Lake, Nev.	Winnemucca, Nev.
SiO_2	—	—	—	22	101	31	103	542	645	36	48	55	1.4	11
Ca	tr[c]	—	640	3	3.9	7	tr	—	—	11	241	—	10	4.2
Mg	34,900	42,400	22,838	20	23	tr	tr	—	—	31	7,200	—	113	4.5
Na	10,900	13,660	7,337	5,360	12,500	8,826	6,567	117,000	119,000	4,090	83,600	18,300	1,630	4,350
K	—	1,570	891	—	—	336	264	8,850	3,890	11	4,070	1,630	134	744
HCO_3	2,400	3,020	6,296	6,090	12,270	4,425	5,916	2,510	—	1,410	251	5,490	1,390	128
CO_3	—	—	—	3,020	5,130	—	—	91,400	60,300	664	—	8,020	—	918
SO_4	160,800	195,710	103,680	2,180	6,020	1,929	695	46,300	9,230	900	16,400	12,100	264	5,290
Cl	200	1,690	1,668	1,360	4,680	6,804	3,039	45,700	115,000	4,110	140,000	9,680	1,960	11,100
Total	209,000	258,000	143,000	18,000	40,700	22,383	16,633	314,000	309,000	10,600	254,000	52,900	5,510	—
pH	—	—	—	—	—	—	—	10.1	9.8	9.2	7.4	9.7	—	8.7
Brine type	14-15	14-15	8-16	1-13	1-7	1-7	1-8	1-7	1-4	1-3	4-1	1-7	4-8	1-3

	15	16	17	18	19	20	21	22	23	24	25	26	27
	Carson Sink, Nev.	Rhodes Marsh, Nev.	Mono Lake, Calif.	Deep Springs Lake, Calif.	Saline Valley, Calif.	Owens Lake, Calif.	Death Valley, Calif.	Searles Lake, Calif.	Soda Lake, Calif.	Bristol Dry Lake, Calif.	Cadiz Lake, Calif.	Danby Lake, Calif.	Salton Sea, Calif.
SiO_2	19	142	14	—	36	299	—	—	—	—	—	—	20.8
Ca	261	17	4.5	3.1	286	43	—	16	—	43,296	4,504	325	505
Mg	129	0.5	34	1.2	552	21	150	—	—	1,061	412	108	581
Na	56,800	3,680	21,500	111,000	103,000	81,398	109,318	110,000	114,213	57,365	22,603	137,580	6,249
K	3,240	102	1,170	19,500	4,830	3,462	4,043	26,000	tr	3,294	1,038	112	112
HCO_3	322	23	5,410	9,360	614	52,463	—	—	—	—	—	tr	232
CO_3	—	648	10,300	22,000	—	—	—	27,100	12,053	—	—	—	—
SO_4	786	2,590	7,380	57,100	22,900	21,220	44,356	46,000	52,026	223	280	13,397	4,139
Cl	88,900	3,070	13,500	119,000	150,000	53,040	140,196	121,000	124,618	172,933	44,764	119,789	9,033
Total	152,000	10,400	56,600	335,000	282,360	213,700	299,500	336,000	305,137	279,150	73,600	271,200	20,900
pH	7.8	9.5	9.6	—	7.35	—	—	—	—	—	—	—	—
Brine type	1-1	1-3	1-7	1-3	1-2	1-7	1-2	1-3	1-2	5-1	2-1	1-1	4-2

[a] Concentrations in ppm. Listed in geographical succession from north to south (see Figure 3).

[b] Analyses 1, 2, 3, 4, 5, 13, 27 from Livingstone (1963); 6, 7, 20 from Clark (1924); 8, 9, 10, 12, 14, 15, 16, 17 from Jones (1966); 11 from Whitehead and Feth (1961); 18 from Jones (1965); 19 from Hardie (1968); 21, 23, 24, 25, 26 from Ver Planck (1958); 22 from White et al. (1963).

[c] tr, trace.

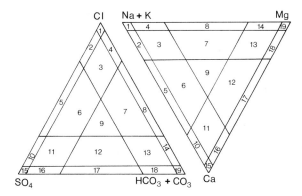

FIGURE 4.   Brine classification scheme in terms of the major anions Cl, SO₄, HCO₃ + CO₃ and cations Na + K, Ca, Mg. Placement of boundaries is explained in text. Compositions in mol%. The following notation is used: *anion field:* 1, Cl; 2, Cl–(SO₄); 3, Cl–(SO₄)–(CO₃); 4, Cl–(CO₃); 5, Cl–SO₄; 6, Cl–SO₄–(CO₃); 7, Cl–CO₃–(SO₄); 8, Cl–CO₃; 9, Cl–SO₄–CO₃; 10, SO₄–(Cl); 11, SO₄–(CO₃)–(Cl); 12, SO₄–CO₃–(Cl); 13, CO₃–(SO₄)–(Cl); 14, CO₃–(Cl); 15, SO₄; 16, SO₄–(CO₃); 17, SO₄–CO₃; 18, CO₃–(SO₄); 19, CO₃. *cation field:* 1, Na; 2, Na–(Ca); 3, Na–(Ca)–(Mg); 4, Na–(Mg); 5, Na–Ca; 6, Na–Ca–(Mg); 7, Na–Mg–(Ca); 8, Na–Mg; 9, Na–Ca–Mg; 10, Ca–(Na); 11, Ca–(Mg)–(Na); 12, Ca–Mg–(Na); 13, Mg–(Ca)–(Na); 14, Mg–(Na); 15, Ca; 16, Ca–(Mg); 17, Ca–Mg; 18, Mg–(Ca); 19, Mg.

(350–900 ppm). Livingstone (1963, pp. 41–52) and Hem (1970) have discussed trace element components in lake and river waters, but there are few comprehensive reports on trace elements in saline lake brines. Lombardi (1963) measured several heavy metals in the Saline Valley, California, brines, Smith (in press) reports analyses of trace elements in Searles Lake, California, brines, Neev and Emery (1967, p. 68) give data for several trace elements in the Dead Sea brines, and Baumann *et al.* (1975) for Lake Shala, Ethiopia. Friedman *et al.* (1976) have measured deuterium variations with evaporation of the brines in Owens Lake, California.

Brine evolution

The evolution of the chemical composition of saline lake waters consists of two steps: (1) solutes are acquired by the dilute inflow waters principally through chemical weathering reactions, and (2) subsequent evaporative concentration leads to the precipitation of minerals and this profoundly affects the composition of the remaining waters.

Acquisition of solutes

Acid waters are the most effective agents for weathering of the carbonates and silicates which form the bulk of the surface rocks. The main types are: CO_2-charged rainwaters, soil waters, acid "mine" waters, and volcanic hot springs.

Rainwater in equilibrium with atmospheric CO_2 ideally has a pH of 5.7 (Krauskopf, 1967, pp. 39–40). Near industrial or volcanic areas, the pH may be considerably lower due to the addition of gases such as SO_2. For instance, the pH of rainwater near Baltimore has been reported as 4.6 (Cleaves *et al.*, 1970). In addition to dissolved CO_2 species (H_2CO_3 and HCO_3^- mainly) rainwater contains significant amounts of other solutes. Some examples are shown in Table 2. In order of abundance the most common cations in rainwater are Na^+, Ca^{2+}, Mg^{2+}, K^+, while the major anions, in addition to HCO_3^-, are Cl^-, SO_4^{2-}, and NO_3^-. The main sources are dissolution of atmospheric dust and sea salt aerosols such as $CaCO_3$, $CaSO_4$, and $MgSO_4$. In industrial areas, NH_4^+, H^+, SO_4^{2-}, and NO_3^- may dominate in rainwater (for example, Cleaves *et al.*, 1974, p. 439) because of dissolved industrial gases. A more complete discussion of the rainwater solute problem is given in Carroll (1962), Junge and Werby (1958), and Smith and Drever (1976).

Soil waters—rainwater that has infiltrated into porous surface soils—often show lower pH values than rainwater, having absorbed additional CO_2 produced by bacterial decay of organic matter in the upper A-horizon. p_{CO_2} is commonly an order of magnitude higher than that of the atmosphere. Very low pH values have been measured near roots in the soil zone due to biochemical activities of the living roots (Williams and Coleman, 1950; Keller and Frederickson, 1952). For these reasons, soil waters are far more effective agents for chemical weathering than is unmodified rainwater.

Acid mine waters derive their acidity by oxidation of sulfides to sulfates in conjunction with precipitation of metal oxides or hydroxides, by reactions such as

$$4FeS_{2(s)} + 15O_{2(g)} + 8H_2O_{(l)} \rightarrow \\ 2Fe_2O_{3(s)} + 8SO_{4(aq)}^{2-} + 16H_{(aq)}^+. \quad (1)$$

Waters produced in this manner may have pH values of 4 or less (White *et al.,* 1963, Table 24). Volcanic hot springs usually show pH values of less than 3 due to the presence of volcanogenic HCl and H_2SO_4 (White *et al.,* 1963, Table 19). Although extremely potent as weathering agents, acid mine waters and volcanic spring waters are of local importance only.

Quantitatively by far the most important weathering reactions are thought to be soil water–bedrock interactions, to which our discussion will be limited. Garrels and Mackenzie (1971, pp. 142–174) and Stumm and Morgan (1970, pp. 385–411) have discussed the chemical and mineralogical aspects of weathering reactions in considerable detail. Here we present a brief synopsis.

The highest solute load is acquired by the dissolution of saline minerals such as halite or gypsum. Dissolution of halite in soil water at 25°C can yield a maximum of 6.1 mol of NaCl/1000 g of H_2O. This corresponds to approximately 138,000 ppm Na and 212,000 ppm Cl. Dissolution of gypsum can produce 0.0158 mol of $CaSO_4$/1000 g of H_2O, that is about 600 ppm Ca and 1400 ppm SO_4. Anhydrite gives similar values.

The dissolution of calcite is strongly p_{CO_2} dependent. At 25°C and a p_{CO_2} of $10^{-3.5}$ atm (atmospheric CO_2) about 20 ppm Ca is taken up into solution which now will have a pH of 8.3 and 61 ppm HCO_3^-. In soil waters with p_{CO_2} of 10^{-2} atm, Ca concentration can be as high as 65 ppm. Dolomite will react in a similar fashion except that equal molar proportions of Ca and Mg will result.

Quartz solubility at 25°C and pH below 9 is roughly 6.5 ppm SiO_2, but at higher pH it can go up to over 100 ppm. The solubility of other silicates is more complex because many dissolution reactions are incongruent, that is they involve the precipitation of another silicate, such as a clay mineral. The weathering of feldspars is a prime example. Judging from the very low aluminum concentrations in natural waters—usually less than 0.5 ppm (White *et al.*, 1963, Tables 1–5)—aluminum is conserved in the solid phases. Therefore, reactions can be balanced on aluminum, such as that for the alteration of albite to kaolinite:

$$NaAlSi_3O_{8(s)} + CO_2 + \frac{11}{2} H_2O \rightarrow \frac{1}{2} Al_2Si_2O_5(OH)_{4(s)}$$

albite   kaolinite

$$+ Na_{(aq)}^+ + HCO_{3(aq)}^- + 2H_4SiO_{4(aq)}. \quad (2)$$

This reaction can be viewed as an acid–base titration. It produces for each mole of albite destroyed 1 mol each of Na^+ and HCO_3^- and 2 mol of silicic acid. Starting with a typical soil water with a p_{CO_2} of 10^{-2} atm, the final water will be nearly neutral (pH = 6.72) and will contain about 100 ppm SiO_2, 19 ppm Na^+, and 50 ppm HCO_3^- (Stumm and Morgan 1970, pp. 399–400). For an intermediate plagioclase, the sodium value would be lower, but the water would now also contain Ca^{2+}, the Na/Ca ratio being a function of the plagioclase Na/Ca ratio. Equivalent relationships involving K instead of Na hold for the weathering of potassium-bearing feldspars.

Other reaction products such as montmorillonite or gibbsite may take the place of kaolinite. Because they have different Si/Al ratios, the silica to cation ratios of the final waters will be different. For instance, albite weathering to montmorillonite will release Si/Na in the molar ratio of 1:1, while albite to gibbsite will produce Si/Na of 3:1. Which clay mineral forms in a particular weathering situation depends primarily upon the local drainage conditions, with large drainage volumes and rates favoring gibbsite formation and small drainage volumes producing montmorillonite, with kaolinite in between (for specific field examples see Barshad, 1966, and Cleaves *et al.*, 1970, p. 3021).

Iron-bearing silicates present a special case because of the redox reactions involved. The solubilities of ferric oxyhydroxides are so low at normal soil pH and Eh values (pH > 4, Eh > 0) that iron is usually precipitated quantitatively in the soil zone as goethite, lepidocrocite, etc., and does not go into the water.

The weathering of nonaluminous silicates can best be illustrated by considering forsterite, Mg_2SiO_4. In the presence of CO_2, forsterite may convert to chrysotile by the following reaction

$$2Mg_2SiO_4 + 3H_2O + 2CO_2 \rightleftharpoons$$
$$Mg_3Si_2O_5(OH)_4 + Mg^{2+} + 2HCO_3^-. \quad (3)$$

TABLE 2.   Chemical Analyses of Atmospheric Precipitation[a]

	Snow; N. Mex. (Miller, 1961)		Rain; N.C. (Gambell and Fisher, 1966) (yearly ave.)	Rain; Baltimore (Cleaves et al., 1976)	Rain; Rothamsted, England (Carroll, 1962)	Rain; Northern Europe (Carroll, 1962) (ave.)	Rain; SE Australia (Carroll, 1962) (ave.)	Rain; San Diego, Calif. (Carroll, 1962)	Rain; Grand Junction, Colo. (Carroll, 1962)
	Lake Peak	Jicarilla Peak							
SiO_2	n.d.[b]	0.1		0.1					
Ca	0.3	0.2	0.65	0.3	1.7	1.42	1.20	0.67	3.41
Mg	n.d.	n.d.	0.14	0.1	0.3	0.39	0.50		
Na	0.5	0.1	0.56	0.2	1.3	2.05	2.46	2.17	0.69
K	0.3	0.3	0.11	0.2	0.3	0.35	0.37	0.21	0.17
HCO_3	3.2	1.9		0.3					
SO_4	n.d.	n.d.	2.18	1.7	1.8	2.19	tr	1.66	2.37
Cl	0.2	0.2	0.57	0.6	2.7	3.47	4.43	3.31	0.28
NO_3	0.1	n.d.	0.62	—	—	0.27	—	3.13	2.63
Σ	4.8	2.8	>2.83	3.5	>8.1	>10.14	>8.96		
pH	6.1	5.3	4.8–5.9	4.6	4.9	5.47	—	—	—

[a]In ppm.

[b]n.d., not detected; tr, trace.

If magnesium and bicarbonate reach high enough values, magnesite may also precipitate according to

$$Mg^{2+} + HCO_3^- \rightleftharpoons MgCO_{3(s)} + H^+. \qquad (4)$$

It has been observed in profiles of weathered rocks that silicate minerals have greatly differing resistance to weathering attack (see discussion in Pettijohn, 1975, pp. 499–500). For instance, olivine weathers more quickly than biotite and plagioclase more quickly than K-feldspar. These different rates have a major influence on the final solute load of the soil waters. Finally, sulfides such as pyrite, FeS_2, through oxidation reactions like Eq. (1), are probably the most important sources for sulfate in weathering solutions.

In summary, the final composition of a ground- or springwater depends on the minerals present in the bedrocks, their relative abundances, their weatherability, the actual weathering reactions involved, and the drainage conditions. A test of the validity of a particular set of weathering reactions is possible by using the final groundwater compositions as a starting point and by calculating backward to the individual reactions responsible for that particular composition. This approach has been used very elegantly by Garrels and Mackenzie (1967) in their interpretation of the Sierra Nevada spring water compositions. They were able to demonstrate not only the nature of the silicate weathering reactions but also their relative importance.

Using the weathering reactions outlined above, we can now briefly review the principal sources of the major solute species present in groundwaters.

Silica is derived from the weathering of silicates rather than the dissolution of quartz, and hence most natural waters are supersaturated with respect to quartz. The silica to cation ratio depends on the stoichiometry of the fresh minerals and that of the clay mineral which is precipitated.

Calcium stems from the dissolution of gypsum, anhydrite, calcite, dolomite, and the hydrolysis of silicates such as plagioclase and pyroxene. Minor contributions are from rain water.

Magnesium comes from dolomite and the weathering of Mg-silicates. Locally basic and ultrabasic rocks are a major source of magnesium.

Sodium is derived locally from the dissolution of halite and more generally from the weathering of feldspars. Atmospheric contributions may also be significant.

Potassium is derived chiefly by weathering of feldspars and micas. The low K/Na ratios of most dilute natural waters must reflect the slower weathering of K-feldspar compared with that of plagioclase.

Iron and aluminum have very low concentrations in most natural waters, because they are retained in precipitates in the soil profile.

Bicarbonate is the principal anion in most dilute natural waters. This reflects the importance of carbonic acid in weathering reactions. Carbonate is not important except for alkaline brines (pH > 8.5).

Sulfate is an important constituent of rain water but can also be derived by dissolution of gypsum and anhydrite. Oxidation of sulfides, however, may be the most widespread source.

Chloride comes from rain water, from dissolution of halite, and from fluid inclusions.

Hydrogen ion; weathering reactions, being mainly acid–base reactions, tend to consume hydrogen ions, so that most natural waters have a pH near neutral. The obvious exceptions are the acid mine waters and the volcanic hot springs.

A more comprehensive compilation of solute sources can be found in Hem (1970). The strong lithologic control on water compositions is evident from the following summary, based mainly on the analyses assembled by White *et al.* (1963).

Limestone waters are characterized by high Ca (Ca/Na molar ratios as high as 20) and HCO_3 and by low SiO_2 (around 10 ppm). The pH is normally slightly alkaline. *Dolomite* waters are similar, except that Ca and Mg are present in near equal molar amounts. Waters in contact with *shales* also have high HCO_3, but some are very rich in sulfate. Either Ca or Na is the dominant cation. The pH may be as low as 4 (sulfate rich) and as high as 9 (carbonate rich). Total dissolved solids may be quite high, especially for those rich in sulfate and chloride. *Sandstone* waters are all dominated by HCO_3, but the cations are very variable. Silica is low and pH is near neutral. The weathering of *acid igneous rocks* produces waters rich in HCO_3, SiO_2, Na, and Ca, with a near-neutral pH. *Basalt* waters are similar, except that Ca and Mg are the dominant cations. In *ultrabasic* waters, Mg and HCO_3 are usually dominant and pH is slightly alkaline. *Metamorphic* waters also have dominant HCO_3, while the cation ratios vary greatly from one rock type to the next.

Early stages of brine evolution

Because of the selective removal of ions, mineral precipitation profoundly influences the composition of waters flowing into a closed basin. Four major processes may lead to supersaturation and consequent precipitation: evaporative concentration, loss of gases such as CO_2, mixing of waters, and temperature changes. Of these, evaporative concentration is by far the most effective in saline lakes. It is convenient to discuss evaporative concentration in two stages: early precipitation of the relatively insoluble carbonates, sulfates and silicates, and subsequent precipitation of the very soluble saline minerals.

Alkaline earth carbonates are usually the first minerals to form. Typical precipitates in saline lakes are aragonite, low-magnesian calcite, high-magnesian calcite, protodolomite, huntite, hydromagnesite and magnesite (see Müller *et al.*, 1972; Graf *et al.*, 1961; Callender, 1969; Nesbitt, 1974). Most of these minerals are obviously formed under metastable conditions and the detailed conditions that govern their formation are not yet resolved (Bathurst, 1971, p. 243–253; Berner, 1975; DeBoer, 1977). Nevertheless it is instructive to consider how the equilibrium precipitation of first pure calcite, and then magnesian calcite, will modify the water compositions.

Equilibrium precipitation of calcite is governed by two conditions which must be met concurrently (Hardie and Eugster, 1970, p. 277.):

"1. Ca^{2+} and CO_3^{2-} must be lost from solution in equal molar proportions, and

2. the IAP ($aCa^{2+} \cdot aCO_3^{2-}$) of the solution must remain constant at constant P (total) and T.

Now, because the initial molar proportions in general will not be equal, the first restriction implies that the Ca^{2+} to CO_3^{2-} proportions in the solution must change as calcite precipitates. The second restriction allows only antipathetic changes in Ca^{2+} and CO_3^{2-} concentrations, that is, if Ca^{2+} increases then CO_3^{2-} must decrease, and *vice versa*. Clearly, then, early calcite precipitation is a critical evolutionary step: it will immediately determine whether an evaporating water will become carbonate-rich or carbonate-poor."

The effect of early calcite precipitation on the subsequent development of water compositions cannot be overemphasized. We have calculated the compositional evolution of natural waters during the early precipitation phase using a computer program modelled after Garrels and Mackenzie (1967) (Hardie and Eugster, 1970). In this study we found that many natural spring waters were already supersaturated

with respect to calcite at atmospheric p_{CO_2} before any evaporative concentration had occurred, obviously due to the elevated p_{CO_2} of most groundwaters. Such waters, on reaching the surface, lose their excess CO_2 and may force calcite to precipitate at exceedingly low ionic strength (below 0.01). For waters not supersaturated upon emergence, we found that very little evaporative concentration (often less than a twofold enrichment) was necessary to reach supersaturation.

Because of the low Mg/Ca ratios (< 1) found in all but ultrabasic dilute inflow waters, the calcite formed contains less than 5 mol % $MgCO_3$ in solid solution (Füchtbauer and Hardie, 1976). As calcite continues to be precipitated, the Mg/Ca ratio in the water increases, and, in turn, the Mg content of the subsequent carbonate precipitates rises. Katz (1973) and Füchtbauer and Hardie (1976) measured Mg distribution coefficients for calcite precipitated from aqueous solution and have shown the manner in which magnesium is enriched preferentially in the solution.

For kinetic reasons, aragonite may precipitate instead of calcite as happens in the Dead Sea (Neev and Emery, 1967). The overall effect on the water composition evolution remains the same.

At this point three evolutionary paths are open, as shown schematically in Figure 5. If the waters initially had a very high HCO_3/Ca+Mg mole ratio, such as 3 or greater (path I), alkaline earths are removed rapidly with evaporative concentration and magnesium enrichment sufficient to produce magnesium-rich carbonates like protodolomite is not likely. The product is an alkaline brine of the type Na–CO_3–SO_4–Cl or Na–CO_3–Cl–(SO_4). Such brines are known for example from Alkali Valley, Oregon (Jones, 1966; Phillips and Van Denburgh, 1971). On the other hand, if the water initially had a very low HCO_3/Ca+Mg mole ratio (path II), bicarbonate is removed rapidly, while

FIGURE 5. Flow diagram for brine evolution. Solid rectangles represent critical precipitates; rectangles with dashed borders are typical water compositions. Final brine types together with examples of salt lakes are surrounded by dash–dot rectangles. All paths are numbered and referred to in the text. Mg-silicate precipitation and SO_4 reduction are possible for most paths.

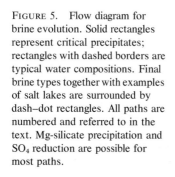
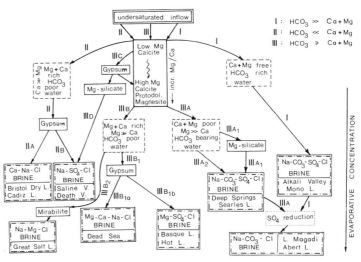

the alkaline earths become enriched. Because of the rapid loss of HCO_3, such waters probably never produce magnesium-rich carbonates, and they become Ca–Na sulfate–chloride brines.

The importance of the third path (path III) has been stressed by Nesbitt (1974). It is taken by waters with intermediate $HCO_3/(Ca+Mg)$ ratios. Such waters initially precipitate low-magnesium calcite, then, with progressive magnesium enrichment, protodolomite; they ultimately may produce magnesite. At this stage these waters will be either poor in alkaline earths and rich in bicarbonate or vice versa. These different waters follow different paths on further evaporative concentration. If bicarbonate predominates after protodolomite precipitation (path IIIA), a brine of the type $Na–Cl–(CO_3)–(SO_4)$ or $Na–Cl–SO_4–(CO_3)$ eventually results, such as those found at Deep Springs (Jones, 1965). On the other hand, if alkaline earths prevail over bicarbonate, an $Mg–(Ca)–Na–SO_4–Cl$ water is formed (path IIIB).

Those brines enriched in alkaline earths, and impoverished in bicarbonate (paths II and IIIB), will, with continued evaporative concentration, reach saturation with respect to gypsum. Gypsum precipitation imposes compositional constraints analogous to those of calcite precipitation, except that the residual waters will become either calcium rich and sulfate poor or sulfate rich and calcium poor, as discussed by Hardie and Eugster (1970, p. 279). For those waters in which calcium initially was enriched over magnesium (path II), if alkaline earths predominate over sulfate, then a $Na–Ca–(Mg)–Cl$ or $Na–Ca–Cl$ brine results (path IIA). Such brines have been described from Bristol Dry Lake (Ver Planck, 1958, p. 123). In contrast, if sulfate dominates over alkaline earths (path IIB), a $Na–Cl–(SO_4)$ brine such as that of Death Valley, California, is produced.

For bicarbonate-poor waters in which magnesium was enriched over calcium (path IIIB1) gypsum precipitation will produce a $Mg–Na–Cl$ or $Mg–Na–(Ca)–Cl$ brine (path IIIB1a), such as that found in the Dead Sea (Neev and Emery, 1967), provided alkaline earths predominate over sulfate. If sulfate dominates (path IIIB1b), $Mg–Na–SO_4–Cl$ or $Mg–Na–SO_4–(Cl)$ brines form. Such brines have been reported from the Basque Lakes, B.C. (Nesbitt, 1974) and from Little Manitou Lake, Saskatchewan (Livingstone, 1963), among others.

Another path (path IIIC) is possible for waters with initially high SO_4 to Ca ratios. Such waters, after having precipitated low-magnesium calcite will become saturated with respect to gypsum before the Mg/Ca ratio is high enough for high-magnesian calcite to form. The precipitation of gypsum removes calcium nearly quantitatively, abruptly raising Mg/Ca, so that protodolomite or even magnesite may precipitate

next. Upon subsequent evaporation, such waters most likely will follow path IIIB. An example is Spotted Lake, B.C. (see Nesbitt, 1974).

The ionic strength of waters saturated with respect to gypsum, as calculated by Hardie and Eugster (1970, p. 279) from a large number of different inflow waters, ranges from 0.1 to 0.7. This is still relatively dilute, and yet the fate of the water compositions upon further evaporation is completely sealed at this point.

Up to now we have not taken into account the effect of direct silicate precipitation. Because of the initial low Al and Fe contents of the water, we need to consider only Mg silicates such as sepiolite or talc and Na silicates such as magadiite. Precipitation of such silicates are important for the removal of magnesium and/or silica, as for example at Saline Valley, California, where sepiolite is formed (Hardie, 1968, path IIID). It is probably also important at Liwa, a saline deposit associated with Lake Chad, where clay minerals have been found to remove Mg (Tardy et al., 1974; Gac et al., 1977, path IIIA1).

Some of the waters following paths II or IIIB,C,D leading to sulfate-rich brines may never precipitate gypsum. This is because SO_4 may be removed by two very effective processes: freezing out of mirabilite during cold winter months and sulfate reduction by bacterial action. At Great Salt Lake, Utah, mirabilite forms when brines reach a temperature of 4–6°C, a common occurrence (path IIIB2). Most of this mirabilite is redissolved during the spring, but considerable accumulations have been found in the subsurface sediments (Eardley, 1962). Bacterial SO_4 reduction has been invoked by Neev and Emery (1967) to account for the absence of gypsum in the Dead Sea sediments and by Jones et al. (1977) for the paucity of sulfate in the Lake Magadi brines (paths IIIA1 and 2).

Precipitation of silicates such as sepiolite or magadiite cannot account for the large silica deficiency observed in many concentrated brines of closed basins (Eugster and Jones, 1977). At Lake Magadi, for instance, " . . . budget calculations indicate more than 99% of the SiO_2 is lost between inflow and the groundwater reservoir represented by the hot springs. Thus alternate wetting and drying in recharge areas may be a major agent of solute fractionation" (Jones et al., 1977, p. 66). We believe this loss to be due to the formation of surface or intrasediment crusts as a consequence of capillary evaporation. Such crusts, formed by complete evaporation of interstitial waters, contain all solutes previously present in the waters. This would be principally silica, perhaps in the form of opal, alkaline earth carbonates, and the more soluble salts such as gypsum, halite, and the sodium carbonates or sulfates. Rainwater and dilute runoff will redissolve the most soluble salts and return their constituents to the interstitial waters, while the least soluble minerals remain in the crusts and thus are permanently removed from the brine evolution. The efficacy of this removal mechanism has been tested experimentally by Drever and Smith (1977, p. 50). Salts from Sierra Nevada-type waters were deposited in a vadose zone by artificial evaporation, using quartz sand as substrate. Upon leaching, "the relative rates of dissolution were Na^+ and Cl^- most rapid, then K^+, SO_4^-, Mg^{++}, Ca^{++}, carbonate species, and finally SiO_2."

Another effective mechanism for silica removal is based on diatoms. They are found in many lakes, even some quite saline ones. They are important in Lake Manyara (Stoffers and Holdship, 1975), Lake Kivu (Degens et al., 1972), Abert Lake (Phillips and Van Denburgh, 1971), and perhaps also in Great Salt Lake, Utah (Quinn, 1966), where silica levels are very low (Hahl and Handy, 1969). At Magadi, on the other hand, diatoms were found only in the inflow deltas of a more dilute precursor lake (Eugster and Chou, 1973).

Potassium is another element which is removed in large amounts during evaporative concentration, but its removal is not coupled to silica (Eugster and Jones,

1977). As Jones et al., (1977) have demonstrated for Lake Magadi, the early removal of potassium is of nearly the same order as that of silica (78% of K is removed between inflow and springs). Obvious candidates for removal mechanisms are exchange reactions on clay minerals, alkali alumina silicate gels such as those described by Eugster and Jones (1968) and Surdam and Eugster (1976), and volcanic glass.

The efficiency of the removal mechanisms differs from basin to basin. Silica is removed most effectively where extensive wetting and drying occurs, while screening out of potassium depends on long-term contact with fine-grained sediments (Eugster and Jones, 1977).

Quantitative tests of the early evaporation stages

Starting with the compositions of the perennial spring waters of the Sierra Nevada, Garrels and Mackenzie (1967) calculated the effect of evaporative concentration, coupled with precipitation of calcite, sepiolite, and gypsum. They were able to show that an alkaline

TABLE 3.   The Major Saline Minerals of the Different Brine Types

Brine type	Saline minerals	
Ca–Mg–Na–(K)–Cl	Antarcticite	$CaCl_2 \cdot 6H_2O$
	Bischofite	$MgCl_2 \cdot 6H_2O$
	Carnallite	$KCl \cdot MgCl_2 \cdot 6H_2O$
	Halite	$NaCl$
	Sylvite	KCl
	Tachyhydrite	$CaCl_2 \cdot 2MgCl_2 \cdot 12H_2O$
Na–(Ca)–SO₄–Cl	Gypsum	$CaSO_4 \cdot 2H_2O$
	Glauberite	$CaSO_4 \cdot Na_2SO_4$
	Halite	$NaCl$
	Mirabilite	$Na_2SO_4 \cdot 10H_2O$
	Thenardite	Na_2SO_4
Mg–Na–(Ca)–SO₄–Cl	Bischofite	$MgCl_2 \cdot 6H_2O$
	Bloedite	$Na_2SO_4 \cdot MgSO_4 \cdot 4H_2O$
	Epsomite	$MgSO_4 \cdot 7H_2O$
	Glauberite	$CaSO_4 \cdot Na_2SO_4$
	Gypsum	$CaSO_4 \cdot 2H_2O$
	Halite	$NaCl$
	Hexahydrite	$MgSO_4 \cdot 6H_2O$
	Kieserite	$MgSO_4 \cdot H_2O$
	Mirabilite	$Na_2SO_4 \cdot 10H_2O$
	Thenardite	Na_2SO_4
Na–CO₃–Cl	Halite	$NaCl$
	Nahcolite	$NaHCO_3$
	Natron	$Na_2CO_3 \cdot 10H_2O$
	Thermonatrite	$Na_2CO_3 \cdot H_2O$
	Trona	$NaHCO_3 \cdot Na_2CO_3 \cdot 2H_2O$
Na–CO₃–SO₄–Cl	Burkeite	$Na_2CO_3 \cdot 2Na_2SO_4$
	Halite	$NaCl$
	Mirabilite	$Na_2SO_4 \cdot 10H_2O$
	Nahcolite	$NaHCO_3$
	Natron	$Na_2CO_3 \cdot 10H_2O$
	Thenardite	Na_2SO_4
	Thermonatrite	$Na_2CO_3 \cdot H_2O$

brine rich in sodium carbonate was the end product. We have applied their approach with the aid of a computer to many inflow waters of closed basins (Hardie and Eugster, 1970). Despite the very obvious shortcomings of the model, we were able to derive the broad compositional spectrum found in natural saline lake waters. We were also able to reproduce individual evolutionary paths observed in several specific closed basins, demonstrating the basic power of the approach. Most shortcomings were built into the method. Because of the computational procedures used, we could not handle precipitation of double salts, such as dolomite, glauberite, and gaylussite or solid solutions such as magnesium calcite. Neither could we treat properly the silica problem and the precipitation of silicates. Obviously, a more refined program which can take these factors into account is necessary before satisfactory quantitative tests are possible with respect to both brine compositions and precipitates.

Late stage concentration processes and products

After carbonate and gypsum precipitation most natural brines must be concentrated many fold before saturation with respect to the more soluble salts occurs. For instance, for the Saline Valley brines (Hardie, 1968), after gypsum precipitation has been initiated, a 25-fold concentration is needed for halite to form. Similarly at Magadi (Jones *et al.*, 1977), after alkaline earth carbonates have been precipitated, trona saturation is not reached until a further 250-times concentration is accomplished.

Two processes are available for producing such large concentration increases, both based ultimately on evaporative concentration: (1) the straight-forward evaporative concentration, either subsurface or from open brine bodies, including evapotranspiration, and (2) recycling of solutes through the fractional dissolution of efflorescent crusts. The latter turns out to be a powerful mechanism for increasing the solute load, particularly for brines of the most concentrated ephemeral salt lakes (Hunt *et al.*, 1966; Eugster and Hardie, 1975, p. 329; Jones, *et al.*, 1977). Because of the differential solubilities of the minerals present in the efflorescent crusts, the brine compositions are affected drastically, so that the same initial waters will produce entirely different brines from those predicted by the paths of Figure 5. For instance, at Saline Valley, nearly pure NaCl surface brines and pure halite deposits are produced by this mechanism, while in the subsurface $NaCl-Na_2SO_4-CaSO_4$ brines form from which glauberite, thenardite, and halite precipitate (Hardie, 1968). Recycling of soluble salts can take place at any stage in the evolution of the brines, that is during surface and subsurface flow as well as in the

lake itself. Flood water runoff is the chief agent for dissolution.

The eventual saline mineral products of continued concentration of the main brine types shown in Figure 5 are listed in Table 3. These brine types coincide with the four types discussed by Hardie and Eugster (1970), who have also analyzed the fate of the most concentrated brines using solubility diagrams. Some examples will be presented under the discussion of individual salt lakes.

Quantitative tests of the late stages

The results of the phase diagram tests used by Hardie and Eugster (1970) were quite useful in interpreting the accumulation of saline minerals and the concurrent evolution of the brine compositions. However, the phase diagram approach is severely limited for natural waters of complex compositions. A more versatile approach has been formulated by Wood (1975). It is purely thermodynamic and based on calculating mineral solubilities in concentrated brines using the Scatchard deviation function coupled with Harned coefficients. In carbonate-free systems it is surprisingly effective from an ionic strength of 2 to over 20. At that point, saturation has occurred with respect to even the most soluble salts. This obviously is potentially the most powerful approach since it is independent of the number of components present. Unfortunately, at the present time the link between dilute solutions which can be treated by an extended Debye–Hückel approach and the more concentrated solutions amenable to Wood's methods is missing. Another potential model for testing concentrated brine evolution is that of Reilly *et al.* (1971) (see also Lafon, 1975). However, this model is not yet fully developed.

Modes of occurrence and accumulation of saline minerals

Saline minerals may occur in four different modes: (1) surface efflorescent crusts, (2) subsurface intrasediment growth from interstitial brines, (3) settle-out of crystals and crystal aggregates precipitated from a surface brine body, deep or shallow, and (4) clastic deposits of eroded and transported saline minerals precipitated in other parts of the basin (intraclasts). We will discuss the early and late stage saline minerals separately.

Early precipitation products

The early stages of saline mineral precipitation may take place from the inflow waters before they reach the lake and/or in the lake itself. The products are located at the surface or in the subsurface vadose zone.

Precipitation from subsurface inflow waters normally will occur in the coarse sediments fringing the lake in the form of either void-filling calcite cements in alluvial fan debris or displacive, poikilitic, or vug-filling crystals, crystal aggregates, and nodules of alkaline earth carbonates and gypsum in the sandy playa- or lake-edge sediments (see Hardie, 1968; Barnes and O'Neil, 1971). This intrasediment precipitation produces a lateral zonation where carbonates occupy the zone nearest to the source of the inflow, and gypsum, if present, a zone closer to the lake (Hardie, 1968, Figure 2). The carbonates themselves may exhibit a progressive zonation from Ca to Mg rich, as has been observed at the Basque Lakes (Nesbitt, 1974). If the water table is close enough to the surface, evaporation may be sufficiently intense for the subsurface water to be drawn to the surface (evaporative pumping of Hsü and Siegenthaler, 1969) where saline minerals will precipitate as efflorescent crusts. Such crusts may consist of alkaline earth carbonates and gypsum as well as the more soluble minerals such as sodium chlorides, sulfates, and carbonates. These exposed surface crusts are susceptible to reworking by storm runoff. The soluble constituents will be dissolved, either completely or partially, and the solute load will be added to the brines, as discussed earlier. The less soluble alkaline earth carbonates and gypsum can be broken up and washed into the lake or playa as detrital particles of pebble, granule, sand, or mud size. These intraclasts may be distinguished from the primary precipitated settle-outs by their abraded form, current deposited fabrics, and peloidal texture (see Hardie and Eugster, 1971; Eugster and Hardie, 1975; Smoot, 1976, 1977; Hardie *et al.,* in press).

During overland flow of inflow waters alkaline earth carbonates may precipitate as spring and stream travertine (and algal tufa) mounds and crusts (Hardie, 1968; Barnes, 1965; Slack, 1967) which are also subject to reworking into detrital particles, particularly the highly fenestral, loosely cemented tufas (Smoot, 1977, in press). This is thought to have been a major carbonate-producing mechanism in the Eocene Green River formation (Smoot, 1976, 1977, in press).

Direct precipitation of alkaline earth carbonates or gypsum out of standing lake waters would seem to produce the simplest record, one of finely laminated crystal settle-outs on the bottom of the lake, such as is found in the Dead Sea (Neev and Emery, 1967) and its Pleistocene precursor, Lake Lisan (Begin *et al.,* 1974; Neev and Emery, 1967). Such finely laminated carbonate lacustrine sediments usually have been interpreted as varves (e.g. Bradley, 1929). Carbonate is thought to be precipitated (inorganically or biochemically) in the summer months and then to be covered

by a thin muddy organic-rich sludge that settled out in the winter so that an annual couplet is deposited. This may well be true for temperate nonevaporitic lakes like Lake Zürich (Nipkow, 1920) but does not seem to apply to the Dead Sea, where only 15–20 laminae have been deposited in the last 70 years (Neev and Emery, 1967, p. 107). Instead of a seasonal precipitation there is a continuous year-round rain of carbonate and gypsum from the constantly evaporating surface waters of the Dead Sea (Neev and Emery, 1967, pp. 88–92). The laminated structure of the bottom sediments is due to the alternation of saline-rich with detrital-rich laminae and so must be the result of *aperiodic* introduction of detrital mud by storm-floods, which punctuate the background deposition of the precipitated salines. An analogous mechanism has been found to produce the laminated deposits of the deep basins of the Gulf of California. Here, the background sediments raining to the floor are diatom tests and the aperiodic, lamination-producing events are Colorado River floods which bring in detrital mud (Calvert, 1966). For saline lakes precipitating both carbonates and gypsum, the mass ratios of carbonate to gypsum in each laminae should reflect the original water composition and the evolutionary stage. However erosion and selective transportation by bottom currents, bioturbation, or bacterial reduction of sulfate (e.g., the Dead Sea, Neev and Emery, 1967, pp. 94–95) may modify the mineral ratios as well as the sedimentary structures.

Late precipitation products

The most spectacular features of ephemeral lake-playa complexes with groundwater brine bodies are the hard blocky efflorescent salt-crusts up to a meter in thickness that cover the dried lake bottom and surrounding playa flats (Figure 6a). Efflorescent crusts are formed by *complete evaporation to dryness* of brine films that have been drawn up from the water table to the surface through the vadose zone by evaporative pumping (Hsü and Siegenthaler, 1969). This is easily shown in model experiments using heat lamps set up over a porous sediment that overlies a subsurface brine reservoir. As a result of this complete dehydration, efflorescent crusts are not equilibrium assemblages and tend to be dominated by one mineral, such as halite or trona, because the brines of the lake area have evolved into waters dominated by only a few major ions, as discussed in some detail above. Efflorescent crusts are dry, very porous (circular to elongate vugs up to several mm wide), and fine grained (crystals barely discernible with the naked eye). Newly formed efflorescences have a bulbous "pop-corn" surface but after several years' exposure these surfaces become ragged, fluted, and rilled by rainwash (Figure 6A). The thicker crusts are so hard that they can be broken only

(a)

FIGURE 6.   (a) Saline Valley salt crusts. View, looking NW, of typical blocky, ragged halite efflorescent crust surface that covers most of the Saline Valley playa. The crust, about 45 cm thick here, is so hard that a pick must be used to break through to the soft silty sediment below. (b) Saline Valley salt crusts. View of the edge of layered halite of the ephemeral lake shown in Figure 7a. The dark upstanding ridges in the foreground are remnants of a polygonally cracked efflorescent crust that have survived dissolution by floodwater runoff that temporarily covered the low-lying lake area. The "shoreline" of this ephemeral lake is sharply defined against the undissolved efflorescent crust in the upper-middle of the photograph. Brunton compass for scale.

(b)

with a hammer. Continued growth of the crust causes rupture into irregular polygons and upward displacement of the polygon edges, ultimately producing an exceedingly blocky and rugged surface (Figure 6a, and also photographs in Hunt *et al.,* 1966; Stoertz and Ericksen, 1974).

Efflorescent crust-covered playas are subject to sporadic violent storm flooding and the freshwater runoff partially or completely dissolves the very soluble minerals in the crusts (Figure 6b). This produces a concentrated brine that collects in the hydrographic low of the playa, making a shallow ephemeral saline lake (Figure 1). After the storm the muddy sediment suspended in the ponded waters settles out as a thin storm layer (in the order of several cm thick at the most). Then in the following weeks and months (or even years) the brine slowly evaporates and a thin layer of salt (halite, trona, etc., commonly less than 10 cm thick) precipitates out. A single storm will leave a couplet of a mud layer overlain by a salt layer. Repeated storms will superimpose couplet upon couplet in the hydrographic low, building up a salt deposit that could be tens or even hundreds of meters thick. The mineralogy of these salt layers will depend on the kind of efflorescent crust minerals that were dissolved by the floodwaters. The layers tend to be monomineralic because the dissolution is very selective and so a chemically simple brine, such as nearly pure NaCl, is produced (Hardie, 1968, pp. 1293–1294). Like the efflorescent crusts, these salt layers are very porous crystalline aggregates, but they differ from the crusts in their texture and fabric. For example, the layered halite in Saline Valley has relatively large crystals (several mm in width) with euhedral outlines oriented into rough vertical columns of superimposed crystals in structural continuity. Here, crystallization was observed to begin with surface films of hopper-shaped crystals that float like rafts. As the rafts grow (mainly by accretion from below) they become heavy enough to sink to the bottom of the very shallow brine pool (only a few tens of cm deep). Once on the bottom these flat hoppers act as nuclei for epitaxial growth of new halite laminae. This accretionary fabric is possible because of the shallowness of the brine pool which allows surface supersaturated brine to be circulated to the bottom before nucleation occurs. The accretionary growth may be periodically interrupted by new settle-out of hopper rafts which form very quickly on windy days when evaporative concentration is accelerated. Shearman (1970) shows some fine illustrations of accretionary halite fabrics formed in ephemeral brine pools on the supratidal flats of the northwest Gulf of California. The salt layers here are precipitated from both seawater and freshwater floods that dissolve halite-rich efflorescent crusts (Hardie, personal observation). Shearman (1970) notes that penecontempora-

neous diagenesis modifies the texture of these crusts by dissolution and reprecipitation of sparry halite. Eugster (1970) made a similar observation for the layered trona in Lake Magadi; he observed that the top of each trona layer is partially dissolved with each flood and trona reprecipitated in the pores.

After each storm in these ephemeral lake systems, the surface brine pool may evaporate completely leaving a smooth, hard salt-flat covered with a thin efflorescence (Figure 7a). The surface of this salt-flat will be dry but below the surface the voids in the salt and sediment layers are filled with saturated brine. At Magadi the brine level within the trona of the salt-flat fluctuates seasonally but even during the driest season does not drop more than 4 m below the surface. In Saline Valley the brine level stays within 0.5 m of the surface. Valyashko (1972) gives data on seasonal brine level fluctuations in Lake Inder, Russia. At Searles Lake, Pleistocene brines still occupy the voids in the salt layers and are being pumped out for commercial purposes. Because of their density such brines are not readily replaced by encroaching groundwater and tend to be preserved until diagenesis obliterates the porosity. If a long period without flooding ensues then the hard dry surface salt layer may crack into large (1–2 m) irregular polygons (Figure 7a), probably due to continuing crystallization of salt and resultant lateral "growth" stresses. The cracks act as channels for subsurface brine to be drawn to the surface by evaporative pumping and growth of a ridge of efflorescent salt occurs along the cracks (Figure 7a). If this process continues uninterrupted for several years, the edges of the polygons become buckled upward by thick efflorescent growth in the cracks to produce an astonishing landscape of upturned crust plates (Figure 7b and see also photos in Hunt *et al.,* 1966).

Precipitation of soluble salts out of the surface waters of deep brine pools like that of the Dead Sea is likely to give salt layers with somewhat different textures and fabrics from those described above for very shallow brine pools. Settle-out of individual crystals or aggregates rather than accretionary bottom growth seems likely in deep basins but we have no modern examples to use as guides. In the present Dead Sea halite is only precipitating out behind dams in the shallow South Basin. But even here, where the brine depth is only a few meters at its maximum, interestingly different features are found. Wind-driven currents have resulted in the growth of loose halite ooids that are rippled (Weiler *et al.,* 1974), so that a clastic rather than a primary crystallization texture results.

In playa-ephemeral lake systems, like Saline Valley, where the main brine body is confined to the subsurface, intrasediment precipitation of even the most soluble salts occurs. In this mode of occurrence the saline minerals may be found as large euhedral crys-

(a)

FIGURE 7.   (a) Saline Valley salt
crusts. Flat but polygonally cracked
surface of a 7-cm-thick halite layer
deposited from a standing surface
brine in the ephemeral lake area of
Saline Valley. The complete
evaporation of the brine has left a fine
efflorescent halite film on the surface.
Evaporation of subsurface brine
drawn up along the cracks has
produced the ridges of fluffy
efflorescent halite. Pick, for scale, is
about 1 m long. (b) Saline Valley salt
crusts. View, looking south toward
the ephemeral lake area, showing the
spectacular buckling of layered halite
polygon edges produced by
efflorescent growth within the cracks
of the polygons. Note the banding of
the efflorescence beneath the
upturned edge (seen below hammer),
which might reflect summer pulses of
accelerated efflorescent growth from
below.

(b)

tals or crystal aggregates that either push the soft sediment aside (displacive growth) or enclose the sediment poikilitically (''sand crystals''). Or they may appear simply as patches of pore-filling sparry cements. Where larger holes occur (open burrows, rootholes, sheetcracks, shrinkage fenestrae, mudcracks, etc.) the salines will come out as large sparry vug linings and fillings.

For most soluble minerals, such as halite, thenardite, and bloedite, precipitation simply involves removal of H_2O, but this is not the case for trona ($NaHCO_3 \cdot Na_2CO_3 \cdot 2H_2O$), which has a solubility that is strongly dependent on p_{CO_2} (see Bradley and Eugster, 1969). As the work at Magadi has shown, trona precipitation is essentially limited by the kinetics of CO_2 addition. Because of their high pH, the lake brines are low in bicarbonate. Precipitation of trona removes HCO_3 and CO_3 in equal molar proportions, thus further depleting HCO_3. Some of the residual brines may be undersaturated with respect to atmospheric CO_2 by one order of magnitude (see Jones *et al.*, 1977, Table 2). Rapid evaporation of such brines may produce thermonatrite ($Na_2CO_3 \cdot H_2O$) or natron ($Na_2CO_3 \cdot 10H_2O$), depending upon temperature. This has been observed in evaporating ponds at Lake Magadi and during the drying-up process of Owens Lake (see Smith, in press).

Diagenetic reactions

Saline minerals

A number of saline minerals, such as gaylussite ($Na_2CO_3 \cdot CaCO_3 \cdot 5H_2O$), pirssonite ($Na_2CO_3 \cdot CaCO_3 \cdot 2H_2O$), glauberite ($CaSO_4 \cdot Na_2SO_4$), and anhydrite ($CaSO_4$), may not form by direct precipitation from brine but by interaction of the interstitial brine with the sediment or by mixing of interstitial brine with fresher waters percolating through the sediment. If there is any calcite present, gaylussite will form readily from sodium carbonate-rich brines by a reaction such as

$$CaCO_3 + 2Na^+ + CO_3^{2-} + 5H_2O \rightarrow$$
$$Na_2CO_3 \cdot CaCO_3 \cdot 5H_2O. \quad (5)$$

If the brine is very concentrated, that is a_{H_2O} is low, pirssonite will form instead. The boundary conditions have been defined by Hatch (1972). Dilute runoff and groundwater usually contains some Ca and HCO_3 and, if such waters come in contact with alkaline brines, gaylussite or pirssonite will form. At Magadi these minerals are very common and are found in the unconsolidated sediment as a loose sand of individual, well-formed crystals (Surdam and Eugster, 1976, p. 1750).

Hardie (1968) has interpreted glauberite at Saline

Valley as an authigenic mineral. It forms at the expense of gypsum deposited earlier, by reaction with Na-rich brines:

$$2CaSO_4 \cdot 2H_2O_{(s)} + 2Na^+_{(aq)} \rightleftharpoons$$
$$CaSO_4 \cdot Na_2SO_{4(s)} + Ca^{2+}_{(aq)} + 4H_2O_{(aq)}. \quad (6)$$

It is probable that many other double salts, such as burkeite ($Na_2CO_3 \cdot 2Na_2SO_4$) or aphthitalite ($K_3Na(SO_4)_2$), form in a similar manner. Generally there will be a precursor mineral, except when mixing of waters is the agent, and this precursor was usually deposited from a less saline brine. This evolutionary aspect is shown dramatically by the mineral zonation characteristic of every playa deposit which contains interstitial brines. Figure 8 illustrates the relations at Saline Valley. The geochemical center of the playa is represented by the most soluble minerals in contact with the most saline brines. As Hardie (1968) pointed out, these minerals are the saline minerals *within* the unconsolidated sediments and not those of the efflorescent crusts. The latter are formed by complete desiccation of groundwaters brought to the surface by evaporative pumping and represent nonequilibrium conditions.

The geochemical center of a playa is usually also a

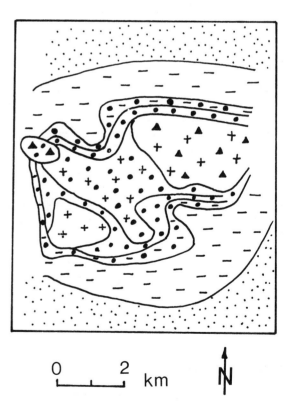

FIGURE 8.   Mineral zonation in the sediments of the Saline Valley playa. Redrawn from Hardie (1968). Small dots, carbonates; dashes, gypsum; large dots, glauberite; triangles, mirabilite; crosses, halite.

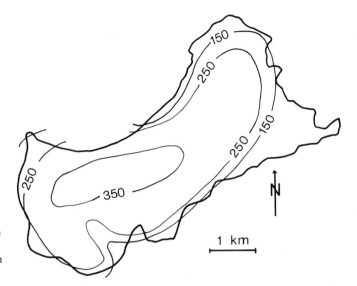

FIGURE 9.   Total dissolved solids in the Teels Marsh playa, in g/liter. The solid line indicates the edge of the playa. From Smith (1974).

topographic low. Not only is evaporation most intense there, but, more important, it is the final receptacle of the storm runoff which has acquired a very heavy solute load by dissolution of efflorescent crusts. As the playa evolves, the body of the brine grows from the center out and the gradient from dilute inflow on the periphery to the central brine steepens. Minerals which formed earlier from more dilute brines are overridden by more concentrated brines and give way to more saline authigenic products. This evolution continues until the water supply is shut off. Some of the steepest lateral gradients observed have been described by Maglione (1974) from the interdunal depressions bordering Lake Chad. In some of these depressions, less than 100 m wide, trona precipitates in the center, while at the margins drinking water is drawn from wells. Another example, Teels Marsh in Nevada (from Smith, 1974), is shown in Figure 9. It is important to note that similar concentration gradients also exist vertically, with the most concentrated brines near the top. This has been documented for Magadi (Jones et al., 1977) and Searles Lake (Eugster and Smith, 1965; Smith, in press). Although hydrologically unstable due to the heavy surface brines, this condition may persist for thousands of years, because solute acquisition occurs at or near the surface and because circulation is strongly inhibited by the crystal framework itself and by the many impervious sediment layers found in such deposits.

Authigenic silicates

The best known authigenic products of saline lakes are zeolites. Their occurrence has recently been summarized by Surdam and Sheppard (in press). They are found principally within the tuffaceous layers of saline alkaline lake deposits and they form by reaction of the volcanic glass with the occluded brine. As Sheppard and Gude (1968, 1969, 1973) have demonstrated, a zonal arrangement exists within these tuff layers, reflecting the lateral salinity gradients discussed above. The peripheral areas are characterized by unaltered glass. They border on a zeolite zone, to be followed by analcime and, in the very center, by potassium feldspar. These relations are clearly exhibited in Figure 10 from Lake Tecopa. The paragenetic sequence unaltered glass → alkalic zeolite → analcime → potassium feldspar has been documented by textural studies. The type of alkalic zeolite formed depends on the nature of the glass and the composition of the brine.

Surdam and Eugster (1976) have described zeolites and zeolite reactions observed at Magadi and its Pleistocene precursors. The sodium and silica-rich zeolite erionite is the most abundant authigenic silicate. It is isochemical with the trachyte glass and can form simply by the addition of water. Ca and Mg are very low. If alteration takes place in the presence of those dilute groundwaters which carry alkaline earths, clinoptilolite forms, while phillipsite, another common zeolite of alkaline deposits (Hay, 1964), represents environments low in alkaline earths and silica. As Mariner and Surdam (1970) have demonstrated, these zeolites probably form from a gel precursor rather than directly from the glass.

Analcime represents an environment of higher salinity. This is compatible with the fact that zeolite → analcime reactions release H_2O. For instance, the erionite → analcime conversion at Magadi has been formulated by Surdam and Eugster (1976) as

$$Na_{0.5}K_{0.5}Si_{3.5}O_9 \cdot 3H_2O + 0.5Na^+ \rightarrow$$
$$\text{erionite}$$
$$NaAlSi_2O_6 \cdot H_2O + 0.5K^+ + 1.5SiO_2 + 2H_2O. \quad (7)$$
$$\text{analcime}$$

There is considerable textural evidence (Sheppard and Gude, 1969) that analcime forms from the volcanic glass directly. Analcime may, however, form by a second pathway as suggested by Eugster and Jones (1968). In the presence of alkaline brines, volcanic glasses may alter to Na–Al-silicate gels, some of which have compositions close to analcime, and crystallization of such gels may give rise to monomineralic analcime beds (Hay, 1970). Analcime has a variable Si/Al ratio and particular analcimes seem to inherit their Si/Al ratios from their precursors (Sheppard and Gude, 1969; Boles, 1972). In this manner, compositions can be used to trace the nature of the precursor.

As mentioned earlier, potassium feldspar may replace analcime as the common authigenic silicate in the most saline center (Sheppard and Gude, 1968, 1969, 1973; Surdam and Parker, 1972). Potassium feldspar may form directly from analcime or from another zeolite precursor (Iijima and Hay, 1968; Sheppard and Gude, 1969). It replaces the hydrous phases not only in response to the still further lowering of a_{H_2O} but also because K in these residual brines often increases dramatically (Eugster and Jones, 1977). However, there must also be a kinetic factor, because none of the active saline lakes contain authigenic feldspars, whereas they are common in many Pleistocene deposits.

In addition to zeolites, a number of other silicates are also found as authigenic minerals in salt lake deposits. The most spectacular list has been compiled

for the Green River formation of Wyoming and will be discussed later.

Magadi-type chert

Another common product of saline alkaline lakes are bedded cherts. Such cherts have been reported from Africa (Eugster, 1967, 1969; Hay, 1968; Maglione and Servant, 1973) and America (Surdam *et al.*, 1972; Sheppard and Gude, 1974). They have been shown to form from a sodium silicate precursor, magadiite, $NaSi_7O_{13}(OH)_3 \cdot 3H_2O$ (Eugster, 1967, 1969). Magadiite and the associated minerals kenyaite, makatite, and kanemite have been reported from the same types of environments (Maglione, 1970; Rooney *et al.*, 1969; Sheppard *et al.*, 1970).

At Magadi, magadiite principally occurs in a bed up to 60 cm thick within the Pleistocene High Magadi beds and is thought to have formed by lake-wide precipitation. Because of the polymerization of silica at high pH, up to 0.4% SiO_2 can be stored in alkaline brines (Jones *et al.*, 1967). Precipitation mechanisms are not yet clear, but lowering of pH due to temporary stratification with a layer of more dilute surface waters has been suggested (Eugster, 1967). Magadiite can also form within the sediment column near the groundwater table by capillary evaporation (Maglione, 1970, 1974).

Two mechanisms have been suggested for maga-

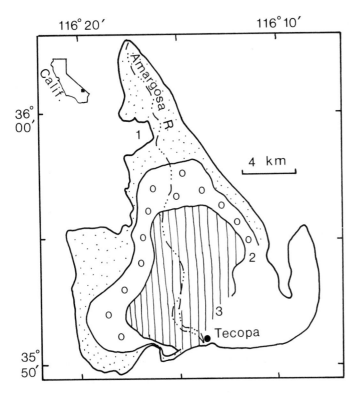

FIGURE 10.   Mineral zonation in the tuffs of Pleistocene Lake Tecopa: dots (1), fresh glass; circles (2), zeolites; lines (3), K-feldspar.

diite–chert transformation. One mechanism assumes leaching of sodium by more dilute surface or near-surface waters and is based on the *in situ* conversion observed in shallow pits (Eugster, 1969). O'Neill and Hay (1973), on the other hand, have postulated the spontaneous crystallization of quartz in the presence of concentrated brines.

Other authigenic minerals

The authigenic saline minerals and zeolites discussed so far are found in many deposits. They form rapidly under surface conditions and do not require unusual compositions. There is a large list of other minerals of authigenic derivation (see for instance Milton, 1971) which are found only in a limited number of places because of either chemical or physical constraints. Good examples would be searlesite, $NaBSi_2O_6 \cdot H_2O$, or shortite, $Na_2CO_3 \cdot 2CaCO_3$. Searlesite needs a source of boron and hence is found only in certain localities, such as at Searles Lake (Smith and Haines, 1964), Teeles Marsh (Surdam and Sheppard, in press), and the Green River Formation (Milton, 1971), while shortite needs the slightly elevated temperatures of burial and later diagenesis (Bradley and Eugster, 1969). Among the many other authigenic minerals falling into these categories are northupite $Na_2Mg(CO_3)_2 \cdot NaCl$ (Fahey, 1962), dawsonite $NaAlCO_3(OH)_2$ (Smith and Milton, 1966), and fluorite CaF_2 (Sheppard *et al.*, 1970; Surdam and Eugster, 1976). The occurrence of a particular authigenic mineral can usually be accounted for by local conditions.

Biological effects

Although we are not concerned here with the biological aspects of salt lakes, there are some indirect effects of biological processes on the precipitation of minerals which must be mentioned briefly. As is evident from the color of brines in evaporating ponds, biological activity extends into the most concentrated, saturated brines. This includes lake brines at Magadi with a pH of up to 11. Some bacteria, algae, and even higher forms, such as the brine shrimp *Artemia,* appear to have an astounding tolerance for high-solute concentrations. The presence of organisms and organic matter can modify mineral reactions in saline lakes in several ways. Two examples will be discussed here briefly: sulfate reduction and CO_2 production.

Sulfate reduction, briefly alluded to earlier, can be accomplished by bacteria belonging to the genera *Desulfovibrio* and *Desulfotomaculum* (Trudinger *et al.,* 1972). Although microbial oxidation of sulfur species can be accomplished by genera such as *Sulfolobos* (Brock *et al.,* 1976), it is probably of minor importance in saline lakes. Extensive sulfate reduction has been invoked by Jones *et al.* (1977) to account for the disappearance of the bulk of the sulfate during evaporative concentration between dilute inflow and saturated lake brines at Magadi. Direct evidence for sulfate reduction is found in the black, H_2S-rich muds found interbedded with the trona. Neev and Emery (1967) call on bacterial reduction of sulfate to account for the disappearance of gypsum from the laminated bottom sediments of the Dead Sea.

Bacterial decay of organic matter is an important source of CO_2 and it is probably responsible for the fact that most subsurface waters contain more CO_2 than waters equilibrated with the atmosphere. If CO_2 production takes place in the presence of sodium carbonate-rich brines, minerals such as nahcolite ($NaHCO_3$) or trona ($NaHCO_3 \cdot Na_2CO_3 \cdot 2H_2O$) may grow within the sediments because the solubilities of nahcolite and trona decrease strongly with an increasing p_{CO_2} (Eugster, 1966; Hatch, 1972). Bradley and Eugster (1969) have used this mechanism to account for the authigenic trona rosettes found within Green River sediments and a similar mechanism probably also applies to the nahcolite frequently found in the Green River formation of Utah and Colorado. Other minerals responsive to p_{CO_2}, such as dawsonite, will behave in a similar manner. Even the surface precipitation of trona is assisted by biogenic CO_2. Precipitation of trona leads to brines strongly depleted in CO_2 and further precipitation can take place only by addition of CO_2 either from the atmosphere or biological processes. The latter seems to be much more rapid and effective.

Examples of active saline lakes

The general principles applying to salt lakes presented here have been derived from a number of specific salt lakes of the western U.S. and Africa which we have studied in detail. Generalizations are valid up to a point, but beyond that point departures become relevant and it is these departures which define the uniqueness of a particular basin. To understand any basin, we feel it is important to be able to separate the generally valid from that which is of local significance. To this end we present brief sketches of seven active salt lakes which represent a variety of hydrological, mineralogical, and chemical conditions: Lakes Magadi and Chad in Africa, the Deep Springs and Saline Valley playas of California, Basque Lakes in British Columbia, Dead Sea in Israel and Jordan, and Great Salt Lake of Utah. The selection is somewhat arbitrary and based mainly on availability of data and personal acquaintance, but it covers a wide range of brine compositions and physical settings.

Lake Magadi

The eastern or Gregory Rift Valley in East Africa contains about two dozen closed-basin lakes, stretching from Ethiopia to Tanzania (see Figure 11). Some of these are fresh, like Naivasha, but most of them are quite saline, with sodium carbonate–bicarbonate the major solute. Hydrologic closure is provided either by volcanic craters (e.g., Lake Bogoria) or by block faulting of the lavas forming on the floor of the Rift Valley. The most concentrated brines are found at Lake Magadi, one of the smaller members, located in Kenya close to the Tanzania border (Figures 12 and 13). Magadi is about 2° S of the equator, at an elevation of 600 m. Evaporation is intense during the dry season as the Loita Hills and the Mau Escarpment to the west shield the valley floor from rainfall.

The first detailed study of the chemistry of the springs and lake waters was provided by Stevens (1932) in an unpublished report of the Magadi Soda Company. Most of this information can be found in the study of the geology of the Magadi area by Baker (1958). In it Baker discusses the geochemistry and mineralogy of the lake itself, as well as the petrology and geology of the Rift Valley. Additional investiga-

tions of the lake and its precursors have been published by Eugster (1967, 1969, 1970), Eugster and Jones (1968), Surdam and Eugster (1976), and Jones *et al.* (1977). Magadi is a valuable study object, not only because of its unusual setting and composition, but also because it is a lake in which deposition of saline minerals is taking place at the present time. In this brief synopsis we will focus on three aspects: the geochemical evolution of Magadi waters and brines, the geologic history of the precursor lakes, and the authigenic mineral reactions between sediments and interstitial brines. Magadi contains $Na–Cl–CO_3$ brines.

The Magadi trough is about 40 km long and has several arms, each 3–4 km wide, representing grabens in the thick sequences of trachyte lava flows which filled the floor of the Rift Valley 1–1.9 million years ago (Baker *et al.*, 1971). It contains a deposit of bedded trona ($NaHCO_3 \cdot Na_2CO_3 \cdot 2H_2O$) up to 50 m thick, called the Evaporite Series, which has accumulated since High Magadi time, dated at 9100 years (Butzer *et al.*, 1972). This deposit, which thins towards the edges, has a high porosity and contains a concentrated alkaline brine. Trona continues to form at the present time.

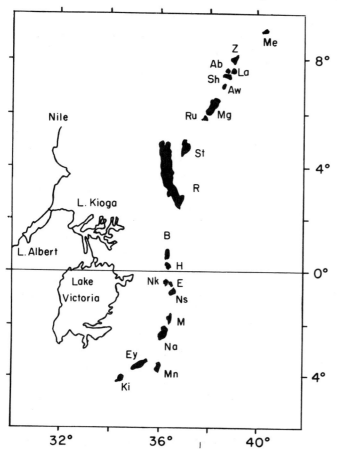

FIGURE 11.   Closed basin lakes in the East Rift in Ethiopia, Kenya, and Tanzania. From north to south: Me, Metahara; Z, Zwei; Ab, Abiata; La, Langano; Sh, Shala; Aw, Awassa; Mg, Margherita; Ru, Ruspoli; St, Stephanie; R, Rudolph; B, Baringo; H, Bogoria; Nk, Nakuru; E, Elmenteita; Ns, Naivasha; M, Magadi; Na, Natron; Mn, Manyara; Ey, Eyasi; Ki, Kitangiri; Lake Victoria is given for reference. From Eugster (1970).

There are no permanent rivers entering the Magadi basin and solutes are supplied mainly by a series of alkaline springs with temperatures up to 86°C, which are located around the perimeter of the lake. During the rainy seasons, storm runoff may flood the lake to several meters depth, but during the dry period the lake surface consists of a hard, porous crust of trona. The level of the interstitial brine never falls far below that surface. The springs feed lagoons, which are perennial water bodies at the lake margins (see Figure 13). These lagoons support a thriving colony of fish, *Tilapia alcalica* (for references see Beadle, 1974), which can tolerate a pH of 10.5 and temperatures of up to 39°C (Reite *et al.*, 1974). Through evaporation from the surface, lagoon waters are concentrated and their solutes contributed to the main lake deposit. Judging from the time available, trona must have accumulated at an average rate of about 5 mm/year, in good agreement with rates for the Green River formation (Bradley and Eugster, 1969). However, because of dissolution and reprecipitation, banding in the deposit itself is more in the range of 1–3 cm, represented by the size of trona single crystals growing from the mud-rich interface of the previous band.

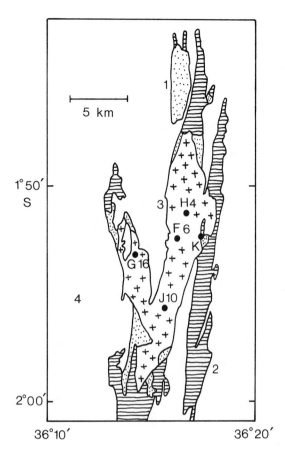

FIGURE 13. Simplified map of Lake Magadi. Locations H4, F6, K, J10, and G16 are drill holes mentioned in the text. 1, Surface brines; 2, High Magadi and Oloronga beds; 3, trona; 4, lava.

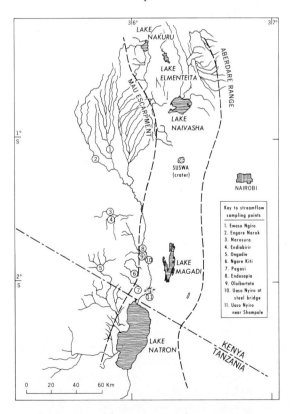

FIGURE 12. Perennial inflow into the East Rift between lakes Nakuru and Natron. The two dashed lines are the approximate locations of the East and West scarps of the Rift Valley. From Jones *et al.* (1977).

The alkaline springs have been constant in composition over the last 45 years and they are assumed to be fed by a groundwater reservoir of hot saline water. Using Na and Cl as tracers, Eugster (1970) and Jones *et al.* (1977) have established that the streams which flow from the western escarpment into the Rift Valley and disappear before they reach the floor could be the major recharge of this reservoir. Because of the largely volcanic nature of the bedrocks, these waters are all of the Na–Ca–HCO_3 type. Lake Naivasha, 100 km to the north (see Figure 12), may be another important supply, as is the occasional storm runoff.

The hydrologic model described above is based on the constancy of the Na/Cl ratio during evaporative concentration from dilute inflow to concentrated lake brines (see Figure 14), a process which spans four orders of magnitude. This constancy is most dramatic for the hot springs, for which log Cl lies between 1.5 and 2.5. The hottest and most concentrated spring is taken to represent uncontaminated reservoir brine, while the more dilute springs are thought to be fed by various mixtures of reservoir brine with dilute inflow. For some of the cooler and very concentrated brines, a third input has to be assumed, consisting of surface brine seeping down into the circulation system (Eugster, 1970). The points for which log Cl > 2.5 belong to surface brines of the lagoons and the lake which are derived mainly by surface evaporation from the spring inflow. The most concentrated brines exhibit a relative enrichment in Cl caused by precipitation of trona, $NaHCO_3 \cdot Na_2CO_3 \cdot 2H_2O$.

The Na/Cl ratio of the dilute inflow (log Cl < 0) is more variable, as one would expect, but in the same range as that of the hot springs and lake brines. The concentration step from inflow to hot spring is not accessible to direct observation and it is represented only by three samples (log Cl between 0 and 1) which belong to shallow ground waters. Their Na/Cl ratio is compatible with the general trend. The principal mechanism thought to operate here is the dissolution of efflorescent crusts by rain and storm runoff mentioned earlier. Such crusts develop extensively during the dry season, especially on the alluvial flats and the surrounding Pleistocene lake beds. The soluble salts consist mainly of halite and thermonatrite ($Na_2CO_3 \cdot H_2O$), and, since both dissolve easily, the constancy of the Na/Cl ratio is preserved. On the other hand, many other constituents remain in the crusts and are lost to the interstitial brines.

The elements lost most readily during the concentration are Ca and Mg. The springs, because of their alkalinity (pH of 9.2–10.2), are essentially free of these elements. However some of the more dilute groundwaters which occur seasonally within the alluvium

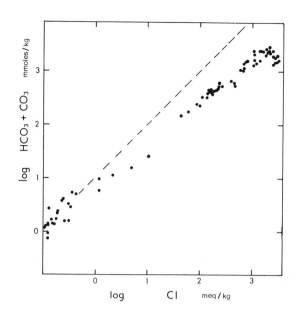

FIGURE 15. $HCO_3 + CO_3$ vs Cl in Lake Magadi waters. From Eugster and Jones (1977).

fringing the lake do carry Ca and Mg (Jones *et al.*, 1977).

$HCO_3 + CO_3$ are lost more gradually, although eventually only 7% of the initial amount reaches the most concentrated brines. Degassing and carbonate precipitation (Ca, Mg, and Na) are the main removal mechanisms. Figure 15 illustrates the loss of $HCO_3 + CO_3$ with respect to chloride. SiO_2 and K, shown in Figures 16 and 17, behave similarly. Both are lost rapidly at first, the former presumably by precipitation in the crusts and the latter by ion exchange (for details see Eugster and Jones, 1977), but both eventually are enriched in the lake brines by evaporative concentration. Overall losses are 99.7 and 96%, respectively. Since no clay minerals are present, K must be fixed either on the surfaces of the ubiquitous trachyte glass or the Na–Al–silicate gels described by Eugster and Jones (1968) and Surdam and Eugster (1976). Sulfate, which is more abundant in the inflow than chloride, is lost even more rapidly than SiO_2. The detailed mechanisms are not clear, though organic reduction may be a major cause. Of the lesser elements Br, B, and PO_4 are all essentially conserved in the solutions during concentration. Fluorine is also enriched to unusually high levels—saturation with respect to NaF—but some F has been removed as fluorite (CaF_2).

Evaporation calculations on Magadi inflow waters were carried out by Hardie and Eugster (1970). The resulting brines agree well with the natural brines, except for sulfate, which should be higher. This again points to the extensive sulfate removal during evaporative concentration.

Recently, four drill holes were placed in the lake:

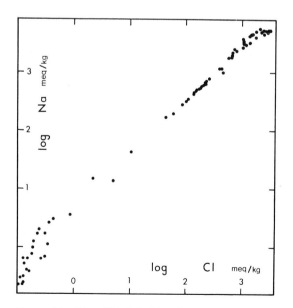

FIGURE 14.   Na vs Cl in Lake Magadi waters. From Eugster and Jones (1977).

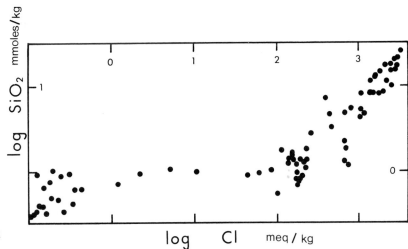

FIGURE 16. SiO₂ vs Cl in Lake
Magadi waters. From Eugster and
Jones (1977).

F6, G16, J10, and H4 (see Figure 13). The Evaporite Series is 18, 10, 7.5, and 28 m thick, respectively, and the brines associated with it are similar to the surface brines, containing 250–300 g of dissolved solids per kg brine. Several meters below the lowest trona unit, these brines are replaced by brines only half as concentrated (average of 127 g/kg), although of the same chemical character. A similar brine was collected by artesian flow from a deep hole (K in Figure 13) at 297 m, which had penetrated mainly trachytes. Thus concentrated brines are not simply a surface feature of the Magadi basin, but they are involved in very deep circulation within the lava flows and are presumably driven in large part by density contrast. Evaporative concentration must have been effective over a very long period of time.

The Magadi trough contains sediments deposited from two older, somewhat larger and more dilute lakes: Lake Oloronga dated at > 780,000 years and High Magadi Lake dated at 9100 years (Surdam and Eugster, 1976). Table 4 shows the stratigraphic relations. The sediments are principally of volcanogenic origin in addition to the magadiite-derived chert beds which are ubiquitous throughout the section. In the center of the basin the total sediment thickness is greater than 130 m (drill hole F6).

Shore lines of High Magadi time are still visible some 15 m above the present lake level, while Oloronga must have been considerably deeper, because its sediments are covering some of the shallower trachyte horsts near the lake and can be found from the foot of Shompole at the south to the northern-most extension of the trough. At their maximum, Oloronga sediments probably amount to 100 m and High Magadi

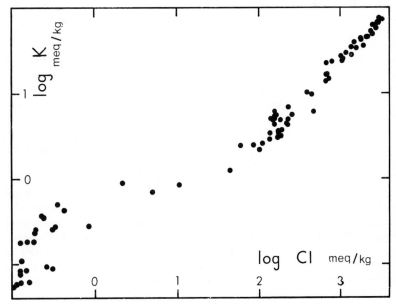

FIGURE 17. K vs Cl in Lake
Magadi waters. From Eugster and
Jones (1977).

TABLE 4.   Stratigraphic Units, Tectonic Events, and
Absolute Ages of Formations Found in the Magadi Basin

Units	Age	Lake
Evaporite series (slight tilting)	0	Magadi
High Magadi Beds (minor faulting?)	9,100	High Magadi
Trachyte flows (minor) caliche	780,000	
Oloronga Beds (extensive grid faulting)	>780,000	Oloronga
Plateau trachyte flows (extensive)	~1,000,000 to 1,700,000	

Data from Eugster (in preparation).

sediments to some 60 m (Surdam and Eugster, 1976). As mentioned above, horizons of bedded chert occur commonly. In the High Magadi outcrops marginal to the lake there is one chert horizon and this horizon is part of the principal magadiite. ($NaSi_7O_{13}(OH)_3 \cdot 3H_2O$) layer. The transformation of magadiite to chert in this layer can be observed over a lateral distance of less than 1 m. Although no continuous magadiite horizons are preserved in the Olorongo beds, it is reasonable to assume that the older cherts were also derived from magadiite. This means that Lake Oloronga frequently became a saline alkaline lake like its successors. The Oloronga sediments are capped basin-wide by a thick (75-cm) caliche horizon rich in calcite, indicating that there may have been a long dry period between Oloronga and High Magadi times.

Considering the abundance of highly reactive volcanic material and alkaline brine, it is not surprising that a variety of authigenic minerals have been observed in the Magadi sediments (Surdam and Eugster, 1976). Most common are gaylussite, fluorite, magadiite, Na–Al-silicate gel, erionite, clinoptilolite, and analcime. Gaylussite is found in unconsolidated surface sediments and probably forms by interaction of interstitial alkaline brines with dilute runoff bringing in some Ca. The high fluorine content of the Magadi brines (up to 0.2% by weight) is not due to unusual inflow waters, but rather to the fact that in these HCO_3-rich waters Ca is removed quantitatively before saturation with respect to fluorite, CaF_2, occurs. Hence fluorine is stored in the surface waters throughout the concentration process until NaF, villiaumite, precipitates. Within the older lake sediments, on the other hand, there are enough sources for Ca, and hence fluorite is a very common mineral in the drill cores. Erionite is the most abundant zeolite. Compositional comparisons have shown that it can form directly from tuffaceous rocks of trachyte composition by the addition of water only. Erionite has the lowest alkaline earth and the highest Na content, which explains why it is the dominant zeolite at Magadi. Clinoptilolite and chabazite are common in the Oloronga

beds, a testimony to the more dilute nature of Lake Oloronga (Surdam and Eugster, 1976). Analcime is ubiquitous and it forms either at the expense of erionite in the presence of concentrated brines or directly from Na–Al-silicate gels. Such gels, first encountered by Eugster and Jones (1968), are found throughout the drill cores (Surdam and Eugster, 1976). They are thought to form by reaction of trachytic material with alkaline brines and they have, except for their higher H_2O content, essentially the composition of analcime. Authigenic K-feldspar has not been found at Magadi and this is interpreted as due to kinetic factors. The many large anorthoclase fragments derived from the lavas remain unaltered. Zonation of zeolites so common in other alkaline lakes is developed only in a most rudimentary fashion. Magadi is situated in a steep-sided trough and does not have the wide playa fringes so essential for the establishment of lateral concentration gradients.

In summary, in terms of water chemistry and mineralogy, Lake Magadi is a typical example of an alkaline saline lake at the stage of maximum evaporite productivity. It is located in the rain shadow of substantial mountains with a large catchment area. Bedrocks are largely volcanic, in addition to some metamorphic basement, and hence dilute inflow is of the Ca–Na–HCO_3 type. Evaporation is intense and no perennial overland flow reaches the lake. Solutes in the saline, hot, groundwater reservoir are increased substantially by dissolution of efflorescent crusts formed by capillary evaporation of ephemeral runoff and near-surface ground water. This process has acted over an area 100 km long (up to Lake Naivasha), 30 km wide, for at least 10,000 years. Final evaporative concentration occurs on the surface from hot springs to lagoon waters to lake brines. Trona will keep accumulating as long as the streams entering the Rift Valley from the west scarp continue to recharge the ground water reservoir.

In accounting for the trona beds of the Green River formation and devising a depositional model for the Wilkins Peak Member (Eugster and Hardie, 1975), Lake Magadi has been used as example of a lake actively precipitating trona. It is important, therefore, to point out some of the crucial differences between Lakes Magadi and Gosiute. Lake Magadi is a Rift Valley lake, essentially a tub with steep sides. Circulation between inflow and springs is largely subsurface. Lake Gosiute, on the other hand, was extremely broad, with a shallow gradient, and fringed by wide mud flats, particularly during its trona precipitating stage. These mud flats were composed principally of a micritic Ca–Mg carbonate mud derived from surface capillary crusts and from travertine-tufa deposits (Smoot, 1976, 1977, in press). Similar Ca–Mg carbonate crusts have been postulated for Magadi but there is no place for them to accumulate.

Salt lakes and evaporites associated with Lake Chad

Lake Chad is a very large (20,000 km²), closed lake in the center of Africa. Its waters are essentially fresh and it is fed mainly by the river Chari and its tributaries, which drain the highlands of Cameroun and the Central African Republic to the south and of Chad and the western Sudan to the east (Figure 18). Precambrian basement predominates in the highlands. The geologic history, hydrology, and biology have been ably presented by Beadle (1974). In this brief summary we will restrict ourselves to the brines and evaporites which occur to the northeast of the lake in a region known as the Kanem. These deposits have been studied in detail by Maglione and his associates, and the results have been presented in Maglione (1974).

The level of Lake Chad, presently at 280–284 m above MSL has fluctuated substantially during recent geological history (Servant, 1973). Some 6000 years ago the level stood at 320 m and the lake occupied an area of 350,000 km², about five times the area of Lake Victoria. This included the Bodélé depression, 500 km NE of Chad, with its lowest point at 166 m and connected to Chad through the Bahr el Ghazal. Prior to this high stage, Chad must have been nearly desiccated. This is evident from the broad belt of completely or partially flooded dunes, trending NW–SE, which make up the extremely complicated NE shore of the lake (see Figure 19). These dunes continue to

the NE of the shore line in the Kanem region, where they isolate hundreds of interdunal depressions, 1–2 km² in size. These depressions are floored by several meters of clays (kaolinite, montmorillonite, illite), diatomites, and calcite laid down presumably during the high stage of the lake. They are now either dry, contain evaporites formed by capillary evaporation of shallow groundwater (natronières), or they may contain a small, perennial lake (see interdunal lakes, Figure 19). The levels of the interdunal lakes close to Chad fluctuate with the level of the main lake but isotopic evidence shows (Roche, 1973) that they are only partially fed by infiltration from Chad. On the piezometric surface, Chad occupies a high, but the Kanem is dominated by a higher groundwater mass, which reaches above 300 m. This is presumably a remnant of the high stage of the lake. Isotopic data show that the interdunal depressions also receive a considerable amount of recharge from recent meteoric waters. Evaporation is intense and Lake Chad is losing yearly some 2.3 m of water, 90% of which is by surface evaporation.

Three environments were investigated in detail by Maglione (1974): (a) the interdunal lakes Djikare, Bodou, Moïla, Mombolo, and Rombou, (b) the salt pan of Liwa, which is an interdunal depression without standing water, but with a shallow water table, and (c) the groundwater and lake brines of two small lakes (Napal and Kangallom) located on an island within

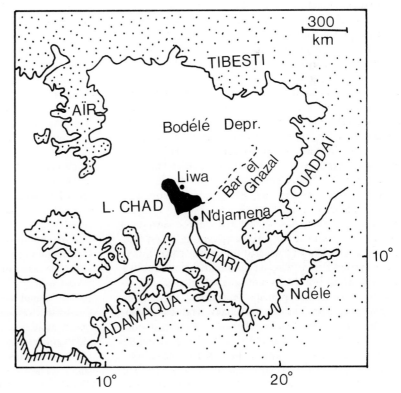

FIGURE 18.   Location map of Lake Chad. From Maglione (1974).

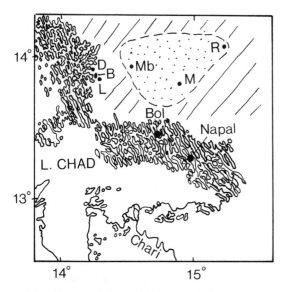

FIGURE 19.   Location map of the Kanem region, NE of
Lake Chad. Diagonal lines show the area of the interdunal
depressions and the dotted area is where the perennial
interdunal lakes are located. The locations of the following
lakes are shown: D, Djikare; B, Bodou; Mb, Mombolo; M,
Moïlo; R, Rombou. L is the depression of Liwa. The island of
Napal, on which lakes Napal and Kangallom are situated, is
also shown.

Lake Chad itself. The location of these study areas is
shown in Figure 19.

The small interdunal lakes close to Lake Chad are
presumably controlled by the composition of the
water of the main lake, while the groundwater in the
area of the interdunal lakes has distinctly higher Na/Cl
and HCO$_3$/Cl ratios, presumably inherited from Paleochad. Servant (1973) also cites evidence for dissolution of evaporite lenses, as indicated by locally high
groundwater salinities not connected to surface evaporation. Such deposits could have formed in interdunal depressions during the low stages preceding the
6000 year B.P. expansion. They may be responsible
for some of the compositional variability of the
groundwater. The small interdunal lakes further removed from Chad, such as lakes Bombou, Moïla,
Mombolo, and others, have essentially the composition of the local groundwater.

Magione (1974) has studied in detail the natronière
of Liwa. Waters at the periphery have less than 1000
ppm dissolved solids, while at the center, 250 m away,
the solutes rise to 300,000 ppm and the pH to 10.3
(Na–CO$_3$–Cl brines). A similar gradient exists vertically. Trona is the principal mineral of the surface
crusts which are harvested annually. Halite and nahcolite are also present and show a zonal distribution.
Occasionally   encountered   were   thermonatrite
(Na$_2$CO$_3$· H$_2$O), gypsum, and natron (Na$_2$CO$_3$·
10H$_2$O). Within the unconsolidated muds underneath,
a number of authigenic minerals form through capil-

lary evaporation. Most common are Mg-calcite, gaylussite, magadiite, and nahcolite. Tardy *et al.* (1974)
reported the formation of Mg-montomorillonite in
these same muds, and Maglione (1974) found mordenite. Most of the muds are in a reducing environment
and hence sulfate is low.

A very different brine and mineral evolution was
encountered by Maglione (1974) on the island of Napal, situated in Lake Chad some 30 km SE of Bol (see
Figure 19). This island, representing the crest of one of
the many flooded dunes, has very gentle topographic
depressions, 2–3 m deep, near its center, and two of
these depressions are occupied by the small lakes
Napal and Kangallom, which normally dry up yearly.
The groundwater table, obviously fed by Lake Chad,
is 1.3–4.2 m below the surface and is recharged
through an acquifer of sand. Evaporation in this well-
aerated environment leads to loss of CO$_2$ (calcite precipitation and atmospheric control), sulfate is not reduced, and hence the residual brines are Na–Mg–Cl–
SO$_4$ brines. Precipitation of thenardite (Na$_2$SO$_4$), halite, northupite (Na$_2$CO$_3$· MgCO$_3$· NaCl), and bloedite
(Na$_2$Mg(SO$_4$)$_2$· 4H$_2$O) results. A surface crust forms,
15–20 cm thick, consisting mainly of finely laminated
thenardite and some halite. Thus this environment is
in sharp contrast with the conditions at Liwa.

This contrast can be illustrated more clearly by
plotting some of the solutes against chloride, considered to be conserved during evaporative concentration (see Figures 20, 21, and 22). Figure 20 indicates,
as mentioned earlier, that the interdunal lakes and
most of the groundwaters have a distinctly higher Na/
Cl ratio than the ground and lake waters of the island
of Napal. The latter presumably represents Lake Chad
water subjected to evaporative concentration, while
the former compositions must be inherited from Paleochad. This evolution from a carbonate to a chloride-
rich lake, with time, has been observed frequently.
This may be due to one of two causes: (a) gradual
enrichment of Cl in the brine through fractional crystallization of other salts or (b) recycling of salts by
fractional dissolution of efflorescent crusts.

The groundwaters of Liwa are presumably derived
from Paleochad, as are some of the other groundwaters. This is in good agreement with isotopic studies
(Roche, 1973). Figure 21 presents the fate of carbonate. As at Magadi (Jones *et al.,* 1977), HCO$_3$ + CO$_3$ is
lost gradually, mainly through precipitation of calcite
and CO$_2$ degassing; however, the loss in the Napal
Island waters is much more pronounced than it is in
the interdunal lakes and at Liwa. This is presumably
due to the fact that calcium from fresher waters infil-
trates more readily at Napal. In consequence, the
most concentrated brines at Napal do not become
alkaline, but instead are dominated by chloride and
sulfate. The behavior of sulfate further enhances this
difference (see Figure 22). As Maglione (1974) and

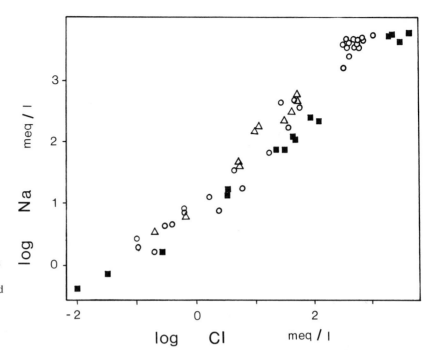

FIGURE 20. Na vs Cl for waters of the Chad area. Squares are waters of Lake Chad and the island of Napal, triangles are interdunal lakes, and circles are groundwaters, including those of Liwa.

Cheverry (1974) pointed out, Napal and the interdunal lakes are oxidizing, while the Liwa groundwaters are in an anaerobic environment, in which much sulfate is lost by bacterial reduction.

Thus, the differences in the brine compositions and evaporite minerals between Liwa and Napal are accounted for by the higher initial carbonate at Liwa, the more rapid carbonate loss at Napal, and the greater sulfate loss at Liwa.

Maglione (1974) has also faced the problem of the salt balance at Chad. He estimates that the total annual solute input amounts to 3.5×10^6 tons, 35% of which is silica. The lake loses about 2 m of water annually, but the water is still fresh. The loss of solutes by infiltration into the Kanem erg and their fixation in saline minerals by evaporative concentration in the interdunal depressions are thought to account for this. Hence, Lake Chad by itself is not a closed basin, and its surrounding areas must be included in the hydrologic closure.

Droubi et al. (1976) have tested some of the mineral reactions inferred for the Chad evaporites by a computer simulation of evaporation of Chad waters and have found good correlation with observed mineral assemblages. Gac et al. (1977) evaporated Chari water and found a Mg-silicate to be an early precipitate.

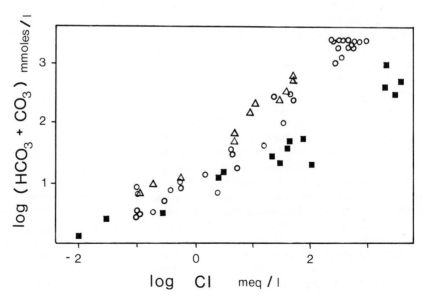

FIGURE 21. $HCO_3 + CO_3$ vs Cl for waters of the Chad area. Symbols are as in Figure 20.

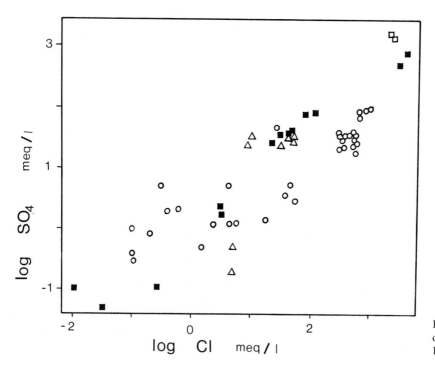

FIGURE 22.   SO$_4$ vs Cl for waters of the Chad area. Symbols are as in Figure 20.

Deep Springs Lake

Deep Springs Lake is a small playa in eastern California located in a basin between the Inyo and White Mountains just east of Owens Valley. Holocene faulting has dropped the floor of the basin to 1500 m in the SE corner, where the playa, occupying 5 km^2, is located. Near the center, a highly saline lake with Na–Cl–(CO$_3$)–(SO$_4$) brines exists, covering 1 km^2. The mineralogy and geochemistry of this playa have been studied by Jones (1965, 1966), with isotopic data on the carbonates provided by Petersen *et al.* (1963, 1966) and Clayton *et al.* (1968). Relic shore lines clearly visible in the SW corner indicate that the basin was occupied by a deeper lake in the not too distant past. This event has been dated by Lustig (1962) as 700–1000 years B.P.

Inflow onto the playa floor is from three sets of springs: Bog-mound Springs to the north, Corral Springs to the east, and Buckhorn Springs to the southeast. The latter two groups are clearly controlled by young fault zones. Recharge of the springs is primarily through two systems of perennial streams: the Wyman–Crooked Creek system in the north and northeast and the Birch Creek–Antelope Creek system in the northwest and north. The river and spring locations are given in Figures 23 and 25. Crooked Creek is located entirely within granitic rocks, Wyman Creek originates in metasedimentary rocks and then traverses granitic rocks, while Birch and Antelope Creeks are located essentially within metasedimentary rocks. The water compositions reflect these bedrock

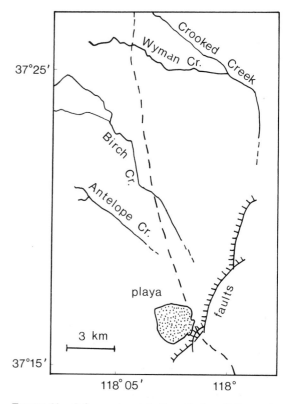

FIGURE 23.   Inflow waters into Deep Springs Valley and maximum extent of the playa lake. The dashed line represents a major lithologic change, west of which sedimentary and metasedimentary rocks dominate. Granitic rocks are the bedrocks east of it. Faults shown are Holocene.

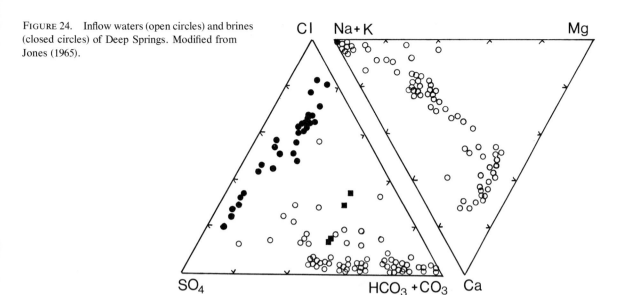

FIGURE 24.   Inflow waters (open circles) and brines (closed circles) of Deep Springs. Modified from Jones (1965).

differences. Crooked Creek is a Ca–Na–(Mg)–HCO₃ water, whereas Wyman Creek is a Ca–Mg–Na–HCO₃ and Birch Creek a Ca–Mg–(Na)–HCO₃–SO₄ water. Major sulfate sources are the sulfide zones associated with contact aureoles. Birch Creek, in particular, follows such a contact for 2 miles.

Jones (1965) has shown that the eastern and central Bog-mound Springs and the Corral Springs are recharged by the Wyman–Crooked Creek systems. A considerable compositional change occurs between rivers and springs. As Figure 24 shows, the change initially consists of enrichment in Na, SO₄, and Cl and,

finally, in the lake brines of Cl over SO₄. Jones (1965) mentioned two mechanisms responsible for the initial changes leading to depletion of Ca, Mg, and HCO₃:

"The major cause of the compositional changes downchannel is evaporation coupled with alkaline earth carbonate precipitation and re-solution of capillary salts" (p. A38).

These are the concentration mechanisms discussed earlier in general terms. They can be observed in almost every closed-basin setting. Carbonate precipitation occurs in the bed of Birch Creek, as has been described by Barnes (1965) and Slack (1967). Alkaline

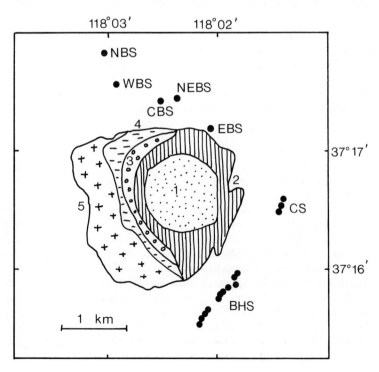

FIGURE 25.   Major inflow springs and mineral zonation of the Deep Springs playa. Modified from Jones (1965). NBS, WBS, CBS, NEBS, and EBS are, respectively, NW, W, central, NE, and E Bog-mound Springs; CS are Corral Springs; BHS are Buckhorn Springs. 1, burkeite; 2, thenardite; 3, gaylussite; 4, dolomite; 5, calcite, aragonite.

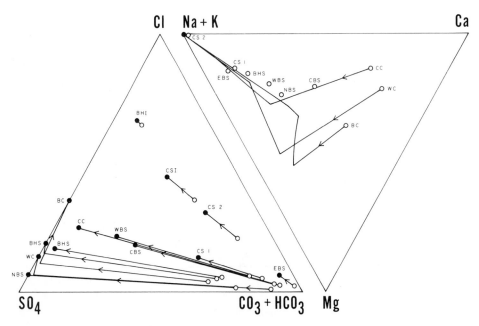

FIGURE 26.   Evaporation paths calculated from Deep Springs inflow waters. Analyses from Jones (1965). BC, Birch Creek; CC, Crooked Creek; WC, Wyman Creek; BHS, Buckhorn Springs; Bog-mound Springs are NBS (north-west), WBS (west), CBS (central), EBS (eastern); CS 1 and CS 2 are Corral Springs 1 and 2, CSI is an inflow channel below CS 1 and CS 2, and BHI is an inflow channel below the Buckhorn Springs. The cation diagram shows paths for the creeks, and starting compositions only for springs. In mol%. From Hardie and Eugster (1970).

earth carbonate cements and travertines are common throughout the valley and can be found also at the spring orifices. By far the largest amount of carbonate, however, is found as unconsolidated mud on the playa floor. Figure 25 shows the mineral zones described by Jones (1965), with calcite at the periphery, followed by proto-dolomite and then gaylussite. This zonation reflects the lateral concentration gradients in the interstitial brines.

The growth mechanism of the ordered dolomite found in the playa sediments has been studied by Petersen et al. (1963, 1966) and Clayton et al. (1968), using isotopic analysis. Dolomite grows very slowly (Petersen et al., 1963). Using leaching experiments, Petersen et al. (1966) argued that growth from solution is accomplished through a magnesian calcite precursor stage, represented by a thin Ca-rich surface layer, and that conversion to ordered dolomite takes place through cation exchange. Clayton et al. (1968) disputed their evidence and concluded that dolomite forms by direct crystallization from solution. They also noted the presence of coarser grained detrital dolomite which is isotopically distinct from the authigenic dolomite. A third carbonate phase, a magnesian calcite with an average content of 3.9 mol % $MgCO_3$, is present and is presumably also formed authigenically.

The center of the playa is occupied by soluble, Na-rich salts, mainly thenardite (Na_2SO_4), burkeite ($2Na_2SO_4 \cdot Na_2CO_3$), trona ($NaHCO_3 \cdot Na_2CO_3 \cdot 2H_2O$),

and halite (NaCl). This zonation documents the final step in the brine evolution: chloride enrichment and sulfate depletion through thenardite and burkeite precipitation. By analogy with Great Salt Lake, much of the thenardite may actually precipitate as mirabilite ($Na_2SO_4 \cdot 10H_2O$) during the cold winter months. At Great Salt Lake, this takes place when the brines reach temperatures of 4–6°C. Unlike Great Salt Lake, however, the residual brines of Deep Springs are depleted in Mg but contain enough CO_3 to precipitate trona. Removal of potassium is less effective than at Magadi and hence it is enriched in the final brines. This presumably is due to shallow circulation and rapid flow-through which does not give the clay minerals sufficient time for K removal (Eugster and Jones, 1977). Consequently, aphthitalite ($K_3Na(SO_4)_2$) and sylvite (KCl) are present in the salt crusts in small amounts.

The chemical evolution of the Deep Springs waters has been tested by Hardie and Eugster (1970), using calcite, sepiolite, and gypsum precipitation by computer simulation. In spite of the inadequacy of the model (sepiolite instead of dolomite), the brines actually found could be duplicated surprisingly closely. Figure 26 shows the calculated evaporation paths for some of the major inflow sources. Wyman Creek (WC), Crooked Creek (CC), and Birch Creek (BC) all produce Na–SO₄–Cl brines, with Wyman Creek (surprisingly) giving the most SO₄-rich waters. The Buckhorn Springs and one of the Bog-mound Springs

(NBS) also yield Na–SO₄–Cl brines. These springs can be derived compositionally from the Wyman–Crooked Creek system by calcite precipitation and twofold concentration, as is shown both in the anion and cation diagrams. BHI is a sample from an inflow channel between the Buckhorn Springs and the lake, and it clearly relates to the springs through mirabilite precipitation. Birch Creek water is rich enough in sulfate to precipitate considerable amounts of gypsum but does not, presumably because of early mixing with the other springs poorer in sulfate and richer in sodium. The Corral Springs (especially CS 2) and Bog-mound Springs (EBS, CBS, WBS) give mixed brines. They must draw on sources other than the streams, a conclusion reached by Jones (1965) through hydro-logic arguments. CSI is from an inflow channel below the Corral Springs. It cannot obtain its composition solely by evaporation of the Corral Spring water but must have dissolved substantial amounts of efflores-cent crusts consisting of halite and thenardite.

Figure 27 gives the comparison of the calculated with the natural brines. Immediately obvious is the connection between the sag pond and the Corral Springs. A mixture of CS 1 and CS 2, combined with evaporation and precipitation of calcite and sepiolite, yields the sag pond water at its high stage (low Cl values). This brine precipitates mirabilite and trona and moves toward the composition of the low stage (high Cl values), at which time burkeite and trona precipitate.

The lake brines are a different matter. Their compo-sitions correspond to synthetic brines derived from Buckhorn and N Bog-mound Springs, with a small addition from the other sources. Evaporation leads to

mirabilite precipitation, with corresponding enrich-ment in chloride. The surface brines have a surpris-ingly constant carbonate + bicarbonate content, which is probably due to loss of CO_2 to the atmo-spheric reservoir. Intercrustal brines cluster near point P, representing the assemblage brine + thenar-dite + burkeite + halite. If we consider that final evaporation proceeds above 20°C, say at 25–30°C, the correspondence is better still, as shown by point P, drawn for brine + thenardite + burkeite + halite at 35°C. The sequence mirabilite (or thenardite) → bur-keite → halite predicted for the Buckhorn Springs from Figure 27 is precisely the sequence observed by Jones (1965) for the horizontal zonation of the lake deposits and in the vertical sequence of the salt crusts. Missing is the gaylussite zone, which occupies the area surrounding the thenardite zone. Gaylussite ($Na_2CO_3 \cdot CaCO_3 \cdot 5H_2O$) probably forms by reaction of calcite or dolomite with the alkaline lake brines and therefore could not be dealt with in the computer model.

Figure 27 demonstrates that the simple model is capable of explaining the compositions of brines and evaporites found at Deep Springs, if we accept the Buckhorn and NW Bog-mound Springs as the domi-nant inflow. The contribution from the Corral Springs can be at most 20% of the total inflow. This is at variance with the estimated inflow rates for the major spring systems (Jones, 1965) but may simply empha-size the importance of seasonal flow variation. The intercrustal brines can be derived from the lake brines by precipitation of mirabilite, thenardite, and burkeite. The burkeite production is lower than it would be in a closed system because of CO_2 loss to the atmosphere.

FIGURE 27. Calculated and actual brines for Deep Springs. Abbreviations are as in Figures 25 and 26. Solid phase boundaries are for 20°C and dashed curves are for 35°C in the vicinity of the "peritectic" point P. In mol%. From Hardie and Eugster (1970). L, liquid; tr, trona; m, mirabilite; tn, thenardite; h, halite.

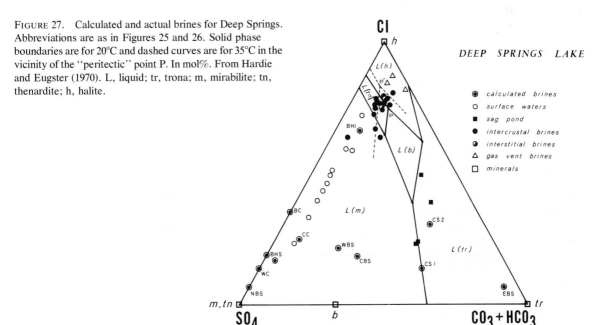

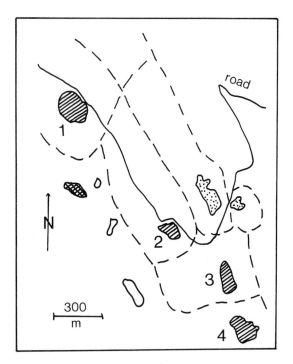

FIGURE 28.   Location map of Basque Lakes (for general location see Figure 3). Lakes 1 through 4 contain epsomite and bloedite, the cross-hatched lake mirabilite and the stippled lakes hydromagnesite. Dotted lines are watershed boundaries. From Nesbitt (1974).

Deep Springs is important to our understanding of closed-basin processes not only because it was one of the first playas to be studied in detail but also because it represents a common brine type and because calcite and dolomite are precipitating actively on the playa floor. It has been used (Eugster and Hardie, 1975; Surdam and Wolfbauer, 1975) as a model for brine evolution and carbonate production in the Green River Formation, though, because of its limited size, it is not comparable to Lakes Gosiute and Uinta with respect to sedimentation processes.

Basque Lakes

The Basque Lakes of British Columbia represent a brine type (Mg–(Na)–SO$_4$) which is quite common in areas underlain by basic and ultrabasic rocks. Inflow waters in such terranes are rich in Mg and SO$_4$ and eventually lead to the precipitation of minerals such as bloedite (Na$_2$SO$_4$·MgSO$_4$·4H$_2$O) and epsomite (MgSO$_4$·7H$_2$O). Most of the Mg presumably is derived from weathering of serpentines, olivines, and pyroxenes, while the sulfate comes from the oxidation of sulfides.

The Basque Lakes are very small, but they have been well studied by Goudge (1924) and Nesbitt (1974) and exhibit the essential features of MgSO$_4$-rich lakes.

This account relies heavily on Nesbitt's unpublished data. Figure 3 gives the location of the area and Figure 28 is a detailed map of the Basque Lakes 1–4, as well as some other ponds with their associated watersheds, all of which are extremely local. Some lakes are dominated by hydromagnesite, others by epsomite + bloedite, and one by mirabilite. Nesbitt (1974) studied Basque Lake 2, because it contains the most concentrated brines. Spotted Lake, a similar lake 200 miles to the south, has conical salt pods, and such pods also exist at the Basque Lakes.

The Basque ponds are located in small valleys at an elevation of 670 m in an area where annual precipitation is less than 30 cm. They are 60–130 m wide and 130–180 m long. Basque Lake 2 covers no more than 8000 m². There is normally no surface inflow and recharge must be by groundwater. The flanks of the valley are steep with bedrocks exposed, represented by the Carboniferous Lower Cache Creek Group, which consists of greenstones, siliceous volcanics, argillites, and limestones. The boundary between lakes 1 and 2 is formed by basic volcanic rocks and limestone. The valley floor is underlain by dense, impermeable clays and located within these clays is a major aquifer: a bed, 3–10 cm thick, of unaltered volcanic glass. This glass has been identified as Mazama glass associated with a Crater Lake event, 6600 years ago (Steen and Fryxell, 1965). The surface of the valley is densely populated by grasses with roots reaching into the ash horizon. There are no efflorescent crusts and groundwater concentration apparently occurs through evapotranspiration.

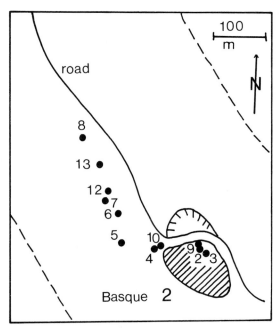

FIGURE 29.   Basque Lake number 2. Sample locations. From Nesbitt (1974).

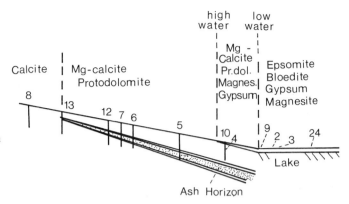

FIGURE 30. Schematic section through the Basque Lake 2 valley, showing the ash horizon, sample locations, and principal carbonate minerals. From Nesbitt (1974).

The lake itself contains numerous circular salt cones or pods which consist mainly of epsomite and bloedite. They are separated by and embedded in mud rich in gypsum crystals.

Figure 29 gives the sample locations. Figure 30 is a partial cross-section, showing the ash horizon as well as the carbonates found in association with that horizon and the minerals in the lake surface. Table 5 gives the chemical compositions of the brines. Concentration of solutes increases dramatically over a distance of less than 200 m from stations 6 and 7 in the valley to station 24 near the center of the lake. This increase can best be monitored by chloride, because it is not involved in any mineral reactions even in the most concentrated brines. Figure 31 shows species concentrations as a function of a concentration factor based on chloride conservation. Of the elements analyzed, only potassium is conserved as completely as chloride. Considering the rapid removal of K in most closed-basin settings (Eugster and Jones, 1977), this is somewhat of a surprise. It may indicate that the surfaces of the volcanic glasses in the aquifer are saturated with K^+ and have long since lost their effectiveness.

Silica values are low, not more than 12 ppm. This is barely supersaturated with respect to quartz. Never-

theless, silica drops still further during evaporative concentration, and it again is the element which is removed most extensively and early.

Total carbonate increases only fourfold during a nearly 60-fold concentration increase of chloride, testimony to the formation of magnesian calcites and protodolomites. Nesbitt (1974) has observed magnesian calcite, protodolomite, and magnesite within the lake muds as well as in a zone 15 cm above and below the ash horizon in the valley. The type of carbonates found is shown in Figure 30. A magnesian calcite with 4–11 mol % $MgCO_3$ is dominant near the ash horizon and smaller amounts of magnesian calcite with 32% $MgCO_3$ are present, while the near-surface muds of the lake area contain a protodolomite with 43 mol % $MgCO_3$ as a major phase, and some magnesian calcite with 30% $MgCO_3$ and magnesite. Concurrently with this change, the atomic Mg/Ca ratio in the waters increases from 20 at station 7 to 129 at station 3, reflecting the preferential extraction of Ca by magnesian calcites. Because it acts as the principal inflow conduit, extraction is most efficient near the ash horizon and diminishes away from the lake. At station 8, some 230 m from the lake, only a minor amount of low Mg calcite was found and the ash horizon was not encountered.

TABLE 5.   Compositions of Waters of the Basque Lake No. 2 Area (see Figure 30) and of Spotted Lake[a]

	7	6	5	4	3	24	SP-2
HCO_3^-	11.60	15.47	15.88	21.96	46.16	48.5	2.26
$SO_4^=$	146.78	142.62	185.30	1249.20	2529.63	2424.6	8.12
Cl^-	2.71	1.89	3.47	15.15	99.30	155.8	0.22
F^-	0.38	0.33	0.41	0.84	0.89	n.d.	0.05
Ca^{2+}	8.86	9.08	9.76	43.17	21.88	n.d.	3.50
Mg^{2+}	117.63	115.17	150.13	970.67	1711.01	1749.0	2.68
Na^+	51.33	51.33	66.12	452.40	1683.45	1347.8	6.09
K^+	2.40	2.56	3.07	21.04	127.08	163.7	0.38
Sr^{2+}	0.09	0.09	0.23	0.32	0.46	n.d.	—
Al^{3+}	3.4	3.7	4.8	35.0	59.0	n.d.	—
SiO_2	0.146	0.200	0.183	0.067	0.00	n.d.	0.03
pH	7.3	7.0	7.0	6.9	8.1	n.d.	7.6
Temperature (°C)	11.5	11.5	11.0	17.0	35.0	n.d.	12.0

[a]Concentrations in millimoles/liter, except for Al, which is in ppm. n.d., not determined. From Nesbitt (1974).

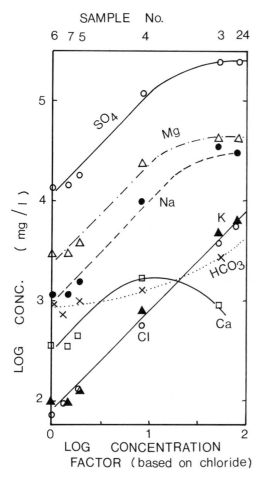

FIGURE 31.   Solute species as a function of concentration, based on chloride. From Nesbitt (1974).

Nesbitt (1974) has made some simple mass balance calculations to determine the amounts of carbonates precipitated between stations 7 and 4 during evaporative concentration. He found a loss of 81×10^{-3} mol/liter of carbonate, 37×10^{-3} mol/liter of Mg. All alkaline earths and carbonate extracted from solution can be accounted for by precipitation of carbonates, and there seems to be little loss of CO_2 to the atmosphere.

Below the low water mark in the lake area, Ca, Mg, Na, and SO_4 are removed, as Figure 31 clearly shows. This is obviously caused by the precipitation of gypsum, epsomite, and bloedite, with gypsum accumulating in the lake muds and the most soluble salts in the salt cones.

No dilute inflow waters are available for the Basque Lake system, so that brine evolution cannot be followed from its inception. However, the observed water compositions are in harmony with the inferred mineral precipitations and the observed mineral assemblages. Using published equilibrium constants at 25°C for calcite, dolomite, magnesite, gypsum, and

epsomite, Nesbitt (1974) has calculated the diagram for the reciprocal system $Ca-Mg-CO_3-SO_4-H_2O$ shown in Figure 32. Protodolomite is metastable with respect to ordered, stoichiometric dolomite, and its field boundaries with magnesian calcite and magnesite were estimated using the Basque Lake water compositions. The Mg/(Ca+Mg) ratio derived for Mg-calcite + protodolomite is 0.80, and that for protodolomite + magnesite is 0.94. For simplicity, the boundaries have been assumed to be straight in the reciprocal system. An inflow water of composition A, assuming perfect equilibrium, would produce the following mineral sequence upon evaporation: Mg-calcite $\rightarrow$ Mg-calcite + protodolomite $\rightarrow$ protodolomite $\rightarrow$ protodolomite + magnesite $\rightarrow$ protodolomite + magnesite + gypsum $\rightarrow$ magnesite + gypsum $\rightarrow$ magnesite + gypsum + epsomite. The brine would evaporate to dryness while in equilibrium with the latter assemblage. This sequence, deduced from the diagram, agrees quite well with the observed mineral zonation, except for the exclusion of bloedite, which contains Na. Spotted Lake waters, on the other hand, would precipitate gypsum before protodolomite, because they are initially richer in sulfate. This is confirmed by preliminary studies which show a calcite + gypsum zone surrounding the lake.

To be able to include bloedite, another reciprocal system must be considered: $Na-Mg-Cl-SO_4$. Field boundaries for 25°C are shown in Figure 33 and are

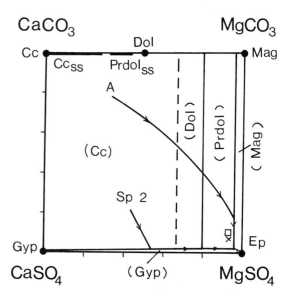

FIGURE 32.   Reciprocal system $Ca-Mg-CO_3-SO_4$ at 25°C, based on thermodynamic data and field relations at Basque Lakes. Solid carbonate boundaries are for protodolomite; equivalent boundaries for ordered, stoichiometric dolomite are dashed. The square and cross are for Basque waters 6 and 7, respectively, and Sp 2 for a Spotted Lake water (see Table 5). Cc, calcite; Prdol, protodolomite; Mag, magnesite: Ep, epsomite; Gyp, gypsum. From Nesbitt (1974).

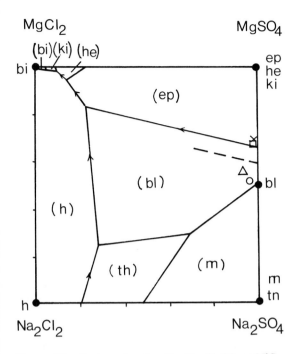

FIGURE 33.   Reciprocal system Na–Mg–Cl–SO$_4$ at 25°C. Field boundaries from Hardie and Eugster (1970). The cross, square, circle, and triangle are waters 7, 4, 3, and 24, respectively (see Table 5). h, halite; tn, thenardite; m, mirabilite; bl, bloedite; ep, epsomite; he, hexahydrite; ki, kieserite; bi, bischofite. The dashed line is the epsomite–bloedite field boundary for 20°C. From Nesbitt (1974).

taken from Hardie and Eugster (1970) and Wood (1975). The bloedite field is quite large. The groundwaters (stations 4 and 7) plot in the epsomite field and the lake waters (stations 3 and 24) in the bloedite field. This does not conform with the observation that epsomite and bloedite occur together in the lake. The most plausible explanation lies in a temperature effect: lower temperatures shrink the bloedite field considerably and at 15°C the lake brines may plot close to the epsomite–bloedite boundary, where they should be. At such a temperature, epsomite would first precipitate from the groundwaters and the water compositions would move away from the MgSO$_4$ corner until they intersect the epsomite–bloedite boundary. Next epsomite and bloedite coprecipitate and the water composition moves towards the MgCl$_2$ corner. Halite would be the next mineral to join, but brine evolution never goes this far at Basque Lake 2.

In summary, the Basque Lake inflow waters owe their high Mg and SO$_4$ contents to weathering of basic and ultrabasic rocks and oxidation of sulfides. After this initial difference, brine evolution proceeds by steps very similar to those followed by the more common waters. Alkaline earths and carbonates are precipitated as calcite, Mg-calcite, and protodolomite and finally even magnesite, as the Mg/Ca ratio increases.

The remaining Ca is removed in gypsum, leaving a brine rich in Mg, Na, SO$_4$, and Cl. Evaporation then continues to the most soluble salts, such as epsomite and bloedite, and finally halite. The extreme product upon evaporation to dryness would be halite + kieserite (MgSO$_4 \cdot$H$_2$O) + bischofite (MgCl$_2 \cdot$6H$_2$O). Meanwhile, some Na and SO$_4$ may be lost by mirabilite freezing out during the cold winter months.

The Dead Sea

The most complete published study of the Dead Sea is that of Neev and Emery (1967). Other papers focusing on geochemical aspects of the Dead Sea system are those of Bentor (1961), Loewengart (1962), Mazor (1962), Neev (1962), Lerman (1967), Lerman and Shatkay (1968), Mazor and Mero (1969), Mazor et al. (1969), Lerman (1970), and Kaufman (1971).

The Dead Sea is an example of a deep stratified chloride lake in an active rift valley, flanked by alluvial fans and fed continuously by a large perennial river.

The Dead Sea lake lies in the deepest depression of the Jordan–Arava graben between Israel and Jordan; the graben walls rise some 500 to 3000 m above the surface of the lake, which is about 397.5 m below sea level. The Dead Sea is about 80 km long, 17.5 km wide at its maximum, and covers an area of 940 km^2 with a volume of 136 km^3 (Neev and Emery, 1967). Maximum depth is about 400 m.

Physiographically the lake is divided into two parts: (1) the shallow South Basin which occupies 27% of the lake area and is only 10 m deep at its maximum, and (2) the deep North Basin, which covers more than twice the area of the South Basin and is essentially a flat-bottomed trough over 300 m deep with steep sloping walls. Chemically the lake waters are very saline, with total dissolved solids around 300,000 ppm, and are of the unusual Na–Mg–(Ca)–Cl type. Sulfate and bicarbonate are very low; together they make up less than 0.4% by weight of the anions. The North Basin waters are notably density stratified into an Upper Water Mass (the top 40 m), a Transitional Member Mass, 100–400 m).[1] The density stratification is due mainly to salinity differences, the U.W.M. having a salinity around 300‰, the transitional zone 320‰, and the L.W.M. about 332‰. Chemical changes accompany these salinity changes, at top of p. 272 (calculated from Neev and Emery, 1967, Table 6):

[1]Since 1975 the density of the Upper Water Mass has gradually increased and the density stratification is no longer discernible. In March 1977, the Dead Sea level stood at −401.50 m and the Southern Basin was almost dry (M. Beyth, personal communication). See also Assaf and Niessenbaum (1977).

(mole ratios)	Mg/K	Na/K	Ca/K	Cl/K	Br/K	SO₄/K	HCO₃/K	pH
U.W.M.	8.952	10.090	2.464	33.458	0.343	0.036	0.023	6.4
L.W.M.	8.995	8.902	2.211	31.876	0.340	0.021	0.019	6.2

Calcium, sulfate, bicarbonate, sodium, and chloride are lower relative to K in the L.W.M. while bromine and magnesium show insignificant changes ($< 1\%$).

At the present time both aragonite and gypsum are found to be precipitating from the surface waters (Neev and Emery, 1967, pp. 88–92). Sediment traps suspended in the lake collected gypsum and aragonite in about a 7:1 mass ratio although the tiny aragonite needles (up to 11 μm long) outnumbered the larger euhedral gypsum plates (up to 95 μm long) by 10 to 20:1. The average concentrations of precipitates were found to increase in the summer and to be somewhat greater in the South Basin than in the North Basin. The proportion of aragonite increased by a factor of over 2 during a "whitening" in August 1959 (Neev and Emery, 1967, p. 90). Cores taken of the bottom sediment show beautifully laminated dark- and light-colored carbonate-rich mud. The light laminae consist mainly of aragonite with small amounts of calcite and gypsum; the dark laminae consist of nearly equal amounts of aragonite and calcite with some quartz, clays, gypsum, and pyrite. Two interesting facts emerge about these mm-laminated sediments: (1) they are not annual, only 15–20 laminae have been deposited in the last 70 years (Neev and Emery, 1967, p. 107), and (2) the gypsum–aragonite ratio in the bottom sediments is considerably smaller than the measured precipitation ratio and it decreases with increasing depth. Neev and Emery's (1967, pp. 94–95) interpretation of this second observation is that sulfate-reducing bacteria in the bottom sediment cause dissolution of gypsum, precipitation of calcite and iron sulfides, and release of H_2S. In this way the bottom sediment becomes carbonate rich and the sulfate ions are recycled as the H_2S oxidizes as it diffuses upward.

No halite is precipitating from the lake waters of the North Basin today and in the South Basin halite comes out only where the basin has been artifically dammed, producing some interesting sedimentary features such as crusts, ripples, and ooids (Weiler *et al.*, 1974). However, cores taken in the bottom sediment of the North Basin showed that below the 40-m depth contour there is hard halite underlying 10–80 cm of the laminated carbonate mud discussed above. Neev and Emery (1967) estimate this halite to have precipitated from the lake in sub-Recent times, over 1500 years ago. This sub-Recent halite can help explain the chemistry of the L.W.M. As pointed out above, the Br/K and Mg/K ratios in the L.W.M. are the same as those in the U.W.M., suggesting that the L.W.M. was derived from the U.W.M. Within the variation of the analyses the L.W.M. chemistry can be accounted for

by precipitating roughly 0.003 mol of gypsum, 0.0005 mol of aragonite, and 0.019 mol of halite from 1 liter of U.W.M. to produce 1 liter of L.W.M.[2] In support of this idea, Lerman (1967) has shown that the L.W.M. is in fact just saturated with respect to halite. The L.W.M., then, seems to be a relict of sub-Recent times when the evaporation/inflow ratio was higher than now and high enough to reach supersaturation with respect to halite.

The final problem concerns the source of the solutes in the Dead Sea lake waters. The Jordan River, flowing south from the Sea of Galilee, has been estimated to provide 80% of the water received by the Dead Sea, with about 8% provided by storm runoff and the rest from saline springs at the periphery of the Dead Sea. However, because the springs are so much more saline than the Jordan River (up to 300 times, see Bentor, 1961, Table 1), the bulk of dissolved solutes must be provided by the springs. This is supported by the comparison of the Jordan River water composition with that of the U.W.M. The Jordan River at first glance has the right general composition to be the parent of the Dead Sea brines. Like these brines the Jordan River is of the unusual Na–Ca–Mg–Cl–(SO₄)–(HCO₃) type, a composition it has inherited from the hot springs around the Sea of Galilee (see Bentor, 1961, Table 1). However, when we compare the conservative ions we find that Br/Cl, Mg/Cl, Mg/K, and Cl/Na mole ratios are too low in the Jordan River, as follows:

(mole ratios)	Br/Cl	Mg/Cl	Mg/K	Cl/Na
Jordan River	0.005	0.182	4.77	2.21
U.W.M.	0.010	0.267	8.95	3.31
Zohar Springs	0.010	0.251	26.75	2.93
Sdom Springs	0.005	0.245	4.19	6.47

Bentor (1961, pp. 252–253) suggested that Sdom Springs, mixing with the Jordan River waters, could after precipitation of aragonite and gypsum account for the U.W.M. However, as the table shows Br is too low and K is too high in the Sdom Springs. Zohar Springs would perhaps be a better candidate. In any event the solutes reaching the Dead Sea lake do not have a simple source but rather must have come from complex mixing of multiple source waters.

---

[2]The best mass balance was obtained using the Dow Chemical Co. analyses given in Table 4 of Neev and Emery (1967) although the U.W.M. value for Mg seems too low. If the average analyses given in their Table 6 are used then too much Ca is lost and Na and Cl losses do not balance.

Saline Valley, California

Saline Valley, Inyo County, California, is an example of a small salt-encrusted playa-ephemeral lake complex, surrounded by very high steep mountains, fringed by large alluvial fans, with no perennial stream inflow but fed instead by subsurface waters.

Early work on the salt deposits and brines of Saline Valley was limited to a few grab-samples and exploratory boreholes (Gale, 1914; King, 1948, p. 190; Tucker, 1926, p. 527; Ver Planck, 1958, p. 25). Lombardi (1963) did the first comprehensive study of the chemical compositions of the inflow waters and playa brines, with particular emphasis on the trace element geochemistry. Hardie (1968) described the mineral–brine relations in the playa system and interpreted them using experimental data for the analogous synthetic system $CaSO_4–Na_2SO_4–NaCl–H_2O$. The following summary is based mainly on this last paper.

Description of the evaporite system.   Saline Valley is a small, closed, intermontane basin in the Basin-and-Range Province, about 24 km northeast of Owens Lake, California (Figure 3). It is about 56 km long and 32 km wide, and bounded to the west by the Inyo Mountains, which tower more than 3000 m above the playa (Figure 1), and to the east by the Panamint Range, which rises 2000 m above the playa. These enclosing mountains, composed of Paleozoic limestones and marine siliciclastics intruded by Mesozoic quartz monzonite, are block-fault mountains formed by massive crustal extension which began in the Eocene. Tertiary and Quaternary basalt flows, originating in the fault zones, drape the eastern walls of the valley. Huge coalescing alluvial fans, up to 700 m high with slopes up to 25 km long, form a continuous fringe or apron around the base of the mountains (Figure 1).

The lowest part of Saline Valley is a flat, salt-encrusted playa which covers a roughly circular area of about 40 km². A very shallow body of open brine a few cm deep, saturated with respect to halite, covers less than 2.5 km² of the playa surface at the southwestern corner. Outward from this, salt lake brine is found in sand or mud 30 cm to 5 m below the playa surface. This subsurface brine is relatively dilute at the playa margins (10,000–30,000 ppm dissolved solids) but rapidly increases in concentration toward the center of the playa (270,000–290,000 ppm dissolved solids), setting up a steep concentration gradient (see Lombardi, 1963, Figure 15).

Drainage in Saline Valley is entirely subsurface except when rare flash floods cause tremendous runoff and temporarily inundate the lowest part of the playa, producing an ephemeral saline lake. Springs rise in the deep, narrow, winding canyons of the enclosing mountains, particularly the Inyos, and along the fault-lines at the base of the mountains where they meet the alluvial fans. These spring and canyon stream waters on reaching the alluvial fans disappear into the coarse porous sediment after travelling no more than a few meters. On the northeastern edge of the valley are a series of hot springs which are depositing travertine, but water from these springs also disappears downslope into the fan sediment.

Evaporation vastly exceeds precipitation so that the playa is extremely arid. Although no formal records are available, Hardie (personal observations) noted that periods of more than a year have passed without rain on the playa and that annual rainfall probably averages less than 8 cm (compare evaporation and rainfall pattern in nearby Death Valley measured by Hunt et al., 1966, p. 5).

The concentrated brines of the playa are Na–Cl–(SO_4) waters whereas the dilute spring and stream inflows are Ca–Na–SO_4–HCO_3 waters. Figure 34 depicts the water compositions in terms of major cations and anions as a function of total dissolved solids. This diagram brings out two very clear trends in composition: (1) as concentration begins to increase there is a dramatic decrease in Ca, Mg, HCO_3, and SiO_2, and (2) during the later stages of concentration SO_4 decreases with respect to Cl.

Evaporite minerals are found in three different modes in the playa: (1) surface efflorescent crusts (Figure 6A), (2) layered crystal-accumulates (Figure 7A), and (3) crystals and crystal aggregates that have grown within the sediment as displacive, poikilitic, or vug-filling precipitates. The major evaporite minerals found in the playa are listed in Table 6. With the exception of the salt-lake area, the entire surface of the playa is covered with a rough blocky porous efflorescent salt-crust which ranges in thickness from 1 to 100 cm. This crust is dominantly halite but small amounts of thenardite, gypsum, glauberite, and mineral X are commonly present. The ephemeral salt-lake in the southwest corner of the playa (the topographic low of the playa) is floored by a smooth layer of halite (Figure 7A), a crystal-accumulate which precipitated out of the brine pond. This surface layer of halite is 3 cm thick and overlies a thinner (1–2 cm) layer of black H_2S-rich mud. This mud–halite couplet formed after the last storm when sediment-charged surface run-off dissolved part of the playa efflorescent crust (Figure 6B) and became ponded in the topographic low of the playa. The mud settled out first, then as the brine evaporated halite crystallized out. This couplet is repeated in thin beds (less than 10 cm thick) for several meters below the salt lake floor. The halite layer is cracked into large (1–2 m) irregular polygons, and efflorescent halite growth in these cracks has produced massive buckling in places (Figure 7B).

Beneath the efflorescent crust of the playa are silici-

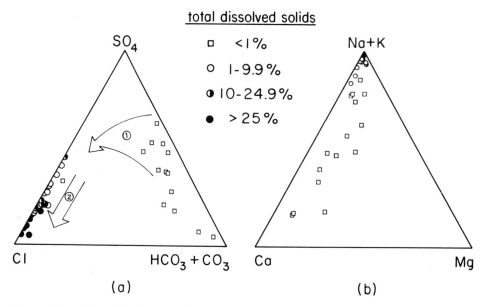

FIGURE 34.   Trilinear diagrams of Saline Valley waters showing relation between compositions (in wt%) and total ion concentration (also in wt%). Major anions are shown in (a) and major cations in (b). In (a) the arrows emphasize the trends (1) bicarbonate decrease, and (2) sulfate decrease, with increasing total ion concentration.

clastic sands and muds. On the margins of the playa thin (2–30 cm) interbedded sands and muds overlie gravelly sand and sandy gravel of the alluvial fan toes, but toward the center of the playa the sediment is mainly of mud (clayey silt). The sands consist chiefly of quartz and plagioclase with smaller amounts of calcite and dolomite. The muds are composed of quartz, plagioclase, 14-Å chlorite, 10-Å mica, and montmorillonite with a little calcite and dolomite invariably present. Within these playa sands and muds isolated crystals or crystal aggregates up to 2 cm across of gypsum, glauberite, and halite have precipitated. These intrasediment precipitates are not randomly distributed but occur as a sequence of assemblages *systematically arranged in laterally concentric zones*. The sequence from the periphery in, to the center of the playa, is gypsum → gypsum + glauberite → glauberite → glauberite + halite. This zonal structure is shown in Figure 8, which is a map of the evaporite mineral distribution within the upper 5 m of playa sediments. Nothing is known of the actual depth

to which the zones might reach, but it does not seem likely to be more than a few tens of meters. The steep, lateral concentration gradient in the present brine body suggests that some impermeable layer at not too great a depth effectively seals the bottom of the present evaporating pan. The record of marked temporal variations in activity of H_2O in the Searles Lake evaporite deposit (Eugster and Smith, 1965, see particularly their Figure 22) testifies to this idea: the Searles Lake deposit seems simply to be a pack of such watertight evaporating pans piled one atop the other.

Development of the brines.   All of the spring and stream waters, on reaching the fans, sink into the alluvium within a few meters so that the playa is fed by subsurface flow only. Evaporation through the fans must occur during passage of these groundwaters to the playa because the waters at the playa edge are considerably more concentrated than the inflow waters. This increase in concentration during transport is accompanied by considerable changes in chem-

TABLE 6.   The Saline Minerals in the Saline Valley Evaporite System

Mineral	Occurrence
Halite (NaCl)	Efflorescent crusts; crystalline layers; intrasediment precipitates
Thenardite (Na_2SO_4)	Efflorescent crusts; intrasediment precipitates
Mirabilite ($Na_2SO_4\cdot 10H_2O$)	Intrasediment precipitates (ephemeral)
Glauberite ($CaSO_4\cdot Na_2SO_4$)	Efflorescent crusts; intrasediment precipitates
Gypsum ($CaSO_4\cdot 2H_2O$)	Efflorescent crusts; intrasediment precipitates
Calcite ($CaCO_3$)	Travertine, intrasediment precipitates
Sepiolite ($Mg_2Si_3O_8\cdot nH_2O$)	Intrasediment precipitates

istry: the relative compositions of the playa waters are significantly different from those of the inflow waters. The most striking change is the drastic reduction in bicarbonate (+ carbonate) proportion in the playa brines (trend 1 of Figure 34). This could be accounted for by precipitation of calcite (or any other carbonate) from the groundwaters before they reach the playa. In the hot spring region of the valley, travertine deposits provide ample evidence of calcite precipitation. However, for the remaining inflow areas no surficial carbonate deposits were observed and hence precipitation of calcite, if it does occur, must take place at subsurface within the voids of the sediment of the alluvial fans. Support for this is twofold. First, McAllister (1956) reports that in the southeast corner of the valley "the fanglomerate in traces of places is well-cemented with calcite," and second, the brines at the margin of the playa are either just saturated or somewhat supersaturated with respect to calcite (Hardie, 1968, p. 1289). Because the main inflow waters have Ca^{2+}/HCO_3^- mole ratios close to 1 and the precipitation of calcite according to the reaction $Ca^{2+}_{(aq)}$ + $HCO^-_{3(aq)} \rightarrow CaCO_{3(s)} + H^+_{(aq)}$ takes out Ca^{2+} and HCO_3^- in equal molar proportions, then *both* Ca^{2+} and HCO_3^- will be maintained at relatively low, and near equal, concentrations, in the order of 10^{-2} to 10^{-3} during progressive evaporation, as the actual brine analyses show (see Hardie, 1968, Tables 4 and 5). In this way, then, SO_4^{2-} and Cl^- become the major anions in the playa brines, while HCO_3^-, once dominant, becomes virtually an "accessory" ion species (Figure 34). Also, the loss of Ca^{2+} as calcite produces a significant increase in the Na^+/Ca^{2+} ratio in the brines.

With SO_4^{2-} as an abundant species in the Saline Valley inflow waters, saturation with respect to gypsum is soon reached with evaporative concentration of the groundwaters, as is directly evidenced by the zone of gypsum-bearing sands at the toes of the fans and fringing the playa (Figure 8). IAP calculations (Hardie, 1968, pp. 1290–1291 and Table 4) support the idea that equilibrium with gypsum was attained by all of the marginal playa brines found in contact with gypsum. This early precipitation of gypsum (ionic strengths of the brines near the calcite–gypsum zone boundary, Figure 8, are as low as 0.3) controls the increase in SO_4^{2-} concentration so that the Cl/SO_4^{2-} ratio climbs significantly (Figure 34). At the same time, because the SO_4^{2-}/Ca^{2+} ratio was initially high, precipitation of gypsum leads to a further increase in the SO_4^{2-}/Ca^{2+} ratio.

During evaporative concentration of the playa brines Mg^{2+} is lost, as is well demonstrated by $Mg^{2+}/$ Na^+ and Mg^{2+}/Cl^- ratios (Hardie, 1968, Tables 1 and 2). The mechanism for Mg^{2+} loss is not quite certain but Mg^{2+} seems to be taken out as sepiolite rather than Mg-calcite or protodolomite (Hardie, 1968, pp. 1291–

1292), a mechanism that would also help to explain the loss of SiO_2 from the brines.

In summary, the brines at the playa margins have developed by progressive evaporative concentration of dilute groundwater inflow, leading to the precipitation of calcite, gypsum, and sepiolite (and/or "dolomite"). These precipitates control the Ca^{2+}, Mg^{2+}, $HCO_3^-(+CO_3^{2-})$, SO_4^{2-}, and SiO_2 contents of the brines at relatively low values so that further evaporation during subsurface flow in toward the playa center leads to brines dominated by Cl^- and $Na^+(+K^+)$. The further evolution of these central playa brines is taken up below. Hardie and Eugster (1970, pp. 285–286), using their computer model, confirmed that early precipitation of calcite, gypsum, and sepiolite from the main group of waters flowing into the Saline Valley playa would indeed yield brines dominated by Na^+ and Cl^-.

The system $CaSO_4$–Na_2SO_4–$NaCl$–H_2O as a model. The main zonal sequence of evaporite mineral assemblages below the efflorescent crust of the playa can be readily accounted for using the available experimental data in the quaternary system $CaSO_4$–Na_2SO_4–$NaCl$–H_2O, as was shown by Hardie (1968, pp. 1294–1298). The phase relations in this system at 25°C and 1 atm total pressure (D'Ans, 1933, pp. 221–222) are given in Figure 35. This is a Jänecke projection (Ricci, 1951, p. 395) of the saturated solution surfaces from the H_2O apex onto the anhydrous base of the composition tetrahedron. In Figure 35 the stability fields have been distorted to show more clearly their relationships; in the quantitative plot, the gypsum field crowds the other fields against the Na_2SO_4–$NaCl$ join (see Figure 36).

In Figure 35 the dotted line beginning at the composition X traces a crystallization path (under isothermal, isobaric evaporation) that produces, *in proper order,* the exact zonal sequence of mineral assemblages observed in the Saline Valley playa, i.e., gypsum $\rightarrow$ gypsum + glauberite $\rightarrow$ glauberite $\rightarrow$ glauberite + halite. This particular crystallization path, which must ultimately end at the eutectic glauberite + halite + thenardite + solution (point d in Figure 35), would be precisely that followed on evaporation of all bulk compositions like X that fall within the composition triangle *abc* (Figure 35).

If a solution of composition X were to be evaporated in a crucible (slowly enough to ensure equilibrium and stirred to ensure solution homogeneity), the crystallization path would be that shown in Figure 35, but one would observe only a single assemblage at a time. The crystallization sequence would be a temporal one. In the Saline Valley playa, however, the sequence is a *spatial* one. All crystallization steps take place at the same time and the whole sequence is

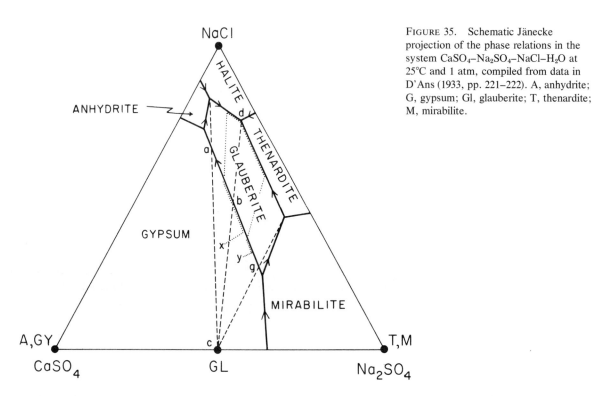

FIGURE 35.   Schematic Jänecke projection of the phase relations in the system $CaSO_4$–Na_2SO_4–$NaCl$–H_2O at 25°C and 1 atm, compiled from data in D'Ans (1933, pp. 221–222). A, anhydrite; G, gypsum; Gl, glauberite; T, thenardite; M, mirabilite.

laid out, in proper order, in concentric zones, the result of the existence of a lateral concentration gradient. This concentration gradient was established (and is maintained) by continuous subsurface flow of brine in toward the center of the pan coupled with continuous evaporation of H_2O. The dilute brines of the playa edge are at the head of this gradient. They are precipitating gypsum and so play the role of the "parent" solutions in the experimental model (X of Figure 35).

Quantitative test of the model.   For the experimental system only those solutions whose bulk compositions fall into the triangle *abc* of Figure 35 would produce on evaporation the desired crystallization sequence. The critical quantitative test is simply that the natural waters also have initial bulk compositions that fall within the composition triangle *abc* of Figure 35. This test was made by Hardie (1968) by expressing the chemical analyses of the Saline Valley brines in terms of the system $CaSO_4$–Na_2SO_4–$NaCl$–H_2O. The compositions of these brines closely approximate this quaternary system: Na^+, Cl^-, and SO_4^{2-} account for over 90% of the total dissolved species. Of the remaining major ions only calcium is an essential constituent of the coexisting evaporite minerals. The small quantities of K^+, Mg^{2+}, CO_3^{2-}, and HCO_3^- were neglected. The natural brine analyses recalculated to the system $CaSO_4$–Na_2SO_4–$NaCl$–H_2O were plotted on the appropriate part of the *quantitative* Jänecke projection as shown in Figure 36. The result was unequivocal:

those brines which are precipitating gypsum and so play the role of the "parent" waters of the model, all plot within the composition triangle *abc*. The usefulness of the experimental system as a quantitative model is thus confirmed.

Great Salt Lake

The Great Salt Lake of Utah is the largest saline lake of North America. At its highest historic stand in 1873, it covered 6200 km² and was 12.5 m deep, while in 1963 it had shrunk to 2400 km², with a maximum depth of 8.5 m. Its brines are of the Na–(Mg)–Cl and Na–(Mg)–Cl–(SO₄) types. The lake is thought to be the remnant of a much larger Pleistocene precursor, Lake Bonneville, which was first studied in detail by Gilbert (1890), and more recently by Eardley (1938), Morrison (1966), and Eardley *et al.* (1973).

Great Salt Lake is located in a structural depression just west of the Wasatch fault and thus belongs to the Basin and Range Province. The lake is fed primarily from the east by runoff from the Uinta and Wasatch Mountains and there is little inflow from the west. The west shore receives much less precipitation than the east shore does, 11 cm as compared with 40 cm.

The inflow waters have been studied by Hahl and Mitchell (1963), Hahl and Langford (1964), Hahl (1968), and Mundorff (1971). Table 7 shows the esti-

FIGURE 36.   Quantitative plot of part of the phase diagram given in Figure 35. Solid circles are the anhydrous compositions of those Saline Valley brines found coexisting with gypsum. Values in wt%.

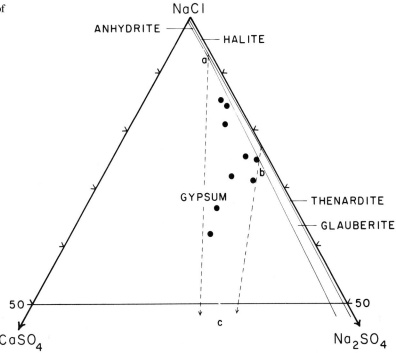

mated contributions from different sources for the years 1959–1961. The three perennial inflow rivers, the Bear River in the NE, the Weber River in the E, and the Jordan River in the SE (Figure 37), account for the bulk of the inflow, both with respect to the amount of water they bring in and their solute load. However. a significant amount of solutes is contributed also by saline springs and by drains and sewage canals. The chemical compositions of the inflow waters have been characterized in Figure 37, taken from Hahl and Langford (1964). In their upper reaches, the Bear and Weber Rivers both are Ca–HCO$_3$ waters with minor amounts of sulfate and chloride, but, as they approach

the lake, they become enriched in Na and Cl. A particularly dramatic change is noticeable in the Bear River between stations 35 and 39 (see Figure 37). The Malad River, a concentrated NaCl water, joins the Bear River upstream of station 39 and must, in part, be responsible for this change. Irrigation and evaporative concentration also contribute to this change through precipitation of alkaline earth carbonates (Hardie and Eugster, 1970) and dissolution of efflorescent crusts. This evolution, which can be monitored by increases in the Cl/HCO$_3$ and Mg/Ca ratios, is reinforced as the waters reach the mud flats fringing the lake. The Weber River shows the same effect, if somewhat less

TABLE 7.   The Relative Importance of the Six Major Inflow Sources to Great Salt Lake, October 1959–September 1961

Unit	Water (% weight)	Solute load (% weight)	Average solutes (ppm)	Water type
Bear River	53	35	870	Sodium chloride bicarbonate
Weber River	14	5	460	Calcium sodium magnesium bicarbonate
East shore	2	1	400	Calcium sodium magnesium bicarbonate
Jordan River	15	15	1300	Sodium calcium magnesium sulfate chloride
Springs around the lake	4	18	6200	Sodium chloride
Drains and sewage canals	12	26	3000	Sodium chloride

From Hahl and Langford (1964).

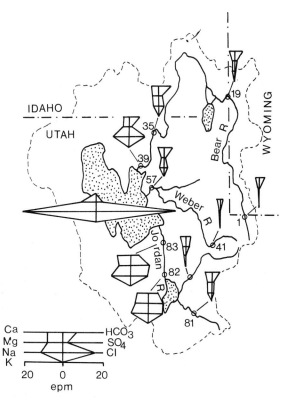

FIGURE 37.   Composition of inflow waters, Great Salt Lake. From Hahl and Langford (1964).

extreme. Initially, it has a much higher SO_4/Cl ratio than the Bear River (see Figure 37), but eventually its composition is quite similar. The Jordan River, on the other hand, is rich in sulfate even in its upper reaches (see Figure 37) presumably through weathering of sulfate or sulfide deposits. After precipitation of alkaline earth carbonates, sulfate becomes the dominant anion, and inflow from the Jordan River water shed may well have been the principle source of the large amount of sulfate now found in the Great Salt Lake brine.

As Hahl and Handy (1969) point out, the yearly input of solutes into the lake is negligible compared

TABLE 8.   Some Analyses of Brines of Great Salt Lake, 1850–1960[a]

	1850	1869	1892	1913	1930	1960
Ca	—	250	2,400	325	360	300
Mg	600	3,800	2,800	5,600	5,780	7,190
Na	85,300	50,000	75,800	67,000	69,200	80,800
K	—	2,400	3,900	3,400	3,380	4,230
SO_4	12,400	9,800	15,000	13,600	11,500	16,300
Cl	125,000	84,000	128,000	113,000	120,000	138,000
Total	223,300	150,250	227,900	202,925	210,220	246,820

[a]Concentrations in ppm.

with the total solute load present, but the input of water is not. For 1964, considered to be an average year, the total solute contribution was less than 0.1%, while water addition amounted to 17%.

The evolution of the Great Salt Lake brine in space and time is complex and has been monitored carefully only during the last 10 years (Hahl and Handy, 1969; Whelan, 1973; Whelan and Petersen, 1975). Before 1959, the lake brine was essentially homogeneous and its salinity depended largely on its volume. The brine became saturated with respect to halite when it reached an altitude of 1279 m above sea level. In historic time, this occurred only twice, during 1933–34 and 1959–63. Some representative brine compositions between 1850 and 1960 are given in Table 8. Mirabilite, $Na_2SO_4 \cdot 10H_2O$, is precipitated frequently during the winter months and it accumulates as thick banks particularly on the west shore. It dissolves during the spring and summer months. However, a substantial bed of mirabilite has been found below 7 m of lake sediments near Promontory Point (Eardley, 1962).

In 1959 a causeway was built from Promontory Point to Lake Side and this causeway has profoundly modified the brines. It was built of permeable material and has two 4.5-m-wide culverts allowing free exchange, but circulation between the N and S arm has been severely restricted. Consequently, since all of the dilute inflow is into the S arm, three different brines have developed: a concentrated N-arm brine, essentially saturated with respect to halite, a dense deep S-arm brine, and a less saline S-arm surface brine. In other words, the S arm has become stratified. In 1972 (Whelan, 1973), the shallow S-arm brine contained 150 g/liter of solids, the deep S-arm brine 190 g/liter, and the N-arm brine 320 g/liter. The chemocline was located at 7 m, but its position varies and depends upon the amount of inflow. The N-arm contained a

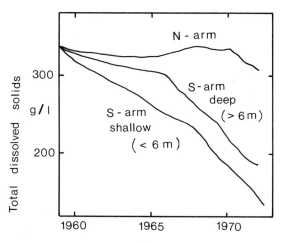

FIGURE 38.   Total dissolved solids (g/liter) in N-arm, deep S-arm, and shallow S-arm brines, Great Salt Lake. From Whelan and Petersen (1975).

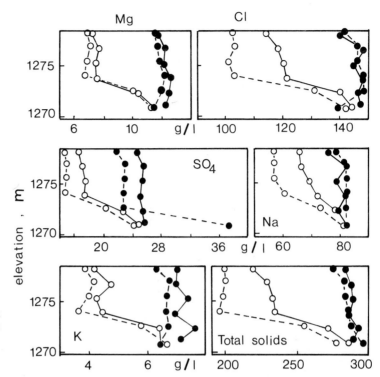

FIGURE 39. Solute concentrations in N-arm (solid circles) and S-arm brines (open circles) (in g/liter). Solid lines are for October 1965, dashed lines for May 1966. From Hahl and Handy (1969).

halite layer 1.5 m thick. The higher salinity of the N-arm brine is due to lack of dilute inflow but also to more intense evaporation. Whelan (1973) has estimated that yearly N-arm evaporation is 1.5 m, while S-arm evaporation is 1.1 m. Part of this is due to the dry winds from the west. Because of this, there is a difference in lake level between N and S of 60 cm. This hydraulic head causes a northward flow of surface brine, which is compensated by a deeper S-ward flow through the culverts of N-arm brine. The N-arm brine is much less affected by the dilution from inflow, and this is shown clearly in Figure 38. Inflow has increased since 1960, but the dilution is restricted effectively to the S-arm. The concentration of the major constituents are shown in Figure 39. The stratification is very apparent. The future development of the brines will depend largely upon the amount of inflow received.

Brine evolution needs to be studied in more detail. As Hardie and Eugster (1970) pointed out, the Great Salt brines can be obtained from the dilute inflow by evaporative concentration coupled with precipitation of calcite, sepiolite, and gypsum. Calcite is present in the sediments in great abundance, sepiolite has been reported (Eardley, 1938), but some of the magnesium is present not in silicates, but in magnesian calcites and dolomite. Gypsum, although reported, is not important in sulfate removal, but mirabilite apparently is.

The sediments of Great Salt Lake have been studied by Eardley (1938). They consist primarily of clay minerals (kaolinite, illite, montmorillonite) and carbonates (calcite, dolomite). Much of the carbonate is present in the form of brine shrimp fecal pellets. Eardley (1938) has also described the occurrence of ooids and calcareous algal bioherms. More recently Sandberg (1975) has reexamined the ooids.

The sediments of Lake Bonneville are similar to those of Great Salt Lake and they have been studied in two cores (Eardley and Gvosdetsky, 1960; Eardley et al., 1973).

The cores represent 800,000 years of depositional history and within them 28 periods of desiccation have been reported. No salt layers have been reported and it is likely that Great Salt Lake brines have reached their maximum concentration at the present time.

Fossil salt lakes

Saline lakes must have existed throughout most of geologic history, but their deposits are often ephemeral and are recycled rapidly (Garrels and Mackenzie, 1971). Not many well-documented evaporitic lake deposits are preserved, some of the better known examples being Pleistocene Searles Lake, Eocene Green River formation, Pleistocene Lake Bonneville, Pleistocene Lake Lisan, Triassic Popo Agie, and Triassic Lockatong. We will restrict ourselves to brief summaries of Searles Lake and the Green River formation, both of which carry significant soluble saline deposits.

Searles Lake

Much interest has focused on Searles Lake in eastern California, not only for economic reasons, but also because it contains an invaluable record of Pleistocene climates. Past and current work has been summarized in an extensive report by Smith (in press) and our synopsis is based largely on this work.

During Pleistocene time, Searles Lake was a member of a chain of lakes located E of the Sierra Nevada which included Mono, Owens, China, Panamint, and Manly (Death Valley) Lakes (see Figure 40). During its highest stage, the lake level stood as much as 200 m above the present playa floor, and Searles and China Lakes coalesced to occupy about 1000 km², some 10 times the size of the present playa. Of lake deposits, 260 m have been cored, representing the last 500,000–1,000,000 years of history, but geophysical evidence indicates that bedrock may be as much as 1000 m below the present surface.

The stratigraphy of the cored section is shown in Figure 41. As the alternation between "muds" and saline layers shows, a series of more or less saline lakes occupied the area, depositing the main stratigraphic units: Mixed Layer, Bottom Mud, Lower Salt, Parting Mud, Upper Salt, and Overburden Mud. The muds consist principally of alkaline earth carbonates (aragonite, calcite, and dolomite) with siliciclastic and diagenetic minerals forming the balance (15–40%). The saline layers contain a variety of minerals such as halite, trona, nahcolite, burkeite, borax, then-

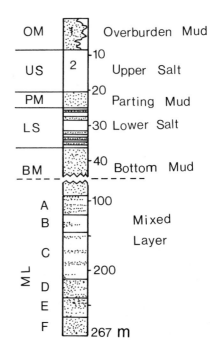

FIGURE 41.   Subsurface stratigraphy of Searles Lake. Note change in scale at 45 m. From Eugster and Smith (1965). 1, mud; 2, salts.

ardite, and hanksite in sizable amounts, while aphthitalite, northupite, sulfohalite, tychite, and schairerite are less common. Gaylussite, pirssonite, analcime, searlesite, K-spar, and phillipsite are common authigenic products. The complete list of minerals is shown in Table 9.

Close similarities exist between the ages of the muds and the advances of glaciers in eastern and western North America and between the saline layers and the retreats. The Overburden Mud and Upper Salt are correlated with the Holocene and Valderan deposits of the Laurentide ice sheet, the Parting Mud with Twocreekian and Woodfordian deposits, and the Lower Salt and Bottom Mud with Farmdalian and Altonian deposits. The lower part of the Bottom Mud probably represents Sangamon and Illinoian ages, while most of the Mixed Layer must be Yarmouth deposits. During these fluctuations the lake level rose and fell and the shore lines moved in and out, with the maximum and minimum extents shown in Figure 40. At its most saline, such as when it precipitated trona and halite, Smith (in press) believes that the lake must have been very shallow or seasonally dry. During the wettest periods, the lake was probably reasonably fresh with inflow provided principally by Owens River, draining the east flank of the Sierra Nevada. However, except for remains of the brine shrimp, *Artemia*, few identifiable fossil remains have been found in the cored section.

As mineralogical studies show (Eugster and Smith, 1965), there has been little mixing of interstitial brines

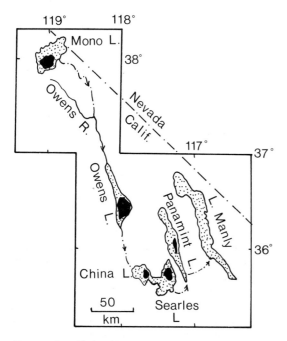

FIGURE 40.   Chain of lakes, eastern California. From Smith (in press).

TABLE 9. Authigenic Minerals of the Searles Lake Deposit

Adularia	$KAlSi_3O_8$	Nahcolite	$NaHCO_3$
Analcime	$NaAlSi_2O_6 \cdot H_2O$	Northupite	$Na_2CO_3 \cdot MgCO_3 \cdot NaCl$
Aphthitalite	$K_3Na(SO_4)_2$	Phillipsite	$KCa(Al_3Si_5O_{16}) \cdot 6H_2O$
Aragonite	$CaCO_3$	Pirssonite	$CaCO_3 \cdot Na_2CO_3 \cdot 2H_2O$
Borax	$Na_2B_4O_7 \cdot 10H_2O$	Schairerite	$Na_2SO_4 \cdot Na(F,Cl)$
Burkeite	$2Na_2SO_4 \cdot Na_2CO_3$	Searlesite	$NaBSi_2O_6 \cdot H_2O$
Calcite	$CaCO_3$	Sulfohalite	$2Na_2SO_4 \cdot NaCl \cdot NaF$
Dolomite	$CaMg(CO_3)_2$	Teepleite	$Na_2B_2O_4 \cdot 2NaCl \cdot 4H_2O$
Galeite	$Na_2SO_4 \cdot Na(F,Cl)$	Thenardite	Na_2SO_4
Gaylussite	$CaCO_3 \cdot Na_2CO_3 \cdot 5H_2O$	Tincalconite	$Na_2B_4O_7 \cdot 5H_2O$
Halite	$NaCl$	Trona	$Na_2CO_3 \cdot NaHCO_3 \cdot 2H_2O$
Hanksite	$9Na_2SO_4 \cdot 2Na_2CO_3 \cdot KCl$	Tychite	$2Na_2CO_3 \cdot 2MgCO_3 \cdot Na_2SO_4$
Mirabilite	$Na_2SO_4 \cdot 10H_2O$		

From Smith (in press).

across mud partings, which are almost impervious, but there is some diffusional transfer at the interfaces. At the present time (Hardt et al., 1972) the hydrostatic head of the brines is larger than that of the more dilute waters surrounding the deposits, indicating that some brine must be moving down and out beyond the edges, mixing with the more dilute waters.

Smith (in press) has given a clear account of the gradual evolution of the lakes with time. Crucial to this account is the assumption that throughout much of the time these lakes were chemically stratified with a saline hypolimnion overlain by a freshwater epilimnion. The concept of a stably stratified lake is attractive, because it can account for the intimate association of very soluble minerals, such as halite and trona, with the Ca–Mg carbonates. Through stratification a large amount of solutes can be stored in the bottom of the lake without interfering with the dilute waters needed to bring in Ca and Mg.

Beginning with the oldest deposits, the Mixed Layer, it is clear that the lake initially was quite fresh, with dolomite and calcite predominating in the muds. Then salinity increased and beds of nahcolite, trona, and halite interrupt the muds. Trona and in particular halite become dominant toward the top of unit C. This gradual enrichment in NaCl can be seen in many salt lakes, such as Magadi, Chad, Saline Valley, or Deep Springs. There is yet no enrichment in K and B, and SO_4 is still very subordinate. In units B and A, trona and nahcolite again dominate, pointing to a distinct shift in brine compositions. Pirssonite and K-spar are the most common authigenic minerals, and searlesite, analcime, and gaylussite are also present.

The Bottom Mud, some 30 m thick, consists mainly of dolomite, aragonite, and calcite and is not normally bedded or laminated. The bottom is about 130,000 years old and the unit took some 100,000 years to accumulate, probably in a larger, fresher lake which may have occupied the major portion of the basin. Saline episodes are represented by thin interbeds of nahcolite and mirabilite, which are believed to have been frozen out during cold winter months. Evapora-

tive periods are also indicated by the presence of interstitial brine which was involved in the formation of the abundant gaylussite and of K-spar, analcime, and searlesite. Some tuff layers have altered to phillipsite, pointing to fairly dilute waters. It is reasonable to assume that inflow and evaporation, and hence salinity, varied considerably during the long time span of the Bottom Mud.

The remaining deposits, the Lower Salt, Parting Mud, Upper Salt, and Overburden Mud, represent the last 30,000 years. The lake was dominantly saline to very saline and, according to Smith (in press), stably stratified. The Lower Salt is estimated to be 56% salines and 44% muds, with the latter being mainly aragonite + calcite (no dolomite). Gaylussite and pirssonite are common in the muds and again are diagenetic in origin. The salines are dominated by trona, halite, and burkeite, with northupite, thenardite, hanksite, and borax of lesser abundance. There are some systematic lateral and vertical variations in the seven salt units (S_1–S_7), which are an expression of relative solubilities. Bottoms and fringes are usually rich in trona, while centers and tops are enriched in halite, just like active evaporating pans. K is usually enriched toward the top, while B is more abundant near the bottom. Sulfate remains fairly constant. The Lower Salt is thought to have been deposited from a sequence of lakes which alternated between large perennial character and small, saline or even dry character. There seems to be successively greater desiccation from S_1 to S_5 and lesser desiccation in S_6 and S_7.

The Parting Mud is 4 m thick and carries mainly dolomite, though the upper part contains many thin aragonite laminae. In outcrop it can be traced over an area of 1000 km². Gaylussite and pirssonite are present, as is some borax, analcime, and phillipsite. Laminae are in the 0.3- to 3-mm range and ^{14}C dates show that they are less frequent than annual. The Parting Mud is thought to represent a long period of deposition in a fluctuating but perennial lake.

In contrast, the Upper Salt records almost uninterrupted desiccation. It is 15 m thick and carries mainly

TABLE 10. Amounts of Solutes Carried by Owens River in 24,000 Years in Comparison with Amounts Now Found in Owens and Searles Lakes

Component	Present concentration in Owens River (ppm)	Amount carried annually by Owens River ($\times 10^9$ g)	Amount carried by Owens River in 24,000 years ($\times 10^{12}$ g)	Amount now in Upper Salt, Searles Lake ($\times 10^{12}$ g)	Amount in Owens Lake in 1912 ($\times 10^{12}$ g)	Total amount now found in Searles and Owens Lakes ($\times 10^{12}$ g)
Na	26	10.9	262	462	54	516
K	3.4	1.4	34	28	3	31
Total CO$_3$	137	57.5	1380	163	30	193
SO$_4$	17	7.1	170	192	15	207
Cl	14	5.9	142	448	38	486
B	0.77	0.32	7.7	7.9	0.8	8.7
Li	0.11	0.046	1.1	0.06	0.0005	0.06

From Smith (in press).

halite, trona, and hanksite, with much of the latter thought to be of diagenetic origin, forming for instance from aphthitalite and burkeite or aphthitalite and thenardite and trona. Less abundant are borax, burkeite, thenardite, aphthitalite, and sulfohalite. Deposition begins with a 1- to 3-m-thick trona layer, but subsequently, halite dominates, much more so than in the Lower Salt. Concurrently, the brines are higher in K and lower in B.

The Overburden Mud is very different from the other mud units, in that it consists mainly of clastics and clays, rather than carbonates. The clastics are much coarser, much of it sand. Salt beds are present, rich in halite.

Average depositional rates for the mud intervals are 0.025 cm/yr (38 years/cm), based on many ^{14}C dates. Maximum rates estimated for salts are 25–40 cm/yr. Judging from the work at Magadi (Eugster, 1970), the latter figure seems very high and does not take into account salt recycling. The full documentation of the evolution of the Searles Lake will only be possible when the evidence from the outcrops contemporaneous with the lake deposits becomes available.

The stratified lake concept invoked by Smith (in press) is based mainly on the intimate association of Ca–Mg carbonates with saline minerals and the presence of aragonite laminae thought to have formed in a manner similar to the aragonite laminae of the Dead Sea (Neev and Emery, 1967). For these same reasons, the stratified lake concept was also invoked for the Green River formation by Bradley and Eugster (1969). More recently, however, this concept has been challenged (Eugster and Surdam, 1973; Eugster and Hardie, 1975), principally on sedimentological grounds, and we suggest that the Searles Lake deposits should also be examined with this possibility in mind.

The playa-lake model of Eugster and Surdam (1973) applies to a lake-carbonate mud flat complex in which Ca–Mg carbonates accumulate in the mud flats surrounding a saline lake. In other words, rather than putting the Ca–Mg source on top of the salt lake, it coexists laterally. During high-water stages, Ca–Mg carbonates can be moved into the central lake, either as clastics or by dissolution and reprecipitation. Through dissolution of capillary and efflorescent crusts, the mud flats also act as solute accumulators.

During the accumulation of saline minerals, if the playa-lake model applies, the central lake would have been relatively small and shallow and surrounded by wide, carbonate-rich mud flats. It was seasonally dry, with perennial water present only in peripheral ponds fed by springs. Thus sheets of run-off would have covered the playa during wet periods and flooded part of the wide carbonate mud flats surrounding the lake. Particularly to the south, these mud flats could have been up to 10 km wide. Strong spring activity is indicated in the south by the tufa mounds. During the dry periods, the saline layers accumulated, which here, as at Magadi, consist of a very porous hard framework of interlocking crystals bathed in the concentrated interstitial brine. During the wettest periods, the lake may have expanded to the full size of the basin.

Table 10 from Smith (in press) supports this view. It compares the total amount of some solutes brought in by a river such as Owens River during Upper Salt time and compares this with the actual amounts found in the Upper Salt. K and SO$_4$ balance roughly, but Na and Cl are more abundant in the deposit. This is not surprising, because much NaCl will be added by dissolving efflorescent crusts on the mud flats and these crusts are derived from groundwater and not from

Owens River. More startling is the large deficiency in CO_3. This can be accounted for readily by precipitation of Ca–Mg carbonates in the mud flats, only a small amount of which will eventually reach the central lake. The fluorine deficiency noted by Smith (in press) points to fluorite precipitation in the muds. Similar balance problems were encountered at Magadi (Eugster, 1970; Jones *et al.*, 1977). With respect to the composition of its saline minerals and brines, Searles Lake is very similar to Deep Springs, except that Deep Springs is much smaller. Deep Springs contains a central saline lake fed by springs, dries up annually, and is surrounded by mud flats. The muds are mainly Ca–Mg carbonates, but contain also saline minerals, such as gaylussite, thenardite, burkeite, and nahcolite. Efflorescent crusts consist mainly of trona, thenardite and halite and the lake crusts also carry burkeite and aphthitalite. Because of these similarities, it is likely that Deep Springs' hydrology and sedimentation also fit Searles Lake during deposition of its salines, except for scale.

Green River Formation

The Eocene Green River formation of Colorado, Utah, and Wyoming has been made famous by Brad-ley (1929, 1931, 1964, 1970). It is the largest and most studied lacustrine deposit in the world. It covers nearly 100,000 km^2 and has an aggregate thickness of 3 km in Utah and 1 km in Wyoming, deposited during a time span of up to 12 million years during early-middle Eocene. It consists dominantly of carbonate rocks, including the kerogen-rich oil shales, which are also carbonate rich. Oil has been encountered recently in the Uinta Basin, Utah (Fouch, 1975). Saline minerals, especially trona ($NaHCO_3 \cdot Na_2CO_3 \cdot 2H_2O$), are present in vast quantities and are exploited commercially. An unusual suite of authigenic minerals has been encountered in Green River rocks, many of them sodium rich and of considerable scientific interest. Finally, there is a rich Eocene fauna and flora present, best known perhaps for its unusual fish (McGrew and Casilliano, 1975). The saline minerals, with which we are primarily concerned in this synopsis, are described in Milton and Eugster (1959), Fahey (1962), Bradley and Eugster (1969), Culbertson (1971), Milton (1971), and Deardorff and Mannion (1971), while recent sedimentological work and the relevant literature have been summarized in Eugster and Hardie (1975), Surdam and Wolfbauer (1975), Ryder *et al.* (1976), and Smoot (1977, in press).

During early-middle Eocene, saline minerals, principally trona, nahcolite, and halite, were deposited in

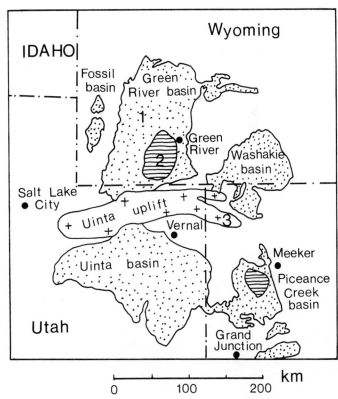

FIGURE 42.   Green River Formation basins. 1, Green River Formation; 2, bedded salts; 3, basement.

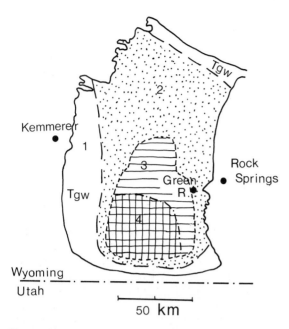

FIGURE 43. Saline minerals in the Wilkins Peak Member. After Culbertson (1971). 1, Wilkins Peak free of saline minerals; 2, shortite present; 3, trona present; 4, trona + halite present.

two large lakes: Lake Gosiute in Wyoming, N of the Uinta Mountains, and Lake Uinta in the Uinta and Piceance Creek Basins of Utah and Colorado, S of the Uinta Mountains (see Figure 42). Because of their economic importance, more is known about the trona beds in Wyoming and we will rely in this summary on the excellent studies by Culbertson (1971) on the trona beds in general and by Deardorff and Mannion (1971) on beds 17, 19, 20, 24, and 25.

The Green River formation is divided, from bottom to top, into the Tipton, Wilkins Peak, and Laney Members, the latter two making up the bulk of the formation. Trona was deposited exclusively during Wilkins Peak time. It is interesting to note that the

area in which evidence of interstitial brine exists (shortite, $Na_2CO_3 \cdot 2CaCO_3$, or calcite pseudomorphs after shortite) is almost coincident with the maximum extent of Wilkins Peak outcrops (Figure 43). Trona occupies a much smaller area and bedded halite is still more restricted. A total of 42 trona beds can be distinguished, covering an area of more than 3300 km², occurring at depths between 120 and 1000 m. Their thickness varies from a few cm to a maximum of 11 m, representing a total reserve of some 100 billion tons of trona and trona + halite, of which more than half is minable. Beds exceeding 1 m in thickness have been numbered 1–25 by Culbertson (1966) and their stratigraphic position is given in Figure 44. Initial trona deposition was concentrated asymmetrically in the south towards the Uinta Mountains boundary fault, but subsequently, as Figure 44 shows, the depositional center moved to the N and NE in response either to tilting of the floor or to a sediment wedge advancing from the south.

Details of thickness and shape of bed 17 are presented in Figure 45. It shows an interesting relationship between halite and trona deposition. Halite, mixed with trona, is found only in the southern L-shaped part of the basin, where the bed reaches its maximum thickness of 6 m. Halite is almost coincident with the 3-m contour. However, in two marginal basins, to the N and E, trona also reaches a thickness of 4 m, but halite is absent. These marginal basins are separated from the main basin by a barrier ridge area where trona is less than 2 m thick. The trona bed extends over 60 km in a N–S direction, so that gradients are extremely gentle, and yet they suffice to separate halite-producing from halite-free areas.

Deardorff and Mannion (1971) clearly understood the role of efflorescent crusts in solute acquisition:

". . . brines, trapped in the muds, migrated to the surface by capillary action, and there evaporated to leave an efflorescence of trona on the surface. With each period of rainfall this efflorescence was washed into the deeper parts of the basin." (p. 30).

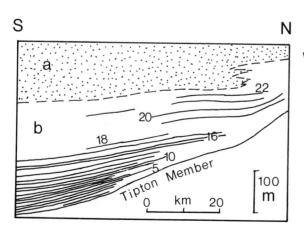

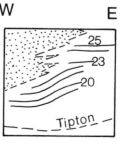

FIGURE 44. The trona beds of the Wilkins Peak Member, Wyoming. After Culbertson (1971). a, sandstones; b, dolomitic mudstones.

Trona seems to have accumulated very rapidly, leaving little record in the laterally equivalent strata. However, there is a consistent vertical succession: trona beds are underlain by organic-rich carbonates (oil shales). Carbonate layers, mainly dolomite, also occur within the massive trona beds (Bradley and Eugster, 1969, Figure 14; Deardorff and Mannion, 1971, Figure 8). Many of these layers are not internally laminated and could represent a single depositional event (Deardorff and Mannion, 1971, p. 35).

To account for the large amount of trona present in the Wilkins Peak Member and the intimate association of trona with dolomite, Bradley and Eugster (1969) invoked the existence of a lake chemically stratified for very long intervals, with the hypolimnion a concentrated brine and the epilimnion dilute water. Eugster and Surdam (1973) suggested a playa-lake model as a more appropriate depositional model. Eugster and Hardie (1975) have presented what we think is compelling evidence for frequent exposure to the air of the carbonate rocks with which the trona beds are associated. The sedimentary cycles we found are not compatible with a stratified lake, but are strong support for the playa-lake model.

The essence of the playa-lake model, which can also be characterized as a "lake-carbonate mud flat complex," is shown in Figure 46. A wide carbonate mud flat, fringed by alluvial fans, surrounds a central lake. During wet periods this lake is large and shallow and the locus for oil shale deposition. During dry periods, on the other hand, the lake shrinks drastically and dries up seasonally, and trona begins to accumulate. Inflow now is principally from springs. The carbonate mud flats which fringe the central lake are alternately wet and dry but do not normally have perennial water bodies. They are the storage area for the carbonate production which can take place by a number of mechanisms, such as direct precipitation by capillary evaporation within the sediment, dolomite duricrusts formed as caliche and surface crusts, travertine associated with springs and ephemeral streams, and algal tufa and direct precipitation in standing water. Smoot (1976, 1977, in press) has beautifully demonstrated, using petrographic evidence, the overwhelming importance of a travertine-tufa source in the fans and fringing sandflats and a surface capillary crust source on the mudflats for the Wilkins Peak carbonate. The large amount of carbonate sediment produced by these mechanisms in the fringing fans and flats is in harmony with the evolution of alkaline brines, as discussed earlier. Judging by the amount of trona present, inflow waters must have been dominated by HCO_3-rich waters for several million years, and for the principal source areas we must look to the two

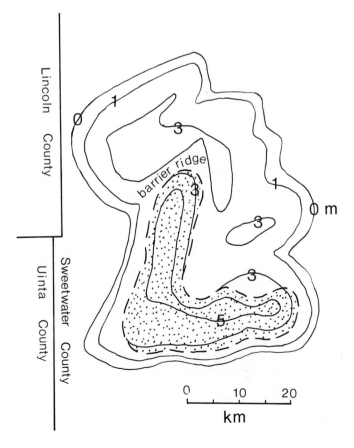

FIGURE 45.   Trona-halite distribution in bed 17. After Deardorff and Mannion (1971). Thickness of bed in meters. Dots, halite + trona; open, trona.

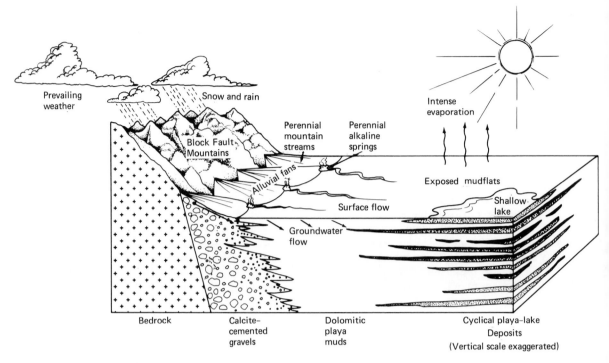

FIGURE 46.   Schematic block-diagram of the depositional environment envisaged in the playa-lake complex. A shallow perennial central lake is surrounded by carbonate mud flats which are normally exposed to air and are in turn fringed by alluvial fans. The lake deposits are either oil shale (black) or trona (trona stage not shown). Oil shale deposition follows either upon flat pebble conglomerates (short dashes), lime sands (dots), or trona. The bulk of the deposits are carbonate muds (no signature). From Eugster and Hardie (1975).

high mountain chains surrounding the basin: the Windriver Mountains in the NE and the Uinta Mountains in the south. The Windrivers consist of Precambrian granites and metamorphics, an ideal lithology for $NaHCO_3$ water, while the Uintas contain a thick section of Precambrian metasediments and Paleozoic sediments.

During trona precipitation stages, the lake must have been seasonally dry, except for spring activity around the perimeter, which represented the major inflow in addition to the seasonal runoff. A considerably scaled-up version of Deep Springs might serve as a useful model. However, K-enrichment in the brines was never sufficient to produce K-bearing saline minerals. Thus the brines are more akin to those of Lake Magadi, with K being removed during subsurface circulation. Silica must have accumulated in the high-pH brines, but, unlike Magadi, chert beds are rare (Surdam et al., 1972). This can be accounted for by the extremely gentle gradients in Lake Gosiute topography. Flooding of the silica-rich brines by more dilute waters produced mixing rather than the stable stratification thought to be essential for lake-wide magadiite precipitation (Eugster, 1969). Sulfides are quite common in the oil shales (Bradley and Eugster, 1969; Milton, 1971), pointing to sulfate reduction in the anaerobic muds.

While Wilkins Peak time was characterized by trona precipitating intervals, the subsequent Laney Member is dominated by oil shale. The central lake was larger and fresher, presumably due to climatic changes, and the lake is thought to have had an outlet into Lake Uinta late in Laney time (Surdam and Stanley, 1976). Nevertheless, the lake remained very shallow and surrounded by mud flats, but evaporation was not

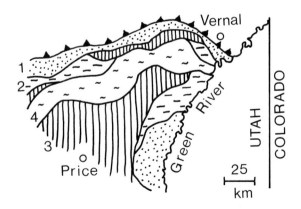

FIGURE 47.   Facies map of the Green River Formation in Utah. After Ryder et al. (1976). Facies: 1, alluvial; 2, siliciclastic mud flats; 3, carbonate mud flats; 4, open lacustrine.

TABLE 11. Authigenic Minerals of the Green River
Formation and Their Relative Abundance[a]

Sulfur S	5

Sulfides

Pyrite, FeS_2	2
Marcasite, FeS_2	6
Pyrrhotite, $Fe_{1-x}S$	4
Wurtzite, Zns	5

Halides

Halite, NaCl	4
Fluorite, CaF_2	6
Cryolite, Na_3AlF_6	6
NEIGHBORITE, $NaMgF_3$[b]	5

Oxides

Quartz, SiO_2	1
Chalcedony, SiO_2–H_2O	1
Anatase (?), TiO_2	?

Carbonates

Nahcolite, $NaHCO_3$	4
Trona, $Na_2CO_3 \cdot NaHCO_3 \cdot 2H_2O$	4
WEGSCHEIDERITE, $Na_2CO_3 \cdot 3NaHCO_3$	5
Thermonatrite, $Na_2CO_3 \cdot H_2O$	6
Natron, $Na_2CO_3 \cdot 10H_2O$	6
Calcite, $CaCO_3$	1
Magnesite, $MgCO_3$	6
Strontianite, $SrCO_3$	5
Witherite, $BaCO_3$	5
Siderite, $FeCO_3$	6
Aragonite, $CaCO_3$	5
Dolomite, $CaCO_3 \cdot MgCO_3$	1
Dawsonite, $NaAl(CO_3)(OH)_2$	4
EITELITE, $Na_2CO_3 \cdot MgCO_3$	7
SHORTITE, $Na_2CO_3 \cdot 2CaCO_3$	1
Pirssonite, $Na_2CO_3 \cdot CaCO_3 \cdot 2H_2O$	4
Gaylussite, $Na_2CO_3 \cdot CaCO_3 \cdot 5H_2O$	4
Barytocalcite, $CaCO_3 \cdot BaCO_3$	3
NORSETHITE, $MgCO_3 \cdot BaCO_3$	5
McKELVEYITE, $(Na_2Ca_1)(Ba_4R.E._{.1.7}U_{0.3})(CO_3)_9$	7
EWALDITE, $(Na_2Ca_1)(Ba_4R.E._{.1.7}U_{0.3})(CO_3)_9$	7
Burbankite, $Na_2(Ca,Sr,Ba,Ce)_4(CO_3)_5$	5

Compound Carbonates with other ions

BRADLEYITE, $MgNa_3CO_3PO_4$	5
Northupite, $Na_2Mg(CO_3)_2 \cdot NaCl$	4
FERROAN NORTHUPITE, $Na_2(Mg,Fe)(CO_3)_2 \cdot NaCl$	6
Tychite, $Na_2Mg(CO_3)_2 \cdot Na_2SO_4$	7
Burkeite, $Na_2CO_3 \cdot 2Na_2SO_4$	7

Silicates

Clay Minerals, Kaolinite, $H_4Al_2Si_2O_9$	4
Illite	1
Montmorillonite: hydrous magnesium aluminum silicate	4
LOUGHLINITE, $H_{16}Na_2Mg_3Si_6O_{24}$	4
Nontronite (?)	
Sepiolite, $H_4Mg_2Si_3O_{10}$	5
Stevensite, H–Mg-silicate	6
Talc, $Mg_3(OH)_2Si_4O_{10}$	6
Chlorite: hydrous iron magnesium aluminum silicate	6
Lazurite, $Na_4(NaS_3 \cdot Al)Al_2(SiO_4)_3$	7
GARRELSITE, $(Ba,Ca,Mg)B_2SiO_6(OH)_3$	5

Searlesite, $NaBSi_2O_6 \cdot H_2O$	4
Leucosphenite, $CaBaNa_3BTi_3Si_9O_{29}$	5
Labuntsovite, $(K,Ba,Na,Ca,Mn)(Ti,Nb)(Si,Al)_2(O,OH)_7H_2O$	5
Vinogradovite, $Na_5Ti_4AlSi_6O_{24} \cdot 3H_2O$	7
Acmite, $NaFeSi_2O_6$	5
Riebeckite, (magnesio-) $Na(Fe,Mg)_3Fe_2(OH,F)(Si_4O_{11})_2$	5
Elpidite, $H_6Na_2ZrSi_6O_{18}$	7
Natron–catapleite, $H_4(Na_2Ca)ZrSi_3O_{11}$	7
Biotite, $K(Fe,Mg)_3AlSi_3O_{10}(OH)_2$	7
Hydrobiotite, $(K,H_2O)(Mg,Fe,Mn)_3AlSi_3O_{10}(OH,H_2O)_2$	7
Orthoclase, $KAlSi_3O_8$	2
Albite, $NaAlSi_3O_8$	2
REEDMERGNERITE, $NaBSi_3O_8$	5
Analcite, $NaAlSi_2O_6 \cdot H_2O$	2
Harmotome–wellsite, $(Ba,Ca,K_2)Al_2Si_6O_{10} \cdot 6H_2O$	6
Natrolite, $Na_2Al_2Si_3O_{10} \cdot 2H_2O$	6
Clinoptilolite–mordenite, $(Ca,Na_2,K_2)(AlSi_5O_{12})_2 \cdot 6H_2O$	6

Sulfates

Barite, $BaSO_4$	6
Celestite, $SrSO_4$	7
Gypsum, $CaSO_4 \cdot 2H_2O$	6
Siderotil (rozenite), $FeSO_4 \cdot 4H_2O$	6

Phosphates

Fluorapatite, $Ca_{10}(PO_4)_6F_2$	6
Collophanite, $Ca_{10}(PO_4)_6CO_3 \cdot H_2O$	3

Hydrocarbons

Gilsonite, uintahite, utahite, tabbyite, ozokerite, ingramite, albertite, etc.

[a] 1 is most abundant, 7 is least abundant.
[b] Capitalized minerals are found only in the Green River Formation.
From Milton (1971).

intense enough for saline minerals to accumulate (Stanley and Surdam, in press).

Lake Uinta, south of the Uinta Mountains, was of a size similar to Lake Gosiute, but it existed for a considerably longer time (see Wolfbauer, 1971, plate 1). The first lacustrine sediments date from late Cretaceous; in the Paleocene the lake was well established, and it lasted to Upper Eocene time. The sedimentary facies are very similar to those of Lake Gosiute, with a central lake surrounded by carbonate mud flats (Ryder et al., 1976), as is shown in Figure 47. Oil shales in the Uinta and Piceance Creek basins are as abundant and even richer in kerogen than they are in the Laney member. However, there is no equivalent mass of trona as there is in the Wilkins Peak. There is a saline facies in the upper part of the Green River formation, but the major saline minerals are nahcolite and halite, rather than trona and halite. Nahcolite occurs either as concretions, disseminated or in thin beds and it is present in vast quantities. Dyni (1974) and Dyni et al. (1970) have described thinly bedded nahcolite interbedded with halite.

The mode of formation of nahcolite is not yet fully understood. Its presence, rather than trona, was originally used as argument that Lake Uinta was deep, while Lake Gosiute was shallow (Milton and Eugster, 1959), because nahcolite needs a higher p_{CO_2} for its formation (Eugster, 1966). We now believe that the presence of nahcolite does not necessarily signal greater water depths. The rise in p_{CO_2} can be accomplished by decomposition of organic matter in very shallow water, because the exchange of CO_2 across the water–air interface is notoriously slow. Furthermore, much of the nahcolite in concretions presumably grew during diagenesis from occluded brines. It is obvious, however, that Lake Uinta did not desiccate to the extent that Lake Gosiute did during Wilkins Peak time and hence was able to support a more abundant biota. Lake Uinta must have received considerable inflow from the south, from the Uncompahgre Uplift, the Henry Mountains, and the Wasatch Plateau, and this contribution apparently was larger than the Windriver contribution to Lake Gosiute. Both basins were asymmetric, with the lakes pushed against the Uinta Mountains, one from the N and the other from the S.

There is one final aspect: authigenic minerals. Milton (1971) has listed some 70 minerals formed by diagenetic reactions in the Green River formation of Colorado, Utah, and Wyoming (see Table 11). Considering the composition of Green River brines (Bradley and Eugster, 1969), it is no surprise that minerals rich in sodium and carbonate dominate. As Figure 43 shows, the presence of shortite is a good indicator of the wide distribution of such brines. More surprising is the abundance of dawsonite, $NaAlCO_3(OH)_2$, in Uinta sediments (Smith and Young, 1969), which is present in amounts large enough to have economic potential for aluminum. Although the details of its formation are not yet clear, the increased solubility of Al in alkaline brines must play a role. Of the silicates, searlesite, albite, K-feldspar, and zeolites are most abundant. These have been studied by Surdam and Parker (1972) in Wyoming and they exhibit a zonal pattern: K-feldspar–analcime–clinoptilolite or mordenite. K-feldspar is abundant in the tuffs near the center of the Wilkins Peak formation, representing the most saline environment. Other silicates look strange in this association at first glance, such as the Ti minerals leucosphenite, labuntsovite, and vinogradovite, the Fe minerals acmite and riebeckite, and the Zr minerals elpidite and Na-catapleite. All are rich in sodium and present in very small amounts and they must form where local supplies of Ti, Fe, or Zr are available from either volcanic or clastic sources. It is surprising, however, that tourmaline is absent (Milton, 1971).

Our understanding of the Green River rocks is still very limited and the different aspects from hydrology, geochemistry, mineralogy, and sedimentation to pa-leontology must become better integrated. While we have a fair concept of trona deposition, the environment of oil shale formation is still conjectural. We now recognize a number of basin edge mechanisms for producing the abundant Ca–Mg carbonates in the Wilkins Peak Member (Smoot, 1976, 1977, in press), but their applicability to other members of the formation has yet to be tested. The interrelation between fauna, flora, and depositional environments deduced from sedimentary structures remains to be elucidated. Finally, compaction and diagenesis effects are little understood. Meanwhile, the Green River formation represents the largest and most varied deposit of saline lakes yet encountered in the geologic record and as such continues to stimulate research in a wide variety of disciplines.

Conclusions

In this chapter we have stressed the chemical and mineralogical aspects of saline lakes and we have presented some general principles as well as a number of case studies. The equally important subject of sedimentation and sedimentary environments has been touched upon, but it is treated more fully elsewhere (Hardie et ál., in press). We must emphasize that the chemical and sedimentological aspects of saline lakes are inextricably linked through the hydrological processes. Saline lake basins are not simple evaporating dishes but complex hydrological systems with spring, stream, and groundwater inflow that is tied to patterns of sediment packaging and to the climatic and tectonic regimes. Saline lake chemistry cannot be fully understood unless the depositional framework is properly known.

Saline lakes are dynamic systems. They respond rapidly to changes in external conditions, mainly climatic and tectonic. Once the evolution of salt lakes is better understood, we should be able to characterize the stage a particular salt lake occupies within that evolutionary chain and to predict the effect a given set of changes will have. To achieve this goal, we must study active salt lakes more carefully and over an extended period of time. Saline lakes help us understand processes which are important in the evolution of all natural waters, including those exposed to less extreme conditions.

Finally, we would like to point out that deposits of ancient saline lakes carry a significance way beyond their size and abundance in the geologic record. This is because they signal severe climatic and topographic restrictions. The use of saline minerals as climatic indicators is well known, but as tectonic indicators saline lake deposits remain to be tapped.

ACKNOWLEDGMENTS.   Blair F. Jones of the U.S. Geological Survey shares all of the credit but none of the blame for this paper. The ideas expressed here have been developed during the many years of fruitful cooperation, for which we want to express our deep gratitude. This work was supported by Petroleum Research Fund Grant No. 7653-AC2, of the American Chemical Society, and by National Science Foundation Grant No. EAR 76-17587.

References

Assaf, G. and Nissenbaum, A. (1977). The evolution of the Upper Water Mass of the Dead Sea, 1819–1976. In: Desertic Terminal Lakes, D. C. Greer, ed., Utah Water Research Lab., Logan, Utah: 61–72.

Baker, B. H. (1958). Geology of the Magadi area. Rep. Geol. Surv. Kenya, 42. 81 pp.

Baker, B. H., L. A. J. Williams, J. A. Miller, and F. J. Fitch. (1971). Sequence and geochronology of the Kenya rift volcanics. *Tectonophysics* 11:191–215.

Barnes, L. (1965). Geochemistry of Birch Creek, Inyo County, California, a travertine depositing creek in an arid climate. *Geochim. Cosmochim. Acta*, 29:85–112.

Barnes, L., and J. R. O'Neil. (1971). Calcium–magnesium carbonate solid solutions from Holocene conglomerate cements and travertines in the Coast Range of California. *Geochim. Cosmochim. Acta*, 35:699–718.

Barshad, I. (1966). The effect of a variation in precipitation on the nature of clay mineral formation in soils from acid and basic igneous rocks. *Proc. Int. Clay Conf.*, 6:167–173.

Bathurst, R. G. C. (1971). *Carbonate Sediments and their Diagenesis: Developments in Sedimentology*. Vol. 12. Elsevier, New York, NY. 620 pp.

Baumann, A., U. Förstner, and R. Rhode. (1975). Lake Shala: Water chemistry, mineralogy and geochemistry of sediments in an Ethiopian rift lake. *Geol. Rundschau*, 64:593–609.

Beadle, L. C. (1932). Scientific results of the Cambridge expedition to the East African Lakes 1930–31. *Linnean Soc. (Zool.) J.*, 38:157–211.

Beadle, L. C. (1974). *The Inland Waters of Tropical Africa*. Longman, London. 365 pp.

Begin, Z. B., A. Ehrlich, and Y. Nathan. (1974). Lake Lisan, the Pleistocene precursor of the Dead Sea. *Geol. Survey Israel Bull.* 63. 30 pp.

Bentor, Y. K. (1961). Some geochemical aspects of the Dead Sea and the question of its age. *Geochim. Cosmochim. Acta*, 25:239–260.

Berner, R. A. (1975). The role of magnesium in the crystal growth of calcite and aragonite from sea water. *Geochim. Cosmochim. Acta*, 39:489–504.

Boles, J. R. (1971). Synthesis of analcime from natural heulandite and clinoptilolite. *Am. Mineral.*, 56:1724–1734.

Bonython, C. W. (1955). The area, volume and salt content in Lake Eyre, South Australia. Rept. Lake Eyre Comm., Royal Geog. Soc. Australia.

Bradley, W. H. (1929). The varves and climate of the Green River epoch. Pp. 87–110. U.S. Geol. Survey Prof. Paper 158-E.

Bradley, W. H. (1931). Origin and microfossils of the oil shale of the Green River Formation of Colorado and Utah. U.S. Geol. Survey Prof. Paper 168. 58 pp.

Bradley, W. H. (1964). Geology of the Green River Formation and associated Eocene rocks in southwestern Wyoming and adjacent parts of Colorado and Utah. U.S. Geol. Survey Prof. Paper 496-A. 86 pp.

Bradley, W. H. (1970). Green River oil shale—concept of origin extended. *Geol. Soc. Am. Bull.*, 81:990–993.

Bradley, W. H., and H. P. Eugster. (1969). Geochemistry and paleolimnology of the trona deposits and associated authigenic minerals of the Green River Formation of Wyoming. U.S. Geol. Survey Prof. Paper 496-B. 71 pp.

Brock, T. D., S. Cook, S. Peterson, and J. L. Mosser. (1976). Biogeochemistry and bacteriology of ferrous iron oxidation in geothermal habitats. *Geochim. Cosmochim. Acta*, 40:493–500.

Butzer, K. W., G. L. Isaac, J. L. Richardson, and C. Washbourn-Kamau. (1972). Radiocarbon dating of East African lake levels. *Science*, 175:1069–1076.

Callender, E. (1969). Origin and diagenesis of lacustrine carbonate minerals. Geol. Soc. Amer. Abstracts with Programs, part 7, 29.

Calvert, S. E. (1966). Origin of diatom-rich varved sediments from the Gulf of California. *J. Geol.*, 74:546–565.

Carroll, D. (1962). Rain-water as a chemical agent of geologic processes—a review. U.S. Geol. Survey Water-Supply Paper 1535-G.

Cheverry, C. (1974). Contribution à l'étude pédologique des polders du lac Tchad. Dynamique des sels en milieu continental subaride dans des sédiments argileux et organiques. Thèse, O. R. S. T. O. M., Strasbourg. 275 pp.

Clarke, F. W. (1924). The data of geochemistry: U.S.G.S. Bull. 770, 783 pp (see pp. 156–180).

Clayton, R. N., B. F. Jones, and R. A. Berner. (1968). Isotope studies of dolomite formation under sedimentary conditions. *Geochim. Cosmochim. Acta* 32:415–432.

Cleaves, E. T., A. E. Godfrey, and O. P. Bricker. (1970). Geochemical balance of a small watershed and its geomorphic implications. *Bull. Geol. Soc. Am.*, 81:3015–3032.

Cleaves, E. T., D. W. Fisher, and O. P. Bricker. (1974). Chemical weathering of serpentinite in the eastern piedmont of Maryland. *Bull. Geol. Soc. Am.*, 85:437–444.

Culbertson, W. C. (1966). Trona in the Wilkins Peak Member of the Green River Formation, southwestern Wyoming. U.S. Geol. Survey Prof. Paper 550-B, B159-B164.

Culbertson, W. C. (1971). Stratigraphy of the trona deposits in the Green River Formation, southwest Wyoming. *Wyoming Univ. Contr. Geol.*, 10:15–23.

Cummings, J. M. (1940). Saline and hydromagnesite deposits of British Columbia. British Columbia Dept. of Mines, Bull. No. 3. 160 pp.

D'Ans, J. (1933). Die Lösungsgleichwichte der Systeme der Salze ozeanischer Salzablagerungen. Kaliforschungsanstalt.

Deardorff, D. L., and L. E. Mannion. (1971). Wyoming trona deposits. *Wyoming Univ. Contr. Geol.* 10:25–37.

DeBoer, R. B. (1977). Stability of Mg–Ca carbonates. *Geochim. Cosmochim. Acta,* **41**:265–270.

Degens, E. T., R. P. Von Herzer, H-K. Wong, W. E. Deuser, and H. W. Jannasch. (1972). Lake Kivu: Structure, chemistry and biology of an East African Rift lake. *Geol. Rundschau,* **62**:245–277.

Drever, J. I., and C. L. Smith. (1977). Repeated wetting and drying of the soil zone as an influence on the chemistry of ground water in arid terrains. 2nd IAGC Symp. Water-Rock Interaction, Strasbourg, **II**:50–55.

Droubi, A., C. Cheverry, B. Fritz, and Y. Tardy. (1976). Géochimie des eaux et des sels dans les sols des polders du lac Tchad: Application d'un modèle thermodynamique de simulation de l'évaporation. *Chem. Geol.,* **17**:165–177.

Dyni, J. R. (1974). Stratigraphy and nahcolite resources of the saline facies of the Green River Formation in northwest Colorado. Pp. 111–121. Guidebook Rocky Mountain Assoc. Geol.

Dyni, J. R., R. J. Hite, and O. B. Raup. (1970). Lacustrine deposits of bromine-bearing halite, Green River Formation, northwestern Colorado. *3rd Symp. Salt, Northern Ohio Geol. Soc.,* **1**:166–180.

Eardley, A. J. (1938). Sediments of Great Salt Lake, Utah. *Am. Assoc. Petrol. Geol. Bull.,* **22**:1305–1411.

Eardley, A. J. (1962). Glauber's salt bed, west of Promontory Point, Great Salt Lake. Utah Geol. Mineral. Survey Special Studies 1. 12 pp.

Eardley, A. J., and V. Gvosdetsky. (1960). Analysis of Pleistocene core from Great Salt Lake, Utah. *Geol. Soc. Am. Bull.,* **71**:1323–1344.

Eardley, A. J., R. T. Shuey, V. Gvosdetsky, W. P. Nash, M. Dane Picard, D. C. Grey and G. J. Kukla. (1973). Lake cycles in the Bonneville basin, Utah. *Geol. Soc. Am., Bull.,* **84**:211–216.

Eugster, H. P. (1966). Sodium carbonate–bicarbonate minerals as indicators of P_{CO_2}. *J. Geophys. Res.,* **71**:3369–3377.

Eugster, H. P. (1967). Hydrous sodium silicates from Lake Magadi, Kenya. Precursors of bedded chert. *Science,* **157**:1177–1180.

Eugster, H. P. (1969). Inorganic bedded cherts from the Magadi area, Kenya. *Contrib. Mineral. Petrol.,* **22**:1–31.

Eugster, H. P. (1970). Chemistry and origin of the brines of Lake Magadi, Kenya. Pp. 215–235. Mineral. Soc. Amer. Spec. Paper No. 3.

Eugster, H. P., and I-Ming Chou. (1973). The depositional environment of Precambrian bedded iron-formations. *Econ. Geol.,* **68**:1144–1168.

Eugster, H. P., and L. A. Hardie. (1975). Sedimentation in an ancient playa-lake complex: the Wilkins Peak member of the Green River Formation of Wyoming. *Bull. Geol. Soc. Am.,* **86**:319–334.

Eugster, H. P., and B. F. Jones. (1968). Gels composed of sodium aluminum silicate. Lake Magadi, Kenya. *Science,* **161**:160–164.

Eugster, H. P., and B. F. Jones. (1977). The behavior of potassium and silica during closed basin evaporation. 2nd IAGC Symp. Water-Rock Interaction, Strasbourg, **II**:1–12.

Eugster, H. P., and G. I. Smith. (1965). Mineral equilibria in the Searles Lake evaporites, California. *J. Petrol.,* **6**:473–522.

Eugster, H. P., and R. C. Surdam. (1973). Depositional environment of the Green River Formation of Wyoming: A preliminary report. *Geol. Soc. Am. Bull.,* **84**:1115–1120.

Fahey, J. J. (1962). Saline minerals of the Green River Formation. U.S. Geol. Survey Prof. Paper 405. 50 pp.

Fouch, T. D. (1975). Lithofacies and related hydrocarbon accumulations in Tertiary strata of the western and central Uinta Basin, Utah. Pp. 163–173. In: D. W. Bolyard (ed.), *Symposium on Deep Drilling Frontiers in the Central Rocky Mountains.* Rocky Mtn. Assoc. Geol.

Friedman, I., G. I. Smith, and K. G. Hardcastle. (1976). Studies of Quaternary saline lakes. II. Isotopic and compositional changes during desiccation of the brines in Owens Lake, California, 1969–1971. *Geochim. Cosmochim. Acta,* **40**:501–511.

Füchtbauer, H., and L. A. Hardie. (1976). Experimentally determined homogeneous distribution coefficients for precipitated magnesian calcites: application to marine carbonate cements. *Geol. Soc. Am.,* Abstracts with Program, 876–877.

Gac, J. Y., A. Droubi, B. Fritz, and Y. Tardy. (1977). Geochemical behavior of silica and magnesium during the evaporation of water in Chad. *Chem. Geol.,* **19**:215–228.

Gale, H. S. (1914). Salt, borax and potash in Saline Valley, California. *Bull. U.S. Geol. Surv.,* **540**:416–421.

Gambell, A. W., and D. W. Fisher. (1966). Chemical composition of rainfall, eastern North Carolina and southeastern Virginia: U.S. Geol. Survey Water-Supply Paper 1535-K. 41 pp.

Garrels, R. M., and F. T. Mackenzie. (1967). Origin of the chemical composition of some springs and lakes. Pp. 222–242. In: *Equilibrium Concepts in Natural Water Systems.* Am. Chem. Soc., Advances in Chemistry, No. 67.

Garrels, R. M., and F. T. Mackenzie. (1971). *Evolution of Sedimentary Rocks.* Norton, New York, NY. 397 pp.

Gilbert, G. K. (1890). Lake Bonneville, U.S. Geol. Survey Monogr. 1. 438 pp.

Glennie, K. W. (1970). Desert Sedimentary Environments. Elsevier, New York, N.Y. 222 pp.

Goudge, M. F. (1924). Magnesium sulfate in British Columbia. Canada Dept. Mines Rep. 642.

Graf, D. L., A. J. Eardley, and N. F. Shimp. (1961). A preliminary report on magnesium carbonate formation in glacial lake Bonneville. *J. Geol.,* **69**:219–223.

Hahl, D. C. (1968). Dissolved-mineral inflow to Great Salt Lake. Utah Geol. Mineral. Survey, Water Resour. Bull. 10. 35 pp.

Hahl, D. C., and A. H. Handy. (1969). Great Salt Lake, Utah: Chemical and physical variation of the brine, 1963–1966. Utah Geol. Mineral. Survey, Water Resour. Bull. 12. 33 pp.

Hahl, D. C., and R. H. Langford. (1964). Dissolved-mineral inflow to Great Salt Lake and chemical characteristics of the salt lake brine; Part II. Utah Geol. Mineral. Survey, Water Resour. Bull. 3. 40 pp.

Hahl, D. C., and C. G. Mitchell. (1963). Dissolved-mineral inflow to Great Salt Lake and chemical characteristics of the Salt Lake brine. Part I: Selected hydrologic data. Utah. Geol. Mineral. Survey, Water Resour. Bull. 3. 40 pp.

Hardie, L. A. (1968). The origin of the recent non-marine evaporite deposit of Saline Valley, Inyo County, California. *Geochim. Cosmochim. Acta,* **32**:1279–1301.

Hardie, L. A., and H. P. Eugster. (1970). The evolution of closed-basin brines. *Mineralog. Soc. Am.,* Spec. Pub., **3**:273–290.

Hardie, L. A., and H. P. Eugster. (1971). The depositional environment of marine evaporites: a case for shallow, clastic accumulation. *Sedimentology,* **16**:187–220.

Hardie, L. A., J. P. Smoot, and H. P. Eugster. (In press). Saline lakes and their deposits: A sedimentological approach. Int. Assoc. Sedimentol. Special Publ.

Hardt, W. F., R. W. Moyle, and L. C. Dutcher. (1972). Proposed water-resources study of Searles Valley, Calif. U.S. Geol. Survey open-file rept.

Hatch, J. R. (1972). Phase relationships in part of the system sodium carbonate–calcium carbonate–carbon dioxide–water at one atmosphere pressure. Ph.D thesis, Univ. Illinois, Urbana, Ill. 85 pp.

Hay, R. L. (1964). Phillipsite of saline lakes and soils. *Am. Mineral.,* **49**:1366–1387.

Hay, R. L. (1968). Chert and its sodium-silicate precursors in sodium-carbonate lakes of East Africa. *Contr. Mineral. Petrol.,* **17**:255–274.

Hay, R. L. (1970). Silicate reactions in three lithofacies of semi-arid basin, Olduvai Gorge, Tanzania. Pp. 237–255. In: B. A. Morgan (ed.), *Mineralogy and Geochemistry of Non-marine Evaporites.* Mineralog. Soc. America Spec. Paper 3.

Hem, J. D. (1970). Study and interpretation of the chemical characteristics of natural water. U.S. Geol. Survey Water Supply Paper 1473. 363 pp.

Hsü, K. J., and C. Siegenthaler. (1969). Preliminary experiments on hydrodynamic movement induced by evaporation and their bearing on the dolomite problem. *Sedimentology,* **12**:11–25.

Hunt, C. B., T. W. Robinson, W. A. Bowles, and A. L. Washburn. (1966). Hydrologic basin, Death Valley, California. U.S. Geol. Surv. Prof. Paper 494-B.

Hutchinson, G. E. (1937). Limnological studies in Indian Tibet. *Int. Rev. Hydrobiol.,* **35**:134–177.

Iijima, A., and R. L. Hay. (1968). Analcime composition in the Green River Formation of Wyoming. *Am. Mineral.,* **53**:184–200.

Jones, B. F. (1965). The hydrology and mineralogy of Deep Springs Lake, Inyo County, California. U.S. Geol. Survey Prof. Paper 502-A. 56 pp.

Jones, B. F. (1966). Geochemical evolution of closed basin waters in the western Great Basin. Pp. 181–200. Ohio Geol. Soc. Symposium on Salt, 2nd, Ohio Geol. Soc. Cleveland 1966, 1.

Jones, B. F., H. P. Eugster, and S. L. Rettig. (1977). Hydrochemistry of the Lake Magadi Basin, Kenya. *Geochim. Cosmochim. Acta,* **41**:53–72.

Jones, B. F., S. L. Rettig, and H. P. Eugster. (1967). Silica in alkaline brines. *Science,* **158**:1310–1314.

Junge, C. E., and R. Werby. (1958). The concentration of chloride, sodium, potassium, calcium, and sulfate in rain water over the United States. *J. Meteorol.,* **15**:417–425.

Katz, A. (1973). The interaction of magnesium with calcite during growth at 25–90° C and one atmosphere. *Geochim. Cosmochim. Acta,* **37**:1563–1586.

Kaufman, A. (1971). U-series dating of Dead Sea basin carbonates. *Geochim. Cosmochim. Acta,* **35L**:1269–1281.

Keller, W. D., and A. F. Frederickson. (1952). Role of plants and colloidal acids in the mechanism of weathering. *Am. J. Sci.,* **250**:594–603.

King, C. R. (1948). Soda ash and salt cake in California. *Calif. J. Mines Geol.,* **44**:189–200.

Krauskopf, K. B. (1967). *Introduction to Geochemistry.* McGraw–Hill, New York, NY. 721 pp.

Lafon, G. M. (1975). The calculation of chemical potentials in natural waters. Application to mixed chloride-sulfate. Pp. 97–111. In: T. M. Church (ed.), *Marine Chemistry in the Coastal Environment.* Am. Chem. Soc. Symposium Series 18.

Lerman, A. (1967). Model of chemical evolution of a chloride lake—The Dead Sea. *Geochim. Cosmochim. Acta,* **31**:2309–2330.

Lerman, A. (1970). Chemical equilibria and evolution of chloride brines. *Mineral. Soc. Am.,* Spec. Publ., **3**:291–306.

Lerman, A., and A. Shatkay. (1968). Dead Sea brines: degree of halite saturation by electrode measurements. *Earth Planet. Sci. Lett.,* **5**:63–66.

Livingston, D. A. (1963). Chemical composition of rivers and lakes: U.S. Geol. Surv. Prof. Paper 440-G. 64 pp.

Loewengart, S. (1962). The geochemical evolution of the Dead Sea Basin. *Res. Counc. Israel Bull.,* **11G**:85–96.

Löffler, H. (1956). Ergebnisse der Österreichischen Iran Expedition 1949–50: Limnologische Untersuchungen an Iranischen Binnengewässern. *Hydrobiology,* **8**:1–252.

Lombardi, O. (1963). Observations on the distribution of chemical elements in the terrestrial saline deposits of Saline Valley California. U.S. Naval Ordnance Test Station, China Lake, Tech. Publ. 2916. 42 pp.

Lustig, L. K. (1962). Clastic sedimentation in a bolson environment. Ph.D thesis, Harvard Univ. 102 pp.

Maglione, G. (1970). La magadiite, silicate sodique de néoformation des faciès évaporitique du Kanem. *Bull. Serv. Carte Geol. Als. Lorr.,* **23**:3–4, 177–189.

Maglione, G. (1974). Géochimie des évaporites et silicates néoformés en milieu continentale confiné. Thèse Univ. Paris VI. 331 pp.

Maglione, G., and M. Servant. (1973). Signification des silicates de sodium et des cherts néoformés dans les variations hydrologiques et climatiques holocènes du bassin tchadien. *C. R. Acad. Sci. Paris* **277**:1721–1724.

Mariner, R. H., and R. C. Surdam. (1970). Alkalinity and formation of zeolites in saline alkaline lakes. *Science,* **170**:977–980.

Mazor, E. (1962). Radon and radium content of some Israeli water sources and a hypothesis on underground reservoirs of brines, oils and gases in the Rift Valley. *Geochim. Cosmochim. Acta,* **26**:765–786.

Mazor, E., and F. Mero. (1969). Geochemical tracing of

mineral and fresh water sources in the Lake Tiberias basin. *Israel. J. Hydrol.,* 7:276–317.

Mazor, E., E. Rosenthal, and J. Ekstein. (1969). Geochemical tracing of mineral water sources in the Southwestern Dead Sea Basin. *Israel. J. Hydrol.,* 7:246–275.

McAllister, J. F. (1956). Geology of the Ubehebe Peak quadrangle. U.S. Geol. Surv. Map GQ 95.

McGrew, P., and M. Casilliano. (1975). The geological history of Fossil Butte National Monument and Fossil Basin. U.S. Natl. Park Service Occasional Paper, 3:1–37.

Miller, J. P. (1961). Solutes in small streams draining single rock types, Sangre de Cristo Range, New Mexico. U.S. Geol. Surv. Water-Supply Paper 1535-F.

Milton, C. (1971). Authigenic minerals of the Green River Formation. *Wyoming Univ. Contr. Geol.,* 10:57–63.

Milton, C., and H. P. Eugster. (1959). Mineral assemblages of the Green River Formation. Pp. 118–150. In: P. H. Abelson (ed.), *Researches in Geochemistry.* John Wiley, New York, NY.

Morrison, R. B. (1966). Predecessors of Great Salt Lake. Pp. 77–104. In: Wm. Lee Stokes (ed.), *Guidebook to the Geology of Utah.* Vol. 20. Utah Geol. Soc.

Müller, G., G. Irion, and V. Förstner. (1972). Formation and diagenesis of inorganic Ca–Mg carbonates in the lacustrine environment. *Naturwissenschaften,* 59:158–164.

Mundorff, J. C. (1971). Nonthermal springs of Utah. Utah Geol. Mineral. Survey, Water Resources Bull. 16. 70 pp.

Neev, D. (1962). Recent precipitation of calcium salts in the Dead Sea. *Res. Counc. Israel Bull.,* 11G:153–154.

Neev, D., and K. O. Emery. (1967). The Dead Sea. Depositional processes and environments of evaporites. *Israel Geol. Survey Bull.,* 41. 147 pp.

Nesbitt, H. W. (1974). The study of some mineral–aqueous solution interactions. Ph.D. thesis, Baltimore, Johns Hopkins Univ. 173 pp.

Nipkow, F. (1920). Vorläufige Mitteilungen über Untersuchungen des Schlammabsatzes im Zürichsee. *Zeitschr. Hydrol.,* 1:100–122.

O'Neil, J. R., and R. L. Hay. (1973). $^{18}O/^{16}O$ ratios in cherts associated with the saline lake deposits of East Africa. *Earth Planet. Sci. Lett.,* 19:257–266.

Peterson, M. N. A., G. S. Bien, and R. A. Berner. (1963). Radiocarbon studies of recent dolomite from Deep Springs Lake, California. *J. Geophys. Res.,* 68:6493–6505.

Peterson, M. N. A., C. C. Von der Borch, and G. S. Bien. (1966). Growth of dolomite crystals. *Am. J. Sci.,* 264:257–272.

Pettijohn, F. J. (1975). *Sedimentary Rocks.* 3rd ed. Harper & Row, New York, NY. 628 pp.

Phillips, K. N., and A. S. Van Denburgh. (1971). Hydrology and geochemistry of Abert, Summer and Goose Lakes, and other closed-basin lakes in South-central Oregon. U.S. Geol. Survey Prof. Paper 502B. 86 pp.

Quinn, H. G. (1966). Biology of the Great Salt Lake. Pp. 25–34. In: Wm. Lee Stokes (ed.), *Guidebook to the Geology of Utah* Vol. 20. Utah Geol. Soc.

Rawson, D. S., and J. E. Moore. (1944). The saline lakes of Saskatchewan. *Can. J. Res.,* Sect. D., 22:141–201.

Ricci, J. E. (1951). *The Phase Rule and Heterogeneous Equilibrium.* Van Nostrand. 505 pp.

Reilly, P. J., R. H. Wood, and R. A. Robinson. (1971). The prediction of osmotic and activity coefficients in mixed electrolyte solutions. *J. Phys. Chem.,* 75:1305.

Reite, O. B., G. M. O. Maloiy, and B. Aasehaug. (1974). pH, salinity and temperature tolerance of Lake Magadi tilapia. *Nature,* 247:315.

Roche, M. A. (1973). Traçage naturel salin et isotopique des eaux du système hydrologique du lac Tchad. Thesis, Univ. Paris VI. 385 pp.

Rooney, T. P., B. F. Jones, and T. J. Neal. (1969). Magadiite from Alkali Lake, Oregon. *Am. Mineral.,* 54:1034–1043.

Ryder, R. T., T. D. Fouch, and J. H. Elison. (1976). Early Tertiary sedimentation in the western Uinta basin, Utah. *Bull. Geol. Soc. Am.,* 87:496–512.

Sandberg, P. (1975). New interpretations of Great Salt Lake ooids and of ancient non-skeletal carbonate sedimentology. *Sedimentology,* 22:497–537.

Servant, M. (1973). Séquences continentales et variations climatiques. Evolution du bassin du Tchad au Cenozoique supérieur. Thesis, Univ. Paris VI. 348 pp.

Shearman, D. J. (1970). Recent halite rock, Baja California, Mexico. *Trans. Inst. Mining Metall.* (Section B), 79:155–162.

Sheppard, R. A., and A. J. Gude, 3d. (1968). Distribution and genesis of authigenic silicate minerals in tuffs of Pleistocene Lake Tecopa, Inyo County, California. U.S. Geol. Survey Prof. Paper 597. 38 pp.

Sheppard, R. A., and A. J. Gude, 3d. (1969). Diagenesis of tuffs in the Barstow Formation, Mud Hills, San Bernardino County, California. U.S. Geol. Survey Prof. Paper 634. 35 pp.

Sheppard, R. A., and A. J. Gude, 3d. (1973). Zeolites and associated authigenic silicate minerals in tuffaceous rocks of the Big Sandy Formation, Mohave County, Arizona. U.S. Geol. Survey Prof. Paper 830. 36 pp.

Sheppard, R. A., and A. J. Gude, 3d. (1974). Chert derived from magadiite in a lacustrine deposit near Rome, Malheur County, Oregon. *J. Res. U.S. Geol. Surv.,* 2:625–630.

Sheppard, R. A., A. J. Gude, 3d., and R. L. Hay. (1970). Makatite, a new hydrous sodium silicate mineral from Lake Magadi, Kenya. *Am. Mineral.,* 55:358–366.

Slack, K. V. (1967). Physical and chemical description of Birch Creek, a travertine depositing stream, Inyo County, California. U.S. Geol. Survey Prof. Paper 549 A. 19 pp.

Smith, C. L. (1974). Chemical controls on weathering and trace element distribution at Teels Marsh, Nevada. Univ. Wyoming, Ph.D. thesis. 96 pp.

Smith, C. L., and J. I. Drever. (1976). Controls on the chemistry of springs at Teels Marsh, Mineral Co. Nevada. *Geochim. Cosmochim. Acta,* 40:1081–1093.

Smith, G. I. (In press). Subsurface stratigraphy and geochemistry of late Quaternary evaporites, Searles Lake, California. U.S. Geol. Survey Prof. Paper.

Smith, G. I. and D. V. Haines. (1964). Character and distribution of nonclastic minerals in the Searles Lake evaporite deposit, California. *U.S. Geol. Surv. Bull.,* 1181-P:1–58.

Smith, J. W., and C. Milton. (1966). Dawsonite in the Green River formation of Colorado. *Econ. Geol.,* 61:1029–1042.

Smith, J. W., and N. B. Young. (1969). Determination of dawsonite and nahcolite in Green River formation oil shale. U.S. Bureau Mines Report Invest. 7286.

Smoot, J. P. (1976). Origin of the carbonate sediments in the Wilkins Peak Member, Green River formation (Eocene), Wyoming. *Geol. Soc. Amer., Abstr. with Programs,* **8,** 6:1113.

Smoot, J. P. (1977). Sedimentology of a saline closed basin: The Wilkins Peak Member, Green River formation (Eocene) Wyoming. Ph.D. thesis, Johns Hopkins University, Baltimore, MD. 296 pp.

Smoot, J. P. (In press). Origin of the carbonate sediments in the Wilkins Peak Member of the lacustrine Green River Formation (Eocene) Wyoming. Int. Assoc. Sedimentol. Spec. Publ.

Stanley, K. O., and R. C. Surdam. (In press). Sedimentation on the front of Eocene Gilbert-type deltas, Washakie Basin, Wyoming, *J. Sed. Petrol.*

Steen, V. C., and R. F. Fryxell. (1965). Mazama and Glacier Peak pumice glass: Uniformity of refractive index after weathering. *Science,* 150:878–880.

Stoertz, G. E., and G. E. Ericksen. (1974). Geology of Salars in Northern Chile. U.S. Geol. Surv. Prof. Paper 811. 65 pp.

Stoffers, P., and S. Holdship. (1975). Diagenesis of sediments in an alkaline lake: Lake Manyara, Tanzania. IXth Intern. Confr. Sediment., Nice.

Stumm, W., and J. J. Morgan. (1970). *Aquatic Chemistry.* Wiley, New York, NY. 583 pp.

Surdam, R. C., and H. P. Eugster. (1976). Mineral reactions in the sedimentary deposits of the Lake Magadi Region, Kenya. *Bull. Geol. Soc. Am.,* 87:1739–1752.

Surdam, R. C., H. P. Eugster, and R. H. Mariner. (1972). Magadi-type chert in Jurassic and Eocene to Pleistocene rocks, Wyoming. *Bull. Geol. Soc. Am.,* 83:2261–2266.

Surdam, R. C., and R. D. Parker. (1972). Authigenic aluminosilicate minerals in the tuffaceous rocks of the Green River Formation, Wyoming. *Geol. Soc. Am. Bull.,* 83:689–700.

Surdam, R. C., and R. A. Sheppard. (In press). Zeolites in saline, alkaline-lake deposits.

Surdam, R. C., and K. O. Stanley. (1976). Evolution of an ancient playa-lake complex. *Geol. Soc. Amer.,* Abstracts with Programs, **8,** 6:1130.

Surdam, R. C., and C. A. Wolfbauer. (1975). Green River formation, Wyoming: A playa-lake complex. *Bull. Geol. Soc. Am.,* 86:335–345.

Talling, J. F., and I. B. Talling. (1965). The chemical composition of African lake waters. *Int. Rev. Hydrobiol.,* 50:421–463.

Tardy, Y., C. Cheverry, and B. Fritz. (1974). Néoformation d'une argile magnésienne dans les dépressions interdunaires du lac Tchad: Application aux domaines et stabilité des phyllosilicates alumineux, magnésiens et ferrifères. *C.R. Acad. Sci.,* Sér. D, 278:1999–2002.

Tomkins, R. V. (1954). Natural sodium sulfate in Saskatchewan. (2nd ed.). Saskatchewan Dept. Mineral Resources, Indust. Minerals Research Board Rept., No. 6. 71 pp.

Trudinger, P. A., I. B. Lambert, and G. W. Skyring. (1972). Biogenic sulfide ores: A feasibility study. *Econ. Geol.,* 67:1114.

Tucker, W. B. (1926). Inyo County. Calif. *Min. Bur. Rep.,* 22:453–530.

Ver Planck, W. E. (1958). Salt in California. *Cal. Dept. Nat. Res. Mines Bull.,* **175.** 168 pp.

Valyashko, M. G. (1972). Playa lakes—a necessary stage in the development of a salt-bearing basin. Pp. 41–51. In: G. Richter-Bernburg (ed.), *Geology of Saline Deposits.* UNESCO, Paris.

Weiler, Y., E. Sass, and I. Zak. (1974). Halite oolites and ripples in the Dead Sea, Israel. *Sedimentology,* 21:623–632.

Whelan, J. A. (1973). Great Salt Lake, Utah: Chemical and physical variations of the brine, 1966–1972. Utah Geol. Mineral. Survey, Water Resources Bull. 17. 24 pp.

Whelan, J. A., and C. A. Petersen. (1975). Great Salt Lake, Utah: Chemical and physical variations of the brine, water—year 1973. Utah Geol. Mineral. Survey, Water Resources Bull. 20. 29 pp.

White, D. E., J. G. Hem, and G. A. Waring. (1963). Chemical composition of surface waters. U.S. Geol. Surv. Prof. Paper 440-L. 67 pp.

Whitehead, H. C., and J. H. Feth. (1961). Recent chemical analyses of waters from several closed-basin lakes and their tributaries in the western United States. *Geol. Soc. Am. Bull.,* 72:1421–1426.

Williams, D. E., and N. T. Coleman. (1950). Cation exchange properties of plant root surfaces. *Plant Soil,* 2:243–256.

Wolfbauer, C. A. (1971). Geologic framework of the Green River Formation in Wyoming. *Wyoming Univ. Contr. Geol.,* 10:3–8.

Wood, J. R. (1975). Thermodynamics of brine-salt equilibria I. The systems $NaCl–KCl–MgCl_2–CaCl_2–H_2O$ and $NaCl–MgSO_4–H_2O$ at 25°C. *Geochim. Cosmochim. Acta,* 39:1147–1163.

Chapter 9

Freshwater Carbonate Sedimentation

K. Kelts and K. J. Hsü

Introduction

Carbonate minerals are a common constituent of lacustrine sediments. The great variability with respect to geological setting, climatic environment, water chemistry, and biological activity limits generalizations about mechanisms of carbonate sedimentation. On the whole, in constrast to an oceanic environment, the bulk of primary lacustrine carbonates are inorganic chemical precipitates. Two distinctly different geological settings can be recognized: (1) carbonate and evaporite deposition in brine lakes or on playas in arid regions (see Chap. 8, this volume), and (2) carbonate sedimentation in fresh- and brackish-water lakes in humid regions. Occurrences of lacustrine chalks and marls in young geological formations of temperate regions have been described since the time of Lyell (1830). In northern America and Europe, Late Quaternary chalks were found near still existing lakes and their genesis was related to a postglacial period of climatic amelioration (e.g., Heim, 1919). Typically, these deposits are fine grained, either rhythmically laminated or massive, white to dull-yellowish gray chalks to marls. This distinction is qualitative based on a bulk carbonate content boundary around 60%. The dominant mineral is calcite. Similar varve-like carbonate or marl sediments were found in older lacustrine deposits (e.g., Bradley, 1929). Nipkow (1920) described recent analogies to laminated lacustrine carbonates in Lake Zurich; the light laminae are rich in CaCO$_3$. Forel (1901) early recognized a biological role, but Minder (1922, 1926) developed the concept of inorganic, biogenically induced calcite precipitation. Meanwhile lacustrine marls in regions of Quaternary glaciation around the Great Lakes in North America were studied (e.g., Davis, 1901; Pollock, 1918). Calcite precipitation in those biologically active hardwater lakes (e.g., Halbfass, 1923; Ruttner, 1962; Pia,

1933; Ohle, 1952; Hutchinson, 1957; Wetzel, 1975) was soon related to extraction of CO_2 during photosynthesis by algae.

During the last decade, there has been a widened interest in lacustrine carbonate sedimentation (Table 1). Seasonal clouding of the epilimnion by CaCO$_3$ (see Figure 1) (or "whitings") has been observed (e.g., Schäfer and Stapf, 1972; Brunskill, 1969; Strong and Eadie, 1978), and the chemistry of lake waters and its relation to carbonate deposition have been investigated (e.g., Stumm and Morgan, 1970; Brunskill, 1969; Otsuki and Wetzel, 1974; Santschi, 1975). The mineralogy and sedimentology of Holocene lake sediments were documented (e.g., Müller et al., 1972; Thompson and Kelts, 1974; Stoffers, 1975a).

We shall attempt in this article to summarize some recent advances concerning carbonate sedimentation in large fresh- and brackish-water lakes, with particular emphasis on our studies of the Lake Zurich sediments. This provides an example of what we refer to as a "deep-lake-lacustrine-carbonate model" (Figure 2). Freshwater chalks are a common feature of many shallow ponds and lakes less than 30 m deep. Their geological life-span is usually short, whereas chalks deposited in large or deep basins such as the Black Sea may eventually become a significant part of the geological record.

Source of carbonate clastics

Calcareous sediments are formed as a combination of four processes:

1. Clastic input from the erosion and transport of allochtonous carbonates.
2. Production of calcareous skeletons, structural parts, and internal waste products within living organisms.

TABLE 1.   Some Recent Case Studies of Authigenic Calcium Carbonate
Sediments in Dilute Lakes

Lake	Reference
Swiss Lakes	
Geneva	Serruya (1969a); Vernet et al. (1971)
Morat	Davoud (1976)
Biel	Santschi (1975)
Lucerne	O'melia (1972); Bloesch (1974)
Greifensee	Emerson (1976)
Zurich	Gyger et al. (1976)
German Lakes	
Constance	Müller (1966, 1969, 1971b);
(including Gnadensee,	Schöttle and Müller (1968); Schäfer (1972);
and Untersee)	Schäfer and Stapf (1972); Schäfer (1973);
	Rossknecht (1977)
Schleinsee	Geyh et al. (1971)
North American Lakes	
Fayettville Green Lake	Brunskill (1969)
Minnesota Lakes	Dean and Gorham (1976); Megard (1968)
Great Lakes	Kramer (1967); Dell (1972); Strong and Eadie
	(1977)
Michigan Lakes	Otsuki and Wetzel (1974); Wetzel (1975)
Fossil Rita Blanca, Texas	Anderson and Kirkland (1969)
Pleistocene	
Other	
Plitvice, Yugoslavia	Stoffers (1975a)
Balaton, Hungary	Müller (1969)
Compilation	Müller et al. (1972)
African Rift Valley Lakes	Stoffers (1975b)

3. Primary inorganic precipitation and sedimentation of carbonate minerals.
4. Postdepositional changes or early diagenetic reactions.

Which mechanism is dominant varies widely both spatially within an individual lake and from lake to lake (Figure 2).

Detrital carbonates

Detrital carbonates may constitute a significant portion of the sediments in lakes if their drainage basins are underlain by carbonate rocks. In many regions, particularly where the carbonate terraines have been or are being eroded by glaciers, carbonate detritus may occur as silt- or clay-size grains and is carried as suspensions by rivers emptying into the lakes. The suspensions may either spread out as overflows onto, or as interflows injected into, the epilimnion. The suspended particles eventually settle out as widespread, blanket-like pelagic sediments. At times, the density of suspensions or rivers, especially during their flood stage, may exceed that of standing lakewater; those suspensions would continue as turbidity underflows and carry their load for very long distances

(e.g., Lambert et al., 1976). Turbidity current deposits are characterized by graded bedding, and they are commonly ponded in the central depressions of lake basins.

Distinguishing detrital from primary lacustrine carbonates is often a difficult problem. One method uses the assumption that dolomite in freshwater lakes is commonly detrital. Variations of mineral ratios (calcite/dolomite) should be related to calcite precipitation if the detrital influx has a constant composition (e.g., Müller, 1971b). Also carbonates precipitated in freshwater lakes have commonly very negative values of δ_C^{13} and δ_O^{18}; isotopic data may thus permit some estimate of the detrital component. Furthermore, a comparison of the absolute age and the apparent ^{14}C age gives clues as to the percentage of detrital carbonate in young lacustrine chalks (Geyh et al., 1971). Finally, the surface morphology of carbonate grains and shapes may also yield evidence as to their origin.

Some detrital carbonates may be resedimented precipitates that accumulated originally on macrophytes in the litteral zone; these detritus should be similar to pelagic chemical precipitates, except for their sedimentary structures which should indicate deposition by penecontemporaneous slumping or by turbidity currents.

Detrital carbonate may constitute the bulk of many

lacustrine marls (Sturm and Matter, 1972; Lambert *et al.*, 1976; Thomas *et al.*, 1973; Müller, 1971b).

Bioclastic carbonates

In lakes, planktonic organisms which produce calcareous shells are extremely rare. One exception is the green algae, *Phacotus* (Figure 3). Charophytes, chlorophytes, and other benthic, littoral, or free-floating macrophyte flora all form extracellular calcium carbonate precipitate due to photosynthesis. Only the tiny oogonia cyst of a charophyte may be an exception (Hutschinson, 1975).

Some faunal species, mainly benthic in the littoral realm, have calcareous skeletons. Gastropod shells are commonly aragonitic, while ostracods are calcitic. Bivalves may be aragonite, calcite, or Mg-calcite. The inner-ear bones of many fish (otoliths) consist of calcite. All of these may contribute, in a small way, to carbonate sedimentation in hardwater lakes. They commonly represent the major source in softwater lakes.

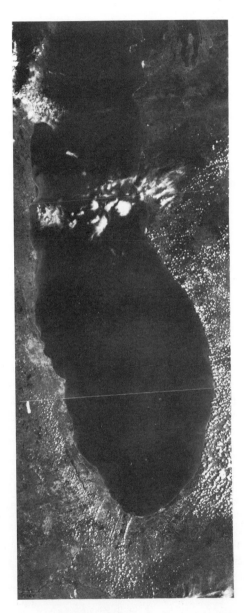 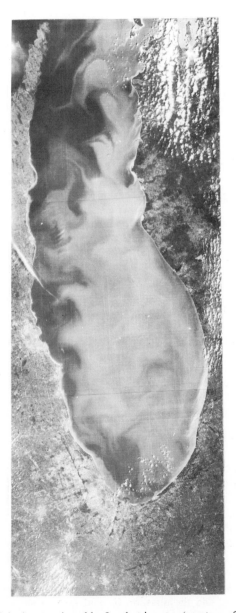

FIGURE 1.   Summer "whitings" in Lake Michigan due to calcite precipitation, as viewed by Landsat imagery (courtesy of NOAA, Strong and Eadie, 1977). Left image shows conditions on July 16, 1973; on the right surface current patterns are outlined on August 21, 1973. The effect of this precipitate is lost in the sediments which are dominated by detrital processes.

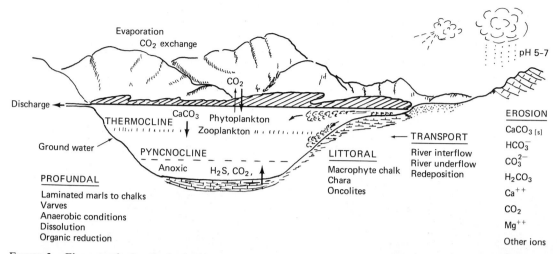

FIGURE 2.   Elements of a deep-basin, freshwater lacustrine carbonate model as seen from spring to autumn during periods of stratified water masses. Depending on the amount of overturn or river underflow, the pyncnocline (boundary to anoxic bottom water) may not always be present.

Chemistry of calcite precipitation

Equilibrium considerations

The condition for calcite precipitation is thermodynamically defined by the relation

$$Ca^{2+} + CO_3^{2-} = CaCO_3 \qquad (Ca^{2+})(CO_3^{2-}) = K_c \qquad (1)$$

where (Ca^{2+}) and (CO_3^{2-}) are ionic activities of these ions at equilibrium and K_c is the equilibrium constant and is at a given pressure only a function of temperature. The pressure dependence can be neglected at depths less than 1000 m. To determine whether a natural water is supersaturated, saturated, or undersaturated with respect to calcite, the activities of the calcium and of the carbonate ions in this water are multiplied to give an ionic activity product (IAP) = $(Ca^{2+})(CO_3^{2-})$. The condition for saturation or supersaturation is

$$IAP \geq K_c.$$

The chemical composition of the dissolved constituents in natural waters can be analyzed. A typical example is illustrated by a routine analysis of Lake Zurich waters, shown in Table 6. The analytical results commonly include values for pH, temperature, p_{CO_2}, alkalinity, total CO_2, and calcium ion concentration of the water. In order to calculate the values of ionic activities from these data, one needs to consider the carbonate equilibria, alkalinity, and activity coefficients, and the question of complex ion or neutral species in natural waters.

Since carbonate-ion activity is rarely obtained by direct measurements, its value must be calculated on the basis of its equilibrium relation to that of bicarbonate ions. Total dissolved inorganic carbon in a solution includes various species: $H_2CO_3^*$, which is defined as $CO_{2(aq)} + H_2CO_3$, HCO_3^-, and CO_3^{2-} (Figure 4a). The distribution of these species is governed by the carbonate equilibria

$$CO_2 + H_2O = H_2CO_3^*$$
$$\frac{(H_2CO_3^*)}{p_{CO_2}} = K_H \qquad \text{(Henry's law)}$$

$$H_2CO_3^* = H^+ + HCO_3^-$$
$$\frac{(H^+)(HCO_3^-)}{(H_2CO_3^*)} = K_1 \qquad (2)$$

$$HCO_3^- = H^+ + CO_3^{2-}$$
$$\frac{(H^+)(CO_3^{2-})}{(HCO_3^-)} = K_2 \qquad (3)$$

where (H^+), $(H_2CO_3^*)$, (HCO_3^-), and (CO_3^{2-}) are ionic activites and K_1 and K_2 are the first and second dissociation constants of carbonic acid (Stumm and Morgan, 1970) given in Table 2.

The analytical results are usually given as concentrations. The relation of activity of any ion to its concentration is defined as activity = concentration × activity coefficient. For the bicarbonate-ion activity

$$(HCO_3^-) = [HCO_3^-] \cdot \gamma_{HCO_3^-} \qquad (4)$$

In dilute solution (less than 10^{-1} mol/liter), where the formation of complex ion or neutral species is insignificant, the activity coefficient can be estimated from the extended Debye–Hückel relation, namely,

$$\log \gamma = \frac{-A\,Z^2\sqrt{I}}{1 + a_i B\sqrt{I}} \qquad (5)$$

where A and B are constants for a given solvent at a specified temperature, Z is the valence of the ion, a_i is

FIGURE 3.   Scanning electron micrograph (SEM) of *Phacotus,* one of the rare nannoplankton (green algae) secreting a calcareous test in freshwater lakes. Sample from Lake Zurich (August 1975, 15 m depth).

the effective diameter of the ion in the solution, and I is the ionic strength of the solution and is equal to

$$I = \Sigma m_i Z_i^2, \qquad (6)$$

m_i being the molar or molal concentration of the component in solution. For practical purposes, the hydrogen-ion activity is defined through the measured pH values as

$$\mathrm{pH} = -\log (\mathrm{H^+}). \qquad (7)$$

Alkalinity is defined by the sum of all titratable weak acids. In practice it is measured by determining the number of equivalents of strong acid necessary to titrate 1 kg of natural waters to the second end equivalence point of carbonic acid, at about a pH of 4.3. In seawater, and particularly anoxic bottom waters in lakes, this titration alkalinity (T_{alk}) may include the following (Gieskes, 1974):

$$T_{\mathrm{alk}} = \Sigma\{[\mathrm{HCO_3^-}] + 2[\mathrm{CO_3^{2-}}] + [\mathrm{HS^-}] + 2[\mathrm{S^{2-}}]$$
$$+ 2[\mathrm{HPO_4^{2-}}] + 3[\mathrm{PO_4^{3-}}] + [\mathrm{NH_3}] + [\mathrm{SI(OH)_3O^-}]$$
$$+ [\mathrm{OH^-}] - [\mathrm{H^+}]\}.$$

It has been common practice to assume that the concentration of other components in freshwater lakes is negligible compared to that of the carbonate and bicarbonate ions. Then the titration alkalinity is for all practical purposes equal to the carbonate alkalinity, or

$$\mathrm{Alk} = [\mathrm{HCO_3^-}] + 2[\mathrm{CO_3^{2-}}] + [\mathrm{OH^-}] - [\mathrm{H^+}]. \qquad (9)$$

Where freshwaters have pH values between 6.5 and 8.5, the concentrations of all other carbonate species are negligible compared to that of bicarbonate ion (Figure 4b). Therefore, one usually assumes that

$$T_{\mathrm{alk}} \cong [\mathrm{HCO_3^-}]. \qquad (10)$$

Note, however, that when considering the mass balance of calcite precipitation and dissolution, all factors

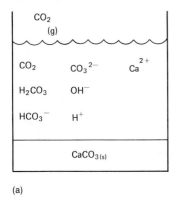

(a)

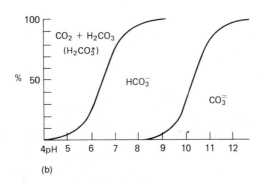

(b)

FIGURE 4. (a)   Simplified carbonate-water system (b) Proportions of the carbonate species $H_2CO_3^*$ (i.e., $H_2CO_3 + CO_2$), HCO_3^-, and CO_3^{2-} in solution at different pH values (after Hutchinson, 1957).

affecting alkalinity must be checked. In some of the European literature the alkalinity of lake waters is expressed as carbonate hardness which gives the weight of $CaCO_3$ precipitate derived from the carbonates in solution. To further complicate the matter, the unit of carbonate hardness given in German literature (dH^0) is defined differently from that given in French and Swiss literature (fH^0):

1 dH^0 = 10 mg of CaO/liter = 18 mg of $CaCO_3$/liter
1 fH^0 = 10 mg of $CaCO_3$/liter
= 0.1 mol of $CaCO_3$/liter.

Since alkalinity is expressed in milliequivalents per liter, we have, therefore, for freshwater with pH = 6.5 to 8.5, a convenient conversion

$$[HCO_3^-] = C_{alk} = 2 \times 0.1 \, fH^0 = 0.2 \, fH^0. \quad (11)$$

The calcium concentration of lake waters is obtained analytically. However, as we mentioned previously, the analyzed concentration [Ca] theoretically may include not only that of the calcium ion but also some calcium in neutral species and in complex ions (e.g., Brunskill, 1969):

$$\Sigma[Ca] = [Ca^{2+}] + [CaHCO_3^+] \quad (12)$$
$$+ [CaCO_3^0] + [CaSO_4^0].$$

In most fresh-water lakes, except for humic waters, the complex and neutral species are negligible in quantity. For example, Stumm and Morgan (1970, p. 151) state that water with $[Ca^{2+}]$ less than 2 mmol/liter and $[HCO_3^-]$ less than 4 meq/liter does not form bicarbonate of carbonate complexes of Ca^{2+} exceeding 5% of the total. It has been a common practice to estimate the activity coefficients of the calcium and other ions in natural fresh waters by the application of the Debye–Hückel formula [Eq. (5); Berner, 1971; Hsü,

1963; Stumm and Morgan, 1970]. Meanwhile carbonate ion $[CO_3^=]$ concentrations are computed from analytical measurements of alkalinity.

The product of the computed (Ca^{2+}) and (CO_3^{2-}) is the IAP, and a comparison of the IAP with the equilibrium constant K_c (at temperature of the lake water analyzed) indicates if the lake water is undersaturated, saturated, or supersaturated with $CaCO_3$.

Several avenues for determining saturation are open (see Berner, 1971, or Stumm and Morgan, 1970, for a complete discussion). One convenient relationship for the computation of IAP of the calcium and carbonate ions from the alkalinity and pH measurements is:

$$IAP = (Ca^{2+})(CO_3^{2-})$$
$$= \{\gamma_{Ca^{2+}}[Ca^{2+}]\gamma_{HCO_3^-} \times K_2 \times Alk\}/(H^+) \quad (13)$$

where K_2 is the second dissociation constant of carbonic acid, defined in Eq. (3), and other parameters are as defined in the preceding equations.

The characterization of the carbonate system by alkalinity and pH is in some instances less precise than another characterization by alkalinity and CO_2-acidity. The CO_2-acidity can be determined by titration with NaOH and its value is conservative in lake waters within the pH range of 5.7 to 7.6 (Stumm and Morgan, 1970, p. 142). We could also, therefore, determine the degree of the saturation by a consideration of the equilibrium expression

$$CaCO_3(s) + H_2CO_3^* = Ca^{2+} + 2HCO_3^- \quad (14)$$

which is defined by the relation

$$\frac{(Ca^{2+})(HCO_3^-)^2}{(H_2CO_3^*)} = K \quad (15)$$

where K is an equilibriun constant and is related to other equilibrium constants of the carbonate system by relating Eqs. (1), (2), and (3)

TABLE 2. Carbonate Equilibria[a]

$CaCO_{3(s)} = Ca^{2+} + CO_3^{2-}$	$\log K_c = 13.870 - 0.04035T - 3059/T$
$H_2CO_3 = H^+ + HCO_3$	$\log K_1(T) = 14.8435 - 0.032786T - 3404.71/T$
$HCO_3^- = H^+ + CO_3^{2-}$	$\log K_2(T) = 6.498 - 0.02379T - 2902.39/T$
$CO_2 + H_2CO_3 = H_2CO_3^*$	$\log(H_2CO_3^*) = \log p_{CO_2} - 14.0184 + 0.015264T -$
	$\quad 2385.73/T - I\,(0.84344 - 0.004471T +$
	$\quad\quad 0.00000666T^2)$

$H_2CO_3^* = p_{CO_2} \cdot K_H$
$CaCO_{3(aragonite)} = Ca^{2+} + CO_3^{2-}$ $\log K_{A(25°C)} = -8.22$

	0°	5°	10°	15°	20°	25°	Centigrade
$Log\,K_H$	-1.11	-1.19	-1.27	-1.32	-1.41	-1.47	
$Log\,K_1$	-6.576	-6.518	-6.466	-6.421	-6.383	-6.352	
$Log\,K_2$	-10.62	-10.556	-10.490	-10.430	-10.376	-10.331	
$Log\,K_c$	-8.35	-8.35	-8.36	-8.37	-8.39	-8.42	

[a]Temperature dependency expressions for calculating the carbonate equilibria constants in dilute waters. Temperature in °K. Numerical expressions after Plummer (1975). K_c (Jacobson and Langmuir, 1974), K_1 (Harned and Davis, 1943), K_2 (Harned and Scholes, 1941). ($H_2CO_3^*$) from Truesdell and Jones (1974). The Henry law solubility coefficient K_H from Stumm and Morgan (1970).

$$K = \frac{K_2}{K_1 K_c}. \qquad (16)$$

For each mole of calcite precipitated, 2 moles of alkalinity should be consumed.

In some anaerobic basins the assumption of $T_{alk} = [HCO_3^-]$ must be corrected for $[HS^-]$ which can approach a value equal to $[HCO_3^-]$. Furthermore, we must consider, especially in the sediment pore waters, that some carbonate alkalinity will be produced by direct bacterial activity rather than by calcite dissolution (Abd-el-Malek and Rizk, 1963). This is governed by the equations for (e.g., Berner et al., 1970):

(a) Sulfate reduction using carbohydrates

$$2CH_2O + SO_4^{2-} = S^{2-} + 2CO_2 + 2H_2O \qquad (17)$$
$$S^{2-} + 2CO_2 + 2H_2O = H_2S + 2HCO_3^- \qquad (18)$$

(b) ammonia formation plus CO_2 from amino acids

$$CH_2NH_2COOH + 2(H) = NH_3 + CH_4 + CO_2 \qquad (19)$$
$$NH_3 + CO_2 + H_2O = NH_4^+ + HCO_3^- \qquad (20)$$
$$NH_3 + HCO_3^- = NH_4^+ + CO_3^{2-}. \qquad (21)$$

In rare cases up to 50% or more of the carbonate alkalinity may be produced by such reactions.

Kinetic considerations

The value of IAP-$(Ca^{2+})(CO_3^{2-})$ of a lake water compared to the equilibrium constant K_c determines if the calcite should precipitate or dissolve. The IAP should be equal to K_c if equilibrium is achieved instantly. Several computer programs are now available to compute equilibrium states from natural water compositions (Truesdell and Jones, 1974; Plummer, 1975). In fact, lake waters are hardly ever found to be in equilibrium: Stumm and Stumm-Zollinger (1968) found that the Lake Zurich waters were undersaturated during the winter and supersaturated during the summer with calcite; Brunskill's (1969) computation led him to conclude that the Green Lake of New York was always supersaturated with calcite. There are many sources of possible errors in computed results. Analytical measurements, especially the pH, are sensitive to CO_2 changes. The chemical composition of the solution in the laboratory may no longer be the same as in situ or suspended particulate $CaCO_3$ present in unfiltered samples. However, the evidence for supersaturation in some lakes is manifold and the IAP far exceeds that of the equilibrium value. Independent measurements, through the use of a saturometer (Brunskill, 1969) or with conductivity measurements (Figure 20), provide additional confirmation. It seems, therefore, very likely that equilibrium is seldom achieved in lake waters, and the precipitation or dissolution of calcite is governed to some extent by kinetic mechanisms.

Commonly inorganic calcite precipitation begins only after a lake water has reached a high level of supersaturation. Supersaturation results from nucleation barriers: the necessary seed crystals may be absent (de Boer, 1977), or magnesium ion, phosphate, or organic compounds may act as surface inhibitors for nucleation. Where the magnesium ion concentration is high, the supersaturation may reach such a degree that magnesian calcite or aragonite would precipitate metastably (e.g., Berner, 1975). The presence of these same inhibitors may also affect the rate of dissolution and prevent equilibrium of undersaturated lake waters with sinking calcite precipitates (Berner and Morse, 1974). In some cases the usually conservative parameter, alkalinity, is inadequate in itself to monitor calcium carbonate budgets in detail.

Factors affecting calcite saturation

In lakes the calcium ion mainly derives from river or groundwater input and sediment refluxing, whereas carbonate ions may also be derived from direct atmospheric equilibria, respiration, and bacterial reduction of organic matter. Two possible mechanisms which can induce supersaturation with respect to calcite are (1) biogenic, through assimilation of carbon dioxide by photosynthesizing plants, and (2) physical–chemical, through seasonal temperature effects on the solubility of carbon dioxide and calcite along with other factors as listed in Tables 3 and 4.

Biogenic factors

Plant activity controls the overall CO_2 budget in a lake. The photosynthesis by algae, for example, uses up large quantities of CO_2. Stumm and Morgan (1970, p. 429) suggest the following approximate stoichiometry:

$$106CO_2 + 16NO_3^- + HPO_4^{2-} + 122H_2O \qquad (22)$$
$$+ 18H^+ = C_{106}H_{263}O_{110}N_6P_1(algae) + 138O_2$$

For comparison, recently, Santschi (1975) found a bulk plankton composition in Lake Biel equal to: $(SiO_2)_6(CH_2O)_{87}(NH_3)_{17}(H_3PO_4)_1$. Because the exchange equilibrium of atmospheric CO_2 with water is a comparatively slow reaction (e.g., Verduin, 1975; Emerson, 1975), carbon dioxide in surface waters during active photosynthesis may become very depleted in eutrophic lakes within a short time, and the waters become supersaturated with respect to calcite. Photosynthetic activities of both macrophyta and microphyta can thus induce precipitation of carbonates. Macrophytes are generally sessile, benthic forms most abundant along the littoral zones. Some macrophytes become encrusted with calcium carbonate amounting to more than their own weight per growth season; pure chalk deposits can form after they decay (Schöttle and Muller, 1968; Stoffers, 1975a; Hutchinson, 1975; Wetzel, 1960, 1975). Sedimentation rates of the order of meters per hundreds of years may result.

TABLE 3.   Sources of Carbonate Sedimentation in Fresh to Brackish Lakes

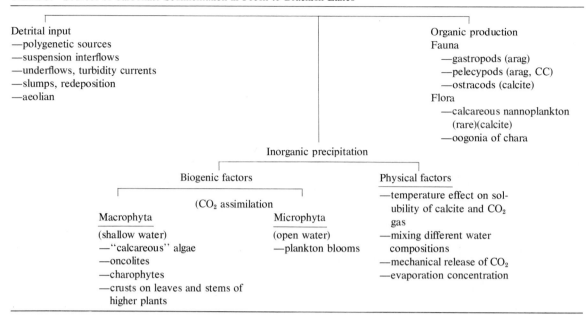

Certain forms such as the various species of *Chara, Potamogeton, Ruppia,* and *Najas* are molded and entombed in these deposits. *Chara* varieties almost always contain more calcite than other plants, probably because they more efficiently utilize bicarbonate in photosynthesis (cf. Hutchinson, 1975, p. 300; Wetzel, 1975). Shallow ponds may be entirely filled with so-called *Chara* lime deposits. As these rhizopod plants decay, an undersaturated microenvironment produced by CO_2 and recrystallisation at point contacts can result in welding of calcite grains to form a very porous, massive, but fragile structure typical of littoral chalks ("Seekreide" in German).

Algal oncolites sometimes form in shallow, shelf

TABLE 4.   Summary of Factors Affecting the Chemical Sedimentation of Calcium Carbonate

Precipitation
    Saturation index (T, Alk, p_{CO_2}, pH); IAP/K_c
    Rate of supersaturation
    Rate of nucleation; seeding
    Inhibitors (Mg, phosphate, organic films)
    Mg/Ca molar ratio
    Ionic strength
    Seeding
Sedimentation
    Aggregation, floculation, size
    Ingestion
    Epilimnion turbulence and residence
    Density and viscosity boundaries
    Dissolution kinetics
    Settling rate
    Residence time sediment/water interface
    Anaerobic conditions, bacterial activity
    Organic decay

environments in freshwater lakes (Logan *et al.,* 1964; Schöttle and Müller, 1968). They result from seasonal precipitation of calcium carbonate over filamentous blue–green algal mats (e.g., *Schizothrix, Calothrix, Rivularia*) which begin their growth as coatings around seed objects such as gastropod shells.

Many authors attribute basinal chalks in deep lakes mainly to redeposition of littoral deposits (e.g., Schäfer, 1973). The role of macrophytes may be commonly overestimated. Seasonal blooms of pelagic microphytes may sufficiently deplete dissolved CO_2 in lake waters to induce significant calcite precipitation (e.g., Minder, 1926; Ohle 1952). Although plankton are usually present throughout the year, a given species may experience very narrowly defined periods of maximum growth. In particular, after spring circulation, nutrients are regenerated in the epilimnion, often resulting in mass blooms of diatoms or other planktonic algae. Megard (1968) found, for example, that calcium carbonate saturation in some Minnesota lakes is probably controlled entirely by the balance between carbon dioxide consumption during photosynthesis and its release during respiration. He plotted calcium depletion against photosynthesis and found an empirical linear relationship. For every mole of calcium precipitated 4 mol of carbon were consumed. The correlation suggested that temperature changes did not have an important role in directly causing calcite precipitation in those lakes. This view was also supported by Otsuki and Wetzel (1974). Bacteria may also play a similar role in calcium carbonate precipitation (e.g., Lalou, 1957).

Organic matter sinking to the bottom of a lake commonly decays to release CO_2 into the hypolimnion. The CO_2 is eventually carried back to the epilimnion by eddy diffusion (e.g., Li, 1973) or by mass circulation and serves as a major source of carbonate needed for further calcite precipitation. That the source of carbon in lacustrine chalks is largely derived from the breakdown of organic matter is indicated by their negative ^{13}C values, to be discussed later.

Physical–chemical factors

The physical–chemical factors influencing calcite saturation include temperature changes, release or solution of CO_2, and mixing of two different waters. In spite of the biological evidence given above, temperature is undoubtedly an important physical factor, as the solubility of calcite is temperature dependent. An increase of temperature decreases its solubility (Table 2). Warming of seasonal low temperature waters brought up to the surface during spring overturn in some stratified lakes is sufficient to result in their supersaturation. Another aspect of the temperature effect is indirect, but no less important: a temperature increase decreases the dissolved CO_2, or $H_2CO_3^*$. This in turn leads to supersaturation as indicated by Eq. (13).

When the dissolved CO_2 in lake water is not in equilibrium with atmospheric CO_2, physical agitation and aeration by wave action, especially during violent storms, could lead to release of excess CO_2 (Minder, 1926). Although ooliths are uncommon in freshwater lacustrine environments, the role of such wave action is emphasized in the formation of ooliths in marine environments (Ball, 1967).

Mixing of two waters, both of which are saturated or undersaturated with respect to calcium carbonate but which have different pH values, can lead to supersaturation (Wigley and Plummer, 1976). Calcite solubility also increases nonlinearly with increasing ionic strength. Mixing of two different waters may explain the origin of the clouds of white aragonite precipitates bellowing from the mouth of some rivers in Lake Van (Irion, 1973).

A good case for lacustrine calcite precipitation as a sequence of physical changes has been made by Brunskill (1969) in his study of Fayettville Green Lake, New York. He monitored seasonal variations of temperature, pH, alkalinity, total carbon dioxide, and calcium concentration in lake waters and computed the activity product $(Ca^{2+})(CO_3^{2-})$ as a function of water depth and of time. The Green Lake waters have an ionic strength of about 0.06 and appreciable H_2S in the monolimnion. His computations indicated that the waters in the mixolimnion were always supersaturated and there was a three- to fourfold increase of the IAP/ K_c ratio from 2 to 4 in winter months to a maximum of more than 8 during summer. Harvesting of suspended calcite crystals revealed that massive precipitation of calcite in the epilimnion occurred from late May to August at a rate of about 2 g m^{-2} day^{-1}, and that the calcite precipitation and sedimentation were greatly reduced during fall, winter, and early spring. Sediment trap data yielded an annual sedimentation of 300 g of dry matter m^{-2} and 240 g of $CaCO_3$ m^{-2}; the sediments occur as annual couplets resulting from seasonal sedimentation of calcite in summer and deposition of organic matter throughout the year.

Brunskill's study also showed that the calcite precipitates are crystals 7–8 μm long or 2–3 μm Stokes settling diameter; they settled as calculated from the Stoke's Law, at a rate of about 2–4 m/day. Aggregation of the crystals by zooplankton ingestion hastened sedimentation. Some crystal rounding was observed suggesting that dissolution took place during the fall.

The major conclusion reached by Brunskill (1969) is that temperature is the direct factor in the initiation of calcite precipitation in Green Lake, with photosynthesis playing a secondary, and probably a minor, role. Precipitation was a consequence of supersaturation caused by an increase of (CO_3^{2-}), while the calcium activity changed little throughout the season. A decrease of 2 moles of CO_2 occurred in the epilimnion 1 month after the onset of crystal precipitation in May and persisted into October. This is equivalent to precipitation of 230 g of $CaCO_3$ m^{-2} year^{-1} and compares closely to the 240 g m^{-2} year^{-1} figures obtained from sediment-trap data.

Chemistry of other carbonate minerals

Calcite is the dominant carbonate precipitate in fresh- and brackish-water lakes. However, other lacustrine carbonate minerals are known, namely, low magnesian calcite, high magnesian calcite, aragonite, monohydrocalcite $CaCO_3 \cdot H_2O$, dolomite, magnesite, huntite $CaMg_3(CO_3)_4$, nesquehonite $MgCO_3 \cdot 3H_2O$, hydromagnesite $Mg_4(CO_3)_3(OH)_2 \cdot 3H_2O$, siderite $FeCO_3$, manganosiderite, and others (Table 5.).

Magnesian calcite and aragonite

The Mg/Ca ratio in the water appears to control the carbonate phase precipitated in a lake. Most freshwater lakes have Mg/Ca molar ratios well below 3. Müller et al. (1972) found the following generalized empirical relationships:

Mg/Ca	Primary precipitate	Sediments
< 2	Calcite	Calcite
2–12	Mg-calcite, aragonite	Dolomite, Mg-calcite
> 12+	Aragonite	Aragonite

TABLE 5.   Mineralogy of Lacustrine Carbonates

A. Primary precipitates
  Calcite $CaCO_3$
  Mg-calcite $Mg_xCa_{(1-x)}CO_3$
    Low Mg-calcite $x = 0.005$ to 0.07
    High Mg-calcite $x = 0.07$ to 0.3
  Monohydrocalcite $CaCO_3 \cdot H_2O$
  Aragonite $CaCO_3$
B. Diagenetic in sediments
  Dolomite $Ca_{45-55}\,Mg_{55-45}\,(CO_3)_2$
  Huntite[a] $CaMg_3(CO_3)_4$
  Magnesite[a] $MgCO_3$
  Hydromagnesite[a] $Mg_5(OH(CO_3)_2)_2 \cdot 4H_2O$
  Nesquehonite[a] $MgCO_3 \cdot 3H_2O$
C. Origin uncertain
  Siderite $FeCO_3$

[a]These minerals only occur in association with concentrated brines and dessicated lakes.

In many cases Mg/Ca ratios follow rising salinities. One exception is shallow Lake Balaton, Hungary, where Mg-calcite with up to 6–8% $MgCO_3$ precipitates in dilute waters (10^{-2} m/liter, Mg/Ca = 2.4) and aragonite crusts occur on macrophyte leaves (Müller, 1971a).

The role of magnesium in determining crystal shape has been explained in terms of an inhibitor. Magnesium ions appear to act as a selective "surface poison" which tends to inhibit the formation of the calcite lattice structure (e.g., Lippman, 1973; Folk, 1974; Folk and Land, 1975). Aragonite appears unaffected. In waters with very high Mg/Ca ratios the primary precipitate is almost invariably aragonite (Müller *et al.*, 1972).

An alternate explanation suggests that Mg^{2+} ion is incorporated into the initial crystal structure. The equilibrium problem then becomes the solubility of a magnesian calcite rather than pure calcite. With increasing magnesium content, the solubility of calcite rapidly increases until at about 6–8.5 mol% a point is passed where aragonite becomes the stable phase (Berner, 1975). It becomes reasonable to make the arbitrary distinction between low and high magnesium calcites at the point close to aragonite solubility, that is, 7 mol % Mg.

Monohydrocalcite

Monohydrocalcite is a very unstable carbonate which, if precipitated, should rapidly convert to calcite or aragonite (Hull and Turnbull, 1973). Reported occurrences are rare (Stoffers, 1975b; Krumbein, 1975; Sapozhnikov and Isvetkov, 1959; Taylor, 1975). Monohydrocalcite from Lake Kivu (East Africa) occurs as laminae of trigonal bipyramid crystals and spherules sandwiched between thin diatom laminae just above

sapropel layers (Stoffers and Fischbeck, 1974). Presently, Lake Kivu is a stratified, deep lake (400 m) with a Mg/Ca molar ratio of about 30 : 1 in surface waters, 8 : 1 at 200 m, and 4 : 1 near the bottom. Its epilimnion has a high pH of about 9.5, while the hypolimnion is anaerobic with a pH around 7.1. Aragonite is otherwise the dominant carbonate mineral in the sediments. Although subrecent in age, it is believed that monohydrocalcite laminae formed when (1) the Mg/Ca ratio was high, (2) the water temperature was less than 40°C, (3) some inhibitor such as magnesium ion, phosphate ion, or organic compounds hindered calcite and aragonite formation, and (4) waters were supersaturated with respect to monohydrocalcite. A scenario for monohydrocalcite might begin when the lake was stagnant for some period forming a sapropel layer. High CO_2 concentrations dissolved any crystal carbonate rain. Following a circulation event, which also caused an explosive diatom bloom, sudden and high carbonate supersaturation leads to precipitation of monohydrocalcite. The crystal rain survives due to a lack of calcite or aragonite seed crystals and less aggressive bottom waters.

Siderite

Siderite is not uncommon in ancient nonmarine sediments. It is apparently forming diagenetically in the brackish sediments of the Chesepeake Bay (Bricker and Troup, 1975), but, as far as we know, not precipitating in any lakes today. Competition is the main problem. The formation of siderite requires that the sulfide and calcium concentrations are sufficiently low so that the iron is not taken up by the pyrite and that calcium and carbonate is not taken up by calcite. Since siderite is formed in an anaerobic environment where the redox potential is low, a low sulfide concentration requires that the sulfate influx be extremely low. The formation of iron carbonate instead of calcium carbonate requires an Fe/Ca ratio greater than 0.05 (Berner, 1971).

Siderite should be forming in the sediments of Greifensee, Switzerland, where the interstitial waters are believed to reach 10 times the saturation concentrations for siderite (Emerson, 1976), but no siderite has been detected by X-ray diffraction analyses. Siderite-rich mud has been reported from the Late Quaternary deposits of Lake Kivu, Africa (Stoffers, 1975b). Siderite laminae, some possibly primary, and nodules are also present in the Plio-Quaternary sediments of the Black Sea, formed at the time when it was a brackish or fresh-water lake (Ross, Neprochnov, *et al.*, in press). At that time the climate was much warmer than today, rivers were draining a deeply weathered terrain, and they possibly had a higher Fe/Ca ratio than those discharging today.

Dolomite

No unequivocal proof of primary dolomite precipitation has been given for fresh to brackish lakes. Yet dolomite does occur in some lake sediments. Formation of dolomite as a replacement of calcium carbonate in lake sediments requires that the water has an Mg/Ca greater than the equilibrium ratio K_{dz},

$$CaMg(CO_3)_2 + Ca^{2+} = 2CaCO_3(s) + Mg^{2+} \quad (23)$$

$$K_{dz} = \frac{(Mg^{2+})}{(Ca^{2+})}. \quad (24)$$

However, field and experimental studies have indicated that very high magnesium-ion concentration actually inhibited dolomite formation (Hsü, 1967; Müller et al., 1972). Perhaps one should consider, instead of a reaction of ionic substitution, the reaction of calcite with Mg^{2+} and H_2CO_3.

$$CaMg(CO_3)_{2(s)} = CaCO_3 + Mg^{2+} + CO_3^{2-}$$
$$\log K_{s0} = -16.7 \quad (25)$$

$$CO_3^{2-} + 2H^+ = H_2CO_3^*$$
$$-\log (K_1 K_2) = +16.6 \quad (26)$$

$$CaMg(CO_3)_{2(s)} + 2H^+ = CaCO_{3(s)} + Mg^{2+} + H_2CO_3$$
$$\log K = -0.1 \quad (27)$$

$$K = \frac{(Mg^{2+})(H_2CO_3^*)}{(H^+)^2} \quad (28)$$

Eq. (28) illustrates the importance of the pH. An increase of the $(H_2CO_3^*)/(H^+)^2$ ratio should shift the equilibrium toward dolomite formation. The relations of carbonate equilibria require that

$$\frac{(H_2CO_3^*)}{(H^+)^2} = \frac{(CO_3^{2-})}{K_1 K_2}. \quad (29)$$

It follows therefore that an increase of (CO_3^{2-}) might favor dolomite formation. This conclusion is in agreement with the general observation that dolomite occurs in high pH and alkaline lakes (Müller et al., 1972; Eugster and Hardie, Chap. 8, this volume). The reaction kinetics is still poorly understood; one requirement seems to be the presence of initial Mg-calcite.

Lacustrine dolomites, commonly calcium rich, are present in Quaternary deposits, but these were formed mainly when a lake was saline or desiccated (West Texas Playa, Deep Springs Lake, Great Salt Lake).

Folk and Land (1975) suggest that dolomite can form in freshwaters with an Mg/Ca ratio as low as 1 : 1, providing crystallization rates are sufficiently slow to allow ordering. Müller (1970) reported protodolomite in the clay fraction of sediments of Lake Balaton, Hungary (Mg/Ca = 2) and Neusiedler See (Müller et al., 1972). Possibly it formed during an earlier drier stage. The presence of dolomite in sediments of ancient brackish lakes is not uncommon (Green River, Black Sea). The association of dolomite with trona, and other alkaline-carbonate minerals in the Green

River formation, suggests that dolomite might replace calcite deposition as the lake water becomes increasingly alkaline. Whether the lacustrine dolomite was a primary precipitate or was formed diagenetically is a problem not yet resolved.

Other magnesian carbonates

Huntite, nesquehonite, and magnesite are common as secondary minerals mainly in saline playa deposits, although their genesis is not well known. High Mg/Ca ratios and high Mg concentrations are necessary (Müller et al., 1972).

Case history of Lake Zurich calcite deposition

Lake Zurich, as a model, well illustrates many aspects of chalk formation in deep lacustrine basins. The lake is relatively deep (142 m) with a narrow littoral zone. It is located in a glaciated valley which drains a carbonate terrain. Systematic limnological studies since the 1880s provide a wealth of historical data (e.g., Nipkow, 1927; Minder, 1943; Thomas, 1969; Zimmermann, 1961; Zimmermann, 1975). The presence of nonglacial varves in Lake Zurich is well known and has long been cited as a modern analogy for ancient laminated lacustrine chalks (e.g., Bradley, 1929, 1937, 1948; Brunskill, 1969; Calvert, 1966; Welten, 1944; Anderson and Kirkland, 1960).

Geographic settings

Lake Zurich is located in a humid, temperate region, and has an elevation of 406 m above sea level (Figure 5). The main tributary is the Linth, which delivers an average inflow of 38 m³/sec, or more than half of the total discharge (Table 6). Prior to the construction of the Linth Canal the bulk of the detritus carried down by the Linth was left behind on its alluvial plain before it emptied into the Obersee. Now the Linth sediments are deposited mainly in the Lake of Walenstadt; the Linth water flowing out of that lake has a suspended-matter content of less than 4 mg/liter. A second major tributary is the Jona which forms a delta in the Obersee basin near Rapperswil. The Lake of Walenstadt and the Obersee have been such excellent sediments traps, that most coarser terrigenous detritus to Lake Zurich was fed mainly by high-gradient creeks draining steep side valleys of the lake. During the last 100 years, detrital input into the Lake Zurich was further curtailed after a series of small dams were built on those creeks for the sake of flood prevention. This peculiar geographical framework of Lake Zurich sets

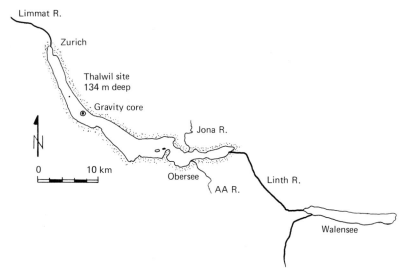

FIGURE 5.   Index map of Lake Zurich, Obersee Basin, Lake of Walenstadt, and environs.

the stage for recent chemical sedimentation. Lake Zurich is now eutrophic and meromictic. The lake water turns over annually in spring, mixing water down to 100 to 120 m. The pycnocline depth varies from a few meters to 30 m above bottom. The temperature below the thermocline is very constant and has remained at about 4°C at least during the last 75 years. The surface temperature varies greatly from about 0°C in deep winter to over 22°C in high summer (Figure 6). These annual temperature variations, as we shall discuss later, may be important for the precipitation of lacustrine chalks.

Holocene sedimentary history

The Lake Zurich basin was excavated in the Molasse formations of the Swiss Plateau. Seismic investigations revealed that Quaternary infill has a maximum

TABLE 6.   Some Physical Parameters for Lake Zurich[a]

Lake Zurich	47°11′ to 47°22′ N/8°36′ to 8°49′ E
Elevation	406 m above sealevel (mSL)
Surface area (SA)	88 km² (67.3 km²)
Volume (V)	3.9 km³ (3.4 km³)
Discharge (D)	2813 m³ × 10⁶ yr⁻¹
Linth inflow	38 m³ sec⁻¹, 2400 m³ × 10⁶ yr⁻¹
Residence (D/V)	1.5 to 3 years
Maximum depth	137 m
Average depth	44 m
Temperature epilimnion	0 to 22°C
Temperature hypolimnion	4 to 6°C
Eddy diffusion	0.1 to 1.0 cm² sec⁻¹

[a]Volume and area given in parentheses refer to the part of the lake excluding the Obersee behind the Hurden barrier. Eddy diffusion coefficient from Li (1973).

thickness of about 300 m (Finckh and Kelts, 1976). Piston cores taken from the deep part in the lake basin sampled laminated sediments of the Bölling Stage (13,300 years) at about 10 m, indicating that the bulk of the lake sediments are pre-Holocene in age.

The postglacial sediment stratigraphy of Lake Zurich can be divided into five units from the top down: (A) nonglacial varves (10–50 cm), (B) marls (100–300 cm), (C) chalk (200–1200 cm), (D) black sulfide mud (10–300 cm), and (E) glacial-lacustrine muds (300–1500 cm).

It is noteworthy that shortly after the rapid retreat of glaciers from the lowlands, detrital calcareous, moraine-derived sediments suddenly give way to a basin-wide pure chalk layer 2–12 m thick. There is a close positive correlation between calcite content in the sediments and warm, dry, climatic trends, particularly around 10,000 to 5,000 years ago. Conditions favorable to chemical sedimentation have been recurrent, but nonglacial varve formation is most prominent in the latest epoch of chalk deposition (Züllig, 1956; Thompson and Kelts, 1974).

Nonglacial varves: descriptions

Nonglacial varves form the sediments in profundal areas since 1885. These sediments, as shown by the photograph of a recent gravity core (Figure 7), have a rhythmic sequence of dark and light laminations. The core is in a slightly oxidized state some 2 hr after it was cut open. When a core is freshly cut the surface is coal-black to dark gray. The partial oxidation of unstable iron sulfides reveals the laminated appearance.

The term varve was originally introduced by De Geer (1912) to describe annual couplets resulting from seasonal variations of detrital input from melting gla-

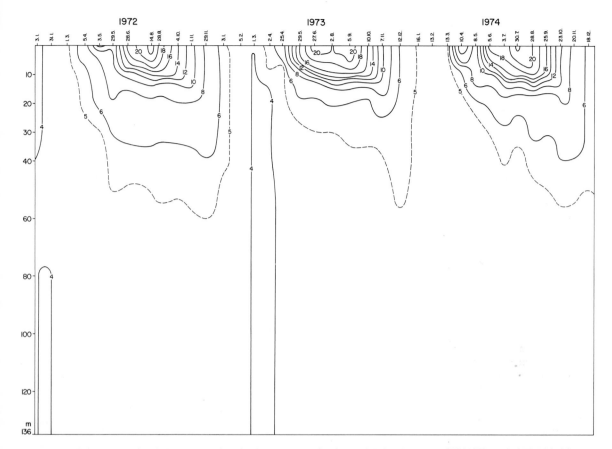

FIGURE 6.   Temperature isopleths measured at the deepest part of Lake Zurich for the years 1972, 1973, and 1975. Monthly measurements noted along top axis. In degrees centigrade.

ciers. The laminated sediments of Lake Zurich sediments are not detritus derived from melting glaciers, but they form annual couplets. Nipkow (1920, 1927) proved the annual nature of these varves by comparing detailed stratigraphy with well-dated records of species blooms and their annual succession in the water column (see also Stumm and Morgan, 1970, p. 412).

The core as shown by Figure 7 contains a continuous record of events from about 1885 to 1965. The chronologic divisions of this core are based on a correlation with Nipkow's core. A counting of varve couplets after 1920 has confirmed their annual layering. Macroscopically, the following zones show well-developed couplets: I, 0–138 mm; II, 149–213 mm; III, 238–243 mm; and IV, 266–288 mm. The average couplet is about 3–4 mm; the water content of this core varies from 70 to 90%, and the bulk organic content varies from 3 to 6% of dry weight. From 1900 onward there has been a trend for the white calcareous bands to increase and the dark (organic plus diatom) laminae to diminish in thickness. The basic pattern is interrupted by four fine-grained, light-gray luttitic turbidite horizons with the designations: A, 138–149 mm; A2, 168–173 mm; B, 214–238 mm; and C, 244–266 mm.

These are deposits from near shore slumps in the years 1908, 1906, 1900, and 1898, respectively. These turbidite layers thicken toward the central part of the basin and form good long-distance marker horizons. In addition to these chronostratigraphical horizons, the layer M denotes a characteristic greenish black, flocculated mass comprising almost solely frustules of the diatom species, *Melosira islandica helvetica*. This cold-water diatom experienced its last population explosion in the late winter to early spring of 1906 and then rapidly waned. Other diatoms, typical in this core, include *Synedra*, *Stephanodiscus*, *Cyclotella*, *Fragilaria*, and *Tabularia*.

The thickness of calcite layers shows an imperfect correlation with climate. The thick laminae of the 1921 summer were formed during one of the hottest, driest summers on record, when extensive "whitings" were observed in the lake (Minder, 1926). On the other hand, we found no correlation between peak years of plankton production and varve thickness, although most organic remains are not peserved in the sediment record. Using the calcite/dolomite ratios from X-ray mineralogy, it is apparent that even the pure white layers may contain up to 10% detrital calcite (see Table 7).

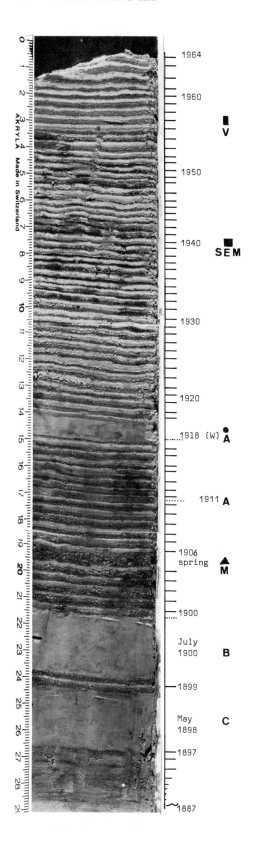

Varve cycles

In general a varve consists of three main parts (Figure 8). Cyclic sedimentation begins with (I) an anastomosed mesh of organic sludge containing algal threads, iron-sulfide pigments, a sprinkling of clay-size detrital minerals, as well as some calcite and diatoms. This is followed by (II) a lacy framework of diatom frustules plus some mineral detritus and organic threads. Cold water species dominate. Higher up, in a transition zone, large calcite polyhedra (up to 30 μm) suddenly set in, mixed with diatom frustules. The diatom predominance gives way across this diffuse boundary to a zone (III) of moderately pure calcite and only scattered frustules which are derived in part from species different from those in zone (II). Within the calcite layer the grain-size mode rapidly decreases from 8 to 16 μm to less than 2 to 4 μm. The cycle ends with a sharp contact with the next zone of organic sludge, which may include some fine-grained calcite near its base. A similar microtextural succession, similar to a typical cycle shown in Figure 8, has also been reported in subrecent varves from other lakes (e.g., Schleinsee, Germany, Geyh *et al.*, 1971).

The sedimentary cycle corresponds well to seasonal variations of biological and physical parameters in the epilimnion of Lake Zurich.

Close examination of some of the couplets with the aid of X-ray radiography (Figure 9) reveals a finely laminated microstructure within the couplet. As many as eight microlaminations have been identified in the varve of 1923. These dark microlaminae are diatom rich and they resulted from discrete diatom blooms of that year (Nipkow, 1927).

Microtextures of varved sediments

The microtextures of varved sediments are illustrated by a scanning electron microscope (SEM) photograph of varve couplets (Figure 10). Specimens are prepared by scraping a tiny chip from each laminae on a dried core section. Note that the micrographs are reproduced at the same scale. At the beginning of each cycle is the dark autumn–winter layer. The frustules of the diatom species *Stephanodiscus* and irregular to platy organic matter are the predominant sediments. Most of the decaying organic matter consists of algal threads of *Oscillatoria*. Some fine-grained calcite is present (2–5 μm). Scattered sheetlaths may be mica

FIGURE 7.   Short gravity core taken from the central plain of Lake Zurich (see Figure 5) near Nipkow's (1920) original site. 134 m water depth. Light layers, calcite rich; dark layers, diatom and organic rich. Location of couplet in Figure 10 given as SEM. A, A-2, B, and C are fine-grained redeposited shoreline sediment layers. M is a *Melosira* bloom in winter 1905/6. See Table 9 for composition.

TABLE 7. Mineral Composition of Lake Zurich Varves and Index Layers from X-ray Diffraction Data[a]

Sample	CC*	QTZ*	DOL*	CLY*	FEL*	AMORPH*	cc/dol*	Ill/K+CH*	PL/K-f*
Varve-8 light	70	7	6	5	5	(11)	12:1	1.5	1.5
Varve-8 dark	69	13	6	6	6	(9)	12.	2.0	2.0
A	50	15	16	7	12	(2)	3	1.1	1.0
A-2	44	18	12	9	15	(2)	3.6	0.9	0.9
M Melosira bloom	43	13	15	8	16	(15)	2.9	1.25	2.1
M-5 Varve	58	14	10	6	10	(5)	5.8	0.8	2.1
B	45	15	13	16	11	(1)	3.4	0.8	4.0
C	41	13	21	15	10	(1)	2.0	0.9	2.2
C-1 Varve	55	17	15	6	8	(1)	3.6	1.0	3.0
S-1* Sand-H (352 mm)	35	13	14	12	23	—	2.5	1.1	6.8
BS* Brown silt (540)	24	15	28	8	24	—	0.8	1.1	2.3
SM* Marl (475 mm)	29	15	25	8	21	—	1.2	1.0	1.7
GL* Green layer (421)	51	14	15	4	15	—	3.3	0.9	2.0

[a]Samples marked with an asterisk are from deeper layers than are visible in Figure 7, other layers marked on the photo. Results from fine-grained powder mounts were converted to semiquantitative percentages using the following intensity absorption factors for peaks (degree 2θ); calcite (CC, 29.4°), 1.65×; quartz(QTZ, 27.6°), 1.00×; dolomite(DOL, 30°), 1.53×; clay (kaolinite + chlorite + illite), 1.00×; feldspars (FEL = Plagioclase, 2.80×, +K-feldspar, 4.0×). Amorphous components are mainly diatom frustules estimated from background swell around 20°.

minerals. Higher above are allochthonous lutitic sediments slumped from nearshore areas. The sample shows a mixture of fine-grained inorganic matter with a few scattered diatom frustules. Still higher up are the spring sediments from the transition zone between dark and light laminae. They include large diatoms, some fine-grained organic and detrital minerals, and a few scattered calcite grains. Finally, at the base of the light calcite layer, large calcite crystals appear (15–20 μm) predominantly accompanied by a few frustules from a changed diatom flora. The calcite crystals are not perfect rhombs but typically stubby, equant, or blocky polyhedra with some well-developed faces and a porous layer-cake structure (see detail Figure 11).

Nonglacial varves: interpretations

We examined the annual succession of events in the water column of Lake Zurich in order to interpret the genesis of the nonglacial varves on its bottom. The understanding of the genesis and preservation of the calcite sediments in Lake Zurich helps to develop criteria for recognizing ancient lacustrine chalk deposits of similar origin. Surprisingly, in spite of large size variations, components in the sediment reflect their respective position in an annual succession.

Preservation of an annual cycle in the sediments requires a delicate balance. Annual layering is not found in all eutrophic lakes with anaerobic bottom conditions. Four main criteria must be satisfied.

(1) Processes in the epilimnion produce a flux of seasonally differentiated particulate matter which settles through a stagnant, stratified water mass.

(2) No bottom dwellers are present to homogenize the sediment. Usually, this is due to anoxic conditions and toxicity of sulfides.

(3) Bottom current activity is minimal or absent, and excessive detrital inflow does not overprint or dilute the seasonal cycle.

(4) Degradation of organic matter does not produce excessive gas bubbles.

In Lake Zurich varved sedimentation is present throughout relatively flat areas below 50 m depth. On slopes, varves are destroyed by slow creep of the

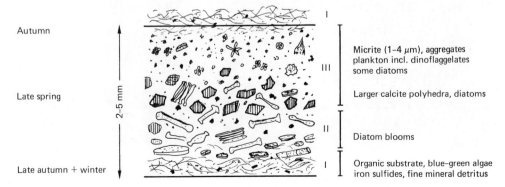

FIGURE 8. Schematic representation of a typical nonglacial varve. Units I and part of II form the dark part, Unit III the light.

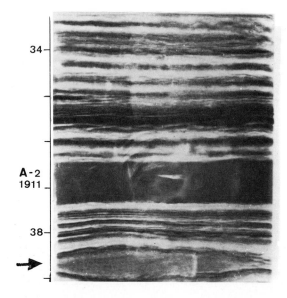

FIGURE 9.   Radiograph of a portion of a Lake Zurich short gravity core covering the time span 1907 to 1920. Scale on the left in cm. Layer A-2, 1911, is a lutite layer of redeposited shoreline sediment. The arrow indicates cross-bedding due to current reworking of pelagic sediments. Other layers are nonglacial varve laminations. Note that due to the X-ray absorption characteristics calcite layers are black and organic and diatom layers appear white. Microlaminations are clearly visible in several couplets.

FIGURE 10.   Scanning electron micrograph (SEM) of a varve couplet from 1941 illustrating the textural variations within a yearly cycle. Note that all are at the same scale (bar = 20 μm). (a) Transition layer, dark. (b) White, late spring. Large, blocky calcite crystals and diatom frustules. (c) Late autumn with *Stephanodiscus* frustules and fine white calcareous specks. (d) For comparison, a sample of nearshore, redeposited lutite layer (A).

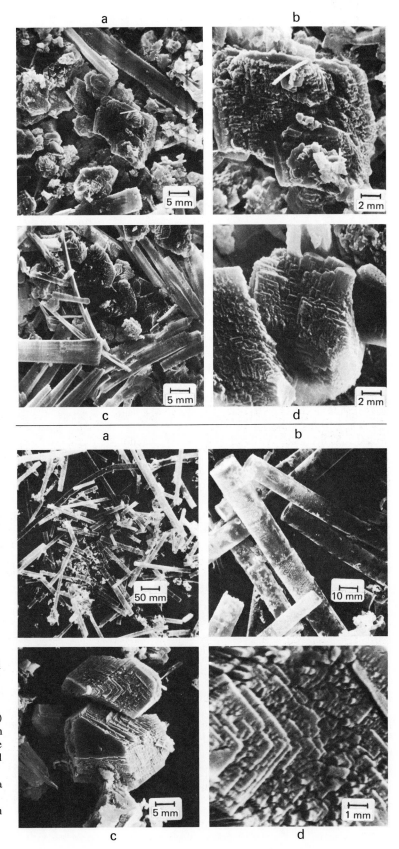

FIGURE 11.   Top. Detail of individual calcite crystals. (a) and (b) From white summer layer of 1950, delicate differential surface etching features. (c) and (d) Blocky polyhedra along with frustules from spring 1950. Note the preservation of some crystal faces. Bottom. (a) and (b) Frustules of *Melosira islandica helv.* from winter–spring bloom 1905/6. This massive monospecific laminae is not accompanied by any significant calcite precipitate. (c) and (d) Calcite crystals, polyhedra, from a 1901 varve. Note surface etching and differential dissolution fluting features on the grain. All samples were freeze-dried before SEM studies.

gelatinous, fragile mass. Bottom fauna is severely restricted in spite of short-term annual overturn which may carry up to 2 mg/liter of oxygen down to depths below 110 m. Possibly, a stable toxic boundary layer exists above the sediment–water interface below 50 m. Gases in lake sediments pose a special problem: in nearby Lake Greifensee, where eutrophic and anaerobic conditions are more intense than in Lake Zurich, varves are poorly developed. However, CO_2, CH_4, and H_2S bubbles escaping from highly reducing sediments contribute to the destruction of delicate layering.

Chemistry of Lake Zurich waters

Chemical analyses of the Lake Zurich waters have been carried out by the Chemical Laboratory of the City of Zurich Water Agency for many years. The results for the years 1948–57 were published (Zimmermann, 1961), and the more recent data are routinely compiled by the Agency. Stumm and Stumm-Zollinger (1968) computed the values of the activity ratio $(Ca^{2+})(HCO_3^-)/(CO_2)$ of the waters on the basis of Zimmermann's averaged data and compared their calculated results with the equilibrium ratio; they found that the Lake Zurich waters were undersaturated at temperatures of 10°C or less and were supersaturated at temperatures of 15°C or more. The water was near saturation in the temperature range of 10–15°C. Selected analytical data for the year 1975 are included in Table 8; these were some of the days when calcite precipitates were collected. The values of activity ratio were calculated, using the approach discussed in a previous section. Several salient features of the chemical results are:

(1) The near surface water (at 5 m) was supersaturated throughout the year. The supersaturation increased from 1.26 times the equilibrium value on April 9 to a maximum of 11 times on June 11.

(2) The bottom water (at 130 m) was undersaturated throughout the year. The degree of undersaturation did not vary very greatly, except that the water was definitely more undersaturated during the months of June and July.

(3) The most remarkable change of surface-water chemistry was the increase of pH from a low 7.91 on April 9 to 8.85 on June 11. This almost 10-fold decrease of hydrogen-ion activity accompanied a 13-fold increase of supersaturation during the same period.

(4) The pH values (7.42–7.62) of the bottom waters stayed fairly constant throughout the year, with a minimum pH (7.43–7.45) during the June and July period of maximum undersaturation.

(5) The calcium concentration of the surface waters varies slightly during the year (2.0–2.5 meq/liter) and a 10–20% calcium depletion during the summer months of calcite precipitation was detected.

(6) The calcium concentration (2.4–2.5 meq/liter) of the bottom water was practically constant throughout the year.

(7) The magnesium content of the lake waters was low: Mg/Ca mole ratio = 0.25.

(8) The alkalinity of the surface waters was appreciably higher (2.5 meq/liter) during the winter and early spring, decreased steadily during the summer, and reached a minimum of 1.94 in August, before rising again to 2.06 in September.

(9) The alkalinity of the bottom waters was practically constant (2.50–2.64 meq/liter) throughout the year, the slight maximum (2.64 meq/liter) being detected during early July.

(10) The dissolved CO_2 of the near surface waters was always comparatively low, the highest content on April 9 being only 0.07 meq/liter.

TABLE 8.   Selected Major Ion and Geochemical Data Used to Estimate the Calcite Saturation Ranges for Days on Which Suspended Calcite Samples Were Collected in 1975 [a]

		12 February		9 April		6 May		11 June		2 July		30 July		27 August		25 September	
		5 m	130 m	5 m	130 m	5 m	130 m	5 m	130 m	5 m	130 m	5 m	130 m	5 m	130 m	5 m	130 m
T(°C)		5.1	4.4	4.9	4.5	11.4	4.4	15.8	4.4	16.5	4.4	19.9	4.4	18.7	4.4	17.8	4.4
pH		8.07	7.54	7.91	7.53	8.7	7.62	8.85	7.52	8.74	7.43	8.73	7.45	8.54	7.62	8.75	7.4
CO_2	meq/liter	0.03	0.12	0.07	0.18	0.0	0.15	0.0	0.32	0.0	0.20	0.0	0.25	0.0	0.28	0.0	0.3
Ca^{2+}	meq/liter	2.4	2.4	(2.4)	(2.4)	(2.4)	(2.4)	(2.2)	(2.5)	2.2	2.6	2.0	2.4	(2.0)	(2.4)	(2.4)	(2.4)
Mg^{2+}	meq/liter	0.4	0.4	(0.4)	(0.4)	(0.4)	(0.4)	(0.4)	(0.4)	0.3	0.3	0.4	0.4	(0.4)	(0.4)	(0.4)	(0.4)
Alk	meq/liter	2.50	2.54	2.50	2.54	2.40	2.58	2.40	2.58	2.22	2.64	2.08	2.56	1.94	2.56	2.06	2.60
PO_4-P	10^{-3} meq/liter	67	.127	75	146	31	139	4	151	2	179	1	171	1	178	1	249
NO_3^-	meq/liter	0.05	0.053	0.053	0.053	0.021	0.052	0.024	0.056	0.027	0.061	0.022	0.060	0.022	0.058	0.021	0.04
Cl^-	meq/liter	0.122	0.099	0.087	0.082	0.127	0.111	0.071	0.082	0.068	0.093	0.048	0.076	0.054	0.090	0.048	0.08
O_2	mg/liter	11.1	5.1	9.6	4.0	13.4	5.3	13.6	4.1	11.3	1.1	12.5	3.6	9.5	3.5	11.5	0.8
Saturation index $CaCO_3$ (IAP/K_c):		1.61	0.54	1.24	0.55	8.9	0.59	11.00	0.46	7.86	0.38	7.92	0.39	4.76	0.58	9.8	0.35

[a] Courtesy of Dr. U. Zimmermann of the City of Zurich Water Agency. Saturation parameters were calculated for an ionic strength of $I = 5 \times 10^{-3}\ M$ mole/liter and the activity coefficients:

$\gamma Ca^{2+} = 0.79$ (5°C), 0.74 (20°C)
$\gamma HCO_3^- = 0.93$ (5°, 20°C)

Analytical values for calcium used in calculations on days with poor control are given in parentheses.

FIGURE 12.   Calcite precipitate from 1955 varve viewed under crossed-nicols. Bar scale is 4 μm.

(11) The dissolved CO_2 of the bottom waters was always higher and varied considerably from a low of 0.12 meq/liter in February to a high of 0.32 meq/liter in June.

(12) The bottom temperature at 130m remained constant at 4.4°C, while the near surface temperature increased from 4.9°C on April 9 to 11.4°C on May 6, to a maximum of 19.9°C on July 30.

Suspensoids in Lake Zurich waters

Calcite was found in most samples of suspended material. Figure 13 outlines the annual development of the biomass in similar samples. Although no quantitative measurements were made, visual estimates indicated that the greatest amount of calcite grains was harvested during the late spring and the summer months, at times of most active calcite production. Mineralogically, all are pure calcite, devoid of magnesium in solid solution. Optically, filtrate samples include some grain aggregates in apparent optical continuity. Commonly, the crystals are subhedral and show rhombic or polyhedral faces (Figure 12). Twinning is rare.

The February to April samples contained no positively identifiable calcite precipitate and very little other suspended matter. One deep-water (134-m) sample taken in mid-March harvested mass diatom frustules but no calcite. *Stephanodiscus* species dominated the early spring diatom production shortly after the overturn of the lake waters (Figure 14).

The May 6th sample harvested an appreciable amount of large subhedral blocky crystals, signifying that the annual calcite production had begun. The crystals are rhombic or polyhedral in shape, but they have a very porous and imperfect structure resulting in a very large surface area per unit volume. Sheet-like calcite units are bound together haphazardly into a optically continuous layer-cake structure. The layered appearance suggests growth in a turbulent fluid medium similar to that of hailstones. In rare instances, molds of organic remains were observed (Figure 15).

In June and July, porous aggregates of smaller calcite crystals are predominant (Figure 16). In one case, we found large well-formed polyhedral crystals which nucleate around diatom frustules. Figure 17 shows, for example, the different development of calcite crystal faces growing around a Synedra frustule in the June 2 sample from the epilimnion. Samples from late August (15 m, 16°C) mainly contained aggregates of tiny polyhedral crystals. Individual particles are 0.5 to 1 μm

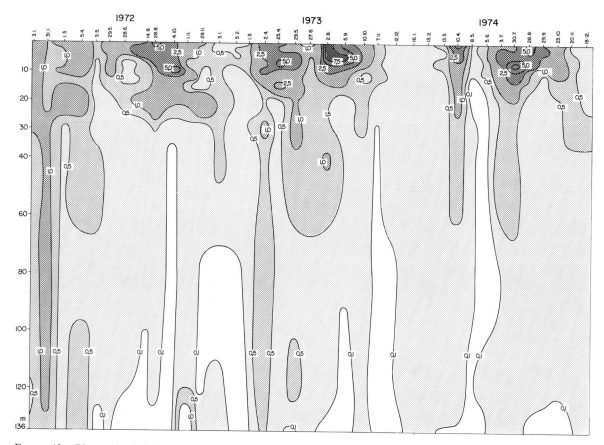

FIGURE 13.   Biomass isopleth diagram for the years 1972, 1973, and 1974 from the deepest part of lake Zurich. Values given in mg/liter weight of wet phytoplankton samples. (Zimmermann, 1975, courtesy of the City of Zurich Water Agency).

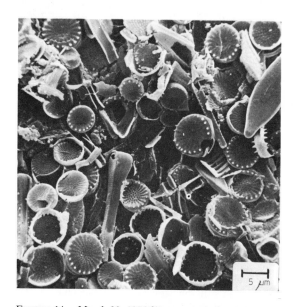

FIGURE 14.   March 22, 1975 filtrate sample from 130 m water depth. Diatom frustules without calcite precipitate comprising mainly *Stephanodiscus* pill boxes with scattered *Navicula* and *Diatoma*.

cristallites. They appear to be point-welded into aggregates up to 30 μm in size (Figure 18). Grains of those aggregates show no optical continuity and they disintegrate easily during ultrasonic treatment. The aggregates form micritic sediments most similar to those which constitute the bulk of fossil lacustrine chalk. In addition to those tiny crystals a few sphaeroid tests of a calcareous phytoplankton *(Phacotus lenticularis)* are present (Figure 3).

In addition to those precipitates formed in the open waters of the lake, calcite crystals were produced on nearshore macrophytes. Those calcareous coatings tend to have poorly developed crystal form and extraordinarily fine-grained sizes of less than 1 μm (see also Gyger *et al.,* 1976). The precipitation of such tiny crystals appears to be typical of the microenvironment in the vicinity of plants where sudden increases in calcite supersaturation during photosynthesis are possible.

The morphology of calcite crystals may give a clue as to their genesis. A misconception is that calcite precipitated in fresh waters should form perfect rhombs. Some irregular rhombs have been harvested but most are polyhedral crystals. Possibly calcite morphology is controlled by its rate of crystallization and

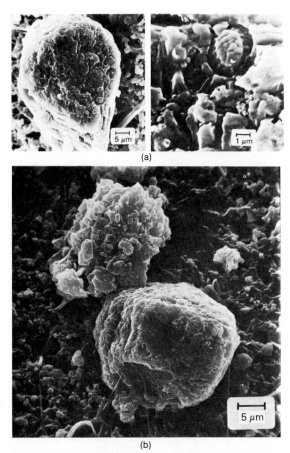

(a)

(b)

FIGURE 15.   Large initial calcite precipitate from May 16, 1975, 5 m depth. (a) Overview of grain with layer-cake texture. (b) Detail of surface irregularity.

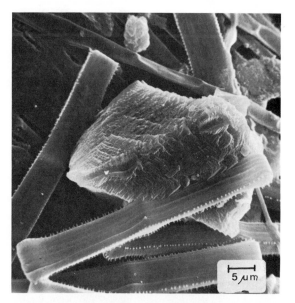

FIGURE 17.   (a) Rare example of a calcite crystal growth attached to a diatom frustule *(Diatoma elongata)*. (b) Detail of the surface texture showing step-like growth features. Sample filtered from 5 m water depth, June 20, 1975.

FIGURE 16.   Irregular calcite crystal aggregates (June 20, 1975, 5 m water depth).

by the chemical composition of the water (cf. Folk, 1974), for it is well known that magnesium may act as a surface inhibitor hindering the growth of some crystal faces. According to a model advanced by Folk (1974), rapid crystallization favors the formation of micritic crystals (2–4 μm or finer). Lakes with low salinities and low Mg/Ca ratios should produce polyhedra, rhombohedra or hexagonal crystals with basal pinocoids. Crystals larger than 10 μm are mostly polyhedral (cf. Davoud, 1976). In magnesium-rich waters, more prismatic crystals of magnesian calcite are pre-

316   K. Kelts and K. J. Hsü

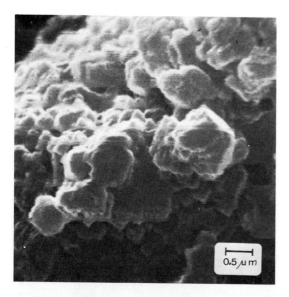

FIGURE 18.   Calcite micrite aggregates typical of filtrate samples (August 28, 1975, 15 m water depth). Note the presence of some well-developed faces on these tiny, polyhedral grains.

cipitated. Our observations of the harvested calcite are in general accord with this model. Tiny crystals were probably formed very rapidly at a time of great supersaturation. Flat and blocky calcite crystals are also common, as the lake waters are low in magnesium. The loose layer-cake structure of imperfect grains may have resulted from rapid growth in the absence of Mg-poisoning. Crystals larger than 10 μm are also predominantly polyhedral. However, we did observe many hexagonal platelets. As a result of the open structures, in layer-cake or sloppy brickwork fashion, surface areas of the chalk particles far exceed their nominal size. For example, particle grain size predicted from surface area measurements in Lake Zurich chalk beds ranged from 0.01 to 0.1 μm (Gyger *et al.*, 1976).

Dissolution of precipitates during settling

Examinations by scanning electron microscope show evidence of dissolution of calcite crystals, as they fall through the undersaturated hypolimnion. Samples harvested from 70 m depth include some platelets which appear somewhat more ragged or more lacy than those from the surface waters. This same tendency is even more pronounced in samples harvested from 130 m depth, especially in the case of smaller crystals (Figure 19). Some rounding of the outline of the platelets has taken place, and edges of small microlites have been trimmed off. Surface etching features are not uncommon; the etching emphasizes the tabular pinacoid structure of many etched crystals. A visual estimate based upon those observations sug-

gests that some 10% of a crystal is dissolved as it falls through the water column. The slight enrichment of calcium concentration in the bottom waters, during the calcite production season, is related to such dissolution. The chemical and visual data both indicate that most calcite crystals probably survive the fall through undersaturated waters to the bottom due to slowed dissolution kinetics.

Deposition of precipitates

A comparison of the harvested calcite precipitates and the sedimentary particles in well-defined seasonal par-

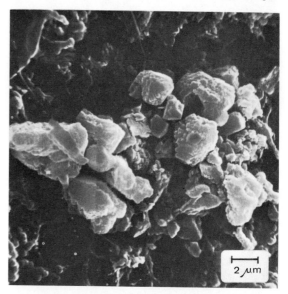

FIGURE 19.   Filtrate sample from 130 m water depth on August 28, 1975 illustrating dissolution features on fine calcite grains. Etching occurs preferentially along certain lattice plains highlighting the layered crystal structure.

TABLE 9.   Settling Rates of Calcite Particles[a]

Stokes diameter $2r$ (μm = 10^{-4} cm)	Settling velocity U_s (cm/sec)	Daily fall distance (m)	Residence time in 110-m-thick hypolimnion (days)
2	0.0003	0.25	440
4	0.0015	1.29	85
8	0.006	5.18	21
16	0.024	20	5
32	0.095	82	1.5

Agal settling rate estimates[b]

Species	Rate (m/day)
Fragilaria crotonensis	7–20
Tabularia fenestrata	11–30
Stephanodiscus hantzschii	1–9
Cyclotella	1–6
Phacotus lenticularis	1–5

[a]Sedimentation of calcite grains is calculated according to a stoke's equivalent diameter. Ranges of settling rates for diatoms and *Phacotus* are based on the observed shifts in an individual species isopleth.
[b]From Bloesch (1974).

ticles of varve couplets indicates that calcite precipitates formed during the various different stages have reached the bottom, with only a moderate time lag with respect to precipitation. It seems surprising as many of the calcite grains are less than 1 or 2 μm in size. Such particles can be held in a turbulent epilimnion indefinitely if currents with a vertically upward component velocity of only 0.085 cm/sec are present. Effects of viscosity or density changes and the exit of a particle from the epilimnion were discussed by Lerman *et al.* (1974).

Our observations confirm the theoretical deduction that the fall of the very fine particles has been hastened because of their aggregation, either as fecal pellets or due to flocculation. Other mechanisms, such as eddy diffusion (e.g., Li, 1973) and possible vertical density currents (Bradley, 1965) are apparently of less importance. Once a particle or an aggregate reaches the quiet hypolimnion, its settling velocity is controlled by gravity. The different settling velocities for particles of various sizes could explain grain sizes in a varve couplet. However, the results of our harvesting experiments have shown that the gradation could also be caused by seasonal difference in production.

In early May, the water was not greatly supersaturated, and the condition favored the slow and regular growth of calcite, nucleated around relatively few available seeding crystals. Later in the season supersaturation increased, the temperature also increased, and rapid nucleation at many seeding centers could produce many uniformly small and imperfect crystals. Large and small grains all seem to have settled fairly soon after their formation, and their position in the

varve couplet reflects more the chronological sequence of their production and less the difference in their settling velocity.

Diatom frustules also seem to have settled fairly rapidly after their production, despite their low bulk density and their high form resistance (Table 9).

Genetic interpretation of calcite production and deposition

The chemical data show that the Lake Zurich surface waters are slightly supersaturated during the winter, and the supersaturation decreases after the spring overturn, when undersaturated bottom waters were brought up to the surface and when the chemistry of the epilimnion and hypolimnion becomes similar. The saturation reached a maximum in early June. The rather rapid increase in the degree of supersaturation corresponded mainly to an increase of the pH, which in turn is caused by the decrease of dissolved CO_2 in surface waters.

Minder (1926) related supersaturation to the phytoplankton activity; Stumm and Stumm-Zollinger (1968) attributed increasing algal photosynthesis as the cause of raising the pH. Phytoplankton growth is distributed throughout the year. Although the total biomass does not show extreme variations, peaks occur. Blue-green algae are dominant in the winter spectrum and low in summer. In 1975 diatoms bloomed mainly in March and April when spring overturn brought up nutrients and when calcite saturation was at its minimum. The maximum biomass peak tends to fall in late summer when green algae, pyrophytes, and zooplankton flourish. The supersaturation maximum does not correlate directly with a biomass maximum but occurs shortly after the April–May diatom peak.

Monitoring the photosynthetic activity in other lakes suggests that planktonic photosynthesis also plays an active role in raising supersaturation and causing calcite precipitation (Megard, 1968; Otsuki and Wetzel, 1974). Material balance considerations suggested that calcite precipitation in Lake Biel, Switzerland, was mainly attributed to the assimilation of dissolved CO_2 by algal photosynthesis (Santschi, 1975). However, a significant amount of CO_2 was unaccounted for and was believed to be lost to the atmosphere. The plant intake is eventually released after death, sedimentation, and decay, which also released dissolved CO_2 to the hypolimnion. Biogenic CO_2, transported by eddy diffusion and during the annual overturn to the surface, is again in part assimilated by photosynthesis and in part precipitated as calcite. Our isotopic analyses of Lake Zurich chalk showed a significantly high negative ^{13}C value, between -4 and $-5\%_o$, indicating the existence of a large component of biogenically recycled carbon in the calcite (cf. Stiller and Magaritz, 1974).

The increased supersaturation can also be related to physical factors such as temperature increases. Brunskill (1969), in his study of Green Lake, found only moderate evidence of CO_2 uptake by algae; he believed that the dissolved CO_2 was largely lost to the atmosphere as a consequence of temperature changes. We do not know if the situation at Lake Zurich is comparable to that of Green Lake. However, the importance of temperature changes is evident if we note that when the April deep waters circulate to the surface, the saturation index can change from 0.55 to 1.24 merely because of the shift of $CaCO_3$ and CO_2 solubilities caused by a temperature rise from 4 to 20°C.

Although the lake surface waters were apparently always supersaturated, calcite precipitation began in May (in 1975). Earlier occurrences, in April, have been reported in some years (Minder, 1926). The onset of precipitation corresponds to the steep climb of the degree of supersaturation, shortly after the main diatom bloom (Figure 20). There was also a steep climb of temperature from 4.9°C on April 9 to 11.4°C on May 6. Meanwhile, the spring diatom bloom and the flourishing of other phytoplankton rapidly depleted the dissolved CO_2 from a maximum of 0.07 meq/liter to amounts too small to be detected, when the pH rose from 7.91 to 8.7. The earliest crystals were large, ranging from 5 to 15 μm, with the largest reaching 40 μm. The supersaturation reached a maximum on June 11 and declined gradually afterward, but still maintained a high level through the summer. A late autumn peak corresponds to the biomass maximum. The summer precipitates are very fine-grained calcite, 1–4 μm on the average, and not uncommonly less than 1 μm in size. Calcite precipitation slowed down after the autumn and may have stopped altogether during the winter to early spring months.

In the summer of 1975, the alkalinity of the surface

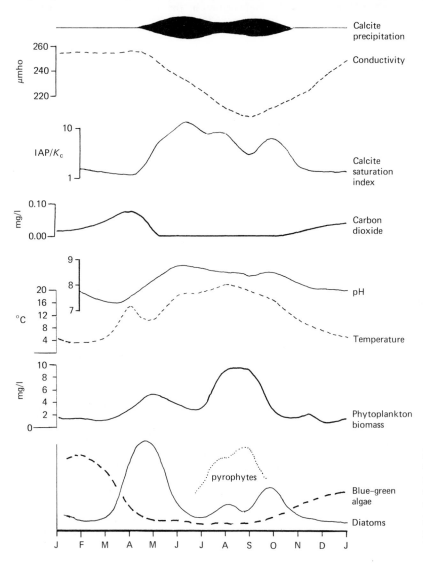

FIGURE 20.   Schematic correlation of several parameters observed in the seasonal cycle of the epilimnion water at 5 m depth. Data based on values from 1974 and 1975 from Lake Zurich (courtesy of U. Zimmermann of the City of Zurich Water Agency).

waters dropped from 2.05 to 1.95 meq/liter. Assuming that there was no net influx of bicarbonate ions into the epilimnion, the annual calcite precipitation can be estimated, as every millimole of calcite precipitated resulted in a drop of 2 meq of alkalinity [Eq. (14)]. This implies that 27.5 mg/liter or 0.55 mg/cm^2 of calcite should have precipitated from a 20-m epilimnion to account for the observed decrease in alkalinity. Due to supersaturation, possibly less than this is actually precipitated. Similarly, a seasonal shift of 0.06 meq/liter alkalinity in the hypolimnion suggests a 3 mg/liter dissolution, or about 10% as we have estimated visually. The calcite precipitates should then form a 4 mm-layer of sediments of 1.3 g/cm^3 density. The observed calcite sedimentation averages about 1–3 mm/year, in general accordance with the computed quantity, considering the simplifying assumptions.

Postdepositional changes

A comparison of the young nonglacial varves with the Boreal chalks deposited some 5,000 to 10,000 years ago in Lake Zurich reveals some distinct differences. The present varves are evenly laminated, and the varved calcite shows size grading reflecting variations in seasonal production. The Boreal chalks are on the whole structureless and very fine grained (1–4 μm), with very few scattered large crystals. The uppermost part of the chalk unit includes paper-thin organic laminae, which form couplets (about 0.2 mm thick) with intervening calcite. Boreal chalks had a sedimentation rate of only 0.3 mm/year, whereas for the present varved couplets the rate is almost a factor of 10 greater when compacted to comparable levels. The present varves contain considerable numbers of well-preserved diatom frustules and the Boreal chalks contain little or none. It is not certain if these textural and compositional differences are due to some primary differences in the formation mechanism, or if the Boreal chalks were similar to the present nonglacial varves before the postdepositional changes took place. The transition is masked by a detrital overprint.

Davaud (1976) studied the sediments of Lake Morat, Switzerland, and observed a similar decrease of calcite grain size from a 16 μm average at the sediment water interface to almost 2 μm at 150 cm depth below bottom. He interprets the change as a result of continuing corrosion after sedimentation. Postdepositional calcite dissolution is indeed possible, particularly in view of the fact that the bottom waters of Lake Zurich are undersaturated. However, the interstitial water chemistry is not yet known in detail. Once the crystal load reaches the sediment it enters a reducing environment. The balance of bacterial alkalinity versus CO_2 production in anaerobic systems is difficult to predict but, at least initially, net CO_2 production appears to prevail. Scanning electron micro-

scope photographs show that the bottom sediments seem to have been subjected to somewhat more dissolution than the precipitate harvested from the hypolimnion (Figure 11a). However, calcite grains from 10 cm and from 30 cm depth below bottom show about the same extent of dissolution.

Chemical analyses of interstitial waters of the sediments of many lakes (Müller, 1969; Brunskill and Hariss, 1969; Emerson, 1976, Santschi, 1975) reveal the trend that calcium concentration increases rapidly in pore waters with depth until a constant and presumably equilibrium value is obtained below a critical depth. Emerson (1976) showed that equilibrium between calcite and interstitial waters of the Greifensee sediments is established at 3 cm subbottom, or within 1–2 years after deposition. It seems, therefore, that we can hardly assume diagenetic dissolution alone to account for the size differences between the young and old calcite precipitates of Lake Zurich. Indeed, SEM photographs suggest that the original grain size of the old chalks were not much smaller than those present, despite evidence of considerable dissolution (Figure 21).

We have observed similar types of chalks in early Quaternary Black Sea sediments: the laminated diatomaceous nonglacial varves and the structureless fine-grained chalk. They represent deposits under different environments and not different stages of diagenetic alterations (Hsü, 1978). Therefore, the difference between the two chalk deposits of Lake Zurich most probably also resulted from some differences in their depositional environments. The calcite production

FIGURE 21.   SEM view of older, Boreal, chalk from approximately 8000 years B.P. Sample from 396 cm subbottom depth in a mid-lake piston core. Dissolution has reduced some crystals to platty remnants. Overall, very fine grain size dominant.

rate during Boreal time was less than the present, as suggested by the slow sedimentation rates then. Climates were warmer and water chemistry may have been somewhat different. Possibly calcium ion was replenished at a slower rate. At times burrowing by bottom-dwelling animals under aerobic conditions may have destroyed laminations except for the few faint traces mentioned above. Diatoms were also produced then, but apparently not as abundantly as now. Their role in calcite precipitation was subordinate. Another possibility is that precipitation at that time was more temperature controlled than biologically controlled, perhaps closer to conditions in the Green Lake situation (Brunskill, 1969).

Summary

A geologist often turns to recent analogues to interpret the geologic record. The preceding discussions have provided some guidelines for the examination of chalk formation in a deep lacustrine freshwater basin. In the following summary we focus on criteria which may be helpful in recognizing this environment in fossil lacustrine deposits. In contrast to the oceans the main source of primary carbonates in these lakes is inorganic precipitation. The carbonate production and phase are determined by the water chemistry. Equilibrium relations permit considerations of factors leading to supersaturation and precipitation. Calcite is most common in freshwater. At higher Mg/Ca ratios and salinities, high magnesium calcites or aragonites apparently precipitate preferentially.

In a deep and dilute hardwater lake, not dominated by detrital input, thick massive pure chalks tend to accumulate in the littoral zone, while nonglacial varves might be more commonly preserved in the deep part where anaerobic conditions prevent burrowing by benthos. In the littoral zones, higher sedimentation rates of authigenic carbonate are possible due to the assimilating activity of macrophytes. Encrustation and entrapment of plants lead to porous, fragile, usually nonbedded structures. Freshwater gastropods and molluscs are common. In the open waters, microphyta and changing physical conditions may cause supersaturation and initiate a seasonal (or even continuous) pelagic rain of calcium carbonate particles. Once formed, crystals tend to persist, but a part of this rain may dissolve in undersaturated bottom waters. Less extreme conditions and the lack of seed crystals early in a season tend to promote the formation of larger grains. High supersaturation levels apparently cause high nucleation rates which favor the formation of micrite. Fine-grained micrite is also particularly characteristic of calcium carbonate from macrophyte encrustations. The morphology of some calcium carbonate crystals tends to reflect their environment of formation. Lacustrine precipitates rarely form perfect rhombs. In freshwater lakes with very low magnesium concentrations crystals are commonly subhedral to euhedral polyhedra. Specific crystallographic directions and faces are favored. In some instances they may be flattened, tabular, and untwinned hexagons. Although exceptions are common, micrite grains (1–4 μm) tend to form more blocky shapes, 5–10 μm sizes are more tabular, and crystals over 15 μm are usually polyhedral, without inclusions, and untwinned. Aggregate crystals commonly show optical continuity. Freshwater lacustrine chalk crystals are typically porous, built up in a "layer-cake" or sloppy brickwork fashion. Specific surface areas can be very large. Surface steps and knobby protrusions abound. Prismatic calcium carbonate crystals are more typical of lakes with higher magnesium concentrations (Folk, 1974).

As lacustrine chalk crystals settle they often pass through undersaturated bottom waters and settle on an anaerobic bottom. Partial dissolution etches away crystal structures in a differential manner. Some faces are preferentially fluted while others remain smooth or even act as the sites of crystal growth. If conditions are balanced, the seasonal cycle can be preserved in the sediments as nonglacial varves.

Varve microstructures and algal remnants are important as indicators of the environment. Diatoms, if initially important, may have dissolved but possibly leave their trace on bulk silica composition. Detailed examination of crystal phases and structures in laminated carbonates should determine whether calcareous components are authigenic, diagenetic, or detrital in origin. Stable isotope studies (e.g., Stuiver, 1970) yield clues as to the source of calcium carbonate. In lakes precipitating calcite, interstitial waters are equilibrated with the sediments after a few centimeters of burial. There seems to be little continuing postdepositional dissolution during the early diagenesis. In lakes precipitating Mg-calcite or aragonite, early diagenetic reactions may lead to dolomite in the same environments. Minor differences in lacustrine chalk textures and structures may be indicative of separate subenvironments.

ACKNOWLEDGMENTS. We wish to acknowledge André Lambert, Judy McKenzie, Euan Nisbet, Peter Stoffers, Michael Sturm, Helmut Weissert, and Dick Wright in particular for their comments on the manuscript. Fruitful ideas and encouragement also derive from discussions with W. H. Bradley, Greg Brunskill, Hans Bürgi, Steve Emerson, Hans Eugster, Y.-H. Li, Abraham Lerman, Albert Matter, Peter Santschi, Werner Stumm, and H. U. Zimmermann. In addition, we thank Urs Gerber, Kurt Ghilardi, Helmut Franz, Carolina Hartendorf, and Judy McKenzie for invaluable technical assistance. The research was supported in part by the Swiss National Fund Project Nr. 2.420-0.75

References

Abd-el-Malek, Y, and S. G. Rizk. (1963). Bacterial sulfate reduction and the development of alkalinity. *J. Appl. Bacteriol.*, **26**:7–26.

Anderson, R. Y., and D. W. Kirkland. (1960). Origin, varves and cycles of Jurassic Todilto Formation, New Mexico. *Am. Assoc. Petrol. Geol. Bull.*, **44**:37–52.

Anderson, R. Y. and D. W. Kirland. (1969). Paleoecology of an Early Pleistocene Lake on The High Plains of Texas. *Geol. Soc. Am. Memoir*, **113**, 211 p.

Ball, M. M. (1967). Carbonate sand bodies of Florida and the Bahamas. *J. Sed. Petrol.*, **37**:556–591.

Berner, R. A. (1971). *Chemical Sedimentology*. McGraw–Hill, New York, NY. 240 pp.

Berner, R. A. (1975). The role of magnesium in the crystal growth of calcite and aragonite from sea water. *Geochim. Cosmochim. Acta*, **39**:489–504.

Berner, R. A. (1976). The solubility of calcite and aragonite in sea water at atmospheric pressure and 34.5‰ salinity. *Am. J. Sci.*, **276**:713–731.

Berner, R. A., and J. W. Morse. (1974). Dissolution kinetics of calcium carbonate in sea water: IV. Theory of calcite dissolution. *Am. J. Sci.*, **274**:108–135.

Berner, R. A., M. R. Scott, and C. Thomlinson, (1970). Carbonate alkalinity in the pore waters of anoxic marine sediments. *Limnol. Oceanogr.*, **15**:544–549.

Bloesch, J. (1974). Sedimentation und Phosphathaushalt im Vierwaldstättersee, Horwer Bucht und im Rotsee. *Schweiz. Z. Hydrol.*, **36**(1):71–186.

Bradley, W. H. (1929). The varves and climate of the Green River Epoch. *U.S. Geol. Sur. Prof. Pap.*, **158**:87–110.

Bradley, W. H. (1937). Non-glacial varves, with selected bibliography. Pp. 32–42. In: *Rept. Comm. on Geol. Time*. Natl. Res. Conc. Ann. Rpt. App. A.

Bradley, W. H. (1948). Limnology and the Eocene lakes of the Rocky Mountain region. *Geol. Soc. Am. Bull.*, **59**(2):635–648.

Bradley, W. H. (1965). Vertical density currents. *Science*, **150**(3702):1423–1428.

Bricker, O. P., and B. N. Troup. (1975). Sediment–water exchange in Chesapeake Bay. *Estuarine Res.*, **1**:1–28.

Brunskill, G. J. (1969). Fayetteville Green Lake, New York. II: Precipitation and sedimentation of calcite in a meromictic lake with laminated sediments. *Limnol. Oceanogr.*, **14**(6):830–847.

Brunskill, G. J., and R. C. Hariss. (1969). Fayetteville Green Lake New York. IV: Interstitial water chemistry of the sediments. *Limnol. Oceanogr.*, **14**:858–861.

Calvert, S. E. (1966). Origin of diatom-rich, varved sediments from the Gulf of California. *J. Geol.*, **74**:546–565.

Davis, C. A. (1901). A second contribution to the natural history of marl. *J. Geol.*, **8**:491–506.

Davoud, E. (1976). Evolution diagenetique du carbonate de calcium dan les sédiments holocenes du lac de Morat (Suisse). *Eclogae Geol. Helv.*, **69**:190–196.

Dean, W. E., Jr., and E. Gorham. (1976). Major chemical and mineral components of profundal surface sediments in Minnesota lakes. *Limnol. Oceanogr.*, **21**:261–268.

de Boer, R. D. (1977). Influence of seed crystals on the precipitation of calcite and aragonite. *Am. J. Sci.*, **277**:38–61.

De Geer, G. (1912). A geochronology of the last 12,000 years. Pp. 241–253. 11th. Int. Geol. Cong. Stoklm. Proc. S.

Dell, C. J. (1972). The origin and characteristics of Lake Superior sediments. Pp. 361–370. Great Lakes Res. Conf. 15th Proc.

Emerson, S. (1975). Chemically enhanced CO_2 gas exchange in a eutrophic lake: a general Model. *Limnol. Oceanogr.*, **20**(5):743–753.

Emerson, S. (1976). Early diagenesis in the sediments of an eutrophic lake. *Geochim. Cosmochim. Acta*, **40**:925–934.

Finckh, P., and K. Kelts. (1976). Geophysical investigations into the nature of Pre-Holocene sediments of Lake Zurich. *Eclogae Geol. Helv.*, **69**(1):139–148.

Folk, R. L. (1974). The natural history of cristalline calcium carbonate: effect of magnesium content and salinity. *J. Sed. Petrol.*, **44**:40–53.

Folk, R. L., and L. S. Land. (1975). Mg/Ca ratio and salinity: two controls over the crystallization of dolomite. *Am. Assoc. Petrol. Geol.*, **59**:60–68.

Forel, F. A. (1901). *Handbuch der Seenkunde*. J. Engelhorn Verlag, Stuttgart. 247 pp.

Geyh, M., J. Merkt, and H. Müller. (1971). Sediment, Pollen and Isotopenanalysen an jahreszeitlich geschichteten Ablagerungen im zentralen Teil des Schleinsees. *Arch. Hydrobiol.*, **69**(3):366–399.

Gieskes, J. (1974). The alkalinity: total carbon dioxide system in seawater. Pp. 123–151. In: E. Goldberg (ed.), *The Sea*. Vol. 5.

Gyger, M., M. Muller-von Moes, and C. Schindler. (1976). Untersuchung zur Klassification Spät und nacheiszeitlicher Sedimente aus dem Zürichsee. *Schweiz. Min. Petrog. Mitt.*, **56**:387–400.

Halbfass, W. (1923). *Grundzüge einer Vergleichenden Seenkunde*. Borntraeger, Berlin. 337 pp.

Harned, H. S., and R. Davis, Jr. (1943). The ionization constant of carbonic acid in water and the solubility of carbon dioxide in water and aqueous salt solutions from 0 to 50°. *J. Am. Chem. Soc.*, **65**:2030–2037.

Harned, H. S., and S. R. Scholes. (1941). The ionization constant of HCO_3^- from 0° to 50°C. *J. Am. Chem. Soc.*, **63**:1706–1709.

Heim, A. (1919). *Geologie der Schweiz: Molasseland und Juragebirge*. Tauchnitz, Leipzig. 704 pp.

Hsü, K. J. (1963). Solubility of dolomite and composition of Florida groundwaters. *J. Hydrology*, **1**:288–310.

Hsü, K. J. (1967). Chemistry of dolomite formation: Pp. 169–191. In: G. V. Chilingar, H. J. Bissell, and R. W. Fairbridge eds.), *Carbonate Rocks, Physical and Chemical Aspects*. Elsevier, Amsterdam.

Hsü, K. J. (1978). Stratigraphy of the lacustrine sedimentation in the Black Sea. In: D. Ross and Y. Neprochov, *et al.* (eds.), *Initial Reports of the Deep Sea Drilling Project*. Vol. 42B. U.S. Govt. Printing Office, Washington, D.C., pp. 509–524.

Hull, H., and A. G. Turnbull. (1973). A thermochemical study of monohydrocalcite. *Geochim. Cosmochim. Acta*, **37**:685–695.

Hutchinson, G. E. (1957). *A Treatise on Limnology*. I and II. J. Wiley, London. 1015 pp.

Hutchinson, G. E. (1975). *A Treatise on Limnology*. III. J. Wiley, New York, NY. 660 pp.

Irion, G. (1973). Die anatolischen Salzseen, ihr Chemismus

und die Entstehung ihrer chemischen Sedimente. *Arch. Hydrobiol.*, **71**(4):517–557.

Jacobson, R. L., and D. Langmuir. (1974). Dissociation constants of calcite and CaHCO₃⁺ from 0°–50°C. *Geochim. Cosmochim. Acta*, **38**:301–318.

Kramer, J. R. (1967). Equilibrium concepts in natural water systems. *Adv. Chem. Ser.*, **67**:243–254.

Krumbein, W. E. (1975). Biogenic monohydrocalcite spherules in lake sediments of Lake Kivu (Africa) and the Solar Lake (Sinai). *Sedimentology*, **22**:631–635.

Lalou, C. (1957). Studies on bacterial precipitation of carbonates in sea water. *J. Sed. Petrol.*, **27**:190–195.

Lambert, A., K. Kelts, and N. Marshall. (1976). Measurements of density underflows from Walensee, Switzerland. *Sedimentology*, **23**:87–105.

Lerman, A., D. Lal, and M. F. Dacey. (1974). Stokes settling and chemical reactivity of suspended particles in natural waters. Pp. 17–47. In: R. J. Gibbs (ed.), *Suspended Solids in Water*. Plenum, New York, NY.

Li, Y. H. (1973). Vertical eddy diffusion coefficient in Lake Zurich. *Schweiz. Z. Hydrol.*, **35**:1–7.

Lippmann, F. (1973). *Sedimentary Carbonate Minerals*. Springer-Verlag, Berlin. 196 pp.

Logan, B. W., R. Rezak, and R. N. Ginsburg. (1964). Classification and environmental significance of algal stromatolites. *J. Geol.*, **72**:68–83.

Lyell, Ch. (1830). Principles of Geology. Vol. 1, J. Murray, London. 519 pp.

Megard, R. O. (1968). Planktonic photosynthesis and the environment of calcite carbonate deposition in lakes. Interim Rept. 2. Limnol. Res. Center. U. Minn.

Minder, L. (1922). Ueber biogene Entkalkung im Zürichsee. *Verh. Int. Verein. Limnol.*, **1**:20–23.

Minder, L. (1926). Biologische-chemische Untersuchungen im Zürichsee. *Rev. Hydrol.*, **3**(3):1–70.

Minder, L. (1943). Der Zurichsee im Lichte der Seetypenlehre. Neujahrsblatt. *Nat. Forsch. Ges. Zürich*, **145**:1–83.

Müller, G. (1966). Die Sedimentbildung im Bodensee. *Naturwissenschaften*, **53**:237–247.

Müller, G. (1969). Diagenetic changes in interstitial waters of Holocene Lake Constance sediments. *Nature*, **224**:258–259.

Müller, G. (1970). High magnesian calcite and protodolomite in Lake Balaton (Hungary) sediments. *Nature*, **226**:749–750.

Müller, G. (1971a). Aragonite inorganic precipitation in a freshwater lake. *Nature Phy. Sci.*, **229**:18.

Müller, G. (1971b). Sediments of Lake Constance. Pp. 237–252. In: *Sedimentology of Parts of Central Europe*. Guidebook, VII Int. Sed. Congress, Heidelberg. 1971.

Müller, G., G. Irion, and U. Foerstner. (1972). Formation and diagenesis of inorganic Ca-Mg carbonates in the lacustrine environment. *Naturwissenschaften*, **59**(4):158–164.

Nipkow, F. (1920). Vorläufige Mitteilungen über Untersuchungen des Schlammabsatzes im Zürichsee. *Z. Hydrol.*, **1**:1–27.

Nipkow, F. (1927). Ueber das Verhalten der Skelette planktischer Kieselalgen im geschichteten Tiefenschlamm des Zürich und Baldeggersees. Diss ETH Zurich, 445.

Ohle, W. (1952). Die Hypolimnetische-Kohlendioxyd Akku-
mulation als productionsbiologischer Indicator. *Arch. Hydrobiol.*, **46**:153–285.

O'Melia, C. R. (1972). An approach to the modeling of lakes. *Schw. Z. Hydrologie* **34**(1), 1–33.

Otsuki, A., and R. G. Wetzel, (1974). Calcium and total alkalinity budgets and calcium carbonate precipitation of a small hard-water lake. *Arch. Hydrobiol.*, **73**:14–30.

Pia, J. (1933). *Die rezenten Kalksteine*. Leipzig. 418 pp.

Plummer, L. N. (1975). Mixing of seawater with calcium carbonate ground water. *Mem. Geol. Soc. Am.*, **142**:219–236.

Pollock, J. B. (1918). Blue-green algae as agents in the deposition of marl in Michigan lakes. *Rept. Mich. Acad. Sci.*, **20**:247–261.

Ross, D., *et al.* (1978). *Initial Reports of the Deep Sea Drilling Project*. Vol. 42B. U.S. Govt. Printing Office, Washington, D.C. 1244 pp.

Rossknecht, H. (1977). Zur Autochthonen Calcitfällung im Bodensee-Obersee. *Arch. Hydrobiol.* **81**:35–64.

Ruttner, F. (1962). *Grundriss der Limnologie*. Gruyter, Berlin. 314 pp.

Santschi, P. (1975). Chemische Prozesse im Bielersee. Ph.D. thesis, University of Bern, Switzerland 307 pp.

Sapozhnikov, D. G., and A. J. Isvetkov. (1959). Precipitation of hydrous calcium carbonate on the bottom of lake Issyk-Kul. *Dokl. Acad. Nauk. SSSR*, **124**:402–405.

Schäfer, A. (1972). Petrographische und Stratigraphische Untersuchungen an den rezenten Seesedimenten des Untersees/Bodensee. *Neues Jahrb. Min. Abh.*, **117**:118–142.

Schäfer, A. (1973). Zur Entstehung von Seekreide. *Neues Jahrb. Geol. Pal. Mh.*, 1973(4):216–230.

Schäfer, A., and K. R. Stapf. (1972). Calcite whitings in Bodensee–Untersee. *Natur. Mus.*, **102**(8).

Schöttle, M., and G. Müller. (1968). Recent carbonate sedimentation in the Gnadensee (Lake Constance) Germany. Pp. 148–156. In: G. Müller and G. Friedman (eds.), *Recent Developements in Carbonate Sedimentology in Central Europe*. Springer-Verlag, Berlin.

Serruya, C. (1969a). Le dépot du lac Léman en relation avec l'evolution du bassin sédimentaire et les caractéres du milieu lacustre. *Arch. Sci. Geneve*, **22**:125–254.

Serruya, C. (1969b). Problems of sedimentation in the Lake of Geneva. *Verh. Int. Verein. Limnol.*, **17**:208–217.

Stiller, M., and M. Magaritz. (1974). Carbon-13 enriched carbonate in interstitial waters of lake Kinneret Sediments. *Limnol. Oceanogr.*, **19**(5):849–853.

Stoffers, P. (1975a). Recent carbonate sedimentation in the lakes of Plitvice (Yugoslavia). *Neues Jahrb. Min. Mh.*, 1975(9):412–418.

Stoffers, P. (1975b). Sedimentpetrographische, geochemische und paläoklimatische Untersuchungen an Ostafrikanischen Seen. Habilitationschrift, Univ. Heidelberg. 118 pp.

Stoffers, P., and R. Fischbeck (1974). Monohydrocalcite in the sediments of Lake Kivu (East Africa). *Sedimentology*, **21**:163–170.

Strong, A., and B. J. Eadie. (1978). Satellite observations of calcium carbonate precipitation in the Great Lakes. *Limnol. Oceanogr.* (In press).

Sturm, M., and A. Matter. (1972). Sedimente und Sedimentationsvorgänge im Thunersee. *Eclogae Geol. Helv.*, **65**(3):563–590.

Stumm, W., and J. Morgan. (1970). *Aquatic Chemistry*. Wiley Interscience, New York, NY. 563 pp.

Stumm, W., and E. Stumm-Zollinger. (1968). Chemische Prozesse in natülichen Gewässern. *Chimia,* **22**:325–337.

Stuvier, M. (1970). Oxygen and carbon isotope ratios of fresh-water carbonates as climatic indicators. *J. Geophys. Res.,* **75**:5247–5257.

Taylor, G. F. (1975). The occurrence of monohydrocalcite in two small lakes in the southeast of South Australia. *Am. Mineral.,* **60**:690–697.

Thomas, E. A. (1969). Kultur beinflusste chemische und biologische Veränderungen des Zürichsees im Verlauf von 70 Jahren. *Mitt. Int. Verein. Limnol.,* **17**:226–239.

Thomas, R. L., A. L. Kemp, and C. F. M. Lewis. (1973). The surficial sediments of Lake Huron. *Can. J. Earth Sci.,* **10**:226–271.

Thompson, R., and K. Kelts. (1974). Holocene sediments and magnetic stratigraphy from Lakes Zug and Zurich, Switzerland. *Sedimentology,* **21**:577–596.

Truesdell, A. H., and B. F. Jones. (1974). WATEQ, a computer program for calculating chemical equilibria of natural water. *J. Res. U.S. Geol. Survey,* **2**(2):233–248.

Verduin, J. (1975). Rate of carbon dioxide transport across air–water boundaries in Lakes. *Limnol. Oceanogr.,* **20**:1052.

Vernet, J. P., M. Meybeck, A. Pachoud, and G. Scolari. (1971). Le Léman: Un synthese bibliographique. Bull. Bur. Res. Geol. Mine. (Ser. 2), **IV**(2):47–84.

Welten, M. (1944). Pollenânalytische, stratigraphische und geochronologische Untersuchungen aus dem Faulenseemoos bei Spiez. Veroeffentl. Geobot. Inst. Ruebel. in Zurich, 21. 201 pp.

Wetzel, R. G. (1960). Marl encrustations on hydrophytes in several Michigan lakes. *Oikos,* **11**:223–228.

Wetzel, R. G. (1975). *Limnology*. W. B. Saunders, Philadelphia, PA. 743 pp.

Wigley, T. M. L., and L. N. Plummer. (1976). Mixing of carbonate waters. *Geochim. Cosmochim. Acta,* **40**:989–995.

Zimmermann, P. (1961). Chemische und bakteriologische Untersuchungen im unteren Zürichsee während der Jahre 1948–1957. *Schweiz. Z. Hydrol.,* **23**:343–395.

Zimmermann, U. (1975). Limnologische Untersuchungen am Trinkwasserspeicher Zürichsee. *Gas-Wasser-Abwasser,* **55**(9):473–480.

Züllig, H. (1956). Sedimente als Ausdruck des Zustandes eines Gewässers. *Schweiz. Z. Hydrol.,* **18**. 487–529.

Chapter 10
Stable Isotope Studies of Lakes

F. J. Pearson, Jr. and Tyler B. Coplen

Introduction

There are natural variations in the ratios of the stable isotopes of many light elements. Isotope ratio differences in substances containing hydrogen ($^2H/^1H$, usually written D/H), carbon ($^{13}C/^{12}C$), nitrogen ($^{15}N/^{14}N$), oxygen ($^{18}O/^{16}O$), and sulfur ($^{34}S/^{32}S$) have been used or have potential use in studies of various aspects of lakes. We give here a general overview of the processes which bring about changes in stable isotope ratios, using studies of lakes as examples of their operation. We have by no means exhausted the literature on isotopes in lake studies.

Stable isotope ratio variations result from isotopic fractionation processes which occur during chemical reactions and some physical processes. Physical fractionation during gaseous diffusion through a membrane or in a thermal gradient comes about because molecules containing the lighter isotope move more rapidly than those containing the heavier isotope. Likewise, during evaporation or ultrafiltration by a membrane (Coplen and Hanshaw, 1973), the residual liquid is enriched in the molecule containing the heavier isotope because the lighter molecule moves more rapidly and hence has a greater tendency to escape from the liquid phase or through the membrane. Although in liquids the amount of fractionation cannot be quantitatively predicted, Graham's law of diffusion is obeyed by gases. This law predicts that the ratio of the translational velocities of the gas molecules is inversely proportional to the square root of their masses. Fractionation during evaporation is discussed in more detail in the section on hydrogen and oxygen isotopes in water, below.

Chemical fractionation effects occur because a chemical bond involving a heavy isotope will have a lower vibrational frequency than the equivalent bond with a light isotope. The bond with the heavy isotope will thus be stronger than that with the light isotope.

The amount of fractionation occurring in reactions involving relatively simple molecules can be predicted from statistical mechanics (Bigeleisen and Mayer, 1947).

Fractionation may occur during both equilibrium and irreversible chemical reactions. The result of kinetic fractionation, which takes place during irreversible reactions, is to enrich the lighter isotope in the reaction product because of the greater ease with which light isotope bonds can be broken. During the acidification of calcium carbonate, for example, the product calcium hydroxide is enriched in ^{16}O and the CO_2 enriched in ^{18}O due to greater ease with which C–^{16}O bonds in the reactant carbonate can be broken. Kinetic fractionation of sulfur isotopes during oxidation–reduction reactions, another example of this effect, is mentioned below.

Chemical equilibrium exchange reactions can be discussed using the reaction

$$\tfrac{1}{3}CaC^{16}O_3 + H_2^{18}O \rightleftarrows \tfrac{1}{3}CaC^{18}O_3 + H_2^{16}O. \quad (1)$$

The equilibrium constant for this reaction is

$$K = \left(\frac{CaC^{18}O_3}{CaC^{16}O_3}\right)^{1/3} \Big/ \frac{H_2^{18}O}{H_2^{16}O}. \quad (2)$$

If the isotopic species of oxygen are distributed randomly among the three positions within the carbonate ion, we can write

$$K = \alpha_{CaCO_3-H_2O} = \frac{(^{18}O/^{16}O)_{CaCO_3}}{(^{18}O/^{16}O)_{H_2O}} \quad (3)$$

where α is the isotopic fractionation factor defined in terms of the ($^{18}O/^{16}O$) ratios. If the isotopic equilibrium reaction is not written for the exchange of one atom, K and α are related by

$$\alpha = K^{1/n} \quad (4)$$

where n atoms are exchanged, again assuming random distribution of isotopes over all sites.

326   F. J. Pearson, Jr. and Tyler B. Coplen

Because bonds with ^{18}O are stronger than those with ^{16}O, the chemical properties of the molecules containing the different isotopes are not identical, and the value of α is not 1. In fact, ^{18}O is enriched in the calcium carbonate, relative to water with which it is in equilibrium at 25°C, by 2.88%, and the value of α in Eq. (3) is 1.02880 (O'Neill *et al.*, 1969).

Stable isotope compositions are reported in δ values in parts per thousand (termed per mil and noted as ‰) enrichment (or depletion if negative) relative to an agreed upon standard. Therefore,

$$\delta^{18}O \text{ (in ‰)} =$$
$$\left(\frac{(^{18}O/^{16}O)_{sample} - (^{18}O/^{16}O)_{standard}}{(^{18}O/^{16}O)_{standard}} \right) 1000. \quad (5)$$

In the same manner δD, $\delta^{13}C$, $\delta^{15}N$, and $\delta^{34}S$ are reported from D/H, $^{13}C/^{12}C$, $^{15}N/^{14}N$, and $^{34}S/^{32}S$ ratio measurements, respectively. The standards chosen for these isotopes are reported in Table 1. The relation between α and δ values then becomes

$$\alpha_{A-B} = \frac{1 + \dfrac{\delta_A}{1000}}{1 + \dfrac{\delta_B}{1000}} = \frac{1000 + \delta_A}{1000 + \delta_B}. \quad (6)$$

One of the primary reasons for reporting isotopic compositions as differential measurements is that the mass spectrometer employed to measure light-stable isotope ratios (McKinney *et al.*, 1950; Nier, 1947) measures differences between the ratios of two gaseous samples, rather than measuring the absolute ratio of a sample. This technique allows a precision of

TABLE 1.   Light Stable Isotope Standards[a]

Element	Standard	Abbreviation
H	Vienna Standard Mean Ocean Water[b]	V-SMOW
C	*Belemnitella americana* from the Cretaceous Pee Dee formation, South Carolina	PDB
N	Atmospheric nitrogen	
O	Vienna Standard Mean Ocean Water[b,c]	V-SMOW
S	Troilite (FeS) from the Canyon Diablo iron meteorite	CD

[a]After Hoefs (1973)

[b]V-SMOW and a second water standard, SLAP (Standard Light Antarctic Precipitation), are distributed by the International Atomic Energy Agency. The recommended δ values for hydrogen and oxygen of V-SMOW are 0 and 0 ‰ and for SLAP are −428 and −55.5 ‰, respectively (Gonfiantini, 1977).

[c]The PDB standard used as the carbon isotope standard is also used for oxygen when involved in paleotemperature studies. To relate the two scales Friedman and O'Neil (1977) provide: $\delta_{SMOW} = 1.03086 \, \delta_{PDB} + 30.86$.

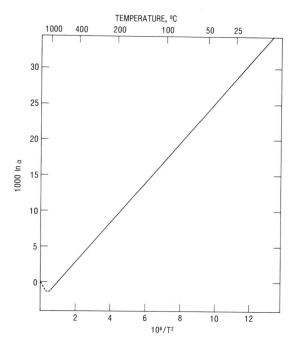

FIGURE 1.   Temperature variation of oxygen isotopic fractionation between calcium carbonate and water.

better than 0.1‰ to be obtained in oxygen and carbon isotope analyses.

The value of α for any reaction is temperature dependent, as are the values of all chemical equilibrium constants. Urey (1947) suggested that if the temperature dependence of α for reaction (1) were known, it might be possible to measure the temperature of past oceans by analyzing $^{18}O/^{16}O$ ratios of shells of animals living in those oceans. McCrea (1950) developed a method to extract carbon dioxide from calcite with reproducibilities of 0.1‰, and Epstein *et al.* (1953) calibrated this paleotemperature scale. The temperature coefficient was found to be 0.00024/degree at 16°C; consequently, an analysis of shell calcite with a precision of ± 0.1‰ yields a "temperature" with a precision of about 0.5°. The use of this technique for the study of past climates is discussed later in this paper.

The temperature dependence of isotopic equilibrium constants was discussed by Urey (1947) and Bigeleisen and Mayer (1947). Isotopic equilibrium constants for perfect gases can be calculated from molecular vibrational frequencies. For liquids and solids no satisfactory theoretical treatment yet exists, although certain generalizations can be made. At low temperatures, generally much below room temperature, the natural logarithm of α is inversely proportional to absolute temperature, T: $\ln \alpha \propto 1/T$. At higher temperatures $\ln \alpha$ is inversely proportional to T^2: $\ln \alpha \propto 1/T^2$. The definition of low or high temperature depends upon the vibrational frequencies of the molecules involved. The pressure effect upon α is negligible (Clayton *et al.*, 1974); thus, the stable isotope geothermometry technique can be applied to minerals that have isotopically equilibrated at depth in the earth's crust.

Reactions involving water and a mineral usually show a straight line relationship over the geologic range of temperature when plotted as $\ln \alpha$ or $1000 \ln \alpha$ versus $1/T^2$; consequently, fractionation factors are usually plotted in such a manner. The value $1000 \ln \alpha$ is chosen because it is almost identical to the per mil fractionation. Therefore, we can define Δ by the equation

$$\Delta_{A-B} = \delta_A - \delta_B \cong 1000 \ln \alpha_{A-B}. \qquad (7)$$

As an example, Figure 1 shows a plot of the calcite–water system. The empirical equation which fits the straight line portion of the data is (O'Neil *et al.*, 1969; revised in Friedman and O'Neil, 1977)

$$1000 \ln \alpha = 2.78(10^6)T^{-2} - 2.89. \qquad (8)$$

In theory (Bigeleisen and Mayer, 1947), at very high temperatures α should approach 1. Thus the dashed portion of the line on Figure 1 has been extended from the end of the experimental data to pass through $\alpha = 1$ ($1000 \ln \alpha = 0$) at $10^6/T^2 = 0$. A compilation of stable isotope fractionation factors of geochemical interest is given by Friedman and O'Neil (1977).

Hydrogen and oxygen

The relative terrestrial abundances of the two stable isotopes of hydrogen H (^{1}H) and D (^{2}H) are 99.985 and 0.015%. Oxygen has three stable isotopes, ^{16}O, ^{17}O, and ^{18}O, with relative abundances of 99.759, 0.037, and 0.204%. Only ^{18}O/^{16}O ratios of naturally occuring materials are usually measured. No more information would be gained from measuring ^{17}O as well. Analytical methods for oxygen isotopes and their abundances in various materials are discussed by Garlick (1969).

Natural distribution in water

The common isotopic species of water are $H_2^{16}O$, $HD^{16}O$, and $H_2^{18}O$. In the standard V-SMOW (Table 1), which represents mean surface ocean water, they are in the proportions 99.768:0.032:0.200.

Thousands of samples of meteoric waters have been analyzed for deuterium and ^{18}O, and the principles governing their distribution are reasonably well known. The first work on these isotopes (Friedman 1953; Epstein and Mayeda, 1953) noted a relationship between δD and δ^{18}O for many samples. Craig (1961),

based on his analysis of many more samples, formalized this relationship in the expression

$$\delta D = 8\delta^{18}O + 10, \qquad (9)$$

the well-known meteoric water line which is found to hold for many samples throughout the world except those which have been heavily evaporated (Figure 2). The geographic distribution of water isotope ratios has been discussed in a number of papers, the first and most comprehensive being those of Friedman *et al.* (1964) on deuterium and Dansgaard (1964) on both deuterium and ^{18}O. The International Atomic Energy Agency, as part of its series on environmental isotope data, sponsors and publishes compilations of the isotopic composition of atmospheric precipitation at stations throughout the world (IAEA, 1969, 1970, 1971, 1973, 1975).

Fractionation of the isotopic species of water occurs during changes of state, from liquid to vapor during evaporation, for example. Because of their different masses, the several isotopic species have different vapor pressures, the lighter species having higher vapor pressures. Consider liquid water containing mole fractions X_{HDO} and X_{H_2O}, with D/H ratio $R_{liq} = X_{HDO}/X_{H_2O}$. The partial pressures of the two species in the vapor phase in equilibrium with this liquid can be found from Raoult's law:

$$P_{HDO} = X_{HDO} P^0_{HDO} \qquad (10a)$$
$$P_{H_2O} = X_{H_2O} P^0_{H_2O} \qquad (10b)$$

where P^0 is the vapor pressure of the pure species, H_2O or HDO, at the temperature of interest. The D/H ratio in the vapor, R_{vap}, is simply P_{HDO}/P_{H_2O}. Thus the fractionation factor, α, for equilibrium between liquid and vapor is:

$$\alpha = \frac{R_{vap}}{R_{liq}} = \left(\frac{X_{HDO} P^0_{HDO}}{X_{H_2O} P^0_{H_2O}}\right) \bigg/ \frac{X_{HDO}}{X_{H_2O}} = \frac{P^0_{HDO}}{P^0_{H_2O}}, \qquad (11)$$

which is simply the ratio of vapor pressures of HDO to H_2O. A similar expression can be written for $H_2^{18}O$ and $H_2^{16}O$.

The relative concentrations of the isotopic species in each phase may vary during the course of a reaction if the vapor phase as it forms is swept out of contact with the liquid, for example. If the vapor phase continues to form under equilibrium conditions, the process can be described as a Rayleigh distillation in which

$$R = R_I f^{(\alpha-1)} \qquad (12)$$

where R_I is the initial isotope ratio in the phase being reacted, α is the fractionation factor, f is the fraction of the reacting phase remaining at any stage of the process, and R is the isotope ratio in the phase at stage f.

A number of measurements of equilibrium fractionation factors between water liquid and vapor have

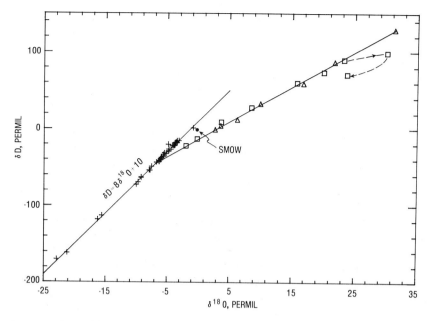

FIGURE 2. Deuterium and ^{18}O in meteoric waters. Crosses represent the amount-weighted mean annual isotopic composition of precipitation at selected sites throughout the world from IAEA (1969) data. They describe the meteoric water line (Craig, 1961). Squares and triangles are the composition of two evaporating lakes in the northwestern Sahara (Fontes and Gonfiantini, 1967). Their slope ($\delta D/\delta^{18}O = 4.6$) is typical of evaporating water. As the lake represented by squares reaches high salinities, its isotopic composition change reverses direction as the dissolved salts begin to affect the activity of free water.

been made and are summarized by Friedman and O'Neil (1977, Figures 7, 8, 34, and 35). Most recent measurements between 0 and 100°C agree within 0.15‰ for ^{18}O and within 2‰ for D. Some representative values are given in Table 2.

Although a Rayleigh process is an oversimplified representation of most natural processes, it can be used to model certain aspects of the hydrologic cycle. Dansgaard (1964), for example, used a Rayleigh model for atmospheric evaporation and condensation based on the overall temperature drop between the region of evaporation (usually the low-latitude ocean) and the mean annual temperature where the precipitation occurs. He predicted that in maritime climates, there should be a regular change of $\delta^{18}O$ with mean temperature of 0.69‰/°C. His measurements on precipitation at sites with maritime climates with mean annual temperatures of 10°C or below showed that the change was indeed 0.7‰/°C. In continental, more temperate

regions he predicted and found lower slopes. Based on a variety of data, Sheppard et al. (1969) have compiled a map showing the deuterium distribution in meteoric water throughout North America (Figure 3).

Lake balances

A common application of stable isotopes to lake studies is an aid in determining the water balance of lake systems. In a lake water balance study, it is usually possible to measure the lake inflow and the lake surface outflow, but it may be difficult or impossible to estimate ground-water inflow or outflow from a lake as well as evaporation from the lake surface. Stable isotope balances have long been used either by themselves or in conjunction with solute balances to estimate evaporative losses from lakes.

A general expression for the water balance of a mixed lake during a time Δt can be written:

$$\frac{\Delta V}{\Delta t} = \Sigma I + P - \Sigma O - E \qquad (13)$$

where V is the total lake volume, ΣI and ΣO are the total surface and ground-water inflow (I) and outflow (O), P is the precipitation on the lake, and E is the evaporation from the lake. A similar expression can be written for a stable isotope balance:

$$\frac{\Delta (V\delta_L)}{\Delta t} = \Sigma I \delta_I + P \delta_P - \Sigma O \delta_O - E \delta_E \qquad (14)$$

where δ_X is the isotopic concentration in the flux X. Because water contains 55 mol of oxygen and 110 mol of hydrogen per liter, neglecting mineral–water and biological effects in Eq. (14) is permissible. Ratio con-

TABLE 2. Equilibrium Fractionation Factors between Water Liquid and Vapor at Several Temperatures[a]

Temperature (°C)	1000 ln α_D	1000 ln α_{18_O}
0	106.4	11.65
20	81.6	9.75
40	62.5	8.20
60	47.6	6.93
80	35.9	5.87

[a]Calculated from expressions (T in K):

$10^3 \ln \alpha_D = 24.844 \ (10^6 \ T^{-2}) - 76.248 \ (10^3 \ T^{-1}) + 52.612$
$10^3 \ln \alpha_{18_O} = 1.137 \ (10^6 \ T^{-2}) - 0.4156 \ (10^3 \ T^{-1}) - 2.0667$

given by Friedman and O'Neil (1977, Figures 7 and 34) based on data of Majzoub (1971).

centrations (R values) should be used in this expression for mathematical rigor, but there is little loss in numerical accuracy if δ values are used as this is usually done.

Eqs. 13 and 14 can be combined in a number of ways to solve for parameters difficult or impossible to measure. Reviews of approaches taken to the use of isotopes in lake balance studies have been given by IAEA (1968) and by Dincer (1968).

Early deuterium balances on lakes were those of Lake Maracaibo, Venezuela, by Friedman et al. (1956) and of several Great Basin lakes (California and Nevada) by Bonner et al. (1961). To make the balances and solve for evaporation, it was assumed that the fractionation accompanying evaporation was an equilibrium process [Eq. (11)] and thus that $\delta_E = \delta_L + \Delta$, where $\Delta = 1000 \ln \alpha$ from the equilibrium Eq. (11).

If chemical data on a lake are available, they may aid in interpreting stable isotope data. If C_I is the concentration of salts entering a lake and C is the concentration in the lake itself ($C > C_I$ due to evaporative concentration), the fraction of water remaining at any time in a lake with no outlet [f, in Eq. (12)] will be C_I/C. From the measured isotope ratios R_I and R corresponding to C_I and C, an apparent α, α', can be found:

$$\frac{R}{R_I} = \left(\frac{C_I}{C}\right)^{(\alpha'-1)} \tag{15}$$

which can be compared with the theoretical fractionation factor at the temperature of evaporation. Fried-

man et al. (1964) report data from a number of lake systems and find that in areas such as the Great Basin where the relative humidity is very low, there is good agreement between the theoretical and apparent fractionation factors. Friedman and Redfield (1971) have used an apparent fractionation factor developed for closed lakes in the western U.S. to model the hydrology of the lakes of the lower Grand Coulee in Washington state. Friedman et al. (1976) again used the salt balance technique to develop an apparent α factor (α') for deuterium during evaporation from Owens Lake, California, which satisfactorily reproduced the measured deuterium values and was in good theoretical agreement with the ratio of vapor pressure fractionation factors.

In fact, evaporation occurs by a much more complicated set of processes than are represented by simple equilibrium models. Craig and Gordon (1965) developed a model which, in addition to equilibrium fractionation effects, accounts for kinetic fractionation during isotope transport through the air–water interface, and for back reactions with water vapor initially present in the atmosphere. The equation they developed for the isotopic composition of evaporating moisture as required in the isotope balance expression [Eq. (14)] can be written:

$$\delta_E = \frac{\alpha \delta_L - h \delta_A - \epsilon}{1 - h + \Delta\epsilon} \tag{16}$$

where δ_L = isotopic composition of the liquid, δ_E = isotopic composition of the evaporating vapor, δ_A =

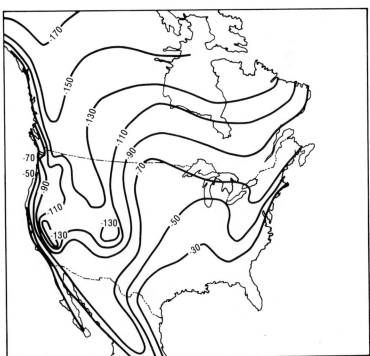

FIGURE 3. Variation in δD in meteoric waters in North America (after Sheppard et al., 1969, Figure 4).

isotopic composition of moisture in the atmosphere into which evaporation is occurring, h = relative humidity, α = equilibrium fractionation factor (R_{vap}/R_{liq}), $\epsilon = (1 - \alpha_{eff})$, $\Delta\epsilon = (\alpha - \alpha_{eff})$ = kinetic enrichment factor, and α_{eff} = effective fractionation factor. Equilibrium effects are accounted for in the $\alpha\delta_L$ term, effects of atmospheric moisture in the h and $h\delta_A$ terms, and nonequilibrium fractionation effects in $\Delta\epsilon$. The original model also includes terms to account for fractionation due to differing diffusion rates of the isotopic species through liquid water to reach the evaporating surface. This is a small effect, however, and can be neglected unless strong isotope ratio gradients exist in the lake of interest (Gat, 1970; Zimmermann and Ehhalt, 1970). Eq. (16) can be written for either oxygen or hydrogen isotopes, and the terms would be written $\Delta\epsilon_{18}$ or $\Delta\epsilon_D$, for example, to specify which isotope pair is being referred to.

The principal difficulties with using Eq. (16) are the experimental problems in measuring h and δ_A with sufficient precision over a lake (Zimmermann and Ehhalt, 1970) and a lack of knowledge of the nonequilibrium fractionation terms. Laboratory work by Craig and Gordon (1965) suggested values of $\Delta\epsilon_{18} \simeq 5\%_0$ and $\Delta\epsilon_D \simeq 20\%_0$, but more carefully controlled studies (Gat, 1970) showed that $\Delta\epsilon_{18} \simeq 16(1 - h)\%_0$ and that $\Delta\epsilon_D$ ranged from $\simeq 2\Delta\epsilon_{18}$ to very small or even negative numbers and was very sensitive to experimental conditions. Merlivat (1970), however, found that $\Delta\epsilon_D \simeq 0.85\Delta\epsilon_{18}$ during evaporation into a laminar flow of air.

Fontes and Gonfiantini (1967) successfully used such a model in their study of closed-basin lakes in the northwestern Sahara. They followed the evolution of the isotopic and chemical composition of two lakes as they evaporated to dryness over a period of 4 to 6 months and were enriched by more than $30\%_0$ in ^{18}O and by more than $100\%_0$ in deuterium. Their data are shown in Figure 2. They describe a straight line with a slope of 4.6 and an intersection with the meteoric water line giving the isotopic composition of the rainfall which initially fed the basin. To interpret their data, they used the equation for the change in isotopic composition of an isolated water body (Gonfiantini, 1965; Craig and Gordon, 1965):

$$\frac{d \ln (1 + \delta_L)}{d \ln f} = \frac{h(\delta_L - \delta_A)/(1 + \delta_L) - \epsilon}{1 - h + \Delta\epsilon} \quad (17)$$

where f = volume fraction remaining, (V/V_0), and the other terms are as in Eq. (16). Assuming h, δ_A, and the fractionation factors were constant, they integrated this equation to:

$$\delta_L - \delta_L^0$$
$$= \frac{h(\delta_A - \delta_L^0) - \epsilon(1 + \delta_L^0)}{h + \epsilon} [1 - f^{(h+\epsilon)/(1-h)}]. \quad (18)$$

By fitting their field data (δ_L as measured and f calculated from salt concentration measurements) to an equation of the form:

$$\delta_L - \delta_L^0 = a(1 - f^b) \quad (19)$$

they found values for:

$$a = \frac{h(\delta_A - \delta_L^0) - \epsilon(1 + \delta_L^0)}{h + \epsilon}, \text{ and} \quad (20)$$

$$b = \frac{h + \epsilon}{1 - h}. \quad (21)$$

Their field data fit Eq. (19) extremely well, supporting their assumption that the atmospheric and fractionation terms in the parameters a and b were essentially constant. Unfortunately, there were no measurements of h and δ_A from which $\Delta\epsilon$ could be evaluated.

In order to evaluate $\Delta\epsilon$ for a study of Lake Tiberias, Gat (1970) used evaporating pan data and the transient Eq. (17). From measured values of δ_L, δ_A, and h, values for $\Delta\epsilon$ were found for both D and ^{18}O. Over the entire period of the experiment, $\Delta\epsilon_{18}/(1 - h)$ values ranged between 13 and 16$\%_0$, but there was much greater spread in $\Delta\epsilon_D$ values.

Whelan and Fritz (1977) have also used evaporation pan data to evaluate $\Delta\epsilon$ and δ_E as part of an isotope balance study of Perch Lake, Ontario. Using Gat's (1970) method, they found values of $\Delta\epsilon_{18}/(1 - h)$ ranging from 11 to 17$\%_0$. They also proposed and tested a method of using pan data for direct estimation of δ_E for a lake without the necessity of measuring humidity and atmospheric moisture isotope composition. As Gonfiantini (1965) and Craig and Gordon (1965) point out, under constant atmospheric conditions, δ_L in the transient Eq. (17) approaches a steady-state value δ_S as f approaches zero:?

$$\delta_S = \frac{h\delta_A + \epsilon}{h - \epsilon}. \quad (22)$$

From this and Eq. (16), Whelan and Fritz (1977) derive the expressions:

$$\frac{\delta_{pan}^0 - \delta_{S_{pan}}}{\delta_{pan}^0 - \delta_{S_{pan}}} = (f)^{m_{pan}} \quad (23)$$

where

$$m_{pan} = \frac{\delta_{E_{pan}} - \delta_{pan}}{\delta_{pan} - \delta_{S_{pan}}}. \quad (24)$$

m_{pan} is a function of conditions at the pan surface, and, if it is assumed that conditions at the lake's surface are the same,

$$\delta_{S_{lake}} \simeq \delta_{S_{pan}}, \quad (25)$$

and

$$m_{lake} \simeq m_{pan} \quad (26)$$

so that, from Eq. (24),

$$\delta_{E_{lake}} \simeq m_{pan}(\delta_{lake} - \delta_{S_{pan}}) + \delta_{lake}. \quad (27)$$

Using these relations, Whelan and Fritz (1977) found δ_E values for Perch Lake which agreed within $2‰$ in ^{18}O with δ_E values calculated using atmospheric data, and Eq. (16) as done by Gat (1970). However, Whelan and Fritz (1977) found that because of high humidity and frequent precipitation in Ontario, evaporation from the pans was not extensive so the range of f values in their experiments was small and did not permit very precise fits to Eq. (23) or precise determinations of m. They suggest that their method might be better suited to arid or semiarid climates than to humid ones.

The models previously described predict that at some stage of evaporation, the isotopic composition of the liquid will reach a steady state [Eq. (22)], which represents a balance between the fractionated evaporative flux and back transport and reequilibration with atmospheric moisture. However, laboratory (Gonfiantini, 1965) and field (Lloyd, 1966; Fontes and Gonfiantini, 1967) studies show that in some cases an evaporating water does not reach a steady isotopic composition, but rather, after an initial period of enrichment, with continuing evaporation, the water becomes depleted. This effect is shown on Figure 2.

The models predict steady-state isotopic composition because, in their formulation, they assume the classic Raoult's law dependence of vapor pressure of an isotopic species on the mole fraction of that species in the liquid. In a more general statement of Raoult's law, vapor pressure is dependent on the thermodynamic activity of the species in solution, rather than on its mole fraction. In a saline solution, as evaporation proceeds, the salt concentration will increase, decreasing the activity of the evaporating solute species, thus lowering its vapor pressure, and not, in general, permitting the attainment of an isotopic steady state. The changes in fractionation factor with salt concentration have been used to study the activity of water in solutions by Taube (1954) and Truesdell (1974). Gonfiantini (1965) theoretically and experimentally related this to the change in the isotopic composition of an evaporating solution. Sofer and Gat (1972, 1975) and Stewart and Friedman (1975) have investigated the effects of various types of solutes on oxygen and hydrogen fractionation factors, respectively. The work of these and other authors is summarized by Friedman and O'Neil (1977, Figures 34, 35, and 38).

While the simple model as used by Friedman or simplifications of the Craig and Gordon model as used by Fontes and Gonfiantini (1967) seem to work well in areas of low humidity, in areas of high humidity the various parameters necessary to use the Craig and Gordon model are, in general, not easily measurable. Zimmermann and Ehhalt (1970) studied the water balance of Lake Neusiedl near Vienna where, in addition to the various input and lake water measurements, they also measured the isotopic composition of water

vapor above the lake. Theoretically, and practically, as a result of their study, they show that in such a humid temperate region as Austria even with data of the best possible accuracy it is difficult to determine the evaporation rate of a lake using isotopes to an accuracy better than about 50%. Their error analysis of the model equations shows that most of this error is due to an inability to measure relative humidities to the precision needed for use in Eq. (16).

Fontes and Gonfiantini (1970) have shown that the isotopic composition of atmospheric moisture over Lake Geneva varies regularly with distance from the lake's surface. They interpret this as mixing between evaporation and regional atmospheric moisture and suggest that this effect would be useful to estimate areal influence of the lake on the atmosphere.

Due to the theoretical and experimental difficulties pointed out by Zimmermann and Ehhalt (1970) in using isotopes to estimate the evaporation of lakes in humid regions, most recent work has been restricted to lakes in arid regions, and the results even there have been a mixed success. Gonfiantini et al. (1973) describe the isotopic composition of waters from several lakes in the Danakil depression of Ethiopia. They find a correlation between $\delta^{18}O$ and chloride content but are unable by any reasonable combination of parameters to reproduce this correlation on the basis of evaporation alone. They therefore conclude that the correlation is due to mixing of waters from various sources within the lake rather than strictly to evaporation.

One of the more fascinating water balance problems in present-day study of lakes involves Lake Chad. A number of isotopic and chemical studies of the lake have been made, among which may be mentioned those of Fontes et al. (1970) and of Roche (1975). Lake Chad is very large—about 20,000 km^2—and is in an area where the evaporation rate is over 2 m/year. Thus, isotopic concentration effects should be large and, indeed, isolated portions of the lake are found to be enriched by as much as $20‰$ in ^{18}O and $110‰$ in deuterium. That the total solute concentration in the lake water does not seem to be increasing with time is accounted for by the production of minerals which remove most of the solutes in solution in the lake proper and in the highly evaporated regions along the lake shores.

Paleotemperatures

As described in the introduction, when calcite ($CaCO_3$) slowly precipitates from water, $\delta^{18}O_{CaCO_3}$ will differ from $\delta^{18}O_{H_2O}$ by an amount which depends on the temperature at which precipitation occurs. This is the basis of the carbonate paleotemperature scale, which has been extensively applied in oceanic sediments, in speleothems, and, to a more limited extent, in lake sediments.

The difficulty in interpreting carbonate stable oxygen isotope data is that one has only a single measured parameter ($\delta^{18}O$) from which to deduce two variables, the temperature and $\delta^{18}O$ of the water from which the carbonate precipitated. To extract at least relative paleotemperature information from freshwater carbonate $\delta^{18}O$ data, Hendy and Wilson (1968) and Stuiver (1968) used the following reasoning. As mentioned in the preceding section, Dansgaard (1964) has shown theoretically and experimentally that at present, $\delta^{18}O$ in precipitation varies by $0.7‰/°C$ with mean temperature. In a long-term climate shift, it is not unreasonable to expect the same relationship to hold, that is:

$$\Delta^{18}O_p = 0.70 \, \Delta(t - t_{oc}) \qquad (28)$$

where $\Delta^{18}O_p$ is the change in $\delta^{18}O$ of precipitation during a climatic shift and $\Delta(t - t_{oc})$ is the change in temperature gradient between the ocean (t_{oc}) and the point of precipitation (t). The change in ^{18}O fractionation between water and carbonate with temperature must also be included (Figure 1). At temperatures between 5 and 30°C, this is close to $-0.24‰/°C$. Finally, changes in $\delta^{18}O$ ($\Delta^{18}O_{oc}$) of the surface ocean, the source of moisture to the atmosphere, must be included. During glacial maxima, enough ^{18}O-depleted water was contained in glaciers to have raised $\delta^{18}O$ of the ocean by as much as $1.2‰$ (Dansgaard and Tauber, 1969). Stuiver (1968), and similarly Hendy and Wilson (1968), combined these considerations in the expression

$$\Delta^{18}O = \Delta^{18}O_{oc} + 0.70 \, \Delta(t - t_{oc}) - 0.24 \, \Delta t. \qquad (29)$$

If one is concerned only with changes since the close of the last glacial maximum (the last 9000 years or so), $\Delta^{18}O_{oc}$ and ΔT_{oc} will be essentially zero, and the expression simplifies to $\Delta^{18}O = 0.46 \, \Delta t$.

Stuiver (1968, 1970) has measured the ^{18}O content of marls and mollusk shells from sediments of lakes in Maine, New York, Indiana, and South Dakota. Age control on his samples was based on ^{14}C measurements or pollen studies. Carbonates deposited during the hypsithermal interval have increased ^{18}O contents suggesting higher mean temperatures then than now. Likewise, there is a marked decrease in the carbonate ^{18}O content beginning at about 9000 years before present, presumably corresponding to the ending of the last glaciation. Stuiver (1968, 1970) also reports the ^{13}C content of these carbonates, to be discussed below.

Fritz *et al.* (1975) were able to follow the climatic history and evolution of Lake Erie since deglaciation from ^{13}C and ^{18}O measurements on ostracode and mollusc shells from a sediment core. The core chronology was inferred from specific pollen boundaries in the core, correlated with ^{14}C-dated pollen records

elsewhere in the region. Two episodes of ^{18}O enrichment occurred, one at about 12,500 and the other at about 9000 years before present.

The isotopic composition of precipitation varies seasonally, being depleted in the heavier isotopes in winter and enriched in summer (Dansgaard, 1964). If the volume of a lake is large compared to the annual flow of water through it, these seasonal variations in precipitation will be smoothed out, and the lake will have a nearly constant isotopic composition. In smaller lakes, however, seasonal variations are to be expected and would appear as well in carbonate precipitating from them. Stuiver (1968) found less than $1‰$ seasonal variation in shells from Linsley Pond, Connecticut, though lake surface waters varied by $3‰$, and concluded that seasonal noise should not seriously obscure long-term trends. Fritz and Poplawski (1974) report similar results and attribute the smoothing of the shell record to the growth patterns of the molluscs which permit them to deposit carbonate at the same times each year when lakes are likely to have the same oxygen isotope compositions.

Where temperatures are likely to have been reasonably constant, changes in the ^{18}O content of carbonate will reflect changes in lake water ^{18}O values from other effects. Covich and Stuiver (1974) report marked $\delta^{18}O$ changes in core from Laguna Chichancanab, Yucatan, Mexico. They attribute these variations to differences in lake level due to changing rainfall and evaporation patterns. The most ^{18}O-enriched shells correspond to periods when evaporation was high and, hence, the lake waters were enriched in ^{18}O by evaporation.

Although the temperature variation of the ^{18}O fractionation factor between water and carbonate is the most widely used paleothermometer, the use of other reactions has been explored. Friedman and O'Neil (1977) have compiled temperature-dependent fractionation factor data for several systems of potential interest in limnology, including the sulfate–water and phosphate–water system. The phosphate–water system has not been explored in detail. The sulfate–water system may be of limited utility because times of the order of 10^3 to 10^5 years are required to approach isotopic reequilibrium at earth surface temperatures (Lloyd, 1968).

Oxygen isotope fractionation factors between water and various silicate minerals are known (Friedman and O'Neil, 1977, Figures 16–25) but are not useful in lake studies because of sluggish reaction rates below several hundred degrees Celsius. O'Neil and Hay (1973), though, find over $10‰$ $\delta^{18}O$ difference in cherts formed in East African, alkaline, saline lakes. This suggests that the fluids in which the cherts formed were of widely varying salinities.

In highly saline lakes, a variety of hydrous minerals may precipitate, permitting the use of deuterium paleothermometers. Matsuo *et al.* (1972) measured the temperature-dependent deuterium fractionation factors between water and the minerals borax ($Na_2 B_4O_7 \cdot 10H_2O$), gaylussite ($Na_2 CO_3 \cdot CaCO_3 \cdot 5H_2O$), nahcolite ($NaHCO_3$) and trona ($Na_2 CO_3 \cdot NaHCO_3 \cdot 2H_2O$). Deuterium is depleted in all these minerals, except for borax, where no significant fractionation occurred. The temperature dependence of trona fractionation was marked. It should be possible to use borax, which does not fractionate, to find the deuterium content of the water from which it precipitated, and the coexisting trona to estimate the temperature of precipitation.

Carbon

The relative terrestrial abundances of the two stable isotopes of carbon, ^{12}C and ^{13}C, are 98.89 and 1.11% (Schwarcz, 1969). Craig (1953), Schwarcz (1969), and Hoefs (1973) discuss the geochemistry of the stable isotopes of carbon and present information on isotopic variation of natural substances and on analytical methods. The average $\delta^{13}C$ of atmospheric carbon dioxide is about $-7‰$ and may vary locally as a function of such factors as the abundance of vegetation and combustion of fossil fuels (Keeling, 1958). Lacustrine plankton, lacustrine plants, and terrestrial plants are major sources of carbon in lake sediments; their average $\delta^{13}C$ values are approximately -30, -21, and $-24‰$, respectively. Mineral carbonate of marine origin has an average $\delta^{13}C$ of about $0‰$ (Schwarcz, 1969).

Carbon isotopes fractionate among the several common oxidized carbon species—gaseous and dissolved CO_2, dissolved bicarbonate, and dissolved and mineral carbonate. Mook et al. (1974) measured the fractionation between dissolved bicarbonate and gaseous CO_2. They found a value of ~ 1.008 at 20°C which implies that bicarbonate of lake water isotopically equilibrated with atmospheric CO_2 should be about $+1‰$. The carbon fractionation factor between dissolved carbonate ion and carbon dioxide is about 1.013 at 25°C (Thode et al., 1965). Therefore, as pH and temperature change, the isotopic composition of total dissolved carbon varies greatly owing to changes in the relative amounts of dissolved carbon-bearing species. However, dissolved CO_2 is about $1‰$ lighter than gaseous CO_2 over the temperature range of lakes. Carbon isotope fractionation factors of inorganic reactions are given by Friedman and O'Neil (1977, their Figures 27–33).

^{12}C is enriched in plants by photosynthesis. Plants using the most common (the Calvin or C_3) photosynthetic pathway have a mean $\delta^{13}C$ of about $-27‰$, $20‰$ depleted in ^{12}C relative to atmospheric CO_2 (Park and Epstein, 1960, 1961). Grasses and other plants using the Hatch–Slack (or C_4) pathway have a mean $\delta^{13}C$ of about $-14‰$ (Hatch and Slack, 1970). A third group of plants, mostly succulents, use the CAM (Crassulacean Acid Metabolic) pathway and have $\delta^{13}C$ values which range from -9 to $-29‰$ with no well-defined peak in the distribution of values. Troughton (1972) reviews carbon isotope fractionation in higher plants.

There is also fractionation between oxidized and reduced carbon species. Both methane and CO_2 are structurally simple molecules and Bottinga (1969) has theoretically calculated carbon isotope fractionation factors between them. At 25°C, methane is depleted in ^{13}C by $68‰$ relative to CO_2 (see also Friedman and O'Neil, 1977, Figure 29). Games and Hays (1976) and Rosenfeld and Silverman (1959) studied the carbon isotope fractionation during bacterial conversion between methane and CO_2. The fractionation is dependent upon microbial ecology which is a function of nutrient availability.

Stable carbon isotope measurements may be useful adjuncts to studies of the carbon cycle in and carbon mass balances of lakes. Carbonate species dissolved in lake waters may have several sources with $\delta^{13}C$ values ranging from $\approx 0‰$ (marine mineral carbonate) to $> -27‰$ (dissolved CO_2 from plant respiration and decay), and the $\delta^{13}C$ value of the dissolved carbonate will reflect the proportions of its various sources. As an aid in providing information for carbon isotope balances, several authors have investigated anaerobic sediments and the monimolimnian (noncirculating bottom waters) of meromictic lakes (Deevey et al., 1963; Stiller and Magaritz, 1974; Koyama et al., 1973; Deuser et al., 1973; Nissenbaum et al., 1972; Oana and Deevey, 1960).

Oana and Deevey (1960) noted ^{12}C enrichment in the bottom layer relative to the surface layer in dimictic lakes in Connecticut. They attribute this to the presence in the bottom water of dissolved CO_2 derived from the oxidation of ^{12}C-enriched plant debris on the bottom. This source dominates over the other sources they consider, which include surface CO_2 exchange, CO_2 production from respiration, and CO_3^{2-} addition from carbonate-bearing rocks. Deevey and Stuiver (1964) and Deevey et al. (1964) developed a carbon isotope balance for Linsley Pond, Connecticut. Its carbon balance, they point out, is dominated by the influx of bicarbonate in surface runoff and by the fact that contributions of carbon from ground-water and the atmosphere are small. Metabolism is a nearly closed cycle within the lake. Takahashi et al. (1968) undertook a chemical and isotopic study of meromictic Green Lake. They account for the lake's carbon chemistry as an interplay between the carbonate in the inflow water, $CaCO_3$ precipitation, photosynthesis, bacterial activity, and gas exchange between the lake's surface and the atmosphere. They conclude that

Green Lake is permanently stratified due to a salinity difference between the deep and surface layers. Water entering below the chemocline is nearly twice as saline as that entering the surface layer. They suggest that there is no possibility that the meromixis was generated by biological activity. Mook (1970) discusses carbon isotope balance in Lake Ijssel, Netherlands. He observes that ^{13}C increases with increasing distance from the mouth of the river Ijssel and concludes that one-half of the increase is due to photosynthetic activity initiating precipitation of calcium carbonate while the other half is due to exchange with atmospheric CO_2.

The use of stable oxygen isotope ratios of shell and other solid carbonate material in lake sediments to estimate paleotemperatures has been discussed. The stable carbon isotope ratios in the same material can also be used to assess some aspects of a lake's history. Stuiver (1970) analyzed freshwater carbonates and mollusks from sediments for carbon and oxygen isotopic composition. He observed that ^{13}C correlates with climate but appears to be a less useful indicator than ^{18}O content. Fritz et al. (1975) measured $\delta^{18}O$ and $\delta^{13}C$ values of mollusk and other shells from a Lake Erie core. They found that the $\delta^{13}C$ values reflect variations in aquatic vegetation and water depth. Fritz and Poplawski (1974) analyzed the isotopic composition of freshwater mollusks and of specimens grown under laboratory conditions. They report that the ^{13}C content of mollusk shells is primarily controlled by that of the aqueous carbonate species. Biological fractionation and the isotopic composition of the mollusk's food are of only minimal importance.

The isotopic composition of organic carbon in lake sediments may also reflect lake conditions at the time of deposition. Stuiver (1975) in a study of late Quaternary lake sediments points out that several factors influence the long-term ^{13}C record. The two predominant factors are changes in the organic productivity and in the hardness of the water. In general, during colder climatic episodes $\delta^{13}C$ values are more positive, with organic sediments being derived nearly entirely from phyto- and zooplankton. More negative $\delta^{13}C$ values indicate an influx of terrestrial and/or floating material.

Nitrogen

Nitrogen isotope abundances in a variety of natural substances have been measured. Studies by Dole et al. (1954) and Hoering (1956) indicate that the ratio of the two naturally occurring stable isotopes of nitrogen, ^{14}N and ^{15}N, is constant in air. This ratio was measured as 273 ± 1 by Nier (1950) and 272 ± 0.3 (Junk and Svec, 1958). Nitrogen in air has been chosen

as the nitrogen stable isotope standard (zero in the per mil scale) because of its constant $^{15}N/^{14}N$ ratio.

Other investigations of the nitrogen isotopic composition of natural substances include studies of groundwater (Jones, 1973; Kreitler and Jones, 1975), of precipitation (Hoering, 1957), of the marine environment (Miyaka and Wada, 1967; Injerd, 1973a, 1973b; Cline and Kaplan, 1975; Wada and Hattori, 1976), of petroleum and coals (Hoering, 1956; Hoering and Moore, 1958; Bokhoven and Theeuwen, 1966; Eichmann et al., 1971), and of soils (Cheng et al., 1964; Delwiche and Steyn, 1970; Rennie and Paul, 1974).

The nitrogen isotopic composition of biological materials is dependent in large degree upon the biological processes of the nitrogen cycle. Delwiche (1970) reviewed the nitrogen cycle. Keeney (1973) discusses sediment–water systems and points out the importance in the nitrogen cycle of fractionations by N-mineralization and immobilization, denitrification and nitrification, and N-fixation (incorporation into compounds that plants and animals can utilize). Cook et al. (1973) present a discussion of nitrogen isotope fractionations in the nitrogen cycle. Although Urey (1947) and later Scalan (1959) calculated equilibrium isotopic fractionation factors between NH_3, NH_4^+, and N_2, biological reactions in nature are kinetically controlled, and the fractionation factors must be experimentally measured. The magnitude of the isotopic fractionation is dependent upon the specific biological process (Delwiche and Steyn, 1970). For instance, a large nitrogen isotope fractionation (~ 1.02) occurs during denitrification (Wellman et al., 1968; Delwiche and Steyn, 1970; Cline and Kaplan, 1975). The direction of the isotopic fractionation is determined by the fact that microorganisms utilize ^{14}N over ^{15}N, causing the substrate to be enriched in ^{15}N. Ammonium oxidation and ammonium assimilation were studied by Delwiche and Steyn (1970). Hoering (1958) investigated fixation of atmospheric N_2 and found ^{14}N being used 1.0022 ± 0.0010 times faster than ^{15}N. Shearer et al. (1974) modelled the isotopic fractionation during biological reactions in soils.

A number of investigators have undertaken nitrogen isotope studies to evaluate sources and sinks of nitrogen in the environment (Hoering, 1957; Kohl et al., 1971; Hauck et al., 1972; Jones, 1973; Edwards, 1973, 1974; Rennie and Paul, 1975; Freyer and Aly, 1975). Because of the large number of sources and sinks of nitrogen any nitrogen isotope study of a particular segment of the cycle, such as lakes, should be aimed at obtaining information to construct a nitrogen isotope mass balance. Research should be directed toward quantifying the (1) isotopic fractionation factors of biological processes, (2) isotopic composition of the nitrogen-bearing phases present, and (3) masses of the nitrogen-bearing constituents involved.

In their nitrogen isotope study of lakes, Pang and

Nriagu (1976) measured the $\delta^{15}N$ of nitrogen-bearing phases in sediments of the eutrophic Bay of Quinte, Lake Ontario. They point out that the sources of nitrogen in lake water include:

(1) solution of atmospheric nitrogen,
(2) introduction of nitrogen-bearing compounds in recharging streams, which might consist of naturally or industrially produced phases,
(3) mineralization of organic nitrogen in sediments to ammonium ion, followed by oxidation to nitrate and diffusion into overlying water (Pang and Nriagu, 1976), and
(4) fixation of nitrogen by microorganisms.

The sinks of nitrogen include:

(1) diffusion of NO_3^- to the anaerobic zone, followed by biological denitrification to N_2, N_2O, or NH_4^+ and loss to groundwater systems, and
(2) burial in sediments as organic nitrogen derived from lacustrine plankton and organic debris.

Pang and Nriagu (1976) observed a range in $\delta^{15}N$ of +5 to +10‰ in exchangeable NH_4^+ and of +3.5 to +5.5‰ in 6 N HCl hydrolyzable total N and 6 N HCl hydrolyzable ammonium nitrogen. These results are in accord with the observation that the incomplete transformation of organic nitrogen $\rightarrow NH_4^+ \rightarrow NO_3^-$ is accompanied by depletion of NO_3^- in ^{15}N. During the incomplete nitrification of NH_4^+, NO_3^- is depleted in ^{15}N, concomitant with an increase in ^{15}N of NH_4^+. The abundance of NO_3^- is too low for $\delta^{15}N$ analysis.

$\delta^{15}N$ values of plankton and bottom sediments in Lake Superior measured by Pang and Nriagu (1977) range from +1.6 to ±5.7‰. They demonstrate that nitrogen isotopes are fractionated by biogeochemical processes in lakes, and that quantification of fractionation factors for each process is required before the nitrogen system can be modelled. Clearly, more biochemical laboratory experiments to measure isotopic fractionation factors of biological reactions are needed in order to employ nitrogen isotopes to study lacustrine environments.

Sulfur

There are four stable sulfur isotopes, ^{32}S, ^{33}S, ^{34}S, and ^{36}S, which occur naturally in the proportions 95.0:0.76:4.22:0.014. Only $^{34}S/^{32}S$ ratios are usually measured and discussed because no additional information would be gained by measuring the other isotopes in naturally occuring samples. Hoefs (1973) discusses measurement techniques and the general geochemistry of stable sulfur isotopes.

The dominant cause of isotope ratio differences among various types of sulfur-bearing compounds is fractionation during sulfur oxidation or reduction. The equilibrium enrichment factor between sulfate and hydrogen sulfide is about 66‰ at 25°C (Sakai, 1957). This is a calculated value; however, the rate of sulfur exchange between sulfate and sulfide is so slow below a few hundred degrees that other fractionation mechanisms dominate the distribution of sulfur isotopes at earth's surface temperatures.

Generally, natural sulfide is depleted in ^{34}S relative to the sulfate from which it is being reduced, but by much less than the equilibrium 66‰. This is a result of kinetic fractionation during irreversible sulfate reduction, for which Harrison and Thode (1957) measured an enrichment factor of 22‰. Because natural sulfate reduction commonly accompanies bacterial activity, many studies of bacterial effects on sulfur isotopic fractionation have been made. These have recently been reviewed and summarized by Goldhaber and Kaplan (1974, 1975).

The isotope ratios of coexisting sulfate and sulfide have been extensively used in studies of reducing marine sediments. The approaches taken are reviewed by Goldhaber and Kaplan (1974, 1975) and should be equally applicable to lakes.

Sulfur isotope work in lakes is usually combined with stable carbon isotope measurements because, in reducing environments where sulfur isotope fractionation is marked, oxidation of ^{13}C-depleted organic carbon accompanies sulfate reduction. Deevey and Nakai (1962) and Deevey et al. (1963) describe such studies on two lakes. In dimictic Linsley Pond, Connecticut, they found that while $\delta^{34}S$ of the dissolved sulfate was usually about +7‰ during the autumn, toward the end of the lake's period of stratification, the bottom water sulfate concentration decreased and its $\delta^{34}S$ increased to +13‰. At the same time, sulfide extracted from bottom muds had $\delta^{34}S$ of −7‰. The ^{34}S enrichment in the dissolved sulfate, coupled with its lower concentration, was interpreted as a result of sulfate reduction to ^{34}S-depleted sulfide. The measured $\delta^{34}S$ values suggest a fractionation during the reduction of about 20‰, in agreement with the kinetic fractionation of Harrison and Thode (1957).

Deevey et al. (1963) have measured sulfur isotopes in the meromictic Fayetteville Green Lake, New York. While the accompanying carbon isotope measurements permit an interpretation of the carbon cycle in the lake, as discussed above, interpretation of the sulfur isotopes is not straightforward. There is a decrease in the concentration and the ^{32}S content of the dissolved sulfate with depth and corresponding increases in the concentration and ^{32}S content of the dissolved sulfide. However, the sulfide is depleted in ^{34}S by about 56‰ relative to the sulfate, too large to be due to simple kinetic fractionation alone, and implying either a complex reflux mechanism operating within the lake or some not well-defined bacterial fractionation mechanism.

Nissenbaum and Kaplan (1976) find a similar pattern of sulfate and sulfide concentration and isotope contents in the water and sediments of the Dead Sea. The sulfate and sulfide isotope differences there are less than 37‰. Laboratory bacteria experiments have produced fractionations as large as 46‰ (Kaplan and Rittenberg, 1964).

Variations other than those due to local reduction occur in the ^{34}S content of sulfate, which have potential use in lake studies. The ratios of the other isotopes discussed here have been essentially constant in a given material through geologic time. The ^{34}S content of marine sulfate minerals, however, has varied through time. At present, the $\delta^{34}S$ of marine sulfate is +22‰, but it has varied from +30‰ in the early Paleozoic to +10‰ in the late Paleozoic (Holzer and Kaplan, 1966). This variation might be of use in determining which of several potential geological sources of sulfate are entering a system of interest.

Summary

(1) Variations in the ratios of the stable isotopes of hydrogen (D/H), carbon ($^{13}C/^{12}C$), nitrogen ($^{15}N/^{14}N$), oxygen ($^{18}O/^{16}O$), and sulfur ($^{34}S/^{32}S$) are of use in lake studies.

(2) Isotope ratio variations are due to isotope fractionation during some physical processes, such as diffusion, as a result of chemical equilibria, or accompanying irreversible chemical reactions.

(3) Fractionation among the isotopic species of water, $H_2^{16}O$, $HD^{16}O$, and $H_2^{18}O$ takes place during evaporation. The amount of evaporative fractionation is a function of many factors and frequently cannot be determined with much precision. Nonetheless, in favorable circumstances, isotope balances are useful in estimating lake water balances.

(4) The oxygen and hydrogen in slowly precipitated minerals may be in isotopic equilibrium with the precipitating solution. Isotope ratios in sedimentary minerals have been used to infer paleotemperature and paleosalinity changes.

(5) Carbon, nitrogen, and sulfur isotopes fractionate during the oxidation–reduction reactions which figure prominently in the natural cycles of these elements. These reactions are bacterially mediated, and their fractionation factors may vary widely. Relative isotope ratio changes in coexisting oxidized and reduced species may, nevertheless, suggest reaction mechanisms, and, in favorable cases, isotope balances may lead to elemental cycle balances.

(6) Carbonate isotope fractionation factors among gaseous, dissolved, and mineral carbonate and CO_2 are known, as are the relatively constant differences between such carbon-bearing compounds as plants, marine carbonate minerals, and atmospheric CO_2. Carbon isotopes can frequently be used to estimate the relative proportions of various potential sources and sinks of carbon in a lake system.

References

Bigeleisen, J., and M. G. Mayer. (1947). Isotopic exchange reactions. *J. Chem. Phys.,* **15**:261–267.

Bokhoven, C., and H. J. Theeuwen. (1966). Determination of the abundance of carbon and nitrogen isotopes in Dutch coals and natural gases. *Nature,* **211**:927–929.

Bonner, F. T., E. Roth, O. A. Schaeffer, and S. O. Thompson. (1961). Chlorine-36 and deuterium study of Great Basin lake waters. *Geochim. Cosmochim. Acta,* **25**:261–266.

Bottinga, Y. (1969). Calculated fractionation factors for carbon and hydrogen isotope exchange in the system calcite–carbon dioxide–graphite–methane–hydrogen–water vapor. *Geochim. Cosmochim. Acta,* **33**:49–64.

Cheng, H. H., J. M. Bremner, and A. P. Edwards. (1964). Variations of nitrogen-15 abundance in soils. *Science,* **146**:1574–1575.

Clayton, R. N., J. R. Goldsmith, K. J. Karel, T. K. Mayeda, and R. C. Newton. (1974). Limits on the effect of pressure on isotopic fractionation. *Geochim. Cosmochim. Acta,* **39**:1197–1201.

Cline, D. J., and I. R. Kaplan. (1975). Isotopic fractionation of dissolved nitrate during denitrification in the eastern tropical North Pacific Ocean. *Marine Chem.,* **3**:271–299.

Cook, F. D., R. P. Wellman, and H. R. Krouse. (1973). Nitrogen isotope fractionation in the nitrogen cycle. Pp. 49–64. In: E. Ingerson (ed.), *Proc. Symp. on Hydrogeochemistry and Biogeochemistry,* Tokyo (Washington, D. C., The Clark Co.)

Coplen, T. B., and B. B. Hanshaw. (1973). Ultrafiltration by a compacted clay membrane. I. Oxygen and hydrogen fractionation. *Geochim. Cosmochim. Acta,* **37**:2295–2310.

Covich, A., and M. Stuiver. (1974). Changes in oxygen-18 as a measure of long-term fluctuations in tropical lake levels and molluscan populations. *Limnol. Oceanogr.,* **19**:682–691.

Craig, H. (1953). The geochemistry of the stable carbon isotopes. *Geochim. Cosmochim. Acta,* **3**:53–92.

Craig, H. (1961). Isotopic variations in meteoric waters. *Science,* **133**:1702–1703.

Craig, H., and L. I. Gordon. (1965). Deuterium and oxygen-18 variations in the ocean and the marine atmosphere. Pp. 9–130. In: E. Tongiorgi (ed.), *Stable Isotopes in Oceanographic Studies and Paleotemperatures.* Laboratorio de Geologia Nucleare, Pisa.

Dansgaard, W. (1964). Stable isotopes in precipitation. *Tellus,* **16**:436–468.

Dansgaard, W., and H. Tauber. (1969). Glacier oxygen-18 content and Pleistocene ocean temperatures. *Science,* **166**:499–502.

Deevey, E. S., and N. Nakai. (1962). Fractionation of sulfur isotopes in lake waters. Pp. 169–178. In: M. L. Jensen (ed.), *Symposium on Biogeochemistry of Sulfur Isotopes.* Yale Univ., New Haven, CT.

Deevey, E. S., N. Nakai, and M. Stuiver. (1963). Fractionation of sulfur and carbon isotopes in a meromictic lake. *Science,* **139**:407–408.

Deevey, E. S., and M. Stuiver. (1964). Distribution of natural isotopes of carbon in Linsley Pond and other New England lakes. *Limnol. Oceanogr.,* **9**:1–11.

Deevey, E. S., M. Stuiver, and N. Nakai. (1964). Isotopes of carbon and sulfur as traces of lake metabolism. *Verh. Int. Verein. Limnol.,* **15**:284–288.

Delwiche, C. C. (1970). The nitrogen cycle. *Sci. Am.,* **223**:137–146.

Delwiche, C. C., and P. L. Steyn. (1970). Nitrogen isotope fractionation in soils and microbial reactions. *J. Environ. Qual.,* **4**:929–935.

Deuser, W. G., E. T. Degens, G. R. Harvey, and M. Rubin. (1973). Methane in Lake Kivu: new data on its origin. *Science,* **181**:151–154.

Dincer, T. (1968). The use of oxygen-18 and deuterium concentrations in the water balance of lakes. *Water Resources Res.,* **4**:1289–1306.

Dole, M., G. A. Lane, D. P. Rudd, and D. A. Zaukelies. (1954). Isotopic composition of atmospheric oxygen and nitrogen. *Geochim. Cosmochim. Acta,* **6**:65–78.

Edwards, A. P. (1973). Isotopic tracer techniques for identification of sources of nitrate pollution. *J. Environ. Qual.,* **2**:383–387.

Edwards, A. P. (1974). Isotope effects in relation to the interpretation of ¹⁵N/¹⁴N ratios in tracer studies. Pp. 455–468. In: *Isotope Ratios as Pollutant Sources and Behavior Indicators.* Internat. Atomic Energy Agency, Vienna.

Eichmann, R., A. Plate, W. Behrens, and H. Kroepelin. (1971). Das isotopenverhältnis des Stickstoffs in einigen erdgasen Erdölgesen und Erdölen Nordwestdeutschlands. *Erdöl Kohle,* **24**:2.

Epstein, S., and T. Mayeda. (1953). Variations of O¹⁸ content of waters from natural sources. *Geochim. Cosmochim. Acta,* **4**:213–224.

Epstein, S., R. Buchsbaum, H. A. Lowenstam, and H. C. Urey. (1953). Revised carbonate–water temperature scale. *Geol. Soc. Am. Bull.,* **62**:417–426.

Fontes, J. Ch., and R. Gonfiantini. (1967). Comportment isotopique cours de l'evaporation de deux bassins Sahariens. *Earth Planet. Sci. Lett.,* **3**:258–266.

Fontes, J. Ch., and R. Gonfiantini. (1970). Composition isotopique et origine de la vapeur d'eau atmospherique dans la region de Lac Léman. *Earth Planet. Sci. Lett.,* **7**:325–329.

Fontes, J. Ch., R. Gonfiantini, and M. A. Roche. (1970). Deuterium et oxygene-18 dans les eaux du Lac Tchad. Pp. 387–404. In: *Isotope Hydrology 1970.* Internat. Atomic Energy Agency, Vienna.

Freyer, H. D., and A. I. M. Aly. (1975). Nitrogen-15 studies on identifying fertilizer excess in environmental systems. Pp. 21–33. In: *Isotope Ratios as Pollutant Sources and Behavior Indicators.* Internat. Atomic Energy Agency, Vienna.

Friedman, I. (1953). Deuterium content of natural water and other substances. *Geochim. Cosmochim. Acta,* **4**:89–103.

Friedman, I., and J. R. O'Neil. (1977). Compilation of stable isotope fractionation factors of geochemical interest. Chapter KK. Pp. KK1–KK12. In: *Data of Geochemistry,* 6th ed.. U.S. Geol. Surv. Prof. Paper 440-KK.

Friedman, I., and A. C. Redfield. (1971). A model of the hydrology of the lakes of the lower Grand Coulee, Washington. *Water Resources Res.,* **7**:874–898.

Friedman, I., D. R. Norton, D. B. Carter, and A. C. Redfield. (1956). The deuterium balance of Lake Maracaibo. *Limnol. Oceanogr.,* **1**:239–246.

Friedman, I., A. C. Redfield, B. Schoen, and J. Harris. (1964). The variation of the deuterium content of natural waters in the hydrologic cycle. *Rev. Geophys.,* **2**:177–224.

Friedman, I., G. I. Smith, and K. G. Hardcastle. (1976). Studies of Quaternary saline lakes—II. Isotopic and compositional changes during dessication of the brines in Owens Lake, California, 1969–1971. *Geochim. Cosmochim. Acta,* **40**:501–511.

Fritz, P., and S. Poplawski. (1974). ¹⁸O and ¹³C in the shells of freshwater molluscs and their environments. *Earth Planet. Sci. Lett.,* **24**:91–98.

Fritz, P., T. W. Anderson, and C. F. M. Lewis. (1975). Late Quaternary climatic trends in history of Lake Erie from stable isotope studies. *Science,* **190**:267–269.

Games, L. M., and J. M. Hayes. (1976). On the mechanisms of CO_2 and CH_4 production in natural anaerobic environments. In: J. O. Nriagu (ed.), *Environmental Biochemistry.* Ann Arbor Science Publishers, Ann Arbor, MI.

Garlick, G. D. (1969). The stable isotopes of oxygen. Section 8-B. Pp. 8-B-1–8-B-26. In: K. J. Wedepohl (ed.), *Handbook of Geochemistry.* Springer-Verlag, New York, NY.

Gat, J. R. (1970). Environmental isotope balance of Lake Tiberias. Pp. 109–127. In: *Isotope Hydrology 1970.* Internat. Atomic Energy Agency, Vienna.

Goldhaber, M. B., and I. R. Kaplan. (1974). The sulfur cycle. Pp. 569–655. In: E. D. Goldberg (ed.), *The Sea, Vol. 5, Marine Chemistry.* John Wiley and Sons, New York, NY.

Goldhaber, M. B., and I. R. Kaplan. (1975). Controls and consequences of sulfate reduction rates in recent marine sediments. *Soil Sci.,* **119**:42–55.

Gonfiantini, R. (1965). Effetti isotopici nel l'evaporazione di acque salate. *Atti della Soc. Tosc. Sc. Nat.,* Series A, **74**:1–22.

Gonfiantini, R. (1977). *Consultants' meeting on stable isotope standards and intercalibration in hydrology and in geochemistry, final report.* Internat. Atomic Energy Agency 77-3977, Vienna. 22 pp.

Gonfiantini, R., S. Borse, G. Ferrara, and C. Panichi. (1973). Isotopic composition of waters from the Danakil depression (Ethiopia). *Earth Planet. Sci. Lett.,* **18**:13–21.

Harrison, A. G., and H. G. Thode. (1957). The kinetic isotope effect in the chemical reduction of sulfate. *Trans. Faraday Soc.,* **53**:1648–1651.

Hatch, M. D., and C. R. Slack. (1970). Photosynthetic CO_2 fixation pathways. *Ann. Rev. Plant Physiol.,* **21**:141–162.

Hauck, R. D., W. V. Bartholomew, J. M. Bremner, F. E.

Broadbent, H. H. Cheng, A. P. Edwards, D. R. Keeney, J. O. Legg, S. R. Olson, and L. K. Porter. (1972). Use of variations in natural N-isotope abundance for environmental studies. A questionable approach. *Science,* **177**:453–456.

Hendy, C. H., and A. T. Wilson. (1968). Paleoclimatic data from speleothems. *Nature,* **219**:48–51.

Hoefs, J. (1973). *Stable Isotope Geochemistry.* Springer-Verlag, New York, NY. 140 pp.

Hoering, T. (1956). Variations in the nitrogen isotope abundance. *Proc. 2nd Conference on Nuclear Processes in Geologic Settings,* p. 85.

Hoering, T. (1957). The isotopic composition of the ammonia and nitrate ion in rain water. *Geochim. Cosmochim. Acta,* **12**:97–102.

Hoering, T. C. (1958). Cosmological and geological implications of isotope ratio variations. P. 161. In: *Isotopic Abundances of Lighter Elements.* U.S. National Academy Science–National Research Council Publication 572.

Hoering, T., and H. E. Moore. (1958). The isotopic composition of the nitrogen in natural gases and associated crude oils. *Geochim. Cosmochim. Acta,* **13**:225–232.

Holzer, W. T., and I. R. Kaplan. (1966). Isotope geochemistry of sedimentary sulfates. *Chem. Geol.,* **1**:93–135.

I.A.E.A. (1968). Atmosphere–surface water interrelations: Evaporation from lakes. Chap. 1. In: *Guidebook on Nuclear Techniques in Hydrology.* Internat. Atomic Energy Agency, Technical Report Series No. 91. 213 pp.

I.A.E.A. (1969). *Environmental Isotope Data No. 1: World Survey of Isotope Concentration in Precipitation (1953–1963).* Internat. Atomic Energy Agency, Vienna, Technical Report Series No. 96. 421 pp.

I.A.E.A. (1970). *Environmental Isotope Data No. 2: World Survey of Isotope Concentration in Precipitation (1964–1965).* Internat. Atomic Energy Agency, Vienna, Technical Report Series No. 117. 402 pp.

I.A.E.A. (1971). *Environmental Isotope Data No. 3: World Survey of Isotope Concentration in Precipitation (1966–1967). Internat. Atomic Energy Agency, Vienna, Technical Report Series No. 129. 402 pp.*

I.A.E.A. (1973). *Environmental Isotope Data No. 4: World Survey of Isotope Concentration in Precipitation (1968–1969).* Internat. Atomic Energy Agency, Vienna, Technical Report Series No. 147. 334 pp.

I.A.E.A. (1975). *Environmental Isotope Data No. 5: World Survey of Isotope Concentration in Precipitation (1970–1971).* Internat. Atomic Energy Agency, Vienna, Technical Report Series No. 165. 309 pp.

Injerd, W. G. (1973a). *Determination of non-exchangable ammonium in marine clays, 2. Isotope-ratio analysis of ammonium and organic nitrogen.* Univ. of California, Los Angeles, Calif., Rep. Chem. 199 JW.

Injerd, W. G. (1973b). *Determination of non-exchangable ammonium in marine clays, 3. Depth profile of Gulf of California and Saanich Inlet, B.C. cores.* Univ. of California, Los Angeles, Calif., Rep. Chem. 199W. 22 pp.

Jones, D. C. (1973). *An investigation of the nitrate problem in Runnels County, Texas.* U.S. Environmental Protection Agency Technical Series EPA-R2-73-267. 214 pp.

Junk, G., and H. S. Svec. (1958). The absolute abundance of the nitrogen isotopes in the atmosphere and compressed gas from various sources. *Geochim. Cosmochim. Acta,* **14**:234–243.

Kaplan, I. R., and S. C. Rittenberg, (1964). Microbiological fractionation of sulphur isotopes: *J. Gen. Microbiol.,* **34**:195–212.

Keeling, C. D. (1958). The concentration and isotopic abundances of atmospheric carbon dioxide in rural areas. *Geochim. Cosmochim. Acta,* **13**:322–334.

Keeney, D. R. (1973). The nitrogen cycle in sediment–water systems. *J. Environ. Qual.,* **2**:15–29.

Kohl, D. H., G. B. Shearer, and B. Commoner. (1971). Fertilizer nitrogen: Contribution to nitrate in surface water in a corn belt watershed. *Science,* **174**:1331–1334.

Koyama, T., M. Nikaido, T. Tomino, and H. Hayakawa. (1973). Decomposition of organic matter in lake sediments. Pp. 512–535. In: E. Ingerson (ed.), *Proc. of a Symp. on Hydrogeochemistry and Biogeochemistry,* Tokyo (Washington, D.C., the Clark Co.).

Kreitler, C. W., and D. C. Jones. (1975). Natural soil nitrate: the cause of nitrate contamination of groundwater in Runnels County, Texas. *Ground Water,* **103**:53–61.

Lloyd, R. M. (1966). Oxygen isotope enrichment of seawater by evaporation. *Geochim. Cosmochim. Acta,* **30**:801–814.

Lloyd, R. M. (1968). Oxygen isotope behavior in the sulfate–water system. *J. Geophys. Res.,* **73**:6099–6110.

Majzoub, M. (1971). Fractionnement en oxygen-18 et en deuterium entre l'eau et sa vapeur. *J. Chim. Phys.,* **68**:1423–1436.

Matsuo, S., I. Friedman, and G. I. Smith. (1972). Studies of Quaternary saline lakes—I. Hydrogen isotope fractionation in saline minerals. *Geochim. Cosmochim. Acta,* **36**:427–435.

McCrea, J. M. (1950). On the isotope chemistry of carbonates and a paleotemperature scale. *J. Chem. Phys.,* **18**:849–857.

McKinney, C. R., J. M. McCrea, H. A. Allen, S. Epstein, and H. C. Urey. (1950). Improvements in mass spectrometers for the measurement of small differences in isotope abundance ratios. *Rev. Sci. Inst.,* **21**:724–730.

Merlivat, L. (1970). L'Etude quantitative de bilans deracs a l'aid des concentrations en deuterium et oxygene-18 dans l'eau. Pp. 89–107. In: *Isotope Hydrology 1970.* Internat. Atomic Energy Agency, Vienna.

Miyaka, Y., and E. Wada. (1967). The abundance ratio of $^{15}N/^{14}N$ in marine environments. *Records Oceanogr. Works Japan,* **9**:37–53.

Mook, W. G. (1970). Stable carbon and oxygen isotopes of natural waters in the Netherlands. Pp. 163–190. In: *Isotope Hydrology 1970.* Internat. Atomic Energy Agency, Vienna.

Mook, W. G., J. C. Bommerson, and W. H. Staverman. (1974). Carbon isotope fractionation between dissolved bicarbonate and gaseous carbon dioxide. *Earth Planet. Sci. Lett.,* **22**:169–176.

Nier, A. O. C. (1947). A mass spectrometer for isotope and gas analysis. *Rev. Sci. Inst.,* **18**:398–411.

Nier, A. O. (1950). A redetermination of the relative abundances of the isotopes of carbon, nitrogen, oxygen, argon, and potassium. *Phys. Rev.,* **77**:789.

Nissenbaum, A., and I. R. Kaplan. (1976). Sulfur and carbon isotopic evidence for biogeochemical processes in the

Dead Sea ecosystem. Pp. 309–325. In: J. O. Nriagu (ed.), *Environmental Biogeochemistry, Vol. 1, Carbon, Nitrogen, Phosphorus, Sulfur and Selenium Cycles.* Ann Arbor Science Pub., Ann Arbor, MI.

Nissenbaum, A., B. J. Presley, and I. R. Kaplan. (1972). Early diagenesis in a reducing fjord, Saanich Inlet, British Columbia—I. Chemical and isotopic changes in major components of interstitial water. *Geochem. Cosmochim. Acta,* **36**:1007–1027.

Oana, S., and E. S. Deevey. (1960). Carbon-13 in lake waters and its possible bearing on paleolimnology. *Am. J. Sci.,* **258-A**:253–272.

O'Neil, J. R., and R. L. Hay. (1973). $^{18}O/^{16}O$ ratios in cherts associated with the saline lake deposits of East Africa. *Earth Planet. Sci. Lett.,* **19**:257–266.

O'Neil, J. R., R. N. Clayton, and T. K. Mayeda. (1969). Oxygen isotope fractionation in divalent metal carbonates. *J. Chem. Phys.,* **51**:5547–5558.

Pang, P. C., and J. O. Nriagu. (1976). Distribution and isotopic composition of nitrogen in Bay of Quinte (Lake Ontario) sediments. *Chem. Geol.,* **18**:93–105.

Pang, P. C., and J. O. Nriagu. (1977). Isotopic variations of the nitrogen in Lake Superior. *Geochim. Cosmochim. Acta,* **41**:811–814.

Park, R., and S. Epstein. (1960). Carbon isotope fractionation during photosynthesis. *Geochim. Cosmochim. Acta,* **21**:110–126.

Park, R., and S. Epstein. (1961). Metabolic fractionation of ^{13}C and ^{12}C in plants. *Plant Physiol.,* **36**:133–138.

Rennie, D. A., and E. A. Paul. (1975). Nitrogen isotope ratios in surface and sub-surface soil horizons. Pp. 441–453. In: *Isotope Ratios as Pollutant Source and Behavior Indicators.* Internat. Atomic Energy Agency, Vienna.

Roche, M. A. (1975). Geochemistry and natural ionic and isotopic tracing; two complementary ways to study the natural salinity regime of the hydrological system of Lake Chad. *J. Hydrol.,* **26**:153–171.

Rosenfeld, W., and S. Silverman. (1959). Carbon isotope fractionation in bacterial production of methane. *Science,* **130**:1658.

Sakai, H. (1957). Fractionation of sulfur isotopes in nature. *Geochim. Cosmochim. Acta,* **12**:150–169.

Scalan, R. S. (1959). *The Isotopic Composition, Concentration and Chemical State of Nitrogen in Igneous Rocks.* Ph.D. Thesis, Univ. Arkansas.

Schwarcz, H. P. (1969). The stable isotopes of carbon. Section 6-B. Pp. 6-B-1–6-B-16. In: K. H. Wedepohl (ed.), *Handbook of Geochemistry.* Springer-Verlag, New York, NY.

Shearer, G., J. Duffy, D. H. Kohl, and B. Commoner. (1974). A steady-state model of isotopic fractionation accompanying nitrogen transformations in soil. *Soil Sci. Soc. Am. Proc.,* **38**:315–322.

Sheppard, S. M. F., R. L. Nielsen, and H. P. Taylor. (1969). Oxygen and hydrogen isotope ratios of clay minerals

from porphyry copper deposits. *Econ. Geol.,* **64**:755–777.

Stewart, M. K., and I. Friedman. (1975). Deuterium fractionation between aqueous salt solutions and water vapor. *J. Geophys. Res.,* **80**:3812–3818.

Sofer, Z., and J. R. Gat. (1972). Activities and concentrations of oxygen-18 in concentrated aqueous salt solutions: Analytical and geophysical implications. *Earth Planet. Sci. Lett.,* **15**:232–238.

Sofer, Z., and J. R. Gat. (1975). The isotopic composition of evaporating brines: Effects of the isotopic activity ratio in saline solutions. *Earth Planet. Sci. Lett.,* **26**:179–186.

Stiller, M., and M. Magaritz. (1974). Carbon-13 enriched carbonate in interstitial waters of Lake Kinneret sediments. *Limnol. Oceanogr.,* **19**:849–853.

Stuiver, M. (1968). Oxygen-18 content of atmospheric precipitation during last 11,000 years in Great Lakes region. *Science,* **162**:994–997.

Stuiver, M. (1970). Oxygen and carbon isotope ratios of fresh-water carbonates as climatic indicators. *J. Geophys. Res.,* **75**:5247–5257.

Stuiver, M. (1975). Climate versus changes in ^{13}C content of the organic component of lake sediments during the Late Quaternary. *Quat. Res.,* **5**:251–262.

Takahashi, T., W. Broecker, Y. H. Li, and D. Thurber. (1968). Chemical and isotopic balances for a meromictic lake. *Limnol. Oceanogr.,* **13**:272–292.

Taube, H. (1954). Use of oxygen isotope effects in the study of hydration of ions. *J. Phys. Chem.,* **58**:523–528.

Thode, H. G., M. Shima, C. E. Rees, and K. V. Krishnamurty. (1965). Carbon-13 isotope effects in systems containing carbon dioxide, bicarbonate, carbonate, and metal ions. *Can. J. Chem.,* **43**:582–595.

Troughton, J. H. (1972). Carbon isotope fractionation by plants. Pp. E39–E57. In: T. A. Rafter and T. Grant-Taylor (eds.), *Proc. 8th Internat. Conf. on Radiocarbon Dating.* Roy. Soc. New Zealand, Wellington.

Truesdell, A. H. (1974). Oxygen isotope activities in concentrations in aqueous salt solutions at elevated temperatures. *Earth Planet. Sci. Lett.,* **23**:387–396.

Urey, H. C. (1947). The thermodynamic properties of ionic substances. *J. Chem. Soc.,* 562–581.

Wada, E., and A. Hattori. (1976). Natural abundance of ^{15}N in particulate organic matter in the North Pacific Ocean. *Geochim. Cosmochim. Acta,* **40**:249–251.

Welhan, J. A., and P. Fritz. (1977). Evaporation pan isotopic behavior as an index of isotopic evaporation conditions. *Geochim. Cosmochim. Acta,* **41**:682–686.

Wellman, R. P., F. D. Cook, and H. R. Krouse. (1968). Nitrogen-15: microbiological alteration of abundance. *Science,* **161**:269–270.

Zimmermann, U., and D. H. Ehhalt. (1970). Stable isotopes in study of water balance in Lake Neusiedl, Austria. Pp. 129–138. In: *Isotope Hydrology 1970.* Internat. Atomic Energy Agency, Vienna.

Chapter 11

Chemical Models of Lakes

Dieter M. Imboden and Abraham Lerman

Introduction

The purpose of a chemical model of a lake is an accurate and concise description of the chemical processes taking place within the lake. A lake and its sediments represent an open system which interacts with its environment (that is, with the drainage basin and the atmosphere) in different ways by exchanging energy and matter. Since some of the most important chemical transformations in the system are linked to biological processes such as photosynthesis and decomposition, most chemical models include biological processes at least in the form of stoichiometric equations between organic matter and its decomposition products (see also Chapter 4).

A discussion of lake models can begin with the description of a lake in the language of control theory. We define $\mathbf{x}(t)$ as the state vector of the lake containing all essential physical, chemical and biological variables, such as temperature and concentrations of chemical and biological constituents as a function of space within the water and sediments. A set of input functions, denoted $\mathbf{u}(t)$, includes hydraulic loading, input of chemical and biological constituents by inlets and from the atmosphere, and energy input by the sun, by wind, or in the form of sensible heat by the inlets. The essential difference between state variables $\mathbf{x}(t)$ and input functions $\mathbf{u}(t)$ lies in the fact that $\mathbf{x}$ depends on $\mathbf{u}$, whereas $\mathbf{u}$ is independent of $\mathbf{x}$. In addition, a lake is characterized by a set of system parameters $\mathbf{a}$ describing lake morphology.

The time evolution of the system can be described by a general vector differential equation

$$\frac{d\mathbf{x}}{dt} = f(\mathbf{x}, \mathbf{u}, \mathbf{a}, \mathbf{p}) \qquad (1)$$

where f is a functional relationship representing the internal system processes, $d\mathbf{x}/dt$ is the rate of change of the set of state variables, and $\mathbf{p}$ is a set of stochastic processes which cannot be treated in a deterministic way. Biological processes, such as the invasion of a new species into a lake, are unpredictable and thus stochastic in nature.

Systems which include transport processes are the so called "distributed parameter systems" (Koppel, 1968); they lead to partial differential equations. Only in very special cases do systems of distributed parameter equations have analytical solutions. Techniques for numerical solutions in one way or another break the continuous system apart into a set of discrete functions as described by Eq. (1). For instance, the continuously varying temperature in a lake is replaced by a finite number of temperature values at given points. One can visualize the lake as being divided into a finite number of boxes each described by a temperature value and by values for different chemical and biological constituents. The so-called n-box models are highly popular and convenient instruments to treat complex systems. If $n = 1$, that is if the parameter distribution is replaced by one single value (for example, the mean), the lake is treated as a one-box model.

The difficulties in the construction of a function f are obvious. Not only do they originate from mathematical reasons but also from a basic inability to collect all necessary information concerning the system and to express chemical and biological processes by mathematical expressions. An explicit construction of f is called a model of the system. Since obviously the number of elements in the state and parameter vector has to be finite, one may characterize a model by saying it replaces the infinite-dimensional state equation by a finite set of relations.

The choice of a model depends on the type of problems which are to be treated, and the usefulness and success of the model can be measured only by the questions asked of the model and the answers produced by it. In general, in more refined models, there are more variables $\mathbf{x}$, and the stochastic influence $\mathbf{p}$ becomes correspondingly smaller. On the other hand, mathematically elaborate models often cannot be adequately used with the available field data.

The models discussed in this chapter are aimed at the chemical processes in lakes. Biological processes affecting the lake water chemistry and depending on it are treated only with respect to their ultimate chemical results but not as a separate set of processes. Also, the major physical processes in lakes do not depend (or, at least, depend only weekly) on the chemical and biological reactions, whereas the dependence in the opposite direction is strong; the chemical and biological processes are much influenced by the physical mechanisms.

Chemical models can be divided into *empirical* and *conceptual* models. In the empirical models we include those which describe various observed relationships among lake parameters, without explicitly taking into account the underlying causes and mechanisms. For example, a relationship between the trophic state of a lake, its mean depth, and the rate of phosphorus input (Vollenweider, 1968) is an empirical model. Another example of an empirical model is a relationship between the mean depth of a lake and the rate of vertical mixing across the thermocline (Snodgrass and O'Melia, 1975).

In the class of conceptual models we include those which describe *time-dependent* behavior of a lake system, taking into account at least some of the more fundamental mechanisms that are behind the processes operating within the system.

Time scales

The simplest possible statement about time-dependent changes in the chemical composition of a lake can be written as

$$V \frac{dC}{dt} = \text{input rates} - \text{removal rates} \quad (\text{g year}^{-1}) \quad (2)$$

where C is concentration (g cm^{-3}), dC/dt is its rate of change (g cm^{-3} year^{-1}), and V is the volume of the lake (cm^3) taken as constant.

Inputs to a lake include dissolved and solid materials that can either be introduced from outside or generated within the lake. Removal mechanisms include water outflow, sedimentation, biological uptake, chemical reactions (adsorption, precipitation), gas exchange at the water surface, or radioactive decay. Eq. (2) can be rewritten by distinguishing between external and internal processes

$$V \frac{dC}{dt} = Q_{in} - Q_{out} + VR \quad (3)$$

where Q_{in} and Q_{out} (g year^{-1}) include all input and output rates which result from transport of the constit-

uent through the system boundaries, and R (g cm^{-3} year^{-1}) is the net reaction rate per volume within the system, that is, the algebraic sum of all *in situ* reaction or removal processes. The relative change in concentration of the chemical constituent is

$$\frac{1}{C} \frac{dC}{dt} = \frac{1}{\tau_{in}} - \frac{1}{\tau_{out}} + \frac{1}{\tau_r} \quad (\text{year}^{-1}) \quad (4)$$

where $\tau_{in} = VC/Q_{in}$, $\tau_{out} = VC/Q_{out}$, and $\tau_r = C/R$ are characteristic residence times for mixing with respect to the input, mixing with respect to the outflow, and *in situ* reactions, respectively. This can easily be seen if we apply Eq. (4) to the balance of water and put $C = 1$. Q_{in} and Q_{out} become inflow and outflow rates of water, and τ_{in} and τ_{out} the so-called water renewal times which are equal for constant volume when $Q_{in} = Q_{out}$.

The length of the mixing time τ_{in} and τ_{out} compared to the reaction time τ_r determines how homogeneously the substance of interest is distributed within the lake and thus it also determines the complexity of the model needed to describe this property. One can think of two adjacent boxes in steady state, the exchange of mass between which is represented by some mixing time τ_{mix}. Alternatively one can think of an internal mixing time required to homogenize the contents of the box.

If the following relationship holds

$$\tau_r \gg \tau_{mix} \quad (5)$$

then the concentration in both boxes will be approximately equal. The relationship means that the chemical removal processes are much slower than the rates of transport between the boxes. If, on the other hand,

$$\tau_r \ll \tau_{mix} \quad (6)$$

the distribution of the species may or may not vary in space depending on the location of the sources and sinks of the substance.

In Figure 1 ranges of characteristic times of mixing and chemical reactions are shown. A characteristic mixing time is effectively determined by major physical forces operating in the system, whereas the chemical reaction time τ_r is to a large extent a function of the chemical species. The diagram shows that a given lake (that is, a given τ_{mix}) can be chemically homogeneous with respect to some long-lived substances (large τ_r) and chemically inhomogeneous with respect to some other rapidly reacting substances (small τ_r).

In a lake, horizontal turbulence and currents are usually stronger than vertical mixing. Therefore, a horizontal mixing time for an entire lake or its part ($\tau_{mix,h}$) is usually shorter than the vertical mixing time ($\tau_{mix,v}$). In Figure 2 three possible combinations between the chemical reaction time (τ_r) and the horizontal and vertical mixing times, each of which leads to a different pattern of chemical inhomogeneity, are

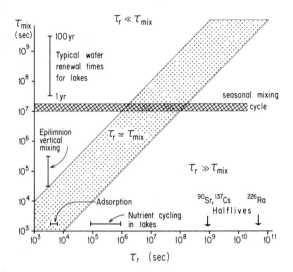

FIGURE 1.   Typical times of mixing (τ_{mix}) and reaction (τ_r) in lakes. See Eqs. (5) and (6).

shown. Examples applying to Figures 1 and 2 are concentrations of nitrate and phosphate entering a lake with river inflow and being reduced by biological uptake over some distance from the river mouth. Radon gas, forming in sediments and being transported upward through the water, decays, and its concentration decreases from the bottom up. Oxygen in a eutrophic lake can decrease in concentration strongly over some vertical distance within the hypolimnion. In a lake undergoing seasonal stratification and complete mixing every 5 to 9 months, a homogeneous distribution of chemical species can be interrupted with a frequency on the same time scale, if the reaction rates of the species in the lake epilimnion and hypolimnion are different. A "permanently" stratified lake has an "infinitely" long mixing time. However, the mixing times within the epilimnion and hypolimnion can be short. With regard to the concept of a "permanent stratification," no chemical stratification in water can be truly permanent, unless there are permanent sources and sinks removing the chemical species from solution. Many of the lakes in which a more dilute epilimnion rests on top of a more concentrated hypolimnion are probably transient features, and mixing of the two layers takes place slowly, by molecular diffusion, or faster, by eddy turbulence (see also section on Two-box models).

In a lake, the movement of water and of the species dissolved or suspended in it is dominated by advection and turbulence. The mixing rates τ_{in} and τ_{out} in Eq. (4) are then approximated by the mixing time of water. In the case of advective motion, a characteristic mixing time can be defined as

$$\tau_{\text{mix}} = \frac{L}{U} \quad \text{(years)} \tag{7}$$

where L is a characteristic linear dimension (cm), such as the box size, and U is the flow velocity (cm year^{-1}). In the case of dispersal by eddy turbulence,

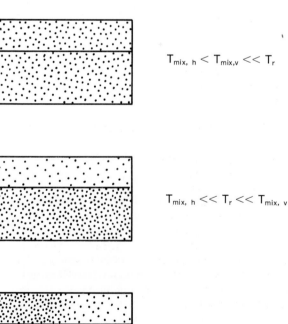

FIGURE 2.   Different types of vertical and horizontal inhomogeneity in a lake. Density of dots indicates concentration. Different relationships between the times of horizontal ($\tau_{\text{mix},h}$) and vertical ($\tau_{\text{mix},v}$) mixing, and time of chemical reactions (τ_r), lead to different degrees of concentration inhomogeneity.

characterized by an eddy diffusion coefficient D (cm^2 year^{-1}), a characteristic mixing time can be taken as

$$\tau_{\text{mix}} = \frac{L^2}{D} \quad \text{(years)}. \qquad (8)$$

One-box models

Theory

A simplest representation of a lake is a well-mixed box of volume equal to the lake volume (Figure 3). The lake receives inputs from surface inflow, groundwater, and the atmosphere. It is convenient to reduce external inputs to a mean concentration

$$C_{\text{in}} = \frac{\Sigma \, (\text{input rates})}{q_{\text{in}}} \quad \text{(g cm}^{-3}\text{)} \qquad (9)$$

where q_{in} is the rate of total water inflow to the lake (cm^3 year^{-1}).

When the lake is well mixed (on the time scale of reaction or observation) then removal by the outflow is Cq_{out}, which is a first-order process. The function of net removal per unit volume R (g cm^{-3} year^{-1}) includes the difference between *in situ* removal and production, radioactive decay, and fluxes through the system boundaries to the atmosphere or sediments. R can be a negative number for species which have a net source within the lake.

A simple mass balance for the concentration of any species can be written as

$$\frac{d}{dt}(VC) = q_{\text{in}} C_{\text{in}} - q_{\text{out}} C - RV \quad \text{(g year}^{-1}\text{)}. \qquad (10)$$

For constant volume V and $q = q_{\text{in}} = q_{\text{out}}$, Eq. (10) reduces to

$$\frac{dC}{dt} = \frac{1}{\tau}(C_{\text{in}} - C) - R \quad \text{(g cm}^{-3}\text{ year}^{-1}\text{)} \qquad (11)$$

where

$$\tau = V/q \quad \text{(years)} \qquad (12)$$

is the mean residence time of the water within the system. The steady-state solution of Eq. (11) is

$$C_{\text{ss}} = C_{\text{in}} - R\tau \quad \text{(g cm}^{-3}\text{)}. \qquad (13)$$

It follows that the steady-state concentration C_{ss} of a species which is removed within the lake ($R > 0$) is smaller than the mean input concentration, C_{in}. The retention factor r is defined as the ratio between net removal by sedimentation or *in situ* reaction and the total input:

$$r = \frac{RV}{C_{\text{in}} q_{\text{in}}} \qquad (14)$$

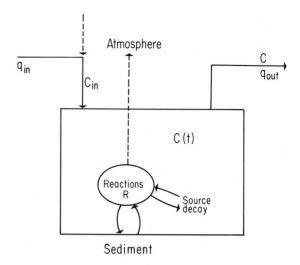

FIGURE 3.   One-box model of a lake.

At the steady state, the retention factor r_{ss} is, using Eq. (13),

$$r_{\text{ss}} = 1 - \frac{C_{\text{ss}}}{C_{\text{in}}} = \frac{R\tau}{C_{\text{in}}}. \qquad (15)$$

In general, the coefficients of Eq. (10), q, τ, and R, are time dependent. In addition, the removal function R depends on the concentration in the lake C. Cases in which R is assumed to be a linear function of C

$$R = kC + R_0 \quad \text{(g cm}^{-3}\text{ year}^{-1}\text{)} \qquad (16)$$

have received special attention. k is a first-order reaction rate constant (year^{-1}) and R_0 is a zero-order rate (g cm^{-3} year^{-1}), both being independent of C.

In reality, the linear model is seldom valid in the strict sense, especially if C is varying over a broad range. However, as a first approximation, Eq. (16) is a very useful step since it transforms Eq. (11) into a linear first-order differential equation which has a well-known analytical solution even for time-dependent coefficients:

$$\frac{dC}{dt} = \left(\frac{C_{\text{in}}}{\tau} - R_0\right) - \left(k + \frac{1}{\tau}\right)C. \qquad (17)$$

For constant coefficients, the solution is

$$C(t) = (C_0 - C_\infty)\exp\left[-\left(k + \frac{1}{\tau}\right)t\right] + C_\infty \qquad (18)$$

$$C_\infty = \frac{C_{\text{in}}/\tau - R_0}{k + 1/\tau}. \qquad (19)$$

The rate of removal of suspended material (inorganic or organic) to the sediments is controlled by the settling velocities of the particles. Dissolved species can be removed from lake water by adsorption on settling particles or at the sediment surface. A simple distribution relationship for adsorption can be written as

$$C_g = K'C \quad \text{(g g}^{-1}\text{)} \qquad (20)$$

where C_g is the species concentration on solids (g g^{-1}), C is the concentration in solution (g cm^{-3}), and K' is a distribution coefficient (cm^3 g^{-1}). The rate of removal by sedimentation R_s is

$$R_s = \frac{U_s C_p K' C}{h} \quad \text{(g cm}^{-3}\text{ year}^{-1}) \qquad (21)$$

where U_s is the settling velocity (cm year^{-1}), C_p is the particle concentration in lake water (g cm^{-3}), and $h = $ volume/area is the mean depth of the lake (cm).

If U_s, K', and C_p are independent of the species concentration C, then Eq. (21) describes a linear removal mechanism for the dissolved species with the rate constant

$$k_s = \frac{U_s C_p K'}{h} \quad \text{(year}^{-1}). \qquad (22)$$

Examples will be discussed later, where the above assumptions do not hold and sedimentation becomes a nonlinear process. Furthermore, if there is a slow exchange between the solid and dissolved phase, then the immediate equilibrium Eq. (20) has to be replaced by a kinetic equation. The case of nutrients, where such a transition is mainly a result of photosynthetic activity, will be discussed in a subsequent section.

Additional linear removal processes are radioactive decay (λC), gas exchange [$k(C_{eq} - C)$], and removal by first-order chemical reactions [$\pm k (C_{eq} - C)$] [λ is decay constant (year^{-1}), k is the gas exchange or reaction rate coefficient (year^{-1}), and C_{eq} is an equilibrium concentration]. Zero-order processes are zero-order chemical reactions ($R_0 > 0$), and *in situ* production of the species by radioactive decay of a long-lived mother nuclide ($R_0 < 0$).

Application to trace metals

Concentrations of certain chemical species transported into the lake by rivers and from the atmosphere are controlled by their adsorption on particulate matter and subsequent removal to the sediments. In most cases, equilibration between the dissolved and adsorbed phase is a fast reaction compared to other processes within the lake (Figure 1). Based on this

TABLE 1. Distribution Coefficients K' of Different Metals[a]

Metal	K' (cm^3 g^{-1})
Cd	7×10^4
Cu	$(3 \text{ to } 4) \times 10^4$
Pb	15×10^4
Zn	$(3 \text{ to } 20) \times 10^4$

[a]Distribution coefficients K' = concentration on solids (g g^{-1})/aqueous concentration (g cm^{-3}). From Schindler (1975) and J. Tschopp (private communication).

assumption, Schindler (1975) has developed a one-box model for trace metal steady-state concentrations in natural water systems. For a metal present at concentration M_{in} in inflow and total concentration M in the lake at steady state, Eq. (13) gives

$$M = M_{in} - R_s \tau \quad \text{(g cm}^{-3}). \qquad (23)$$

M and M_{in} refer to total (aqueous plus particulate) concentrations. The removal rate by sedimentation R_s is defined in Eq. (21) which we rewrite as

$$R_s = \sigma C_p K' M_{aq} \quad \text{(g cm}^{-3}\text{ year}^{-1}) \qquad (24)$$

where

$$\sigma = \frac{U_s}{h} \quad \text{(year}^{-1}) \qquad (25)$$

is the removal rate of particulate matter C_p (g cm^{-3}) by sedimentation and K' (cm^3 g^{-1}) is the distribution coefficient as introduced earlier.

The relation between M_{aq} (concentration of metal in solution) and M follows from Eq. (20)

$$M = (1 + K' C_p) M_{aq} \quad \text{(g cm}^{-3}). \qquad (26)$$

Inserting these equations into Eq. (23) gives

$$M = M_{in} \frac{1 + K' C_p}{1 + K' C_p (1 + \tau \sigma)}. \qquad (27)$$

Given fixed input concentration M_{in}, the total concentration in the lake M decreases with increasing K', C_p, τ, or σ. Distribution coefficients K' of different metals are listed in Table 1. The retention factor r follows from Eq. (15) as

$$r = \frac{K' C_p \tau \sigma}{1 + K' C_p (1 + \tau \sigma)} \qquad (28)$$

and r increases with increasing K', C_p, τ, or σ.

For a further discussion it is convenient to include a model which describes particulate matter in the lake. In fact, not all the parameters appearing in Eqs. (27) and (28) are independent, but C_p depends on τ and σ.

The equation for particulate matter in the lake is

$$\frac{dC_p}{dt} = \frac{(C_{p,in} - C_p)}{\tau} - \sigma C_p - R_p \quad \text{(g cm}^{-3}\text{ year}^{-1}) \qquad (29)$$

where R_p is *in situ* net removal of particulates by biological or chemical processes. For steady state, C_p becomes

$$C_p = \frac{C_{p,in} - \tau R_p}{1 + \tau \sigma} \quad \text{(g cm}^{-3}). \qquad (30)$$

Now, either the removal rate of particulate matter by sedimentation σ or the particulate concentration C_p can be replaced in Eq. (27):

$$M = M_{in} \cdot \frac{1 + K' C_p}{1 + K' C_{p,in} - K' \tau R_p} \quad \text{(g cm}^{-3}) \qquad (31a)$$

or

$$M = M_{in} \cdot \frac{1 + \dfrac{K'C_{p,in} - K'\tau R_p}{1 + \tau\sigma}}{1 + K'C_{p,in} - K'\tau R_p} \quad \text{(g cm}^{-3}\text{).} \quad (31b)$$

In both cases, the relationships contain the *in situ* net removal of particulate matter R_p, a quantity which cannot easily be determined although it is important to the particulate matter budget of the lake, at least in productive (eutrophic) lakes during the summer. Among the different parameters in Eqs. (31a, b), only K' depends on the trace metal concentration, whereas $C_{p,in}$, τ, R_p, σ, and C_p are characterized by the system under consideration. Typical ranges of the lake parameters are listed in Table 2.

For a given lake, the ratio M/M_{in} lies between 1 (for $K' = 0$) and $(1 + \tau\sigma)^{-1}$ (for $K' = \infty$):

$$1 \geqslant \frac{M}{M_{in}} \geqslant \frac{1}{1 + \tau\sigma} = \frac{C_p}{C_{p,in} - \tau R_p}. \quad (32)$$

The biggest change in M/M_{in} occurs for adsorption coefficients in the vicinity of $(C_{p,in} - \tau R_p)^{-1}$ (Figure 4a).

In all the equations derived in the preceding section we have assumed $q_{in} = q_{out}$ and constant volume. Lakes which lose their water merely by evaporation may still have constant volume, but the equation of mass balance for dissolved and suspended constituents, Eq. (11), has to be replaced by

$$\frac{dC}{dt} = \frac{C_{in}}{\tau} - R \quad \text{(g cm}^{-3}\text{ year}^{-1}\text{)} \quad (33)$$

For trace metals, an analogous derivation using Eq. (33) instead of Eq. (11) yields

$$M = M_{in} \frac{1 + K'C_p}{K'C_{p,in} - K'\tau R_p}$$

$$= \frac{1 + \dfrac{K'}{\tau\sigma}(C_{p,in} - \tau R_p)}{K'(C_{p,in} - \tau R_p)}. \quad (34)$$

The ratio M/M_{in} lies between ∞ (for $K' = 0$) and $(\tau\sigma)^{-1}$ (for $K' = \infty$) (Figure 4b):

$$\infty > \frac{M}{M_{in}} \geqslant \frac{1}{\tau\sigma} = \frac{C_p}{C_{p,in} - \tau R_p}. \quad (35)$$

In lakes without any outlet, concentration in the lake may exceed M_{in} many times. This is especially true for the ocean. However, in reality the ratio M/M_{in} will always remain finite, since at high concentrations the removal of the dissolved species is not limited to adsorption but may include precipitation of minerals.

Application to nutrients

Application of a one-box model to nutrients will be demonstrated for phosphorus, present in two main forms—dissolved and particulate. In detail, distribu-

tion of the different nutrient elements among different chemical species can be very complex owing to the presence of numerous inorganic and organic species. For example, a model of several nitrogen species treated simultaneously has been developed by Brezonik (1968). The Redfield reaction describing the stoichiometric relationships between the nutrients in solution and organic matter produced by photosynthesis (Stumm, 1964) is a classic example of a short-hand expression for an array of chemical species involved in the life cycles of organisms:

$$106CO_2 + 16NO_3^- + HPO_4^{2-} + 122H_2O + 18H^+$$
$$+ \text{ trace elements} + \text{energy}$$
$$\underset{\text{respiration}}{\overset{\text{photosynthesis}}{\rightleftharpoons}} C_{106}H_{263}O_{110}N_{16}P_1 + 138O_2. \quad (36)$$

In the above reaction, formation of 1 g of organic material requires changes in concentrations of the aqueous species in certain defined proportions. If the rate of organic matter production by photosynthesis is denoted Φ, in units of g of C cm^{-3} year^{-1}, then the rates of change in the concentrations of dissolved phosphorus [OP], nitrogen [NO], and oxygen [O$_2$] become

$$\frac{d[OP]}{dt} \quad \text{(g of P cm}^{-3}\text{ year}^{-1}\text{)} = -0.025\Phi \quad (37a)$$

$$\frac{d[NO]}{dt} \quad \text{(g of N cm}^{-3}\text{ year}^{-1}\text{)} = -0.18\Phi \quad (37b)$$

$$\frac{d[O_2]}{dt} \quad \text{(g of O}_2\text{ cm}^{-3}\text{ year}^{-1}\text{)} = +3.5\Phi. \quad (37c)$$

The inverse reaction, respiration or the decomposition of dead plankton (mineralization), may be expressed by the release of carbon from organic material, Ψ (g of C cm^{-3} year^{-1}). Obviously, the corresponding stoichiometric equations follow from Eq. (37) if Φ is replaced by Ψ and the sign is reversed.

The construction of a specific model reduces to the question of how the two governing rate functions, Φ and Ψ, depend on light, temperature, nutrient concentration, plankton density, and other parameters.

In many lakes, the productivity is controlled by the availability of one specific nutrient, the so-called limiting nutrient which very often is phosphorus. From a mathematical point of view this means that Φ depends on the availability of phosphorus, but not on other dissolved nutrients. The system of differential equations [Eqs. (37)] consists therefore of independent equations, and a solution for phosphorus alone can describe the system.

A simple approach is to define the rate of photosynthetic productivity with respect to phosphorus Φ_p as

$$\Phi_p = \alpha[OP][PP] \quad \text{(g of P cm}^{-3}\text{ year}^{-1}\text{)} \quad (38)$$

where Φ_p has the significance of Φ but it expresses uptake of phosphorus instead of carbon, [OP] and [PP] are dissolved and particulate phosphorus con-

TABLE 2.   Range of Variation of Typical Lake Parameters

Mean residence time of water	τ (years)	1 to 100
Removal rate by sedimentation	σ (year^{-1})	0.5 to 50
Removal rate by mineralization	k (year^{-1})	1 to 10
Uptake rate of P, Eq. (38), from daily averages	α (g^{-1} cm^3 year^{-1})	(5 to 100) x 10^9
Uptake rate appearing in Eq. (44)	$\bar{\mu}$ (year^{-1})	50 to 500
Michaelis constant	K_P (g of P cm^{-3})	(1.5 to 10) x 10^{-9}
Extinction coefficient of water without biomass	ϵ_0 (cm^{-1})	(1 to 4) x 10^{-3}
Specific extinction coefficient of biomass	β (g^{-1} cm^2)	(1 to 2) x 10^5

centrations (g cm^{-3}) representing the nutrient pool and the biomass, and α (g^{-1} cm^3 year^{-1}) is a rate constant which depends on light and temperature but not on the nutrient concentrations. Eq. (38) states that the specific growth rate $\Phi_p/[PP]$, that is, productivity per unit biomass, is proportional to the concentration of the limiting nutrient. This is only true as long as [OP] is small with respect to some critical concentration.

For the respiration function Ψ_P we chose the first-order reaction

$$\Psi_p = k[PP] \quad \text{(g of P cm}^{-3}\text{ year}^{-1}) \quad (39)$$

where the rate of respiration k (year^{-1}) may depend on the water temperature and the chemical redox potential, especially on the concentration of dissolved oxygen. However, if [O$_2$] is larger than some critical

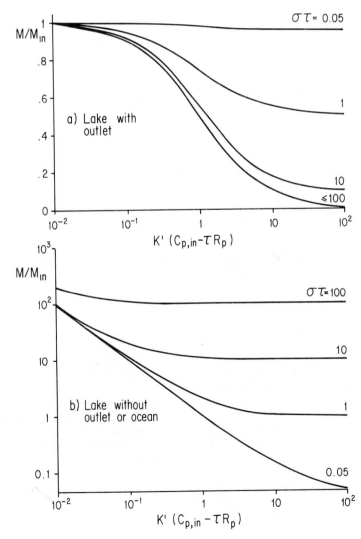

FIGURE 4.   Ratio of the total metal concentration in the lake and in inflow M/M_{in} as a function of dimensionless parameters representing outflow and removal by sedimentation, as defined in Eqs. (31)–(34). Upper figure, lakes with outlet; lower figure, lakes without outlet.

value, only temperature remains as a major influence on k.

The system of differential equations become

$$\frac{d[OP]}{dt} = \frac{[OP]_{in}}{\tau} - \frac{[OP]}{\tau} - \alpha\,[OP][PP] + k[PP] \tag{40a}$$

$$\frac{d[PP]}{dt} = \frac{[PP]_{in}}{\tau} - \frac{[PP]}{\tau} + \alpha[OP][PP] - k[PP] - \sigma[PP]. \tag{40b}$$

If $[PP]_{in} = 0$, then the steady-state solution of Eq. (40a), provided that $\alpha\,[OP]_{in} > (1/\tau + k + \sigma)$, is given by

$$[OP] = \frac{1}{\alpha}\,[1/\tau + k + \sigma] \tag{41a}$$

$$[PP] = \frac{[OP]_{in} - \dfrac{1}{\alpha}(1/\tau + k + \sigma)}{1 + \tau\sigma} \tag{41b}$$

$$[PT] = [OP] + [PP]$$

$$= \frac{[OP]_{in} + \dfrac{\sigma}{\alpha}(1 + k\tau + \tau\sigma)}{1 + \tau\sigma} \tag{41c}$$

where $[PT]$ is the total phosphorus concentration. In case of $\alpha[OP]_{in} \leq (1/\tau + k + \sigma)$ we have

$$[OP] = [PT] = [OP]_{in} \tag{42a}$$

$$[PP] = 0. \tag{42b}$$

Eq. (40) reveals an interesting feature inherent to the nonlinear one-box model: there exists a finite critical input concentration $[OP]_{crit} = (1/\tau + k + \sigma)/\alpha$ below which the plankton community collapses to zero value as a consequence of the combined removal effects of outflow, sedimentation, and decomposition.

In Table 2 are listed some typical ranges of variation for the different parameters appearing in this model which apply to lakes in general. The phosphorus uptake parameter α depends strongly on climatic conditions and the season. The listed values are daily aver-

ages (α would be zero during the night). If we take an extreme case (small α, τ; large k, σ), we see that the critical loading concentration may become as high as 10^{-8} g of P cm^{-3} = 10 mg of P m^{-3}. Lakes with high flushing rates (τ small) belong to these critical cases. In fact, in rivers the free-floating plankton is often of minor importance with respect to benthic communities. Complete loss of biomass by flushing from an activated sludge process used in sewage treatment may also occur.

Two-box models: stratified lakes

In Figure 5 a two-box model consisting of the epilimnion (E) and the hypolimnion (H) is shown (Imboden, 1974). The two boxes are considered to be completely mixed while vertical mixing between the boxes is slow.

The vertical subdivision of the water column can be caused either by surface heating and wind-induced turbulence, or by higher concentrations of dissolved salt in the deeper layer, as well as by combinations of these processes. A more or less pronounced density gradient usually exists between the upper (E) and lower (H) layers. In a two-box model, the layer of the density gradient (pycnocline) is divided between the two boxes. In freshwater lakes in temperate climates, stratification of the water column is mostly seasonal. In saline lakes, stratification can be permanent, at least on a time scale of the age of the lake (10^3 years).

In seasonally stratified lakes, the thermocline forms and descends during the period of seasonally rising temperatures, such that a two-box model made of boxes of fixed dimensions is in itself an approximation for the warm period. In salt-stratified lakes, the existence of a difference in concentration is a driving force for the transport of salt from the more to the less

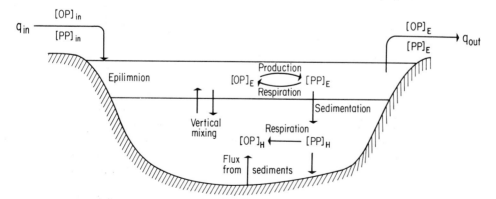

FIGURE 5.   Two-box model of phosphorus in a lake. $[OP]$ is the concentration of dissolved phosphorus, used as indicating the available nutrient concentration; $[PP]$ is the concentration of phosphorus in particulate form, used as a measure of the biomass.

concentrated layer. The slowest transport is due to the driving force of molecular diffusion. Any turbulence at the pycnocline and within the water layers above and below it only accelerates the mixing process.

As an illustration of the rates of transport across the boundary layer between E and H (Figure 5), the following computation will serve the purpose. A concentration gradient between E and H exists within a layer 1 m thick, and transport through it (that is, from the higher concentration reservoir H to the lower concentration reservoir E, along the concentration gradient) takes place by molecular diffusion, with a diffusion coefficient of the order of 10^{-5} cm^2 sec^{-1}. A quantity analogous to a vertical velocity of transport is the ratio (diffusion coefficient)/(layer thickness) or 10^{-5} cm^2 sec$^{-1}/10^2$ cm $= 10^{-7}$ cm sec$^{-1} = 3$ cm year^{-1}. Material transported from H to E at the rate of 3 cm year^{-1} has a characteristic residence time in H (depth 100 m $= 10^4$ cm) of about 10^4 cm/3 cm year$^{-1} = 3000$ years. The figure of 3000 years is about the same as the ages of postglacial lakes. By a similar reasoning, eddy turbulence, characterized by an eddy diffusion coefficient of the order of 10^{-2} cm^2 sec^{-1}, gives the vertical transport velocity of 30 m year^{-1} and a characteristic residence time in H of only a few years. Input of salt with river inflow to the epilimnion accelerates the process by which the salt concentrations in E and H tend to become equal. For different ratios of the epilimnion/hypolimnion values (two boxes) and epilimnion/pycnocline/ hypolimnion (three boxes), the times required to destratify a lake by molecular or eddy diffusional processes can range between 10^0 and 10^3 years. Sample computations and applications to a number of salt-stratified lakes have been discussed in Lerman (1971) and in Toth and Lerman (1975).

Vertical density gradients, caused either by temperature or solutes, inhibit propagation of turbulence in the vertical direction. During the summer, lakes often show very low exchange rates between E and H, leading to larger density gradients in the thermocline. In the winter, depending on the meteorological conditions, lakes may go through a complete turnover (see also Chapter 1). For the model this means that the exchange rate becomes so fast that all vertical inhomogeneities disappear. For this period, the system can be described by a one-box model. However, in some lakes part of the hypolimnion remains permanently stratified either as a result of chemical gradients or insufficient turbulence (protection from wind by topographic relief or ice). In such lakes, part of the water may have a very long residence time; as a result the response of such a system to external changes should be considered as made of two contributions: the faster and slower responding parts.

The essential difference between the epilimnion and hypolimnion is that Φ, the rate of photosynthesis, is zero in the hypolimnion. In fact, we assume that the productive layer does not extend below the thermocline. This may not be the case in lakes with very high transparency where the depth of maximum productivity may sometimes lie well below the thermocline.

As before, phosphorus is considered as the only controlling nutrient. The partition of total P into [OP] and [PP] represents the nutrient and biomass. Only the latter is affected by sedimentation. The rate of photosynthesis can be expressed by Eq. (38), or a refinement of it based on the Monod equation,

$$\Phi_p = \mu \frac{[OP]}{[OP] + K_P} [PP] \quad \text{(g of P cm}^{-3}\text{ year}^{-1}\text{)} \quad (43)$$

where K_P (g of P cm^{-3}) is the Michaelis constant, and μ (year^{-1}) is the maximum specific uptake rate. In fact, for $[OP] >> K_P$, $\Phi = \mu[PP]$, whereas for $[OP] << K_P$, the equation reduces to the linear expression, Eq. (38), with $\alpha = \mu/K_P$.

The parameter μ depends on light intensity, which is a function of depth, because of absorption by water. To determine the mean productivity within the epilimnion, Eq. (43) has to be averaged over depth. Imboden and Gächter (1978) have shown that the productivity per unit of lake area averaged over 24 hours, $\Sigma\Phi_P$, can be written as

$$\Sigma\Phi_P = \bar{\mu} \frac{[OP]}{[OP]+K_P} \times \frac{[PP]}{\epsilon_0 + \beta[PP]}$$

$$\text{(g of P cm}^{-2}\text{ year}^{-1}\text{)} \quad (44)$$

as long as the productivity below the epilimnion can be disregarded. $\bar{\mu}$ (year^{-1}) is a mean rate constant averaged over depth and 24 hr of the day, ϵ_0 (cm^{-1}) is the extinction coefficient of light caused by the water and its constituents other than the biomass, and β (g g^{-1} cm^2) is a proportionality constant relating extinction and biomass density, the latter expressed as particulate phosphorous concentration. Again, typical ranges of the parameters are listed in Table 2.

Eq. (44) shows two kinds of saturation effects, one originating from the overavailability of nutrients and the second from self-shadowing. Indeed, productivity figures from a great variety of lakes confirm that an upper productivity limit around 500 g of C m^{-2} year^{-1} exists.

The two-box model of nutrients in a stratified lake (Figure 5) consists of four coupled differential equations, for each box a pair of equations similar to Eq. (40). Instead of writing them down, we can discuss some typical aspects of the model with the aid of Figure 6, which shows schematically the behavior of the system. (Reference to Figure 6 will help in reading this section.) Starting in April, the beginning of stratification, two yearly cycles are shown. The input of phosphorus, represented by the mean concentration

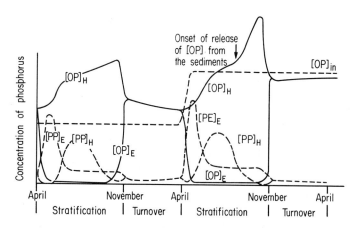

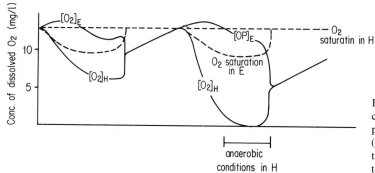

FIGURE 6.   Schematic illustration of changes in the concentrations of phosphorus and oxygen in the epilimnion (E) and hypolimnion (H) of a lake during two annual cycles. For description see text.

$[OP]_{in}$, is taken as larger in the second year than in the first.

With the onset of stratification, the phosphate concentrations in the two boxes, $[OP]_E$ and $[OP]_H$, which are equal after the period of total mixing, are driven by different forces. In E, photosynthetic activity quickly uses up nearly all available phosphate. At the same time, a drastic increase in $[PP]_E$ indicates the development of an algal bloom. After a certain time, the bloom stops. The settling biomass leads to an increase in $[PP]_H$. Part of the organic debris is lost from the system to the sediments, and the rest is mineralized in the hypolimnion leading to a steady increase of the hypolimnetic nutrient pool $[OP]_H$ during the summer. The thermocline prevents a significant backflux of nutrients to the productive layer. Therefore, $[OP]_E$ remains small throughout the rest of the summer. Only at the onset of destratification are the nutrients transported back to E where they may lead to a late algal bloom in fall or become part of the initial nutrient pool responsible for the spring bloom in the subsequent year.

Since photosynthetic activity tends to concentrate phosphorus in the hypolimnion, removal of phosphorus by the outlet is less effective during the summer. Therefore, and in contrast to the results from the one-box model, the mean phosphorus concentration in the lake may exceed $[OP]_{in}$ as can be seen from the period of complete mixing during the winter.

The dynamics of oxygen in the lake is dominated by the stoichiometric linkage of O_2 to phosphorus [Eq. (37c)] and by gas-exchange processes at the lake surface.

The O_2 concentrations are shown in Figure 6b. In the epilimnion, oxygen is supersaturated during most of the summer because of the photosynthetic oxygen production [see Eq. (36)]. In addition, the temperature rise in the epilimnion decreases the oxygen saturation concentration. Gas exchange is often not fast enough to achieve equilibration with the atmosphere.

In the hypolimnion, mineralization of organic material consumes oxygen. As in the case of phosphate, the low vertical diffusivity within the thermocline hinders the vertical flux of oxygen; many eutrophic lakes turn anoxic in their hypolimnion during the summer. In fact, the oxygen hypolimnetic concentration is a very sensitive indicator and a trigger for some drastic chemical changes within the lake. As shown for the second year in Figure 6, the assumed higher phosphorus input is responsible for an anoxic hypolimnion in the second part of stagnation. A striking consequence of this situation consists of an additional increase in $[OP]_H$ resulting from the release of phosphate at the sediment surface. As Mortimer (1941, 1942) has pointed out, anoxic sediments do not retain phosphate originating from the decomposition of organic material. The mechanism of internal P-loading may cause extremely high values of $[OP]_H$ at the end of stagnation. If the flushing time of the lake is long, the concentrations remain high through the winter.

The release of phosphate at the lake bottom leads to large vertical concentration gradients in the hypolimnion. The approach of the box model becomes a crude approximation and overestimates nutrient concentrations just below the thermocline. In a more detailed model, the hypolimnetic box should be replaced by a one-dimensional continuous model (Imboden and Gächter, 1978). In addition, the importance of the flux of nutrients from the sediments stresses the need for including the sediments in the lake model. Exchange processes between sediments and water are not only important for phosphate but also for other chemical species in the lake. The last section of this chapter deals with those processes.

Multi-box models

A mult-box model is an extension of a one-box model to those situations where the inhomogeneity of the lake system cannot be reasonably represented by one box only. One multi-box analogy is a system of interconnected lakes, such as the Laurentian Great Lakes or many other smaller lakes in other parts of the world, where the lakes receive inflow from the surrounding land as well as from the preceding lakes upstream. In such a system, events taking place in any one of the lakes affect the lakes downstream, and the duration and magnitudes of the various events depend to a large extent on the physical characteristics and, among them, on the water residence time in the individual lakes.

A step down the physical scale is a lake distinctly subdivided into a number of basins of different volume and geometry. A diagram of such a hypothetical lake is shown in Figure 7: subdivision of the lake into individual boxes conforms the pattern of two deeper basins separated one from another by a sill, and the

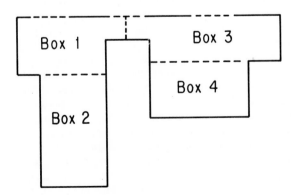

FIGURE 7. Subdivision of a lake into several boxes: two basins separated one from another by a sill.

presence of the shallower and deeper water masses. Lakes of geometrically irregular coastline contours, and lakes with prominent bays and partly restricted communications among the individual parts fall generally in the category of the systems that should be treated as multi-box models. In this category belong, among the better known lakes, Lake Lucerne with its four almost independent bay arms; the Dead Sea with its pronouncedly shallow southern basin and the much deeper bigger norther basin; the Caspian with the Gulf of Kara-Bugaz in the east receiving inflow of brackish water that evaporates and precipitates minerals out of a saline brine; Lake Como with its three basins extending out in the form of long bays away from an area of common junction; and Lake Huron with the Georgian Bay in the northeastern part of the lake from which it is partly shielded by an archipelago of islands.

The one-box model equations, such as Eqs. (2) and (11), apply in principle to each individual box of a multi-box model. For the entire model, the number of equations is as the number of boxes, and this immediately shows that the complexity of the model increases substantially when the boxes are characterized by different physical *and* chemical parameters. For a single lake, the mean water renewal time is relatively easy to determine from measurements of the lake inflow or outflow and the lake volume. For individual basins within a lake, the mean water residence times are as important a parameter as for a one-box model lake, but they are considerably more difficult to determine.

In dividing a lake into boxes, attention should be given to the relative values of the internal mixing and chemical reaction times, as discussed in the section on Time scales. Ideally, a box should be small enough to approach closely a condition of a chemically homogeneous unit, as defined in Eq. (5).

A five-box model for the Great Lakes has been developed to describe the rates of change in concentrations of the man-produced radionuclide ^{90}Sr that enters the lakes with atmospheric fallout, with inflow from the lake drainage basins, and with inflow from each lake upstream (Lerman, 1970). Chains of lakes, such as the chain of five Great Lakes schematically depicted in Figure 8, are more often than not characterized by lakes of unequal size and water residence time. The example of the Great Lakes includes extremes, from a lake with the water residence time of about 200 years (Lake Superior) to a lake with the water residence time of about 3 years (Lake Erie).

One conclusion for chains or systems of interconnected lakes that can immediately be drawn from a diagram of Figure 8 is the controlling potential of each of the lakes on the entire system.

A pronounced change in the chemical composition of any one of the three bigger upper lakes would cause long-term changes in the downstream lakes, that de-

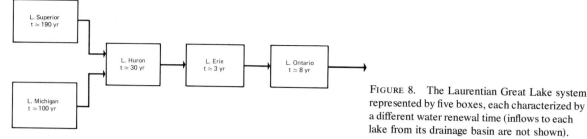

FIGURE 8.   The Laurentian Great Lake system represented by five boxes, each characterized by a different water renewal time (inflows to each lake from its drainage basin are not shown).

rive a major fraction of their water budget from inflow from the bigger lakes. A most pronounced change in water quality within a lake system can be caused by long-term accumulation of substances that remain in solution. Their removal to the lake floor sediments may prevent long lasting effects on the downstream lakes if the residence time with respect to sedimentation is significantly shorter than with respect to lake outflow.

Horizontal inhomogeneity in chemical properties commonly shows in the presence of horizontal concentration gradients of different chemical species entering a lake with surface inflow: from a point source at the river mouth, gradual dispersal and mixing of river and lake waters result in two- or three-dimensional concentration gradients, observable on a scale that may amount to a significant fraction of the physical dimensions of the lake. Sediment introduced by river inflow can form a gradient of thickness and grain size, both decreasing away from the source. Redistribution of sediment by persistent water currents within a lake can also result in mineralogical and chemical inhomogeneity of the lake bottom sediments (see Chapters 3 and 8). Chemical precipitation of calcium carbonate or evaporitic minerals in one part of a lake can be responsible for pronounced horizontal gradients in concentration in lake water. Among the previously mentioned saline lakes, deposition of sodium sulfate minerals along the eastern shores of the Gulf of Kara-Bugaz is nourished by the Caspian water inflow from the west and its strong evaporation; extensive precipitation of salt in the southern part of the Dead Sea is also a result of stronger evaporation and restricted water inflow into the south basin.

In dealing with horizontal inhomogeneity in chemical properties of a lake, it is difficult to draw a line between a case where a multi-box model can be constructed to describe the existing situation and a case where a continuous model should be applied. In the case of point-input sources, such as river inflow or discharge from a pipe, dispersal in two or three dimensions results in the development of a plume, and sophisticated mathematical models have been developed to deal with distribution of dissolved and suspended substances in plumes (see Chapter 2). As an approximation, a grid or an array of unequal boxes in two or three dimensions can be used to deal with

dissolved materials in a plume. At the limit, subdivision of a lake space into very small boxes leads to a continuous model, based on eddy diffusional dispersal, water advection, and chemical reactions in three dimensions. The simpler approximation of "several" boxes, within which the concentration gradients are replaced by mean concentration values, can be justified on heuristic grounds, as such a model is, at least at the beginning, easier to comprehend and analyze by letting some of the parameter values vary and producing answers in response to some scenario questions.

Models for lake water and sediments

Removal of dissolved material from lake water on sediment particles and in biologically produced organic matter was treated as a removal mechanism in the section on One-box models. If no chemical and biological processes affected the settled material after it became sediment on the lake floor, then the sediment would only be a depository for the material removed from lake water, and the sediment below the sediment–water interface would have no effect on lake water. However, there is abundant evidence from lake sediments that chemical and biochemical reactions take place over some distances below the sediment–water interface, and concentrations of several chemical species in the sediment pore waters change in the course of diagenesis. As long as a column of the sediment pore water (interstitial water) is open to the overlying lake water, dissolved chemical species can migrate up or down across the sediment–water interface, in response to the existing concentration gradients. For example, concentrations of silica in pore waters are commonly higher than in lake water, owing to dissolution of diatom skeletons. Bacterial decomposition commonly results in the reduction of sulfate and concomitant production of phosphate, ammonia, and carbon dioxide that are released to pore water. The result of the bacterial activity can often be a decrease in the sulfate concentration in pore water down from the sediment–water interface and an increase in the same direction in concentrations of the produced species, such as sulfide, phosphate, ammonia, and bicarbonate ions.

A chemical species newly introduced in solution into the lake can migrate into sediments by molecular diffusion in pore water, even if it is not taken up by sediment particles or biota. This is, for example, the fate of sodium chloride used for deicing of roads in the winter: runoff introduces sodium chloride into freshwater lakes at input levels high above those of the 19th and early 20th centuries.

In lakes subject to large variations in volume, because of temporal changes in climate or hydrological regime, concentrated saline brines originated during the drier periods can fill the sediment pore space. When the lake volume rises due to influx of fresh water, the dissolved or solid salt minerals in the sediment can act as a long lasting reservoir supplying salt to the overlying lake water.

If the chemical quality of water in the lake is a main objective of modelling, then the role of sediment can be reduced to a question, "what and how much do the sediments remove from, or supply to, the lake?" Figure 9 shows a diagram of a lake represented by a well-mixed box, which exchanges material with the underlying sediment, in addition to having other physical, chemical, and biological removal and input mechanisms discussed in the section on One-box models. Removal to, and supply from, the sediment take place by diffusion of dissolved species in pore water, and by deposition of sediment particles (organic and inorganic). Also material in solution may interact with solids at the sediment surface through adsorption or some other form of a chemical reaction. Relative to the sediment–water interface, transport in the vertical direction, maintained by diffusion and sedimentation, is represented by the one-dimensional flux at the interface ($F_{z=0}$, in units of mass per unit time per unit area of sediment surface)

$$F_{z=0} = \phi\left[-D\frac{\partial C}{\partial z} + UC + U_s C_s\right]_{z=0}$$

$$(\text{g cm}^{-2}\ \text{year}^{-1})\quad (45)$$

where ϕ is the sediment porosity or the fraction of volume occupied by water ($0 < \phi < 1$), z is the vertical distance coordinate, positive and increasing downward from the sediment–water interface taken as $z = 0$ (Figure 9), C is concentration in pore water and C_s is concentration in solids (both in units of g per 1 cm^3 of pore water), D is the diffusion coefficient in pore water solution (cm^2 year^{-1}), U is the rate of downward pore water advection relative to the sediment–water interface (cm year^{-1}), and U_s is the rate of downward sediment advection relative to the sediment–water interface (cm year^{-1}).

Depending on the algebraic sign of the concentration gradient $\partial C/\partial z$ and the relative magnitudes of the terms ($UC + U_s C_s$) and $-D\ \partial C/\partial z$, their sum, which is the flux $F_{z=0}$, can be either positive or negative. In the coordinates of Figure 9, a positive flux ($F_{z=0} > 0$) indicates flux downward into the sediment; a negative flux ($F_{z=0} < 0$) indicates flux out of the sediment.

Two simplifying assumptions can be introduced into Eq. (45). One, if the sediment porosity ϕ changes little with depth, then the sediment particles and pore water do not move *relative to each other* in a growing sediment column, and the advection rates become equal, $U = U_s$. The parameter U can be equated to the sedimentation rate (cm year^{-1}) at the sediment surface. Two, a relationship between concentration in pore water (C) and on solids (C_s) can be written as a simple distribution relationship of the form $C_s = KC$, where K is a dimensionless distribution factor that may generally depend on concentration, nature of the dissolved species and solid substrate, as well as other environmental variables. [Compare the definition of the distribution factor K' in Eq. (20), which is related to K by $K = K'C_p$, where C_p is concentration of

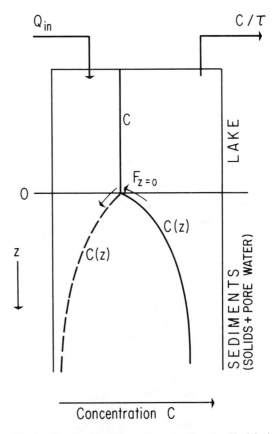

FIGURE 9.   Model of lake water and sediments. The lake is a well-mixed box, characterized by concentration C (time dependent) and water renewal time τ. For sediments and pore water, one-dimensional distribution of concentrations is time and distance dependent, $F_{z=0}$ is the flux at the sediment–sediment–water interface, directed upward or downward, depending on the algebraic sign of the concentration gradient in pore water. z is the vertical distance coordinate for sediments.

particles.] With these two simplifying assumptions, Eq. (45) becomes

$$F_{z=0} = \phi \left[-D \frac{\partial C}{\partial z} + U(K + 1)C \right]_{z=0}. \quad (46)$$

The flux at the sediment–water interface given by Eq. (46) can be used in the mass-balance Eq. (2) as input or a removal term. Then the rate of change in concentration of a dissolved species in the lake can be written as

$$\frac{dC}{dt} = \frac{Q_{in}}{V} - \frac{A\phi}{V} \left[-D \frac{\partial C}{\partial z} + U(K + 1)C \right]_{z=0} - C \left(\frac{1}{\tau} + \frac{1}{\tau_r} \right) \quad (47)$$

where Q_{in} is the rate of input of a chemical species to the lake from all external sources and from production (if any) in the lake water column (g year^{-1}), τ is the water renewal time in the lake by outflow, and τ_r is the residence time with respect to removal by chemical processes ($\tau_r = 1/k$ where k is a reaction rate constant of dimensions time^{-1}, or $\tau_r = 1/\lambda$ where λ is the radioactive decay constant). The flux at the sediment–water interface is multiplied by the bottom area A, over which the flux exists, and divided by the lake volume V.

Eq. (47) is of a type combining the mathematical terms of a box model and the terms of a continuous model, insofar as it is concerned with concentration gradients within the sediment pore water.

If the flux $F_{z=0}$ is constant over the lake bottom area then the quotient $AF_{z=0}/V$ in Eq. (47) represents the bottom contribution to lake water. However, if the flux varies over the lake bottom, $F_{z=0}$ has to be averaged over area A. Chemical composition of pore waters in some lakes that have been studied in detail (Tessenow, 1975) shows considerable variation over lake bottom such that horizontal concentration gradients in pore waters are commonly observed. Although the horizontal gradients are generally smaller than the vertical gradients within the upper 10^1 to 10^2 cm of the sediment column, the horizontal variability indicates that the *vertical* flux $F_{z=0}$ is a function of position on the lake bottom. While horizontal fluxes of dissolved species in pore water can be in many cases small in comparison to the vertical fluxes, the vertical fluxes themselves can vary over the two-dimensional bottom space.

Insofar as Eq. (47) treats the lake as a box, the geometric shape of the lake bottom is immaterial to the total flux from the bottom, $AF_{z=0}$ (g year^{-1}). If, however, the lake is treated as a continuous model where dissolved materials are dispersed at different rates in the vertical and horizontal directions, then the shape of the bottom, deviating from a horizontal plane, can be of considerable importance in determining the distribution of concentrations within the lake.

One such example, a basin receiving flux of radon from an irregularly shaped bottom and distribution of radon by horizontal and vertical eddy diffusion in water, has been dealt with by Lietzke and Lerman (1975).

Depending on whether the individual coefficients in Eq. (47) are constants or whether they are functions of time t and concentration C, explicit solutions of the equation may or may not exist. By definition, concentration in lake water C is always equal to concentration at the sediment–water interface $C_{z=0}$ (this means the concentration is continuous across the interface, see Figure 9). Thus Eq. (47) is also a boundary condition for an equation describing concentration changes in pore water of the sediment. For some specific cases of input to a lake, migration to sediments, decay, and removal by outflow, Eq. (47) can be solved explicitly. One such solution gives C as a function of t in lake water, as well as C as a function of z and t in the sediment. This solution applies to the case of a lake of fixed dimensions (A, V, and τ constant), and constant diffusivity in pore water (D), sedimentation rate (U), chemical adsorption (K), and radioactive decay ($1/\tau_r = \lambda$). It has been used to analyze transient distributions of the radionuclides ^{90}Sr and ^{137}Cs in the sediments of the Great Lakes (Lerman and Lietzke, 1975). One-dimensional vertical transport of the diffusing species in sediments under these conditions is given by the differential equation for diffusion, advection, decay, and adsorption

$$\frac{\partial C}{\partial t} = D \frac{\partial^2 C}{\partial z^2} - U(K + 1) \frac{\partial C}{\partial z} - \frac{C}{\tau_r}. \quad (48)$$

For lake water, a steady-state concentration C_{ss} is a function of the transport and chemical parameters appearing in Eqs. (47) and (48)

$$C_{ss} = \frac{Q_{in}}{A} \left\{ \frac{\phi U(K + 1)}{2} \left[1 + \left(1 + \frac{4D}{(K + 1)\tau_r U^2} \right)^{1/2} \right] + h \left(\frac{1}{\tau} + \frac{1}{\tau_r} \right) \right\}^{-1} \quad (\text{g cm}^{-3}) \quad (49)$$

where $h = V/A$ (cm) is the mean depth of the lake.

Eq. (49) can be reduced to specific simpler cases. For example, in a closed lake without outflow and without chemical reactions of the decay type in water (that is, $1/\tau = 0$ and $1/\tau_r = 0$), the only removal process from lake water is adsorption on sediment particles and their deposition. In this case, concentration in pore water is constant with depth and equal to concentration in lake water, which is, from Eq. (49),

$$C_{ss} = \frac{Q_{in}/A}{\phi U(K + 1)} \quad (\text{g cm}^{-3}). \quad (50)$$

The latter equation shows, as may be expected, that the stronger the adsorption on sediment particles (the larger is K), the lower the steady-state concentration in water. This case can be compared to the equation dealing with the adsorption in lake water discussed in the section on One-box models.

Lakes differ from one another considerably in their rates of sedimentation, water residence times, physical dimensions, and the rates of input of a given chemical species (such as, for example, the rates of phosphorus input). Nevertheless it is instructive to compare the magnitudes of the residence times in lakes, with respect to the renewal of a dissolved substance by water outflow, chemical reactions, and diffusional and settling fluxes to sediments. This can be done by considering individually either the terms in the braces of Eq. (49) or the terms on the right hand side of Eq. (47). In Eq. (47), both sides can be divided by C and the ratio V/A can be equated to the mean depth of the lake h, giving

$$\frac{d\ln C}{dt} - \frac{Q_{in}}{VC} = -\frac{\phi D}{h}\frac{\partial \ln C}{\partial z}$$

$$+ \frac{\phi U(K+1)}{h} - \frac{1}{\tau} - \frac{1}{\tau_r} \quad (\text{year}^{-1}). \quad (51)$$

As noted, all the terms in Eq. (51) have the units of year^{-1} or they are reciprocal residence times with respect to the individual input or removal processes. At the steady state, we have $d\ln C/dt = 0$; then each of the terms in the equation gives a rate of renewal per year of the dissolved species concentration in the lake.

By analogy with the rate constants for the water residence time ($1/\tau$) and chemical removal ($1/\tau_r$), rate constants can be defined for the diffusional flux at the sediment–water interface ($1/\tau_d$), and for the sedimentation and pore water advection flux ($1/\tau_u$). The latter two quantities are

$$\frac{1}{\tau_d} = \left|\frac{\phi D}{h}\frac{\partial \ln C}{\partial z}\right|_{z=0} \quad (\text{year}^{-1}) \quad (52)$$

$$\frac{1}{\tau_u} = \frac{\phi U(K+1)}{h} \quad (\text{year}^{-1}). \quad (53)$$

The four rate terms ($1/\tau_d$, $1/\tau_u$, $1/\tau$, and $1/\tau_r$) can take different numerical values, depending on the characteristics of the lake, but some representative ranges of their magnitudes are listed in Table 3. The numbers shown in the table are based on the following limiting values of the individual transport and chemical parameters.

Lake depth h: between 10^3 and 10^4 cm; we use $h = 5 \times 10^3$ cm. Mean rates of sedimentation U, between 0.05 and 1 cm year^{-1}. A value of about 0.1 cm year^{-1} is fairly characteristic of lakes (see Chapter 6).

Sediment porosity at the sediment–water interface $\phi_{z=0}$: between 0.8 and 0.9, $\phi_{z=0} = 0.85$.

Molecular diffusion coefficient of ionic species in pore water D: about 3×10^{-6} cm^2 sec^{-1} = 10^2 cm^2 year^{-1}. This value is characteristic of diffusion of ionic species in pore waters of sediments, where it is lower than the values near 10^{-5} cm^2 sec^{-1} in a bulk solution.

TABLE 3.   Rate Constants[a]

$1/\tau_d$	$1/\tau_u$	$1/\tau$	$1/\tau_r$
		(year^{-1})	
0–0.1	0–0.05	0.01–1	0–35

[a]Rate constants (reciprocal residence times) for a dissolved species in a lake for diffusional flux at the sediment–water interface ($1/\tau_d$), sedimentation and growth of the pore water column ($1/\tau_u$), water outflow ($1/\tau$), and first-order chemical removal or decay processes ($1/\tau_r$).

In detail, the diffusion coefficients depend on the nature of the chemical species, and such physical characteristics of the sediment as porosity and tortuosity.

Adsorption coefficient K: as far as the simplistic relationship $C_s = KC$ is taken to represent equilibrium exchange between a solution and solid, the values of K determined under different experimental conditions or computed from analytical data on pore waters and sediment particles show a large variation. The lowest value possible is $K = 0$, for the case of no adsorption by solids. High values, of the order of 10^2 to 10^4 have been reported for adsorption of various radionuclides by sediments. In oceanic and freshwater sediments, the values of K for such ionic species as sodium, calcium, and magnesium are of the order of 10^0 to 10^1. We use two values, $K = 0$ and $K = 3000$. In the quotient $\phi U(K+1)/h$, a three orders of magnitude variation in K is about the same as can be expected from the range of the U and h values given above.

Relative concentration gradient $\partial \ln C/\partial z$ or $(1/C) \times (\partial C/\partial z)$: if the concentration gradient at the sediment–water interface $(\partial C/\partial z)_{z=0}$ is zero, then diffusional transport in pore water plays no role. A higher value may be represented by a fivefold increase or decrease in concentration within the uppermost 1 cm of the pore water column. A fivefold change corresponds to the relative concentration gradient of $(1/C)(\partial C/\partial z)_{z=0} = \pm 5$ cm^{-1}.

Water residence time in the lake τ: a range of interest is mostly between 1 and 100 years, corresponding to the range of $1/\tau$ from 1 to 0.01 year^{-1}.

The chemical rate term $1/\tau_r$ may range from 0, for a nonreactive species, to relatively high values for rapidly decaying or reacting substances. For example, a renewal rate of 10% per day corresponds to the value of $1/\tau_r \simeq 35$ year^{-1}, although such high values are more characteristic of the periods of intense biological productivity in the photosynthetic zone of lakes.

Comparing the rates listed in Table 3, it should be noted that the ranges of magnitudes are fairly similar for the four types of processes. Diffusional transport in pore water or deposition with sediment particles each can be of a comparable magnitude, either enhancing or canceling one another, depending on the algebraic sign of the concentration gradient in pore water. The potential significance of the sediments as sources or sinks of chemical species in lake waters becomes greater when other removal mechanisms, such as water outflow or evaporation, are relatively slow. Conversely, in lakes that are flushed through relatively fast, inflow and outflow can better compete with the fluxes to and from the sediment. However, even in such lakes, an advanced stage of eutrophication can be reached where the amount of material deposited on the lake bottom and regenerated seasonally to lake water becomes a major fraction of the material balance of a chemical species in the lake. For example, the water residence time in Greifensee (Switzerland) is about 1 year, and the amount of phosphorus regenerated from the lake bottom is comparable to the amount of input from external sources (Imboden and Emerson, 1978).

References

Brezonik, P. L. (1968). Application of mathematical models to the eutrophication process. Pp. 16–30. Proc. 11th Conf. Great Lakes Res.

Imboden, D. M. (1974). Phosphorus model of lake eutrophication. *Limnol. Oceanogr.,* **19**:297–304.

Imboden, D. M., and S. Emerson. (1978). Natural radon and phosphorus as limnologic tracers: Horizontal and vertical eddy diffusion in Greifensee. *Limnol. Oceanogr.,* **23**: 77–90.

Imboden, D. M., and R. Gächter. (1977). A dynamic lake model for trophic state prediction. *J. Ecol. Modelling,* **4**: 77–98.

Koppel, L. B. (1968). *Introduction to Control Theory.* Prentice–Hall, Englewood Cliffs, NJ.

Lerman, A. (1970). Strontium-90 in the Great Lakes: Concentration time model. *J. Geophys. Res.,* **77**:3256–3264.

Lerman, A. (1971). Time to chemical steady-states in lakes and ocean. *Adv. Chem. Ser.,* **106**:30–76.

Lerman, A., and T. A. Lietzke. (1975). Uptake and migration of tracers in lake sediments. *Limnol. Oceanogr.,* **20**:497–510.

Lietzke, T. A., and A. Lerman. (1975). Effects of bottom relief in two-dimensional oceanic eddy diffusion models. *Earth Planet. Sci. Lett.,* **24**:337–344.

Mortimer, C. H. (1941). The exchange of dissolved substance between mud and water in lakes. *J. Ecol.,* **29**:280–329.

Mortimer, C. H. (1942). The exchange of dissolved substances between mud and water in lakes. *J. Ecol.,* **30**:147–201.

Schindler, P. W. (1975). The regulation of trace metal concentrations in natural water systems: A chemical approach. Pp. 132–145. Proc. 1st Speciality Symposium on atmospheric contribution to the chemistry of lake waters. Int. Assoc. Great Lakes Res.

Snodgrass, W. J., and C. R. O'Melia. (1975). Predictive model for phosphorus in lakes. *Environ. Sci. Technol.,* **9**:937–944.

Stumm, W. (1964). Discussion (Methods for the removal of phosphorus and nitrogen from sewage plant effluents by R. A. Rohlich). Pp. 216–229. In: W. W. Eckenfelder (ed.), *Advances in Water Pollution Research.* Proc. 1st Int. Conf., London, 1962, Vol. 2. Pergamon.

Tessenow, U. (1975). Lösungs-, Diffusions- und Sorptionsprozesse in der Oberschicht von Seesedimenten. *Arch. Hydrobiol. Suppl.,* **47**:325–412.

Toth, D. J., and A. Lerman. (1975). Stratified lake and oceanic brines: Salt movements and time limits of existence. *Limnol. Oceanogr.,* **20**:715–728.

Vollenweider, R. A. (1968). Water management research. OECD-Rep. 68.27. Paris. 159 pp.

Subject Index

Index of Lakes

Coastal Sedimentary Environments

Edited by **R.A. Davis, Jr.**
1978. ix, 420p. 247 illus. cloth

Here is a thorough examination of various aspects of the coastal system and each of its component environments. *Coastal Sedimentary Environments* is designed as a text for advanced undergraduate or graduate students interested in coastal environments. Although primarily aimed at students majoring in geology, the book will also benefit students of geography, coastal engineering, ecological- and life sciences.

Coastal Sedimentary Environments is the only book available that covers the major coastal environments. Each is allocated a separate chapter, with additional chapters on relationships and modeling. Since each chapter is the work of a specialist with extensive experience in the particular field under discussion, the reader is provided with insight not usually found in single-authored volumes.

This fascinating new book explores descriptive aspects of coastal environments such as morphology and sediment distribution, with emphasis on physical processes and their interactions with the sediments and sediment body morphology. Primary attention is given to the principles involved and to general considerations. In addition to numerous case histories, the book features a chapter on dunes and one on marshes which constitute perhaps the best comprehensive summaries of these areas available in the literature.

A Springer-Verlag Journal

Environmental Geology
Editor-in-Chief: **L. Jan Turk**

Environmental Geology is an international journal concerned with the interaction between man and the earth. Its coverage of topics in earth science is necessarily broad and multidisciplinary. The journal deals with geologic hazards and geologic processes that affect man, such as management of geologic resources, broadly interpreted as land, water, air, and minerals including fuels; natural and man-made pollutants in the geologic environment; and environmental impact studies.

Springer-Verlag   New York   Heidelberg   Berlin

Handbook of Geochemistry

Executive Editor: K.H. Wedepohl

Editorial Board: C.W. Correns, D.M. Shaw, K.K. Turekian, J. Zemann

This critical selection of important facts on the distribution of the chemical elements and their isotopes in the earth and the cosmos is the work of some 70 specialists under the direction of a distinguished editorial group. The data are set out in the main part of the Handbook (Vol. II) in tables and diagrams as an integral part of extensive discussions on abundance, distribution, and behavior of the elements.

With the exception of the general part (Vol. I), the work is arranged according to the atomic numbers of the elements, each chapter being organized in exactly the same way. Thus, the reader will find such frequently needed information as the crystal chemical properties of an element, or its occurrence in meteorites or metamorphic rocks, under the same section in each of the 65 chapters. The loose-leaf system enables the contributions to be published in random order, regardless of their position in the book, and revisions to be made as desired.

Volume I
1969. xv, 442p 60 illus. cloth

Volume II
Part 1
1969. x, 586p. 172 illus. loose-leaf binder

Part 2
1970. iv, 667p. 105 illus. loose-leaf binder

Part 3
1972. iv, 845p. 142 illus. loose-leaf binder

Part 4
1974. vi, 898p. 103 illus. loose-leaf binder

Part 5
1978. approx. 1500p. approx. 200 illus. loose-leaf binder